1989

Theory and Practice of Social Welfare Policy

ANALYSIS, PROCESSES, AND CURRENT ISSUES

Bruce S. Jansson
School of Social Work
University of Southern California

Wadsworth Publishing Company
Belmont, California
A Division of Wadsworth, Inc.

To Betty Ann

Sociology Editor: Sheryl Fullerton

Production Editor: Hal Humphrey

Managing Designer: Paula Shuhert

Designer: R. Kharibian

Copy Editor: Stephen Bodian

Printed in the United States of America

1 2 3 4 5 6 7 8 9 10—88 87 86 85 84

ISBN 0-534-01469-0

Library of Congress Cataloging in Publication Data

Jansson, Bruce S.
  Theory and practice of social welfare policy.

  Bibliography: p.
  Includes index.
    1. Public welfare—United States. 2. United States—Social policy. 3. Social service—United States.
I. Title.
HV95.J36 1984   361.6′1′0973   83–12430
ISBN 0–534–01469–0

Preface

This book has evolved during years of teaching courses in social welfare policy to social work students. Many entered these courses with foreboding because they believed the discipline to be tangential to direct service interests. The author's central objective, then, has been to provide a text that makes social welfare policy an interesting yet challenging subject to a range of readers—one that underscores the importance of social welfare policy to social workers. Five major strategies have been used to achieve this objective.

First, practical implications of social welfare policy for social workers are discussed in each chapter. Social welfare policy is sometimes discussed as a philosophical or conceptual discipline—or as a descriptive or historical one. In either case, students often perceive it to be removed from daily activities of social workers in direct service or other positions. This book is different. Various policy roles and skills are discussed in part 1 that together constitute the "practice of policy"—a practice that requires development of competencies in a fashion similar to direct service practice. Also, the practice implications of the policy practice of social workers are discussed in a range of agency, community, and legislative settings in each of the succeeding chapters. And at the end of each chapter there is a list of concepts and policies discussed during the chapter, as well as a summary of main points covered, a list of discussion questions, and suggestions for additional reading. Methods for organizing, presenting, and researching policy papers are discussed in chapter 9.

Second, since readers require an overview of

the discipline if they wish to participate intelligently in the policy-making process, this book presents many facets of social welfare policy. Many books emphasize either policy outcomes or products, historical materials, description of programs and policies, policy analysis, or policy processes, thereby frustrating many students in basic courses when large pieces of the social welfare policy puzzle are missing. In this book, an overview of social welfare policy is developed in the first two chapters in part 1. Policy analysis materials are emphasized in chapters 3, 4, and 5 in part 2, ones relevant to identifying and choosing between policy alternatives. Realities of politics and implementation are discussed in part 3 (chapters 6 and 7), since policy outcomes are shaped in decision making and organizational arenas. Alternative methods of assessing or evaluating programs and policies are discussed in part 4 (chapter 8), a relevant topic in the 1980s, when many persons question the effectiveness of social programs. Finally, part 5 (chapters 10 through 13) provides extensive material about current policies, reform possibilities, and professional roles in the four policy sectors that provide "the heart" of the social welfare system: child and family, economic security, health, and mental health. Case illustrations in other chapters provide exposure as well to issues in gerontology, housing, substance abuse, juvenile justice, developmental disability, and employment sectors. While some prior knowledge of the historical evolution of policy in the United States is assumed, an overview of developments in the contemporary period is coupled with brief analysis of the historical evolution of policy in the four policy sectors in chapters 10 through 13. Conceptual and analysis materials, then, are discussed in parts 1 and 2, policy processes in part 3, and policy evaluation in part 4. Concepts, analysis, and policy processes are then applied to policy developments and issues in the four policy sectors in part 5.

Third, a format is used in the various chapters that facilitates application of concepts to current events and social work practice. Extensive use is made of guest editorials and case examples to insert perspectives and concrete policy problems into the text. Further, numerous political cartoons of Paul Conrad and Herbert Block are used. When responding to written and graphic "points of view," the reader is encouraged to analyze personal and professional values and to take an active rather than passive interest in the subject matter.

Fourth, two unifying themes are developed that serve to link or integrate discussion in the various chapters: (1) a policy framework is developed in chapter 2 that is used in the succeeding chapters, and (2) the controversial nature of social welfare policy is also stressed in each chapter, since values, political interests, and economic stakes influence policy choices at numerous points. Emphasis upon the controversial nature of the discipline is particularly important in the current era, when divergence between liberal and conservative perspectives is so obvious. Considerable attention is given in each chapter to patterns of policy discrimination against members of racial and economic subgroups, as well as against women.

Finally, the book has been written so that it can be used in flexible fashion. Specific chapters can be deleted when they overlap with materials from prior or succeeding courses. Chapters can be used in a modified order as when, for example, various of the chapters on current policies are interspersed with preceding chapters on phases of policy formulation. Readers new to social welfare policy can use the book as an introduction to the discipline and to current issues. More advanced readers can use it to extend knowledge of policy concepts and frameworks, the controversial nature of social welfare policy, current issues, and the practice of policy.

A final note to the reader. This book was written during the conservative developments of the 1980s, a period when social programs have en-

countered major cutbacks. I have not hesitated to draw on many examples from this time period, because its issues and challenges expose essential characteristics of social welfare policy, such as its controversial nature and the importance of values and vested interests in shaping policy positions.

Indeed, the emphasis in this book upon the theory *and* practice of social welfare policy stems from realities confronted by social workers in the 1980s. If social workers want to help disadvantaged populations, they need to use concepts to inform their "practice of policy," a practice that is particularly needed when dominant interests in society seek drastic cuts in social programs. Emphasis upon "value clarification" at numerous points in this book also can be attributed to issues posed in the 1980s, when the importance of values to social policy has never been more obvious. Indeed, I have not tried to disguise my own redistributive and social-reform values, in the hope that readers will be able to clarify personal and professional perspectives as they respond to— and criticize—my perspectives.

By emphasizing the controversial nature of social welfare policy and the practice of policy, then, this book may serve a useful function even when the conservative developments of the 1980s have been supplanted by liberal perspectives. It may also remind some liberals that no substitute exists for the development of broad-based support for social programs.

ACKNOWLEDGEMENTS

Countless students in classes at the School of Social Work of the University of Southern California have contributed to this book by criticizing ideas and frameworks. Some ideas evolved in the course of discussions with social policy colleagues including June Brown, Ramon Salcido, Sam Taylor, Madeline Stoner, Frances Feldman, Wilbur Finch, and Harry Engelman. Special thanks are due Professors June Brown and Norman Wyers who respectively commented on chapters 10 and 11.

It has been a pleasure to be associated in this project with Wadsworth Publishing Company. This book has been facilitated in numerous ways by William Oliver, former sociology editor. Curt Peoples prompted me to undertake the project.

They both showed forbearance with flaws of the numerous drafts that preceded the final version and made many suggestions that were incorporated into the book. Editorial assistants Lauren Foodim and Susan Goerss helped along the way. Paula Shuhert and R. Karibian creatively designed the book, and copy editor Stephen Bodian made many editorial improvements. Hal Humphrey expertly shepherded the book through the production phase.

Comments of reviewers at various points in the development of this book greatly improved the final product. They included Sheldon R. Gelman, Pennsylvania State University; Morris Siegel, Rutgers University; and Donald Brieland, University of Illinois, Chicago Circle. Professor David P. Kemple of Boston University made many valuable suggestions when reading the final draft. Suzanne Grebe Kemple of Harvard-Radcliffe's Hilles Library greatly improved the discussion of policy research in chapter 9.

I would also like to thank authors and publications who kindly consented to use of their material in this book, including the *California Journal*; *NASW News*; the *New Republic*; the *New York Times*; the *Washington Post*; the *Los Angeles Times*; *Newsday*; the *National Journal*; *Policy Analysis*; *Grants Magazine*; Random House; Professor Samuel Taylor; the Honorable Patricia Schroeder, Cochairwoman of the Congresswoman's Caucus; the National Urban League; economist and Professor Lester Thurow; James C. Webster, publisher of the *Food and Fiber Letter*; columnist Richard E. Cohen; Joan Claybrook, former administrator of the National Highway Traffic Safety Administration; columnist Colman McCarthy; Marian Wright Edelman, President of the Children's Defense Fund; salesman Alber Reingewirtz; science writer K. C. Cole; columnist Roger Wilkins, former Director of the Community Relations Service in the Department of Justice; Bob Greenstein of the Center on Budget and Policy Priorities; Professor Norman Wyers; Geraldine Dallek of the National Health Law Program; Professor Nancy Humphreys, former President of the National Association of Social Workers; Chauncey Alexander, former Executive Director of the National Association of Social Workers; Daniel S. Greenberg, editor of *Science and Government Report*; Paul Fahri of *Ad Week*; Barbara Deming Lurie of the Patient Rights Office of the Los Angeles County Department of Mental Health; Richard Fiene of the Children's Services Monitoring Consortium; Joanne Gonzalez, director of information and referral for the Senior Citizens Activity Center in Claremont, California; and political cartoonists Paul Conrad and Herbert Block. Thanks are also due social workers Glee Cantilibre, Michele Wilson, Mary Hays, Andrea Karzen, Stacey Stern, Michael Cervantes, Constance Williams, and Marcia Mabee for case material. The Library of Congress facilitated the project by providing me with a research desk at a critical juncture. None of the preceding persons, publications, or institutions are responsible, of course, for errors of omission or commission in this text.

Dean Robert Roberts facilitated my work on this project at numerous points. Lee Angela Thomas, Gloria Byrd, and Sue Redman assisted with typing. Ruth Britton provided expert reference assistance.

Finally, I want to thank some special people. Mary S. Buchtel gave much needed support and encouragement throughout the project. Roger and Stephanie were good sports when my mind was elsewhere. The book is dedicated to my wife, Betty Ann, who was always there.

Contents

PART 1

The Foundations
of Social Welfare Policy

Part 1 of this book is an overview of social welfare policy. A case example of policy turmoil in a social agency is used in chapter 1 to illustrate the scope of social welfare policy, the social problems addressed by it, and recurring policy issues. Issues of social equality are discussed as they pertain to the poor, racial minorities, women, the elderly, the mentally ill, and those persons commonly perceived to violate social norms (e.g., homosexuals). The controversial and political nature of social welfare policy is discussed as well as the roles of social workers as they seek to shape policies in agency, community, and legislative arenas.

A social welfare policy framework is presented in chapter 2 and illustrated by a case example drawn from the juvenile justice system. The framework delineates five phases in the policymaking process: scanning, analysis, politics, implementation, and assessment. Cultural, economic, political, and technological realities that influence policy development are also emphasized. The chapter concludes with discussion of the various policy roles and skills needed by social workers.

An Overview of Social Welfare Policy

Consumers, citizens, and professionals all "breathe" social welfare policy, whether as utilizers, providers, or funders of social services and programs. Even with recent cuts, the market value of noncash benefits like food stamps, medical care, and subsidized housing increased from $2.2 billion in 1956 to $72 billion in 1982. While in prior eras most social workers were employed in income maintenance programs and nonprofit agencies such as family counseling agencies, they now work in a multitude of agencies in child and family, economic security, health, and mental health sectors, among others. It is not possible to help consumers navigate the complex social welfare system without knowledge about existing programs and policies.

Other, equally compelling reasons exist for studying social welfare policy. The well-being of social workers and consumers is importantly affected by policies. Sometimes participation is partially defensive, as when social workers or consumers oppose funding cutbacks that endanger jobs or programs. Social workers also take the offensive in seeking better programs for consumers who are the ultimate beneficiaries (or victims) of social welfare policy. In this and subsequent chapters, elements of the practice of social welfare policy are discussed to underscore the relevance of policy for professional activities.

To participate in the fashioning of social welfare policy, social workers need to be able to:

Define social welfare policy

3

Identify groups in the population who are disadvantaged by existing policies

Discuss recurring issues in social welfare policy

Understand processes that are used to develop social welfare policies

These various topics are presented in this chapter, providing a foundation to undergird discussion in the remaining chapters.

To facilitate our discussion of social welfare policy, a case study of an agency in turmoil is presented in case example 1.1. This case does not portray a typical social agency; turmoil of this magnitude is unusual. The case nonetheless facilitates examination of the nature of the discipline, basic policy issues, policy arenas, the relationship of social welfare policy to direct service, and social work policy roles.

In case example 1.1, the agency is in turmoil because staff members disagree about policy strat-

CASE EXAMPLE 1.1

Agency in Policy Turmoil

Exactly one year ago, Dr. George Breeze came to San Marcos, a metropolitan suburb of Los Angeles with a population of 60,000 people, to direct the recently established San Marcos Community Mental Health Center. Dr. Breeze had previously worked in Philadelphia, where he had acquired a reputation as the innovative, inspiring, and flexible director of Manford University's Outreach Mental Health Services Department.

When Dr. Breeze was initially interviewed for his position, several board members expressed some reservations about how he would fit in, since he did not wear a tie and seemed almost overconfident. Dr. Sedgwick, the retiring director, calmed the board by saying that, as a young psychoanalyst, he too had been fairly unconventional. The board had to keep in mind that this was no longer the San Marcos Clinic, it was a new mental health center, and it needed new ideas and the dedication of youth. "He will work out," Dr. Sedgwick reassured them.

Shortly after George Breeze arrived at the San Marcos Community Mental Health Center, he made it clear to the staff that waiting lists, long-term therapy, and supervision were outdated. In the following months, he:

1. urged short-term, crisis-oriented management of cases

2. requested and received permission to establish an advisory board of citizens from the catchment area and another board composed of consumers

3. abolished the supervision system and established a flexible peer-consultation system

4. asked staff members to work evenings in order to see families

5. got into an argument with the Chief of Police about how officers were handling youngsters and emotionally ill persons

6. hired paraprofessionals from a human services program of a community college to serve as community aides

7. told the staff that he wanted to know personally about the service and disposition of each case that involved a racial or ethnic minority client because he suspected that staff members were allowing biases to influence case management

Within six months, the staff in the agency had become deeply divided. Three major groups had formed and developed leadership. First,

egy; i.e., about rules, regulations, procedures, and objectives that shape services and programs. Disagreement in the first instance concerns the agency's priorities and objectives. Dr. Breeze and allies appear to favor marked emphasis on services to low-income and ethnic minority groups and to stress social change and advocacy. By contrast, the traditionalists favor restoring "the traditional mission of the agency—long-term therapy with white and middle-class clients." In light of

these differences about objectives, it is not surprising that marked disagreement exists about the specific policies that together define the agency's strategy. To Dr. Breeze, policy reforms are necessary to accomplish his policy objectives, but traditionalists perceived these objectives as antithetical to their own.

This case study reveals the multiplicity of policies in agency settings. Some *directly* influence services by prescribing their content and form as

---

some of the original clinic staff members (who had helped Dr. Sedgwick prepare the mental health center application) resented Dr. Breeze's nontraditional ways and felt that they had had no chance to introduce their ideas. They rallied behind Dr. Jones, met privately, and decided that they must take their case to other agencies in San Marcos and to local civic leaders and then must present their complaints to the agency board with the support of these other groups and leaders.

The staff hired by Dr. Breeze (young activist professionals and community aides) learned of the strategy and immediately alerted Asian, black, and Chicano groups in San Marcos and rallied behind Dr. Smith, who contacted both the National Institute of Mental Health (the prime federal funder of the center) and the Citizen and Consumer Advisory Boards. They were ready to ask for termination of federal and state funds if Dr. Breeze was fired.

Finally, a number of agency supervisors formed a group behind Dr. Virtue that advocated "responsible change." They were not opposed to all the changes instituted by Dr. Breeze but particularly opposed to those that deprived "professionals" of their rightful positions of authority and prestige within the agency. They wanted restoration of the supervisory system and curtailment of hiring of new careerists.

The issue reached crisis proportions when a patient being cared for by a community aide committed suicide in a most sensational manner. A reporter from the newspaper interviewed a member of the original staff and was told that "this would never have happened if Dr. Sedgwick had been there; Dr. Breeze's ideas just didn't work."

The board decided to hold a meeting to settle the issue, and they agreed to allow representatives of all sides to present their evidence. They felt that Dr. Breeze had introduced some good programs but also felt that he was unconventional. At this meeting, they hoped to reach a final decision as to whether Dr. Breeze should be fired, retained (but only after placing limits on the reforms he had issued), or given a vote of complete confidence.

"Traditionalists," then, rallied behind Dr. Jones and wanted to restore the traditional mission of the agency—long-term therapy with white and middle-class clients. "Insurgents" supported Dr. Breeze and his various reforms with no qualifications. "Advocates of responsible change" wanted some innovations but not at the expense of the traditional prerogatives of professionals. The board wished to bring unity to the agency as soon as possible to avoid further adverse publicity as well as possible loss of funds.

SOURCE: This case was developed by Professor Samuel H. Taylor, Graduate School of Social Work, University of Southern California. Names and locations have been altered.

illustrated by the policy about "short-term, crisis-oriented management of cases." Others *indirectly* shape services by establishing conditions that favor certain kinds of services or clientele. As an example, a policy to open the clinic during evening hours modifies agency clientele by providing services when employed persons can make use of them.

DEFINITION OF SOCIAL WELFARE POLICY

Many definitions of social welfare policy have been advanced by various writers. Despite nuances in their wording and scope, most are similar to the definition used in this book: social welfare policy is collective strategy to address social problems.[1]

Collective Strategy

Strategy consists of specific rules, regulations, procedures, and objectives that shape services and programs.[2] The services of direct service staff are commonly influenced by policies that define which consumers qualify, which service approaches are to be used, what duration services are to be offered, which social problems or needs are to be addressed, and which methods are to be used to evaluate services. In national, state, county, and municipal arenas, strategy similarly consists of specific rules, regulations, procedures, and objectives that are defined in legislation, court rulings, and guidelines issued by government agencies such as the U.S. Department of Health and Human Services. These policies provide central mandates for large social programs that employ large numbers of social workers, e.g., community mental health programs, neighborhood health centers, income maintenance programs, preschool programs like Head Start and daycare, multiservice centers for the elderly, and drug abuse programs.

The word *collective* is used in the policy definition because policy influences activities of groups of persons, agencies, taxpayers, and consumers; even seemingly technical policies can have widespread impact upon consumers and staff in the nation or in specific settings.[3] Policies commit program staff members and administrators, consumers, and legislators to certain courses of action. When legislators or administrators allocate funds to specific programs, they bind themselves and the public to those programs rather than others. When funders and government authorities establish guidelines and objectives for programs, they set parameters for agencies, providers, and consumers who deliver and use program services. In similar fashion, the board of a nonprofit agency that decides to concentrate resources on specific social problems commits agency staff to certain kinds of services.

The collective nature of social policy is well illustrated in case example 1.1. Dr. Breeze and allies sought to translate their policy objectives into specific policies that would shape the collective activities of staff and consumers in the San Marcos agency. Were the tables reversed and Dr. Breeze replaced by a director drawn from the ranks of traditionalists, many resurgents would have become disenchanted.

The collective nature of policy makes it imperative that social workers participate in its formulation in agency, community, and legislative settings. They can try to influence policy *goals* or *objectives* of agencies, as illustrated by the efforts of Dr. Breeze to modify the traditional mission of the San Marcos center. They can propose specific *instrumental policies*, as reflected by Dr. Breeze's effort to encourage evening hours in the center. They can modify *official policy*, as illustrated by efforts to persuade the board of directors of the San Marcos clinic to adopt different intake policies. Or they can try to change *informal procedures* used by agency staff, as illustrated when Dr. Breeze believes that some staff members are using, without official sanction, different service procedures with ethnic minority consumers. Social workers can try to modify collective strategy by focusing upon *internal agency policy* or by modifying policies that are established by *external authorities*, whether funders, government officials, or legislators. (A distinction is sometimes made between administrative policy established within agencies and social policy that derives from legislation; in this book, both are included under the rubric "social welfare policy.")[4]

Many kinds of social welfare policies, then, comprise collective strategy to address social problems. Social workers can examine specific policies in agency, community, or national settings, as when examining eligibility provisions in a piece of legislation. Alternatively, they can give attention to networks or constellations of policies, as when examining the nature of social provision nationwide or those social policies that together inform the services of a specific agency.[5]

Social welfare policies often overlap with other kinds of policies—e.g., public and economic policies. Public policy is established by local, state, and national governments. Although all public policy cannot be considered social welfare policy, many government policies do bear directly upon social problems, and others have important ramifications for social welfare policy and must be considered relevent, if not integral, to the discipline.[6] As an example, use of resources for military programs precludes development or expansion of specific social welfare programs and so indirectly influences the nation's collective strategy for addressing specific social problems.

Similarly, some economic policies can also be classified as social welfare policies because they directly bear upon economic deprivation.[7] For example, taxation that directly influences the extent and nature of poverty—e.g., proposals to increase the proportion of taxes paid by low-income persons—should be included in the discipline. Many other kinds of economic policy, however, have little or no relationship to social problems like poverty and can safely be classified outside social welfare policy.

In short, social welfare policy intersects economic and public policies. In some cases, specific policies can be classified under one or another of these categories; in other cases, under several or more. In yet other cases, boundaries are not clear, and no precise resolution is possible. Policies pertaining to import quotas and tariffs, for example, would not normally be considered social welfare

policy, but they might be so considered when their effects on unemployment are singled out for study.

Social Problems

Social problems are specific conditions in the external world that are perceived as sufficiently bothersome or harmful to merit social intervention. The complexity of social welfare policy stems in part from the sheer number of social problems, which include deprivation of material resources, of adequate psychological and physical development, of interpersonal skills, of economic opportunity, and of personal rights.[8] Persons who have inadequate income, suffer from a form of physical illness, lack any or fulfilling employment, are enmeshed in destructive relationships, or suffer mental discomfort are deprived of basic human needs (see table 1.1).

The complexity of social welfare policy also stems from controversy about what conditions constitute bonafide social problems. Some conservatives believe that poverty exists only when persons are in danger of starvation, a view challenged by those who believe it to exist when some persons have markedly less income than others. Serious forms of deprivation are often ignored, as illustrated by the scant attention given to needs of abused children prior to the 1970s. A host of political, value, and cultural factors influence whether, when, and by whom specific conditions are labelled as social problems.[9]

Differences in the definition and ranking of social problems are illustrated in case example 1.1. Dr. Breeze emphasizes environmental causes of mental health problems and thus favors policies that support advocacy and community involvement by staff, whereas traditionalists place greater emphasis on personal and familial causes. Dr. Breeze gives priority to deprivation of personal rights (e.g., unfair treatment of mentally ill persons by the police) as well as to deprivation of material resources (e.g., blighted conditions in the neighborhood); traditionalists emphasize more traditional forms of mental illness. When participants disagree about the nature and im-

TABLE 1.1 Selected Forms of Deprivation

Material Resources Deprivation	Developmental Deprivation	Physical Deprivation	Interpersonal Deprivation	Deprivation of Opportunity	Deprivation of Personal Rights
inadequate income	various forms of mental illness	various forms of physical illness	marital conflict	lack of education	lack of basic civil rights (voting, free speech, due process)
inadequate food	developmental disabilities	addictions to alcohol and other toxic substances	destructive child-parent relations	lack of access to social services	lack of equal access to employment and promotions
inadequate housing	bereavement and other crises	malnutrition	loneliness	lack of access to medical services	lack of equal access to services
inadequate or blighted community	lack of challenging work	handicaps	lack of adequate recreation	lack of access to employment	commitment to mental or other institutions in absence of procedural safeguards
				lack of "survival skills" (e.g., knowledge of employment markets and job-related skills)	

portance of specific social problems, as in the case of Dr. Breeze and the traditionalists, they are also likely to differ about the policy strategy for addressing them.

Social workers often need specialized knowledge of specific social problems and of the policies that constitute the collective strategy. Specialized agencies provide services or resources that focus on one or more of these problems. Public welfare agencies provide income assistance to the poor, hospitals assist the ill, and community mental health centers help persons with mental health needs. Some agencies also provide services or resources to specific groups in the population that suffer from the kinds of deprivation listed in table 1.1. Child welfare agencies assist children with psychological, physical, and other kinds of deprivation, and other agencies provide services and resources to senior citizens. Only by developing expertise about specific social problems and related policies can social workers participate in reforming existing policies or initiating new ones. In chapters 10 through 13, policies, programs, and issues in the mental health, health, child and family, and economic security sectors are discussed.

A knotty problem of definitions deserves discussion here—namely, what kinds of social problems or deprivation belong under the rubric "social welfare policy"?[10] As one example, social workers often do not place educational deprivation in the domain of social welfare policy, since they tend not to be staff participants in many school districts. However, presence or absence of social workers in particular agencies is an uncertain basis for classifying specific social problems as inside or outside the discipline of social welfare policy. Perhaps more social workers should work within school systems. In contrast, medical policy is usually classified as social welfare policy, despite the fact that physicians and nurses predominate in the medical sector. Problems like environmental pollution are even more difficult to classify, since social workers are not employed in the agencies that address them, and they fall outside the set of traditional social welfare problems. If environmental pollution is a major cause of physical illness, however, no clear basis exists for

excluding it while including medical policy. (One can also imagine a social worker undertaking a community organization assignment to rally citizens to eliminate a source of environmental pollution.)

In short, no objective method exists for defining some social problems as internal and others as external to social welfare policy. This assertion does not imply, however, that social workers ought not to concentrate on or have knowledge of particular kinds of social problems and related policies, since social workers are usually employed in certain kinds of agencies. Chapters 10 through 13 discuss policies in child and family, economic security, medical, and mental health sectors in considerable detail because such policies are most germane to the professional work of most social workers. But the breadth of interests of social workers is acknowledged in the use of case examples drawn from housing, gerontology, substance abuse, juvenile court, and economic sectors.

ISSUES OF EQUALITY

Social problems, then, define the boundaries of social welfare policy. Participants propose or initiate policies because they believe conditions in the external world require social intervention, and they assess specific policies to see if they reduce the severity or incidence of those conditions.

Social problems are not distributed randomly in the population. Certain kinds of persons are more likely than others to experience certain kinds of discrimination. Women are more likely to receive low wages than men. Persons with severe mental illnesses are likely to have difficulty in finding work. Poverty-stricken persons are more likely than others to experience a host of mental, physical, and community problems.

Comparisons are often made to ascertain which kinds of persons suffer disproportionately from specific problems—the poor are contrasted with the nonpoor, women with men, racial minorities with Caucasians, homosexuals with heterosexuals, and the elderly with the nonelderly.[11] Such comparisons assume importance for several reasons. In many cases, relative standards are used to label specific conditions in the external world as social problems. In the case of income, for example, many poverty-stricken Americans are relatively affluent when compared to the poor in India. The American poor compare their economic condition, however, not to Indians but to other Americans. Wide disparities between groups, then, are often used as evidence that social intervention is needed to assist those experiencing relatively severe deprivation.[12]

Many commentators also perceive inequalities as social problems in their own right. In many cases, "problems cause problems"—witness the vicious circle that exists for many unemployed persons (see case example 1.2). As they become

---

CASE EXAMPLE 1.2

Sociologist Links Unemployment, Crime

Disputed Data to Be Used to Push Jobs Bill

By Bill Drummond, Times Staff Writer

WASHINGTON—When the House begins debate on the Humphrey-Hawkins full-employment bill this week, supporters of the controversial measure will be counting heavily on ammunition supplied by a little-known Johns Hopkins University sociologist named Harvey Brenner.

Using complex computer analysis techniques, Brenner has given advocates of vast government action to stimulate employment something they have always wanted—"scientific" evidence that joblessness contributes directly to many social problems, including crime, drug abuse, alcoholism, suicide and heart disease.

The Brenner research points up a trend: Congress and other branches of government have been increasingly tempted to use sophisticated statistical tools derived from the social sciences in their deliberations.

The question raised by the research is whether members of Congress will use the techniques and findings in ways that scientists and scholars consider sound.

Be that as it may, Brenner's controversial findings have been nothing less than startling.

In testimony late last year before a congressional subcommittee, Brenner suggested that a 1% increase in the unemployment rate in 1970 had raised crime rates by the following magnitudes:

- 40,056 narcotics violations of a total of 468,146 cases reported by the FBI that year.
- 8,646 burglary cases of a reported total of 385,785.
- 23,151 larceny cases of a total of 832,624.
- 5,123 embezzlement cases of a total of 85,033.
- 684 homicide victims of a total of 16,848.
- 3,340 state and federal prison admissions of a total of 67,304.

Although the originators of the Humphrey-Hawkins bill have hailed Brenner's work, the question of how valid the new research is remains unanswered.

Some social scientists express skepticism and believe that Brenner's work needs more scrutiny and testing before it is used as a basis for government policy.

Brenner's disclaimer that the research did not show a cause-and-effect link has been

unemployed, they experience stress that, in turn, can trigger mental and physical problems. Lack of resources makes it more difficult to obtain needed food, and lack of food can cause health problems. For some very small minority of the unemployed, income deficits lead to desperation that promotes criminal activity. The interlocking nature of social problems, then, is one important reason for examining systematic differences between groups in society; not to reduce unemployment among blacks is, some argue, tantamount to causing them to have many other problems as well.[13]

Inequalities are also perceived as requiring social intervention because they violate standards of fairness that derive from Judeo-Christian and other ethical codes. If there have to be social prob-

---

drowned out by praise from sponsors of the national jobs bill.

The late Sen. Hubert H. Humphrey called Brenner's work "a highly important, pioneering study" and described it as "new wisdom."

Rep. John Conyers Jr. (D-Mich), chairman of the subcommittee on crime of the House Judiciary Committee, said that Brenner's work was "something new that is coming into its own. . . . Law enforcement people and legislators have not seen this relationship. Brenner will bring it to their attention and they will have to acknowledge the facts." . . .

Brenner's findings were presented to the Joint Congressional Economic Committee, of which Humphrey was chairman, and published Oct. 26, 1976. In the study, Brenner compared unemployment rates from 1940 to 1974 and seven indicators of social stress: suicide, state mental hospital admissions, state prison admissions, homicide, deaths from cirrhosis of the liver, deaths from cardiovascular disease and the total number of deaths in the country.

What Brenner found was that when unemployment went up these stress indicators went up, after a time lag.

For example, he found that a 1% rise in unemployment resulted in a 4.3% rise in admission to state mental hospitals after five years.

Statistical research into the social costs of unemployment goes back to at least 1963. But for the first time, Brenner's study offered an actual body count of how many additional deaths, for example, would result from a given percentage rise in unemployment.

Brenner strongly suggested that, had the unemployment rate in 1970 remained unchanged, 51,570 persons who died would have lived. The 1.4% increase in 1970 joblessness, according to Brenner, induced additional deaths, which included 1,740 homicides, 1,540 suicides, 870 cirrhosis of the liver deaths and 26,440 cardiovascular deaths.

Joblessness means that many people lose group health benefits and do not obtain medical care as often, Brenner said in explaining the increased death rates. The added stress of losing a job causes a greater risk of a fatal heart seizure among persons with borderline heart problems, greater probability of suicide among those prone to suicide and a greater incidence of alcoholism among borderline alcoholics, according to the Brenner theory.

The inducement to crime as a result of joblessness was not as clearly developed by Brenner. He said that jobless workers became criminals to regain lost income.

Also, he said, unemployment causes a person to feel rejected and alienated from society, and such a person is more likely to engage in antisocial acts such as violence against others or theft of property.

The other explanation is the "idle hands" notion—that those without a useful occupation gravitate to crime. . . .

SOURCE: Copyright 1978, *Los Angeles Times*. Reprinted by permission.

lems, they should be distributed randomly throughout the population, so that specific groups, such as women and racial minorities, do not bear a disproportionate burden. To right the imbalances, according to this ethical perspective, Americans need to develop policies for distributing economic, medical, and other resources to such groups.[14]

OUTGROUPS

Groups whose members are particularly likely to experience various kinds of deprivation are termed outgroups in subsequent discussion because they often experience discrimination.[15] The "poor" or "lower classes" are *economic outgroups;* blacks, Hispanics, Native Americans, Puerto Ricans, and some Asian American groups are *racial* or *ethnic outgroups;* women, the elderly, and children are *sociological outgroups* that often occupy residual economic and social roles in society; and the mentally ill, homosexuals, lesbians, criminal offenders, and juvenile delinquents are *nonconformist outgroups.*

Further, Japanese Americans, Jews, and blue-collar Americans are often denied social services and programs because officials believe that they are members of *model outgroups,* i.e., groups that lack serious deprivation. As subsequent discussion makes clear, many policy issues arise when agencies, local units of government, and national officials respond to inequalities experienced by these various outgroups.

Economic Outgroups

Economic inequality can be measured by contrasting the resources of the highest and the lowest quintile (one-fifth) of the population. When compared with other industrial nations, the United States is characterized by wide economic disparities. A ten-to-one discrepancy exists between the average incomes of the highest and lowest quintiles in the United States, compared with seven-to-one and five-to-one ratios in Germany and Japan, respectively.[16]

Americans perpetuate economic inequality in

many ways. The tax system is often regressive, since loopholes, tax deductions, exemptions, and credits disproportionately benefit many affluent persons. Americans do not fund national health insurance and other massive programs common in many Western countries, so many poor Americans need to purchase services. Economic disparities are defended by many Americans on grounds that they stimulate economic productivity by providing the affluent with funds for business investment, funds that ultimately, it is argued, create jobs. Germany and some Scandinavian countries invest a larger portion of their national income in social programs, however, and still have higher rates of economic growth than the United States.[17]

The fact that large numbers of Americans "blame the victims" (illustration 1.1) for their economic problems is hardly conducive to the formulation of policies to redress economic inequality.[18] Many Americans believe that poverty is a

ILLUSTRATION 1.1

"WE'RE to blame for the riots?! . . . Why, I've never been in a ghetto in my life!"

Paul Conrad, © 1982, *Los Angeles Times.* Reprinted by permission.

reflection of laziness, immorality, or other personal faults, a contention disputed by those who cite economic and social causes.

Racial Minorities

The chronicity of poverty among black, Native American, and Spanish-speaking populations is particularly disturbing. If poverty were distributed randomly, it would still constitute a major social problem; its concentration over time among certain groups in the population adds to its severity. Racial minorities perceive themselves as members of groups systematically excluded from economic benefits and prosperity, a perception that increases feelings of alienation.[19] To the extent that others in the population perceive racial minorities as "generally poor," discrimination is perpetuated; these groups, they reason, are unable to "pull themselves up by the bootstraps" and so deserve their low economic status. With respect to the poor and racial minorities, Americans have entered a vicious circle of mutual suspicion. The implications of this vicious circle are discussed by the columnist Colman McCarthy in the context of the 1980 race riots in Miami, Florida (see guest editorial 1.1)

In the case of blacks, Native Americans, Puerto Ricans, and Hispanics, economic inequality is linked to the timing of historical migrations that can usefully be contrasted with those of European immigrants. Irish, Italian, and Eastern European immigrants came to the United States in massive numbers in the nineteenth and early twentieth centuries and experienced appalling poverty in comparison to the rest of the nation. Many, however, arrived when the American economic order was relatively simple. Some were able to develop small businesses, but most became unskilled or semiskilled workers in factories. By incremental degrees their descendants acquired the education, apprenticeships, and other prerequisites for further mobility. A major problem for blacks, Native Americans, and Hispanics, by contrast, was that they were excluded from early access to the industrial order because most lived in agricultural areas in the South, Southwest, and West. When they finally moved to cities in the

1940s and 1950s, key positions in the developed industrial order had already been taken by descendants of European immigrants. Whites controlled building trades and other skilled unions and were reluctant to allow minorities into apprenticeship programs.[20]

Few social and political supports existed for these agricultural immigrants. European immigrants benefited from political machines that distributed jobs to "their own," but these were relics of the past in most cities by the 1950s. Although often living in ethnic communities, European immigrants were not consigned to inner-city neighborhoods ringed by more affluent neighborhoods that contained the major sources of employment. The problems of racial minorities were also exacerbated by physiological differences from the Caucasian population. Children of white ethnic minorities could escape discrimination by merging with the broader population, a remedy hardly possible for blacks and other racial minorities.

Finally, major deficits in educational achievement among nonwhite populations inhibited—and continued to inhibit—their upward mobility, since education and credentials are required for advancement. Teachers are more adept at educating children from middle- and upper-income families. Many children in low-income and segregated areas lack models of economic or educational success, and their parents are ill prepared to support, tutor, and otherwise shepherd their children through the educational system, much less finance higher education. Their school systems also often lack the resources of suburban districts.

Sociological Outgroups

Certain groups, notably women and the elderly, are widely perceived as occupying specialized roles that preempt them from entering the economic and social mainstream. Women have traditionally assumed primary responsibility for child rearing and homemaking and did not enter the labor force in massive numbers until the Second World War. Despite increasing participation in employment, they continue to experience economic inequality, in many cases earning less than

GUEST EDITORIAL 1.1

In Sunny Miami, the Tip of the Iceberg

The Poor Send a Message: One Way or Another, the Rich Are Going to Pay

By Colman McCarthy

One of the questions being asked about the killing, burning and looting in Miami last weekend is: Will it spread? Are the skies of other cities to be blackened by their own explosions of violence and lawlessness?

In the narrow sense, the answer is no, what happened in Miami won't spread. With a special set of incendiary circumstances, this was a one-city, one-time blowup.

The trouble with this explanation is that explosions are only noticed when they go off in one public outburst of inner-city chaos that can be handily captured on news film or described in headlines as "race riots." That shouldn't be the reaction, because in countless U.S. cities the conditions of explosiveness are present even if an actual explosion isn't.

At the core of these conditions is the feeling among the poor and near-poor that injustice has been institutionalized. In Miami, if it had been only a few cases of police brutality that blacks had to think about, the tensions might have been absorbed. They could have been accepted as temporary harassments. But too many permanent harassments were already pressing in, the same kind that the poor feel everywhere in America: high unemployment rates, poor housing, the searing effects of inflation.

The eruptions that cause a city like Miami to be paralyzed are much like the less visible eruptions that occur within individual lives and families of the poor when the addition of one more burden becomes too much and something snaps. Psychiatrists and social workers have been reporting for some time that when families are hit with unemployment, the rates of child abuse, divorce, alcoholism and depression increase. This is even presuming that individuals can make it into adulthood with enough economic security to begin a family.

In a new book, "Mental Health and the

half the wages of men with corresponding responsibilities (see guest editorial 1.2). Women who raise children suffer career penalties because their careers are interrupted for substantial periods. Then, too, many women cannot seek challenging positions if child rearing cannot be shared. Patterns of discrimination against hiring and promoting women are also widespread. As with minorities, many work in unskilled or semi-skilled positions that offer little hope of advancement. Women have been most successful in obtaining access to specialized careers in nursing, teaching in elementary and secondary education,

and social work, but, even in these female-dominated professions, they are often denied administrative posts.[21]

Elderly persons are often consigned to residual roles in society. Many Americans assume the elderly have sufficient resources to finance retirement years, but inflation has seriously eroded fixed pensions and other benefits. While Medicare and some housing programs assist elderly persons, most find government programs inadequate to cover more than a share of total costs. Once they have exhausted short-term Medicare benefits, for example, many elderly persons must

Economy," Robert L. Kahn of the University of Michigan writes that "the pathogenic effects of economic changes are characteristically underestimated . . . More people are affected than are revealed by counts of unemployment. Repeated cycles of job-getting and job-loss are likely to be cumulatively damaging."

This damage seldom shows up in the way that the total costs of a ghetto explosion can be calculated. The fire chief of Miami said that financially the burnings may go into "the billions of dollars." Yet, as Richard Barnet argues in "The Lean Years: Politics in the Age of Scarcity," the "poor extract public money in all sorts of hidden ways . . . Premature babies born to poorly nourished mothers extract from society far more money than decent education, prenatal care or job opportunities would have cost, for it is easy to spend more than $100,000 in the weeks of elaborate care needed to keep a small baby alive."

The message that the poor, not only in Miami, are sending is that one way or another the affluent are going to pay for the privileges of enjoying an economic system that allows power and resources to be excessively accumulated by one part of the population, while another part receives little.

Although America is well short of pushing its poor into the sea as boat people, socially acceptable ways of trying to drown them have been found. In Manchester, Conn., voters recently refused to take $1 million in HUD money because it would have committed the town to a housing program for the poor. This, and other cases like it, prompted President Carter to say that "there is a tone in this nation that is not as committed to civil rights, to human rights, as I would like to see." He neglected to say that his own commitment has been without spine.

The one ally that the poor once counted on, big government, is now in retreat. Few policymakers have the courage now to raise their voices on behalf of the unemployed or unfed. They mistakenly fear being branded as romantics who don't know that the poor had their hour in the '60s and that the country is now in tougher times.

Without doubt, an effort will be made to explain away the Miami outbreak as a fluke occurrence. In that particular city, the body politic may indeed have suffered a random heart attack. But everywhere else, in the budget cuts for social services and programs, the sickness is cancer.

SOURCE: Reprinted by permission of author; this article first appeared in the *Los Angeles Times*.

---

deplete personal assets before they can qualify for Medicaid. Problems of the frail elderly are particularly vexing; these are persons who could often remain independent and avoid nursing homes if they were given a range of homemaker, community housing, and other supports.[22]

Nonconformist Outgroups

Nonconformist outgroups include persons widely perceived to have different life-style preferences (e.g., homosexuals and lesbians), to have violated social norms (e.g., criminal offenders and juvenile

delinquents), and to be experiencing social problems regarded as taboo (e.g., mental health problems). In each case, persons in these groups are often perceived to be outside prevailing norms. Members of nonconformist outgroups experience many of the difficulties of other outgroups, notably discrimination in housing, employment, and promotions. In some cases, they also experience violation of basic civil rights.[23] State and federal laws and court rulings have belatedly given the mentally ill some protections against ill-advised involuntary commitments to mental hospitals. In the case of homosexuals, strong grass-

A Sorry Record on Women's Rights

Reagan Goes Back on His Campaign Promise in a Big Way

By Patricia Schroeder

Ronald Reagan was the only major presidential candidate in the last two elections to oppose the Equal Rights Amendment. While insisting that he supported equal rights for women ("little 'e' " and "little 'r' "), he said that the ERA was not needed because he would push for legislation to advance these rights.

To back up that promise, he issued a "white paper," which stated that he "supports the enforcement of all equal-opportunity laws, and urges the elimination of discrimination against women . . . (and) therefore pledges vigorous enforcement of laws to assure equal treatment in job recruitment, hiring, promotion, pay, credit, mortgage access and housing."

But, in his nine months in office, the President not only has failed to make good on his campaign promise, he also has moved in precisely the opposite direction. The only exception has been his appointment of Sandra D. O'Connor to the U.S. Supreme Court, in fulfillment of another campaign pledge. It is clear that Reagan is actively opposed to programs designed to further or protect women's rights, and that his Administration has all but declared war on women. Here is what the Reagan record shows:

Economics: Earlier this year, the President sought the elimination of the $122 minimum benefit for recipients of Social Security, a proposal that would have had a disproportionate effect on women. All but 700,000 of the persons who receive minimum benefits are women. The proposal was withdrawn after a storm of protest.

The economic package that Reagan pushed through Congress last summer reduced or eliminated benefits for nearly three-quarters of a million recipients of Aid to Families with Dependent Children and prohibited AFDC recipients from owning more than $1,000 worth of assets, half the amount that used to be allowed. Work incentives have been eliminated; consequently, poor women will be forced to choose between keeping their jobs and losing needed additional income or quitting to go on welfare and thereby increase their income. (Eighty percent of all AFDC recipients live in households headed by women.)

Sex discrimination: The Justice Department has abandoned the use of any numerical or statistical formulas in connection with affirmative action, thereby rendering equal-employment goals (for minorities as well as women) meaningless. The Labor Department has proposed reducing by 75% the number of companies that must make written reports and outline recruitment procedures; as a result,

roots movements in a number of jurisdictions have sought to deny them positions as teachers. Community prejudice often takes the form of opposition to halfway houses or other community-based residential facilities for released criminal offenders, the developmentally disabled, and the mentally ill.

Some nonconformist outgroups, of course, do

not want to adopt prevailing norms and may be subjected to unwarranted pressure to make them conform. Homosexuals have only recently been able to persuade many professionals to accept their sexual orientation as a legitimate life-style preference.[24] Some persons are labelled as mentally ill when they are simply "eccentric." For this reason, laws in most states now stipulate that per-

most federal contractors will have less incentive to hire and promote women.

In a move apparently aimed at weakening the Labor Department's Women's Bureau, the primary office charged with promoting equal opportunity for women in the job market, its staff was reduced 28%. By contrast, across-the-board staff reductions in the department amounted to only 5.5%. Similarly, Reagan has left vacant three of the five seats on the Equal Employment Opportunity Commission, the chief federal enforcer of Title 7 of the Civil Rights Act of 1964, which prohibits discrimination in employment. The commission thus lacks a quorum and is limited in the action it can take. At the same time, the Justice Department is seriously considering abolishing class-action discrimination suits.

Other Reagan Administration proposals would affect Title 9 of the Education Amendments Act of 1972, which bans sex discrimination in schools that receive federal aid. The Education Department has proposed narrowing the scope of Title 9 to specific programs receiving direct federal aid; these account for only 4% of the $13 billion in federal funds spent on schools. Vice President George Bush announced in August that his Task Force on Regulatory Relief has targeted for review regulations that protect women from sexual harassment and discrimination in college athletics.

Appointments: Here the President's record is nothing short of dismal. Only 44 of the 398 top-level appointments have gone to women. And the appointments have reflected Reagan's attitudes toward women. For example, Anne M. Gorsuch, head of the Environmental Protection Agency, is well-known to women's groups for her efforts while serving in the Colorado Legislature to dismantle the state Commission on Women. For jobs with particular significance for women, the President named Rex Lee, a leading opponent of the ERA, as solicitor general and Dr. C. Everett Koop, an active opponent of abortion, as surgeon general. Another appointee, Donald J. Devine, director of the Office of Personnel Management, eliminated abortion coverage from all federal employee health-insurance plans. (The decision was struck down by a U.S. district court but is being appealed; meanwhile, Devine has agreed to permit coverage for abortions in a small percentage of the plans.)

The President has yet to appoint a single woman to the federal district or circuit bench or to fill the White House post that oversees the intergovernmental Task Force on Women.

One may quibble with some of these examples. Not every program, just because it seems beneficial to women, is worth maintaining. We need to scrutinize all federal spending as we try to balance the budget.

But there's no question that President Reagan, instead of fulfilling his campaign promise, is moving to weaken, cut back or abolish just about every federal program, law or office designed to advance women.

Patricia Schroeder (D-Colo.) is co-chairwoman of the Congresswomen's Caucus. SOURCE: Reprinted by permission of author; this article first appeared in the *Los Angeles Times*.

sons can be committed to state mental institutions only when they pose a clear danger to themselves or others.

Model Outgroups

Some groups have difficulty in obtaining recognition for serious social problems in their midst because they are widely perceived as problem-free, model outgroups. Asian Americans, Jews, and blue-collar Americans encounter widespread apathy from legislators and the general public when seeking resources for members of their groups who experience income, mental, physical, and housing deprivation.

Certainly, Japanese Americans and Jews have made remarkable economic gains despite profound discrimination. Japanese Americans were consigned to low-income and servile status in the decades following their initial settlements in the late nineteenth century. They were not allowed to vote, were denied property rights, encountered housing discrimination, were placed under immigration bans after restrictive legislation in the wake of the First World War, and were incarcerated in concentration camps during the Second World War. Economic gains after the Second World War were remarkable. A number of factors allowed Japanese Americans to achieve economic and occupational gains even when encountering adversity: the group placed heavy emphasis upon education and mobility, made extensive use of mutual aid, and developed specialized businesses in the agricultural sector.

Many Asian Americans, however, experience serious forms of deprivation. Marked intergenerational tension exists as older and more traditional members find it difficult to communicate with the Americanized younger generation. Waves of Vietnamese, Korean, Filipino, and Thai immigrants have settled on the West Coast and elsewhere during the last decade, uprooted persons who often lack educational, job, and language skills. Staff members of social service agencies often cannot communicate with these immigrants because they lack knowledge of their language and culture. Ominous signs of racial prejudice against Asian Americans exist, particularly as whites and other ethnic groups perceive them as competing for jobs.[25]

Initial and massive immigration of Jews to the United States occurred between 1880 and 1920. Many were impoverished and subject to widespread discrimination. Antisemitism took the form of housing, job, and social discrimination. (Jews are still underrepresented in the managerial ranks of many corporations and encounter housing and social discrimination.) Like Japanese Americans, many succeeded by mobilizing self-help projects, including an array of social and medical agencies. Generations of Jews supplemented public school education with tutoring and after-school educational projects. As with Japanese Americans, educational achievement was

used to obtain access to medical, legal, and other professions. Jewish entrepreneurs developed local businesses in textile, shoe, and other enterprises.

Serious social problems exist in the Jewish community. As one example, many of the Jewish elderly are poor and encounter inadequate housing and community services. Although Jewish families have traditionally been a source of stability, divorce rates are escalating. Jews who are successful in professional and other fields often experience job-related stress that can precipitate mental distress.[26]

Blue-collar Americans are another model outgroup. Social welfare programs constructed during and after the Great Depression were largely designed for the poor to the exclusion of persons near but not below poverty standards. As an example, many Americans from blue-collar ranks lack both medical insurance and eligibility for major public medical programs like Medicaid. Lacking sufficient educational credentials, they encounter job-related discrimination not dissimilar to some racial minorities. Those who work in marginal or vulnerable industries are subject to layoffs during recessions. The tedium of assembly-line positions and the lack of opportunity for advancement can precipitate use of drugs and alcohol as well as mental illness. In addition, blue-collar workers experience on-the-job chemical and other health hazards.[27]

SOCIAL EQUALITY AND POLICY CHOICES

Participants in social welfare policy, then, analyze and seek remedies for social problems in the broader population. They also ponder whether and how to assist specific groups so that their members do not continue to bear a disproportionate share of those problems. Many argue that single programs and policies will not suffice. Combinations of income, job, housing, transportation, medical, and social service programs are needed if the social condition of these various outgroups is to improve. As an example, the income of blacks and women has increased in the past several decades, but gains relative to whites and men have been far less noteworthy.

A difficult problem, then, is how to help specific groups make absolute gains as well as gains relative to society as a whole. It is hardly comforting to tell a black person that he earns double the wages of his father but less than half the wages of the average white worker. Some argue that gains for outgroups will increasingly need to occur by diverting resources from members of the dominant society through major changes in the tax system, affirmative action programs, and other policies. These policies are certain to be resisted, however, by those who believe that they might lose resources or jobs to outgroup members.[28]

Controversy associated with social equality also arises in social agencies. To be candid, staff members in some agencies have little choice as to whom they serve, since public laws that shape services allow little discretion. Many agencies, however, have considerable discretion, as illustrated by case example 1.1. Dr. Breeze favors redistribution of services to ethnic and racial minorities, in contrast to the traditionalists, who want to give priority to white and middle-class clients.

SEVEN CORE POLICY ISSUES

At least seven policy issues recur during social welfare policy deliberations, issues so common that they can aptly be called "core" policy issues: Social workers and others have to decide (1) whether a specific condition in the external world constitutes a social problem, (2) how large or important is a specific social problem, (3) which intervention strategy should be chosen, (4) which consumers should receive program benefits or services, (5) how programs should be designed and financed, (6) who should participate in program decisions, and (7) how the relative success of policies and programs should be gauged.[29] These core policy issues are frequently encountered in agency, community, and legislative settings, where their sheer number often contributes to the controversial nature of social welfare policy.

1. Social workers often seek to convince others that specific external conditions merit social intervention, sometimes in the face of opposition by those who believe that no or little intervention is warranted (*core issue 1*). In some cases, external conditions are not deemed social problems until powerful groups, participants, or interests become convinced they merit attention. Thus, mass unemployment among minority teenagers has not attracted widespread attention because it is a problem distant from more affluent families. In case example 1.1, many differences exist between Dr. Breeze and traditionalists regarding core issue 1. As an example, resurgent and traditionalist groups attach differing degrees of importance to the deprivation of minority rights—Dr. Breeze is much more concerned about police brutality than the traditionalists.

2. Decisions must also be made about the relative importance of specific problems (*core issue 2*). Two participants may agree that child abuse, drug abuse, and incidence of suicide are all important problems but may differ regarding which should receive priority in agency services. Many claimants for scarce funds try to convince others that their problem or issue merits priority. In case example 1.1, members of specific minority groups believe that problems of low-income consumers should receive high priority in services of the San Marcos agency, but the traditionalists emphasize the social needs of more affluent clients.

3. Participants often disagree as well about preferred intervention strategies and the nature of benefits to be given to consumers in social programs (*core issue 3*). In the mental health sector, for example, some persons favor intrapsychic interventions (the traditionalists in case example 1.1), whereas others favor influencing environmental factors (the allies of Dr. Breeze). Controversy is also common when agency staff members consider whether available program resources should be distributed to a relatively large number of consumers in an extensive strategy or concentrated on relatively few in an intensive strategy. Controversy about intervention strategies is particularly likely when agency staff members have radically different perceptions of the causes of social and economic deprivation.

4. Policy choices are also required regarding which consumers receive priority in services and programs (*core issue 4*), particularly when the scarcity of resources requires difficult choices. If eligibility is relatively selective (as when only the

poor are eligible), then others are excluded, and programs lack a broad base of political support because relatively few persons have a personal stake in them. However, broad or universal eligibility diminishes resources that could be concentrated on those most in need of or those who could not otherwise purchase assistance.

Numerous issues arise when deciding how to implement services (*core issue 5*). One source of contention in case example 1.1, for example, is disagreement about proper roles of community aides as compared with professionals. Unlike the traditionalists, Dr. Breeze favors extensive use of such aides. Policy participants often disagree about many program financial and administrative issues, as illustrated by controversy during the past decade about the roles of federal, state, and local agencies in funding and administration of social welfare programs.

Since values influence policy choices, decisions about who participates are crucial (*core issue 6*). In case example 1.1, Dr. Breeze favors establishing consumer advisory boards to inject consumer perspectives into agency decision making. Regulations that shape access by the public to legislative and governmental proceedings and limit campaign contributions and lobbying of powerful interests also enhance policy roles of citizens.

Finally, methods used to evaluate social services and programs can occasion controversy (*core issue 7*). Absence of any evaluative mechanisms gives program providers carte blanche. Overly simplistic or misguided evaluation strategies can also foster ill-advised decisions. For example, it is not clear whether the "sensational suicide" in case example 1.1 stems from the policies or programs of Dr. Breeze, yet some participants use this event to evaluate those programs.

CHARACTERISTICS OF SOCIAL WELFARE POLICY

Our discussion to this point has established parameters, or boundaries, for social welfare policy. It is equally important to analyze characteristics of the process of social welfare policy formulation, since policies emerge in the course of deliberative and decision-making processes in agency, community, and legislative settings. Examination of the characteristics of policy formulation can also serve as an introduction to succeeding chapters, since each of them emphasizes a specific facet of the policymaking process.

Multiple Sources of Controversy

The likelihood of disagreement about preferred policy options increases as cultural, political, economic, and situational factors lead participants to divergent perspectives. Thus, controversy in social welfare policy is likely when participants possess divergent values or ideologies, when they utilize conflicting technical studies, or when they believe they have divergent political and economic interests.

A distinction is commonly made between core and instrumental values.[30] Both describe preferred social and institutional arrangements. Core values describe "the good society," whereas instrumental values describe preferred governmental, administrative, and financing approaches for reaching policy objectives. Core values involve beliefs regarding social equality and the role of government in social and economic affairs. Values about social equality, for example, range from survival-of-the-fittest to egalitarian perspectives. At one extreme, some believe that society has virtually no responsibility to its citizens other than preserving law and order, providing for the common defense, and serving custodial functions. At the other extreme, socialists believe that government should drastically reduce economic and social inequalities by fashioning far-reaching social and economic initiatives that redistribute resources from the haves to the have-nots. A variety of positions exists between these two polar extremes, including positions of persons who believe that society should enhance equality of opportunity by providing job training and social services. In case example 1.1, Dr. Breeze places more emphasis than traditionalists upon redistributing services to low-income citizens, a divergence in core values that precipitated controversy in the agency.

In similar fashion, disagreements about the proper role of government promote social welfare policy controversy. At one extreme, a restrictive notion of government is reflected in the writings of conservative economist Milton Friedman, who places ultimate value on preserving liberty for individual citizens.[31] Friedman argues that liberty increases as citizens pay relatively few taxes, are not required to participate in social programs, and are free to choose where they receive services. By contrast, Richard Titmuss, the late English social welfare theorist, valued social equality.[32] If given unrestricted liberty, Titmuss maintained, some individuals and groups in society emerge with more resources and power than others, whether because they inherit fortunes from their parents, are more lucky than others, or jealously guard their prerogatives against others. Correspondingly, Titmuss believed that government should assume major regulatory and redistributive roles.

Controversy in social welfare policy in the current era is frequently associated with divergent values about the proper role of government, as reflected by disagreements between conservative politicians such as President Ronald Reagan and more liberal politicians who argue that government should expand rather than contract its regulatory and redistributionary roles.

Divergent instrumental values also prompt controversy, as illustrated by comparisons of the perspectives of President Ronald Reagan on the one hand and those of Presidents Lyndon Johnson and John Kennedy on the other. The latter two presidents emphasized federal roles in social welfare policy in which the federal government assumes the major burden of financing and administering social welfare programs. President Reagan, by contrast, extolled localism as the "vision of the Founding Fathers" and feared that federal programs are not as responsive to local needs as programs administered by state or local governments. In similar fashion, President Reagan favored use of the private market in social welfare; i.e., provision of subsidies to consumers who then purchase services. Presidents Johnson and Kennedy placed more emphasis upon direct public provision of services.

These differences about how best to administer

or implement social welfare policies and programs stimulate controversy because, like preferences about "the good society," they rest upon values that lead participants to believe their opponents are misguided. In case example 1.1, Dr. Breeze differs with traditionalists regarding the relative merits of citizen advisory boards and use of paraprofessionals, differences that in turn can be partly attributed to divergent instrumental values of participants in the agency.

The influence of divergent political and economic interests on policy choices is also illustrated by case example 1.1. Some traditionalists probably opposed Dr. Breeze because they feared loss of personal power in the agency, while resurgents feared that his demise could jeopardize their roles within the agency. At the national level, controversy between Democrats and Republicans over many policy issues stems in considerable measure from divergent political interests. Many Republicans represent relatively conservative suburban and agricultural constituencies that do not favor major expansion of social welfare programs. By contrast, many Democrats represent low-income and urban constituents that are more likely to urge maintenance or expansion of social programs.

Scarcity of resources frequently contributes to controversy as well. Resources available for social welfare programs are always limited and only some claimants can find their needs satisfied. In many cases, resources for one program or policy option must be taken from those favored by other persons, a fact likely to promote controversy. Even in discussions of specific programs, controversy can arise when persons disagree about how best or most wisely to use scarce resources. In case example 1.1, traditionalists believe that the programs initiated by Dr. Breeze drew resources from programs that existed prior to his selection as director.

Controversy can also stem from use of divergent technical studies and evidence. In case example 1.1, for example, Dr. Breeze probably believes that the kinds of programs that are favored by traditionalists are not effective in addressing mental health problems of many persons. His advocacy of crisis or short-term services may stem from analysis of research that suggests these approaches are more effective than long-term therapy. Some traditionalists may draw upon different research or believe that studies that suggest that long-term therapy is ineffective are flawed (i.e., they utilize inaccurate measures or poor methodology). Although useful, quantitative studies have not rendered social welfare policy an uncontroversial discipline.

Power Realities Shape Outcomes

Certain participants and groups in policy settings are relatively advantaged because they possess disproportionate power and economic resources. Those who control strategic committees, boards, and other decision-making entities are often able to assume the initiative in deciding which issues receive priority. By shaping the rules of debate and voting, they can often determine outcomes.[33] (Power realities are discussed in more detail in chapters 2 and 6.)

Multiple and Intersecting Arenas

Social welfare policy is not, as some suppose, constructed only in legislative settings; it is also fashioned in government, funding, regional planning, agency, and community arenas.[34] (Various policy-making arenas are depicted in illustration 1.2).

Many policies are devised in congressional or other *legislative arenas,* as illustrated by such social programs as Medicaid, food stamps, federally funded community mental health centers, and countless others. The courts (*legal arenas*) have established procedural limits on delivery of social services, as illustrated by safeguards for mental patients who are admitted involuntarily to mental institutions. Private *nonprofit funding arenas,* most notably the network of United Way, federated Jewish, and other fund-raising drives, provide resources and policy guidelines to nonprofit agencies.

Professional associations such as the National Association of Social Workers, the American So-

ILLUSTRATION 1.2

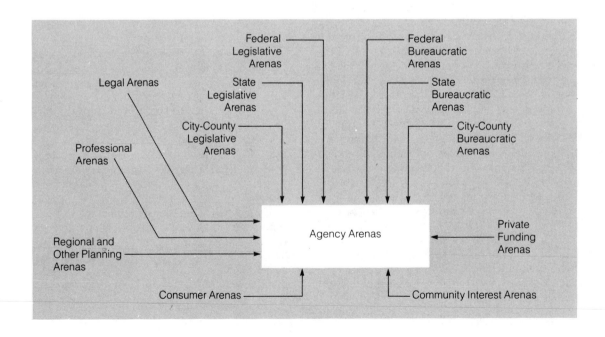

ciety of Public Administrators, and the Child Welfare Association of America (*professional arenas*) establish professional standards, accredit agencies, and issue ethical standards. *Agency network arenas* include regional planning bodies, consortia of agencies, and high-level government officials who provide policy guidelines to agencies; examples include county mental health associations, regional centers for the developmentally disabled, health system agencies (HSAs) and federal officials charged with overseeing the Head Start program. Policy also evolves from *private funding arenas* such as insurance companies. Private insurance companies such as Blue Cross are major funders for mental health and health services.

Policies are also developed in arenas external to agencies, courts, and legislatures. Interest groups assume major importance in legislative proceedings (*community interest arenas*). Groups like the American Medical Association and the American Hospital Association, for example, wield enormous influence in shaping medical policies—and often oppose reforms like national health insurance. Citizen groups and civil rights groups (*consumer arenas*) seek new, reformed, or expanded social programs. Political parties develop policy positions through caucuses and platforms and during campaigns.

Agency arenas must also be considered.[35] For public agencies, laws provide general policies, as in the case of federal legislation establishing Food Stamp, community mental health, and Medicaid programs. These laws are supplemented by regulations and rules that are established by government officials and provide the basis for agency manuals that guide decisions made by direct service and administrative staff. These rules are crucial because they address key policy issues often neglected or ill defined in legislation. Even in the case of public agencies, though, staff sometimes has some discretion in shaping services. For example, federal legislation requires federally funded community mental health centers to provide community services for preventing the incidence of mental illness, but many have not provided such services. Discrepancies between official policy and implemented policy may exist for

many reasons, as discussed in detail in chapter 7.

Nonprofit agencies are not created by public officials, though they must conform to state and federal laws. They have governing boards of directors that establish service priorities and other policies. Both direct service and administrative staff in nonprofit agencies usually possess more discretion in their activities than their counterparts in public agencies because they are not as limited by public laws and regulations. Here, too, discrepancies can exist between official agency policy and implemented policy.

In many cases, social workers seek policy changes in specific arenas, as in efforts to change the service procedures of an agency, amend a federal statute, or modify administrative guidelines of a public agency. Many issues, however, require scrutiny of a web of related policies that derive from many policy arenas. For example, those concerned with discrimination against women in employment can hardly hope to correct this problem by securing modifications of policy in a single agency or arena but must simultaneously seek changes in federal policies, new court rulings, and modification of policies in specific organizational settings.

Processes and Products

Social welfare policy is fashioned in the course of interactions between persons in agency, community, and legislative arenas. These *policy processes* are preludes to final outcomes when legislation, proposals, or recommendations are finally approved—or defeated. Clearly, effective policy practitioners are well versed in policy processes and develop skills that enable them to utilize these processes to secure their policy preferences.

By the same token, social welfare policy involves *policy products*, i.e., formal policies that are approved by decision makers and positions that are developed by policy practitioners. A social worker who develops a policy recommendation has constructed a policy product that may be presented to deliberative bodies (e.g., staff meetings) or to decision makers (e.g., executives). Were the position to be approved, the resulting official policy would represent a policy product as well.

Policy processes and products are both discussed in this book. The practice of social welfare policy is discussed in most chapters, with extended discussion in chapters 3 through 8, where various phases of the policymaking process are analyzed. Chapter 9 discusses policy products and examines the content and varieties of policy positions. Chapters 10 through 13 deal with legislative and administrative policies in mental health, health, economic security, and child and family sectors.

ROLES IN POLICY PRACTICE

Social welfare policy is not exclusively a philosophical, conceptual, or analytical discipline. In policy, as in administration, community organization, and direct service, social workers need to assume various practice-related roles in agency, community, and legislative arenas.[36]

Analytical roles are required because a major portion of social welfare policymaking is devoted to identifying possible policy options and selecting those that are preferred. In recent decades, analytical skills have received justified attention that has led to the development of quantitative approaches for comparing policy options and facilitating choices. (Policy analysis is discussed in chapters 4 and 5.)

At virtually every point in the formulation of social welfare policy, social workers assume *political* roles. Some policy options are not even considered because participants readily perceive that they are not politically feasible. During the implementation of policy, social workers emphasize some policies rather than others because highly placed and influential staff members favor them. No model of policy formulation is adequate that does not acknowledge the role of political factors at many points during the policymaking process. (Political factors are discussed in chapters 2 and 6).

Administrative and *organizational* roles are required because policies are ultimately successful only as the organizational staff implements them.

The nation has witnessed countless policy initiatives that were christened with high hopes but came to naught because of the realities of implementation. Skills are required in identifying factors that impede implementation of policies, including turf rivalries within and between organizations, absence of adequate planning, lack of resources, and lack of technical skills. (Implementation issues are discussed in chapter 7.)

Research and *program evaluation* roles are used at numerous points in the policymaking process. Data is often obtained about the prevalence of specific social problems. Social science and related research is used both in constructing and in assessing intervention strategies. (Policy-related research is discussed in chapters 3 and 8.)

Social workers, then, must assume multiple roles if they are to make effective contributions to social welfare policy. (A list of selected roles is presented in table 1.2.) Various roles are illustrated in case example 1.1 presented at the start of this chapter. Dr. Breeze identifies a series of community needs that are not addressed by the old agency. He assumes the role of change agent to persuade others to modify existing services. As program designer and implementer, he constructs operating programs that translate service objectives into operational reality, and then he addresses morale, logistical, resource, and other barriers that impede implementation. As evaluator, he evaluates programs and makes needed changes. (It is difficult to determine from case example 1.1 whether Dr. Breeze could have achieved more success and averted some opposition had he possessed more skill in designing and implementing programs.)

Direct service social workers also participate in the policymaking process by assuming the various roles described in table 1.2. A line staff member is well situated to detect unmet needs, offer contributions when new programs are devised, detect deficiences in operating programs, and contribute information useful to program evaluation. In some situations, direct service staff members can assume change agent roles by participating in reform projects within agencies or in the broader community. Those who do not participate in policy cast a vote for the status quo

TABLE 1.2   Selected Social Work Policy Roles

as discoverers of unmet needs	proposing new programs
	proposing program expansion
as program designers	devising content of social interventions
	devising organizational structures to be used in service delivery
as implementers	devising policies when existing ones are insufficient
	troubleshooting programs to remedy deficiencies
	weighing relative importance of numerous and often conflicting policies
as evaluators	assessing adequacy of existing policies
	injecting direct service knowledge into assessment deliberations
as change agents	assuming reformer roles when existing policies are misdirected
	increasing monitoring of standards established for services and institutions
	undertaking advocacy for relatively powerless groups

even when existing policies and programs are misdirected.

The practice of policy within agencies is illustrated by policy case 1.1, in which a social work executive contemplates various policy proposals to increase agency responsiveness to the Hispanic population in the surrounding community. The executive identifies specific policy changes that she believes should be considered in the agency but has not yet initiated the change process. Upon further reflection, she may expand the number of policy changes that she wishes to initiate or may focus on one or more of them to enhance the likelihood of obtaining immediate successes.

As "discoverer of unmet needs," the executive uses research to measure the extent to which the agency has met the needs of the local Hispanic population. The disparity between the number

132,628

of Hispanics in the community and the proportion of Hispanics comprising the clientele of the agency suggests that policy reforms are needed if the agency is to be responsive to the Spanish-speaking population.

Even prior to introducing the reforms in agency policy, the executive as change agent is anticipating possible sources of opposition to the proposals. She decides to encourage staff participation in the recruitment and hiring of the new Spanish-speaking member of the staff, for example, to forestall staff opposition. In many cases, of course, the change agent role is a crucial one in social welfare policy practice, since policy ideas come to naught if they are not approved by decision makers in a specific setting. The social worker is already anticipating possible sources of opposition to the policy proposals and devising stra-

Increasing the Responsiveness of an Agency to the Hispanic Population

I am a social worker in an agency located in an area with a considerable Hispanic population. Yet the agency is not very responsive to this population; indeed, one-third of the persons residing in the community surrounding this mental health agency are Hispanic, yet only 10 percent of the clientele of the agency are from this ethnic group. Not one Spanish-speaking person is on the agency's board of directors, nor is there a full-time Hispanic professional on the agency's staff.

Four individuals at the agency are Hispanic and speak Spanish: the receptionist, two social work interns, and the chief psychiatric social worker (CPSW). But the social work students are only at the agency two days a week for eight months, and the CPSW is strictly an administrator and, as such, has no involvement with clients. Further, neither of the two Chicano students work in the evenings, when most Hispanic adults utilize the agency.

My main goal, then, is to improve and expand our services to the Chicano population and to involve clients (including parents and their children) in a feedback evaluatory process in an attempt to provide a more responsive and relevant community agency.

- *Proposal 1:* To immediately hire one full-time Hispanic (Spanish-speaking) therapist, who will work in the evenings with adult Spanish-speaking clients (parents)

- *Proposal 2:* To add one Hispanic citizen to the board of directors

- *Proposal 3:* To hang a visible sign in Spanish on our agency building stating, "We speak Spanish"

- *Proposal 4:* To increase client input by conducting client surveys regarding the services provided by the agency

Our board should represent the entire community, including various income levels and various ethnic groups. Ideally, the board should interpret the community's needs and values to the agency and also communicate to the community the purpose and goals of the agency, which is essentially why a pluralistic approach to board membership is so important. If the board is to interpret community needs and values to the agency, we most certainly need to have our Hispanic constituents represented.

Moreover, if we assume that our agency provides a public service and view our clientele as consumers of that service, then they should have a voice in helping us to make our services and policies more relevant and beneficial to their needs. Therefore, I propose that we conduct client surveys in which some clients fill out a service evaluation form after contact with the agency has been concluded. In this manner, we will be obtaining much-needed consumer input in helping to make our agency more responsive and relevant to the persons we serve.

If we add a full-time Spanish-speaking therapist to our staff, our staff will gain knowledge about Hispanic culture and values, knowledge that is specifically related to the treatment of the Spanish-speaking population. A full-time Hispanic therapist, with whom we can consult on an informal basis, may provide us and our agency with an enriching educational experience.

As I have previously noted, a Hispanic therapist will be able to hold Spanish-speaking adult groups in the evenings, which will enable both husband and wife to come to therapy rather than only the wife. Until now, most of our male Hispanic clients have been unavailable for morning groups because of their jobs.

One of the simpler ways in which we can increase our responsiveness to our Chicano community is to place a sign in front of our agency that indicates that we speak Spanish. In this way, we are actively taking the initiative to serve and respond to our Hispanic consumers. Once again, I think it is important to emphasize our need to be aware of and sensitive to our surrounding community, as opposed to waiting until we are forced to take action. In the long run, we are saving ourselves and our agency from external attacks that might force us to change. We are, in a sense, taking out an insurance policy by taking action now to improve our agency instead of delaying and waiting until we are forced to do so by our funders or the surrounding community.

I think it will be important for the staff to look at some of the difficulties involved in these new proposals. First of all, putting up a sign in Spanish (and making our referral sources aware of our Spanish-speaking abilities) may so increase our Spanish-speaking clientele that we may be unable to accommodate them all. I do not feel, however, that this will be a major problem. We have at many times maintained a waiting list, and, therefore, if for some reason we should receive a barrage of Spanish-speaking clients, we can always institute a Spanish-speaking waiting list. However, I do not predict that a waiting list will be necessary, primarily because we can always use our Spanish-speaking interns to help lessen the load.

Some of the staff members may wonder whether adding a Spanish-speaking therapist to the staff will affect their job, position, or status. They may feel that a Spanish-speaking therapist will have more status because she or he can do something they cannot—speak Spanish. This tension or conflict may be somewhat reduced by allowing them to participate in interviewing Hispanic applicants. It might be possible for the staff to help select those applicants they feel are best suited to the position. (However, I will have to make the final decision.) Furthermore, since the new Hispanic therapist will be someone they may want to consult for information regarding Hispanic culture, it would be very important to allow the staff some measure of choice in the type of therapist they would feel most comfortable consulting.

As for the client evaluation questionnaires, we will be looking for general responses that indicate how we might improve our agency and our services. These forms are not going to be used to criticize a particular therapist's clinical techniques or abilities. Rather, we want citizen input that is useful for planning agency services. In fact, I want to elicit the assistance of all our staff members in helping to design our evaluation questionnaire. Staff members can participate on a voluntary basis by contributing their suggestions either during our staff meeting or directly to my office. In this way, I think the entire staff will play a part in making our agency a more responsive community service organization. Hence, they will hopefully feel less threatened by the utilization and initiation of evaluation questionnaires.

Generally, as I have mentioned, I do not think that the cost factor will greatly impede the initiation of these proposals. One problem, however, may involve placing a Spanish-speaking person on the board of directors. The board is really an elitist group of upper-middle-class professionals, and it might be difficult to get a Chicano added, especially one from a lower economic level. I think that eventually the board might concede to adding a prominent Chicano professional, but even this goal may be difficult to achieve.

SOURCE: This case is adapted from one written by Michele H. Wilson, M.S.W. Names and locations have been altered.

tegies to counter them. She hopes to decrease opposition to the policy changes, for example, by noting the minimal impact of changes on the agency's budget.

When assuming an implementation role, the executive is anticipating possible resistance to consultation with the Hispanic staff member after the hiring process has been completed. She hopes to encourage staff participation in the hiring process not only to defuse opposition but also to create good will that will extend to the implementation process.

Policy change is often not an orderly and predictable process, since unforeseen events and consequences—not to mention sources of opposition—may arise. In this case, the social work executive fears that the board will recruit a prominent Hispanic member who will not seek changes in agency policy. Her challenge is to influence the selection process so that this policy innovation will represent more than symbolic change.

In addition to executives, direct service and other staff members also assume various policy roles within specific policy sectors. Although generic skills are useful, participants require specialized knowledge about programs and policies in these sectors. Discussion in chapters 10 through 13 provides an overview of policies in child and family, mental health, health, and economic security sectors. (Case examples are also provided in other chapters pertaining to juvenile delinquency, substance abuse, family violence, gerontology, and housing sectors.)

SUMMARY

Social welfare policy is collective strategy to address social problems. Participants devise rules, procedures, regulations, and objectives (strategy) to define the direction and content of services and programs. Social problems provide the starting point for social welfare policy, since policies are directed toward redressing specific forms of material, developmental, physical, interpersonal, and opportunity deprivation.

Inequalities encountered by economic, racial and ethnic, sociological, nonconformist, and model outgroups are often addressed in policy deliberations. Seven core issues provide the substance of most social welfare policy debates, as illustrated by controversy regarding which conditions in the external world are social problems, which conditions should receive priority, which intervention strategies are preferred, which consumers should receive priority, how social programs are structured and financed, who receives prominence in decision making, and how staff and administrators are held accountable to funders and society.

Social welfare policy is constructed in an often volatile process where participants favor different policies. Policies are fashioned in multiple and intersecting arenas. Power realities often shape outcomes. Although some portray policymaking as a conceptual or philosophical discipline, effective participation requires interactional, analytical, political, administrative, and evaluative skills.

Key Concepts, Developments, and Policies

Social problems
Collective strategy
Policy objectives
Instrumental policy
Official policy
Informal policy
Agency policy
External or social policy

Public policy
Economic policy
Varieties of deprivation
Equality
Outgroups
Economic outgroups
Racial or ethnic outgroups
Sociological outgroups

Nonconformist outgroups   Scarce resources
Model outgroups   Power realities
Relative inequality   Policy arenas
Seven core policy issues   Policy processes
Instrumental values   Policy products
Core values   Policy practice roles
Policy controversy

Main Points

1. Social welfare policy is "collective strategy to address social problems."

2. Many kinds of policies exist, including policy objectives, instrumental policies, official policies, informal policies, agency policies, and social policies.

3. Social welfare policies overlap with public and economic policies.

4. Social problems are specific conditions in the external world that are perceived as sufficiently bothersome or harmful to merit social intervention.

5. Many kinds of social problems exist, including material, developmental, physical, interpersonal, opportunity, and personal-rights deprivation.

6. It is difficult to determine with precision what kinds of social problems or deprivation should be considered the domain of social welfare policy, but certain traditional ones form the core of the discipline.

7. Social problems are not distributed randomly in the population.

8. Issues of inequality are important in social welfare policy, because persons in groups that deviate from economic, health, and other norms are particularly disadvantaged, likely to experience discrimination, and likely to experience many interacting kinds of deprivation. Marked inequality also can be criticized on moral grounds, i.e., as violating standards of fairness and social justice.

9. Many kinds of "outgroups" exist, i.e., groups whose members are particularly likely to experience various kinds of deprivation.

10. Seven recurring core policy issues often arise during social welfare policy deliberations.

11. Central characteristics of social welfare policy formulation include the prevalence of controversy, the importance of power realities to outcomes, the development of policy in multiple and intersecting arenas, and the importance of processes and products.

12. Multiple practice roles need to be assumed by social workers who participate in the formulation of policy in agency, community, and legislative settings.

Questions for Discussion

1. Review case example 1.1. Identify various sources or causes of controversy in the San Marcos clinic. Even with incomplete knowledge of the case, would you side with traditionalists, advocates of responsible change, or insurgents? Why?

2. In a social agency or organization with which you are familiar, define (a) social problems that are addressed by its staff and (b) collective strategy as influenced by specific rules, regulations, procedures, and objectives. Try to identify a policy that should be reformed or

changed—whether a policy goal, an instrumental policy, an official policy, an informal policy, an internal agency policy, or a policy external to the agency. What kinds of controversy would likely attend efforts to change the policy?

3. Take any of the outgroups discussed in this chapter as your point of departure. Discuss how specific problems often encountered by members of the group interact with or cause other problems. Discuss reasons why this particular outgroup experiences inequality.

4. Discuss the following statement: "Social problems should be distributed randomly in the population so that specific groups do not bear a disproportionate burden."

5. Take any two of the outgroups discussed in this chapter and note similarities and differences between them in (a) kinds of inequality experienced and (b) causes of inequality.

6. In the context of case example 1.1, discuss the following assertions: "Power realities influence policy outcomes"; "Policy is fashioned in multiple and intersecting arenas."

7. Discuss kinds of core policy issues that arise in case example 1.1.

8. Discuss the the kinds of skills used by the social worker in policy practice case 1.1. How does the case illustrate the statement "Policy change is often not an orderly and predictable process"?

Suggested Readings

Boulding, Kenneth. "The Boundaries of Social Policy." *Social Work*, 12 (January 1967): 3–11. A good discussion of distinctions and overlapping between economic, public, and social welfare policy.

Dobelstein, Andrew. *Politics, Economics, and Public Welfare* (Englewood Cliffs, N.J.: Prentice-Hall, 1980): "The Policy Setting," pp. 1–39. (Also see "The Political Process of Welfare Policy Making," pp. 155–194). The author provides an overview of different policy arenas and participants who fashion public welfare policy.

Gilbert, Neil, and Specht, Harry. *Dimensions of Social Welfare Policy* (Englewood Cliffs, N.J.: Prentice-Hall, 1974): "The Field of Social Welfare Policy" and "Framework for Social Welfare Policy Analysis," pp. 1–53. A useful introduction to policy definitions, policy formulation, values, and basic issues in social welfare policy.

Heilbroner, Robert. *The Worldly Philosophers* (New York: Simon and Schuster, 1968): "Adam Smith," pp. 38–67. An excellent presentation of the major economic tenets of Adam Smith, an economist whose theories had extraordinary influence in the United States and served as underpinnings to laissez-faire policies.

Kamerman, Sheila, and Kahn, Alfred J. *Social Services in the United States: Policies and Programs* (Philadelphia: Temple University Press, 1976): "Context and Definition," pp. 3–23. A good overview of the variety of social services provided in social welfare that are of central importance to social workers.

Morris, Robert. *Social Policy of the American Welfare State* (New York: Harper & Row, 1979): "The Scope of Public and Social Policy" and "A Framework for Understanding Social Policy," pp. 1–37. A concise discussion of policy definitions, policy arenas, and policy formulation is provided.

Rokeach, Milton. *The Nature of Human Values* (New York: Free Press, 1973): "The Nature of Human Values and Value Systems," pp. 3–25. The author provides a classification of human values as a prelude to presenting empirical research.

Ryan, William. *Equality* (New York: Pantheon, 1981): "The Equality Dilemma," pp. 3–36. An introduction to basic value components of social welfare policy is presented in this book. The author discusses alternative conceptions of equality and provides a normative position congruent with perspectives of social workers.

Taylor, William. *Hanging Together: Equality in an Urban Nation* (New York: Simon & Schuster, 1971): "The Immigrant Myth," pp. 48–82. The author provides an excellent discussion of the kinds of discrimination encountered by blacks in comparison to the discrimination experienced by white immigrants and their descendants.

Titmuss, Richard. *Essays on the Welfare State* (Boston: Beacon Press, 1969): "Social Administration

in a Changing Society" and "The Social Division of Welfare," pp. 13–34 and 34–56. These excerpts provide an overview of policies and services that fall within the domain of social welfare policy as well as historical perspectives about the emergence of the discipline.

Notes

1. The definition of social welfare policy used in this book is similar to that used by Richard Titmuss: social policies are "collectively provided services deliberately designed to meet certain socially recognized needs." See his book *Essays on the Welfare State* (Boston: Beacon Press, 1969), p. 39. Various definitions are discussed by Martin Rein, *Social Policy* (New York: Random House, 1970). See also Neil Gilbert and Harry Specht, *Dimensions of Social Welfare Policy* (Englewood Cliffs, N.J.: Prentice-Hall, 1974), p. 4.

2. Some policy theorists define social policy as constituting goals or objectives in contrast to "rules, guidelines, standard operating procedures, reporting requirements" and other instrumentalities. See Bruce Gates, *Social Program Administration* (Englewood Cliffs, N.J.: Prentice-Hall, 1980), pp. 8–9. In this book, instrumental policies and policy objectives are both included under the rubric "social welfare policy."

3. The collective attributes of policy are discussed by Gates, *Social Program Administration*, p. 8.

4. A distinction is made by Gilbert and Specht between macro (or societal) and micro (or agency) policy in *Dimensions of Social Welfare Policy*, p. 26. Also see Robert Morris, *Social Policy in the American Welfare State* (New York: Harper & Row, 1979), pp. 11–14.

5. National policies that together describe social response to social needs are discussed by Davil Gil, *Unravelling Social Policy* (Cambridge, Mass.: Schenkman, 1976), pp. 31–56.

6. Complexities of distinguishing public from social welfare policy are discussed by Rein in

Social Policy, p. 13. He also notes how many public policies that are not traditionally placed within social welfare policy have profound implications for consumers who experience problems like unemployment.

7. Titmuss places economic issues and policies squarely within social policy when he argues that "social welfare, fiscal welfare, and occupational welfare policies" should be included within the discipline. See Titmuss, *Essays on the Welfare State,* p. 42.

8. Discussion of cultural and value factors that lead to divergent definitions of social problems are discussed by Arnold Green, *Social Problems: Arena of Conflict* (New York: McGraw-Hill, 1975).

9. Value and cultural determinants of definitions of social problems are also discussed by Richard Titmuss, *Social Policy* (London: Allen & Unwin, 1974), pp. 132–143, and Gilbert and Specht, *Dimensions of Social Welfare Policy,* pp. 39–46.

10. Various kinds of social problems included in social welfare policy are discussed by John Romanyshyn, *Social Welfare: Charity to Justice* (New York: Random House, 1971), pp. 51–80.

11. Issues of inequality are discussed by William Ryan, *Equality* (New York: Pantheon Books, 1981). Also see Titmuss, *Commitment to Welfare* (New York: Pantheon Books, 1968), pp. 188–199.

12. For discussion of relative and absolute poverty, see Victor Fuchs, "Redefining Poverty," *Public Interest,* 8 (Summer 1967): 88–96.

13. See, for example, Thomas Wills and Thomas

Longner, "Socioeconomic Status and Stress," in Irwin Kutash et al., eds., *Handbook of Stress and Anxiety* (San Francisco: Jossey-Bass, 1980), pp. 159–174.

14. Robert M. Veatch, *A Theory of Medical Ethics* (New York: Basic Books, 1981).

15. Varieties of discrimination are discussed by Albert K. Cohen, *Deviance and Control* (Englewood Cliffs, N.J.: Prentice-Hall, 1966), and Joe B. Feagin and Clairece B. Feagin, *Discrimination American Style* (Englewood Cliffs, N.J.: Prentice-Hall, 1978).

16. Lester C. Thurow, "A Look at Trickle Down Economics," guest editorial 4.2, chapter 4.

17. Lester C. Thurow, *Zero-Sum Society* (New York: Penguin Books, 1980), pp. 3–9.

18. William Ryan, *Blaming the Victim* (New York: Pantheon, 1971).

19. Black perspectives are discussed by Barbara Solomon, *Black Empowerment* (New York: Columbia University Press, 1976). Also see Ronald W. Walters, "Race, Resources, Conflict," *Social Work,* 27 (January 1982): 24–30.

20. For discussion of difficulties in achieving equality by racial minorities, see William Taylor, *Hanging Together: Equality in an Urban Nation*.

21. Problems of women in American society are discussed by Constantina Safilios-Rothschild, *Women and Social Policy* (Englewood Cliffs, N.J.: Prentice-Hall, 1974).

22. Discrimination against the elderly and their problems are discussed by R. Butler, *Why Survive? Being Old in America* (New York: Harper & Row, 1975).

23. Discrimination against nonconformist groups is discussed by Nicholas N. Kittrie, *The Right to be Different* (Baltimore: Penguin Books, 1971).

24. See Sandra J. Potter and Trudy Darty, "Social Work and the Invisible Minority," *Social Work,* 26 (May 1981): 187–192, and E. Carrington Boggan, *The Basic ACLU Guide to a Gay Person's Rights* (New York: Discus Books, 1975).

25. See Paul Chikahisa et al., *Asian and Pacific American Curriculum on Social Work Education* (Los Angeles: Asian American Community Mental Health Training Center, 1976), and Stephen M. Lyman, ed., *The Asian in North America* (Santa Barbara, Calif.: ABC–Clio Books, 1976).

26. Gerald Bubis, *Serving the American Jewish Family* (New York: Family KTAV, 1977), and Thomas J. Cottle, *Hidden Survivors* (Englewood Cliffs, N.J.: Prentice-Hall, 1980).

27. Arthur B. Shostak, *Blue Collar Stress* (Reading, Mass.: Addison-Wesley, 1980).

28. Lester C. Thurow, *Zero-Sum Society,* pp. 3–26.

29. Gilbert and Specht define various allocation and financing issues in *Dimensions of Social Welfare Policy,* pp. 30–33. It is also useful to supplement these traditional policy issues with issues pertaining to the analysis of social problems and the construction of social interventions, as discussed by Gil, *Unravelling Social Welfare Policy,* pp. 33–36.

30. Milton Rokeach, *The Nature of Human Values* (New York: Free Press, 1973), pp. 3–12.

31. Milton Friedman, *Capitalism and Freedom* (Chicago: University of Chicago Press, 1962).

32. Titmuss, *Commitment to Welfare,* pp. 124–137.

33. Ronad B. Dear and Rino J. Patti, "Legislative Advocacy: Seven Effective Tactics," *Social Work,* 26 (July 1981): 289–297.

34. See Sheila Kamerman and Alfred Kahn, *Social Services in the United States* (Philadelphia: Temple University Press, 1976), pp. 450–456, and Morris, *Social Policy,* pp. 9–14.

35. Agency arenas are discussed by George Brager and Stephen Holloway, *Changing Human Service Organizations* (New York: Free Press, 1978).

36. For discussion of "policy competencies," see John E. Tropman et al., *New Strategic Perspectives on Social Policy* (New York: Pergamon, 1981), pp. 181–247.

CHAPTER 2

A Social Welfare Policy Framework: Analysis and Processes

In the preceding chapter it was argued that social workers need to assume various practice-related roles in social welfare policy if they are to make contributions to policy in agency, community, and legislative settings. This chapter presents a policy framework to facilitate understanding both of the process of policy development and of the roles and skills of those who engage in it. Social workers need to be able to:

Understand how a preliminary survey is often required before initiating policy proposals

Gauge the extent to which a variety of background, political, economic, ideological, and technical factors suggest a relatively positive or negative prognosis for policy change

Gauge the feasibility of obtaining support for specific policy proposals

Identify and participate in various phases of the policymaking process

Identify specific roles that policy practitioners assume when they participate in the policymaking process

Develop specific policy skills

These topics are discussed in this chapter to provide a basic framework for guiding and informing policy practitioners.

To illustrate concepts discussed in this chapter, case example 2.1 presents issues of policy formulation in the juvenile justice system. While persons who openly advocate harsher treatment want to transfer many juveniles to adult courts, others fear that efforts to rehabilitate juvenile offenders will be sabotaged by such transfers. Both sides in this dispute engage in preliminary surveys of background, political, economic, ideological, and other forces as a prelude to introducing specific policy proposals to decision makers in their jurisdictions.[1]

POLICY TASKS AND PHASES

Social welfare policy evolves in a policy formulation process in which social work practitioners

(1) *survey* the policy landscape in specific settings to ascertain whether and when to initate policy changes; (2) *scan* conditions in the external world to locate and define unmet needs; (3) *analyze* and choose between policy options that can be used to address those needs; (4) *secure approval* or legitimation for preferred options; (5) *implement* policies and programs; and (6) *assess* the effectiveness of operating programs to see if they should be terminated, expanded, or otherwise modified.[2] In most settings, social workers rarely progress through this sequence of activity in such an orderly fashion. An administrator may begin by assessing an operating program (5), seek new staff to make the program more effective (4), reassess

CASE EXAMPLE 2.1

The Adult-Penalty Crackdown on California's Juvenile Criminals

By Stephen Pressman

More than 20 years ago a group of judges reported to the National Council on Crime and Delinquency that the nation's juvenile justice system should be "therapeutic and preventative rather than retributive and punitive, a viewpoint designed to preserve the child's self-respect and spare him the permanent handicap of a criminal record."

But today, with an alarming percentage of violent and serious crimes being committed by juveniles, the theory expressed in that 1957 report is being severely challenged by legislators, judges, prosecutors and even some defense lawyers and social workers. Public attitudes have hardened toward the treatment of youths who wind up in the courts for their criminal activity.

In California, legislative attempts to crack down on juvenile crime resulted in passage last year of SB 840, authored by Democratic Sena-

tor Ruben Ayala of San Bernardino. Ayala's bill, which went into effect January 1st, makes it considerably easier for 16- and 17-year-olds who commit a wide range of serious crimes to be tried in adult criminal courts. California is just one of several states that have taken steps recently to toughen up juvenile-offender laws. The New York Legislature, for example, recently lowered to 13 the age at which a youth can be tried as an adult.

The CYA Critics

Much of the criticism in California has been aimed at the State's Youth Authority which is responsible for housing and treating juveniles referred to the CYA by the courts. Critics of the CYA say the agency has been excessively lenient with some juveniles who have committed serious and sometimes repeated offenses. That, in part, explains the Legislature's desire to make it more likely that a juvenile charged with a serious crime will be tried as an adult. Says one deputy district attorney: SB

the effectiveness of the program (5), design a radically different program in the course of analyzing options (2), and seek approval for the new program (3). Many other sequences are also possible. In these various policy phases, policy practitioners are concerned with processes and products. They interact with others (processes) as they develop and seek support for specific positions or recommendations (policy products).

Legislation to allow judges to refer juvenile offenders to adult rather than juvenile courts illustrates the policy formulation process (see case example 2.1). Partly in response to pressure from those who believe deterrence will decrease crime, legislators measure, during the scanning phase,

increasing incidence of juvenile crime in California. During the analysis phase, some develop the details of legislation that defines which minors (sixteen- and seventeen-year-olds who commit specific crimes) can be tried in adult criminal courts. During implementation, those who advocate deterrence scrutinize actions of judges to see if juveniles are referred to adult courts and given stiff sentences. Social workers who question whether reliance on deterrence is likely to reduce crime (see the social worker's comments at the end of the case example) engage in the program assessment phase.

The term *policy phase* is often used to identify facets of the policy formulation process. Social

---

840 "puts young offenders on notice that they face punishment in line with the gravity of crimes they commit."

But even the juvenile courts are reexamining their traditional reliance on treatment and rehabilitation rather than on punishment. While few juvenile court judges say publicly they have given up on rehabilitation, they make it clear that punishment is a consideration when disposing of juvenile crime cases. "If you disregard the offense and focus on the juvenile's need, then the treatment program may have no relation to the offense, at least in terms that the community really understands," says Los Angeles Superior Court Judge Richard Byrne, who presides over that county's juvenile courts.

Citing an example, Byrne says it is entirely possible that a youth arrested for petty theft could end up spending five years in a CYA facility, while another who commits murder could go home on probation. The difference, he says, is simply in a judge's decision that one youth requires a certain amount of treatment while the other would not benefit from such treatment and is better off on probation.

It is precisely those kinds of sentencing dis-

paraties that have prompted law enforcement groups and legislators to demand harsher treatment of juveniles by the courts. "You just can't have a situation where the offender walks out laughing about the criminal justice system," said state Senator Alan Robbins, a member of the Senate Judiciary Committee. "Murder is not a crime that can be dealt with by having someone spend 90 days in detention." . . .

There are others involved in the criminal justice system who view more cynically the demise of rehabilitation efforts and the growing emphasis on punishment. "What is there about the adult criminal system that is so successful in combatting crime?" defense attorney Clayman wonders. "If you throw in the towel on a kid, you might as well recognize that you're breeding a lifelong criminal." Jon Chambers, a colleague of Clayman's in the LA public defender's office, says the issue has political and economic implications as well as philosophical ones. It is politically expedient to toughen the laws against juveniles. Also, rehabilitation programs cost money. "And right now," Chambers says, "the public mood is not to spend money for any purpose, let alone

workers who survey the policy landscape to determine whether reforms are feasible participate in the preliminary phase of social policy formulation. In similar fashion, they engage in the scanning phase when they identify and define unmet needs, the analysis phase when they choose between policy options, the implementation phase when they examine and seek changes in operating programs, the assessment phase when they evaluate existing policies, and the legitimation phase when they seek approval for specific policies.[3]

The substantive issues addressed in the various phases can be described in the context of the seven core policy issues discussed in chapter 1. The various phases overlap, but each focuses on certain core policy issues (see table 2.1). In the scanning phase, for example, participants decide what conditions in the external world constitute social problems (*core issue 1*) and make judgments about the relative importance of specific problems (*core issue 2*). In the analysis phase, specific policy options are analyzed with regard to the content of services (*core issue 3*), the consumers that will receive priority (*core issue 4*), and the way programs are designed and financed (*core issue 5*). Participants scrutinize many program and financing policies (*core issue 5*) during the implementation phase, as well as decision-making procedures that are used in specific settings (*core issue 6*). Policies are considered germane to evaluation of programs during the assessment phase (*core issue 7*). All policy issues are considered in the legitimation phase when participants seek support or approval for policies that emerge from any of the other phases. As an example, a social worker who

---

spend money on someone who has committed a crime."

But a rehabilitation program that costs, say, $500 for each youth is less expensive than the $18,000 it costs to house someone in a state prison each year. Further calculating the other costs of crimes—including property damage and court time—successful rehabilitation programs can save taxpayers millions of dollars each year.

The only problems are finding rehabilitation programs that work and then convincing legislators and the public of their value. Senator Robbins last year introduced a bill (SB 133) to duplicate in California the well-known "Scared Straight" prison visitation programs at Rahway State Prison in New Jersey. Inmates at San Quentin Prison, meanwhile, have been conducting a counseling program for years which is considered by some to be more successful than the New Jersey "confrontation" approach. But critics of SB 133 say that mass visits to prisons might dilute the impact of such a program.

Adversary Proceedings

The courts have been gradually changing the way they handle juveniles. They are using more of the traditional adversary proceedings that have earmarked adult, but not juvenile, criminal cases. Ever since the U.S. Supreme Court's landmark *In re Gault* decision in 1967, which granted juveniles the right to counsel and other due-process guarantees, criminal proceedings involving minors have shifted away from their earlier, more informal setting to court environments which focus more attention on questions of guilt or innocence. Most defense attorneys applaud that shift, saying it gives minors the same basic constitutional rights enjoyed by adults. But others, while conceding the importance of those rights, say there is something lost for the youths involved in a more adversary system.

Such a system "focuses the attention of the court (away) from the interests and needs of the young person to whether the young person actually is in violation of a law or not," says Laurence Rubin, executive director of Project

wants an agency to devote more resources to a program addressing a specific social problem is progressing from the scanning to the legitimation phase.

POLICY FRAMEWORK

Values, ideologies, political and economic factors, and available technical information influence the activities of participants at numerous points in the various phases. A policy framework is needed, then, that depicts the phases in a systems framework that portrays links between broader societal, community, and agency factors, on the one hand, and the activities of participants, on the other hand (see illustration 2.1). Most important, the framework should provide concepts useful to

those who contemplate initiating policy reforms in specific agency, community, or legislative settings.

It should also facilitate examination of the sources of controversy in social welfare policy, since controversy has never been more obvious than in the current era, a period of scarce resources in which many persons question traditional social reform agendas. (Policy controversy, a topic introduced in chapter 1, is a recurring theme in this and succeeding chapters.)

PRELIMINARY SURVEY OF PREVAILING POLICIES

Current policies and background realities provide a context for policy development. In case example

---

Heavy West, a social service agency in Southern California. Rubin would prefer a system that sends to adult courts juveniles charged with serious crimes and leaves others to get rehabilitative treatment. "We don't even want to deal with real serious offenders," says Rubin, whose agency helps train juveniles and find jobs for them. "A lot of these kids have to be removed from the community, sent away and locked up. Some will never make it."

Before the *Gault* decision, juveniles were often the victims of "railroad jobs" in the courts, say many defense attorneys. "I'm enthusiastic about the adversary system because one thing it does allow is for a kid to be treated as fairly as an adult in a similar situation," says Clayman. "If we really want to rehabilitate, that should be the goal. We have a much better chance if we treat that kid fairly." In fact, Clayman has joined others around the state in supporting legislation that would allow jury trials in juvenile criminal cases. This would be yet another extension of a right accorded adult defendants. . . .

Surviving Differences
Despite the new legislation and the growing belief that juveniles should be treated like adults when accused of crimes, there are some differences that probably will survive. Few, if any, would support death penalty sentences for juveniles who commit capital crimes. And few judges relish the idea of sentencing a 16-year-old to a state prison.

There are still some observers who believe that most juvenile offenders can be aided by treatment and rehabilitation. Exposing these youths to the adult criminal justice system, they say, only encourages more criminal activity because of the ineffective way the adult system in California operates. A number of social workers believe that judges who deal with juveniles should get training in psychology and other fields used in treatment programs. "They're making decisions about these kids' lives," says Project Heavy West's Rubin, "and they really have very little information about what makes a young person tick."

SOURCE: Stephen Pressman, "The Adult-Penalty Crackdown on the State's Juvenile Criminals," *California Journal,* 11 (June 1980), pp. 254–255. Reprinted by permission.

TABLE 2.1　Substantive Issues in Various Policy Phases

Phase	Core Policy Issues	Substantive Issues
preliminary	all core issues	identifying policy issues and then deciding whether it is possible to initiate policy changes
scanning	core issues 1 and 2	identifying specific social problems in external world, assessing their importance, and defining their scope and causation
analysis	core issues 3, 4 and 5	assessing program alternatives pertaining to eligibility, service interventions, the service delivery system, decision making, and evaluation mechanisms
implementation	core issues 5 and 6	examining the service delivery system to ascertain why it does not allow achievement of specific policy objectives
assessment	core issue 7	devising methods of evaluating operating programs and associated policies
legitimation	all core issues	all substantive issues from other phases are relevant to the legitimation phase, i.e., whenever participants seek a mandate or approval for policies that emerge from any of the other phases

2.1, the existing network of juvenile courts, judges, and social agencies, already established and funded, provides the starting point for policy development. Those who develop policies respond to existing policies and programs. When satisfied with prevailing policies, they are likely to resist sweeping reforms, though they may favor incremental modifications. When thoroughly disenchanted, they often urge major reforms certain to be resisted by those who favor the status quo.

As a prelude to participating in policymaking, then, social workers survey existing policies to determine whether those policies are seriously defective. When policy issues are discovered, they have then to decide whether and when to initiate actions that could lead to changes in existing policies. In some cases, they emerge from this preliminary phase with a decision not to proceed further, either because no significant defects in existing policies are discovered or because reforms do

ILLUSTRATION 2.1 Policy Framework

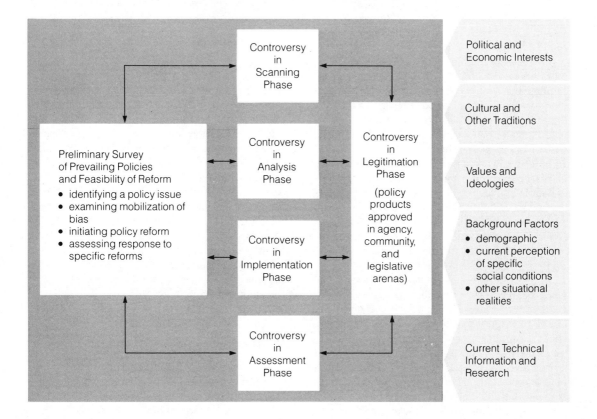

not appear feasible. In other cases, they decide to initiate reform activity at once or to seek changes but wait for a more favorable moment. This preliminary phase of surveying existing policies is thus a vital part of the policymaking process because social workers use it to decide whether to proceed with further action.

When conducting an initial survey, social workers seek answers to at least four kinds of questions. First, does a policy issue exist, and is it sufficiently important to merit attention? Second, what factors, forces, interests, and persons generally support or oppose continuation of the status quo? In other words, to what extent does a "mobilization of bias" exist against basic changes? Third, how and where should reform activity be ini-

tiated?—a difficult question in complex organizations and legislatures. Finally, social workers need to engage in preliminary analysis of the feasibility of specific reform initiatives so that they can gauge, if only in preliminary terms, whether a proposed modification in policy has any chance of success. (More detailed analysis of feasibility is made subsequently during the legitimation phase, once specific proposals or reforms are developed.)

IDENTIFYING A POLICY ISSUE

Social workers must often decide whether existing policies are defective and whether defects are sufficiently serious to warrant investment of time and resources to obtain changes in existing policies. Important policy issues arise when consumers are harmed by existing policies, as illustrated by policies that deprive some consumers of needed services, promote misdirected or inappropriate services, or dictate implementation procedures that preclude effective services. Social workers often oppose existing policies on grounds that they violate basic rights of consumers, as when confidentiality of information obtained by social workers is breached.

Indeed, all the sources of policy controversy discussed in chapter 1 are relevant to the process of defining policy issues in the preliminary or survey phase. Social workers find existing policies to be inadequate when those policies violate basic core and instrumental values, threaten economic and political interests of the profession, or contradict research or technical findings.

In case example 2.1, for example, many social workers find policies that allow the referral of juvenile offenders to adult courts to be defective. Use of deterrence violates core values that define children's rights to institutional and community treatment programs rather than incarceration. Social workers who work in juvenile court settings may oppose referrals of juveniles to adult courts because they do not wish to give program and policy roles to adult courts. They may also wonder on technical or research grounds whether litigation of cases of juveniles in adult courts will truly reduce rates of juvenile crime.

MOBILIZATION OF BIAS

When contemplating changes in existing policies, social workers survey general sources of support to ascertain the extent to which policy changes or reforms are feasible. To the extent that support exists for policy change, what is the nature and source of discontent? In case example 2.1, it is clear that many forces contribute to uneasiness with prevailing policy and that there is widespread support for policies that strengthen deterrent aspects of the current juvenile system.

Various factors that need to be assessed when analyzing the extent of existing bias against reforms are portrayed at the periphery of illustration 2.1.[4]

Background Factors

In case example 2.1, a range of factors influences preferences of policy participants. Some of those factors make basic reforms difficult or even unlikely in the short term. The conservative nature of the current era is hardly promising for those who want to increase jobs and opportunities for youth. Dramatic increases in juvenile crime have made many Americans unsympathetic to nondeterrent approaches. On a more promising note, massive costs of constructing residential facilities housing ever-increasing populations make some legislators willing to consider community services. In addition, the fact that most adult prisons are filled to capacity could lead some persons to question referring large numbers of juveniles to adult courts.

Political and Economic Interests

When examining interests, social workers ask, "Who benefit from the status quo, and who believe their practical interests would better be met by some or major reforms?" Preferences of organized interest groups and of participants who have traditionally assumed important roles in construction of policies need to be examined (illustration 2.2). In the juvenile offender arena, orientations of bar associations, associations of judges, officials in charge of juvenile and adult facilities, consumer groups supportive of deterrent policies, and social reform groups need to be identified and considered. Which are most important in framing policy, and what have been their traditional policy preferences? Which are willing to consider basic reforms, which want incremental changes, and which are satisfied with the status quo?[5] As in many policy sectors, consumers are often the least represented; e.g., in case example 2.1, juveniles and their families are not organized into an interest group.

ILLUSTRATION 2.2

"HE'S QUITE INDEPENDENT — OF POLITICAL LEADERSHIP, THAT IS"

From *Herblock On All Fronts*, New American Library, 1980.
Reprinted by permission of Herblock Cartoons.

Relevant Values and Ideologies

Modification of existing policies becomes more difficult the more that existing policies are consonant with core and instrumental values of influential participants. In case example 2.1, changes toward a deterrent approach in juvenile court policies are precipitated because large numbers of persons find existing policies to be inconsonant with "law-and-order" values. Social reformers often encounter American values that extol localism, define social problems as attributes of "deviants who cause their own demise," and prescribe restricted social welfare roles for government. But values and ideologies can also be supportive of policy changes. Powerful persons may believe current policies are outmoded, perpetuate or reflect discrimination, increase inequality, or are overly costly.

Controversy is likely, of course, when persons have divergent values, ideologies, and interests. In case example 2.1, the balance has swung toward those with values supportive of deterrent policies. Eventually, the pendulum will probably swing toward those who insist that incarceration of young people hardly represents a long-term solution to juvenile crime.

Relevant Technical Evidence

Policy participants often use findings of technical studies to buttress positions. In some cases, technical studies generally support specific policy recommendations, as in the case of medical research that suggests specific public health measures are required to reduce a particular form of disease. In other instances, technical evidence is not clear, as when scant research exists regarding causes or solutions to certain social problems. Evidence may also be conflicting, as when some research studies suggest that social services can prevent juvenile offenses while others provide less sanguine evidence. It is important to analyze the extent to which technical data influence the preferences of persons as they examine existing policies and programs.

INITIATING POLICY REFORMS

Preceding discussion suggests that those who seek changes in policy need to analyze the extent to which a mobilization of bias exists that makes policy reforms difficult. Social workers also need to consider how and where to initiate activity to modify existing policies. In particular, they need to choose a specific policy phase and a specific locus as a starting point in an agency, community, or legislative arena.

Choice of a Policy Phase

A social worker who decides to seek reforms in existing policy must decide whether to initiate activity in the scanning, analysis, implementation, assessment, or legitimation phase—or in some combination of these phases. A social worker in a mental health agency may decide that it does not provide services to members of a specific racial minority group and may suggest that the agency devise a task force to study the needs of this group as well as their current utilization of agency services (the scanning phase). Conversely, she could decide to join others in a committee to scrutinize alternative methods of structuring intake so that persons of the group were not systematically excluded from agency services (the analysis phase). She could discuss with her supervisor logistical or attitudinal factors that appear to limit service to this group during implementation of agency services (the implementation phase). Or she could proceed directly to the legitimation phase by advancing reform proposals even prior to extensive deliberations or activities in one of the other phases. In this case, she might, for example, initiate a suggestion in a staff meeting that "a vigorous recruitment effort be initiated to find a new staff member with background and skills to work with the underserved population."

In many cases, of course, those who seek changes in existing policy must join activity that has already been initiated by others. In this case, for example, the executive director in this agency may already have devised a task force to examine patterns of utilization of agency services. The social worker might decide to join the committee and hope to introduce needs of the excluded group during its deliberations. An important strategy option, then, is to utilize existing activities and committees to accomplish or further specific reforms that might otherwise have been tangential to them.

Locus of Activity

Persons who seek changes in policy must decide where to initiate action.[6] In some cases, they need to choose among the various policy arenas discussed in chapter 1. When confronted with funding cutbacks, for example, a social work executive could decide to (1) join a community co-alition of agencies and community groups to fight the cutbacks; (2) establish a task force of agency executives to scrutinize implications of the funding cuts for community services; (3) participate directly in the legislative process by contacting key legislators to rescind the cuts; or (4) develop internal agency strategies to offset the cuts, perhaps by seeking internal economies. In many cases, of course, social workers decide that they need to participate in policy actions in a number of arenas.

Even within specific arenas, social workers often must choose where to initiate action. Within specific social agencies, for example, a social worker could decide to use low-level strategies by seeking policy changes in an immediate work unit. Alternatively, he might try to initiate change by participating in high-level deliberations, including discussions with the agency executive. In other cases, social workers participate indirectly in the process of changing policies, as when, for example, they sensitize a supervisor to the need for specific policy reforms.

In some instances, social workers change policy by developing precedents even in the absence of high-level and formal approvals. A director of a social work department in a hospital may obtain extension of social work services to new units of the hospital by negotiating arrangements with medical and nursing staff even prior to obtaining high-level clearance from hospital administrators.

Alternatively, of course, social workers can try to initiate change by participating in high-level agency deliberations. In many cases, policy changes are obtained through intermediaries, as when a social worker in a line position sensitizes a supervisor or agency official to the need for specific policy reforms.

In some cases, an appropriate locus of intervention is external to the agency. In the case of funding cutbacks that cause serious deterioration of services within specific agencies, social workers may initiate or participate in coalitions established external to their agencies that propose changes in legislation or governmental regulations.

When initiating change in community or legislative settings, social workers similarly need to decide where to initiate action. In the case of a community problem such as lack of primary-care medical services, a social worker in a public health department could initiate "pressure from below" by developing a communitywide task force of citizens. Alternatively, he might try to develop a high-level task force of public health officials as a prelude to seeking funds from government funders. In legislative settings, many choices also exist. Constituency pressure can be developed and applied to important legislators. Or behind-the-scenes assistance could be obtained from the aide of an important legislator as a prelude to developing a piece of legislation that could then receive extensive constituency support from consumer and professional groups.

FEASIBILITY OF SPECIFIC POLICY PROPOSALS

When seeking reforms, social work participants need to assess the extent to which specific reform measures are likely to attract support or opposition, regardless of which phase or locus has been chosen as the point of initial entry into the policy formulation process. A social worker in an agency who decides to initiate a suggestion to form a task force to examine the relevance of agency services to elderly consumers would need to assess whether others support or oppose a recommendation to form a planning committee. Were the committee established, she would need, at successive points during the scanning phase, to assess relative support for possible recommendations she might want to advance.

Social work participants in the policy process can make policy recommendations even when the prognosis for those recommendations is extremely unfavorable. However, it is unwise to initiate recommendations without assessing both support and opposition. Perhaps other recommendations can be proposed to avoid certain defeat. In addition, timing is often crucial. An unfavorable climate may doom a proposal at one point in time, but the same recommendation may later prove acceptable to decision makers.

When examining the prognosis of specific proposals, social workers need to consider the sources, intensity, and locus of opposition as well as the extent to which prior traditions suggest that the proposals will be met with controversy. When the feasibility of a proposal is being gauged, analysis of the relative balance of support and opposition is also useful.[7]

Sources of Opposition

When proposals in any of the policy phases are perceived to infringe value, ideological, political, and economic interests and preferences of participants, they are likely to be met with controversy. In the case of a hypothetical multibillion dollar proposal to develop federally funded and supervised services and jobs for assisting juvenile offenders, reformers would encounter opposition from (1) conservatives who believe a get tough approach is needed, (2) those who believe programs for juvenile offenders belong in the hands of local government, (3) taxpayer groups that resist development of yet another "social experiment," and (4) representatives of business who believe that a deterrent approach is required to stop shop lifting and burglaries. Widespread opposition is less likely if proposals do not make sweeping changes in the status quo and do not require major new outlays of resources.

Intensity of Opposition

In many cases, objections to policy proposals on value, political, or technical grounds may not be intense. As an example, a legislator who favors rehabilitation for juvenile offenders may object to removing those who have committed murders to adult courts but may find merit in using deterrence in extreme instances of violence. Although she objects to removal, her opposition may be relatively muted. When those who put forward proposals anticipate a shrill and committed opposition, in contrast, they may need to reassess the likelihood of success.

Locus of Opposition

Opposition is not as formidable if it derives from persons who are not strategically placed, i.e., who do not possess the ability to block or sabotage specific policy changes. If the president strongly opposes a scheme to provide jobs for juvenile offenders, its chances decrease markedly. He can mobilize a campaign against it by charging that it represents "a go-easy approach toward criminals" and can orchestrate a congressional strategy that intensifies opposition from committee chairpersons. He can also threaten a presidential veto, distribute rewards to those who oppose it, and threaten sanctions against those who support it. In similar fashion, opposition from strategically placed chairpersons of committees, party officials, important governmental officials, or powerful leaders of interest groups may indicate political trouble.

Prior Traditions

Opposition to a policy proposal is often likely when the proposal is associated with a tradition of controversy. Participants in policy controversy often remember or hear of prior efforts to obtain a specific policy reform. In the case of national health insurance, for example, a rich tradition of legislative effort exists in which conservatives and liberals have confronted one another. The prognosis for such legislation is guarded partly because of the controversial nature of the issue and partly because participants are used to confrontation politics whenever it is introduced. Proposals with a tradition of successive defeats often have a poor prognosis, since allies are difficult to enlist in what is commonly perceived to be a losing cause. Thus, liberals find it difficult to obtain supporters for national health insurance proposals because they have been defeated on so many occasions.

Balance of Forces

Policy practitioners also need to estimate the relative balance of forces in the political organization as well as the resources of likely opponents and proponents of specific measures. In

---

POLICY PRACTICE CASE 2.1

Access by Patients to Their Charts: An Agency Issue

As a staff member in a mental health agency, I believe that patients should have access to written case records. In absence of knowledge about their diagnosis and problems, how can they fully participate in making a treatment plan? Far from causing them to become upset, reading and discussion of case materials is likely to promote thoughtful participation in contract making between social worker and consumer. But I now work in an agency where few patients see their records. This case provides a good example of the preliminary phase of the policymaking process. I assumed a survey role as I examined prevailing policies and identified a policy issue that, I believe, merits further attention in this agency.

The Agency

The agency (henceforth anonymously referred to as "B Center") is located on the grounds of a state hospital and was itself once a ward and part of that hospital. In 1969, B Center negotiated a contract with the county of Los Angeles under the terms of the Short Doyle Act. This new contract meant that B Center, which had been a ward of the state hospital, was now to be separated from the hospital but still partially under its control. B Center was also to maintain its location on the grounds of the state hospital.

B Center's formal mandate comes from both the county and the state. Funding, for example, is shared by both the county (10 per-

some cases, supporters of a position are better organized and more skillful than their opponents, making success likely with even a relatively modest campaign. The outlook is hardly positive, however, if those who support a measure are outorganized or if the balance of forces is relatively even. The relative balance of forces can be estimated in crude terms by summing the factors enumerated in preceding discussions (i.e., sources, locus and intensity of opposition and support, and political resources of each side in a dispute). But such calculations are difficult to make and sometimes lead to erroneous conclusions. Indeed, the policy practitioner must often decide whether and when to seek policy changes in light of insufficient information.

POLICY PRACTICE IN THE PRELIMINARY PHASE

In policy practice case 2.1, a social worker assumes the survey role in the preliminary phase of policy formulation as she explores the issue of accessibility to consumers of patient charts. During this initial stage of policy exploration, she has to decide whether widespread denial of charts represents a policy issue and whether she wants to try to remedy the situation.

After considerable thought, the social worker decides that the existing policy has the effect, with rare exceptions, of denying patients access to records—a policy that, she believes, infringes upon their right to information about their current condition and about treatment alternatives. How can patients participate in the selection of treatment alternatives, she asks, if they do not know what problems they have? She also doubts, on technical grounds, whether divulging records would traumatize most consumers, as many therapists fear, much less cause them to repudiate the staff members who describe their problems in case records.

Mobilization of Bias

The social worker in policy practice case 2.1 examines the extent to which a "mobilization of

---

cent) and the state (90 percent), and the approval of the agency's policies and constitution is also a shared responsibility. Although the mandate is passed down and approved by two sources, the state actually has more direct control over B Center. B Center, for example, although no longer part of the state hospital, must abide by the hospital's administrative manual and policies.

B Center is a community mental health and day treatment facility where patients receive psychiatric treatment only during daytime hours, returning to their own homes in the evening. B Center provides a variety of services: group therapy, individual counseling, occupational therapy, recreational therapy, chemotherapy, and vocational rehabilitation. These services are utilized by individuals with some mental disorder or life crisis who are able to function on at least a minimal level.

Specifically, B Center's patient population consists of individuals who have been hospitalized and do not need full-time care but are not quite ready to adjust to life outside a hospital setting as well as persons who will always need some kind of supportive and therapeutic influence. Such patients would otherwise be hospitalized but can function when provided partial services.

Most of the patients served are in the lower-income bracket, and many must depend on some kind of government assistance —supplemental security income, general assistance, or aid to families with dependent children. Most of the patients have had very little formal education and are between twenty-five to forty-five years of age.

Charts are maintained for each person served by the agency and contain information regarding personal history, a psychiatric evaluation conducted at the initial intake interview, any correspondence that relates to the person, and daily notations charting progress at the center.

The staff is run on an "equalized interdisciplinary" principle, i.e., each staff member funtions as both a group and an individual therapist. All staff members perform basically the same functions in their involvement and treatment of patients.

The staff consists of three social workers, two nurses, four psychiatric technicians, one marriage counselor, one psychologist, and one psychiatrist who functions as the agency's executive director. The entire staff meets formally once a week for an hour and a half. The director has an agenda, and each staff member adds to the agenda before the meeting. The agenda is kept on the secretary's desk, where each staff member has access to it.

The Issue

At B Center, each patient is on some kind of chemotherapy schedule and must walk through B Center's main office to collect his or her medication. When passing through the main office, each patient comes in visual contact with the medical charts, which are located in a three-sided cabinet. Each chart has a patient's name printed in bold letters and is held in a slot that enables easy visual access to the name.

In December of 1974, several staff members at B Center became quite concerned about patients loitering in the main office and, also, about some asking to see their charts. This problem was put on the director's agenda and brought up at a Thursday staff meeting. After much discussion, the entire staff agreed on a proposal to keep patients out of the main office as much as possible. The technicians and nurses were to hand the patients their medication, and the patient was then to be instructed to leave the office area immediately. A patient was only to remain in the office area if he or she had some financial business with the billing clerk. Furthermore, patients who wanted to see their chart were to be referred to their personal staff therapist, who would decide whether to show it to them.

My research was directed toward interviewing a staff member from each of the disciplines represented at the agency to obtain an overall picture of staff attitudes regarding this issue. Of the six staff members I interviewed, all had at one time during the year been asked by a patient to see his or her chart.

All the therapists felt that patients had the right to see their charts, yet they also felt that granting them this right was dependent on the patient's ability to accept, understand, and fully interpret the material he or she read. Controversy centered on the issue of patients' rights versus therapists' discretion.

One of the most frequently used reasons for not allowing a patient to see his or her chart was that it might jeopardize the patient–therapist relationship. Each therapist I interviewed was very much concerned that the patient might become angry, hostile, or intimidated by the therapist's written remarks, and that the therapist would have to start building the relationship all over again or that the patient might not even be willing to continue.

The design of B Center ensures that each patient comes into contact with a number of different therapists each day, although he or she may also have an individual therapist. Patients are considered almost a "community project," meaning that each therapist at the agency can feel free to talk to or help any patient. Because of this unique "community project" design, comments are made in each patient's chart by many members of the staff. Thus, therapists feared that patients might not trust any of them if the patients knew that the therapists shared information with one another. Many therapists also feared that they (the therapists) would not feel free to chart as they wished. Essentially, they were concerned about losing privacy and freedom in the types of notations they would be able to chart.

During my interview with the director, he suggested that patients might be able to file slander suits against either an individual or the entire agency if they felt a comment to be malicious or harmful toward them. Although he felt that this situation was unlikely to occur, his comment suggested yet another rationale for opposing policy change. Some staff also feared a sort of domino effect: as one patient obtained access, others would also seek it.

It was also important to consider the attitudes of the staff toward mentally ill patients. Four out of the six staff members I interviewed felt that a patient's request for his chart was probably a symptom of his illness. Several staff members explained that a request to see a chart might be a sign of paranoia or of feelings of insecurity or distrust toward the therapist or staff. A patient was also not felt to be equipped to read, accept, and understand chart material.

Three of the therapists stated that, when confronted by a patient, they would flatly state that it was agency policy not to show patients their charts.

In fact, patients have exerted little pressure for a change in the access-to-records policy. I think it is important to analyze this situation in a historical context. To begin with, the majority of B Center's patients have been discharged from the state hospital but still need some kind of therapeutic influence and support. At the hospital, patients were expected to follow hospital rules and schedules and were not allowed to disrupt hospital procedures. There was little room for individual freedom.

This approach actually reinforces the concept of mental illness. A patient is seen—not only by the lay person but by professionals as well—as sick, out of control, and dependent. Therefore, patients coming from the hospital are put in a passive role and are seen by hospital personnel as dependent on them for help and treatment. Patients do not create demands to be met by the staff; rather, the staff is seen as setting the rules that the patient must follow. Essentially, patients are the recipients of an agency service over which they have no control.

Staff members as a whole were unwilling to let patients read their charts. As a result, a number of tactics were used to put an end to the issue once it was raised by a patient. The most widely used tactic was to tell patients that agency policy did not allow them to see their charts.

Another tactic was to actually sit down with patients and explain why they could not see their charts.

Another method of dealing with the issue was to allow the patient to read only specific excerpts from his or her chart. Some therapists, for example, would not let a patient read the diagnosis, the correspondence, or the notations of other therapists but would allow the patient to read their own notations. Still another method was to explain to a patient that the therapist wanted to think about letting the patient see his or her chart. In this way, the therapist would put the issue off for an indefinite period of time, even though the issue eventually required a solution.

None of the therapists I interviewed had, at any time during their employment at B Center, allowed a patient to see his or her entire chart, nor had any of the other therapists, as far as they knew.

An interesting aspect of the issue was the legal ambiguity regarding the patient's right to see his or her chart. According to the agency's administrative manual (which is the state hospital's manual as well), the B Center staff did not have to provide access, since the section discussing confidentiality of information does not discuss the issue. A comprehensive list is presented of persons other than the patient who may or may not have access to the chart, but nothing about patient rights is mentioned. The administrative manual interprets its policies from the Welfare and Institutions Code, which also noticeably omits any mention of a patient's right to see his or her chart.

During my research of the issue, I found a lack of information for dealing with the issue not only in the hospital's and B Center's procedures but also in the Welfare and Institutions Code. I did manage to find one source published by the American Medical Association that made some attempt to explicitly state a patient's rights. This source maintained: "In the absence of any statutory or court precedent that gives the patient the right of personal access to the medical record, hospital policy must be followed."

Since neither state statute nor hospital administrative policy makes any provisions, the issue of patients' rights to see their charts is open to agency interpretation. Historical precedent set down by the state hospital has been to not allow patients to see their charts. Within this framework, B Center's director did indeed initiate an innovative policy when he allowed staff members to decide individually whether or not to provide access, yet they have chosen to adhere to traditional practice.

My personal experience with allowing consumers access to records suggests that they benefit from it, i.e., are more likely to become collaborative participants in decision making during their treatment. Further, I believe that these consumers have certain rights that cannot be arbitrarily ignored. At this point, some sentiment exists that prevailing policy is defective. But, if I pursue this issue, I will need to think carefully about how to proceed, since there is relatively little interest in policy change and even considerable sentiment that patients should not obtain access.

SOURCE: This case is adapted from one developed by Michele H. Wilson, M.S.W. Names and locations have been altered.

bias" against policy reforms exists that would make it virtually impossible to modify or clarify existing policies. Clearly, the situation is complex. On the one hand, she notes that many staff members believe that patients would generally be harmed if they were allowed to read all or even part of their records. Some also believe that the reading of records by patients could jeopardize the therapist–patient relationship. In addition, the current policy that enables therapists to decide, on an individual basis, whether patients can read records makes policy change difficult. Even if no staff members avail themselves of this policy, it *appears* that patients are able to obtain access.

On the other hand, an obvious gap exists between the intent of formal policy and existing

practice. Virtually no patients do obtain access, even though official policy gives staff the right to divulge records to them. Indeed, some staff members even refuse access to patients on grounds that agency policy does not allow it. Further, many staff members appear uneasy with existing policy, which could lead some of them to want to participate in efforts to clarify or improve it. Although not mentioned in this case, background court and administrative law rulings fostering patient rights are also leading many executives to scrutinize this issue.

Initiating Policy Reforms

Were this social worker to proceed, she would need to decide whether to try to initiate activity in the scanning, analysis, implementation, assessment, or legitimation phase. As one example, she could try to educate staff about existing policy so that they might more frequently allow patients to see their records (implementation phase). Or she could decide that existing policy gave individual staff too much leeway in making decisions. In this case, she might want to reformulate policy so that staff had to give access unless specific conditions existed. But this would require an intraagency committee or task force to identify alternative options and develop recommended policies (analysis phase).

As important, the social worker would need to decide whether to initiate action inside or outside the agency. She could decide that staff opposition to reform was sufficiently strong that policy changes were needed at the state level, either in the state mental health department or the state legislature. Or she could choose any number of avenues of change within the agency itself, including discussions with other staff members, supervisors, or the executive.

Feasibility of Reform

Even in this preliminary survey phase, the social worker might want to gauge the relative support for or opposition to specific proposals by examining the sources, intensity, and locus of support and opposition. A policy that would require staff to routinely show patients their records would probably encounter intense opposition from most staff members and administrators. By contrast, a proposal "to devise a task force to examine the gap between formal and actual policy" might encounter far less opposition. In this latter case, the balance between opponents and proponents might prove favorable to those seeking clarification of existing policy.

Social workers must frequently assume a survey role in the preliminary policy phase, whether in agency, community, or legislative settings. In one sense, this role is analogous to the early phase of direct service intervention, when the social worker obtains a wide range of background information as a prelude to helping a consumer address specific problems. In policy arenas, the preliminary phase provides a point of access to the policymaking process that often leads to direct participation in one of the policy phases.

CONTROVERSY IN POLICY PHASES

No matter which policy phase or locus is chosen, social workers can expect controversy to be common when they initiate policy recommendations or even when they examine the feasibility of changing existing policies. In policy practice case 2.1, the social worker might disagree about the feasibility of reform with another staff member who believes that policy change is not feasible or desirable. Divergent values, ideologies, interests, and technical opinions often manifest themselves during the various phases, particularly when major changes in existing policies are proposed. The following discussion serves as a brief introduction to the kinds of controversies that often occur in the various policy phases —phases discussed in greater detail in chapters 3 through 8.

Controversy in the Scanning Phase

In the scanning phase, participants try to persuade others that a specific condition in the external world does or does not represent an important social problem. Reformers traditionally seek to generate concern about social problems. Daycare reformers appeal to values, for example, when they argue that no group is more important than children and that society should not abdicate its responsibility to its children by providing inferior services. They utilize evidence to support their reforms by analyzing existing daycare arrangements and arguing that deprivation at an early age can have serious consequences. They then try to show that increased funding for daycare will not encourage women to abdicate parenting responsibilities by encouraging them to work. Women *already* are working in massive numbers, they argue, and should not also encounter moral dilemmas when unable to afford quality daycare. In many cases, reformers seek relatively broad entitlements, as represented by daycare programs that assist middle- as well as low-income families.[8]

Opponents of proposed reforms minimize the importance of specific social conditions. In the case of daycare, they argue that massive daycare programs ultimately harm children by encouraging women to forgo parenting responsibilities, that large expenditures required to fund such programs are not available, and that current arrangements, such as existing daycare facilities and informal services, are sufficient.[9]

Controversy during the scanning phase is illustrated in case example 2.1 by differing perceptions of basic causes of juvenile crime. Some participants believe deterrence will drastically reduce rates of crime, but others, including many social workers, believe that social conditions, lack of job opportunities, and detrimental familial and personal factors are more crucial.[10] If persons disagree about causes of social problems during the scanning phase, they are likely to be at odds in subsequent policy phases.

Controversy in the Analysis Phase

During the analysis phase, participants construct or design social initiatives to address specific social problems.[11] Complex proposals define administrative structures, service delivery strategies, eligibility policies, estimates of required resources, and an evaluation strategy. When child development reformers sought to establish a multibillion dollar national program that would fund daycare and other children's services, they described in legislative form a complex service delivery apparatus that included regional councils, state planning boards, contracting mechanisms, and eligibility procedures.[12] Simpler proposals may emphasize only one or several issues, as illustrated by a proposal to increase citizen participation in decision making in a specific program, change intake procedures in order to give priority to different consumers, or modify existing services by decentralizing them.

Those who construct policy proposals often encounter multiple, often conflicting objectives, which makes their task more complicated than if they encountered only one objective, such as minimizing overall cost.[13] They must also con-

sider whether such proposals are effective in addressing a specific social condition, are politically feasible, and are implementable. A proposal that is relatively inexpensive may not have sufficient scope to allow effective solution of a problem.

In case example 2.1, social workers favoring a rehabilitation strategy might differ in the kinds of proposals they advance to a state legislature. One social worker might emphasize personal counseling services and propose linking the juvenile court with family counseling agencies. Another might desire job training and favor instead development of job-related services under the aegis of the courts. The two proposals might differ markedly in their total cost and ease of obtaining legislative approval.

Controversy in the Implementation Phase

In the implementation phase, social workers seek to identify and modify organizational factors perceived to impede achievement of specific policy objectives. As an example, a social worker in a juvenile court may be dissatisfied with the kinds of rehabilitative services offered by family counseling agencies to juvenile offenders. (The youth are referred by the courts to the agencies, which are paid for services rendered.) She may decide that services are ineffective because staff members in the family counseling agencies lack familiarity with the kinds of problems encountered by the juvenile offenders. Possible solutions include providing in-service training to agency staff and shifting services to court-hired staff.[14]

Controversy is common when persons are confronted with different opinions as to how best to correct shortcomings. In the above example, the social worker may favor placing services under the court but encounter opposition from several judges who do not want to be bothered with administration of court-provided services. Controversy is compounded when participants seek different program objectives. A judge who believes services are ineffective may oppose any policy proposals initiated by a social workers because he believes these professionals to be "do-gooders."

Controversy in the Assessment Phase

Social workers evaluate social programs and policies during the assessment phase. In many cases, judgments are made on the basis of "best guesses" that in turn may stem from professional judgment, feedback from consumers, and perceptions of administrators. In other cases, considerable use is made of empirical data gathered in program evaluation projects. Judgments about the merits of social programs can have considerable significance, since they influence decisions about continuation, expansion, and reforms of operating programs. In case example 2.1, some participants believe that existing juvenile offender programs are not effective, a judgment likely to spawn reform efforts.

Controversy during assessment phases is exacerbated when persons disagree about the relative importance of specific program objectives. In the case of services provided juvenile offenders, should primary importance be given to their effectiveness in reducing recidivism, improving school attendance and performance, strengthening family ties, or helping youth develop understanding of their personal problems? Without agreement about such factors, it would be difficult to develop evaluation strategies, much less agree about findings.[15]

Disagreements are also common about the weighting or importance of criteria to be used in deciding whether a program should be retained or modified. Policy participants often assess programs on the basis of criteria known as the five Es and one F: effectiveness, efficiency, equity, equality, externality, and feasibility outcomes.

Effectiveness outcomes are measured by analyzing whether consumers, on balance, are assisted by social programs, and how much. Effectiveness is not easy to gauge. States of mind, levels of functioning, and other criteria of consumer improvement in the wake of mental health and other interventions are difficult to define, much less measure. Then, too, background factors often influence outcomes to the point that it is difficult to disentangle program from background effects. In case example 2.1, movement toward a deterrent approach is prompted because many believe the rehabilitative approach to

be ineffective in reducing crime and recidivism, a charge countered by those questioning effectiveness of deterrence.

The *efficiency* criterion involves judgments about whether services or programs waste social resources. Cost reductions allow funders and government authorities to use saved resources to expand existing programs or mount new ones. Evaluators often examine effectiveness and efficiency outcomes simultaneously to see if programs and policies can be located that are both effective and efficient. (In some cases, programs that are effective in redressing social problems are prohibitively expensive, just as some programs are inexpensive but do not redress social problems.) A telling argument of those who favor rehabilitation programs for juvenile offenders (see case example 2.1) is that such programs are far less expensive than institutional programs. It costs only $500 per juvenile in many rehabilitation programs but $18,000 per year to house them in prisons. (Savings to society are even larger, of course, if rehabilitation programs prevent recidivism.)

Social reformers are particularly interested in *equity* and *equality* issues. A program is inequitable when two persons identical in other respects receive different services or resources from a program. Differential treatment can be caused by logistical or administrative factors. Many rural persons, for example, cannot receive the same medical care as urban residents because few physicians choose to locate in rural settings.

Inequity can also stem from orientations toward disadvantaged or powerless groups. *Prejudice* is negative orientations toward members of specific groups who are perceived to possess such undesirable characteristics as laziness, dishonesty, stupidity, duplicity, and criminality. Someone who despises blacks, for example, may not wish to extend social welfare benefits to them on grounds that they will become "yet more lazy."

Racism is prejudice directed toward groups whose members are considered physiologically homogeneous. *Institutional racism* is policies, often covert in nature, that discriminate against minorities in community, education, employment, and social service settings. Institutional racism is reflected in agency policies that exclude racial or other minorities from positions of employment; locate facilities in areas that are relatively inaccessible to specific groups; provide services that discourage certain kinds of persons from obtaining them; devise hours of service that make it difficult for certain groups to obtain assistance; or use informal procedures to refer some consumers away from agency services, while at the same time providing those services to others. Such policies may reflect an intent to discriminate or may merely reflect *de facto* discrimination, which exists whenever policies exclude certain groups from service.

Institutional prejudice is policies that systematically restrict any group, whether women, the mentally ill, criminal offenders, homosexuals, lesbians, the elderly, the physically handicapped, or the poor. Sexism, for example, is usually prejudice specifically directed against women; it is reflected in policies in some employment agencies that promote referrals of women to secretarial, clerical, and sales-oriented jobs and not to a broader range of opportunities. Ageism is prejudice against elderly persons; critics allege that many mental health professionals shun work with the elderly, who are often deemed to lack potential for marked personal change. Classism, prejudice against low-income persons, is present when service providers shun poverty-stricken consumers in favor of more affluent persons.

The extent to which a social program promotes *social equality* is ascertained by examining the extent to which it benefits some disadvantaged group, such as poor people, racial minorities, or women. In some cases, analysis of distribution of benefits is combined with scrutiny of methods of obtaining funds. The Social Security program, for example, has relied disproportionately on payroll deductions of the poor and lower-middle classes, a fact that has reduced its redistributive potential.

Equity and equality issues are obvious in case example 2.1. Even some defenders of rehabilitation programs agree that some sentences lack equity when judges have discretion. (A youth committing a petty theft may spend five years in a public facility, while a youth who commits murder may be given probation.) Members of black and other racial groups point to research that indicates discretion often leads to harsh treatment for their youth in comparison to whites. Deterrent approaches that reduce the discretion of judges and require harsh sentences for various crimes can also be criticized. Is the imposition of years of prison on low-income youth likely to facilitate their entry into the economic and social mainstream? (Poverty and lack of opportunity led some to resort to crime in the first place.)

Policy practitioners often assess policies as well in the context of *externalities,* i.e., the extent to which those policies have positive or adverse effects on external entities, such as society or social agencies. By providing less expensive alternatives to institutionalization, community-based service programs for juvenile offenders save government funds. This positive benefit to society is one rationale for increasing funding for these programs.

Finally, policy practitioners examine the extent to which policies meet *feasibility* criteria. Is a specific policy option politically feasible? Does an agency have sufficient budgetary resources to implement it? Do staff members in an agency possess the required technical expertise? These kinds of practical considerations assume crucial importance in many policy deliberations, since the best policy ideas come to naught if they founder on real-world barriers.

Participants often disagree about the relative importance to be given the various criteria.[16] An efficiency expert is likely to emphasize success in terms of reduction of costs (efficiency). Professionals are likely to emphasize the extent to which programs actually benefit consumers (effectiveness). Social reformers are most interested in equity and social equality outcomes. Of course, the ideal program would satisfy all the criteria, but, in many cases, policies and programs that score high on one may not meet the other criteria.

If persons often differ about the relative importance they attach to the various criteria, some also dismiss findings of social or policy research that run counter to deep-seated values or practical interests. In such cases, findings of even the most sophisticated studies or commissions are dismissed, an occurrence not uncommon in social welfare policy controversy. In the case of the juvenile offenders in case example 2.1, those who are convinced of the need for deterrent strategies will be likely to dismiss research findings suggesting that social service or job-finding strategies are viable alternatives.

Controversy in the Legitimation Phase

As discussed earlier, each of the seven core policy issues are germane to the legitimation phase. Ideas or options are considered in the various phases, often in the course of controversy. When persons seek collective approval for policies that emerge from any of the phases, they initiate the legitimation phase. A social worker may seek legitimation for a policy proposal designed in the analysis phase or approval for a new procedure devised during the implementation phase to correct malfunctioning of an operating program. In some cases, social workers use the findings of evaluation studies in the assessment phase to devise changes in existing programs, but they are unlikely to modify the programs until formal approval is obtained during the legitimation phase.

Clearly, then, the legitimation phase is pivotal, since recommendations and options devised during other policy phases cannot be translated into collective commitments until they are ratified by decision makers during this phase. Indeed, it is often not possible even to initiate activity in one of the other policy phases until decision makers agree that task forces, committees, or other kinds of deliberations need to be structured first to address specific policy issues. As an example, a social worker who wants an agency to invest more resources in addressing a specific community need is not likely to obtain a change in agency priorities unless some committee or group decides to consider the issue.

The controversial nature of social welfare policy is most obvious, of course, during the legitimation phase because binding commitments are sought.[17] Some persons may not object to policy options considered during scanning, analysis, implementation, and assessment phases because they are only under discussion but may object when they now see that binding policies could be enacted. In many cases, policy participants suffer losses in prestige, program responsibility, and remuneration when major policy changes are approved, particularly when program resources are diverted to others.

PRACTICE OF SOCIAL WELFARE POLICY

Preceding discussion suggests that social workers require a series of practical skills if they are to participate in the making of policy. At no prior time have staff in the social or human delivery systems encountered more controversy than in the 1980s. Not to participate in social welfare policy is tantamount to acceding to drastic cuts in social programs and in the federal government's role as well as to the narrowing of program eligibility to the point that only restricted groups, such as the very poor, can receive assistance. A rationale for participating in social welfare policy is provided by social work educator Nancy Humphreys in guest editorial 2.1 in the context of restrictive pressures on funding encountered in the 1970s and 1980s.

How can the practice of policy be conceptualized? Roles and skills that describe the practice of policy in the various phases of policy development (see illustration 2.3) need to be added to the policy framework presented earlier in this chapter.[18]

Policy Roles

The concluding section of the first chapter discussed various roles useful to social workers in policymaking. The purpose in introducing those roles even in the first chapter of this book was to underscore the practical relevance of policy to social workers in agency, community, and legislative settings. With that discussion as an intro-

Saving Social Services: Leading the Fight Against Cutbacks

By Nancy Humphreys

Over the next many months (some say years), rally-calls of "diminishing resources," "funding cuts," and "doing more with less" will be heard everywhere. Many states and localities have already cut many social service programs. In my home state of New Jersey, eleventh-hour legislative action following desperate attempts to find administrative remedies will, we hope, forestall a cut of over $600,000 in Medicaid funding—a cut which would drastically reduce basic medical services to thousands of ill people.

The great, underlying fear of social activists who ponder the future under a Reagan Administration is that social programs in particular will fall victim to cost-cutters seeking to slay the favorite political dragon of the day, government spending.

Indeed, it is more probable that we in the social services field are in for some very difficult times. The effects of budget-cutting will not be limited to public programs; the voluntary sector also will suffer. An inflation-ridden economy cannot produce enough philanthropic dollars to offset losses in the public sector. And, as the private voluntary agency becomes even more dependent on public dollars (it has already, through grants, contracts, and purchase-of-service arrangements), it

will very directly feel the pinch of reduced public spending.

Particularly troubling about these events is that they come on the heels of a marked increase in the need for social services. This has come about because of several factors.

Over the last two decades, social service advocates have worked to remove the stigma attached to those who avail themselves of the services. As a result, Americans are slowly recognizing that social services are a necessary cog in our very complex societal machinery.

We have also become more aware of, and have begun to document, the correlation between stress and the need for social services. And, a larger number of our population are now potential social service recipients through such public programs as Title XX.

It is ironic that as the need for social services increases, the money necessary to provide them is being reduced.

The social tensions that accrue from this inverse relationship are obvious, and suggest that social workers, the rightful leaders of the social service industry, need to act decisively to ward off a potentially difficult situation.

Our action must be guided by an awareness that cuts in social service funding, made by anyone at any time or anywhere, represent a conscious choice in the face of options. Cuts

---

duction, policy practice can now be integrated into the policy framework provided in this chapter. Various policy roles were defined in table 1.2 at the end of chapter 1, including discovering unmet needs and designing and implementing programs. These roles correspond to the

various phases of policy development. Thus, a *problem recognition and definition role* is assumed during the scanning phase as social workers identify conditions in the external world that are associated with deprivation or suffering (problem definition). During the analysis phase, social

are not foreordained; public dollars can be spent in any number of ways. The issue, rather, is whether or not the government will commit itself to assuring that social service needs are adequately met. We must not lose sight of this. We must constantly demand more adequate support of the programs that enrich the quality of our society, support that would not now be threatened if the country's priorities, as perceived by its elected leaders, were different.

We cannot, however, afford to be naive. We must also realize the dim prospect for a change in priorities, and must consider ways of dealing with the current choices.

We must be prepared immediately to fight, and fight hard, any attempt to redefine the need (i.e., eligibility) for—and, thus, people's right to—basic-survival social service programs. A characteristic way of reducing spending is to restrict eligibility for participation, and attempt to convince those no longer eligible that they do not need—and have no right to expect—certain social provisions, even such basic provisions as food.

It is widely feared that the Food Stamp program, which is up for renewal this year, will be in deep trouble when it faces the more conservative, cost-conscious and anti-social-program mentality of the new Congress. Probably, its opponents will try to cut it back by imposing a number of eligibility restrictions, including denial of benefits to strikers. NASW must fight these threats.

In leading the fight, we must be aware that the efforts to redefine need and reduce bene-fits afford us an opportunity to organize and mobilize new advocacy groups. The newly disenfranchised (e.g., organized labor and others, in the instance of Food Stamps) can add great power to the call for support of social service needs and programs. And we must be at the forefront in mobilizing these new constituencies to protest cuts.

But, perhaps the greatest danger to social programs' survival lies within. Shrinking resources increase the competition for the remaining funds. Over the last several years, our field has become more specialized (some may call it fragmented) with the emergence of a variety of special or "target" populations. Each of these specialized areas has its own loyal constituency and its advocacy initiatives. Usually, the advocates of one group vie with those of another to gain a share of the meager resources controlled by outsiders increasingly hostile to social service programs.

Because of this vying, much energy is wasted on internal power struggles that only further the objectives of anti-social-service forces, who are spared pressure and confrontation. All elements, constituencies, and advocates in the social services field must recognize this dilemma and work together to overcome it. At the same time, they must not compromise their own special interests.

To paraphrase: United, we stand a much better chance of surviving; divided, we place ourselves in great jeopardy. Our present adversity not only poses us a great challenge, but also offers us great opportunity. Much depends on how we respond to both.

Nancy Humphreys was president of the National Association of Social Workers. SOURCE: Copyright 1981, National Association of Social Workers, Inc. Reprinted by permission, from NASW NEWS, Vol. 26, No. 2 (February 1981), p. 2.

workers assume a *program design role,* in which they identify and choose between policy options for addressing specific social problems. In the implementation phase, they assume a *trouble-shooting role* as they try to locate logistical, administrative, or ideological factors that sabotage or otherwise undermine implementation of specific policies or directions. During the assessment phase, they engage in an *error detection role* as they try to ascertain whether, how, and to what extent operating programs are defective in meeting specific program objectives. When social

ILLUSTRATION 2.3   Policy Skills and Roles

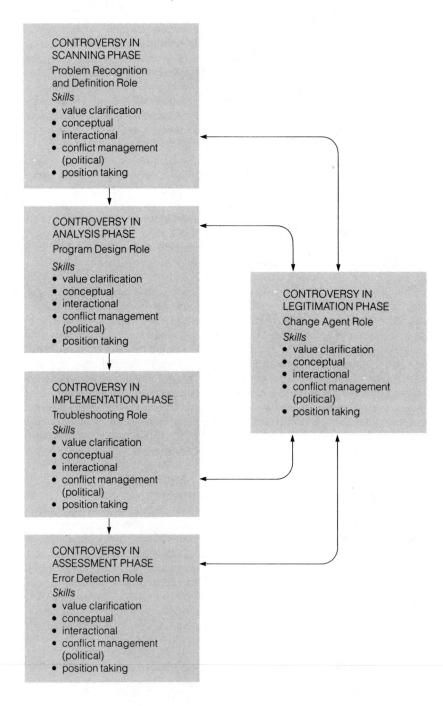

workers seek collective commitments to policies during the legitimation phase, they assume a *change agent role,* in which they devise political strategy to obtain approval of specific policies.

Even prior to assuming these roles, social work practitioners need to make a preliminary exploration of existing policies before deciding whether to participate in changing prevailing policy. As discussed earlier in this chapter, this *survey role* in the preliminary policy phase is directed toward examining (1) whether a policy issue exists, (2) whether a mobilization of bias preempts policy change, (3) which policy phase and locus might be used in initiating policy activity, and (4) which specific kinds of reform proposals are feasible in the context of sources, intensity, and locus of opposition. In one sense, the survey role functions as a gatekeeper, since social workers employ it to decide whether to proceed to one or more of the other policy phases.

When roles are defined in this manner, with titles suggestive of practical activities, it becomes even more obvious that all social workers, including direct service professionals, assume each of the roles. A direct service worker in a mental health program who believes intake procedures erroneously screen out certain kinds of consumers is filling an error detection role in the assessment phase. She may then engage in a program design role in the analysis phase as she seeks alternative methods of restructuring intake and then a change agent role in the legitimation phase as she seeks changes in agency policy. By the same token, an assistant assigned to a state legislator assumes each of the roles when variously helping the politician recognize and define unmet needs in the state, develop legislative proposals, critique the working of an existing state-funded social program, evaluate various social programs, and gauge levels of support for specific legislative provisions.

Policy Skills

We have used the term policy roles to describe the activities that participants undertake during each of the policy phases (preliminary, scanning,

analysis, implementation, assessment, and legitimation phases). Participants need various kinds of skills—which we will call *policy skills*—as they assume these various roles. Five kinds of skills are as important to policy practiconers as diagnostic and interviewing skills are to direct-service staff members in interventions with consumers. (Unlike in direct service, though, the objective in policy practice is to propose, modify, assess, or defend policies that singly or together comprise collective strategy to address social problems.) These policy skills are value clarification skills, conceptual skills, interactional skills, political skills, and position-taking skills. They are needed when assuming any of the various policy roles (see illustration 2.3).

Value Clarification Skills. The discussion in chapter 1 suggested that policy choices are influenced at many points by core and instrumental values. In some cases, underlying values are easily identified, as when a social worker opposes obvious forms of discrimination against specific racial minority or other outgroups. In other cases, social workers may discover that numerous and sometimes conflicting values need to be identified. In the case of a social worker who wants to target scarce program resources for the very poor (he favors redistribution to enhance equality) but who also values provision of resources to a broad spectrum of the population (he favors broadly based rather than narrow social programs), the two values conflict—and he would need to engage in value clarification to decide which takes precedence or how a compromise solution can be found.[19] In many cases, social workers try to make hidden values explicit, as illustrated by arguments that an objectionable policy rests on values that condone social and economic inequality.

Conceptual Skills. Social workers assume the various policy roles because existing policies and programs are inadequate. They need to be able to articulate whether current policies and programs meet efficiency, effectiveness, equity, equality, effort, and feasibility criteria (i.e., the five Es and one F discussed earlier). Then, too, participants must be able to identify a range of policy options to be considered in the various phases. As social workers assume a program design role in the analysis phase, for example, they should be familiar with various financing, administrative, and eligibility options.[20] They also need to be able to make comparisons between policy options as a prelude to taking positions, and they need skills in taking and then defending positions.

Interactional Skills. Person-to-person interaction occurs during each of the policy phases. Social workers need to be able to elicit opinions and information from others, engage in persuasion when they want others to accept a policy recommendation, and decipher the values and positions of others when they are not obvious. A director of a social work department in a major hospital, herself skilled in direct service work, argues that many clinical skills can be converted to policy uses because of the emphasis on person-to-person interaction. Social workers also participate in staff groups, task forces, committees, and coalitions during the various policy phases. They therefore need skills in helping groups accomplish tasks, develop leadership, maintain cohesion, and establish priorities.[21]

Political Skills. During the various phases, social workers need to be able to estimate the extent to which proposals are likely to be associated with conflict. In some cases, particularly in encounters with a well-organized and intense opposition, the only recourse is to withdraw.[22] In other cases, it may be advisable to proceed but to consider making compromises. In still other cases, social workers may decide that there is no recourse but to "fight to the finish" even when confronting formidable opposition. Personal values are crucial when making these decisions. If an issue is relatively unimportant, social workers may decide not to press forward when they encounter opposition. With other issues, they may decide that they must proceed even when defeat seems possible or even likely.

Position-Taking Skills. Social workers need to

be able to devise, present, and defend policy positions in the various phases. No matter how meritorious, positions are not likely to be accepted by others if they are not presented in convincing fashion. As discussed in more detail in chapter 9, many formats can be used when presenting positions, including lengthy documents, oral presentations, visual aids, and brief memoranda. The format, as well as the nature of supporting arguments, must be chosen with the audience in mind. In some cases, a detailed and technical written report may be an effective vehicle for obtaining support. In other cases, an informal oral presentation that highlights arguments likely to be appreciated by the audience may be more effective. Social workers also need to be able to foresee the kinds of arguments that are likely to be used by potential opponents so that they can devise effective counter-arguments in advance.

Combining Roles and Skills

Policy roles and skills are illustrated in policy practice case 2.2, which discusses the activities of a director of planning in the United Way. This case illustrates not only the multiplicity of such roles and skills but also the fact that participants do not proceed from one to another in predictable fashion. Because of the fluid nature of policy development, sequential use of roles and skills often cannot be planned. At the outset, the director of planning in policy practice case 2.2 assumes a problem recognition and definition role in the scanning phase when obtaining information about the problem of displaced homemakers. (Even prior to this, she decides that it is feasible to initiate policy proposals when she assumes a survey role in the preliminary policy phase, since she finds considerable community interest in helping displaced homemakers and decides that lack of employment counseling and training constitutes a serious policy issue.) She then successively assumes roles in analysis, scanning, and legitimation phases. Actions of others in the case force her to modify her strategy, as when some persons unexpectedly question whether the needs of women are as important as the needs of unemployed teenagers.

This social work director uses value clarification, conceptual, interactional, political, and position-taking skills as she engages in the various roles. Core values pertaining to social and economic equality for women prompt the planner to undertake the planning project in the first instance. Instrumental values influence the choice of the YWCA as the implementing agency. *Value clarification* skills are particularly necessary when the planner must decide whether to hold out for a large project or to ac-cept a smaller one in light of scarce resources.

She uses *conceptual skills* during scanning, analytical, and legitimation phases whenever she helps the committee identify and choose between policy options, such as whether to place a career center under the aegis of the YWCA or to use a feminist center. *Interactional skills* are used when forming a task force, when negotiating policy, and when sounding out policy preferences of key participants. Since policy options are chosen during the course of deliberations,

---

POLICY PRACTICE CASE 2.2

Policy Roles and Activities of a United Way Planner

The social work director of planning in a United Way agency had long been concerned about problems of displaced homemakers. A preliminary analysis of the issue in her jurisdiction suggested widespread interest in the issue, so she decided to proceed further (she assumed a *survey role* in the *preliminary policy phase*).

Although she had anecdotal evidence, she did not know the extent or seriousness of the problem and so decided to initiate an inquiry (i.e., she assumed a *problem recognition and definition* role in the *scanning phase*). A first step, she decided, was to form a task force to give prominence to the issue in order to form a base of support. In the first meeting, the committee members decided that they should spend at least a year obtaining information; they foresaw developing specific recommendations to the board of United Way.

The committee gathered considerable information during the year about existing training programs and unemployment rates among women and also convened a number of meetings of residents to obtain information about the seriousness of the problem. Data indicated the existence of a major social problem that agency programs did not address. The committee then explored a variety of pol-icy options (here the planner is assuming a *program design role* in the *analysis phase*). One option was to place a central career center for women under the aegis of the YWCA; another was to use a feminist center. For a variety of reasons, they chose the YWCA option and framed a proposal to the United Way requesting seed money for the center.

At this point, black and Hispanic members of the United Way board questioned whether employment needs of women are as important as those of black and Hispanic unemployed teenagers (the *legitimation phase* was now entered). A meeting of the task force was held at which members engaged in often contentious discussion of this issue. The upshot was submission of the women's career center proposal with an amendment suggesting an expanded committee to devise another proposal for unemployed teenagers. A meeting of the United Way board ensued at which the planner was, in effect, an advocate for the enlarged proposal (here she assumes a *change agent* role in the *legitimation phase*). She presented technical information supportive of the proposal. Sensing that compromise was needed in light of scarce resources, she reluctantly supported a modified and less costly program.

choices are influenced by personal relationships. Therefore, skillful practitioners develop and use interpersonal and group relationships.

Political skills are most evident at the end of the case, when the social worker senses that compromise is needed. Conflict is frequently present in policy deliberations, particularly when participants possess divergent values and interests. Skillful practitioners are able to build support for positions by developing and using power resources, organizing coalitions, and developing strategy.

She uses *position-taking skills* whenever she develops, presents, and defends policy positions. At the end of the case, for example, she "presents technical information supportive of the proposal" to create a women's career center as well as a supporting amendment for a committee that would develop a proposal for unemployed teenagers. Her skill in this position-taking activity facilitates subsequent adoption by the United Way Board of the proposal, a proposal that might otherwise have been rejected because of scarce resources.

SUMMARY

Policies are shaped during a multiphased process. In the scanning phase, social problems are identified, conceptualized, and ranked according to their importance. During the analysis phase, policy options are identified regarding the priority given consumers, intervention strategies, and preferred organizational and funding approaches. Organizational policies are analyzed as they facilitate or impede achievement of policy objectives during the implementation phase. Social workers develop accountability strategies during the assessment phase to demonstrate to funders, government authorities, and consumers that programs are effective—and to facilitate informed choices about retention, deletion, expansion, and modification of social programs.

A policy framework is useful that highlights the importance of politics during each of the phases and whenever participants seek approval for policy choices. In this perspective, politics is not a single phase or an irritating distraction but

is endemic to the entire policy process. (This is particularly true because of the prevalence of sources of controversy discussed in chapter 1, i.e., divergent values, ideologies, political stakes, economic interests, and theoretical orientations.)

Social workers who seek policy reforms in agency, community, and legislative settings need to engage in preliminary analysis of "mobilization of bias" for or against basic changes in policy in order to gauge the extent to which political and economic interests, values and ideologies, and existing technical evidence provide a favorable climate for change. With such analysis as a backdrop, they can then decide how to initiate activity and whether to initiate it in scanning, analysis, implementation, assessment, or legitimation phases. In agencies and legislatures, they must choose a locus for initial intervention.

Once a reform process is initiated, social workers need to gauge the anticipated response to specific policy recommendations. Do multiple sources of opposition exist in the form of background values, ideologies, interests, and technical factors? What is the intensity of opposition? Do opponents outbalance supporters? These kinds of questions are asked by social workers as they participate in the various phases.

To be effective, social workers need to develop skills in the practice of policy. Although many authors emphasize technical or analytical skills, a range of skills is required. A first step is to define task-related activities, including problem recognition and definition (scanning phase), program design (analysis phase), troubleshooting (implementation phase), error detection (assessment phase), and change agent roles (legitimation phase).

Policy practitioners also have to use a survey role in the preliminary policy phase to identify policy issues and to decide whether to initiate policy activity in one of the other policy phases. When undertaking each of these various roles, social workers need to develop value clarification, conceptual, interactional, conflict management or political, and position-taking skills. Policy roles and skills are not usually used in a predictable sequence, since many factors, including activities of other participants, influence the unfolding of policy.

Key Concepts, Developments, and Policies

Policy phases	Effectiveness
Policy issues in policy phases	Efficiency
Policy framework	Equity
Prevailing policies	Equality
Mobilization of bias	Externality
Background factors	Feasibility
Political and economic interests	Policy roles
Relevant values and ideologies	Policy skills
Relevant technical evidence	Prejudice
Initiating policy reforms by locus and phase	Institutional racism
Feasibility of specific reforms	Survey role
Sources, locus, and intensity of opposition	Problem recognition and definition role
Balance of forces	Program design role
Preliminary phase	Troubleshooting role
Scanning phase	Error detection role
Analysis phase	Change agent role
Implementation phase	Value clarification skill
Assessment phase	Interactional skill
Legitimation phase	Conceptual skill
Controversy in phases	Political skill
Alternative criteria for assessing policies	Position-taking skill

Main Points

1. Social welfare policy evolves in a policy formulation process.

2. In the preliminary phase, social workers survey existing policies to determine whether policy issues exist, whether policy changes are possible, and how change-oriented projects can be initiated.

3. In the scanning phase, social workers identify, define, and gauge the importance of specific social problems.

4. In the analysis phase, social workers design programs and delivery systems.

5. In the implementation phase, social workers scrutinize operating programs to see how they can be improved.

6. In the assessment phase, social workers evaluate policies and programs.

7. A policy framework is needed that depicts the various policy phases in a systems framework that links them to broader political, economic, cultural, ideological, background, and technical factors.

8. Prevailing policies provide the starting point for policy development. Social workers use a survey role in the preliminary policy phase to decide whether a policy issue exists and whether they need to proceed to another policy phase. (Various tasks in this preliminary policy phase are described in points 9, 10, and 11).

9. When developing strategy for changing existing policy, social workers often need to determine the extent to which a "mobilization of bias" exists against basic changes.

10. Social workers need to carefully choose a lo-

cus and policy phase when initiating policy changes.

11. When assessing the feasiblity of specific reforms, social workers must often consider the sources, intensity, and locus of opposition, prior traditions of controversy associated with a proposal, and the relative balance of resources of opponents and proponents.

12. Controversy often exists in the various policy phases, as illustrated by different emphases placed on effectiveness, efficiency, equity, equality, externality, and feasibility criteria in the assessment phase.

13. The practice of policy often requires familiarity with six policy roles that correspond to the six policy phases: survey, scanning, program and policy design, change agent, troubleshooting, and error detection roles.

14. When assuming these policy roles, social workers use value clarification, conceptual, interactional, political, and position-taking skills.

Questions for Discussion

1. Review case example 2.1, and assume you are a legislative assistant charged with analyzing the issue of juvenile crime in a specific state. Discuss kinds of tasks and issues you might encounter as you analyze juvenile crime in the state, propose legislation, and analyze and assess existing programs. (Refer to the various policy phases in your discussion.)

2. Discuss the statement "The legitimation phase intersects with each of the other policy phases."

3. Assume that you wanted to resist the trend in case example 2.1 to place juveniles under the jurisdiction of adult courts and that you want instead to create special programs and facilities for youth who have committed homicides. What kinds of background factors, political and economic interests, and technical evidence might you need to examine as you analyze the extent of the "mobilization of bias" against your proposal?

4. When developing a specific proposal for assisting juveniles who have committed homicides, what kinds of factors might you anticipate when gauging its feasibility?

5. Take a policy issue in an agency or organization with which you are familiar.

What options might you wish to consider regarding locus and phase of the policy cycle when initiating policy changes?

6. Discuss the statement "Policies that meet one or several criteria are often not satisfactory on other counts." (Refer to effectiveness, efficiency, equity, equality, and externality criteria.)

7. How might a direct service worker in an agency assume each of the five policy roles discussed in this chapter?

8. In policy practice case 2.1, which discusses the issue of patient access to records, do you think the social worker has identified an important or trivial policy issue? What kinds of considerations should be used to decide whether a policy issue is sufficiently important to merit investment of time and resources?

9. In policy practice case 2.1, do you think that the social worker would be able to obtain modification of existing agency policies? Or was there a strong "mobilization of bias" against change?

10. How does policy practice case 2.2 illustrate the statement "No simple sequential order typifies the policymaking process"?

Suggested Readings

Anderson, James. *Public Policy-Making* (New York: Praeger, 1975). The author discusses various phases of policy formulation, with specific reference to the development of government policies.

Cloward, Richard, and Piven, Frances Fox. *Regulating the Poor: The Functions of Public Welfare* (New York: Pantheon, 1971). The authors discuss how the political and economic interests of corporations and the affluent lead to policies that perpetuate poverty.

Dye, Thomas. *Understanding Public Policy* (Englewood Cliffs, N.J.: Prentice-Hall, 1978): Chapter 2. An overview of policymaking processes delineating interest group, bureaucratic, and legislative factors that influence the choice of policies in American society.

Gil, David. *Unravelling Social Policy* (Cambridge, Mass.: Schenkman, 1976): "A Framework for Analysis and Synthesis of Social Policies," pp. 31–56. The author provides an analytical framework that emphasizes the dynamics of policy choices in the context of assessments of their relative merits. In this sense, his framework applies specifically to the analytical phase of the larger framework presented in this chapter.

Gilbert, Neil, and Specht, Harry. *Dimensions of Social Welfare Policy* (Englewood Cliffs, N.J.: Prentice-Hall, 1974): "Framework for Social Welfare Policy Analysis," pp. 24–53. The authors describe recurring policy issues, or "major dimensions of choice," including those presented in this book and supplemented by others that arise in scanning, implementation, and assessment phases.

Jones, Charles. *An Introduction to the Study of Public Policy* (Belmont, Calif.: Wadsworth, 1970). A useful overview of phases in the policy formulation cycle, with particular reference to development of national policies.

Rein, Martin. "Social Work in Search of a Radical Profession." *Social Work*, 15 (April 1970): 13–29. The author discusses cleavages within the social work profession regarding social reform as well as agency and funding constraints that often impel professionals to take relatively conservative positions.

Rothman, Sheila. *Women's Proper Place: A History of Changing Ideals and Practice, 1870 to the Present* (New York: Basic Books, 1978): "Liberation Politics," pp. 257–290. An overview of contemporary issues and political obstacles confronted by feminists.

Tropman, John, et al. *New Strategic Perspectives on Social Policy* (New York: Pergamon, 1981): pp. 181–257. Assorted readings discuss various "policy competencies."

Notes

1. Dennis Romig, *Justice for Our Children* (Lexington, Mass.: Lexington, 1978).

2. See Alfred J. Kahn, *Theory and Practice of Social Planning* (New York: Russell Sage Foundation, 1969); Gilbert and Specht, *Dimensions of Social Welfare Policy*, pp. 14–20; and Tropman et al., eds., *New Strategic Perspectives on Social Policy*, pp. 257–369.

3. Charles O. Jones, *An Introduction to the Study of Public Policy* (Belmont, Calif.: Wadsworth, 1970).

4. The term "mobilization of bias" is from Eric Schattschneider, *The Semisovereign People* (New York: Holt, Rinehart and Winston, 1960), p. 71. Also see Gil, *Unravelling Social Policy*, pp. 143–156.

5. Analysis of contending interests in specific policy arenas is discussed by Eugene Bardach, *Skill Factor in Politics* (Berkeley: University of California Press, 1972). Also see George Brager and Stephen Holloway, *Changing Human Service Organizations* (New York: Free Press, 1970), pp. 107–128.

6. Brager and Holloway, *Changing Human Service Organizations*, pp. 157–205.

7. Techniques for estimating support and opposition for policies can be found in William D. Coplin and Michael K. O'Leary, *Everyman's Prince* (North Scituate, Mass.: Duxbury, 1976); Jack Rothman et al., *Fostering Participation and Promoting Innovation* (Itasca, Ill.: Peacock, 1978); and Brager and Holloway, *Changing Human Service Organiztions*, pp. 107–128.

8. Florence M. Ruderman, *Child Care and Working Mothers* (New York: Child Welfare League of America, 1968), and Shirley M. Buttrick, "Issues in Day Care," *Social Work*, 17 (March 1972): 106–107.

9. For discussion of the conservative position, see John K. Inglehart, "Welfare Report: Congress Passes Major Child Care Program Despite White House Veto," *National Journal*, 3 (October 23, 1971): 2125–2130.

10. Arnold Green, *Social Problems: Arena of Conflict* (New York: McGraw-Hill, 1975), pp. 209–238.

11. Discussion of competing policy options is found in Gilbert and Specht, *Dimensions of Social Welfare Policy*, pp. 54–177.

12. Inglehart, "Welfare Report," 2125–2130.

13. Multiple objectives in proposals are discussed by Bernard Brock et al., *Public Policy Decision Making* (New York: Harper & Row, 1973), pp. 85–109.

14. See, for example, Jeffrey L. Pressman and Aaron Wildavsky, *Implementation* (Berkeley: University of California Press, 1973), and Robert S. Montjoy and Laurence J. O'Toole, "Toward a Theory of Policy Implementation," *Public Administration Review*, 39 (January 1980): 465–477.

15. Alice Rivlin, *Systematic Thinking for Social Action* (Washington, D.C.: Brookings Institution, 1971).

16. See, for example, Arthur Okun, *Equality and Efficiency: The Big Tradeoff* (Washington, D.C.: Brookings Institution, 1975).

17. Lewis Coser, *Functions of Social Conflict* (Glencoe, Ill.: Free Press, 1956), and Morton Deutsch, *The Resolution of Conflict* (New Haven, Conn.: Yale University Press, 1973).

18. For discussion of policy skills, see Tropman et al., eds., *New Strategic Perspectives on Social Policy*, pp. 181–217.

19. Martin Rein, "Conflicting Goals in Social Policy," in Rein, *Social Policy*, pp. 249–270.

20. A framework for policy analysis is provided by William Dunn, *Public Policy Analysis* (Englewood Cliffs, N.J.: Prentice-Hall, 1981), pp. 34–63.

21. See John Tropman, "The Relationship between Staffer Roles and Policy Committees," in Tropman et al., eds., *New Strategic Perspectives on Social Policy*, pp. 185–202.

22. Brager and Holloway, *Changing Human Service Organizations*, pp. 107–205.

PART 2

Policy Scanning and Analysis:
The Conceptual Phases

The scanning phase is discussed in chapter 3. Policy controversy often stems from disagreement about the relative importance of specific conditions in the external world. Those who seek new or expanded programs to address one or another social problem are often countered by those who give those programs lower priority. Then, too, persons often differ in how they define the scope, nature, and causes of problems—as reflected by a case example of policies regarding alcoholism. The chapter concludes with a discussion of the roles and skills needed by participants who assume a problem recognition and problem definition role during the scanning phase.

Two chapters are devoted to the analysis phase because of the multitude of program design issues in contemporary America. Issues pertaining to the structure of the delivery system and allocation of program resources and services are discussed in chapter 4. Difficult choices have to be made about staffing, location, and content of services, as well as relationships between agencies. A case example is presented that pertains to development of halfway houses and vocational training for the developmentally disabled.

A case example describing President Ronald Reagan's "block grant strategy" is used in chapter 5 to highlight issues pertaining to funding of social programs, a topic particularly crucial during the current era of scarce resources. Issues pertaining to "policy oversight" are also discussed, i.e., methods of regulating and overseeing policy implementation including roles of federal and local governments, courts, and consumers in decision making.

The reader will note that the policy framework discussed in chapter 2 is used again, in somewhat modified form, at the beginning of chapters 3 and 4 to facilitate discussion of the scanning and analysis phases.

CHAPTER 3

The Scanning Phase: Social Needs and Social Problems

The scanning phase undergirds all others, since concepts and definitions of social problems shape the kinds of programs and proposals constructed in the analysis phase as well as the procedures and policies chosen during program implementation. Further, issues raised during the scanning phase are often associated with controversy during the legitimation phase. Those who want more funds and resources directed to specific social needs are often countered by those who argue that a specific problem is not serious or that other problems are more important.

The scanning phase is central to the activities of social workers. The work of direct service staff is influenced by prevailing concepts about the nature and causes of the social problems they encounter. In some cases, they face difficult dilemmas—when, for example, they are asked to participate in relatively harsh or deterrent strategies.[1] In turn, professionals try to alter mistaken or simplistic approaches favored by administrators, legislators, funders, or the general public. Professionals who work in social programs draw on professional experience and training as well as social science research when assuming a problem recognition and definition role in the scanning phase. Social workers need to be able to:

Identify contextual background, political, cultural, and technical factors that influence definitions of specific social problems

Use various technical approaches to gauge the importance and location of social problems and needs

Identify political and economic realities that influence the importance attached to specific problems or needs

CASE EXAMPLE 3.1

ALCOHOLISM

Our No. 1 Drug Problem

By Shelley Wood

Alcoholism is probably as old as alcohol, but in recent years the extent of the social problem it presents has been pushed out of public view by concern over the high incidence of narcotics experimentation. In the meantime, the abuse of alcohol has continued to rise and to increase also among females and teen-agers. Now, officials are beginning to acknowledge that California's number-one drug problem is still alcoholism. What has made the difference is a change in attitude: State agencies, the Legislature and even the police are moving away from treating alcoholics as criminals or degenerates and accepting instead the view that alcoholism is America's most untreated treatable disease.

Yet, this change in attitude hasn't been as far-reaching as it will apparently have to be in order to address the problem squarely state-wide. Despite the fact that public drunkenness has been officially decriminalized and that rehabilitation efforts are being beefed up with some success, anti-alcoholism programs aren't always working out the way planners had hoped.

One of 12 Californians . . .

At least one million Californians—one of every 12 over the age of 20—suffer from alcoholism. Few of these people fit the usual stereotype of the skid-row down-and-outer. In fact, public inebriates comprise only about four percent of the alcoholic population. The problem drinkers look on the surface pretty much like everyone else but while they remain undetected the scope of their problem spreads. As it does, California government and business lose at least $400 million annually in lost wages—and probably a good deal more than that.

Analyze the causes of specific social problems and use this information to devise policies

Understand that specific social problems have different manifestations and causes in subgroups of the population

These topics are discussed in this chapter because they provide conceptual tools used during the scanning phase in agency, community, and legislative settings. The policy practice case discussed at the end of the chapter illustrates scanning concepts and skills used by one social worker.

The problem of alcoholism is used in this chapter to facilitate discussion of issues in the scanning phase (see case example 3.1). No major problem has proven more difficult to solve, much less to conceptualize and address, than alcoholism.[2] It is difficult to determine what behaviors distinguish alcoholism from problem or social drinking. Because many alcoholics hide their problem, researchers find it difficult to measure its prevalence and to identify and weigh the importance of its various genetic, cultural, mental, occupational, and economic causes. Social strategy to address alcoholism is influenced by these various issues. (As will become apparent in chapters 10 through 13, similar issues arise in scanning phases associated with many child and family, mental, physical, and economic problems.)

Even more critical is the cost to the alcoholics themselves. Although as a cause of death alcoholism still ranks tenth in California, the number of fatalities due to alcoholism among those aged 35 to 64 has risen sharply. Taking this figure into account, alcohol becomes the fourth major health threat in this productive age group. It is surpassed only by heart disease, cancer and mental illness. Even worse, recent studies indicate that drinking drivers are involved in at least one-third of all California highway traffic fatalities and in 20 percent of all injury accidents.

Drunkenness Decriminalized

The first big official turn-around in the approach to alcoholism took place in 1971, when the Legislature passed Senator George Deukmejian's bill to decriminalize drunkenness. Although its implementation has been much less than widespread, the possibility now exists for counties to stop "the revolving door" court process of repeated jail sentences for public drunks with no effort at treatment of their drinking problem. Enactment also constituted a decision by the state to treat public

California's Problem Drinkers

Total population	19,953,134
Population over 20	12,251,431
Problem drinkers	1,151,760
Arrests for public intoxication	254,877
Arrests for drunk driving	199,174

Source: Office of Alcohol Program Management

drunkenness as an illness, instead of as a crime, it being thought that the law would provide an impetus for establishing a statewide network of centers to receive and treat people with an alcohol dependency.

Under this law, counties can eliminate public drunkenness as a crime. Instead of arresting a person found inebriated in public, a civil procedure can be followed; under it, an officer can take an inebriate into protective custody and place him in a local health facility for up to 72 hours. After detoxification there, the person is released but encouraged to seek further medical treatment, if necessary. The catch, however, is that drunkenness can only be decriminalized where detoxification centers have been established. And the funds for

CRITICAL TASKS IN THE SCANNING PHASE

Social workers address four related questions during the scanning phase (see illustration 3.1). First, how important are specific social problems, i.e., do they merit investment of social (or agency) resources? Second, what parameters or limits should be used when defining social problems? Third, what causal or precipitating factors are useful in devising interventions to address the needs of persons who already experience specific problems? Finally, how can policies and programs be shaped so that social interventions address the needs of specific populations? (Alcoholism and other social problems are hardly uniform or unvarying phenomena, as illustrated by the differences between suburban housewife, skid-row, teenage, and blue-collar alcoholics, not to mention alcoholics from different ethnic and racial groups.)

These four questions are interrelated, as depicted in illustration 3.1. The relative importance of a social problem, for example, cannot be determined until decisions are made about how to define it. In the case of alcoholism, criteria must be established to decide what drinking behaviors constitute alcoholism as a prelude to measuring its prevalence. Before these central questions are discussed in more detail, it is important to consider the influence of background, cultural, political, and technical factors on scanning activities.

constructing them have so far been made available only in seven of the state's 58 counties—San Diego, Santa Barbara, Sacramento, Monterey, Santa Clara, San Mateo and San Joaquin. No funds have yet gone to the two counties with the highest incidence of drunkenness arrests: Los Angeles and San Francisco. . . .

Detoxification centers have come in for their share of criticism. Detractors point out that they are at best stop-gap measures that may allow the inebriate to sober up safely yet don't attack causes of drunkenness.

Police Attitude

Related to decriminalization is the changed outlook of those who often have the most contact with alcoholics—law-enforcement personnel. According to Dick Iglehart of the California Peace Officers' Association, the police would "love to be rid of the criminalistic approach to public drunkenness. For the police to pick up these people is an administrative hassle," he explained. "If there were some way to avoid it, they would." Iglehart, who represents California law-enforcement officers' interests in Sacramento, believes that detoxification centers are becoming more widely accepted by the police for the practical reason that drunks ought not to be increasing the jail population. Penalties for drunkenness do not deter the chronic public drunk, he observed, and the process of jailing inebriates just drains funds needed elsewhere.

A health problem as extensive and costly as alcoholism must be dealt with on a large scale. So far, the nature of alcoholism and how society views it seem to have precluded such a major state effort. A loosely connected series of treatment programs have existed for some time, but only recently has attention been directed toward the problem from the outside. The consequence of this concern has been an increase in the size, scope and number of programs financed or supervised by the state. . . .

The state's primary role is not to establish the actual alcoholism programs, but to coordinate what Director Loran Archer of the Office of Alcohol Program Management calls the "alcohol system." It is within this system that the alcoholic could find the kind of help most compatible with his needs. The major components of this system of direct assistance are:

- *Alcoholics Anonymous*. Probably the best known of all alcoholism-abuse programs, AA is not funded by the state, but depends on the endeavors of its alcoholic members to help themselves.

- *Out-patient clinics*. Offering such techniques as group therapy and counseling to alcoholics, 19 clinics now operate throughout the state.

- *Recovery houses*. The more than 200 of these facilities provide residential arrangements for alcoholics who need to be in a semi-protective atmosphere. Recovery houses, staffed by non-drinking alcoholics, only recently became recipients of public funding.

OVERVIEW OF THE SCANNING PHASE

Deliberations about the nature and causes of social problems are influenced by a range of contextual, cultural, and technical considerations that often lead to divergent definitions of those problems as well as to divergent assessments of their causes and importance (see illustration 3.2).

Background Factors

Activities of participants in the scanning phase are influenced by many background factors.[3] In the mental health sector, for example, the devel-

- *Detoxification centers.* These serve as entry points into the system for those typically not a part of society's mainstream.

- *Toll-free telephone number.* By calling (800) 372-6450, a person can receive information about available alcohol-treatment programs. The service is sponsored by the state alcoholism office.

- *The Department of Rehabilitation.* Only one of many state agencies involved in alcohol-abuse programs, rehabilitation offers vocational training to those classified as handicapped by alcoholism.

Which of these approaches is most effective depends upon whom one is trying to reach. Detox centers, for example, are suited to down-and-outers, while clinics are better for the working alcoholic. The state has thus shied away from trying to devise one program to take in everyone—an orientation that also prevents creation of a non-duplicative and co-ordinated approach. . . .

Some Success

The major obstacle to coherence faced by the state is the lack of definitive information. No one knows precisely how many alcoholics there are, how they break down by race, sex, and income, or even how many are actually being treated. This problem stems from inadequacies in the methods used for compiling statistics, and it has hampered the delivery of services and allowed local groups to escape

Where Alcoholism Is Greatest

County	Total Population	Number Problem Drinkers	%
1. San Francisco	715,674	145,325	20
2. Sierra	2,365	280	12.2
3. Calaveras	13,585	1,330	9.7
4. Tuolumne	22,169	2,060	9.3
5. Lake	19,548	1,780	9.1

Source: Office of Alcohol Program Management

the kind of control that might draw them into a coordinated system. The concentration of programs at the local level enables services to be close to the alcoholic's daily life, and leaves room to tailor treatment to the individual; but it also prevents offering a uniform level of service in the state.

In spite of the administration and operational problems, however, Archer remains optimistic. "If I could get the same return on stock that this office gets on its rate of success with alcoholics, I could retire," he declared. Much of Archer's optimism stems from a study of 2,000 individuals who had gone through alcoholism programs. When analysts compared how much the subjects were earning before treatment and 18 months later, the increased amount of taxes they now contributed was found to exceed the cost of their treatment. (This finding does not include such indirect savings as the need for fewer hospital beds and decreased family problems.)

SOURCE: Shelley Wood, "Alcoholism," *California Journal* (June 1974), pp. 199–201. Reprinted by permission.

opment of a variety of mood-altering drugs has allowed many mental patients to live in community rather than institutional settings. This reality has forced researchers and practitioners to explore community factors that precipitate and exacerbate mental problems. Demographic realities have also assumed major importance. Dra-

matic increases in the number of senior citizens has led to increased interest in research into their medical, housing, and social needs.

Cultural Factors

Definitions of social problems are influenced by cultural or value factors that change over time.

ILLUSTRATION 3.1   Four Intersecting Issues in the Scanning Phase

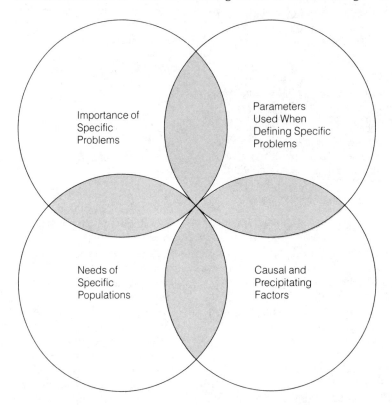

Definitions of drug addiction, for example, vary widely. At the turn of the century, many Americans, including affluent ones, used cocaine, a custom now (but not then) widely perceived as a social problem. Many definitions of alcoholism also exist. The Australians and the French are heavy consumers of alcohol, but drinking beer in pubs or mealtime consumption of wine is not likely to be perceived as alcoholism, even when consumers imbibe heavily. Other people establish low levels of consumption when defining alcoholism, as illustrated by prohibitionists.[4]

Definitions are influenced by cultural and value factors in part because social problems are typically defined in the context of deviations from a social norm. Alcoholics are distinguished from others not just because they drink, but because they drink "far more" than others. Persons are perceived as having mental problems because they exhibit symptoms of anxiety or depression more acutely than others. Persons are perceived to be poverty-stricken because they have significantly less economic resources than others.[5]

Definitions that involve deviations from a social norm, however, rest on an uncertain foundation. As social norms change, established definitions become outmoded, as illustrated by drastic change in marijuana use, a practice so widespread that laws treating usage as criminal behavior have been modified in many jurisdictions. Estimates of how much deviation is required to constitute "deviance" are subject to cultural factors. To some, drastic deviations are required, as when conservatives argue that society should as-

ILLUSTRATION 3.2   An Overview of the Scanning Phase

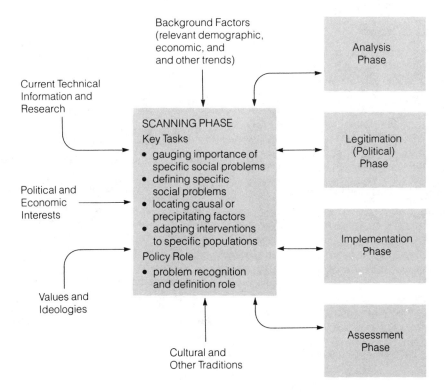

sist only "truly needy" poor persons who have virtually no resources (see illustration 3.3). To others, only minor deviations suggest that social problems exist. Many argue that persons who have relatively minor bouts with anxiety or depression should receive assistance from mental health programs in contrast to others, who believe publicly funded mental health programs should primarily assist persons who are seriously disabled.

Definitions of social need are influenced by values pertaining to social equality. Social reformers seek social programs in part to elevate the income, health, education, and opportunity of those who fall beneath prevailing social norms. Such programs are staunchly opposed by those who insist that it is utopian to seek equality or who believe that marked inequality is neces-

sary for a healthy economy. Some argue, for example, that economic inequality promotes competition for well-paying and demanding jobs, competition that in turn promotes greater productivity. But persons with egalitarian perspectives counter that gross income differentials are not required, since persons seek challenging positions even when incumbents are not paid extraordinarily well.

Political Factors

Some factions profit from the existence of social problems, as reflected by the indifference of manufacturers of alcoholic beverages to excessive drinking, resistance by the cigarette industry to government efforts to decrease smoking, opposition by employers to programs to reduce

ILLUSTRATION 3.3

"YOU DON'T LOOK TRULY NEEDY TO ME ... NEEDY PERHAPS, BUT NOT TRULY NEEDY!"

Paul Conrad, © 1981, *Los Angeles Times*. Reprinted by permission.

occupational hazards, and opposition by the affluent to programs to redistribute economic resources to the poor (see case example 3.2). Political considerations also have a more subtle influence on deliberations in scanning phases. Some persons deny causal factors that imply or require the need for basic social reforms. For example, those who perceive alcoholism as simply a manifestation of the psychological problems of specific individuals are unlikely to analyze occupational, stress, advertising, and other contributing factors. Feminists, in contrast, argue that escalating rates of alcoholism among housewives are partly caused by denial of access to fulfilling jobs in a labor market that discriminates against women. In similar fashion, Americans have been disinclined to mount major programs that address economic and social causes of health problems in low-income communities.

Technical Factors

Many participants in scanning draw on research from the social and biological sciences. In some

CASE EXAMPLE 3.2

Alcoholics' Aid Bill's Chances Slim

Rehabilitation Effort Heavily Opposed by Beverage Lobby

By Bill Billiter

Times Staff Writer

SACRAMENTO—"Drunks are sick and they are hurting, but they have no lobbyists," said Deputy Los Angeles Police Chief Ron Frankle. "They have nothing."

Frankle was describing the legisative odds against a bill designed to help alcoholics, especially those in California's urban areas.

The bill is scheduled to be acted on Wednesday by the Assembly Revenue and Taxation Committee, but it is solidly opposed

by the powerful alcoholic beverage lobby; thus its chances of approval are said to be slim.

The measure, sponsored by Assemblyman Art Torres (D-Los Angeles), would raise about $17 million a year in increased state taxes on alcoholic beverages, including beer and wine. The increased money would be earmarked for a new alcoholism prevention, treatment and rehabilitation fund that cities and counties could draw on for comprehensive help programs for alcoholics.

Among such projects would be help for "public inebriates"—alcoholics who roam city

instances, contradictory research findings complicate their work, as illustrated by controversy in the medical sector over the causes and cures of such ailments as heart disease and cancer. Still, research technology is one method of obtaining systematic evidence about the causes and prevalence of social problems, information that is useful in the development of intervention strategies.[6]

Relationships between Scanning and Other Phases

Activities in the scanning phase influence other phases as well (see illustration 3.1). A social worker who is devising a proposal in the analysis phase to assist alcoholics in a community center would need to ponder the causes of alcoholism in order to develop intervention strategies and service delivery mechanisms. Otherwise, foundation and government funders would likely ask, "Why do you believe your proposal will redress alcoholism in your consumer population?" Social workers in the implementation phase often examine whether specific social programs actually provide consumers with appropriate or needed services, but they draw on theories and definitions of "good service" devised during the scanning phase.

When assessing the effectiveness of operating programs, social workers often ask whether the interventions strike at the root causes of social problems. These assessments are made in the context of definitions and theories developed during the scanning phase. Mental health staff members who accept an intrapsychic framework, for example, are likely to use the counseling skills and training of center staff as major assessment criteria, in contrast to someone using an ecological or public health model, who is more likely to base an assessment on analysis of the extent to which staff members possess and employ community work and preventive skills.

The scanning phase also intersects with the legitimation phase at numerous points. In legislative, community, and agency settings, persons often disagree about the causes and definitions of social problems as well as about preferred inter-

---

streets and who often live in areas such as Los Angeles' Skid Row.

The possible use of such state funds to boost the embryonic El Rey Project in Los Angeles' Skid Row is a major reason Torres' bill has drawn strong support in the city. The El Rey Project calls for renovating the old hotel of that name into an alcoholism treatment facility.

Facility Donated

The Weingart Foundation, former owner of the hotel, donated it to the Volunteers of America with the condition that the facility be established by July 1, 1982.

The Los Angeles Police Department says that without state funds, the El Rey Project may not have enough operating funds.

Torres' bill also has the support of the mayor and City Council, the district attorney's office, the county Board of Supervisors and the county probation officers union.

Torres acknowledged that despite such strong local support, his bill faces an uphill battle in the legislative halls of Sacramento, led by the alcoholic beverage lobby.

"We have offered to help alcohol abuse groups to try to get more money from the general fund, but we oppose earmarking money for this," said Paul de Nio, executive vice president of the California Beer Wholesalers Assn. The industry would help to lobby on behalf of programs that alcoholism groups want, he said.

De Nio said the alcoholic beverage industry generally opposes any dedication of a tax source to one spending purpose.

"If there is to be a tax increase (on alcoholic

ventions. Social welfare policy is typically replete with charges that program staff members "are not addressing the causes of this problem," "have not defined this problem correctly," or "are using the wrong interventions."

IMPORTANCE OF SPECIFIC SOCIAL PROBLEMS

Social workers are often asked to distinguish trivial from important social problems as a pre-

---

beverages), then it definitely should go to the general fund and not be earmarked," said De Nio, arguing that earmarked taxes tend to build up a bureaucracy that lives off the tax, regardless of the need.

Torres argues, however, that earmarking of the tax is required and justified for his proposed alcoholism program.

"Society should require those who help cause the problem to help pay for the solution," Torres said. He added that alcoholism stems from products of the alcoholic beverage industry, and he thinks the industry should help pay for programs to help alcoholics.

The assemblyman said the liquor lobby in Sacramento is furiously working to defeat his bill, in part because of its sensitivity about being linked to a tax geared for alcoholics.

"It's a problem they don't wish to admit to," Torres said.

De Nio, however, said the industry is very concerned about alcohol abusers. "We don't make our living off the alcoholic," he said.

In addition to the alcoholic beverage lobby, Torres' bill may face opposition from Democratic leaders in the Legislature who are trying to work out a new state budget by July 1. Faced with a possible state deficit, the Legislature is considering raising taxes, and an increased tax on alcoholic beverages is a prime candidate.

If Torres' bill earmarks an increase solely for alcoholism programs, the Legislature would lose at least part of the tax increase it hopes to gain for the general fund. The general fund pays for almost all of the state programs, including education.

Gov. Edmund G. Brown Jr. usually opposes a dedicated tax such as Torres' bill proposes.

In 1975 he vetoed a bill similar to the one now being carried by Torres. The 1975 bill, sponsored by then Sen. Arlen Gregorio (D-Menlo Park) would have increased the taxes on alcoholic beverages to raise $34 million annually for alcoholism programs. It was the last bill to increase alcoholic beverage taxes that made it through both houses of the Legislature.

In vetoing the bill, Brown cited his campaign promise to oppose any general tax increase his first year in office. The governor also said the state was spending $27 million annually combatting alcoholism, "yet there is hardly any data to show the impact of so much effort."

Torres admits he does not know how his bill stands with the governor. "I haven't talked directly with the governor on this particular bill," he said.

But Torres said he is banking on Brown's record of being very supportive of alcoholism programs.

The assemblyman added that despite the odds against his bill, he will be fighting Wednesday to get committee approval and bring the bill to the full Assembly.

"I always think I have a chance," he said.

---

lude to deciding how to allocate scarce resources. Few would argue that scarce resources should be diverted to trivial problems when more serious problems exist. Analysis of the location of social problems is also needed so that interventions can be devised to assist consumers. If alcoholism manifests itself in absenteeism, for example, outreach programs should be devised in specific industrial settings where the problem is most acute.

Technical Approaches

Much as the fabled blind man gradually develops a composite concept of an elephant, various technical approaches exist to facilitate understanding of social problems. Different procedures exist for estimating the prevalence of social problems, the extent to which they are addressed by social agencies and programs, their spatial distribution, and their relative importance.

Prevalence of Specific Social Problems. Legislators, funders, and executives are more likely to invest scarce resources in programs if they believe that those programs address widespread problems. Concepts such as *rates, prevalence,* and *incidence* are commonly used as measures of the relative magnitude of social problems (see table 3.1).[7] These measures allow analysis of the distribution of social problems at a given point in time. Trend data are also important because they give information about whether a social problem is increasing or decreasing in magnitude, information useful when deciding whether to initiate, restrict, or expand social interventions.

Various strategies can be used to collect data about prevalence, incidence, rates, and trends.[8] Consumers can be surveyed directly and asked whether they experience specific problems. Since it is rarely financially feasible to conduct a study of all residents even within a relatively small geographic area, smaller samples of respondents can be used. An agency might interview a sample of working mothers with preschool children, for example, to assess the extent to which they need daycare. Or children in day-

care centers might be examined to assess the extent to which they experience various physical or mental problems as a prelude to offering them mental health or health services.

Alternatively, a less direct method can be used that allows informed guesses about the prevalence of specific problems. In some cases, social scientists have discovered associations between specific demographic or economic factors and certain social problems. For example, physical ailments such as sickle cell anemia or Tay Sachs disease have been linked to racial and ethnic characteristics. In such cases, data collected by national census authorities can be used to infer the location of a particularly high incidence or prevalence of a specific problem.

In many cases, income is associated with physical, mental, housing, and other social problems. In the case of housing, low-income consumers lack resources to purchase quality housing, particularly when there are housing shortages. They experience relatively high rates of various medical and mental problems because they lack resources to obtain preventive services, are more likely to be exposed to health risks and occupational hazards, lack the resources for adequate diets, and experience high levels of stress occasioned by economic uncertainty and inequality.

Another approach for analyzing the incidence of social problems is to analyze the help-seeking activities of consumers. In such cases, intake records of agencies are examined to assess how many persons seek help for alcoholism, marital discord, suicidal tendencies, or other problems. Knowledgeable experts can also be polled to gauge the importance of specific social problems. In either case, estimates of the prevalence of problems are based on the extent to which consumers actually seek assistance. In some cases, direct service staff members are able to detect emerging social problems in their clientele.

However, none of these approaches is a foolproof method for obtaining information about the prevalence or incidence of social problems. In the case of alcoholism, consumer surveys may understate its true prevalence because denial is

TABLE 3.1   Measures of Magnitude of Social Problems

Rates	Incidence	Prevalence
$$Rate = \frac{\text{Number of persons who experience a specific social problem}}{\text{Total number of persons in the population "under inspection"}}$$	$$Incidence = \frac{\text{Number of new cases}}{\text{Total number of persons in the population "under inspection"}}$$	$$Prevalence = \frac{\text{Number of persons who currently experience a specific social problem}}{\text{Total number of persons in a specific population at the current time}}$$
Illustration: A policy analyst might want to know the percentage of white males between ages 18 and 25 arrested for drunk driving during a specific year. The rate would be determined by dividing the number of arrestees by the total number of males in the specified population and year.	*Illustration:* A policy analyst might want to know the number of new arrestees in the white male population in the age bracket 18 to 25 during 1982, a figure calculated by dividing new arrestees by the total number of males in the specified population in 1982.	*Illustration:* A policy analyst might want to know the number of persons currently under prosecution for drunk driving in the white male population in the age bracket 18 to 25, a figure obtained by dividing the number of persons in the population under prosecution on, say, November 1, 1982, by the total number of persons in the population.

often associated with the malady. Some alcoholics are transient and unlikely to appear in survey samples. Examination of patterns of consumer use of existing services can similarly understate the magnitude of the problem because many alcoholics do not seek help. And experts may overstate or understate the importance of the problem, depending in part on their definitions of it. An expert who believes problem drinkers *are* alcoholics, for example, is likely to assess the magnitude of the problem differently from one who limits alcoholism to massive and ongoing consumption of alcoholic beverages.

Adequacy of Existing Programs and Services. In some cases, a surplus of services may exist as illustrated by services for the nonelderly blind. Many agencies were established to serve this population when blindness was relatively common. When medical advances strikingly reduced the incidence of blindness, sometimes ill-advised competition for clientele developed between agencies. By contrast, relatively few agencies exist to serve elderly blind persons, despite the fact that blindness is increasing in this population because of rising rates of diabetes among the elderly.[9] Social workers, then, need to couple studies that probe the prevalence of social problems with those that analyze the extent of currently existing services.

Trend Data. Trend data is useful because it gives information about future or impending developments (see guest editorial 3.1).[10] The increasing number of women who work, for example, has obvious implications for the development of daycare services. Population migrations from the North to the South, from urban to rural areas, and from inner-city to suburban areas have many implications for the location of social welfare agencies. An obvious and profoundly important trend is the aging of the American population (see illustration 3.4). This trend suggests the need for major changes in medical services, since elderly consumers have a relatively high proportion of chronic and acute medical problems. New services will need to be developed, including mental health, nutritional, transportation, and community services responsive to elderly persons.

Location of Specific Social Problems. Most social problems are not distributed randomly in the population. The poor, elderly, blacks, women, and children often experience higher rates of specific social problems than other groups. Identification of the locus of problems, both in geographic and group terms, is crucial to development of service strategies.[11] In many cases, good information is lacking, as when "no one knows precisely how many alcoholics there are, how they break down by race, sex, and income, or even how many are actually being treated" (see case example 3.1). Yet, even in this case, available information suggests marked disparities in rates of alcoholism in various counties, e.g., a 20 percent rate in one and a 9.1 percent rate in another.

The locus of problems is determined by surveys, consumer utilization data, and the conclusions of experts, i.e., the same approaches used when examining the prevalence of social problems. But greater emphasis is placed on comparing prevalence, incidence, and rates of different jurisdictions and populations. Further,

census data, vital statistics maintained by health departments, and special surveys commissioned by federal and local authorities can often provide useful information. If a certain social problem is believed to be associated with economic class, census data can be used to define "at risk" neighborhoods or populations. The U.S. Bureau of the Census provides easily accessible information about racial, social class, occupational, size-of-household, age, and other characteristics on a block-by-block and area basis.

Importance of Specific Problems to Society. Data about the prevalence and location of social problems and the adequacy of existing programs or services are crucial to policymaking but hardly sufficient to establish a case that major new resources need to be directed toward a specific problem. A problem may be widespread and services wholly deficient, yet policy participants may be unwilling to recommend initiation of major social programs. An oral surgeon, for example, estimated that 25 percent of the population requires major reconstructive work because their teeth or jaws exhibit major defects. However, a critic might respond that cosmetic imperfections, even if widespread, hardly constitute an important social problem in comparison to major social problems like poverty. (Americans already spend far more than other nations for dental braces.) What is needed, then, are methods for assessing whether specific social problems have serious ramifications for consumers and society.

Persons often inquire about the implications of specific social problems for the broader society. In case example 3.1, Loran Archer, director of the state office of alcohol program management, argues, "If I could get the same return on stock that this office gets on its rate of success with alcoholics, I could retire." Since the state obtains increased taxes because many recovered alcoholics are able to work more regularly, its enhanced tax revenues far exceed the cost of alcohol treatment programs. (Further, some of these recovered alcoholics do not need to collect unemployment insurance or welfare payments.) Less obvious, indirect savings may accrue to society as well. Surely marital, mental health, and physical ailments of alcoholics and family members often decrease when the problem is addressed, problems that in turn would have required state expenditures for programs. And, since alcoholics also account for the majority of automobile-caused fatalities, even minor reductions in alcoholism may lead to reductions in health and court expenditures.

Policy analysts, then, often attempt to gauge the relative importance of a specific social problem's ramifications for society.[12] These consequences are often termed *externalities*, i.e., effects of problems on taxpayers, the social structure, families, and other facets of society. Social workers who seek enlarged or new programs often cite these externalities when seeking support for their proposals.[13] Middle-income persons, for example, may attribute little importance to problems encountered by poor per-

---

GUEST EDITORIAL 3.1

Shifts in Culture Mean Decisive Break with the Past

By Daniel Yankelovich

Through the 1960s, while the news media focused on the ferment in American life—civil rights marches, the assassinations of John and Robert Kennedy and Martin Luther King, protests against the war in Vietnam and other spectacular events—my work in studying cross sections of the public showed the vast majority of Americans going about their daily routines unruffled, their outlook on life hardly touched by these momentous happenings. In the past few years, however, as the media tell us that we have reverted to a 1950s-style normalcy—quiet campuses with well-dressed young people more concerned with finding jobs than bringing the Establishment to its knees, and much talk of a retreat from the liberal social attitudes of the post-World War II era toward more conservative values—our recent studies show evidence of startling cultural changes.

These range from marginal changes (fewer V-8 engines, white wine instead of hard liquor before dinner) to changes that penetrate to the core of American life—into the private spaces of our inner lives, the semipublic space of our lives within the family, at work, in school, in church, in the neighborhood and into the public space of our lives as citizens.

The shifts in culture manifest themselves in many different ways.

Every year throughout the 1970s, a million or so Americans had themselves sterilized. In just one decade, 10 million Americans made sure that they would not have children. This is only one cause of a declining birth rate in a society that seems to have set itself against biological imperatives that prevailed in the past. At an anticipated 1.7 children for each woman of childbearing age, we have fallen below the 2.2 zero population replacement rate needed to keep the population from shrinking, and dramatically below the 3.7 rate of the 1950s. Our studies show that, unlike most American women in the recent past, tens of millions of women no longer regard having babies as self-fulfilling. Large-scale and deliberate childlessness is a new experience for our society.

Among the most startling changes are those in a household composition. In the

sons, but they may accept the need to develop social programs when they believe that such interventions prevent various problems and, in the long run, save social resources.

Political and Economic Realities in Ranking Problems

Pleas by consumer groups, advocates, and professionals for increasing attention to one or another social problem often fall on deaf ears, as illustrated by massive cutbacks in many social programs by the administration of President Ronald Reagan. Technical analysis, then, even when well done, is often superseded by political and economic realities. One method of discussing these realities is to again underscore relationships between scanning and legitimation phases. Issues "bubble up" in scanning phases as participants in specific policy arenas make a case

---

1950s a typical American family consisting of a working father, a stay-at-home mother and one or more children constituted 70% of all households. This was the norm, the familiar American nuclear family.

The Norm Has Collapsed

It shocks most Americans to learn to what extent this norm has collapsed in a single generation. Far from being the dominant mode, the "typical American family" does not now constitute even a large minority of households. Rather, it accounts for only 15% of them. There are fewer "typical American families" today than households consisting of a single person—the fastest-growing category of households counted by the U.S. census. Single households grew from 10.9% of all households in 1950 to 23% in the late '70s. We have moved from a society dominated by one type of arrangement, the husband-provider nuclear family, to a more variegated society with many types of households, no one of which predominates.

Vast shifts are taking place in the composition of the workplace. A generation ago, the typical worker was a man working full time to provide complete support for his wife and children. Today, fewer than one out of five people who work for pay conform to this standard. By the late '70s a majority of women

(51%) were working outside the home. By 1980, more than two out of five mothers of children age 6 or younger worked for pay. In families earning more than $25,000 a year, the majority now depend on two incomes: the husband's and the wife's. Ironically, while women have been clamoring to get in, men have been slowly edging out of the work force. Between 1947 and 1977, the number of men in the prime working years (from ages 16 to 65) who dropped out of the work force nearly doubled, from 13% to 22%.

Most jobs are still organized as if these changes had not taken place: they continue to be full-time, five-day-a-week, regular-hour jobs, with pay and fringe benefits based on the assumption that the jobholder is the sole earner in the family. We can expect vast changes in the future in how paid work and child care are organized.

In 1978, for the first time in our history, more women than men were admitted to U.S. institutions of higher learning. This trend reflects women's determination to achieve parity with men in education, training and job opportunities. But it also reflects a decline in the proportion of male high school graduates going on to college—a reversal of the post-World War II pattern. For many American men, going to college is no longer the royal road to success as they define success.

SOURCE: From *New Rules: Searching for Self-Fulfillment in a World Turned Upside Down* by Daniel Yankelovich. Copyright © 1981 by Daniel Yankelovich. Reprinted by permission of Random House, Inc.

ILLUSTRATION 3.4 Population, by Sex and Age: 1890, 1950, and 2010

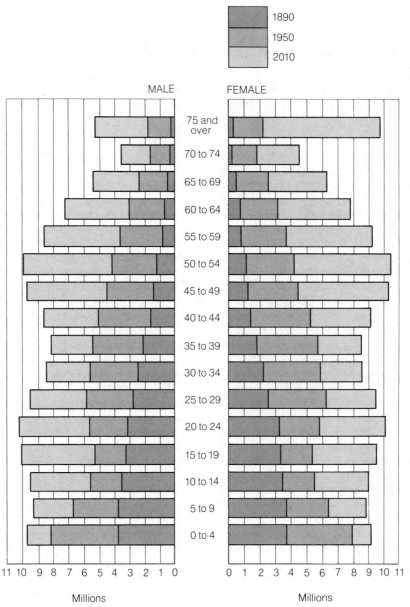

SOURCE: U.S. Department of Commerce, Bureau of the Census, *Social Indicators III*, 1980, p. 13.

for devoting more resources to an issue. Whether or not they succeed depends on the relative strengths of sources of bias against the issue, countervailing forces supporting greater emphasis, and specific precipitating factors that tip the balance for or against social reform.[14]

Sources of Bias. Many social programs have already preempted social welfare budgets of agencies and governments. Hence, major funding increases for new or expanded programs are difficult to obtain, particularly in times of constricting resources, when major funding increases for one program require funding decreases for others. Then, too, since there are many claimants for scarce funds, only issues with strong lobbies are likely to obtain increased resources. In the case of alcoholism, the consumer lobby is relatively weak, since existing and reformed alcoholics do not constitute a strong interest group. Political pressure for a new program increases if many persons believe that social programs can successfully address a social problem or that nongovernment alternatives do not exist. Many politicians (or even agency directors and staff) wonder if it is truly possible to rehabilitate alcoholics. Or they may wonder if nongovernment groups like Alcoholics Anonymous or private, profit-oriented clinics can provide better services than public agencies.

Countervailing Forces. Strong interest group pressure from bureaucracies, professionals, or consumers facilitates funding increases for specific programs. That Social Security escaped initial cuts in the Reagan Administration is testimony to the political clout of the consumer and agency interests that resisted cutbacks. In some cases, previously ignored problems receive prominence because of media campaigns. In the early 1980s, for example, Vietnam veterans used picketing and sit-ins to draw national attention to delayed stress syndrome, the accumulated stress, anxiety, and resentment experienced by veterans even years after participation in the Vietnam War. In similar fashion, child abuse, largely ignored in social reforms of the 1960s, became a popular cause in the 1970s, even, some argued, to the point of drawing attention from long-standing problems like daycare.

Increased spending for specific social problems is sometimes advocated by persons, agencies, or legislators that seek credit and prestige from a new program. In the case of political parties, enterprising politicians often seek personal and party credit for recognizing and addressing a social problem that is perceived to have widespread political support. Northern Democrats have traditionally been initiators of social programs in response to obvious social needs of low-income populations, while Republicans from relatively affluent suburban districts or from agricultural districts have opposed them. (Reform has often been stymied at the national level by a conservative coalition of Southern Democrats and Republicans.)[15]

Precipitating Factors. Attention to specific issues is often triggered by precipitating factors that strengthen the hand of advocates. In some cases, participants believe that there is a "crisis," as when publicity is given an ugly gang war, a sensational suicide, or an expose of prison conditions. Child abuse legislation in the 1970s was promoted on grounds that increasing patterns of intrafamily violence indicated a breakdown in the American family. In other cases, a leader can divert resources to new issues, as when a new executive in a social agency rallies support for new programs. Political campaigns are often used by aspiring politicians to draw attention to neglected issues.[16]

EXAMINING CAUSES OF SOCIAL PROBLEMS

Once participants in an agency, community, or legislative setting have decided that a social problem exists and that it merits social intervention, they must then identify intervention strategies. However, it is difficult to devise interventions in the absence of careful analysis of the problem itself, and, in this process, many difficult questions arise. Is the social problem a single problem or rather a collection of smaller problems placed (perhaps erroneously) under one label? Is it possible to prevent the emergence of a problem by early detection strategies and other preventive programs, or should most (or all) resources be given to curative strategies?

Issues in Causation

These conceptual issues are difficult to resolve by use of technical procedures, and they often become associated with political controversy, as in disagreements about how best to address specific social problems.

Numerous labels are used in social welfare policy to describe phenomena in the external world, including *mental illness, alcoholism,* and *developmental disabilities.* These broad terms are supplemented by others that describe narrow or limited phenomena, e.g., *paranoid schizophrenic, problem drinker,* and *mongolism.* Use of relatively broad or narrow labels to describe social problems can have important consequences for social programs and ultimately for consumers.

Advocates of narrow or limited definitions believe they are more precise because they focus on highly specific conditions.[17] Instead of using terms like *mental illness,* for example, some commentators urge the use of specific terms for specific mental conditions, such as *manic-depressive schizophrenic.* Narrow labels also have the advantage of not stigmatizing large numbers of consumers, as general terms like mental illness have done. Further, they argue, use of highly specific labels encourages professional staff to be more precise not only in describing social conditions but also in refining treatment. If one can identify various kinds of mental illness, interventions can be developed that are effective with each. As an example, a behavioristic strategy, a particular medication, or group therapy may be successful in treating one mental condition but not another.

But a specification strategy, some argue, can be carried to extremes. Many consumers have problems that do not neatly fit classification schemes, as illustrated by the fact that many mental health problems cannot be placed in the specific categories devised by the American Psychiatric Association.[18] Further, some persons exhibit identical symptoms but have different problems, as illustrated by a person whose "situational depression" after losing a spouse is different from another person's severe and chronic depression. Finally, some argue that social programs devised to solve narrow and carefully defined problems exclude many consumers who have problems and need assistance but cannot be neatly categorized.

Issues in problem definition are illustrated by case example 3.3. What threshold of consumption is required before someone is designated an alcoholic? Do varieties of alcoholics exist, and should the general term therefore be discarded in favor of terms like *chronic long-term user, social drinker, binge drinker,* and *chronic sipper?* In analyzing drug usage, one commentator devised a classification system (see illustration 3.5) that describes a variety of users; but one is prompted to ask whether these sub-groups are mutually exclusive.

Conceptual Frameworks

All participants in social welfare policy bring certain biases to the task of identifying causes of social problems, as reflected in differences between persons with public health or ecological perspectives, persons who favor disease or medical approaches, persons who seek intrapsychic explanations, and persons who use deterrent approaches. Frameworks influence the kinds of information sought, the ways in which that information is interpreted, and the kinds of interventions favored.[19]

In *public health* or *ecological* perspectives, social problems are perceived to be caused by misfit between persons and their environments. In the case of alcoholism, a variety of occupational, economic, familial, neighborhood, mass-media (advertising), and peer variables could be seen as increasing the likehood of alcoholism. In some cases, these factors may cause stress that in turn promotes drinking. Certain individuals may also

No 'Best' Cure for Alcoholism, Experts Agree

By Harry Nelson
Times Medical Writer

CORONADO—There is no such thing as "the best" treatment of alcoholism—only treatments that are good for some alcoholics but ineffective for others, experts agreed here Friday.

In fact, said Mark Keller, editor emeritus of the leading journal of alcohol studies in the nation, "they all have about the same success rate—about 33%"

The list of treatments being used today filled three typewritten pages in Keller's speech and included everything from imprisonment to Alcoholics Anonymous, from psychoanalysis to biofeedback.

A review of studies on the efficacy of these treatments reveals roughly the same score, Keller said. One-third of the alcoholics were helped a great deal, one-third somewhat and one-third were not helped.

Keller, who until last summer edited the Journal of Studies on Alcohol published by Rutgers University in New Jersey, was a speaker at a seminar on alcoholism sponsored by the Vista Hill Foundation, a nonprofit organization that operates hospitals and clinics for the mentally and emotionally ill.

Several physicians on the program emphasized that while there is no single optimal treatment for alcoholism, certain treatments work exceptionally well for specific patients. This means, they said, that a wide variety of approaches should be available at all treatment centers to meet the needs of all patients.

"What we need more than a new treatment is the most meticulous evaluation and assessment and a skillful sorting procedure to select the treatment that is best for each patient," said Dr. Sidney Cohen, a UCLA psychiatrist who is former director of the U.S. division of narcotics addiction and drug abuse.

Dr. Robert A. Moore, a psychiatrist who is vice president of Vista Hill, warned doctors to use great caution in prescribing drugs such as Valium or Librium for alcoholism. The two drugs are the most widely prescribed psychoactive drugs in the United States.

These drugs, as well as others that combat depression or manic conditions, may be useful for alcoholics with appropriate types of mental problems but not for the alcoholism itself, he said.

Alcoholics, he said, have a strong desire to shift to drugs other than alcohol and doctors who help them achieve that goal may do great harm.

be exposed to advertising, peer pressure, and parental models that increase their likelihood of drinking. Research suggests, for example, that members of certain professions (e.g., reporters subject to deadline pressures) and children of alcoholic parents are more likely than others to experience alcoholism.

Those using a *medical* or *disease* model explore specific biological factors associated with drink-

ing and other problems. Some alcoholics have metabolic defects that make them crave sugar, a substance obtained through alcohol consumption. Intergenerational studies suggest that genetic factors also assume a role in causing alcoholism.

Those who emphasize *intrapsychic* factors explore personal dispositions of alcoholics as well as relationships with parents, spouses, and oth-

ILLUSTRATION 3.5   Dynamic Model of the Heroin-Using Population

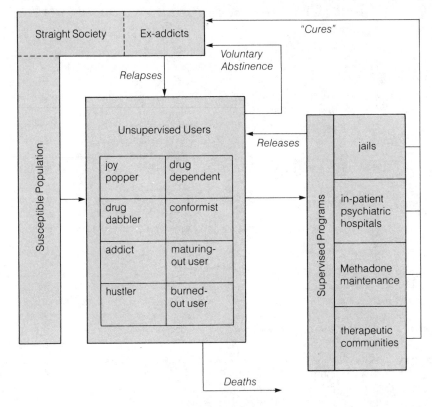

SOURCE: © 1976 by the Regents of The University of California. Reprinted from *Policy Analysis* (vol. 2, no 3, p. 256) by permission.

ers. Perhaps many alcoholics drink to escape personal or familial dilemmas. Some may binge as a form of rebellion against spouses, parents, and others. Others may continue to be dependent on their mothers and use drinking as a substitute form of oral gratification.

An interesting departure from traditional counseling is the use of learning strategies that draw on *behavior modification* frameworks. In this perspective, persons with social problems such as alcoholism can be assisted by aversive conditioning or positive reinforcement. The number of profit-oriented clinics using these approaches with alcoholism, smoking, and obesity has increased dramatically.

Some also emphasize *deterrent* strategies by favoring incarceration or other penalties against alcoholics, particularly those who drive while intoxicated. Recent crackdowns during holiday periods suggest deterrence reduces driving by intoxicated persons, but criminalization of drinking (see case example 3.1) has led to crowded jails with scant evidence of rehabilitation.

Politics of Causation

The politics of causation can best be understood by examining the contention that the definition of social problems dictates their solution. Theoretical formulations have important consequences for operating programs and policies. Those who utilize a public health or ecological perspective, for example, are likely to favor policies considered controversial because they reduce environmental causes of physical and mental illness, such as poverty, occupational hazards, poor diet, and other causative agents. In some fields, modification of prevailing theories would lead to displacement of large numbers of professionals. Were emphasis truly given to public health perspectives in medicine, for example, large numbers of physicians might be displaced by new staff members who placed emphasis on diet, exercise, and community changes. Such reformulation would be resisted by existing providers as well as by drug companies and food manufacturers.

PROBLEM VARIABILITY

"Those services may work for them but not for us" is a commonly heard assertion in social welfare policy. The "us" may be women, racial minorities, members of specific ethnic groups, inner-city or rural residents, or members of any other group that believes itself to have unique or special needs.[20] In some cases, problem labels are inappropriately applied to behaviors or symptoms. Take the case of black school children who lag in educational performance and are placed in special programs because they are diagnosed as developmentally disabled. Rather than developmental disability, blacks charge, many of the children are unable to learn because schools are unresponsive to their needs or because they lack exposure to reading and other cognitive skills in their home environments. In case example 3.4, a black psychiatrist alleges that black patients are more likely to receive serious diagnoses than white patients, even when symptoms are identical.

Members of specific groups also argue that services must be tailored to the characteristics of their culture and community if those services are to be utilized effectively. Services that lack bilingual staff, do not include male heads of households in service transactions, and do not incorporate indigenous or community resources are unlikely, many Hispanics argue, to be effective in their communities. In some cases, the sequencing of services must be drastically changed. As an example, many Asian Americans are unlikely to divulge personal problems in initial sessions because they fear "losing face"; hence, the pace of mental health services must be tailored to this cultural reality. In similar fashion, traditional, long-term, intrapsychic therapies are not likely to be used by low-income persons who want assistance with immediate economic, legal, housing, and employment issues.[21]

Inflexible application of frameworks, then, should be avoided, as well as premature definition of problems or specification of causal factors. Many social scientists note that our knowledge about most social problems—even those that afflict persons within the dominant culture—is still primitive.

POLICY PRACTICE IN THE SCANNING PHASE

No role is more important in policy practice than problem recognition and definition, since choices and concepts developed during the scanning phase influence the kinds of social programs fashioned in succeeding phases. In many cases, defects in programs can be traced to faulty reasoning in the scanning phase, as when definition of social problems is simplistic or erroneous. Policy practice case 3.1 describes the activities of a social worker in a mental health agency who tries to develop a preventive program.

Value Clarification Skills

During the scanning phase, social workers must often choose between various social needs or problems, since scarcity of resources precludes addressing them all. In policy practice case 3.1, the social worker decides that existing and traditional programs of the Hobart Community Mental Health Center (Hobart CMHC) do not address the needs of a large group of families because they do not provide assistance to them until they

Diagnosis: Psychiatrists' Skills with Blacks Questioned

By Lois Timnick

Times Human Behavior Writer

Black patients run a higher risk of being misdiagnosed by psychiatrists than do white patients, an African psychiatrist at the University of Pittsburgh reports.

They are more likely to be labeled "schizophrenic," while their white counterparts are diagnosed as "depressed," and to be viewed as sicker—even when they show identical symptoms, according to Dr. Victor R. Adebimpe, writing in the current issue of the American Journal of Psychiatry.

Those misdiagnoses are then incorporated into flawed statistics that show false ethnic differences for various psychiatric disorders, he says.

Adebimpe says errors may arise when white psychiatrists evaluate black patients because the analysts use standards derived from experience with whites, because they are socially and culturally removed from black or lower class patients and because they tend to accept stereotypes about blacks.

While he stops short of charging that the misdiagnosis of blacks is either widespread or systematic, Adebimpe says "a modest body of circumstantial evidence" points in that direction and warrants a closer look.

Studies at 19 Institutions

He reviewed studies conducted in 19 state hospitals, private institutions and psychiatric units of general hospitals.

In one study, more than 700 depressed patients, with nearly identical psychopathology and matched for age, sex and social class, were found to have been given widely differing pretreatment diagnoses: 39% of the black men were identified as schizophrenic, compared with 23% of the black women and only 18% of the white men.

In another study, follow-up computer diagnosis of more than 100 discharged hospital patients found erroneous "clinical impres-

have relatively serious problems. She decides as well that the small preventive project called the Pre-School and Infant Parenting Service (PIPS) does not address parenting needs of many families with latency and adolescent children.

The social worker begins with a value preference, then, that favors extension of services to new families. This value preference is likely to be questioned by others in this agency, particularly during a period of funding cutbacks when increases in funds for these new programs may require reductions in funds for others. While quantitative data can be assembled to demonstrate that specific social needs exist, decisions about where to allocate scarce resources are importantly conditioned by values.

Another value dilemma during the scanning phase concerns balancing incremental and "basic change" objectives. Most of us agree that many major problems are at least in part caused or exacerbated by injustice in the broader society, including poverty and discrimination. Many social workers want to incorporate social change into social programs by developing projects that seek modifications in existing social policies. Funders, government officials, and taxpayers are often unsympathetic to fusing social welfare services and social change, however, a fact that can lead to

sions" for 46% of the blacks but only 25% of the whites.

When defined criteria, such as those in the American Psychiatric Assn.'s Diagnostic and Statistical Manual of Mental Disorders, are used in diagnoses, Adebimpe says, "there is some evidence that . . . the incidence of psychiatric disorders among white and blacks drawn from the same population is the same."

Racism May Be Factor

Adebimpe, who works at the Northern Communities Mental Health/Mental Retardation Center in Pittsburgh, says racism may be a factor in such errors, but there are other possible causes as well:

—The social and cultural distance between patient and doctor, which includes differences in vocabulary, modes of communication, value systems and how distress is expressed, can color the largely subjective nature of what psychiatrists call "the clinical impression."

(This is less likely to happen when the psychiatrist is black and the patient white, however, Adebimpe says, because most black psychiatrists are trained by whites and the majority of their patients are white.)

—Blacks have been steryotyped, even in the pyschiatric literature, as too jovial to be depressed, too impoverished to experience object loss, hostile, lacking motivation for treatment, having a primitive character structure, not being psychological-minded, and being impulse ridden.

Inadequate Criteria

But one researcher Adebimpe cites suggests that the most common clinical findings related to depression in blacks are physical symptoms, that usual diagnostic criteria may be inadequate and that doctors may not know enough about black culture to judge either the presence or severity of depression.

—The misinterpretation of signs and symptoms, even when based on a checklist rather than intuition, can lead to what are called "false-positive" symptoms.

For example, although hallucinations and delusions rank high on the list of symptoms of schizophrenia, they also occur in mania, psychotic depression, chronic alcoholism and acute organic brain syndrome, and should not be taken as indicating schizophrenia unless certain other symptoms are also present.

termination of funds to change-oriented programs. Many social workers have to make difficult value choices that require balancing social change and political survival objectives, an uneasy tension that is sometimes resolved by devoting nonagency time to political and advocacy projects.

Social workers must also balance preventive and curative interests. In secondary prevention, projects can try to help consumers detect problems at a relatively early stage and thus keep them from becoming serious. Or social workers can try to develop primary prevention programs directed toward eliminating basic causes of social problems, as suggested by efforts to remove blighted housing, provide consumers with educational materials, or obtain improvements in income maintenance programs. As in the instance of social action, however, many funders and officials prefer directing social welfare funds toward existing social problems. In some cases, they fear that primary prevention programs can quickly become social action programs, or they may be dubious that such programs truly prevent the emergence of specific social problems. Here, too, social workers need to balance competing values in the context of economic and political realities that confront their agencies. They should be dis-

Expanding a Preventive Program in a Mental Health Agency

I work for a community mental health center (the Hobart CMHC) attached to a local hospital that provides it with some of its funds. The Hobart CMHC is currently in a state of fiscal crisis because the local hospital is experiencing marked budgetary deficits; indeed, there have been layoffs of clerical and administrative staff.

Thus, Hobart CMHC as a community mental health center has become like Cinderella, a participant in a hospital family that views her as an unwanted stepchild. As with Cinderella, Hobart is becoming aware of her need to look to external sources for deliverance.

It would be too presumptuous of me to consider the program proposal I will set forth in this paper to be Hobart's fairy godmother. However, perhaps it could be like the glass slipper, an instrument for creating inroads into the process of orienting Hobart to the concept of community mental health and a means for educating the local hospital to the validity of that concept.

Proposal

In 1970, the family-child division of Hobart CMHC began a program called the Pre-School and Infant Parenting Service (PIPS). The aim of this program was to reach parents of young children (birth through five years) who had concerns about their children's development and behavior. A "warm line" free telephone service was established. Parents could call into the clinic and within twenty-four hours receive direct assistance from either staff clinical social workers, child development specialists, or volunteer paraprofessionals specifically trained for this program. Medical questions were not in the realm of service; rather, the objective was to provide sug-

gestions, alternatives, information, referrals, and/or reassurance to callers. The name "warm line" denoted the kind of response and the fact that this was not to be correlated with crisis or "hot line" kinds of programs. Calls averaged about forty-five minutes in length, and, generally, families who called received follow-up calls (callers may choose to remain anonymous, however).

In addition to the "warm line," the PIPS program offered a variety of brief services usually about six weeks in length. Mothers and fathers with "normal" concerns about raising their children could rap with other parents in various group settings led by a staff member. A twenty-five dollar fee per family was charged for the six-week groups. The PIPS program was considered an early (secondary) prevention program whose objective was to enlarge the population using Hobart CMHC and at the same time increase the comfort experienced by "normal" families in using this kind of clinic. Every family participating is interviewed and evaluated separately, and families with serious problems are referred to other programs at the local hospital. PIPS was initially funded by a small federal grant, which has expired; it is now funded by the local hospital. It is a small operation that has never been evaluated for its impact and is currently in jeopardy of being eliminated.

In order to provide more comprehensive mental health services and thereby increase community support and participation, I am seeking an expansion of the present PIPS program through increased publicity and staffing and through the addition of a second level that would initiate a similar service for families with children of latency and adolescent ages. With tongue in cheek, I must admit that

I have already accomplished the first task of program development, that of devising an appropriate acronym. The new program is to be called LEAPS (Learning Everything About Parenting Service). Allowing myself the freedom to fantasize, I could envision a LEAPS program with its "warm line" and group technology serving families at all levels of the life cycle, including three-generational problems. (Hobart's catchment area has a large senior citizen population, yet program development for that group has been minimal.)

The idea for a LEAPS program evolved from observations of the "warm line." Each time that PIPS advertised its "warm line" service through the communications media, "warm line" would receive calls from families with children over the age of five. Staff time and availability to respond to these families are limited, so these calls could not be adequately serviced. Professionally, I feel that expansion to a LEAPS program could lead to better services for a larger population.

Four sequential steps are needed before LEAPS can be implemented. One step is to make a comprehensive documentation of the LEAPS program, which would include a definition of the LEAPS mission as it correlates with stated and implied goals for Hobart CMHC and its family-child unit. LEAPS would have to be described as a program able to provide broader services to people needing help with emotional problems and to provide mandated consultation and prevention objectives through an innovative approach to treatment in the family and child mental health field.

Documentation needs to include a description of program operation and specific populations served. It should also anticipate statistics, such as estimates of the numbers who would utilize this service, operational costs, probable space needs, staffing needs and costs, and equipment needs and costs, including telephone and audiovisual materials. Some of these estimates could be based on studies of similar programs, including the PIPS project, suicide prevention, and other hot line services.

A preliminary market research survey could add additional credence to the documenter's sense of "felt need." It would also alert the public to the potential service and provide an avenue for community input in the planning stage. Market research is important because it puts the consumer in the position of contributing to decision making.

The description of staff could strategically emphasize in-house control through appointment of a staff member as clinical administrator. To satisfy attending staff, a psychiatrist could be designated to act as program consultant. This might also serve to reinforce public legitimation of the project.

Because of the present dearth of funds, use of existing staff would be prudent. In order to mitigate conflicts with PIPS personnel, the PIPS staff should be LEAPS core personnel. The validity for hiring a community worker who had additional communications and public relations expertise could be justified in terms of economics, i.e., saving staff time. I feel that infusion of new blood schooled in community work could be an important asset to the LEAPS program. Most of the present staff needs to be educated to the nuances of consultation and community outreach, since few have participated in community projects.

Also, methods for recordkeeping and evaluation need to be improved. One important statistic that PIPS is not gathering is the number of referrals it makes to the family-child unit or other programs at Hobart CMHC. There has been much speculation that PIPS is a viable "feeder" for Hobart CMHC, and information to that effect would point to an additional success of the program. Built-in methods of evaluation and research seem to be needed also as justification for continued funding.

A second step is to obtain approval from internal sources, i.e., people within the agency structure. My first targets would be those whom I perceive to be key personnel. The originator of the PIPS program is the wife of Dr. Jones, an influential physician. He is a pivotal person in terms of his influence as administator at Hobart CMHC and as an envoy for the local hospital to key persons in positions of power. My observation of a parenting project now in existence at Hobart CMHC bears witness to the necessity for seeking support from Dr. Jones for any new proposal. The parenting project, a longitudinal study of children and their families, was funded and staffed independently and was approved by officials at the local hospital without seeking aid from Dr. Jones, the Hobart CMHC chief. Consequently, the project staff is faced with obstacles such as lack of space and is subject to the criticism of Dr. Jones's chief, who publicly questions the validity of the study.

A third step involves community support for the project. I know several influential persons on the advisory council of PIPS who want an enlarged project that serves a larger section of the population. External support may also be obtained from the county child welfare agency, which is understaffed but working to develop a preventive strategy.

A crucial fourth step is to obtain funding from external sources. Informal contacts with officials from several local foundations suggest the possiblity of funding for a larger program, especially if part of the funds can be assumed by Hobart CMHC and the county child welfare department. Hobart CMHC has several ongoing private fund-raising groups, and perhaps one of these groups could be persuaded to dedicate fund raising for a new program. Present financial difficulties preclude asking for a portion of existing funds. This program might need to be presented as a one-year "demonstration" project when funding sources are initially approached.

SOURCE: This case is adapted from one written by Andrea Karzen, M.S.W. Names and locations have been altered.

inclined, however, to accommodate these realities to the point that they do not even consider participation in social action and prevention projects inside or outside their agency of employment. In policy practice case 3.1, the social worker decides to seek new priorities within the Hobart CMHC even at risk of drawing opposition from staff members who are unwilling to develop new programs. But she decides to obtain allies, both within and outside the agency, to obtain support.

Conceptual Skills

The social worker in policy practice case 3.1 needs to devote considerable time to analysis of the social problems that could be addressed by the LEAPS project; i.e., the Learning Everything About Parenting Service. In order to obtain support for the project as well as to develop effective interventions, she needs to identify specific kinds of problems that might be addressed by the telephone service, as well as by special counseling or group services.

The county child welfare department, one possible funding source, will probably not be interested in providing monies, for example, if she does not identify specific child and family problems that could be addressed by the project. Might the project, for example, try to offer services to prevent the incidence of child abuse, neglect, and incest problems? Could the project supplement efforts of the school system to decrease truancy, drug abuse, or disruptive behavior by adolescents?

When pondering any of these (or other) specific problems and needs, the social worker needs to engage in further conceptual work to establish basic definitions. Assume, for example, that she decides that the LEAPS project could provide services relevant to prevention of drug abuse among teenagers. Should different kinds of counseling or group services be provided for users of hard drugs than for those who had merely used marijuana? Should efforts be made to include parents in groups with the adolescents, or should self-help groups of adolescents be formed? These kinds of issues can be addressed only in the course of conceptual work that is based upon practice experience as well as social science literature.

To convince funders that the project was needed in the instance of prevention of drug usage, the social worker needs to use technical tools. Use of research to document and measure social needs can be time-consuming and expensive, particularly if surveys of community residents are used. Indeed, some needs assessment projects take so long to complete that they are no longer relevant to decision makers when they are finally presented. Even when resources and time are lacking, however, less ambitious approaches can be employed: e.g., the use of experts, the use of available statistics, or the scrutiny of service statistics maintained by existing agencies. In this instance, she should obtain considerable information from local schools, drug treatment programs, and existing national surveys.

Interactional Skills

The need for interactional skills in the scanning phase is obvious in policy practice case 3.1. If a task force is established to develop the proposal, the social worker can assist it in its deliberations by using a variety of group skills. Since groups may become overwhelmed if they establish grandiose objectives, the social worker needs to help it develop priorities. In this case, she might help it identify manageable tasks, since the LEAPS project could fail to obtain support from funders and agency staff if specific program priorities are not developed from an array of possibilities.

Indeed, task forces and committees often thrive when they achieve successes in planning and completing tasks. A tension sometimes exists between a healthy desire to identify relatively modest and manageable tasks and the challenge of addressing major and formidable issues. Resolution of this tension depends in part on the nature of the group and its leadership. If the group is not cohesive and lacks leadership, relatively simple and time-limited projects may be chosen.

Leadership of task forces and committees is crucial to task accomplishment. When operating as staff to a group, a social worker does not choose its leader, but he or she can help existing leaders to become more effective, can encourage rotation of leadership, and can facilitate accomplishment of specific tasks. In agency settings, social workers sometimes chair internal task forces or committees that examine community needs and problems. In such leadership roles, they need skills in developing group cohesion, setting priorities, and delegating responsibilities.

Whether they staff, lead, or participate in groups in the scanning phase, social workers need to help others consider innovative approaches to social problems. In some cases, agencies use outmoded or simplistic interventions, and staff members are so wedded to traditional approaches that they reject any alternatives. Or the agency may not serve specific kinds of consumers or may give inadequate attention to primary and secondary prevention. A central challenge for social workers, then, is to introduce new ideas without so antagonizing others that their ideas are immediately dismissed.

Political Skills

In policy practice case 3.1, the social worker confronts political realities that are usually present in the scanning phase. In government and agency settings, many claimants seek scarce resources for their favored programs or populations; thus, policy practitioners who want to establish new or expanded programs need to develop strategies to diminish opposition and mobilize support. The social worker has anticipated opposition to the LEAPS project and has devised stategies for decreasing it, including enlisting the support of a key physician, obtaining support from external funders and residents, and developing technical information. She is also trying to identify positive functions that the project might serve for the Hobart CMHC, such as provision of referrals for ongoing programs of the Center. To decrease opposition from the existing PIPS program, she decides to try to merge the PIPS and LEAPS projects with reliance upon PIPS staff to plan and administer the enlarged preventive program.

In many cases, social workers confront a dilemma when deciding whether to seek major or relatively modest funding for a new program. They may believe, as does the social worker in policy practice case 3.1, that major programs are needed to meet specific community needs, whether as changes in existing services or as the addition of new programs. Political and economic realities during a period of funding cuts often dictate selection of pilot or demonstration projects requiring relatively little funding for limited periods of time. In many cases, these pilot projects appear to be a token innovation, at best. No easy solution to this dilemma exists. In some cases, pilot projects are expanded as their staffs develop quality programs and a political base, but they may also represent minimal commitment by decision makers to important social needs.

Position-Taking Skills

To obtain more resources for preventive services, the social worker in policy practice case 3.1 has to develop a proposal that specifically establishes the need for the LEAPS project. The proposal might be presented to potential funders, as well as to executives and boards in the Hobart CMHC. Depending upon the specific audience, she needs to decide which supportive arguments to emphasize. In the instance of public welfare and local educational institutions, she may wish to obtain data about specific problems that concern them. For Hobart CMHC staff, she may wish to emphasize public relations and referral benefits that could ensue from initiation of the new project.

SUMMARY

Activities in the scanning phase are vitally important to policy development because they influence service priorities and interventions in social welfare policy arenas. These activities are shaped by a variety of background, cultural, political, and technical factors. Controversy is likely when these factors, singly or together, lead participants to attach different levels of importance to specific social problems or to define them in different ways.

The questions addressed in the scanning phase pertain to the relative importance of specific social problems, the labels used to describe them, the causal or precipitating factors, and the extent to which specific groups in the population need interventions different from those used with the broader population.

When analyzing the importance of specific social problems, social workers obtain information from consumers, investigate utilization patterns of social agencies, and examine trends. They also gauge the extent to which specific problems have important consequences for the broader society. Decisions about funding priorities are made in the push and pull of politics, with outcomes often determined by the strength of constituencies who favor increased spending for specific social needs.

Efforts to determine the causes of social problems are shaped by the conceptual frameworks of participants. Those who adhere to ecological or public health frameworks, for example, often differ in their assessments of the causes of problems from persons with intrapsychic, behavioral, disease, or deterrent frameworks. Determination of causation is also controversial when participants seek to redress social causes of such social problems as poverty or alcoholism since vested economic and political interests are likely to resist basic reform.

In many settings, increased attention should be given to the variability of social problems. Single intervention approaches rarely suffice, since specific groups in the population require programs that address their unique needs.

Key Concepts, Developments, and Policies

Interrelated tasks in the scanning phase
Importance of specific social problems
Rates
Incidence
Prevalence
Consumer surveys
Census data
Utilization statistics
Trend data
Locus of problems
Use of experts
Cost-benefit studies
Externalities

Ranking problems
Highly specific definitions
Broad definitions
Causes of social problems
Conceptual frameworks
Public health perspectives
Medical or disease models
Intrapsychic perspectives
Behavioral perspectives
Deterrent strategies
Problem variability
Policy practice in the scanning phase

Main Points

1. Four interrelated tasks or issues are encountered in the scanning phase.

2. Background, cultural, political, and technical factors influence definition and analysis of social problems in the scanning phase.

3. Since social problems are often defined in the context of deviations from a social norm, they are subject to the cultural and value factors that establish norms.

4. Political interests and realities influence which social problems receive attention and which causes are widely recognized and addressed.

5. The scanning phase intersects with the other policy phases.

6. An understanding of specific social problems is often obtained by examining rates, incidence, and prevalence. Consumer surveys, census and demographic data, utilization statistics, and reports of experts are often used to obtain information about specific social problems and to examine trends and their location.

7. The magnitude of economic and other consequences of specific social problems for the broader society (externalities) are often calculated to determine whether major resources should be devoted to programs that address those problems.

8. Political and economic realities influence the importance ascribed to specific social problems.

9. Relatively broad or narrow definitions of specific social problems can be used.

10. Conceptual frameworks—including public health, medical, intrapsychic, behavioral, and deterrent models—influence analysis of the causes of social problems.

11. Manifestations and causes of problems often vary within subgroups in the population, with important implications for services given to persons in the various outgroups discussed in chapter 1.

12. Social workers should develop practice skills in the scanning phase.

Questions for Discussion

1. In case example 3.1, assume you are attached to a state agency charged with developing programs for alcoholics. Discuss issues you would encounter as you:
   a. try to develop an operational definition of alcoholism
   b. attempt to obtain information about its prevalence in the state
   c. try to identify major causes of alcoholism
   d. analyze its causes and manifestations among different groups, such as white suburban housewives and low-income persons in the Hispanic community

2. In the case of alcoholism, what political realities influence the kinds of policies that Americans are willing to approve and fund? What policies are not likely to be enacted?

3. Identify a social problem in some area other than substance abuse. By using either international comparisons or historical information, note how cultural factors influence how persons define the problem and its causes.

4. It is sometimes argued that "the way in which persons define a problem influences how they proceed to solve or address it." Discuss this statement as it applies to alcoholism.

5. In any social agency or organization with which you are familiar, discuss how conceptual frameworks influence how staff perceive and seek to address specific social problems. Disucss conceptual frameworks that are absent in this setting.

6. In the case of alcoholism, what economic and other consequences for the broader society could be gauged to see if the nation should in fact invest more resources in treatment and prevention programs?

7. What political and economic realities influence how Americans address problems of alcoholism?

8. Discuss the statement "Participation in the scanning phase should be integral to the professional practice of all social workers."

9. Discuss how the following dilemmas, tasks, and realities are illustrated in policy practice case 3.1:
   a. Basic change and incremental objectives must often be balanced during the scanning phase.
   b. Preventive and curative objectives often conflict during scanning.
   c. Relatively broad social problems must often be partialized into smaller ones.
   d. Time considerations often limit use of various technical tools during the scanning phase.
   e. Social workers often have to use interactional skills to convince others that a neglected problem needs to be addressed by service providers.
   f. Political and economic realities often influence which social problems receive priority in a specific setting.

Suggested Readings

Bradshaw, Jonathan. "The Concept of Social Need." In Neil Gilbert and Harry Specht, eds., *Planning for Social Welfare* (Englewood Cliffs, N.J.: Prentice-Hall, 1977), pp. 290–297. An excellent discussion of different sources of information that are used to determine the relative importance of specific social problems.

Eyestone, Robert. *From Social Issues to Public Policy* (New York: Wiley, 1978). The author examines why some rather than other social issues receive attention from policymakers in various settings.

Green, Arnold. *Social Problems: Arena of Conflict* (New York: McGraw-Hill, 1975). A provocative analysis of alternative methods of defining social problems in the context of background historical and value factors.

Lindblom, Charles, and Cohen, David. *Usable Knowledge: Social Science and Social Problem Solving* (New Haven: Yale University Press, 1979). The authors discuss various political and technical factors that influence the extent to which social science research is used to inform the making of policy.

Lowry, Ritchie. *Social Problems: A Critical Analysis of Theories and Public Policies* (Lexington, Mass.: Heath, 1974). Alternative ways of defining spe-

cific social problems are discussed that in turn lead to markedly divergent proposals for addressing those problems.

Solomon, Barbara. *Black Empowerment* (New York: Columbia University Press, 1976): "Characteristics of the Nonracist Practitioner," pp. 299–313. An excellent discussion of "traps" that social workers may encounter when they stereotype consumers from specific racial or ethnic backgrounds.

Notes

1. Ethical dilemmas are discussed by Martin Rein, "Social Work in Search of a Radical Profession," in Rein, *Social Policy*, pp. 281–301.

2. Wayne Pley et al., *Alcoholism* (New York: Gardner, 1979), and Ralph Tarter and A. Arthur Sugarman, *Alcoholism: Interdisciplinary Approaches to an Enduring Problem* (Reading, Mass.: Addison-Wesley, 1976).

3. Brager and Holloway, *Changing Human Service Organizations*, pp. 47–50.

4. Green, *Social Problems: Arena of Conflict*, pp. 67–115.

5. See Fuchs, "Redefining Poverty," 88–96.

6. See Martin Rein, "Values, Social Science, and Social Policy," in Rein, *Social Science and Public Policy* (New York: Penguin, 1976), pp. 96–138; Leonard Goodman, *Can Social Science Help Resolve National Problems?* (New York: Free Press, 1975); and Jack Rothman, *Social R and D: Research and Development in the Sciences* (Englewood Cliffs, N.J.: Prentice-Hall, 1980), pp. 59–86.

7. Martin Bloom, *Primary Prevention: The Possible Science* (Englewood Cliffs, N.J.: Prentice-Hall, 1981), pp. 173–174.

8. Jonathan Bradshaw, "The Concept of Social Need," *New Society*, 30 (March 1972): 640–643. See also U.S. National Institute of Mental Health, *A Working Manual of Simple Program Evaluation Techniques for Community Mental Health Centers* (Washington, D.C.:

Government Printing Office, 1976), pp. 99–146.

9. See Robert A. Scott, "The Selection of Clients by Social Welfare Agencies: The Case of the Blind," in Yeheskel Hasenfeld and Richard English, eds., *Human Service Organizations* (Ann Arbor: University of Michigan, 1974), pp. 485–499.

10. William N. Dunn, *Public Policy Analysis* (Englewood Cliffs, N.J.: Prentice-Hall, 1981), pp. 151–170. Also see Mayer Zald, "Demographics, Politics, and the Future of the Welfare State," *Social Service Review*, 51 (March 1977): 110–124.

11. U.S. National Institute of Mental Health, *A Working Manual*, pp. 123–160.

12. Alice Rivlin, *Systematic Thinking for Social Action* (Washington, D.C.: Brookings Institution, 1971), pp. 46–64.

13. See Stanley Masters et al., "Benefit-Cost Analysis in Program Evaluation," *Journal of Social Service Research*, 1 (Fall 1978): 79–93.

14. See Phoebe Hall et al., *Change, Choice, and Conflict in Social Policy* (London: Heinemann, 1975), pp. 475–509.

15. Differences between the two major parties in orientations to social reforms are discussed by Eric F. Schattschneider, *The Semisovereign People* (New York: Holt, Rinehart and Winston, 1960), pp. 78–96.

16. Robert Eyestone, *From Social Issues to Public Policy* (New York: Wiley, 1978), pp. 69–86.

17. See discussion in J. K. Wing, *Reasoning about Mental Illness* (London: Oxford University Press, 1978), chapter 2.

18. David Mechanic, *Mental Health Policy* (Englewood Cliffs, N.J.: Prentice-Hall, 1980), pp. 16–27.

19. See Bloom, *Primary Prevention: The Possible Science*, pp. 103–117; Richard Titmuss, *Social Policy* (London: Allen & Unwin, 1974), pp.

23–33; and Ritchie Lowry, *Social Problems* (Lexington, Mass.: D.C. Heath, 1974).

20. See Wynetta Devore and Elfreda Schlesinger, *Ethnic Sensitive Social Work Practice* (St. Louis, Mo.: Mosby, 1981), and Shirley Jenkins, *The Ethnic Dilemma in Social Services* (New York: Free Press, 1981).

21. August B. Hollingshead and Fredrick Redlich, *Social Class and Mental Illness* (New York: Wiley, 1958).

CHAPTER 4

The Analysis Phase: Service Delivery and Allocation Choices

A challenge in social welfare policy is to develop delivery systems that successfully implement intervention strategies devised in the scanning phase, discussed in chapter 3. During the analysis phase, participants identify and choose between policy options that define who receives program services and resources, who delivers or gives services, who funds programs, and who makes policy decisions required during implementation. These choices have profound implications for consumers, professionals, and members of the broader society.

Community programs for the developmentally disabled provide a useful example of policy analysis (see guest editorial 4.1). In prior times, individuals with developmental disabilities and those with severe and chronic forms of mental illness were often warehoused in large public institutions. However, increasing attention has been given in recent decades to the development of a range of community programs. This community strategy has required policy analysis of a variety of service delivery issues.

TASKS IN THE ANALYSIS PHASE

The central tasks in policy analysis are: to shape the characteristics of organizations that convey resources and services to consumers (*decisions about the structure of the delivery system*); to determine which consumers will receive priority (*allocation decisions*); to decide how services and pro-

Shelter the Handicapped, 'But Not in My Backyard'

By Neal R. Peirce

In Skokie, Ill., the Orchard Assn. runs a group house providing shelter for two mentally disabled young men—both of whom hold stable jobs. A married couple provides supervision. With rooms to spare, the home seeks to take in two more mentally disabled residents. Neighborhood opposition is swift, led by realtors who predict a decline of property values—perhaps even a crime wave. The village board votes 4–3 to deny the required special-use permit. The local mayor, who supported the group home's expansion, is crushed and near tears.

In the District of Columbia's fashionable Cleveland Park, the Joseph Kennedy Jr. Institute seeks to open a group home for six to nine moderately retarded women who hold jobs in sheltered workshops. But the neighbors—a network newscaster, a social worker, a psychiatrist and an attorney with sterling "liberal" credentials—seek to block the move. To its credit, however, the neighborhood did, after unfavorable media coverage, take steps to welcome the group's residents.

Similar not-so-pleasant responses have been reported coast-to-coast as the trend proceeds toward "deinstitutionalization"—taking the physically or mentally handicapped out of huge, impersonal state hospitals and returning them to a close-to-normal neighborhood setting. Sparked by the social-service professionals and then warmly supported by economy-seeking state governments, deinstitutionalization is now public policy in virtually all states.

But some taxpayers who love deinstitutionalization in the abstract often resist group homes with a vengeance when proposals reach local zoning boards. Unrestrained, this "NIMBY" syndrome—"Not in My Back Yard"—has ugly implications. It legitimizes a virulent form of me-firstism; it could easily besmirch the constructive reputation of the nation's burgeoning neighborhood movement. And as communities resist group homes, thousands of deinstitutionalized Americans may be thrown out to wander the streets of our cities.

The most frequently expressed objection to group homes—that they may depress property values—is simply not sustained by experience, according to studies by Princeton University (its report was on White Plains, N.Y.), and by planning departments in Lansing, Mich., and Green Bay, Wis.

---

grams will be funded (*funding choices*); and to determine how services will be monitored (*decisions about policy oversight*).[1] Decisions must also be made about the content of services or program benefits (*decisions about service or program content*).

These various tasks are addressed together when lawmakers construct legislation defining the characteristics of new programs and when administrators and planners develop program proposals. (In grant writing, proposals are also written by a range of direct service, supervisory,

By contrast, a large shelter can trigger serious problems. Neighbors of the First Moravian Church on Manhattan's Lower East Side seem to have had good grounds to ask curbing of the church's program of meals and counseling to 200 "street people." Derelicts invaded doorways and vestibules, leaving bottles, urine and feces behind, and some neighborhood residents were assaulted. Small group homes, by contrast, not only have insignificant impact on property values but also fail to create crime or traffic problems, or change a neighborhood's character. Shelters for a modest number of people rarely become a problem unless they are concentrated in one part of a city—typically a declining neighborhood or an area heavily populated by students. Such "social service ghettos" can be avoided by city ordinances requiring considerable distance between homes.

Recognizing the compelling need to find satisfactory homes for their deinstitutionalized patients, 21 states, including California, have passed statutes declaring that small group residences be considered single-family dwellings for zoning purposes—and can't be excluded by city zoning ordinances. That is an infringement of home rule, but a necessary one. Only an infinitesimal number of cities are willing to enact such rules on their own volition. The Ohio Association of Retarded Citizens tried the town-by-town approach for several years and succeeded in only five of Ohio's 900 municipalities.

Even the state legislators who override local zoning to facilitate homes for the retarded often stop short of aiding the other types of halfway houses desperately needed in our times—for troubled teen-agers, alcoholics and former drug addicts and ex-convicts. Yet what American can say he or she—or perhaps a close relative—might not fall on hard times, and then stand to benefit from shelter in a halfway house instead of some grim state institution, or wandering the streets?

None of this is to say group homes are always ideal environments. Many are warmly and sensitively managed. But others are run by overseers who may overmedicate their mental patients to keep them placid.

But compared to the institutional alternatives, small group homes represent a step forward. In an era of local tax revolts and emaciated federal social-service budgets, they provide dramatic savings. Illinois, for instance, spends about $20,000 a year for each disabled person in an institution. By contrast, the residents of the disputed group home in Skokie cost the state $5,700 a year—actually, only $1,200 yearly if their purchases and taxes are figured in.

But the bottom line really shouldn't be self-interest ("It could happen to me") or tax savings. Rather, it's that a society deserves to be judged on how it treats its least fortunate members. On that test, ours has a long way to go.

Neal R. Peirce writes a column for the National Journal. SOURCE: © 1981, The Washington Post company. Reprinted by permission.

and administrative staff.) Scrutiny of specific policy issues is also common during the analysis phase, as, e.g., when staff in an agency analyze intake procedures or the decentralization of agency services.

Policy analysis is so important to social wel-

fare policy that both this and the succeeding chapter are devoted to it. Service delivery, allocation, and content choices are discussed in this chapter; funding and oversight issues are analyzed in chapter 5.

Social workers need to:

Identify cultural, political, and technical factors that shape policy choices during the analysis phase

Understand how economic analysis and calculation of trade-offs are used to facilitate choices among competing policy options

Develop familiarity with policy options regarding the staffing, locus, service, and interorganizational relationship strategies of social services and programs

Develop familiarity with policy options that pertain to eligibility and coverage issues

These various topics are discussed in this chapter as a prelude to discussion of a policy practice case in which a social worker engages in policy analysis.

OVERVIEW OF THE ANALYSIS PHASE

Policy analysis is influenced by a range of background, cultural and value, political, and technical factors (see illustration 4.1). Indeed, participants often vacillate when making choices because many often conflicting external forces shape those choices. The legislative process provides an excellent illustration; subsequent versions of legislative proposals are often strikingly different from initial versions because of the influence of these factors.

Background, Cultural, and Value Factors

The importance of background factors to program design choices is evident when one examines different choices made in different countries as well as changing preferences in any specific country. As an example, Americans have given local units of government far larger policy roles than most European countries, a choice that can only be understood by analyzing the development of the American federal system, where national social welfare roles evolved belatedly and only subsequent to local and state social welfare roles. Understandably, then, American legislators are more likely than their European coun-

terparts to specify in legislation strong policy roles for local governments. In similar fashion, Americans—because they are more likely to perceive social problems as reflections of deviant life-styles than as integral to society—are more likely than Europeans to restrict eligibility for social programs to highly specific groups, such as the very poor.[2]

Staff members in specific agencies also develop customary methods of designing programs. Social psychologists have identified a phenomenon known as groupthink that can impede the development of policy program innovations.[3] Accustomed to standard operating procedures, some persons believe that traditional policy and program choices are the only ones that should be considered, even to the point of scapegoating or ostracizing dissenters. In guest editorial 4.1, prevailing sentiment in many communities against development of community-based programs for the developmentally disabled is discussed, a sentiment shared until relatively recently by many policymakers as well.

Political Factors

Political factors that influence policy analysis are also evident in guest editorial 4.1. Fearful that halfway and other community facilities will depress property values, outraged citizens pressure legislators and government officials not to give the facilities zoning clearance. Community opposition to such facilities has led many officials to deemphasize them even when considerable evidence suggests that they are cost-effective (i.e., cost less than state institutions while providing services that are as effective or more effective). Choices made during policy analysis often have major importance for persons and groups that in turn seek to protect their roles and funds by pressuring those who frame legislative proposals.[4]

Technical Factors

Policy analysis is often informed by technical studies that compare policy alternatives with re-

ILLUSTRATION 4.1 An Overview of the Analysis Phase

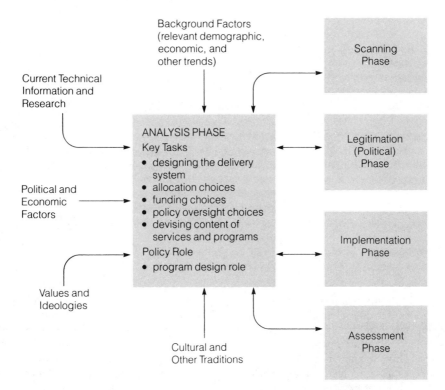

spect to their cost, effectiveness, administrative feasibility, and other criteria.

Economics. Techniques drawn from economics have assumed considerable prominence in recent decades. When initiating a new program for developmentally disabled citizens, for example, policy analysts could probe the extent to which fee charges to consumers would decrease the utilization of services. In this period of scarce resources, when many agencies and programs are increasing the use of fees, it is crucial to assess what levels of fees are likely to discourage utilization and what kinds of consumers will be most affected by fee imposition. In illustration 4.2a a hypothetical consumer use or demand curve illustrates how demand decreases for a specific kind of service as fees increase. Note how virtually no demand exists when relatively high fees are charged (point A) and how demand increases substantially at point B. The supply curve describes in similar fashion how provision of agency services is influenced by level of fees (see illustration 4.2b). In this example, agencies provide more services when fees are raised because of increased revenues (see point C). Conversely, use of relatively low fees curtails revenues and can lead to fewer services (see point D.)

Supply decisions of agencies cannot be made, however, without considering consumer choices (see illustration 4.2c). Were agencies to charge relatively high fees (point E), relatively few consumers would seek their services, and some

**ILLUSTRATION 4.2   Relationship between Supply and Demand in a
Hypothetical Agency**

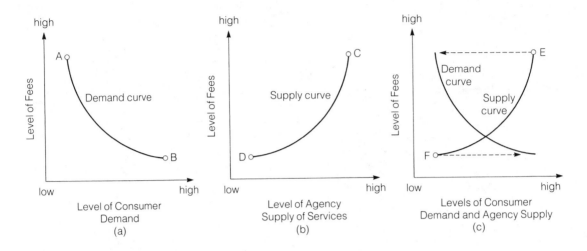

agencies would become insolvent. While lower fees (point F) would increase consumer demand, insufficient income would be generated to pay costs of salaries and other operating costs for these services. Thus, agency administrators often try to set fees at levels near the equilibrium point (point G), a point at which sufficient demand from consumers exists to generate revenue to cover agency costs.

Economic analysis, then, examines the relationships between economic factors as they bear upon economic decisions or on the well-being of consumers. In the preceding agency example, such analysis clarifies the relationships between supply and demand and, more specifically, the effects of the raising or lowering of fees upon agency and consumer decisions.[5] In the absence of any economic analysis, an agency

GUEST EDITORIAL 4.2

A Look at Trickle Down Economics

By Lester C. Thurow

Trickle down economics—immediate tax cuts for the rich that hopefully will eventually lead to future jobs for the middle class—lies at the heart of President-elect Ronald Reagan's tax proposals. Consider the Reagan proposal for lowering or even eliminating the capital gains tax. Since the richest 7½% of the population own 60% of all the privately held physical assets in the United States, 60% of the total tax cut will go to them.

executive might raise fees only to find that his agency clientele had dissipated.

Economic analysis is similarly useful in national settings, as suggested by the economist Lester Thurow's discussion of "trickle down economics" in guest editorial 4.2.[6] He analyzes the relationship between taxation policy, national productivity, and social equality. Advocates of trickle down economics, such as the advisers to President Ronald Reagan, maintain that tax reductions for affluent persons increase monies available to industries and thus promote the creation of new jobs that ultimately benefit the poor. Thurow questions this theory by arguing that other economic factors more powerfully influence economic growth, as reflected by an examination of the economic policies associated with the booming economies of Japan and West Germany. In those countries, funds for industries are obtained not by reducing taxes on affluent persons but by using taxes that reduce personal consumption by all citizens and so increase rates of saving, generating funds that can then be used to finance capital expansion by industries.

Despite its technical appearance, economic analysis is intimately entwined with and influenced by the core and instrumental values discussed in chapter 1.[7] As an example, Thurow finds trickle down economics questionable because, he argues, it does not increase economic growth as effectively as alternative strategies,

such as the use of the value-added tax. He *also* questions trickle down economics because it promotes extraordinary social inequality, which he dislikes—an objection that would not be raised by those among its advocates who favor a relatively inegalitarian society. Economic options, then, are often discarded or rejected when someone finds that they conflict with certain social objectives—even when they promote other economic objectives, such as increased economic growth. In some cases, too, economists overlook or discount factors that conflict with their basic ideology. As an example, advocates of trickle down economics often assume that affluent persons will invest their resources in industry rather than purchasing "antiques, old masters, land, first homes, second homes and a wide variety of other assets that have nothing to do with reindustrialization."

Economics is useful to social welfare policy, then, because it allows exploration of the relationships between economic factors—information necessary for informed policy choices. Economics is, at best, an imperfect science because economic behavior of consumers, businessmen, and others is influenced by many cultural, political, and sociological factors. Further, the discipline of economics does not provide core and instrumental values for defining "the good society." But it does allow the examination of various options for reaching social or policy ob-

---

If lower capital gains tax rates were limited to plant and equipment investment in new, highly risky, venture capital situations—the announced purpose of the tax—one could understand the proposal even if one did not agree with it. But the lower capital gains tax rates are also to apply to antiques, old masters, land, first homes, second homes and a wide variety of other assets that have nothing to do with reindustrialization. For every dol-

lar's worth of reindustrialization incentives offered, there will be several dollars worth of incentives for non-productive investments.

Since non-productive speculative investments usually pay off much faster than productive investments, the net effect of the tax cut may even be to increase the diversion of funds away from productive investments. The capital gains tax should be indexed so that owners only pay taxes on real increases in the

jectives by providing information about the economic consequences of specific choices. In the case of trickle down economics, for example, Thurow provides some evidence that policies that promote it (e.g., tax cuts that disproportionately favor the rich) are undesirable from the vantage point of increasing industrial expansion. These policies might also be rejected on the moral grounds that they increase social inequality—but this line of inquiry would soon take us beyond the realm of technical economic analysis.

Knowledge of economics is also useful in another way. Economists often develop broad theories about economic phenomena, as exemplified by Adam Smith's insistence that "the

---

value of their assets, but a general capital gains tax cut will not meet this objective either.

Is it possible to stimulate investment without generating a more unequal distribution of income and wealth? Or is trickle down the only choice? If we look at our successful international competitors it is clear that there are other choices. Neither Germany nor Japan have been successful using trickle down techniques.

U.S. Next to Last

If industrial countries are ranked in accordance with their economic success, Japan is No. 1. Since 1960 per capita gross national product has grown at an annual rate of 7½% after correcting for inflation. We tend to think of our other major competitor, West Germany, as No. 2 in the growth race, but it was outdone by 6 other industrial countries. Spain was actually No. 2 followed by France, Norway, Italy, Canada, the Netherlands and then West Germany in 8th place.

But 8th place is not to be denigrated if you live in a country (the United States) that came in next to last among industrial countries with a growth rate of 2.5% per year. Only the British did worse. But since the Germans and the Japanese are our main industrial competitors, let's look at them.

While the Japanese government spends a smaller fraction of its GNP than ours does (principally because of defense), the Germans spend more. Government absorbs 32% of the American GNP but almost 50% of the German GNP. And this does not include the spending of Germany's nationalized industries—railroads, utilities, telephones, Volkswagen, and a number of other companies. If they are included, government controls far more than 50% of the GNP.

But perhaps the magic answer is not to be found in fraction of the GNP taken in government spending but in large income differentials that encourage individual initiative to save and work. If that were the magic answer, the United States should have the second most successful industrial economy—only the French have more inequality than we. If you compare the average income of the top 20% of the population with the bottom 20%, there is a 10-to-1 gap in the United States. But the Germans run an efficient economy with a 7-to-1 gap and the Japanese run an even more efficient economy with a 5-to-1 gap.

If the answer is not to be found in government spending or income inequalities, maybe it is to be found in governments that have enough sense to keep out of the economy. But here comes the German government owning a large fraction of its industries and requiring codetermination where union members must by law sit on corporate boards of directors. Hardly an example of governments keeping out of the economy.

invisible hand" of the private market, left to its own devices, engenders economic growth and stability. But these macro theories have profound implications for social welfare policy quite apart from their assertions about supply, demand, and other economic factors.[8] For example, Smith's theories have been used to justify non-intervention by government in the economic

working of society, including the distribution of wealth (illustration 4.3). Acceptance of laissez faire economics is, some would argue, tantamount to acceptance of an inegalitarian society and the persistence of widespread poverty. By contrast, economists John Galbraith, Robert Lekachman, and Lester Thurow insist that government regulations and redistribution of wealth are

---

And the Japanese government is even more intrusive. The Bank of Japan and MITI (the Ministry of Industry and Trade) basically serve as a corporate finance committee allocating capital across the entire economy. Large firms are dependent on indirect government loans for much of their capital. The Japanese do not engage in detailed economic planning, but they certainly do engage in something that might be called economic coordination.

But perhaps Americans are just different. They simply require more inequality and less government than other humans to work hard.

If you look at the American distribution of earnings, fully employed white males—still the dominant work group—work hard with a 5-to-1 gap between the earnings of richest quintile and the poorest quintile—approximately the same gap that exists in Japan. In contrast there is a 27-to-1 gap in the earnings of everyone else.

But perhaps we need more inequality, not to work, but to promote savings. After all, the average American family saves only 4% of its income while the average German family saves 14% and the average Japanese family 20%. These countries do not generate high savings rates with inequality, but let's work out what would have to be done to increase savings with a trickle down approach of cutting taxes on the rich and raising them on the middle class—the approach being used by

Mrs. Margaret Thatcher, prime minister of Great Britain.

$118 Billion Shift

Suppose that households with incomes below $20,000 per year (the bottom 60% of the population in 1979) saved nothing and that households with incomes over $48,000 (the top 5% of the population) saved 100% of their extra income. To raise personal savings from 4% to 9% of the GNP government would have to alter the tax system to transfer $118 billion from the bottom 60% of the population to the top 5% of the population. With such a transfer, the bottom 60% would suffer a 25% cut in their earnings while the top 5% would get a 50% raise. And the actual transfer would have had to be much larger than this since the bottom 60% do some saving and the top 5% do not save 100% of their extra income.

If you look at why savings rates are high abroad, the answer is not to be found in trickle down, but in governments that very actively intervene to reduce consumption. Their principle instrument is a value-added tax—a tax on consumption—that you do not pay if you save.

Trickle down can be evaluated economically—is it necessary—or ethically—is it desirable. Is it necessary? Other successful countries indicated that it is not. Is it desirable? That is a question that every American is going to have to answer in the next few years.

Lester C. Thurow is a professor of economics and management at the Massachusetts Institute of Technology. He served on the staff of the Council of Economic Advisers in the Johnson Administration. Reprinted by permission of author. This article first appeared in the *Los Angeles Times.*

crucial to economic stability and growth.[9] Their economic theories, unlike the laissez faire approach, provide tools for redistributing wealth. Social workers, then, need to develop familiarity with broad economic theories, since such theories have direct and indirect implications for a host of social welfare problems. Choice of economic theories is partly determined by core and instrumental values, even though many economists insist that they possess scientific proof confirming the validity of their particular theory.

Analyzing Policy Trade-Offs. Policy analysts often have to examine both the advantages and the disadvantages associated with specific policy options, as illustrated in table 4.1. Such an analysis requires the identification of trade-offs.[10] In some cases, choices are relatively straightforward, as when someone supports a policy clearly superior to its alternatives. Some choices are preferable to others "in some ways but not in

ILLUSTRATION 4.3

TRICKLE-DOWN THEORY

Paul Conrad, © 1981, *Los Angeles Times*. Reprinted by permission.

others," however, in which case participants cannot easily decide how to make final choices. Advantages and disadvantages of selected policy choices commonly confronting agency staffs are presented in table 4.1. In light of the merits and demerits of each choice, participants must decide which they prefer, on balance, or whether compromise solutions can be found that make it possible to obtain the advantages of each. This process of comparing the relative merits of policy alternatives is common at all levels of policymaking. Were a network of community agencies to assist the developmentally disabled funded by a state or national legislature, many of the issues presented in table 4.1 would have to be addressed by local administrators, local staff, and national funding authorities.

Many policy choices are truly difficult ones, particularly in periods of scarce resources. Take the issue of universal versus selective eligibility in table 4.1.[11] Universal services have the advantage that they maximize *equity*; i.e., all consumers with a specific problem are treated the same. There is no need to refuse services to certain consumers because they do not meet specific economic qualifications. Because they allocate program resources to the affluent as well as the poor, however, universal services do not *redistribute* resources from the affluent to the poor; selective programs, in contrast, target resources to the poor. In this case, then, equity and redistributive objectives conflict, making policy choices difficult.

A similar tension characterizes the choice between intensive and extensive services, a choice encountered by many social agencies (see table 4.1). Scarce program resources can be concentrated on relatively few consumers in hopes that their problems will be significantly redressed. In the case of developmentally disabled youth, for example, a battery of occupational, counseling, residential, and educational services could be provided lasting, say, eight to ten years for each enrollee. This strategy, however, which emphasizes *effectiveness*, would sharply reduce coverage as well as the numbers of consumers served. Again, a catch-22 situation confronts the policy

TABLE 4.1   Selected Trade-offs Associated with Agency Policy Options

Policy Options	Advantages	Disadvantages
Intensive rather than extensive services	Allows provision of in-depth or intensive services with greater impact	Lack of provision of service to large numbers of consumers
Development of community-based rather than institutional services	Decreases stigma of service; facilitates integrating consumers into mainstream	Difficult to orchestrate a range of community services and to involve transient populations
Use of generic rather than specialized services or staff	Attention is given to needs of the whole person	Staff members lack specialized expertise relevant to specific needs of consumers
Provision of preventive rather than curative services	Allows early detection and treatment of social problems as well as education of consumers to forestall development of problems	Existing and serious social problems may be neglected
Universal rather than selective eligibility	Allows staff not to have to reject certain applicants; makes imposition of means tests unnecessary	Makes it difficult to target scarce resources to those with particularly serious problems
Decentralized rather than centralized services	Makes outreach to consumers possible; improves access to services and use of community networks	More expensive to operate than centralized facilities
Use of multiprofessional teams rather than single professions	Allows inputs to services from many professions	Interprofessional conflict and turf rivalry is possible

analyst. Unfortunately, no easy methods exist for resolving policy trade-off dilemmas, though participants often seek compromises to avoid the negative consequences of extreme positions. Thus, a developmental disability agency might offer consumers services characterized as "somewhat intensive."

Many persons argue that social workers should have distinctive perspectives during this choice-making process. Because of their proximity to consumers and the reformist traditions of the discipline, social workers, some argue, should place more emphasis on consumer needs than other policy participants in order to balance the emphasis on efficiency and administrative feasibility objectives.

DECISIONS ABOUT THE STRUCTURE OF THE DELIVERY SYSTEM

Transactions between consumers and program staff occur within the context of a social services or program delivery system. How this system is constructed has important implications for the nature of those transactions. Which kinds of consumers receive priority? What kinds of staff members are hired to provide various services? What kinds of relationships exist between various agencies?

Staffing Issues

Controversy is often associated with decisions about the kinds of staff members that perform specific functions in social welfare.[12] Government authorities influence the use of staff in many ways including using licensing powers to limit who can perform certain tasks, regulating professional titles, and classifying civil service positions. *Licensing of tasks or functions* is illustrated by the restriction of surgical procedures to those who have graduated from an accredited medical school. *Licensing of titles* occurs when the title "licensed clinical social worker" is restricted to those who have graduated from an accredited school of social work, met specific experience requirements, and passed an examination constructed by state authorities. When government authorities require certain credentials for civil service positions, they *classify* the positions, as when only social workers can fill supervisory positions in some child welfare agencies. Social workers have been perturbed by declassification (i.e., removal of the credentialing requirement) of many positions in public welfare and other government agencies. Government authorities also influence staffing decisions by requiring certain credentials for those who provide specific publicly subsidized services. In the Medicare program, for example, federal legislation limits direct government reimbursement to those with medical or psychology degrees.

A rationale for restricting ranks, titles, positions, and reimbursement to specific professions or to those who have also passed required examinations is that regulation is required to protect the public. Were just anyone to provide surgical services, for example, consumers could be subjected to unnecessary risk. While physicians often make mistakes, consumers at least know they have had basic training and internship. Decisions about restriction or regulation of staff become more difficult as mental health and related services are considered. It is difficult to demonstrate definitively that certain rather than other professions harm consumers when providing counseling or clinical services. Further, many more kinds of providers exist in mental health than in surgical services—e.g., faith healers, ministers, psychiatric nurses, psychiatrists, social workers, psychologists, and family counselors. Members of professions excluded from providing various services often argue that regulations promote monopolies by favored professions, drive up fees for consumers, and stifle innovative approaches. The social work profession has often been caught in the middle; i.e., it has sought inclusion in services funded by Medicare, Medicaid, and private insurance companies, yet it has sought to exclude marriage and family counselors and other professions on grounds that they lack sufficient or appropriate training. Within the profession, there has been considerable discussion about the kinds of tasks that should be undertaken by those with B.S.W. and M.S.W. credentials, as well as by those who have not completed undergraduate education (e.g., those with associate in arts degrees).

Locus of Services

As noted in guest editorial 4.1., an institution versus community debate is under way in mental health, correctional, and developmental disability sectors. The issue has also received prominence in gerontology. How many older persons are now in nursing homes who could remain within the community were homemaker, community residential, and other services available?[13]

The range of facilities and programs that must be established in a community strategy includes halfway houses, group homes, apartment complexes, day treatment centers, and emergency care facilities. Funding mechanisms need to be set up for facility construction as well as for program costs, and regional coordinating bodies are needed to orchestrate the various services. Americans have only intermittently been willing to fund fully developed community approaches in any policy sector. More typically, they have been content to turn people from institutions with the assumption that they would survive with scant assistance from community-based programs. In some cases, too, deinstitutionalization has been sold with the argument that it would save vast sums of money. With this mentality, Americans have been unwilling to allocate sufficient funds for community alternatives.

In emphasizing the need for community strategies, many reformers have forgotten that institutions are needed as well. Some consumers with mental health problems benefit from structured settings distant from their place of residence. Institutional settings allow provision of specialized diagnostic services, as illustrated by the services given mental patients in the aftermath of violent episodes. Some persons argue that large county and state hospitals should themselves be reorganized and expanded to include emergency, day treatment, and community services.

Extent of Preventive Services

All too often, critics argue, services and programs address existing problems rather than preventing problems prior to their emergence (primary prevention) or addressing them during early stages of development (secondary prevention). Only a small fraction of social welfare expenditures are directed to programs that provide consumer education or early detection efforts, even less to programs that address the environmental and social class factors that cause specific social problems. These critics argue that an ounce of prevention can truly save billions of dollars in expenditures for unfortunate victims.[14]

Policies that promote prevention often lack political support for a number of reasons. Considerable knowledge is needed about the causes of social problems in order to devise preventive interventions. Most social problems have multiple causes, and it is often difficult to decide which are most important. Preventive programs also compete with existing curative programs; politicians and funders are more likely to support programs for existing problems than those that offer the distant promise of prevention. Many professionals are schooled in curative services and do not know how to use or develop educational and early detection strategies. Then, too, numerous special interests thwart prevention, as illustrated by the resistance of the tobacco industry to regulations that limit cigarette advertising. Many studies document higher rates of mental, physical, drug, and other problems among the poor. Massive programs to rebuild cities, decrease unemployment, and raise the economic status of low-income families would reduce the incidence of many social problems, but political opposition has defeated major reforms. Finally, researchers find it difficult to demonstrate whether preventive programs save money (and, if so, how much) because years may be required to discover whether early intervention or consumer education reduces the incidence of specific problems.

Extent of Use of Deterrence

Social welfare policies are often devised to influence behaviors of consumers perceived to violate social norms. Controversy exists about how best to increase employment among welfare recipients, reduce use of drugs or alcohol, decrease criminal activity by those on parole, and foster independence among the elderly.

Deterrent strategies—e.g., policies that prohibit the use of program resources unless consumers take certain actions, such as seeking employment—are favored by those who attribute evil intent to specific groups like welfare recipients. Proponents of such strategies are also likely to urge stiff penalties to discourage adult and juvenile offenders and those who use drugs. Critics of deterrence argue that it reinforces and reflects punitive orientations toward persons in need, discourages them from seeking needed services, and requires program staff members to assume coercive functions that undermine their credibility.

Incentives take the form of rewards or added benefits that follow specific behaviors or activities.[15] Income maintenance programs frequently use work incentives that allow recipients to retain part of their earnings while continuing to receive financial assistance. In similar fashion, programs can be structured to provide social program benefits to persons who utilize services, who reside in halfway houses, or who take other specific actions. Defenders of incentives argue that they are more humane than deterrence. In some cases, social workers oppose both incentives and deterrence. If women with young children lack sufficient funds and wish to remain at home with children, for example, why offer either incentives or penalties to make them seek employment?

Relationships between Agencies and Programs

When constructing a network of services for the developmentally disabled (see guest editorial 4.1), social workers should address a variety of questions. Which agency should assume the lead in orchestrating services? Should a large number of highly specialized programs be constructed to provide various medical, counseling, educational, and occupational services, or should fewer, multifaceted programs be used? And how should specific services for the developmentally disabled be linked to mental health, educational, job-training, and other services?[16]

Lead Agencies. Programs and agencies are typically classified as belonging to mental health, health, child and family, economic security, and gerontology sectors, among others. These classifications are arbitrary, since it is often unclear whether one or another kind of agency or program should assume specific responsibilities. Do programs for alcoholism belong in mental health or health agencies? Do child abuse programs be-

long in juvenile court, mental health, or health agencies? Do child development programs belong in educational, mental health, or family counseling agencies? Placement of programs in one or another sector is influenced by tradition and political factors. In the case of mental health and health, strange patterns of separation and intermingling exist. Community mental health centers are separate from, and often have little contact with, medical programs and staff, yet many of their services are financed by Medicare, Medicaid, and private health plans.

In the instance of vocational training services for the developmentally disabled, then, planners would need to decide whether to place these services within the existing network of agencies that serve this population, to "funnel them through" existing vocational training services, or to create a new set of agencies. In some cases, policy analysts choose to bypass all existing agencies in order to create new ones that they believe will be more responsive to consumer needs and more capable of innovation.

Regional and Local Government Roles. In some cases, because resources pass directly from federal authorities to local agencies or to consumers, program review or oversight functions of local governments, or regional entities are limited or nonexistent. Many federally funded community mental health centers, for example, apply directly to the National Institute of Mental Health for program funds, with final decisions contingent on federal review of applications. Persons who favor direct funding of projects by federal authorities argue that it renders intervening layers of bureaucracy unnecessary, but critics retort that it gives no role to local units of government. In the case of vocational training for the mentally disabled, federal authorities could themselves fund and review local projects.[17]

Alternatively, funds can be channeled through local or state government units that in turn assume major program review and funding roles. In such cases, federal authorities provide major funding but delegate policy responsibilities to local government bodies. Defenders of this option argue that local representatives are more familiar with local needs than federal authorities, but critics respond that local politicians often are not responsive to the needs of vulnerable and relatively powerless populations.

Another option is to establish regional planning bodies that are given central roles in funding and program development. Indeed, some argue that regional bodies should receive federal and state funds and assume major responsibilities for program development, including distribution of program funds. In this instance, regional agencies for the developmentally disabled (or, more narrowly, for vocational training of this population) would be formed.

In reality, American policy often consists of complicated combinations of policy options. As an example, federal agencies sometimes provide basic funding, but local and state governments are given limited program review and even program veto powers. Or federal authorities may delegate important policy roles to local units but issue detailed guidelines that place restrictions on kinds of agencies and programs to be funded.

Breadth of Programs.   No issue is more perplexing or more important than the breadth of social programs. Many officials in the administration of President Ronald Reagan argue that New Deal and Great Society reformers erred in creating "categorical programs"; i.e., programs directed to specific categories of problems and consumers. A categorical approach to the vocational needs of the developmentally disabled is one that provides a specific training program with its own funding, policy regulations, and agencies.[18] This approach leads, some argue, to a welter of social programs and a complex social welfare system difficult for consumers to navigate. Alternatively, vocational training for the mentally disabled could be linked to related programs, such as vocational training for the mentally disturbed or the physically handicapped; vocational training for this population could be included as but one of many programs to be offered under an omnibus vocational training program.

Advocates of broader programs defend them on grounds of administrative simplicity and efficiency, but critics wonder if needs of specific powerless groups, such as the developmentally disabled, are not overlooked by officials in broader programs.[19] In the case of the developmentally disabled, vocational training officials might not be responsive to the unique needs of this population because they are accustomed to helping persons requiring less intensive and lengthy training.

Linkages between Programs.   Imagine a continuum extending from wholly separate and autonomous programs to merged or consolidated programs. In the former instance, separate categorical programs exist in isolation from one another. True, executives and staff members refer consumers back and forth between programs, but there is no interchange of staff and resources, much less development of joint programs. At the other extreme, separate programs are merged, sometimes in large agencies that pool resources from many separate agencies to fund a variety of programs. An integrated human resources agency might use funds from constituent mental health, developmental disability, health, public health, and substance abuse programs, for example, to establish a network of community agencies. In the separate and autonomous service delivery system, specialized agencies are devised to meet mental health, health, and other needs, but, in these community agencies, a variety of services are offered by staff members whose primary identification is with the umbrella agency rather than with specialty services. Those who support consolidated agencies argue that they foster multidisciplinary programs and simplify the service delivery system. Critics counter that "superagencies" become unwieldly bureaucracies that encounter resistance from those who wonder whether specific populations and social problems will be given due attention and priority.[20]

Less ambitiously, some localities put a host of separate programs under one roof but do not merge them. In this case, a program for the mentally disabled might be placed within a larger agency that contained mental health and many other programs. Multiservice centers are also created so that consumers find a number of specific services in the same facility. Critics argue that multiservice centers do not redress the fragmentation of the social welfare system, since the still separate agencies often do not develop joint programs even when placed together. As an example, staff members in agencies in multiservice centers sometimes resist the use of a common intake system because they fear their program will not receive its share of consumers from such a system.

Another linkage strategy is to provide case manager services. In this option, specific staff members are assigned the task of developing a service plan for each consumer that includes an array of needed services from various agencies. They then follow consumers over time to see if service plans are implemented. In this approach, the service plan of a developmentally disabled child might include vocational, counseling, halfway house, and medical services. A case manager would follow the progress of the case to be certain that planned services were received and to ascertain whether new services were needed.

ALLOCATION DECISIONS

The reality of scarce resources in social welfare policy requires development of allocation policies that determine which consumers receive, and which do not receive, program benefits. Put simply, insufficient resources preclude receipt of services by all consumers who could benefit from or who might desire them. In some cases, formal policy devised in legislation or by agency boards limits access; in other cases, as discussed subsequently, more subtle and sometimes informal policies serve to restrict access. (A host of nonpolicy factors also determine who does or does not receive assistance, as when many consumers do not claim income assistance because they fear stigma.)

Breadth of Coverage

Were vocational training of developmentally disabled persons devised in national legislation, rel-

atively universal eligibility criteria could be devised so that citizens diagnosed as mentally disabled would receive free training. The advantage of this approach would be that most or all persons needing this assistance would be eligible. Universal eligibility would also enhance the visibility of the program and create a broader constituency that in turn could increase political pressure on legislators to fund the program adequately.

Alternatively, legislators could devise selective eligibility policies that use specific criteria to restrict access.[21] As an example, a policy might limit access by *age,* e.g., to mentally disabled consumers between the ages of sixteen and twenty-one. In this instance, some legislators might believe it advisable to provide these services to relatively young persons, since their prognosis is best. This point of view would be countered, however, by those who argue that vocational needs of older consumers ought not to be neglected.

Access could be limited as well by *diagnostic criteria,* such as the extent of mental disability of consumers.[22] Supporters of this approach might seek to limit access to those consumers whose intelligence is above a certain threshold but beneath another to focus program resources on mentally disabled persons who have the potential to learn job-related skills. Opponents of this policy might question the ability of tests to measure "intelligence," a concept that continues to stir controversy. Representatives of black groups, for example, might question whether existing tests are class-biased, thereby excluding many black mentally disabled consumers from the benefits of the program.

Perhaps the most common method of restricting eligibility is by *income,* as when access is limited to persons who meet poverty or other income levels. Here, too, one might expect controversy, since it is not clear how low to set income standards. Persons supporting income restrictions argue that the poor need program resources the most because they lack resources to obtain program benefits from any other source. Others might contend that few programs are available even for developmentally disabled children of the affluent, that fees discourage many parents from using lengthy training programs, and that the designation "welfare program" could deter utilization even by poverty-stricken consumers.

The case for narrow eligibility based on income was never more forcefully presented than by officials in the administration of President Ronald Reagan. Massive and widespread reductions in eligibility for an assortment of social programs were proposed (see case example 4.1) based on core values that defined limited and last resort roles for government. Opponents retorted that this restrictive approach precluded government assistance to millions of citizens who needed assistance but fell outside eligibility limits. As important, critics argued that programs for poor people tend to be poor programs because the nonpoor have no personal stake in them.

Place of residence can also be used in eligibility policy, as when benefits are focused on developmentally disabled persons residing in rural areas. In many cases, a number of criteria are used together, as illustrated by a program that offers free services only to those who fall beneath specific income levels, meet specific diagnostic criteria, and meet specific age qualifications.

Buck passing is common with respect to eligibility. Both to give localities the option to decide what constitutes poverty and to sidestep political controversy associated with allocation decisions, national legislators often give states and localities considerable leeway in devising allocation policies for federally funded programs. This approach has some merit, since standards of living vary in different parts of the country. But critics counter that more conservative and poorer states often restrict eligibility so severely that many persons cannot receive assistance.

Related to eligibility issues are questions as to the extent to which program participation is *mandatory*.[23] Consumers choose voluntarily whether or not to participate in most social programs. Alternatively, legislators or governmental officials can mandate participation, either by threatening sanctions or by linking participation

to other benefits. Sanctions are used when institutionalized juveniles or adults or those on probation are asked to accept counseling or other services, with utilization linked to release from custody or probation. In similar fashion, most Americans are required to participate in Social Security, Medicare, and various proposed versions of national health insurance. Mandatory participation is favored by those who believe that many people could jeopardize personal welfare if not required to participate, as in the case of Social Security, where some fear many citizens would not otherwise save for retirement years. Opponents argue that mandatory programs infringe upon personal liberty.

Indirect Methods of Restricting Access

Social agencies and programs devise policies that indirectly influence the allocation of resources, particularly when the demand for services far exceeds the ability to provide them. In the case of an agency providing training services for developmentally disabled youth, for example, administrators would need to devise a method of rationing scarce resources if they were deluged with training requests.

One method of rationing is to place upper limits on the intensity or duration of program benefits or services. To allow more persons to receive assistance, program administrators might decide, for example, that no trainee could receive more than two years of vocational training under the program. (In the case of programs that distribute resources such as food stamps or income, limits are placed on the amount of resources received by enrolled consumers.) When placing these limits on benefits or services, the obvious dilemma is how to balance effectiveness and equity. If the intensity, duration, or amount of services or benefits is markedly reduced, many consumers receive program benefits (equity is enhanced, since relatively fewer consumers need be denied any service). Resources or services may be distributed so thinly, however, that consumers may receive little, hence ineffective or inadequate, assistance. Were administrators to

Shift for Social Welfare

*Reagan Seeking to Uproot Old Philosophy by Only Providing Aid
for Truly Destitute*

By Robert Pear

Special to The New York Times

WASHINGTON, Oct. 27—The most significant change that has been evolving in social welfare programs this year is not simply the reduction in Federal financing, but a basic shift in purpose and philosophy, separating the poorest people from the "working poor" and middle-income families.

As Reagan Administration officials whittle away at "entitlement" programs and redefine the "social safety net" in the second round of budget cuts, they are searching for ways to distinguish the poorest of the poor, the "truly needy," from lower-middle-class and middle-income families who have other means of support. The officials expect to announce their latest budget cutting proposals next week.

Reductions in spending can always be made up by increased appropriations at a later date, but a change in eligibility rules or in the philosophy of a program is harder to reverse.

Earlier Democratic administrations believed that welfare programs should help not only the destitute, but also people who were attempting to work their way out of poverty. In contrast, the emerging Reagan philosophy is that the purpose of these programs is just to provide basic sustenance for poor people who have no other means of support.

Implications of Philosophy

This principle was inherent in President Reagan's original proposals, but its full implications became evident only recently, as Federal officials prepared to make deeper cuts in the welfare system.

By tightening income eligibility standards, Congress and the Reagan Administration have already cut off welfare, food stamps and other benefits to the more financially secure segment of a relatively poor population. Only by controlling expenditures in these programs and by redirecting benefits to the neediest people can Government insure the programs' survival in the face of a mounting political backlash, say Administration officials.

Other analysts, however, say that if the programs have poor people as their only constituency, they will not remain viable.

Prof. Alvin L. Schorr, a longtime student of welfare policy now at Case Western Reserve University in Cleveland, warns that "programs for poor people tend to become poor programs."

"Because of the way we feel about poor people in the United States," he adds, "we build stigmas and limitations into the programs designed for them. In the end, the programs deteriorate and they are administered in a demeaning and uncaring way."

Programs Are Vulnerable

In addition, Congressional aides note that the poor are among the least potent of political lobbies, so that programs designed exclusively for them are highly vulnerable to further cuts.

Even as the Administration has removed the working poor and middle-income people from welfare programs, it has tried to remove welfare-oriented benefits from the Social Security system. It attacked the minimum benefit of $122 a month on the ground that it was an "unearned benefit," an obsolete "welfare support add-on."

"Safety net" programs, including Supplemental Security Income, provided more than enough to meet the needs of elderly or disabled people receiving the minimum benefit, the Administration said.

These are the basic tenets of the Reagan

Administration philosophy, as articulated by the President and his senior aides: The poor, in some numbers, will always be with us. The purpose of the Federal Government is not to redistribute income or to lift the poor out of poverty. Welfare and food stamp programs should not supplement the income of people who have income, however meager; they should provide assistance only as a last resort to people who are literally unable to support themselves.

Position Is Explained

"The idea that the Federal Government should help all relatively poor people just because they are relatively poor—that is, should help equalize incomes—may be noble in spirit, but it ignores fundamental reality," two White House aides, Robert B. Carleson and Kevin R. Hopkins, write in a forthcoming issue of "Public Welfare," the journal of the American Public Welfare Association.

The Government, they say, does not have the money to help the "relatively poor," nor does it have a popular mandate to do so.

Administration officials say they are returning welfare programs to their original purpose by eliminating the income supplement for the working poor. Senator Daniel Patrick Moynihan, Democrat of New York, says this represents "an extraordinary change in the purpose of public assistance" because it takes away an economic incentive to work.

President Reagan's critics in the Democratic Party might be expected to defend the programs that he has cut and proposes to cut further. More interesting are the doubts now expressed by such advocates of "supply side" economics as Jude Wanniski and Representative Jack F. Kemp, Republican of upstate New York.

Mr. Kemp, who helped popularize the idea of a social safety net in his book "An American Renaissance," says it should not be necessary to keep trimming programs in the net. The original idea, according to Mr. Kemp and Mr. Wanniski, was that economic expansion should make people ineligible for welfare, food stamps, unemployment insurance and other benefits because they would have good jobs and good incomes.

"The proper solution to the growing burden of social spending then is not to lower the safety net so far that it bounces against the ground," Mr. Kemp wrote. "Instead, we must draw people out of the net by expanding attractive opportunities in the private sector."

The idea of a safety net gives the Reagan Administration a more coherent social philosophy than the Carter Administration had, but the enumeration of programs in the net has always been somewhat arbitrary and variable.

In an address to Congress on Feb. 18, Mr. Reagan said that seven safety net programs— Social Security, Medicare, Supplemental Security Income, veterans' pensions, school breakfast and lunch for poor children, Head Start and summer jobs for young people— would be "exempt from any cuts."

Those words have come back to haunt him. David A. Stockman, director of the Office of Management and Budget, said yesterday that the safety net programs were "not exempt from efforts to review, reform or tighten" them. Specifically, he said he believed that in entitlement programs other than Social Security, the Government could cut 15 percent while still supporting those who needed support. Entitlement programs, which Mr. Reagan calls "automatic spending programs," guarantee benefits to groups of people who meet certain eligibility requirements.

The intense pressure to cut domestic spending may drive the Reagan Administration to systematize a chaotic array of welfare programs, a goal that liberal crusaders for "welfare reform" could never achieve. The Administration would like to give states the authority to set a single standard of eligibility for welfare and food stamps. That would represent a major change because for 10 years, the food stamp program has been governed by uniform national standards set by the Federal Government.

SOURCE: *New York Times*, October 27, 1981, p. A 22. © 1981 by The New York Times Company. Reprinted by permission.

decide, for example, that mentally disabled trainees should receive no more than five weeks of training, program services would be ineffective in meeting their vocational or other needs. Policy makers must make difficult choices, then, when considering the relative intensity or amount of program benefits.

Another common method of rationing program resources in social agencies is to adopt a first-come, first-served policy in which consumers are given services in order of application. At first glance, this approach appears to be equitable. But this policy too has drawbacks, particularly when analysis of utilization statistics reveals that certain kinds of persons receive far less service than other segments of the population. Low-income or geographically isolated populations, for example, often are less likely to know about and use specific services or to use them at later points in time than others, as illustrated by low-income persons who seek medical services when physical problems are well advanced.

Hence, critics argue that social agencies should earmark or reserve program resources for underserved populations much as affirmative action and quotas are used in reserving employment slots for women and racial minorites. They should also, according to this argument, develop outreach services to these populations and examine service utilization patterns to provide outreach to consumers who prematurely terminate.

Some social agencies ration services by *discouraging* specific populations from utilizing them. Overt discrimination is probably less serious than subtler forms. In some cases, the service approaches employed are unlikely to be used by low-income populations. As discussed in chapter 3, low-income consumers are unlikely to use the introspective therapies utilized by many psychiatrists and some social workers, since many need and will only use services relevant to immediate situations. In similar fashion, lack of bilingual and ethnic minority staff members can deter use of services by ethnic minority consumers.

Rationing can be effected indirectly in many other ways, including placement of facilities, use of program titles, and selective use of outreach.

Health and mental health facilities placed in low-income areas promote their use by the poor, just as facilities in suburban locations favor affluent populations. The importance of titles becomes obvious when one examines the implications of calling an agency "free clinic" instead of "women's free clinic." Patterns of outreach also influence access; if program staff members make considerable effort to publicize services among certain and not other groups, they shape and bias access in this way.

Use of fees constitutes another method of restricting access. As fees increase, low-income consumers are less likely to seek services or to terminate at the earliest possible point. Waiting lists or queues restrict access by imposing time delays, since many persons drop out of services when asked to wait for them. Finally, informal practices of staff restrict access, as reflected in patterns of differential treatment. In many cases, critics argue, program staff members "cream," i.e., provide encouragement to those who appear motivated to the detriment of those perceived to have a poor prognosis.[24] Members of minority or ethnic groups sometimes allege patterns of informal discrimination that lead their members to terminate prematurely.

Extent of Mainstreaming

When devising social welfare programs, policy planners need to decide whether to create programs that serve a cross-section of the population or programs that provide services only to restricted groups. In the former case, a mainstreaming strategy is employed that can be distinguished from the development of specialized programs. The issue of mainstreaming versus specialization was widely discussed with respect to the developmentally and physically disabled when court rulings and consumer groups required inclusion of disabled children in school programs attended by other children.[25]

Mainstreaming is supported on grounds that inclusion of specific groups in programs used by broader populations allows them to develop skills to cope in the wider society. A physically handicapped child who only relates to other handicapped children, for example, is not likely to develop the range of acquaintances or experiences she needs. Separation of children into specialized programs can reinforce stigma and low sense of self-esteem. In similar fashion, prejudice against the handicapped is likely to be perpetuated when handicapped and nonhandicapped persons do not encounter one another.

Opponents of mainstreaming argue that specialized programs are often needed by specific groups, such as the developmentally handicapped or children with learning problems. Such children need, they argue, teachers and curriculum materials relevant to their specific needs. Is it fair, they ask, to "hold back" other students, in order to give attention to those who learn more slowly?

The mainstreaming debate occurs as well with respect to the poor. Americans have created dual delivery systems in educational, medical, mental health, and other sectors, systems in which poor persons receive different services from their more affluent counterparts. In the case of medical services, for example, poor persons are likely to use public hospitals, emergency rooms, and foreign-born physicians, while more affluent persons tend to use nonprofit hospitals and American-born primary-care physicians. Many critics argue that the poor should be mainstreamed into programs and services used by the broader population, since separate programs often are not equal. But mainstreaming has been an elusive objective, as illustrated by the disinclination of many physicians and hospitals to serve low-income patients subsidized by public programs like Medicaid.[26] Further, residential segregation of poor persons frustrates their use of programs and providers located in more affluent areas.

CONTENT OF SERVICES AND PROGRAMS

In devising policies that shape the content of services and programs, policy practitioners need to answer questions such as the following: What strategies are used by direct service staff members as they address specific problems of consumers? What is the duration and intensity of services? Are consumers given soft services, such as counseling, or tangible resources, such as money or housing? Such questions are critical to social workers, whose professional activity is often shaped by policies that define the content of services and programs, policies formulated both within agencies and by outside authorities and funders.

Concepts discussed in the preceding chapter relevant to the scanning phase are used when devising these kinds of policies, since they require theories about the causes and nature of specific social problems. Indeed, mismatches often occur. Some consumers may be given counseling services, for example, when they most need employment or tangible resources. Others may need a combination of tangible resources and counseling assistance but only receive one of those services. Social workers, then, can make important contributions to policy development by using knowledge of human and social behavior to criticize and develop policies that shape the direction and focus of social services and programs. In the process, they need to decide whether to provide hard or soft, single or multiple, preventive or curative, intensive or extensive, office-based or community services.

Hard and Soft Services and Benefits

Many social programs provide tangible resources to consumers in the form of funds, housing, food, health service, or jobs. These resources are often provided in means-tested programs where consumers must demonstrate that they meet specific eligibility criteria. Such resources alleviate obvious material deprivation and the anxiety or stress deriving from uncertainty. As an example, provision to a runaway youngster of temporary housing, not to mention financial assistance and employment, can forestall development of serious personal problems.

The range of available soft services includes those with therapeutic, educational, navigational, and life-survival orientations. *Therapeutic* services help consumers resolve conflicted emotions and establish personal objectives, as illustrated by the services provided by mental health clinics. An array of therapeutic interventions is offered, including Gestalt, psychodynamic, behavioristic, transactional, and social-psychological approaches, each with its cadre of followers. *Educational* services are used in many preventive programs where consumers are provided information intended to forestall the subsequent development of problems. Social workers may provide new parents with educational materials about parenting, for example, to try to decrease incidence of family pathology. In *navigational* services, consumers are given information and referrals to enable them to find and receive assistance. In some cases, advocacy is provided when consumers find that existing services or programs are not responsive to their needs. *Life-survival* services include job training, job seeking, budgeting, and related services intended to help consumers develop the skills and knowledge required in contemporary society.

Policy controversy often arises in choices of a preferred balance between hard and soft resources and services and preferred kinds of soft services. In some cases, persons argue that specific consumers erroneously receive counseling or other soft services when they need tangible resources. While navigational and survival services can assist consumers in finding jobs, for example, they obviously are ineffective if no jobs in fact exist. Counselors can sometimes impose their interpretations on consumers, as when a staff person in a mental health agency erroneously leads a female consumer to believe that she cannot find work because she has personal conflicts. Conversely, some critics argue that many consumers who need counseling and other services are only given tangible resources. As an example, many recipients of public assistance need navigational, survival, educational, and even therapeutic services but usually find it difficult to find them in the wake of drastic cuts in the size of social service departments in public assistance agencies.

A challenge in many agencies is to find ways of coupling hard and soft resources and services. Recipients of public assistance should not be forced to receive soft services as a condition of receiving financial assistance. However, such services should be offered when they are clearly needed, either at intake or at a subsequent time. Residents of public housing need a variety of personal and community organization services to help them develop positive living arrangements rather than the barren accommodations often found in large public housing developments.

Controversy also often arises when preferred kinds of soft services are chosen. What combinations of therapeutic, navigational, educational, and survival services are needed, and which kinds should be provided to specific kinds of consumers? When therapeutic services are offered, should they emphasize intrapsychic interventions or interventions that also include a range of community and situational factors? Full discussion of these controversies is beyond the scope of this chapter, but they illustrate how policies are often linked to concepts and theories of human behavior and direct service practice.

Single and Multiple Services

In some cases, agencies provide a specific service or resource; indeed, specialization allows staff to develop particular skills and competencies. In many cases, of course, legislative mandates establish the specific focus of agencies.

But consumers often need a variety of services or benefits. They may have complex or multifaceted problems that require different kinds of services and resources, as illustrated by a person with a physical disability who needs counseling, educational services, navigational skills, medical assistance, and housing. Policy practitioners can consider a number of options when providing multiple services. Agencies can sometimes diversify their internal service capabilities by developing staff who can deliver various kinds of services, often in multiprofessional teams. Or they can use interorganizational strategies that include joint programs, referral networks, exchanges of staff, or colocation schemes in which a number of agencies are located in one multiservice center. Some public agencies develop service plans for consumers at intake, use a case manager to oversee and monitor the plans, and contract with other agencies to provide needed services.

Intensive and Extensive Services

As discussed earlier in this chapter, difficult choices between intensive and extensive services or programs are often required. In intensive strategies, staff and program resources are concentrated on a relatively few consumers. A mental health agency might allow staff to see specific consumers many times during the week and for protracted periods of time, a strategy that would obviously limit the numbers of consumers who could be assisted. Conversely, another agency could set limits on the intensity and duration of services, perhaps requiring specific approvals when consumers received more than ten hours of staff assistance.

Controversy is common when policy practitioners decide whether to provide intensive or extensive services or programs. Legislators and public officials often favor extensive strategies because they want to spread scarce public resources to many consumers, an approach useful at election time when they seek support from persons who have received program benefits. Some professionals favor intensive strategies because they allow full use of professional skills during a lengthy helping process. Further, some believe that imposition of time limits on services deprives them of the opportunity to provide extended services when their professional judgment indicates that such services are needed. Legislators often retort, however, that professionals who do not have to honor time or intensity restrictions often err in the direction of intensive services that make their agencies unresponsive to the needs of the many consumers who receive no services. Indeed, some persons argue that far greater use should be made of preventive strategies that provide extensive educational and survival materials to relatively large numbers of consumers.

Service or Program Strategy

A service or program strategy is defined by policies that shape or guide the activities of staff members as they interact with consumers. Such policies define the locus of services, the extent to which preventive or curative interventions are used, the mix of hard and soft services, the intensity of services, and the extent to which multiple services or benefits are provided. In many cases, the various activities are not clearly defined, thereby providing the staff considerable autonomy. In other cases, numerous regulations prescribe service activities of staff in considerable detail. Official or written policies can be supplemented by informal policies in which staff members develop conventional procedures or service approaches, as illustrated by agencies where the staff commonly uses certain kinds of therapeutic approaches.

A challenge to social workers is to identify policies that singly and together shape service or program strategies in a specific setting and to subject those policies to critical analysis. Perhaps conventional strategies need to be challenged because they are outmoded or do not allow staff to meet the needs of specific kinds of consumers. Perhaps service or program strategies are not sufficiently well defined to give agency staff a sense of direction when helping consumers. Or perhaps staff members are overly restricted by existing policies, which stifle innovation and adaptation of services to the particular needs of specific consumers. As social workers identify these kinds of defects in service or program strategies, they need to engage in policy analysis as they devise alternatives and try to obtain changes in existing policy—whether within their agencies or in external policy arenas where legislation or administrative guidelines are fashioned.

POLICY PRACTICE IN THE ANALYSIS PHASE

The program and policy design role during the analysis phase is important to the policy practice of social workers because they can assume leadership roles in designing innovative programs. In policy practice case 4.1, two social workers develop a community emergency services program (CES) that provides emergency services during specific family crises.

A Social Worker Develops Policies for a New Program

I was one of several coordinators assigned to develop an innovative program to provide community emergency services (CES) to families in a large metropolitan area. (The word *we* is used subsequently to describe the coordinators.)

This model for a service system is taken from the program developed in Nashville, Tennessee. Nashville had one large children's institution that housed the majority of the children coming into placement. Public welfare staff members became aware of a lack of any real preventive system or alternatives to placement and developed a program model that incorporated six components (described later in this case) that could help a family in crisis.

In 1977, an unincorporated area was chosen by Region 2 HEW (now the Department of Health and Human Services) as a possible site for the implementation of CES. It was felt that this community had a problem, recognized by many people in the community, in delivering services to certain kinds of families. An initial exploration suggested that the community would be receptive to the program; thus, it was decided by an administrator in the public welfare agency that we should be assigned to the CES program to work with the community on devising policies.

Our initial focus as staff coordinators hired by the public welfare agency was to do a needs assessment in the community, identifying the problem areas, diagnosing causes, and formulating solutions. The next step was to develop a constituency and devise strategies to effect necessary action. The regional administrator of the public welfare agency was helpful in providing two resources at this point. First, we were given a list of various agencies and personnel in the community involved in providing services to families. Key persons were identified who could give information on the community's problems and on existing programs. We used this list and expanded it by contacting people informally to sound out problems experienced by the community. Second, we were given access to records of emergency family situations dealt with by the public welfare agency during the past two years. These records covered both day and evening situations and revealed that major defects existed in the community that could be addressed by the CES program.

During the day, emergencies of families were handled by the public welfare office and various other community agencies in the area. But the various services sometimes overlapped and were not very well coordinated. The most severe problems, however, arose during the evening, when no viable services for families existed. Children from families in crisis were picked up by the sheriff and placed in foster homes in surrounding communities or at Duncan Hall (a county detention facility) because no emergency foster homes were available in the community.

These children, many of whom spoke only Spanish, were traumatized by the experience of placement outside their homes in a strange community where no one understood or could even communicate with them. Often children of a parent hospitalized on an emergency basis went to Duncan Hall because no foster homes were available in the community at night for such families. Adolescents who were having family problems came into the court system because they were found on the streets at night. Some children came into placement because adequate housing was not available for the entire family. Finally, records revealed that service programs among various agencies in the community were not coordinated. In some instances, we found that various agencies were providing the same services to some families and none to others or were competing with one another for clients. And some families fell through the cracks of intake criteria in agencies and were denied services in a crisis.

In the CES program, six components were developed:

1. 24-hour emergency intake

2. Emergency homemaker caretaker

3. Emergency foster-family homes

4. Emergency shelter for adolescents

5. Emergency shelter for families

6. Outreach and follow-up

Our next step was to develop a constituency and devise strategies to effect action. This task was accomplished in several ways. First, we went into the community to meet with various persons and agencies about the problem they had identified and about what could be done from the community perspective. Next, we attended meetings of established groups in the community to learn more about community leaders and agencies, including the Interagency Coordinating Council, a group of ninety agencies that meet on a monthly basis and share resources and new program information. We went to these meetings to begin to establish linkages with already existing agencies.

However, we began to face political problems. People in the community had strong feelings about the public welfare agency, some of which were negative. They asked whether the coordinators were really going to implement the services. In one instance, an agency executive in a small, private, com-

munity-based agency accused our agency of always talking but never producing results. We restated our commitment to the program and asked for community participation in the planning committees in order to make it both a public welfare and community system. Community people responded to our enthusiasm.

After a month and a half of reconnaissance work in the community, a large general meeting was held at a neighborhood center to bring together various community and agency personnel. The general meeting accomplished its goals of imparting information, getting support, gaining legitimacy for the program, and establishing community linkages.

Six planning committees were formed focusing on the six components. People were given sign-up sheets at the general meeting and signed up for whichever component was most closely related to their interests or agency services. Meetings were held on a weekly basis, and we acted as facilitators. In December, two months later, another general meeting was held to inform people of the accomplishments of the various committees with the hope of setting a time for implementation of the program.

After the first CES general meeting, a meeting was set up with administration of the public welfare agency to discuss what resources they would offer. It soon became obvious that, for a number of reasons, the key division chief did not fully support or understand the new CES project, which he described as an extension of an already existing twenty-four-hour hot line program in the public welfare agency. We were not part of the ongoing administrative staff and therefore lacked credibility with this executive and had not developed linkages within the department. Further, the executive had the approval of his superior to explore the program, not to approve it. (We were asking him to approve the plan to implement CES.) We realized we had made a tactical error and resolved to develop intradepartmental support for the CES program.

We spoke at meetings within the agency, informed line staff supervisors and middle management staff about CES, and asked for suggestions. We informally contacted staff in various offices of the public welfare agency to discuss the program and get support. These strategies were so successful that, when we requested a budget for CES, we were told that approval was likely by early January and that CES would begin on a trial basis by March. Resources offered by other community agencies helped keep projected costs relatively low.

It was the planning committee, however, that really influenced the public agency to sponsor the program. The twenty-four-hour intake committee found a twenty-four-hour phone line that CES could use. They set up intake guidelines for families coming into the program, and they established written agreements with agencies in the program as to what services they would provide and who the contact person for each agency would be after regular working hours. Further, the public welfare agency agreed that six children's services workers would be assigned to make home calls for the CES program at night.

For each of the committees, plans were submitted that recommended various resources. The emergency shelter committee was instrumental in getting support from the county board of supervisors. Further, a powerful supervisor helped facilitate working relationships with other county agencies by putting the CES coordinators in touch with key persons in these agencies, i.e., the county medical center, mental health, and the probation department.

By the first week in January, the public welfare agency had assigned eight homemakers to the program, two of whom were available immediately to CES. Emergency foster homes that were bilingual and bicultural were developed in the Hispanic area especially for the CES program. Arrangements were made with already existing adolescent group homes in the community to set aside beds for the CES program. The emergency shelter for families committee, in working with the Chicana center, had found an old church building that they were working to have ready in one month. On the outreach component, various private and public agencies made written commitments to supply services once the program became operational.

In planning the project, responsibility for providing services was divided up between the public welfare agency and the various community agencies. As the project moved closer to implementation, the promise of delivery of services became a basis for attaining legitimacy with community agencies, who maintained or developed closer ties with CES. We built linkages both externally (outside DPSS) and internally (inside DPSS) because we knew that the program could not function in their absence. Service responsibilities among agencies were clearly defined, and community agencies gained prestige through association with the project.

SOURCE: This case is adapted from one developed by Mary Hayes, M.S.W. Names and locations have been altered.

Conceptual Skills

Many program and policy options exist in the designing of programs, options described earlier in this chapter with respect to the structure of the delivery system, allocation decisions, and the content of social programs. As a precursor to making choices, social workers need to help identify a range of policy alternatives that are relevant to a specific policy problem or issue. In policy practice case 4.1, for example, the social workers locate a model of family services designed in Tennessee that includes a twenty-four-hour emergency intake, various emergency services, and an outreach program. This model represents a marked departure from existing policies of the child welfare services of the public agency, a departure that allows more responsive services to a large number of families who do not need traditional foster-care, protective, or adoption services.

Trade-offs must frequently be considered. Although the issue is not discussed in policy practice case 4.1, the social workers have to consider whether to provide most of the homemaker and emergency foster-care services under the direct aegis of the public agency (option 1) or to contract with private agencies to provide them (option 2). The second option would allow more rapid development of services, since existing programs could be used. Yet inclusion of other agencies also requires a more complex planning process that makes deliberations more difficult. On balance, the social workers decide that a significant number of services will be supplied on a contract basis, but it is a difficult choice. (Other considerations also influence this decision.)

Policy choices often require contingency planning that anticipates future events. In policy practice case 4.1, for example, officials in the public agency initially believe that they can best obtain homemaker services by contracting with other agencies but later realize, to their chagrin, that the complex process of obtaining bids means that none are available when the project is initially implemented. Had officals predicted this unforeseen event, they would have been able to consider alternative strategies that might have avoided this problem.

Indeed, policy analysis intersects with the broader discipline of planning, in which various logistical details are analyzed as they influence the implementation of policies. Policy choices need to be grounded in a planning process that includes all relevant administrative, financing, community, and staffing considerations. In some cases, policy practitioners engage in modelling or simulations where they try to anticipate how these various factors may influence subsequent implementation.

Value Clarification Skills

When constructing proposals, social workers often have to make difficult choices between competing values. As an example, program designers often want to implement new programs rapidly, an approach that precludes all but a relatively few persons from participating in the process of designing the program. (As more persons, groups, and institutions are included, the process of choosing often becomes more protracted, particularly when different perspectives and policy preferences exist.) But the social workers in policy practice case 4.1 also want to utilize a range of community contributions because they want to develop a community-based program that citizens and agencies will perceive as different from the traditional bureaucratic services of a public agency. In this instance, the social workers choose to utilize a community process even though it requires delays in development of the project.

In similar fashion, a tension often exists between the objectives of efficiency and effectiveness during the analysis phase. During periods of scarce resources, social workers often want to develop relatively inexpensive projects by limiting the intensity or duration of services. (They can also try to limit eligibility or raise fees, policies certain to conflict with program objectives to make services accessible to consumers.) Carried to an extreme, however, an emphasis on efficiency can imperil the effectiveness of programs or services. Therefore, a balancing of efficiency and effectiveness is often required.

Tensions often exist as well between efficiency and social equality objectives. Service costs can be reduced, for example, by limiting services to in-office locations and to consumers who self-select, i.e., who seek agency services in the absence of outreach by program staff. Neglected low-income and other populations often require costly outreach services as well as decentralized and community-based facilities if they are to use and benefit from programs.

In policy practice case 4.1, the two social workers have to skirmish with some officials in the public agency who prefer merely using a twenty-four-hour hot line to developing a full range of community-based emergency services.

Social workers also experience tension between political or feasibility objectives and their desire to develop innovative programs. In policy practice case 4.1, for example, some administrators in the public welfare department do not envision CES as a community-based program but merely an extension of the hot line service. Were they to fight the new project with determination, the social workers might face a difficult dilemma, i.e., whether to seek a smaller and more traditional program to decrease the likelihood of defeat or to insist on a larger program. Instead, because they invest sufficient time in building departmental support, relatively few concessions are needed.

Political Skills

Program and policy changes often encounter opposition from persons who believe that they will lose resources, prestige, and program roles or who are accustomed to traditional policies and programs. In some cases, of course, opposition can be decreased by making the strategic compromises often needed in the push and pull of negotiations. The process of making compromises returns social workers to value clarification. They need to decide which policies or components of programs are essential and which can be modified or deleted without jeopardizing program objectives. In some cases, defeat is better than victory, particularly if compromises require unacceptable policies.

Social workers often have to decide how specific to make policies and proposals in the analysis phase. It is sometimes easy to obtain passage of a relatively vague proposal because potential opposition cannot find specific provisions to criticize. As an example, policy practitioners in legislative settings often do not include important details in legislation in hopes of avoiding controversy. A conservative lawmaker who favors strong local roles in policymaking in a specific program may be less willing to object to the

entire program if some of these roles are ill defined than if proponents specifically state that local decision-making roles will be minimized. But vagueness can also bring opposition from those who argue that policies in a proposal are insufficiently developed and may give implementers carte blanche.

Interactional Skills

Politics must also be considered when developing task forces, committees, and personal interactions in the analysis phase. In policy practice case 4.1, the social workers attempt to engender widespread support by including a wide variety of persons and institutions in the planning process. In other situations, policy practitioners do not include a broad range of persons because they believe that political considerations require a speedy process, perhaps one in which details of new policies or programs are divulged to only a few persons in order to decrease potential opposition. In their contacts with key decision makers, social workers must also decide in the analysis phase whom to contact and whom not to contact. In policy practice case 4.1, the social workers discuss the project with a range of officials from the public agency not only to inform them about the project but also to obtain suggestions from them. Sometimes, of course, policy practitioners try to coopt others by giving them policymaking and implementation roles in a new project, but, in policy practice case 4.1, the social workers genuinely want policy contributions from staff.

The social workers also have to assume staffing roles with respect to the task force and its various committees. A major task is to infuse the group with confidence that a proposal can be written, approved, and implemented in a setting in which many members distrust a public agency that has made many unfulfilled promises. They have to help the task force develop priorities and delegate tasks to subcommittees, a process that proceeds with minimal problems. Many of the concepts used when helping therapeutic groups are relevant to task-focused groups as well, including cohesion, leadership, and recruitment. In policy practice, however, these concepts are used as they are relevant to the accomplishment of policy-related tasks in the various phases of the policymaking process.

Position-taking Skills

Program proposals are presented to specific audiences such as funders, executives, boards, or foundations. The arguments that are used to defend proposals have to be carefully tailored to the audience. In policy practice case 4.1, the social workers were so successful in explaining and defending the program that support was obtained from many different sources including the public welfare agency, private agencies, and the board of supervisors. While the case does not describe in detail the arguments that the social workers used with these audiences, it suggests that they emphasized fiscal and administrative details to administrators in the public agency, interorganizational issues to officials in private agencies, and their commitment to speedy implementation of reforms to community citizens.

SUMMARY

In the policy analysis phase, participants address a variety of issues pertaining to the structure, funding, and oversight of the social welfare delivery system as well as a variety of consumer eligibility issues encountered in agency, community, and legislative settings.

Policy analysis is influenced by a series of background, cultural and value, political, and technical factors. Customary methods of devising delivery systems often blind participants to innovative approaches. In many cases, those who benefit from existing arrangements oppose reforms. When making choices, participants often use analytical techniques derived from economics and also examine policy trade-offs.

Social workers examine many policy options when analyzing the structure of the delivery system. Policy choices are needed regarding the kinds and training of staff members used and the extent to which institutional or community strategies are employed, preventive or curative services provided, and deterrence or incentives used. Many policy options relate as well to the relationships between agencies in the delivery system, including the use of regional coordinating entities, the development of umbrella or consolidated agencies, and the use of multi-service centers.

Allocation choices determine which kinds of consumers receive priority in the use of social programs. Decision makers have to decide whether programs have relatively universal or selective eligibility policies and whether program participation is mandatory or voluntary. Social agencies use a variety of methods to ration benefits and services, since resources rarely allow provision of assistance to all persons who could use services. Rationing can occur by placing limits on the length or intensity of service, the use of waiting lists or queues, and the placement of facilities.

In some cases, as when agencies do not develop outreach programs to underserved groups, agency policies discriminate against the poor or other groups. Americans need to decide whether to create medical, educational, child and family, and mental health institutions and agencies that provide services to broad sections of the population or to continue to provide separate services and programs for groups like the poor and the developmentally or physically disabled.

Key Concepts, Developments, and Policies

Central tasks or issues in the analysis phase
Groupthink
International comparisons
Economic analysis

Demand curves
Supply curves
Trickle down economics
Broad economic theories

Policy trade-offs	Breadth of programs
Structure of the delivery system	Linkages between programs
Staffing issues	Autonomous programs
Licensing	Merged or consolidated programs
Classification of positions	Multiservice centers
Locus of services	Case managers
Community strategies	Allocation decisions
Institutional services	Breadth of coverage
Prevention	Mandatory and voluntary participation
Curative services	Indirect methods of restricting access
Deterrence	Mainstreaming
Incentives	Tangible resources
Relationships between agencies	Soft services
Lead agencies	Single and multiple services
Regional authorities	Service intensity
Alternative funding patterns	Service and program strategy
Local and federal roles	

Main Points

1. Five major tasks are encountered in the analysis phase: policy practitioners must decide on policies that shape the structure of the delivery system, allocation, funding choices, policy oversight, and the content of programs or services.

2. International comparisions suggest the importance of cultural factors in policy choices.

3. Economic analysis is frequently used to facilitate policy choices during the analysis phase, both within agencies and in the broader society.

4. Policy trade-offs are frequently calculated in comparisons of competing policy options in order to decide which, on balance, are preferable. In many cases, choices are difficult because no specific policy option is wholly satisfactory.

5. Staffing issues frequently arise during the analysis phase, as illustrated by the importance of licensing and classification issues in social welfare agencies and programs.

6. Many issues arise concerning the extent to which institutional or community strategies are used in social welfare.

7. Many critics suggest that more use should be made of preventive programs, but they have been thwarted by many factors, including the pressing needs of persons who already experience major problems.

8. Controversy is common in social welfare over the issue of whether to use deterrence or incentives in social programs.

9. Numerous options exist in the development of linkages between agencies and programs, as illustrated by debates about lead agencies; roles of local and federal governments and regional authorities; the breadth of programs; and various methods of consolidating or linking specific programs.

10. Because of scarce resources, allocation decisions are required to determine which consumers will receive services or benefits from specific social programs.

11. Difficult choices must be made about the breadth of coverage of specific programs,

choices that involve diagnostic, income, place-of-residence, and other criteria. Policy practitioners also have to decide whether to make consumer participation in programs mandatory or voluntary.

12. Various indirect methods of rationing services or resources exist, including placing of upper limits on intensity of services; use of waiting lists; earmarking of resources; overt and covert methods of discouraging specific consumers; program titles; placement of agencies; and use of outreach services.

13. When devising social welfare programs, planners must decide whether to create specialized programs for specific groups or to mainstream those groups into programs used by the broader population.

14. A variety of policy issues need to be considered when devising the content of services or programs, including issues pertaining to the mix of hard and soft resources and services, the use of single or mutiple services, the locus of service, and the extent to which preventive interventions are offered.

Questions for Discussion

1. In case example 4.1, assume you are asked to develop services to meet employment needs of developmentally disabled adults between the ages of seventeen and twenty-one. You have a $5 million budget for a major metropolitan region. Discuss some policy options you might consider when deciding how to staff the services and when considering relationships between your agency and others in the region.

2. To what extent do you think that mental and other institutions can be eliminated in favor of a "community strategy"?

3. Contrast deterrent strategies and the use of incentives as methods of increasing employment among developmentally disabled persons. Which do you favor, and why?

4. Discuss some licensing and classification issues confronted by the social work profession regarding the roles of persons with B.A. and M.S.W. degrees. What issues arise regarding roles of social workers and members of other professions that provide counseling or mental health services?

5. What are the pros and cons of consolidating most social welfare programs into "super-agencies"? Do you think that multiservice centers should be used more widely?

6. When developing employment services for the developmentally disabled in a specific region with a limited budget, you would need to make difficult allocation choices. Discuss alternative methods of rationing services.

7. Take some social problem that interests you, and discuss difficulties in classifying it within a specific policy sector (e.g., within mental health, economic security, child and family, or some other sector).

8. Discuss informal methods used to ration services or resources in some agency or organization with which you are familiar.

9. Discuss policy trade-offs that would need to be considered in an agency wrestling with universal versus selective eligibility criteria.

10. Discuss kinds of policies and issues social workers confront when they try to decide whether to make their services relatively intensive or extensive. Do professional perspectives differ from those of external funders and government officials?

11. How does policy practice case 4.1 illustrate the following dilemmas, tasks, and realities?
    a. Contingency planning is often needed during the analysis phase.
    b. Efficiency and effectiveness objectives often conflict during the analysis phase.
    c. Social workers experience tension between political or feasibility objectives and their desire to develop innovative programs.

d. Opposition to innovations are often encountered from "persons who believe that they will lose resources, prestige, and program roles."

e. Policy practitioners sometimes decide to make proposals relatively vague by not defining certain details.

Suggested Readings

Bloom, Martin. *Primary Prevention: The Possible Science* (Englewood Cliffs, N.J.: Prentice-Hall, 1981). A comprehensive overview of primary prevention strategies is provided. The author believes that far more resources should be devoted to preventive programs but notes political and other barriers that impede their development.

Fretz, Bruce, and Mills, David. *Licensing and Certification of Psychologists and Counselors* (San Francisco: Jossey-Bass, 1980): "Values, Purposes, and Challenges of Licensing," pp. 9–29. The authors discuss the rationale for and criticisms of licensing as it applies to mental health professions.

Gilbert, Neil, and Specht, Harry. *Dimensions of Social Welfare Policy* (Englewood Cliffs, N.J.: Prentice-Hall, 1974): pp. 54–80. Allocation policies and issues are discussed, with specific reference to income maintenance policies and programs.

Lindblom, Charles. *The Policy Making Process* (Englewood Cliffs, N.J.: Prentice-Hall, 1968): "Limits on Policy Analysis," pp. 12–20. The author notes political realities that constrain policy choices but also discusses alternative approaches to analyzing policy options.

Magill, Robert. *Community Decision Making for Social Welfare* (New York: Human Sciences Press, 1979). A concise overview of the development of the new federalism is provided, with discussion as well of the controversy that it engendered.

Murphy, Michael J. "Organizational Approaches

for Human Services Programs." In Wayne Anderson et al., eds., *Managing Human Services* (Washington, D.C.: International City Management Association, 1977): pp. 193–229. Alternative ways of structuring social programs at the local and regional levels are discussed.

Okun, Arthur. *Equality and Efficiency: The Big Tradeoff* (Washington, D.C.: Brookings Institution, 1975). An excellent discussion of two competing objectives in social welfare policy that often conflict and require calculation of trade-offs.

Thurow, Lester. *Zero-Sum Society* (New York: Basic Books, 1980): Chapters 1 and 7. A provocative discussion of economic options as they pertain to redistribution of national resources and economic growth. A good introduction to economic reasoning.

Titmuss, Richard. "Laissez-faire and Stigma." In Brian Abel-Smith and Kay Titmuss, eds., *Social Policy: An Introduction* (London: Allen & Unwin, 1974): pp. 33–46. The author discusses the rationale for mandatory inclusion of citizens in social welfare programs in the light of arguments by conservatives that mandatory policies infringe on personal liberties.

Tobin, Sheldon, and Lieberman, Morton. *Last Home for the Aged* (San Francisco: Jossey-Bass, 1976). With specific reference to elderly populations, the authors discuss adverse consequences of premature or unnecessary institutionalization as well as alternative community strategies.

Notes

1. For discussion of various policy options during the analysis phase, see Gilbert and Specht, *Dimensions of Social Welfare Policy*, pp. 24–177; Kamerman and Kahn, *Social Services in the United States*, pp. 435–456; and Richard

Bolan, "Social Planning and Policy Development in Local Government," in Wayne F. Anderson et al., eds., *Managing Human Services* (Washington, D.C.: International City Mangement Association, 1977), p. 111.

2. See international comparisons in Sheila Kamerman and Alfred Kahn, *Not for the Poor Alone* (Philadelphia: Temple University Press, 1975).

3. Irving L. Janis, *Victims of Groupthink* (Boston: Houghton Mifflin, 1972).

4. Edward Banfield, *Political Influence* (New York: Free Press, 1965).

5. Paul Samuelson, *Economics*, 10th ed. (New York: McGraw-Hill, 1976), pp. 483–508.

6. Lester Thurow and Robert Heilbroner, *The Economic Problem*, 5th ed. (Englewood Cliffs, N.J.: Prentice-Hall, 1978), pp. 443–533.

7. Ibid., pp. 274–288.

8. See John Kenneth Galbraith, *Economics and the Public Purpose* (Boston: Houghton Mifflin, 1973); Robert Lekachman, *Greed Is Not Enough: Reaganomics* (New York: Pantheon, 1982); and Robert Heilbroner, *The Worldly Philosophers* (New York: Simon & Schuster, 1980).

9. Galbraith, *Economics and the Public Purpose*; Lekachman, *Greed Is Not Enough*; and Thurow, *Zero-Sum Society*.

10. See Martin Rein, "Policy Analysis as the Interpretation of Beliefs," in Rein, *Social Science and Public Policy*, pp. 139–170; and Okun, *Equality and Efficiency: The Big Tradeoff*.

11. George Hoshino, "Britain's Debate on Universal or Selective Social Services," *Social Service Review*, 43 (September 1969): 245–258.

12. Discussion of licensing issues is found in Bruce Fretz and David Mills, *Licensing and Certification of Psychologists and Counselors* (San Fransisco: Jossey-Bass, 1980).

13. Sheldon Tobin and Morton Lieberman, *Last Home for the Aged* (San Francisco: Jossey-Bass, 1976), and David Mechanic, *Mental Health Policy* (Englewood Cliffs, N.J.: Prentice-Hall, 1980), pp. 118–137.

14. Martin Bloom, *Prevention: The Possible Science* (Englewood Cliffs, N.J.: Prentice-Hall, 1981).

15. See David Macarov, *Incentives to Work* (San Francisco: Jossey-Bass, 1970), and Bruno Stein and S. M. Miller, eds., *Incentives and Planning in Social Policy* (Chicago: Aldine, 1973).

16. See Michael J. Murphy, "Organizational Approaches for Human Services Programs," in Wayne F. Anderson et al., eds., *Managing Human Services* (Washington, D.C.: International City Management Association, 1977), pp. 193–229.

17. Alvin N. Taylor, "Relations with Other Agencies Delivering Human Services," in Wayne F. Anderson et al., eds., *Managing Human Services*, pp. 37–56.

18. Gilbert and Specht, *Dimensions of Social Welfare Policy*, pp. 45–46.

19. An overview of new federalism is provided by Robert S. Magill, *Community Decision Making for Social Welfare* (New York: Human Sciences Press, 1979).

20. Michael J. Murphy, "Organizational Approaches," in Wayne F. Anderson et al., eds., *Managing Human Services*, pp. 193–229. Also see Martin Rein, "Coordination of Social Services," in Rein, *Social Policy*, pp. 103–137.

21. Hoshino, "Britain's Debate on Universal or Selective Social Services."

22. Gilbert and Specht, *Dimensions of Social Welfare Policy*, pp. 68–70.

23. Conservatives object to compulsory features of Social Security, which they believe violates standards of liberty. See Marc Plattner, "The Welfare State vs. the Redistributive State," *Public Interest*, 55 (Spring 1979): 28–49.

24. See discussion by Richard Cloward in Irwin Epstein, "Private Social Welfare's Disengagement from the Poor: The Case of Family Adjustment Agencies," in Mayer Zald, ed., *Social Welfare Institutions* (New York: Wiley, 1965), pp. 623–644.

25. Mainstreaming issues are discussed by Ronald Wiegerink and John Pelos, "Educational Planning," in Phyllis Magrak and Jerry Elder, eds., *Planning for Services to Handicapped Persons* (Baltimore, Md.: Brookes, 1979), pp. 41–76.

26. Dorothy Kupcha, "Medicaid: In or Out of the Mainstream," *California Journal*, 10 (May 1979): 181–183.

CHAPTER 5

The Analysis Phase: Funding and Oversight Choices

Social programs require funding not only to provide consumers with services and benefits but also to cover administrative, staff, and overhead costs. The issue of funding is inextricably entwined with the issue of authority; "he who pays the piper dictates the tune." Funding and oversight issues are both discussed in this chapter.

Funding and oversight issues have become embroiled in political controversy in the 1980s, as discussed in guest editorial 5.1. President Ronald Reagan led a crusade to restore funding and policy roles to local units of government, to shift major funding responsibilities to the private sector, and to use market forces instead of regulations to make programs responsive to consumer needs. His funding and policy oversight preferences were contested, however, by many liberals, who argued that the needs of powerless groups would be sacrificed in this massive shift away from national and government roles.

Social workers need to:

Understand alternative sources of funding that can be used to finance social welfare programs

Understand relationships between different kinds of funds as well as methods commonly used to determine levels of funding

Have familiarity with methods used to dispense and allocate funds in a complex federal system

Understand policy roles of different levels of government

These various topics are discussed in this chapter. At the conclusion, a policy practice case is presented that allows examination of strategies used by a social worker who seeks funds for a social agency.

FUNDING ISSUES

After several decades of meteoric increases in funding, social programs in the United States and in European countries have encountered major funding cutbacks in the 1980s. The funding crisis in social welfare has raised anew a host of funding issues, including those pertaining to the source of funds, methods of distributing funds to agencies and consumers, and kinds of social agencies chosen to provide social welfare programs.

Sources of Funds

Policy analysts must choose between a variety of potential government and private sources when funding social programs.[1]

General Revenues. The extensive general revenues of local, county, state, and federal governments—representing nonearmarked resources of government collected from income, property, sales, and excise taxes, among other sources—are used to fund many programs. As suggested in guest editorial 5.1, the federal government has emerged since the 1930s as the major funder of social welfare programs because it has greater tax-raising capabilities than state or local governments. Unlike the income taxes of many of those states that even possess them, the federal tax is graduated; i.e., taxable income and

---

GUEST EDITORIAL 5.1

The States Can Sink or Swim

Reagan Adamant in Passing Down Programs without Money

By Neal R. Peirce

No one could fairly deny President Reagan credit for taking a sincere interest in the U.S. federal system and elevating it to its most prominent position in American debate in well over a half-century. Last Thursday the President even took the step—highly unusual if not unprecedented in modern-day White House communications—to designate federal questions as the sole theme for a press briefing covering the better part of an hour.

Yet as the other four correspondents and I walked out of the Oval Office, I felt no small measure of despair. Reagan had come close in the interview to confirming the view of skeptics who say his "new federalism" amounts to little more than reducing the federal role and shipping programs down to the states as fast as possible. I asked him what, in his dream of American federalism, should be the federal government's "domestic functions"? His sole answers: "national security" and, later in the interview, "interstate commerce."

It was not that the President had not expressed the thoughts of many concerned and acute observers of federalism. He had restated the bedrock principle that it's generally far preferable to raise and spend taxes at the same level of government, be it federal, state or local. He had spoken out for block grants over the plethora of smaller categorical grants so often associated with that "extra layer" of federal bureaucracy that can smother locally administered programs. He had spoken out for maximum feasible local control and discretion. He had pointed with pride to his Administration's removal of hundreds of pages of cumbersome federal program regulations. He had pointed to his Administration's active effort to identify potential revenue turnbacks to the states (though he could not say when they might actually materialize). And he had boasted, with legitimate reason, of his personal, ongoing consultations with state and local officials—more than 1,200 during his first 10 months in office.

Why, then, would one feel anything less than unfettered admiration?

First, because the President seems not to appreciate fully the turmoil into which his rapid, successive budget cutting thrusts have thrown state and local budgets. The state-local sector absorbed $13 billion of cuts, many times its proportionate share, in the first budget round. In September the President sought to excise another 12% from this same sector. In his interview he would give no guarantee that state-local aid—even general revenue-sharing and the newly created block grants—might not suffer still more cuts in the fiscal 1983 budget to be released in January.

Despite direct quotes offered by the interviewers, the President pointedly ignored the alarm flags that were raised by the nation's governors in hearings before the Senate intergovernmental relations subcommittee, chaired by David Durenberger (R-Minn.) in early November. The governors had warned of a condition of "disarray and chaos" in state capitols because of the deep and continuing federal cuts. National Governors Association Chairman Richard Snelling (R-Vt.) had cited one Congressional Budget Office scenario suggesting that discretionary federal aid to state and local governments could virtually disappear by 1984, so great are the other pressures on the budget.

So the governors had said that official

Washington simply must, however painful politically, come to grips with the so-far sacrosanct "entitlements," ranging from Social Security to veterans' benefits to Medicare and all indexed to an inflation-driven cost-of-living escalator. The defense budget can also no longer remain sacrosanct, they said, nor can the prospect of modifying the biggest tax cut in U.S. history passed by Congress at Reagan's behest.

But Reagan, in the interview, dismissed Snelling's urgent call for a two-year moratorium on further cuts in aid to states and localities so that they might catch their breath and institute some rational budgeting and planning. "It would be great if we could afford it," he said. The President mentioned no prospect of major budget cuts other than in federal grants to states and localities, even though that aid flow accounts for but 15% of the federal budget and is dwarfed by entitlements and defense spending. (There are reports that an Administration task force has found some potential economies in the multi-hundred-billion-dollar entitlements, however, perhaps $27 billion through 1984.)

There was perhaps one glimmer of hope: Reagan did not completely rule out the proposal of Gov. George Busbee (D-Ga.) for "a domestic summit involving the President, the bipartisan leadership of Congress, and (the governors') leadership so that we might gain general agreement on ultimate prime responsibilities for government programs, the budget targets we should all plan for, and the time frame in which we are going to reach those goals."

But Reagan did not embrace the idea, either. My impression was that he would never submit himself to a true summit of equal constitutional partners unless he became convinced that his own economic program was failing seriously enough to necessitate an emergency bailout and he wanted partners to share the political responsibility.

The President brushed aside one long-cherished goal of the governors—a sorting out of federal-state roles, with welfare and Medicaid becoming federal responsibilities and such fields as education and transportation passing totally to the states. He simply reiterated his long-held opinion that welfare costs are best controlled locally. He showed no openness to negotiating such questions with governors or others who differ with him.

The President also scorned a resolution, passed by the Western governors in Scottsdale, Ariz., Nov. 7, that the governors would flatly oppose further Administration cuts in the discretionary domestic budget unless negotiations begin for "a significant sorting out of functions between the federal government and the states." Said Reagan: "Most of those Western governors are Democrats." In fact, they are divided—seven Democrats, six Republicans.

What the President at least professes not to grasp is that the chorus of protests by the governors—plus demands that they be acknowledged as constitutionally equal partners—is bipartisan, broad-based and growing, a development that may mark a historic turn in federal-state relations.

Finally, the President demonstrated almost no sensitivity to the plight of the losers in the great new gulf of differentials in wealth developing among the states, such as the energy-poor ones versus those in the South and West with vast reservoirs of oil, gas and coal, which they can tax heavily. Sen. Durenberger has asked how such differentials jibe with a New Federalism in which vast program areas will be pushed down to the state level. He questions whether it's at all "fair to expect the states and localities that suffer from a declining economy to provide the same level of public services as those states flush with energy-related revenues?"

The President's response was that an energy-rich state enjoys no greater taxing advantage than, for example, California with its multi-billion-dollar fruit and vegetable crops. Governments perennially tax everything they can touch, he suggested; energy serverance taxes are no different.

Even if one agrees that some level of state energy severance taxes is justifiable, the sweep of that presidential argument is startling. It ignores the fact that energy-rich states are pulling in not just millions but many billions of dollars, based on the spiraling prices of energy brought about by OPEC and deregulation. And that such states can easily absorb the fiscal blows of the Reagan Administration's budget cuts, while the energy-poor states, especially those with declining industrial bases, are pushed to the wall.

Any interstate disparities in wealth, said the President, are strictly the states' own problem. "The built-in guarantee of freedom is our federalism. That makes us unique. That is, the right of a citizen to vote with his feet." Any inequalities should be taken care of by "the marketplace." He apparently feels that the federal government has no obligation to people or states or communities dealt crippling blows by the economic vagaries of the times.

Absent in this, to my mind, is the essential sense of nationhood and nationwide interdependence and mutual responsibility that ought to underpin any federalist philosophy for our times. Thus my feelings of despair at the close of the Reagan interview. Yet I also reminded myself that this is a warm, outgoing man who really means others no ill. A remaining hope is that he is a politician who has shown, as recently as last week in his European nuclear policy, that when an old policy self-destructs, he can become the statesmanlike leader of a new one.

Neal Peirce is a columnist for the *National Journal*. SOURCE: © 1981, The Washington Post Company. Reprinted by permission.

tax rates increase with the level of income. Further, the percentage of income taxed by the federal government far exceeds the percentage taxed by states. The federal income tax raised $200 billion in fiscal year 1980. Further, it has yielded rapidly increasing sums because, with inflation, many citizens and corporations have moved into higher tax brackets as income has increased. (Legislation in 1981 partly offset this so-called bracket creep.)

The crisis described in guest editorial 5.1 occurred because local units of government, charged with administering a host of federally funded social welfare programs, became used to relying on federal largesse in subsidizing large shares of thousands of federal-local categorical programs. But the Reagan administration proposed reducing the federal share without specifying how local units of government could raise funds to make up the difference. General revenues of many local units continue to derive from taxes with relatively small revenue-raising potential, e.g., property, sales, excise, and license taxes. Even with its loopholes for affluent persons and corporations, the federal tax is more progressive than many local taxes that bear disproportionately on the poor. Local tax revenues have also been eroded by taxpayer revolts, as illustrated by statewide referendums in Massachusetts and California that have slashed property tax rates.

The advantage of using general revenues, then, is that they provide large sums of money; the disadvantage is that they are subject to taxpayer revolts. Large numbers of claimants, including those who seek expanded military programs, compete for scarce resources in a complicated authorization and appropriations procedure. This procedure, used in Congress and in state legislatures to decide which programs receive what share of general revenue resources, poses many risks for programs with relatively powerless constituencies. The burden of local taxes in particular falls disproportionately on the poor, and numerous loopholes limit the actual progressiveness of federal taxes.

Payroll Taxes. Payroll taxes are a useful source of revenue precisely because they repre-

sent a stable source of funds not subject to yearly vicissitudes.[2] Also, consumers are likely to perceive programs based on payroll taxes as earned benefits rather than as handouts, a fact that enhances political support for these programs. Payroll taxes can be used only to a point, however, since most Americans do not want their paycheck excessively eroded by taxes. Employers' shares of medical and Social Security taxes are also passed to consumers in the form of higher prices, thereby penalizing low-income consumers, who pay a large share of personal income for consumer goods.

Consumer Payments. Consumer payments in the form of fees or consumer portions of private medical insurance are defended by those who argue that such payments deter frivolous or nonessential use of programs. Critics of free medical services in England, for example, argue that many consumers seek nonessential cosmetic and dental services. Persons opposed to major government funding of mental health services believe that many consumers would seek counseling for relatively trivial conditions, dramatically increasing the cost to government. Critics of consumer payments retort that such payments deter use of needed services, particularly among the less-affluent.[3]

Special Taxes. Special taxes—such as those on marriage licenses for programs to help battered women, on alcoholic beverages to fund alcoholic counseling services, and on auto licenses to fund pollution controls—have the advantage that they, like payroll taxes, are earmarked for special programs that do not need to compete with others for scarce funds from general revenues (see case example 5.1). But Americans are not accustomed to using these special taxes for social welfare programs, nor are special interests, such as the manufacturers of alcoholic beverages, likely to support taxes that could reduce consumer purchases of their goods.

Private Philanthropy. Private philanthropy has long been eclipsed as the major source of funding for social welfare programs. Still, about $50 billion was raised in 1980 from individuals,

Abused-Wife Shelters Get New Funding

By Bill Curry
Times Staff Writer

GREAT FALLS, Mont.—For 35 years she was married, and for 35 years she was battered. It started with a slap, and the last beating was the worst: After being knocked senseless to the floor, the 56-year-old woman now recalls, "I said, 'What are you going to do, kill me?' He said, 'I've got a notion to.' "

So not long after, when she could feel the tension building toward another attack, she packed a few things and drove to Mercy Home, a shelter for battered wives here. "I wouldn't have had anyplace to go," she said of her delayed flight to a new life. "I had left many times and went back many times because there was no Mercy Home.

"If there had been, maybe I wouldn't have stayed all those years."

Marriage Fees the Key

Mercy Home exists today because Montana has joined the small but growing number of states that have found a new and unusual source of money to provide aid to battered wives. Since 1978, Montana and six other

foundations, and corporations, including federated community fund-raising drives like United Way and appeals for Jewish and Catholic agencies. An advantage of private giving, some argue, is that it allows social agencies to escape the restrictions of government authorities. But there is scant evidence that agencies that rely on private philanthropy are more innovative than those using government funds. Indeed, some argue that agencies using public funds are more innovative and more sensitive to low-income consumers than their nonprofit counterparts. Further, critics argue that many foundations and federated appeals are biased against new and innovative agencies. For example, women's groups argue that many foundations do not provide them with funds even when requests are meritorious. Even if private philanthropy is no panacea, however, it offers useful supplementation of public funds. But it hardly serves as a substitute for major social programs, as some persons naively hoped in the wake of major cuts in social welfare programs in the early 1980s.[4]

Mixed Funding Sources. Social programs are rarely funded from only one source, as illustrated by those that make use of federal-local matching funds. In these programs, the federal government provides a certain share of total program costs that is matched according to a specific formula by local public contributions. As an example, the federal government pays a major share of public assistance payments under the Aid to Families with Dependent Children program (AFDC), but each state also contributes a major portion of costs of the program within its boundaries. In many cases, federal and local contributions are also supplemented by use of consumer fees, as in the instance of medical services, where consumers pay a share of costs under the various public programs. In some cases, public and philanthropic funds are used to support certain projects, as when a private foundation supplements government funding.

Determining Levels of Funding

Euphoric in the wake of enactment of legislation that mandates a social program, reformers often discover that the program subsequently receives inadequate funding. (Funding increases are particularly needed during times of high inflation,

states, including California, have increased their marriage license fees to raise money to combat family violence and help its victims. Other states are considering such action.

The result is that hundreds of thousands of dollars have been provided to open shelters and rescue financially endangered ones. Here in Montana, for example there are now four shelters. Shelter workers say flatly there would be none at all in the state—where about 250 incidents of spouse abuse are reported monthly—without the marriage license money.

In California, marriage license fees, which vary from county to county, were increased by $8 statewide in July, 1980, to provide for abuse programs. The fees provided about $1.2 million in the first year. Some $600,000 of that was in Los Angeles County, where there are now 13 abuse shelters, compared to nine last year.

Reliable Source of Money

The use of marriage license surcharges is seen as an especially important development because it finally provides a reliable, long-term source of money for the private, non-profit groups that operate shelters for battered wives. Nationwide, shelters have traditionally been plagued by the annual and un-

predictable whims of government spending, politics and shoestring fund raising.

Nancy Solomon of the now closed Safe House in Denver described the funding problems of many shelters when she lamented: "You get into the business of trying to raise money to provide a needed service, and you spend more time raising money than providing a service."

Two years ago, Colorado turned down a proposal for a marriage license surcharge to fund abuse programs. Today, three of six Denver-area shelters face questionable futures because of financial difficulties. Safe House closed last December when it lost its federal support.

"It's the only stable source of funding," Lonnie Gordon, coordinator of the Los Angeles County Domestic Violence Council, said of the marriage license money.

Fund Raising a Snowball Effect

"Until we had that base, we couldn't get started," said Susan Barrow of the year-old Gateway shelter in Billings, Mont., a city where two battered wives recently killed their husbands. "Fund raising is a snowball effect: The more you have, the more you get."

In one year, Gateway, which was only a telephone crisis line at first, has become a

when program resources dwindle as the real value of benefits decreases and program costs increase.) In some cases, funding for programs is relatively secure, particularly in programs with open-ended appropriations, such as some federal-state public assistance programs and the Food Stamps Program. In these cases, Congress agrees to provide funds to finance services or resources for all consumers who use the program, no matter the cost. Funding can be cut in these programs, however, by decreasing the level of benefits provided to consumers or by devising

more restrictive eligibility standards—policies pursued by the Reagan Administration with many open-ended programs. Further, Congress can establish ceilings, or "caps," for some previously open-ended programs. As an example, a major open-ended social services program (Title XX of the Social Security Act) experienced funding increases as many states drastically increased their use of the matching federal-state funds, but Congress established a national ceiling of $2.5 billion in federal funds in 1972 to counter escalating costs.

comfortable refuge that thus far has temporarily housed 270 women and children. About $16,000 of Gateway's $50,000 budget comes from marriage licenses.

Following Florida's lead in 1978, Montana in 1979 increased its marriage license fee from $15 to $25 to fund educational programs, hot lines, counseling and private, nonprofit shelters for spouse abuse. In addition to California, Michigan, Kansas, North Dakota and Ohio have also adopted marriage license surcharges: Indiana has imposed an anti-abuse fee on divorce filings.

This year, Montana raised its marriage license fee another $5, earmarking the additional money for shelter support. All told, the state expects to extract $115,000 from altarbound couples this budget year for anti-abuse efforts.

"We just couldn't have done a tenth of what we're doing without that state money," said Caryl Borchers, director of Mercy Home here and a driving force in the state's efforts to combat domestic violence. Mercy Home, the state's first shelter for abused wives, opened in May of 1977 with more faith than funds.

Even today with its state money—$18,375 of its $60,000 budget—Mercy Home is still dependent on foundations, churches, the United Way and donations for much of its

support. So eclectic is its funding, in fact, that a $12,495 Presbyterian grant provides stipends for three Jesuit missionaries serving as shelter workers.

Borchers added, "With the state money, we can help twice as many people and we can do the after-care and follow-up. We had hand-to-mouthed it so long, and we have stretched every penny. Everybody says the private sector's going to take care of social programs, but the same private foundations will not be able to keep funding us (indefinitely).

"That's why this marriage license money is so important. (Without it) we wouldn't have any state money, and a private foundation will not support a facility if it's not funded locally and statewide."

Without the marriage license money, Borchers said without hesitation, Mercy Home would not have lasted. And without shelters, many women would remain in their violent surroundings.

Mercy Home housed 277 women and children last year and provided other assistance to 284 more families. It accommodates 16 persons at a secret location for their safety, providing them with food, clothing if necessary, counseling, reassurance, a roof and a respite from constant fear. . . .

SOURCE: Copyright 1981, the *Los Angeles Times*. Reprinted by permission.

In the case of the Social Security program, benefits are sometimes increased without commensurate increases in payroll taxes. Thus, Congress decided in 1974 to "index" social security benefits, i.e., to increase benefits at a rate at least equal to the national rate of inflation. Some but inadequate provision was made to increase payroll taxes, so officials in the Carter and Reagan administrations considered various combinations of payroll tax increases and cutbacks in benefits to finance the automatic benefit increases.[5]

Legislators sometimes mandate diminishing

government funding through the "declining share" approach. Congress may agree, for instance, to pay 80 percent of costs of a specific national program in the first year, 60 percent in the second, and declining shares in subsequent years until no share is paid in eight years. While it may be assumed that local units of government will increase their share to match federal cuts, this increase often does not occur, and some programs are imperiled.

The funding of most social programs is dependent on an authorization and appropriations

process.[6] Congress *authorizes* funds by stipu-
lating in the mandating legislation how much
money (upper limit) can be allocated for a social
program. (Authorizations are given either for
specific years or for a series of years, as illustrated by an authorization that allocates $30 mil-
lion for a specific program in each of the next
three years.) But programs often receive far less
than authorized sums during the annual *appropriations* process. Well in advance of the fiscal
year beginning in October, the president submits
a proposed budget to Congress containing recommended appropriations for specific programs.
After testimony from program administrators
and others, a subcommittee of the appropriations committees of the House and Senate recommends specific funding allotments that cannot exceed authorizations. House and Senate
eventually pass appropriations bills that, once
signed by the president, determine how much
each program receives. Intensely political from
start to finish, the appropriations process is one
that leads to big winners (programs that achieve
authorized funds) and losers (those who receive
funds for less than authorized amounts). Similar
budgeting processes are used in local and state
government units.

Interdependence of Funding Sources

Decisions of specific funders of social welfare
programs have profound implications for others.
Indeed, considerable jockeying occurs among
various levels of government concerning who
should pay for what service when counties urge
state officials to pay larger shares of the local
match in the federal-local programs. In turn,
states sometimes try to make local officials assume larger burdens. Similar jockeying between
state and federal officials occurs when federal
authorities reduce federal funds for social welfare
programs yet simultaneously increase social welfare roles of the states. Understandably, many
state officials are irate when they encounter this
no-win situation (illustration 5.1).

   Case example 5.2 suggests that interdependence of funding can produce tragic con-

ILLUSTRATION 5.1

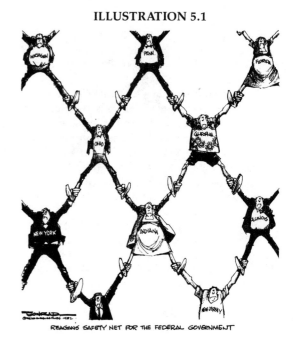

REAGAN'S SAFETY NET FOR THE FEDERAL GOVERNMENT

Paul Conrad, © 1982, *Los Angeles Times*. Reprinted by
permission.

sequences for consumers and agencies when one
set of funders summarily curtails its funds. Many
social agencies rely upon a combination of federal and local contributions, but cutbacks in federal funds mean that localities have to cut their
funding of these agencies in order to pick up the
slack in essential medical, income, and other services. Meanwhile, foundations, federations, and
other private sources are subjected to incredible
pressure to fund now-desperate agencies but
lack the funds to help many of them. Such funding uncertainty, common in the 1980s, precludes
long-term planning in agency or government
settings.

Auspices

Policymakers must determine the kinds of agencies that should implement specific programs as
well as the source of their funds. The complexity

Nonprofit Groups Drop into Aid Gap

By Bruce Keppel
Times Staff Writer

"We're just poor people whose philosophy is, use what you got," said Sister Gloria Davis, who runs a pair of centers to help destitute families in the Pacoima and Compton areas.

What Davis got last week was a check for $600 from Los Angeles County, representing the final distribution of federal funds from the Community Services Agency, which will expire Sept. 30. For Davis, the check also marked the end of the once-widespread "war on poverty" declared by President Lyndon B. Johnson more than 15 years ago, a "war" that once had furnished her a $130,000 grant.

To keep the centers open temporarily, Davis borrowed $28,000 against her home—trusting, she said, that "God will provide."

Davis' organization is among the thousands of private nonprofit organizations caught in the Reagan Administration's budget slashing. They range from child-care centers to soup kitchens to community orchestras, theaters and recreation programs.

$128 Billion Total

Cuts in public aid for social welfare, health, the arts, housing and food programs could total $128 billion by 1984, the Urban Institute estimated last month in projecting funding in the Administration's current economic program. The reduced level of government services will likely increase demand for help from many nonprofit community agencies, the institute observed. But aid to them is expected to decline $27 billion over the next five years.

"These program areas, which accounted for 26% of all outlays in 1980, will absorb 50%

of the projected cuts," said the institute, an independent education and research organization based in Washington, D.C.

The Reagan Administration is trusting in the private sector to rally around and fill some of the huge revenue gaps this will produce through greatly increased philanthropy—at least to those agencies that private donors deem effective in their terms.

Increases Planned

While a number of major firms and foundations do plan to increase their grant programs—and some increased them even before enactment of hefty tax cuts—those familiar with corporate charity and private philanthropy predict an immense shortage in available funds.

"The rhetoric is terrific," said Lloyd B. Dennis, chairman of First Interstate Bank's social policy committee in Los Angeles. "I don't think the private sector is going to take up the slack—not by a long shot."

Even a major effort by corporations would have little overall effect. Total contributions to nonprofit groups by companies and company-operated foundations totaled $2.55 billion in 1980, according to the Conference Board, whose 4,000 members include leading businesses, foundations, government agencies and educational institutions. That sum represents only about 5% of all private giving.

Nonprofit foundations and private individuals contributed the balance—more than $45 billion in 1980, the board reported.

So, despite such examples of corporate largesse as Arco Foundation's doubling of its contributions to $27 million this year and Exxon Corp.'s intention to boost its $38-million philanthropy budget to at least $45 million this year and $50 million next year, the nation's thousands of nonprofit service organizations are going to be squeezed as never before.

Los Angeles County alone counts more than 30,000 such groups, said Jack Shakely, executive director of the Los Angeles-based California Community foundation, which pools philanthropic donations and awards grants in the $15,000 to $30,000 range to scores of Southland agencies.

"Many will not survive the next four years," Shakely said, "I'm afraid that many that don't survive will be the newer community-based organizations that got mostly government money." . . .

While programs like those run by . . . Sister Davis have reflected the ebb and flow of public funding, scores of other nonprofit organizations, supported by local philanthropy as well as public money, also must cope with federal cutbacks.

United Way, which supports 250 agencies serving 2.5 million Los Angeles County residents on a $56-million budget, said its members lost $16 million in federal funds—an average budget cut of 20%.

"Our need is always great, but this year it is exacerbated by the federal cuts," said United Way's fund-drive chairman, Joseph J. Pinola, chief executive officer of First Interstate Bankcorp.

Pinola cited just two examples of what the federal cutbacks have caused United Way–supported agencies to curtail so far:

—The Central City Mental Health Assn. lost $2 million and laid off 25% of its staff.

—The Visiting Nursing Assn., shorted $1 million in anticipated funds, laid off 10 nurses and two office workers and cut its anticipated caseload by 2,000 patients.

United Way's announced 1981–82 fund-raising goal is $60 million, Pinola said, a $4-million increase over last year. That increase won't begin to close the funding gap its membership is facing, he said.

"Over the next six months," Pinola said, "we will be trying to establish priorities as to which programs can be picked up."

While some consolidation and elimination may be beneficial—many in the field say it is long overdue—nothing assures that the most needed organizations will be those spared, observed Jennifer Leonard of the Grants-

of the American social welfare system derives not only from the multiplicity of programs and funding sources but also from confusing patterns of responsibility for program delivery. Nursing homes are largely profit-oriented agencies, for example, whereas most hospitals are nonprofit. Many sectors are comprised of a complicated aggregate of public, nonprofit, and profit-oriented agencies and professionals. In the mental health sector, for example, public state hospitals and federally funded mental health centers are supplemented by nonprofit child guidance and family counseling agencies and an array of private practice professionals drawn from psychiatry, social work, psychology, and other professions.

Opinions differ as to what kinds of agencies should serve as conduits for social welfare programs.[7] The English and many other European countries favor extensive use of *public agencies*. They are, after all, accountable to elected officials who are ultimately elected by consumers and who can seek reforms when alerted to problems. Since public agencies lack a profit motive, they have no incentive to increase profits by deceiving or short-changing consumers. To socialists such as the late social welfare theorist Richard Titmuss, public agencies reinforce public commitment to developing a collective altruism, i.e., to helping strangers who are afflicted with social problems.[8]

manship Center in Los Angeles, which teaches survival skills to such hard-pressed groups.

"There certainly are some that have outlived their usefulness," Leonard said, "but I'm not sure that they correlate with those that may not survive."

Tax Incentive

Meanwhile, the Reagan Administration's tax program attempts to increase corporate giving by doubling the exemption for philanthropic donations from 5% of pretax earnings to 10%. A task force appointed by the President to suggest ways to stimulate private aid for the arts and humanities recommends further tax incentives.

But corporate philanthropy now averages less than 2% of earning, according to the Conference Board. As a consequence, Shakely of the California Community Foundation, among others, looks to another change in the tax laws that will affect the 80% of all individual taxpayers who use the short form—those who do not itemize deductions but take the standard deduction instead.

The large group of smaller taxpayers will have available for the first time an additional 25% deduction on the first $100 of charitable donations they claim.

"Those $10 and $20 gifts to churches and organizations can add up," he observed.

Still, he conceded, private giving would have to increase by 140% a year over the next few years to begin making up lost public funds. Private giving actually increased by 35% annually over the last decade. Moreover, there is concern that the cut in the maximum tax rate, to 50% from 70%, may reduce the incentive for some wealthy individuals to maintain their level of philanthropy.

"So," Shakely concluded, "we're looking for ways to be clever, nimble, and get the job done (with less)."

Not surprisingly, the community foundation and virtually every bank and company with known philanthropic programs are swamped by new applications for grants. First Interstate Bank, for example, received 60% more bids in the first six months of this year, Dennis said. The RCA and General Motors charitable programs report similar increases. . . .

Many participants in policy criticize public agencies, which, they argue, are not responsive to the needs of consumers. Bureaucrats develop political power, which they use to resist efforts to reform services. Employees with union and civil service protection cannot easily be demoted or removed, even when they provide poor services. Because they do not have to compete with other agencies, some argue, public agencies are likely to be inefficient.[9]

Others favor extensive use of *nonprofit agencies*. Many incorporate contributions from citizens and communities in agency deliberations. Further, some citizens are more likely to use nonprofit agencies than public agencies because they

are less likely to be perceived as welfare agencies. These agencies also have their critics, among whom are researchers who question whether they are more innovative than public agencies or more willing to accept community contributions to decision making. As with public agencies, critics argue that they can be inefficient when they are not subject to direct competition.[10]

Both the promise and the limits of nonprofit agencies are illustrated by the fund raising of the national network of United Way drives, which provide resources for many nonprofit agencies. These drives constructively elicit local participation of citizens in social welfare and provide resources to supplement existing public and profit-oriented services. Many conduct local planning projects to identify gaps in services and stimulate innovative programs. Still, critics question whether United Way drives fund innovative services, since many appear to distribute resources to traditional and relatively powerful agencies.[11] In many cases, priorities are established by committees that make primary use of affluent citizens to the detriment of a range of citizens. New agencies arising in response to consumer needs that are not met by traditional agencies often have difficulty obtaining United Way funding. In some cases, blacks and other segments of the population have launched competing drives to provide resources for programs they believe to be underfunded by United Way.

Finally, some support extensive use of *profit-oriented agencies*, either through contracts to provide specific services or through social welfare funds distributed directly to consumers, who then choose agencies or providers on the open market (contracts, vouchers, and vendor payments are discussed subsequently). According to their defenders, profit-oriented agencies have to be responsible to consumers to remain profitable, since consumers would otherwise shun them, and they need to contain costs in order to be able to remain competitive.[12] But critics point to nursing home scandals and poor services in some profit-oriented daycare centers as examples of dangers in wholesale conversion to a market system. When there is conflict between a desire to increase profits and provision of quality services, critics believe, many entrepreneurs opt for profits. Some critics also note that profit-oriented agencies can resort to deceptive advertising, particularly when offering services that are difficult for consumers to evaluate.[13]

The problem of determining which kind of agency works best is made difficult by variations between agencies. Some public agencies conform to stereotyped, hide-bound bureaucracies; others are innovative. Some nonprofit agencies pioneer new services; others are mired in tradition. Profit-mongering entrepreneurs exist, but some profit-oriented agencies provide quality services. On balance, liberals and socialists favor use of public and nonprofit agencies because

they are more likely than conservatives to find an inherent contradiction between profit motives of private entrepreneurs and the altruism implicit in helping relationships.

Funding Channels

Once funds exist for a social program and some combination of nonprofit, public, and profit-oriented agencies has been chosen, funding channels need to be devised to distribute resources from funders. One method of discussing strategies is to portray a number of channels, or routes, that can be used in social welfare policy funding (see illustration 5.2). Government can directly fund local agencies (route 1) or can provide funds directly to consumers (route 5). Numerous additional options are possible, including federal routing of funds to states that then fund local agencies (route 2) or provision of federal funds to state governments that then direct those funds to local governments, which in turn fund local agencies (route 3). Advocates exist for each of these funding channels, as suggested in the following discussion.

Direct Funding of Agencies by Federal Officials (Route 1). Government funders often provide funds directly to agencies to deliver social programs. Agencies or bureaucracies, whether public, nonprofit, or profit-oriented, can be given *project grants*, as when the federal government provides funds to a local vocational training agency to provide services to the mentally disabled. The project grant might come with many regulations that specify the content of services or give relatively wide latitude to local agencies. Alternatively, funders can *contract* for specific services. In this instance, the federal agency might contract for a specified number of days of vocational training or a specified number of trainees. Contracts are usually more specific than project grants in defining the quantity of services or resources to be provided.

The advantage of funding organizations to provide services rather than providing subsidies directly to consumers is that government authorities can monitor their programs during both ap-

ILLUSTRATION 5.2   Selected Funding and Decision Channels, or Routes

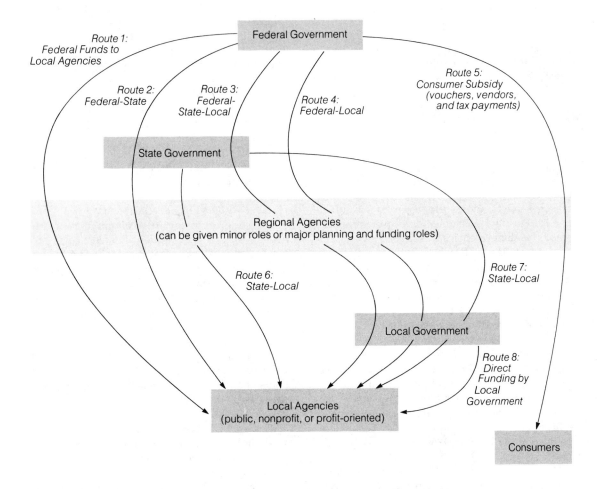

plication and implementation.[14] If an agency is providing inferior services, funds can be terminated and awarded to another agency. (Critics retort, however, that government authorities rarely monitor organizations, particularly when those organizations have strong political resources; thus, discrepancies often exist between program realities and program objectives.) Funders can also promote certain kinds of innovative projects during the application process or can influence the location of services by deliberately funding programs in underserved areas.

Consumer Subsidy Channels (Route 5). Alternatively, some persons argue that federal funders should provide resources directly to consumers.[15] One approach is to give consumers *undesignated funds* that they use as they wish. Some critics of existing categorical programs argue, for example, that they should be abolished and their funds redistributed to consumers, who could then purchase the desired services. Another and more restrictive approach is to provide consumers with funds that they must use for specific social needs, as in the case of educational *vouchers,* health care vouchers, or food stamps. Government can place parameters upon the kinds of services or commodities that can be purchased and can require that agencies or providers meet certain basic licensing standards. Alternatively, government funders can make so-called *vendor payments,* in which consumers receive services from providers who are then reimbursed by the government for services rendered. As an example, the Medicaid program reimburses hospitals and physicians for specific medical services.

Proponents of these various consumer subsidy strategies argue that they promote healthy competition among agencies, which in turn makes services more responsive to consumer needs. Further, consumers are given considerable freedom of choice in selection of services or commodities. Critics, however, point to many defects in market schemes.[16] Although armed with vouchers, many low-income consumers cannot find quality providers because relatively few choose to practice in low-income areas. Providers often deceive powerless or ignorant consumers, as attested by nursing home abuses. In the case of unrestricted cash subsidies, some fear that less important needs of consumers may take priority over basic medical, housing, and nutritional needs. Finally, subsidies to consumers can foster escalation in fees charged for services, as reflected in runaway medical fees in the wake of passage of Medicare in 1965.

Federal-to-State Channel (Route 2). As discussed in more detail later in this chapter, another option favored by many persons is to give federal funds to the states, which are then given relatively broad latitude to fund local agencies. Advocates of enhanced roles for state governments support this policy option because federal officials no longer intrude in local social welfare administration. Opponents argue that state governments are often not responsive to local needs, much less the needs of low-income and powerless groups.

Federal-to-Local Channel (Route 4). Just as federal-to-state "block grants" characterize route 2, in "special revenue sharing" the federal gov-

ernment bypasses state governments and gives funds directly to local units of government, including counties and municipalities (both of which are discussed later in this chapter). As in federal-to-state block grants, relatively broad latitude is given local governments, a policy supported by those who want to diminish policy roles of the federal government. Here, too, however, many persons fear that local units of government are no more responsive to the needs of low-income and powerless populations than state governments and often lack required technical competence to oversee and develop quality social welfare programs.

Local Funding Channels (Routes 6 and 8). Conservatives often favor virtual elimination of federal roles, as when President Ronald Reagan, in 1982, proposed giving states responsibility for administering and funding Food Stamps, Aid to Families with Dependent Children (AFDC), and a myriad other social programs. (He proposed relinquishing several sources of federal funds to states to enable them to have required resources.) This extreme version of localism is opposed by many liberals who believe that important social problems require national solutions and fear that some jurisdictions are less likely to assist powerless groups than others.

Regional Authorities. Regional authorities were discussed in the preceding chapter and are portrayed with dashed lines in illustration 5.2 to underscore their minimal policy functions in most jurisdictions. As intermediaries between higher levels of government and local needs, they could be given expanded policy roles. Indeed, in some versions of national health insurance, funds would be given directly by national officials to regional bodies that would then fund local hospitals and other providers.

Indirect Financing

Preceding discussion has focused upon direct methods of financing social welfare programs and transferring these funds to consumers or agencies. Purchase of social welfare services, however, can be indirectly encouraged through the tax system. Consumers and others are sometimes given tax *deductions* that allow them to deduct specific social welfare and housing expenditures from their taxable income, as reflected in policies that allow consumers to deduct interest payments on their mortgages or to deduct personal health expenditures. The value of tax deductions increases as the taxable income increases; a family that earns $50,000 per year, because it is in a higher tax bracket than one that earns $10,000 per year, receives a greater net benefit from $5,000 in medical care deductions.

Alternatively, social welfare expenditures can be financed through tax *credits* that allow taxpayers to subtract monies from their tax payments to the government. A tax credit is used, for example, to assist many women with financing of daycare costs when they are allowed to subtract a childcare credit from tax payments. Since their value does not increase with the income of the taxpayer, tax credits represent a more equitable method of providing tax assistance than tax deductions. Indeed, in the case of daycare tax credits, ceilings are placed on the incomes of persons who can qualify for them.

Tax *exemptions* allow the taxpayer not to have to pay taxes on specific income. Someone who is allowed to exempt from taxable income a specified sum for each dependent, for example, subtracts that amount from total income and then calculates tax payments due the government. Here, too, the value of exemptions increases with taxable income, since more affluent persons would otherwise pay a higher rate of tax on the exempted income than persons with lower income. Exemptions do not specifically encourage purchase of medical, childcare, or other services, but they are important to social welfare policy because, like deductions and credits, they influence the distribution of income in American society. Some critics argue that these income tax devices, when their cumulative effect is reckoned, disproportionately favor the affluent.

In these various indirect methods of financing social welfare, then, monies are provided to consumers not by direct appropriations from government but by the less obvious route of tax concessions.[17] The advantage of using the tax system is that it does not require appropriations and thus

avoids political uncertainties. But use of the tax system carries serious liabilities. First, since many Americans are not even aware of the magnitude of social welfare tax concessions, the programs and benefits financed by them escape scrutiny. As one example, Americans lose billions of dollars in tax revenues by allowing employers to deduct a large proportion of their contributions to the fringe health benefits of employees, a staggering sum not frequently considered in analyses of how to curtail medical care costs in the United States. Second, use of the tax system renders many middle- and upper-class Americans unaware of the magnitude of the indirect social welfare benefits they receive; therefore, it is understandable that many assume that only poor persons receive welfare benefits. Third, government gives persons who use tax-subsidized benefits carte blanche in choosing which services to use. Persons who receive daycare credits are not asked, for example, whether they used high-quality daycare programs. Finally, as the preceding discussion of tax deductions and exemptions indicates, many benefits financed through the tax system are regressive, i.e., favor the affluent. Policies that allow home owners to deduct mortgage interest payments are particularly inequitable, for example, since renters—often low-income persons—receive no such deduction. (Further, the value of interest deductions for low-income home owners is far less than for more affluent persons.)

An imaginative policy proposal known as the negative income tax represents one possible method of using tax policy to truly help low-income persons. Persons earning less than a specified income would be exempt from paying taxes, and many would also receive specified subsidies from the government through the Internal Revenue Service. Such a policy could eliminate the stigma of welfare programs for many consumers.

POLICY OVERSIGHT

Policy oversight is important because many policy issues are not resolved by enacted social welfare legislation. While legislation sets some parameters, who gets what, when, and where is partly determined in the push and pull of groups and interests during implementation. Sometimes specific provisions are not implemented. In the case of the federal community mental health legislation of 1963, which funded a national network of community mental health centers, investigators analyzing who was served by the centers a decade after its passage found that many centers emphasized services to middle- and upper-class consumers despite the obvious needs of low-income persons. Services to patients released from state hospitals, preventive services, outreach, and citizen participation in center governance were also deemphasized. In part, the legislation itself was too vague—but implementers also ignored key provisions of the legislation that mandated preventive services and assistance to consumers recently released from state mental institutions.[18]

Policy Roles of Different Levels of Government

As illustrated in guest editorial 5.1, the administration of President Ronald Reagan sought to radically shift policy oversight roles from national to local units of government. A major strategy of the administration was to collapse hundreds of categorical, or single-purpose, programs into nine *block grants*. Under this approach, state governments are given blocks of funds by federal authorities to be spent on community development, health, housing, and other broad areas. (Under the prior categorical arrangement, federal authorities gave funds largely for specific programs, such as neighborhood health centers, community mental health centers, and a myriad others.) President Reagan not only proposed that states decide which programs should be established but also eliminated vast numbers of federal regulations that specified minimum standards and other program details. This emphasis on localism represented not only a continuation of long-standing conservative interest in localism but also an extension of the new federalism of President Richard Nixon, who established general and special revenue-sharing programs that gave local units of government relatively un-

restricted funds.[19] Defenders of localism believe that local officials are best situated to know local needs.

The Reagan perspectives can be contrasted with those of the political scientist Theodore Lowi. In his view, delegation of policy setting to local government is tantamount to ignoring the needs of the poor, racial minorities, and other relatively powerless groups—groups that have more power at the national level than in local arenas often dominated by business and agricultural interests. Better, he argues, to write national legislation that specifies all major policies and leaves little discretion to local government.[20] Some theorists believe as well that national strategies should be developed for major social problems that transcend state boundaries. If juvenile delinquency, venereal disease, drug addiction, and countless other problems exist in many jurisdictions, why not address them with well-developed national programs so that each jurisdiction does not have to "reinvent the wheel"? True, some localities with enlightened leadership could well develop innovative programs, but this history of the new federalism suggests, according to these critics, that many localities use scarce resources for frivolous problems or ill-conceived programs.

Some persons favor coupling federal funding with delegation of major policy oversight roles to regional boards. In this view, state governments are often not responsible to local needs and the welter of local municipalities and counties unable to develop programs extending beyond their restricted boundaries. Many regional bodies were developed in the 1960s and 1970s, but relatively few were given major funding or planning roles. Still, regional bodies are used extensively in many European nations as intermediaries between national governments and local service providers.[21]

Role of the Courts

Courts have assumed marked importance in virtually every policy sector by prescribing safeguards for consumers as well as substantive policies regarding abortions, school busing, location of housing, and many other issues. To many con-

servatives, courts have overstepped their jurisdiction, whereas liberals, who sought to restrict
the role of the courts in the 1930s when the courts
threatened to rule major New Deal initiatives unconstitutional, have more recently welcomed a
variety of rulings protecting minorities from police harassment, mandating desegregation of
schools, and declaring state statutes outlawing
abortions unconstitutional.[22]

Decision-Making Controversies

Whether in the form of legislation, court rulings,
or pronouncements by boards of agencies, official policy is almost always riddled with loopholes and ambiguities, in part because insistence
on defining all fine points can jeopardize passage. Many decisions regarding the content, nature, and recipients of services must be made
during the course of implementation. Should
consumers, professionals, administrators,
boards, high government officials, technical evaluators, planners—or some combination of
these—make key decisions?[23] Community control advocates want major program decisions to
be made by consumers or community representatives. Many professionals favor a central role
for those who actually deliver services. In many
agencies, top administrators make key program
decisions, often with little formal participation
from agency staff or consumers. Many insist that
program evaluators and others with technical
skills should be given central roles in decision
making to offset professionals who, they claim,
use "hunches and traditions."

Exclusive reliance upon any of these specific
contributors to decision making can lead to faulty
decisions. It is difficult, for example, to decide
who should represent the community. All too
often, parochial or narrow interests emerge and
then use community credentials to direct social
benefits and policies to parochial constituencies.
Boards of some social agencies are dominated by
business, legal, and professional elites who have
little interest in low-income residents. Professionals have knowledge and experience on their
side but often prefer working with specific kinds
of consumers to the exclusion of others. In many
community mental health centers, for example,

professionals work with middle-class "neu-
rotics" rather than with multiproblem, low-
income families. Administrators often become so
preoccupied with efficiency and fund raising that
they no longer favor risk taking, innovative programs, or service to hard-to-reach clientele. Program evaluators have impressive technical credentials but can lack personal acquaintance with
the complexities of the work of professionals. No
single set of participants can, by its presence,
ensure the "right" decisions, a finding that returns discussion to the inherently controversial
nature of social welfare policy.

ACCOUNTABILITY
CONTROVERSIES

Opposition to social welfare programs in the contemporary era has been fueled by the belief that
they are not effective or that they have grown
beyond original objectives. Many states have enacted "sunset legislation" that hinges continuation of programs upon periodic evaluations.
Technical and other issues associated with the
assessment of social programs are discussed at
length in chapter 8.

POLICY PRACTICE IN THE
ANALYSIS PHASE

Policy practice in the analysis phase is discussed
in the concluding section of chapter 4. Realities
of funding shortages in the 1980s suggest that
social workers need familiarity with policy practice skills pertinent to fund raising and budget
cuts, skills discussed in this chapter. Policy practice case 5.1 describes a social worker's determined and successful efforts to obtain funding
for a center for battered women.

Conceptual Skills

A central problem for social workers is to locate
potential sources of funding as a prelude to developing funding proposals.

The social worker in policy practice case 5.1
encounters a confusing array of funding options,

A Social Worker Obtains Funding for a Shelter for Battered Women

I work for Family Crisis Center (FCC), a shelter for women who have been subjected to physical abuse in their homes and who seek assistance for themselves and their children. As this case demonstrates, many social service agencies have such a precarious source of funding that their staff members have to devote a great deal of time and energy to fund-raising activities, while still trying to educate the public, seek policy changes, help consumers, build coalitions, and handle daily work roles and administrative tasks. While we often find this disheartening, those of us who work in such agencies know that people who experience extremely grave problems would be left with no resources if we did not expend considerable energy in fund raising. Therefore, we grit our teeth and try to become increasingly knowledgeable about funding sources and strategies.

Since its inception in November 1975, FCC's major funding source has been Preston County revenue sharing monies allocated by the board of supervisors for social programs. An elaborate evaluation process takes place yearly when programs reapply for grants for the next funding year. Although FCC has always maintained a high evaluation (second in the county last year), we still have to adjust to the annual screening process used by the board of supervisors and must also find private sources or engage in fund-raising activities that will allow our services to continue. A 10 percent cut in last year's budget required staff cuts, since our core program essentials (rent, utilities, food, salaries, payroll taxes) were not subject to reduction. Negotiations with the city of Oakdale provided us with two additional CETA employees (i.e., from the federal public service positions under the Comprehensive Employment and Training

Act) to supplement the one CETA worker we already had, and we were able to survive the staffing crisis. Our efforts coincided with a field memorandum sent from the Department of Labor to all regional administrators that encouraged the funding of jobs and services for battered women. With a larger facility, we could even provide training and placement services for our clients under new Title I CETA provisions. No shelter has tried to implement this concept as yet but many shelters are staffed *entirely* by CETA employees. Through creative interpretation and numerous memorandums, the Department of Labor has quietly assisted the shelter programs and provided priority training and placement for battered women.

In November 1978 we began to negotiate for United Way funds. (An agency must have survived for three years before United Way will consider funding it.) The United Way was planning its 1981–82 budget at that time and had never funded a woman's organization other than the Girl Scouts. There is presently a split within the agency on the traditional policy of funding only conservative programs, and we find ourselves "walking on egg shells" to maintain relations with both factions and to appear as respectably conservative as possible. The shelter is still in limbo with United Way after many months of meetings and seemingly endless negotiations.

Although we have been told repeatedly to obtain funds from corporations, foundations, and the private sector, we have discovered that these grants actually involve relatively small amounts of money ($500–$5,000) and require a great deal of public relations work. Many will not give money to organizations who do not own their own facility (indicating stability), and the majority of donations have to be earmarked for special projects or purchases. Most corporations, foundations, and service clubs do not give money that can be used to fund salaries, pay the rent, or purchase office supplies. After many appeals, we were able to capitalize on the "Year of the Child" and obtained $1,200 from Hope Corporation and $4,800 from a professional organization to reinstate our children's activities director to full-time status. Obtaining these grants required much telephone and personal contact, tours of the shelter (which we are reluctant to allow), photographs with our donors, press releases, speaking engagements, solicitation of letters of support, and many hours of grantwriting. We constantly have to compromise other priorities to pursue small sums of money that could never sustain the cost of a twenty-four-hour crisis/live-in facility. Although we continue to write grants, promote fund-raising activities, and solicit these smaller contributions, we have formulated a long-range plan to work toward obtaining our own facility, provide more stable funding, and bring eventual economic self-sufficiency.

My first investigation into federal Title XX funds, used to subsidize a variety of services, have proven frustrating. In Preston County, the public welfare department, mental health department, public health department, child protective services, and some smaller agencies have recently been combined into one large conglomerate agency named Human Resources Agency (HRA). Since Title XX also pays many HRA staff salaries, HRA officials are not willing to consider funding new programs when they are trying to cope with cutbacks resulting in understaffing and underfunding in their own agency. I was told by an official of the public welfare department to inquire about Title IV-B money (child welfare services), which is always budgeted but never completely used on the state or federal level. This official believes that these monies are being used as a contingency fund but could be allocated to counties to fund shelter programs. I spoke with a high-ranking federal official on this subject when she visited our area, but she skirted the issue and stated that we would have to talk to Governor Rice about funding shelters. She also stated that the federal Department of Health and Human Services would encounter much public opposition for advocating anything interpreted as interfering with the family.

Attempts to interest Governor Rice in battered women over the past few years have failed, in contrast to the state of Minnesota, whose governor addressed the issue of domestic violence in his inaugural address and promised to use his influence to create support for shelters. Avenues for funding began to open up soon after he took office. Agency regulations were changed and interpretations were broadened. At the present time, Minnesota is the only state where shelters are on solid footing, since they receive both vendor and purchase-of-service funds through Title XX for their residents. Shelters are designated as day-care facilities, which makes them eligible for funding as child-care centers. They are provided with special education teachers because of the special needs of the resident's traumatized children, can receive state funding through the Department of Agriculture as a group family day-care home, and receive Housing and Community Development Block Grant money from the federal Department of Housing and Urban Development (HUD) to pay off mortgages and rehabilitate property. Clearly, the interest and influence of the state's chief executive opens many doors.

Minnesota's efforts to obtain Block Grant money resulted in a change in HUD regulations. Last fall, shelters were specifically designated as eligible to receive Housing and Community Development (HCD) Block Grant and discretionary funds through HUD. As a preliminary measure to applying for these funds and in order to gain additional information on the political process, one of our staff members applied and was appointed to the Oakdale HCD Citizens Advisory Committee. In November, we approached the Preston County HCD office for information. They appeared eager to work with us and offered technical assistance by providing a college intern to research HUD regulations and assist us in writing the grant. Although we were pleased with their commitment to help us, we became apprehensive about their lack of knowledge and their conflicting information on HUD's funding procedures, available grants, application deadlines, and timelines. In mid-January, our frustrated intern abandoned the project, mumbling about inscrutable bureaucracies and his increased workload in school.

In December, a sixteen-room facility came on the market, less than ten blocks away from our present shelter. Formerly a convalescent hospital, Liberty House had not been in use for many years and had been purchased a few months earlier, partially renovated, and offered for sale again. After a tour of Liberty House, we decided that although it looked like an institution, it would provide much-needed space. We felt we could "junk it up" with plants, posters, our old furniture, and a house full of kids. The location was ideal— close to bus lines, a hospital, a park, the police station, a grocery store, and a shopping area. Zoning would not be a problem since the area was not considered residential. We decided we wanted Liberty House and began to incorporate it into our plans for the future.

One of our most valuable contacts proved to be a staff person at the Oakdale HCD office. She advised us about how to get support for our HUD grant applications and indicated that there were many different funding sources we could tap for a building, facility rehabilitation, and services. Each source would require different political and community support. We could apply directly to the county for HCD Block Grant funds, as well as to the individual cities who have their own HCD allocations. There are twenty-two cities plus unincorporated areas in Preston County. Since we are the only existing shelter and serve all areas of the county, we were eligible for funds from each jurisdiction. The enormity of the problem of gaining sponsorship in all these areas was frightening, but we started our task of contacting mayors, city managers, council members, HCD staff members, citizen advisory boards, supervisors, legislators, and congressmen. Many of these people wanted to visit the shelter, and our no-tour policy was again given up for political expediency.

Our Oakdale HCD contact had informed us that local HCD money went for "bricks and mortar" projects. Administrative costs and salaries were frowned on by officials who would have to support our grant. Our present shelter has twenty-four beds (in five bedrooms). We would clearly have to increase staff to manage an additional eleven bedrooms. We learned through our contact we could apply for discretionary funds through HUD in Washington with an Innovative Grant, which would cover salaries and costs for a demonstration project and was renewable up to three years. Since FCC had been in operation since November 1975, our present program could not be considered a demonstration project. Liberty House divided itself easily into three wings and we concluded it could accommodate our regular thirty-day program in one wing, a three-day crisis intervention center for women who did not need or want the thirty-day program in another wing, and a day-care center for our thirty-day clients and ex-clients who are in school, training programs, or starting back to work, in the third wing. Our HCD contact promised to contact Frank Jones, a lobbyist for the city of Oakdale, and ask him to "grease it" for us, since discretionary funds are very competitive. Frank Jones would be instructed to watch over it and lobby for it once it got to

Washington. We would also need the blessing of our congressman.

While scouring voluminous federal regulations, we discovered we could apply for a National Business Revitalization grant that would allow us to start our own business and perhaps eventually become self-supporting. We decided that we were already trying to juggle too many things at once and tabled that idea until we could secure the new facility and services.

In addition to making political contacts, we began to investigate day-care licensing so we could qualify for public welfare DPSS day-care vouchers. We also enlisted community support from several police departments, hospitals and service agencies for an expanded crisis facility. We took the fire chief, planning commissioner, and city engineers through Liberty House.

When our HUD intern withdrew from the agency in mid-January, we began to investigate the information he had given us on the grant with a deadline in early February. After many phone calls and conflicting information from Oakdale and Preston County HCD offices, we finally discovered that we could apply for reallocation Block Grant funds that had been turned back to the federal government by the Preston County cities of Elwood, Smithville, and Cyprus. This money was earmarked by HUD for low- to moderate-income housing, and these three cities had refused to consider low-income projects within their borders. The amount of money to be reallocated was $1.5 million with grants limited to $250,000. Preston County HCD would select one project to recommend to the HUD state clearing house as deserving of these funds. Other cities within Preston County might also elect to submit a project to HUD officials, which would put us in the awkward position of competing with potential supporters for HUD's reallocated funds. During a visit with Joe Thomas, an official with Preston County HCD, he revealed that

he would be on the screening committee that would sift through all proposals submitted to the county and make three recommendations to the Preston County Board of Supervisors, who would make the final choice. If our project was chosen we would then have to lobby for it on a much larger scale to indicate widespread community support for the shelter project.

Meanwhile, our center had obtained funds to make a contingency offer to the seller of Liberty House, through a fund-raising party that had attracted many local celebrities. Our bid was for $465,000, with the seller carrying the mortgage which he had previously agreed to do for any buyer. (Nonprofit agencies have great difficulty securing mortgage loans). The bid was submitted to the seller on February 10. Our grant proposal was submitted to the county HCD office on February 11. On February 14, the seller refused our offer! He stated that he could not afford to wait for the federal grant. He had decided to open a board-and-care facility of his own in Liberty House. Although we were extremely disappointed, we began to investigate other properties in the event that we were selected to receive the grant.

Late in the afternoon of February 21 we received word that FCC had been selected by the screening committee as one of the three projects to be voted on by the board of supervisors at their meeting on the twenty-third. We had to start lobbying for our project! We spent all day of the twenty-second visiting with the supervisors and their aides, trying to negotiate a commitment for the important vote. (Unless a program has the support of the supervisor of its district, the other supervisors will not vote for you—out of courtesy to their colleague.) At the shelter, staff members were busy contacting some of our key supporters, asking them to send telegrams before their meeting on the following morning. They decided unanimously that our proposal to purchase a permanent shelter would be the county project they would present to HUD officials. The support we had developed in the community and with our own supervisor was a crucial factor in this positive outcome.

Since our methods had proved so successful on the county level, we continued to use them with state officials to ensure the selection of our proposal in the final competition with fifteen other projects submitted to HUD. At one point we received a call from the office of Governor Rice asking us to call off some of our supporters because they couldn't handle all of the mail they were getting in support of our project! In late May we were notified by an aide to our congressman that we had been selected by HUD to receive $250,000 toward the purchase of a permanent shelter for battered women in Preston County.

Our work has just begun. We must now get the Innovative Grant proposal designed, written, and off to Washington, or we could end up with a large facility and no staff to operate it. The work must continue on the HCD Block Grant proposals to be submitted to the cities of Preston County starting in September. If everything falls into place, we

could pay off the remaining mortgage with these smaller grants and cover staffing and program for three years with the Innovative Grant. In the meantime, we will be researching ideas for a business venture that could contribute to our eventual independence. It will be brinksmanship all the way.

Some fallout from our struggle is that we are getting much recognition within the county as a hard-working, creative, politically astute, ambitious program. Many unexpected benefactors have suddenly appeared and are becoming involved in seeing that we succeed. We recently learned that Manning Corporation has written a proposal to their regional office asking for $20,000 to support our new shelter. They are also writing letters to other corporations suggesting that they support us in a similar way.

In retrospect, most of our time and effort over the past few months has gone into political strategy. Since FCC was one of the first shelters in the nation to open and has become a model program, we are considered experts in providing services for battered women. We have no problem defining the problem or veri-

including county revenue-sharing funds, United Way, corporations, professional associations, Title XX funds, federal child welfare funds, state funds, and block grants. (The center currently receives in-kind contributions as well, i.e., staff funded by the Comprehensive Employment Training Act.)

When selecting potential funders, social workers must try to discover their specific program priorities and requirements. As noted in policy practice case 5.1, funders variously provide monies for "bricks and mortar," ongoing costs of running programs, monies for staff, and start-up costs for innovative programs. Funders also have different program interests, such as programs for children, medical programs, and educational institutions. The social worker in

policy practice case 5.1 spends considerable time trying to locate funders who are specifically interested in programs for battered women or in programs for the children of these women, who are dislocated and traumatized by the family crisis. Funders differ as well in their administrative requirements and preferences. Some are willing to fund new agencies, others prefer traditional ones. Some require elaborate fiscal and accounting controls, others deemphasize these management techniques. It is important, then, to explore a number of funding options so that time is not spent pursuing sources that are not likely to be interested in a specific project.

Foundation, corporate, and government sources of funds often differ markedly. (Such sources are described in more detail in readings

fying it, since we have accumulated much data over the past few years. Our telephone log also documents a much greater need exists than we can respond to with our present facility and staff. We receive over 200 calls monthly from women needing shelter and assistance. We are presently able to serve only forty to fifty clients per month with shelter care, including children. We are still the only shelter in Preston County and the only agency attempting to provide a solution or alternatives to the problem of domestic violence within the county. We know how to implement a program and have done that from scratch, on shoestring budgets. Evaluation is not a problem for us, since we have been accustomed to providing the accountability demanded by Preston County Revenue Sharing. Clearly, we have to fight our future battles in political arenas until solid funding is provided for shelters.

In advising a new shelter seeking financial stability, I would recommend that it learn as much as possible about the political process in its community—or it will not survive very long. I scan newspapers systematically, clip-ping articles on political figures, community people, agencies, and corporations we may have to deal with in the future. Becoming an astute listener is also necessary. Knowing key persons within a bureaucracy will save wasted time and much frustration when information or assistance are needed. Such persons can also keep a programs informed when new regulations and policy changes occur.

To those seeking funding for their shelter, I would say: You must be flexible enough to deal with unexpected contingencies (there will be many) and creative enough to form alternative plans. Read everything you can find on other shelters and their funding sources. Compare notes with other shelter people and visit their programs whenever possible. Develop and maintain strong community support systems. Be aware of proposed legislation, write letters, send telegrams, visit lawmakers in person. Follow up on any potential funding source, take plenty of vitamins, and nurture yourself on every possible occasion! If all else fails, try bingo. Sometimes it sounds like the easiest solution.

SOURCE: This case is adapted from one developed by Glee Cantalibre, M.S.W. Names and locations have been altered.

suggested at the end of this chapter.)[24] *Corporate funders* are often willing to consider donations to cover costs of administration and salaries and to give in-kind contributions, such as office equipment. They usually want to be certain that programs are administered efficiently and with adequate fiscal controls. *Foundations* often favor innovative projects rather than ongoing programs —projects that are clearly needed in a community and do not duplicate existing programs. Their officials often want to talk personally with applicants and make on-site visits. Each foundation is also likely to have specific program interests, as described in the publications that identify their assets and their funding priorities (see grantsmanship readings at the end of this chapter). *Government funders* are guided by legislative and administrative mandates that specify the way that funds are to be allocated, the specific methods to be used to apply for grants, and the administrative procedures to be used during implementation. In some cases, government grants or contracts are awarded on the basis of political contacts of applicants; in other cases, relatively technical criteria assume major importance. In many cases, as in policy practice case 5.1 with respect to some federal sources, strategic contacts with agency personnel, legislators, or lobbyists can be important.

In many cases, social workers seek funds from numerous sources, whether simultaneously or sequentially. Funders often like to make joint contributions, since no single funder has to bear the exclusive burden. They are also more likely to believe a project to be meritorious if other funders have contributed to it.

Social workers also need skills in proposal writing (skills described in more detail in chapter 9). Before ideas can be effectively communicated in proposals, however, they must be clearly developed. Why is an innovative project needed in the context of needs assessment materials discussed in chapter 4? Have relevant policy options been identified and sensible choices made? Does a clear set of program objectives exist, as well as some method of determining whether the project will meet those objectives during the implementation phase? Are implementation policies clearly articulated? These questions suggest

that proposals rest upon concepts pertinent to the various phases of the policymaking process.

Value Clarification Skills

Value dilemmas are often encountered during the fund-seeking process, as suggested by policy practice case 5.1. In some cases, social workers have to decide whether the fund-seeking game is worth the effort, especially when its heavy requirements of time divert attention from ongoing programs. The social worker in policy practice case 5.1 wonders at times whether she will be successful in obtaining funds, which in turn makes her question her preoccupation with fund

---

CASE EXAMPLE 5.3

Cutback Options Considered by State Officials in a Planning Meeting

Session 2: Identification of Options for Funding Reductions

During this second session, the participants discussed all the possible scenarios for where and how to reduce the current $68 million in daycare funding by the 17 percent required by federal cutbacks. These options are outlined below. It was noted that a single option or combination of options could result in the needed reductions.

1. Obtain Funding from Alternate Sources

Participants identified other funding sources to replace the federal money, e.g., Title IV-B for the teenage parenting program and crime prevention monies for certain services in the city of Philadelphia. Also, Title IV-A for AFDC recipients as eligibles was discussed.

2. Increase Revenues from Services

In this category are a number of options:

Increase fees for all children. The primary issue here is to determine what the market will bear. Another consideration is whether so many children will leave the program that increased fees will not result in increased revenues.

Increase fees selectively. The office can increase fees by type of service, by setting (i.e., center versus home), or by income level.

Charge those not currently paying a fee. Parents who make less than 50 percent of the state median income currently do not pay a fee for services. This option would change that policy.

raising. On the other side of the coin, however, social workers often realize that lack of fund raising can deprive certain consumers of needed services, a realization that leads the social worker in policy practice case 5.1 to renew her fund-raising efforts.

Social workers also have to decide whether they wish to expand their programs in light of funding, quality control, and administrative problems often associated with growth. The executive of the agency and some board members in policy practice case 5.1 wonder if the program should obtain the new facility; only the aggressive commitment to expansion by the social worker and her allies enables the acquisition to

take place. In some cases, too, social workers wonder if expansion of their program occurs at the expense of other, equally meritorious programs, particularly during a period of funding cutbacks. When they believe that they are meeting important community needs, however, social workers realize that a "small is beautiful" philosophy can lead to suffering for those excluded from service.

Social workers also confront difficult policy choices when funds are cut. In the case of funding cuts of daycare programs in Pennsylvania, for example, state officials have to identify alternative strategies (see case example 5.3). The critical task is to locate the best among a number of evils,

3. Cut Underutilized Contracts

This option would allow the concentration of limited resources on those contracts with the most impact. However, a problem will arise if the targeted contract is the only one in a geographical area.

4. Lower Eligibility Requirements

Services would no longer be offered to children with parents in the upper-income group (i.e., those making close to 115 percent of the state median income). However, in considering this option, one must balance the cost reduction with fees lost from this group, since these consumers pay relatively high fees. Therefore, all fees may have to be raised to make up for this income loss.

5. Eliminate or Reduce Specific Types of Services

Under this option, funding would be reduced or stopped entirely for one or more types of service (e.g., the crime prevention service or school-age care).

6. Eliminate or Reduce Services by Age of Child Involved

This option is closely linked to option 5. However, using age specifically as a criterion can produce somewhat different results. For example, if the office eliminates infants from all services under which they are currently covered, this would have an impact not only on infant/toddler but also on group and family daycare.

7. Reduce Funding Across the Board

With this option, the office would cut funding a specified percentage for all types of services.

8. Consolidate Contracts by County

This option would help increase the efficiency and reduce the costs of daycare delivery in certain areas. For example, there are thirty individual contracts for preschool programs in Philadelphia and, therefore, thirty different directors.

SOURCE: Dr. Richard Fiene et al., *Cutback Planning: An Interim Report on Assistance to the Pennsylvania Office of Children, Youth, and Families in Planning for Reductions in Federal Funding* (Washington, D.C.: Children's Services Monitoring Transfer Consortium, 1981).

i.e., the policy strategy that will have the least harmful effect on consumers. Selective raising of fees for more affluent consumers, for example, is preferable in some settings to diminishing of services to low-income consumers. No simple formula exists, however, for deciding which cutback strategy is the best; indeed, values condition choices.

Political Skills

The fund-raising process is inextricably entwined in political realities both within specific agencies and in their relations with external agencies, communities, and funders. Within agencies, numerous clearances are often required prior to and during the process of writing proposals, as illustrated in policy practice case 5.1 by the disinclination of some staff and board members to purchase the new facility. The social worker has to convince others that the project is needed and that it is consonant with the existing programs and objectives of the shelter.

In many projects, clearances and support must also be obtained from others in the community. Informal and formal agreements often exist concerning the kinds of services provided by various agencies. The staff in one agency may fear that a proposal by another violates its program's turf. Many foundations require evidence of community support for proposals and will sometimes make informal contacts to gauge whether it exists.

Political skills are also needed when presenting proposals to funders. Informal contacts with key staff persons prior to, during, and after formal submission can be invaluable in approaching some funders. In policy practice case 5.1, for example, the social worker obtains assistance from local elected officials, a key contact in a public program, and a Washington lobbyist when seeking the federal grant from the Department of Housing and Urban Development.

Political skills are rarely a substitute, however, for creative ideas and well-formulated proposals. In some cases, funds are allocated on the basis of contacts, but the competitive nature of fund raising in the 1980s suggests that political savvy is insufficient for most grants. Since informal overtures can be counterproductive with some funders, care must be exercised in using them.

Interactional Skills

At numerous points in policy practice case 5.1, the social worker uses interactional skills. She needs to establish informal contacts in political and funding arenas to provide her with information and support. She must persuade others within her agency that a new facility is needed and that proposals have to be prepared and submitted. She needs skills in presenting expert testimony at critical points in the funding process when funders require information about specific facets of the new facility or programs of the shelter. In many cases, funding proposals are developed by task forces or committees where social workers use knowledge of group dynamics to facilitate task accomplishment and resolution of differences.

Position-taking Skills

When seeking resources, social workers often have to make presentations to budget committees and boards within their agencies, to foundations, or to specific donors. The length, form, and substance of proposals needs to be tailored to the specific audience. In policy practice case 5.1, the social worker encounters numerous audiences as she seeks funds for the shelter, each with its own interests and funding preferences. If many foundations are interested in funding innovative projects, for example, other ones only consider "bricks and mortar." As discussed in more detail in chapter 9, formal proposals to foundations and governmental funders need to include specific kinds of content and be written in a prescribed format.

SUMMARY

A variety of policy issues commonly encountered in the analysis phase have been discussed in this and the preceding chapter. Funding issues are critically important in this period of declining resources. The various sources of funds—

including payroll taxes, consumer fees, special taxes, and private philanthropy—have their advantages and disadvantages. General revenues of government units, particularly those of the federal government, will remain the major source of funds for most social welfare programs. Americans have created a complex funding system that uses resources derived from these various sources. As events of the early 1980s suggest, cuts in one source, such as federal funds, place severe strains on other sources, such as local governments and private philanthropy.

Whatever their source, choices must be made between consumer and agency subsidy strategies. Some favor subsidizing consumers who purchase their services; others favor the use of government grants or contracts with agencies. Authorization and appropriations processes are used to determine the level of funding given specific programs. Social programs often receive scant funding because they lack organized constituencies.

In the contemporary period, Americans have debated the merits of federal and local roles in social welfare policy. In a major reversal of a trend toward greater federal roles, many categorical programs were ended with development of nine block grants that provided state governments with relatively unrestricted funds. Liberals feared that substitution of block grants for categorical programs would imperil distribution of program resources to relatively powerless groups. Oversight issues are also encountered by staff in social agencies as they consider how to evaluate social programs and whether to include consumers in agency deliberations.

Social workers need value clarification, conceptual, interactional, and political skills when assuming a program design role. These skills are needed when shaping legislation, writing grants, and proposing specific changes in agency policies.

Key Concepts, Developments, and Policies

Funding issues
Alternative sources of funds
General revenues
Payroll taxes
Consumer payments
Special taxes
Private philanthropy
Mixed sources
Levels of funding
Authorizations
Appropriations
Indexing
Declining shares
Open-ended authorizations
Ceilings, or caps
Interdependence of funding sources
Auspices
Nonprofit agencies
Public agencies
Profit-oriented agencies
Funding channels

Funding of agencies by government
Project grants
Contracts
Vouchers
Direct cash payments
Vendor payments
Indirect financing
Tax deductions
Tax exemptions
Tax credits
Negative income tax
Policy oversight
Block grants
Categorical programs
Localism
Federal roles
Regional authorities
Courts
Decision-making controversies
Accountability
Policy practice in the analysis phase

Main Points

1. Many alternative sources of funds exist for social welfare programs, each with advantages and disadvantages.

2. Because they are so vast, general revenues are used to fund many social programs. General revenues of federal authorities have become important because revenue-raising capabilities of the federal income tax exceed those of local jurisdictions.

3. Payroll taxes are used to fund the Social Security program and other public insurance programs.

4. Consumer payments, special taxes, and private philanthropy are important sources of funds that can supplement payroll and general revenue sources.

5. Many programs are funded by combining funds from a variety of the above sources.

6. When general revenues are used, authorization and appropriations processes are employed to determine the level of funding.

7. Since complex patterns of interdependence exist between different funding sources, cuts in any single source often have important ramifications for others.

8. Divergent opinions exist about the relative merits of public, nonprofit, and profit-oriented agencies.

9. Government can provide funds directly to social agencies through project grants or contracts or can use vouchers, direct cash payments, or vendor payments to subsidize consumers.

10. Many social welfare services and benefits are financed indirectly through tax concessions as deductions, exemptions, or credits. This kind of financing, like others discussed in this chapter, has both desirable and undesirable features.

11. Opinions differ as to the relative merits of block grants and categorical programs as well as the respective policy roles of federal and local authorities.

12. Courts have assumed a major role in social welfare policy, a development that has occasioned considerable controversy.

13. Controversy exists about roles of consumers, professionals, administrators, evaluators, and others in decision making.

14. Social workers should develop skills pertinent to the practice of policy in the analysis phase.

Questions for Discussion

1. Review guest editorial 5.1. Discuss problems of interdependence of funding sources, as illustrated by cuts in federal spending.

2. Discuss positive and negative features of the use of general revenues, payroll taxes, consumer payments, and special taxes.

3. Some conservatives believe that private philanthropy should assume far larger roles in social welfare policy. Do you agree?

4. Critically discuss the following assertion: "Profit-oriented agencies are more efficient and responsive to consumer needs than public or nonprofit agencies."

5. Describe various kinds of social welfare benefits received by yourself and family members. To what extent is it desirable that the tax system be used to indirectly finance social welfare services and needs?

6. Why might some government officials favor funding social agencies directly rather than funding consumers through cash payments or vouchers?

7. Discuss the merits of federal categorical programs in contrast to block grants. How meritorious, do you think, were policies of the Reagan Administration to shift from categorical programs to block grants?

8. Critically discuss the following assertion: "Local units of government are more responsive to citizens and their needs than distant federal authorities."

9. In some agency or organization with which you are familiar, discuss patterns of decision making, and describe groups that are excluded? What kinds of persons or groups should be given larger roles?

10. Discuss how the following dilemmas, tasks,

and realities are illustrated by policy practice case 5.1:

a. Much time can be lost in pursuing funders who are not likely to support a specific project.

b. Social workers often have to decide whether the fund-seeking game is worth the effort.

c. A "small is beautiful" philosophy is often questioned by those who want to markedly expand specific programs.

d. Many political and economic realities influence the proposal-writing process within social agencies.

e. "Political skills are rarely a substitute for creative ideas and well-formulated proposals."

Suggested Readings

Fenno, Richard. *The Power of the Purse* (Boston: Little, Brown, 1966). This classic study of the appropriations process in Congress probes political and institutional factors that influence who gets what.

Horowitz, David. *The Courts and Social Policy* (Washington, D.C.: Brookings Institution, 1977): "Social Policy and Judicial Capacity," pp. 1–21. A good introduction to issues and controversies pertaining to the expanding role of the courts in social policy issues.

Kramer, Ralph. "Voluntary Agencies and the Use of Public Funds: Some Policy Issues." *Social Service Review*, 40 (March 1966): 15–27. An overview of issues associated with the use of voluntary agencies to provide social services, issues still relevant in contemporary America.

Lowi, Theodore. *End of Liberalism* (New York: Norton, 1969): "Federal Urban Policy—What Not to Do and What to Do About Apartheid," pp. 250–283. An excellent case example that supports Lowi's contention that strong national policy roles are needed if the rights of powerless groups are to be defended.

Manser, Gordon, and Higgins, Rosemary. *Voluntarism at the Crossroads* (New York: Family

Service Association of America, 1976). An overview of private philanthropy in the United States is provided, as well as discussion of current issues.

Meltsner, Arnold. *Policy Analysts in the Bureaucracy* (Berkeley: University of California Press, 1976): "Analysts," pp. 14–49. The author describes alternative styles, including political and technical styles, for engaging in policy analysis.

Pechman, Joseph. *Federal Tax Policy* (Washington, D.C.: Brookings Institution, 1977). An overview of the tax system is provided, including discussion of individual, corporate, and payroll taxes as well as state and local tax structures.

Smith, Craig, and Skjei, Eric. *Getting Grants* (New York: Harper & Row, 1981). A good introduction to grantsmanship. The authors outline alternative sources of funding and strategies for the proposal-writing phase.

Terrell, Paul. "Financing Social Welfare Services." In Gilbert, Neil, and Specht, Harry, eds., *Handbook of the Social Services* (Englewood Cliffs, N.J.: Prentice-Hall, 1981): pp. 380–411. The author discusses various sources of revenues for social welfare programs and benefits.

Wildavsky, Aaron. *Politics of the Budgetary Process*

(Boston: Little, Brown, 1964). A description of the budgeting process at the national level.

Wildavsky, Aaron. *Speaking Truth to Power: The Art and Craft of Policy Analysis* (Boston: Little, Brown, 1979): "Analysis as Art," pp. 1–19. Wildavsky discusses various skills and issues associated with policy analysis, including ethical problems and difficulties in using quantitative information.

Notes

1. General discussion of financing issues is found in Paul Terrell, "Financing Social Welfare Services," in Neil Gilbert and Harry Specht, eds., *Handbook of the Social Services*, pp. 380–413.

2. Eveline Burns, *Social Security and Public Policy* (New York: McGraw-Hill, 1956), pp. 155–171.

3. Karen Davis, *National Health Insurance* (Washington, D.C.: Brookings Institution, 1975), pp. 59–68.

4. See Eleanor L. Brilliant, "Private or Public: A Model of Ambiguities," *Social Service Review*, 43 (September 1973): 384–396.

5. Discussion of financing issues in Social Security is found in Martha Derthick, *Policymaking for Social Security* (Washington, D.C.: Brookings Institution, 1979).

6. See Aaron Wildavsky, *Politics of the Budgetary Process*. Also see Fenno, *The Power of the Purse*.

7. Kramer, "Voluntary Agencies."

8. Titmuss, *The Gift Relationship* (New York: Pantheon, 1971).

9. Alain Enthoven, *Health Plan: The Practical Solution to the Soaring Cost of Medical Care* (Reading, Mass.: Addison-Wesley, 1980).

10. Bruce Jansson, "Public Monitoring of Contracts with Nonprofit Agencies: Organizational Mission in Two Sectors," *Journal of Sociology and Social Welfare*, 6 (May 1979): 362–375.

11. Stanley Wenocur, "A Pluralistic Planning Model for United Way Organizations," *Social Service Review*, 50 (December 1976): 586–601.

12. Enthoven, *Health Plan*.

13. Maureen Orth, "Child Care: The American Disgrace," *MS* (May 1974): 89–90, 94–95.

14. Karen Davis, *Medicine's War on Poverty* (Washington, D.C.: Brookings, Institution, 1978), pp. 14–18. Also see Paul Terrell, "Public Alternatives to Public Human Services Administration," *Social Service Review*, 53 (March 1979): 56–74.

15. Enthoven, *Health Plan*.

16. Use of market mechanisms is criticized by Titmuss, *The Gift Relationship*.

17. Extended discussion of the tax system, including use of deductions, exemptions, and credits, is found in Pechman, *Federal Tax Policy*.

18. Franklin Chu and Sharland Trotter, *The Madness Establishment* (New York: Grossman, 1974).

19. See Robert S. Magill, *Community Decision Making for Social Welfare* (New York: Human Sciences Press, 1979).

20. Theodore Lowi, *End of Liberalism*.

21. Alvin N. Taylor, "Relations with Other Agencies Delivering Human Services," in Wayne F. Anderson et al., eds., *Managing Human Services* (Washington, D.C.: International City Management Association, 1977), pp. 193–229.

22. Donald Brieland and John Lemmon, *Social Work and the Law* (St. Paul, Minn.: West, 1977).

23. Gilbert and Specht, *Dimensions of Social Welfare Policy*, pp. 178–199.

24. For extended discussion of fund raising and grantsmanship, see Smith and Skjei, *Getting Grants*.

PART 3

Legitimation and Implementation: The Action Phases

A case example of the political strategy of social reformers who seek expanded subsidies for low-income housing in the Congress is used in chapter 6 to illustrate political strategy in social welfare policy. The role of external pressures on decision makers, power and procedural realities in legislative and agency settings, and decision makers' predisposing orientations toward specific issues are discussed as a prelude to analysis of political strategy.

Official policies are sometimes sabotaged or otherwise deflected during the implementation process, as illustrated in chapter 7 by a case example of programs for the elderly. A systems framework is used in this chapter to explore a variety of societal, policy, regional, and organizational variables that impede implementation of policies. Also discussed are troubleshooting skills needed by social workers who intervene in implementation processes.

In both chapters 6 and 7, the policy framework developed in chapter 2 is used in modified form to facilitiate understanding of legitimation and implementation phases. Both phases are discussed in the context of background forces and their relationships to the other policy phases.

The Legitimation Phase: Change Agent Roles

Social welfare policy as collective strategy for addressing social problems becomes collective only as participants in specific policy arenas approve specific policy proposals. During the legitimation phase, formal approval is sought from decision makers. Some proposals are successful, but many are deferred, modified, or defeated.

Social workers need to:

Understand ethical issues that often arise during the legitimation phase

Be able to identify various kinds and sources of external pressures that often influence policy choices during the legitimation phase

Have familiarity with power and procedural realities that influence outcomes during legitimation

Understand how orientations and perceptions of key decision makers shape their choices and activities during legitimation

Possess knowledge of different kinds of power that can be used to obtain support for a specific proposal

These various topics are discussed in this chapter, as well as common dangers or errors committed by policy practitioners during the legitimation phase. A policy practice case is presented at the conclusion of the chapter in which a social worker assumes a change agent role.

ETHICAL ISSUES

Value and ethical judgments are required at numerous points in the legitimation phase. Political realities often lead participants to support less-than-perfect proposals because they fear that better ones cannot be obtained. In case example 6.1, some housing reformers would like housing subsidies that assist poor and middle-income renters but reluctantly emphasize the former because they fear that funds are insufficient to assist both groups.

Decisions about investing time and political resources in specific issues are also influenced by values. In some settings, support of unpopular issues can lead to demotion, loss of pay increases, or even loss of employment. In many cases, such as the instance of the welfare recipients in case example 6.1, political success is unlikely because constituencies are not powerful enough to persuade decision makers that action is required. Reformers have to decide whether to invest time and resources in important but unpopular causes and whether to encounter the

CASE EXAMPLE 6.1

Beleaguered Lobbyists for the Poor—Taking Allies Where They Can Find Them

*The Battle Against Federal Subsidies for Middle-income Housing Is a
Case in Point: Supporters of Low-income Housing Joined with
Conservatives in Opposition*

By Rochelle L. Stanfield

When Jake Garn and the ADA are on the same side of an issue, that's news.

And when organizations that purport to speak for the poor break ranks with their traditional allies in Congress, that also suggests something is up.

What's up is a new willingness on the part of lobbyists for the poor to form alliances of convenience to repulse attacks on their favorite programs. In this case, the liberal Americans for Democratic Action is working with Garn, the outspoken conservative Republican Senator from Utah, to fight legislation that would provide federal subsidies for middle-income housing.

What's true for housing is true for other social programs that are coming under increasing attack at a time of budgetary retrenchment.

"If you want to get a thing done, you've got to link up with people not normally in your camp," said Nancy Amidei, director of the Food Research and Action Center, a coalition that lobbies on food stamps. "When we talk to people, we don't just talk to the people we support."

Lobbyists for the poor are waiting for better times—which, they are convinced, are only a few years away—to press for such costly goals as welfare reform. Right now, said Sandra B. Solomon, government affairs director of the National Urban Coalition, "every fight is defensive, and you lose two battles for every one you win."

In the case of the housing bill, advocates for the poor are trying to defend low-income housing subsidies from encroachment by proponents of federal subsidies for middle-income renters. Hence their alliance with Garn who, while he may not be a vigorous supporter of low-income housing subsidies,

personal risk sometimes associated with losing causes.

A policy victory for one group often represents a defeat for others, since funds for new or expanded programs must often come from other programs. In case example 6.1, those supporting middle-income housing subsidies know that low-income housing subsidies will be reduced; their judgment to proceed is value-laden and hotly contested by those who are principally interested in low-income subsidy programs.

Ethical decisions are also required when de-

vising political tactics. Ideally, all participants are utterly candid with one another and agree on and use "fair rules of the game." But this ideal hardly describes rough-and-tumble political realities (illustration 6.1). Participants often surprise opponents with unexpected parliamentary rules and use deception, distortion, and half-truths.[1] In some cases, they support positions of others not because they truly believe in them but because they have constructed *quid pro quo* arrangements. Sometimes they even divulge confidential information to others. At a minimum,

---

adamantly opposes aid for middle-income families.

Ironically, the authors of the controversial housing legislation apparently share the same basic objectives as their liberal critics. They agree on the nature of the problem: a scarcity of rental apartments, particularly for the poor but for middle-income families as well.

There is already a large federal program that subsidizes the rent payments of low-income families, paying all of the rent that exceeds 25 percent of the renters' income. But there's a long waiting list for subsidized apartments.

Even for those who can afford apartments without benefit of a government subsidy, the shortage is acute, especially as the trend to conversion of apartment houses into condominiums accelerates.

More money to subsidize the poor and incentives for developers to build apartment buildings for middle-income people might alleviate the problem. But Congress would prefer to trim the housing budget, not increase it, and it is in no mood to spend billions of additional dollars to benefit middle-income people.

This is where the congressional leaders in the housing field came in. Why not, they suggested, shift some money from low-income

housing subsidies and spend it to encourage builders to erect middle-income apartments—which in turn would open up more apartments for the poor?

Surprisingly, perhaps, the proposals split the housing lobby, with advocates for the poor—led by the National Low Income Housing Coalition—joining with congressional conservatives to fight them because the money for the new middle-income program would have to come from funds allocated to the poor.

"It wasn't an argument between the goodies and the baddies," said Cushing N. Dolbeare, president of the coalition. "It was about what you perceive the housing problem to be and how to deal with it." . . .

For the middle-income housing fight is another in a long string of liberal battles not to add new social programs but to hold on to existing programs and the support levels achieved in the past. The low-income housing coalition was not, in this case, asking for more money but merely trying to hold the line on the current level.

The liberal lobbyists blame the declining economy for the miserly national mood. "The country is tired of progress," said Shull. "So we're having a rough time now protecting as many of the good programs as possible."

Stiff competition for every federal dollar has forced advocates of aid for low-income families to adopt more sophisticated lobbying techniques. It's no longer enough simply to describe terrible conditions in poor areas and ask a sympathetic Administration or Congress for money to combat them.

Now they must offer more complex remedies, present elaborate cost-benefit justifications for their proposals and try to document how more spending would actually save money in the long run—by stimulating the economy, for example.

So when a housing construction or rehabilitation program is suggested, for example, its job-creating potential is stressed. And the food stamp lobby goes to some analytical lengths to show the positive effect of food stamps on the economies of agricultural states.

That's a radical change from the late 1960s and early 1970s, when George Wiley brought welfare mothers from his National Welfare Rights Organization to Washington to demand welfare reform.

"George Wiley took welfare reform about as far as it ever got," said Matthew H. Ahmann, associate director of the National Conference of Catholic Charities. "But that was still in the period of economic growth. We're working in a substantially changed climate now." . . .

Getting Together

These changes in congressional procedures and attitudes put a premium on close collaboration among advocates of any cause.

The National Low Income Housing Coalition typifies the liberal response. It is one of a new breed of informal networks, formal associations and loose coalitions established in specific policy areas.

In some respects, the new coalitions resemble the civil rights and welfare rights movements of the 1960s. But they have a broader base, employ more sophisticated lobbying techniques and take a more pragmatic approach to achieving their goals.

The housing coalition, like similar groups supporting food stamp benefits and children's programs, combines some of the traits of the traditional liberal organizations—the ADA, the unions, the churches and the civil rights groups—with some of the characteristics of the special-interest lobbies.

Like the former, it is dedicated to getting a better deal for the poor. Like the latter, it concentrates its energies on a single subject, housing.

"It's not so much how many dollars—although that's certainly important—but what they get used for," Dolbeare explained. "Our whole focus is adequate housing for low-income people, not just more money for housing."

Because of their narrower goals, groups like the housing coalition have an advantage over the traditional liberal forces that deal with social issues across the board: they can concentrate on the increasingly complicated programs and processes and develop the considerable expertise required to lobby for them.

The issues involved in the middle-income assistance proposal were subtle and complex. Because Dolbeare specializes in low-income housing issues, she was able to deal with them. And because she is an expert on housing issues in general, she was able to gather the facts, the figures and the allies to mount an effective campaign. . . .

Another way in which the new breed of coalition differs from the old-line liberal lobbies is its ability to mobilize the poor.

"We think it's very important that poor people speak for themselves, that they are involved in the decision making and determination of the issues," said Amidei. She attributed the success of this spring's effort to prevent an impending cutoff of food stamps to the involvement of the poor.

"The congressional offices told us they had never seen so much activity before," she said. "They said people never bothered to write them before." . . .

Forging Alliances

Flexibility was the key to the housing coalition's initial victory in the middle-income fight when it found itself thrown into an unlikely alliance with Garn and the Senate Banking Committee conservatives.

"The amazing thing is that the conservatives often are on our side on the issue of targeting programs to the poor," Dolbeare said. "They want the least government aid, and so any aid that is given out, they want to go only to the very neediest. We, of course, are concerned that the neediest get adequate aid because they are the most neglected. I wouldn't be surprised if we see this kind of thing happening more often in the future." . . .

The welfare reform movement, by contrast, has been unable to hook up successfully with any unlikely allies; and welfare reform, the liberal lobbyists agree, is in the deepest trouble of all the federal social programs. President Carter's recent failure to move on welfare reform, one of his top priorities when he came into office, is only the latest instance. Apparently Wiley was attempting to forge some links through his Movement for Economic Justice when he died in 1973. Since then, no one has even tried, say the lobbyists.

"People on welfare are the most unpopular people in the world," said Shull. "They have no political clout. Nobody gives a hoot about them. How can they make an alliance? What can they give in return? I don't see what they have to offer."

Holman agrees that "this country doesn't like welfare; it has a deep bias against the dole." But he isn't convinced that all efforts to build alliances for welfare reform are doomed to failure. Success, however, would require radical changes in the nature of the program.

"You've got to get business involved, the cities and the women's movement," Holman said. "I think you can pull together people from areas of different strength and do something about welfare reform—probably wind up calling it by a different name."

The Right Issue

So far, the crusaders for social programs agree that in a time of budgetary stringency, you've got to have the right issue. And welfare reform isn't that issue.

This year, food stamps and housing are two of the right issues. Even when the public is in an ungenerous mood, it approves the provision of basic necessities for the poor. And those programs can be sold because they help other constituencies.

"There's no question we're liable to do more because food stamp money goes for food," said Amidei. "People balk at putting cash in the hand of a welfare mother but are willing to see her get food. It's the old booze versus baby food argument."

Housing is another issue of the moment. "Housing means jobs during a recession. That's got to be one big factor" in the relative good fortune the housing lobby has had this year, said Edson. "Another factor is that we're about to have a real housing crisis for the first time since World War II."

The "right" issue also changes with the times. "Causes have their moments," said Holman. "Welfare rights had its day, too, as we sometimes forget."

But he also recalled that even the best times for social programs are not altogether bright. "Everybody looks back to the '60s and remembers only the victories. They ignore all the defeats—and there were many." . . .

SOURCE: Rochelle L. Stanfield, "Beleagured Lobbyists—Taking Allies Where They Can Find Them," *National Journal* (September 20, 1980), pp. 1556–1560. Reprinted by permission.

ILLUSTRATION 6.1
Haunted House

From *Herblock's State of the Union*, Simon & Schuster, 1972. Reprinted by permission of Herblock Cartoons.

such value dilemmas should be examined forthrightly and resolved with careful deliberation.

OVERVIEW OF LEGITIMATION

Useful to social workers in the legitimation phase is a framework that facilitates understanding of external forces, distribution of power, and political strategies that influence who wins and who loses. The framework presented in illustration 6.2 depicts background and other contextual realities that influence political strategy. An ultimate objective during legitimation is to devise strategies that increase the likelihood that personal policy preferences are reflected in legislation, in positions by boards, in policy rulings by executives, and in policy positions of agency staff. In some cases, social workers seek approval for procedural steps as a prelude to policy development, as when someone wants an agency to initiate a task force to explore the need to establish a new agency program to assist the Hispanic population. In this example, success in securing legitimation to initiate the task force could be a crucial and necessary first step, to be subsequently followed by efforts to secure support for a policy that requires hiring bilingual staff.

In an examination of the politics of an issue, then, attention is given to the question, "Who won and who lost?" In case example 6.1, proponents of subsidies to low-income consumers are able to defeat legislation that extends these subsidies to middle-income consumers. In many cases, as in the instance of stalemate between those who favor two versions of legislation, no one is successful—or both sides may be unhappy when they are required to devise compromise legislation that requires all parties to make significant concessions.

Perceptions that the other side was successful often fuel new efforts to overturn or modify legislation or other policies. In some cases, as noted in the next two chapters, participants may decide that the best method of recouping losses is to sabotage policy successes of others during implementation and assessment phases. Government officials who favor subsidies to middle-income rather than low-income consumers, for example, might seek to delay implementation of the low-income subsidy programs or restrict funding to them. Or they might seek new empirical evidence that low-income housing subsidies are less efficient than alternative use of the funds for middle-income consumers and then use the evidence to buttress proposals to expand middle-income subsidies.

BACKGROUND FACTORS

Some proposals are doomed from the start, no matter how skillful their proponents in devising political strategy. Difficulties in obtaining welfare reforms in the 1980s, for example, are discussed

ILLUSTRATION 6.2   An Overview of the Legitimation Phase

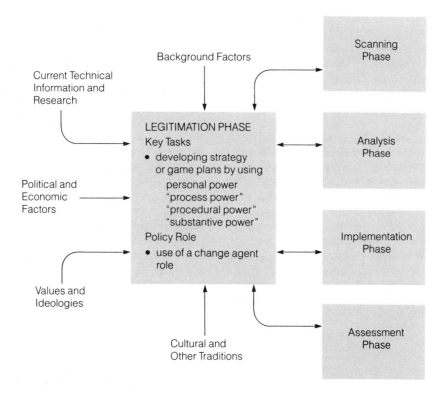

in case example 6.1 in the context of the absence of powerful consumer constituencies as well as widespread distrust of welfare recipients. By contrast, more favorable, if still not promising, background realities favor retention of food stamps and low-income housing subsidy programs.

Policymakers are often influenced by external pressures that can predispose them to support or oppose specific policy proposals. In discussion of background factors, it is useful to analyze the source, direction, and amount of external pressure associated with specific measures.[2]

Sources of External Pressure

Politicians are subject to many pressures—from interest groups, from beneficiaries of existing or proposed social programs, from professionals and administrators who provide or administer program benefits, from constituents, and from officials from their own political party. They are dependent on the technical expertise of lobbyists who in turn are associated with any of a myriad interest groups. These lobbyists provide technical information to harassed legislators who lack the time or resources to master the multitude of issues before them.[3]

These various groups and persons possess power over decision makers precisely because they can give or withhold tangible resources. The general public can vote out of office those politicians that choose unpopular policies. Consumers who directly benefit from existing or proposed programs can similarly reward or punish politicians by voting for or against them, as re-

Surrendering in the War on Hunger

Food Aid for Needy Women, Children Faces Sharp Cut

By James C. Webster

The Reagan Administration claims that its proposed cuts in food assistance would not deny the "truly needy." The evidence is otherwise, even granting the Administration's bare-bones definition of true need. This became clear when Budget Director David A. Stockman went after the Special Supplemental Food Program for Women, Infants and Children, which targets prescribed food packages (infant formula, fruit, eggs and dairy products) to 2.2 million pregnant women, nursing mothers and infants with identified high nutrition risks.

Advocates argue that the program's rapid growth, from a $50 million pilot in 1974 to its present $1 billion budget, has come about because of overwhelming evidence that it's one of the few federal projects that serve their purpose and are cost-effective, too. Even the conservative Heritage Foundation recommended keeping the program at current spending levels because "there is evidence that (it) does in fact improve nutrition." Stockman's analysts at the Office of Management and Budget will be hard put to refute the evidence.

One of the late Sen. Hubert H. Humphrey's most passionate arguments for the program, which he authored, was the surprisingly poor infant mortality rate in the

flected in case example 6.1 where politicians experience pressure from those who want continuation of low-income housing subsidies and various nutritional programs. In the case of large interest groups, such as the American Medical Association and the National Education Association, politicians risk forfeiture of campaign contributions when they oppose favored legislation.

As the leader of his party and the ultimate executive of massive government bureaucracies, the president can reward or punish politicians in numerous ways. He can reward allies by locating new projects, facilities, and grants in their jurisdictions, support politicians when they request appointments to key congressional committees, and campaign for incumbents during hard-fought elections. Leaders of political parties in the Congress, in states, and in localities can pressure party members to vote with their party on key issues as a prerequisite for party support at election time. (Multiple sources of external pres-

sures supportive of the Food Stamp program are discussed by James Webster in case example 6.2.)

In social agencies, decision makers are also influenced by many external factors.[4] Government legislation that establishes specific programs and ensuing administrative guidelines define services or benefits to be provided and include many procedural details. Government agencies often issue detailed guidelines when engaging in contracts with nongovernment agencies. A state mental health department can contract with local nonprofit agencies, for example, for 1,000 hours of clinical services and can specify in advance the kinds, duration, and cost of services. Since funders are often vague or silent on many key policy issues, however, some agencies have considerable discretion in developing their programs.

Agency decision makers are subject to pressures from the external community as well. Public agencies often experience pressure not only

United States—at 15 per thousand, almost double that of Japan or the Scandinavian countries. A frequently cited study by Harvard University's School of Public Health has since found that women in the program gave birth to low-weight babies only 6% of the time, compared with 10.1% for women in the study's control group. The study concluded that every $1 spent on the program for pregnant mothers saved $3 in hospital costs for their babies, because low-birth-weight babies are prone to illness and long-term medical complications such as retardation and poor eyesight.

Now Secretary of Agriculture John R. Block has the unenviable job of selling cuts in the program to Congress, despite his own department's studies of the program and infant mortality. A Department of Agriculture analysis of seven Indian reservations in Montana reports that infant mortality dropped from 31.5 per thousand to 16.6 after the program was begun on the reservations.

To propose cutting almost one-third from a program with proven results and popular acceptance, on top of major surgery on food stamps and school lunches, while leaving some farm subsidy programs untouched will risk giving credibility to the charge that Reagan wants to balance the federal budget on the backs of the poor, the disabled, the elderly, even the hungry.

Even the strongest advocates of the food stamp program will concede that it is marred by fraud, waste and abuse. Carter Administration appointees in charge of food stamps spent much of their time tightening error rates and improving management. But the Reagan proposal for $1.8 billion in cuts in the $12.4 billion program does not attack fraud and abuse. Instead, it seeks to deny eligibility to so-called "non-needy" families at the upper

from distant officials in Washington but also from local politicians. As an example, administrators of public welfare and public housing agencies often report to county or municipal elected officials who in turn appoint their directors. Nonprofit agencies are required by law to establish boards of directors who possess the power to hire and fire the executive and to ratify the agency budget. Various community or consumer groups may pressure the agency to provide certain kinds of services. Agency administrators are also subject to many legal precedents that may influence recordkeeping, quotas or affirmative action in hiring, and grievance procedures for clients and staff.

Amount of External Pressure

Identification of the sources of external pressure must be supplemented by analysis of their strength. Groups or individuals that apply ongoing and intense pressure are more likely to influence decisions than those who apply infrequent or negligible pressure. It is also useful to distinguish between actual and potential pressure. Decision makers respond to pressure but also anticipate it because they believe specific groups or interests could apply it. For example, a legislator may know from prior experience that groups representing agribusiness would not like marked reductions in the Food Stamps program, which may influence him to oppose reductions in the program even in the absence of major pressure. The perception of power, then, can be as important as its application.

It is also important to analyze the amount of pressure that emanates from specific sources in agency settings.[5] Government officials may not adequately monitor the public or private agencies that they fund, allowing some agencies to deviate from official policy. Agency boards may not sufficiently scrutinize agency operations to

end of the eligibility list—mostly the elderly on pensions or people working at low-wage jobs.

The proposed reduction of $1.7 billion in the $4.1 billion school-lunch and child-nutrition programs also would hit the "truly needy," notwithstanding a White House declaration to maintain free school lunches for lowest-income families. Those families would be affected by Reagan's proposals in two ways. (1) The value of their free lunches, $1.02 a meal this year, would be counted as income in determining their eligibility for food stamps, thus reducing the food-stamp coupons that they receive for meals prepared at home. (2) Big cuts in federal aid for reduced-price and fully paid meals are likely to boost per-meal prices and cause students to drop out of the school-lunch program, either threatening the very existence of the program at many schools or turning the lunch room into an economic ghetto of poor and minority youngsters.

Stockman's zeal in trimming the food-assistance programs, and Block's acquiescence in cutting them rather than farmers' programs, may have bought more political trouble for their boss, the President, than he bargained for. While antagonizing the poor, who don't have much political clout, the Administration also has gored the ox of several special-interest lobbies with considerable muscle in Congress:

Farmers. All told, Department of Agriculture food programs this year are budgeted at $18.5 billion. Because farmers get 38 cents of every retail food dollar, the food programs represent $6.8 billion in farm income.

Grocers and manufacturers. Because they get most of the rest of the retail food dollar, they too stand to lose from a possible overall cut of $4.3 billion from Department of Agriculture programs.

Farm-commodity organizations. They support programs under which the department buys surplus commodities (peanuts, raisins, flour, vegetable oil, potatoes, poultry) to give to schools and institutions.

influence agency policy, even when agency programs are of dubious quality. And external pressures from consumers and community groups may not be sufficiently intense or frequent to assume importance in many agencies.

Direction of External Pressure

Social workers who seek legitimation for a policy proposal are delighted when they find little or no opposition, particularly when the lack of opposition is coupled with intense and supportive pressure from numerous sources. In the early round of social program cutbacks in the Reagan Administration, for example, many programs for the elderly escaped serious cuts precisely because, unlike many other groups of needy persons, the elderly were widely perceived as deserving assistance. Interest groups such as the American Association of Retired Persons also resisted cuts. The chances that a policy proposal will be enacted within a social agency also increase as there is widespread consensual support. Staff or board members may already believe, for example, that an agency should provide a new kind of service desired by a social worker.

Many issues, however, are associated with some or major polarization between competing factions. Ideological polarization is illustrated by conflict between congressional conservatives and liberals over merits of initiating a new social program. Interest polarization may result if one

The dairy lobby. It stopped cold the efforts of the last three administrations to eliminate or cut the school-milk program that puts $120 million into the dairy market.

If the food-assistance budget cuts become symbolic of the political difference between the Administration's laudable goal of restraining federal spending and the wild-spending Democrats in Congress, it would be a tragedy, for feeding the hungry has never been a partisan issue. While President Kennedy's New Frontier and President Johnson's Great Society invoked compassion for the poor, the greatest expansion of food programs happened during Nixon's presidency. Nor was it Carter who in his first year in office declared war on hunger; that, too, was done by Nixon.

Political lines in Congress likewise have blurred when the issue is feeding hungry people. Former Sen. Herman Talmadge of Georgia, conservative chairman of the Agriculture Committee, was proud of his contribution to the expansion of the school-lunch program;

Sen. Robert Dole (R-Kan.) stood shoulder to shoulder with Sen. George McGovern (D-S.D.) in almost every legislative improvement of the food-stamp program.

One of the principal engines behind the commitment to end hunger in this land of food abundance was a study by Field Foundation doctors who visited several poor rural counties in the late 1960s and shocked the conscience of the nation with their findings of starvation and malnutrition reminiscent of famine-plagued Africa. In the late 1970s they went back to the same poverty pockets, and reported "far fewer grossly malnourished in this country than there were 10 years ago." They credited federal food programs for the turnaround.

Unless Ronald Reagan wants to be known as the Republican who surrendered the war that Nixon launched on hunger, he had better rein in his zealous budget-cutters and point them in another direction.

James C. Webster, assistant secretary of agriculture in the Carter Administration, is now publisher of the Food & Fiber Letter, a weekly Washington report on trends and developments in food and farm policy. SOURCE: This article first appeared in the *Los Angeles Times.* Reprinted by permission of the author.

group believes their political or economic interests will be furthered by a specific proposal but another fears that the proposal will harm its interests.[6] In case example 6.1, proponents of housing subsidies are divided, with each faction believing that subsidies to the other income group would threaten the subsidies it favors.

A number of factors determine why some and not other issues are associated with polarization. Politicians anticipate ideological cleavages when issues are introduced that are traditionally associated with conflict.[7] The chances of obtaining major changes in welfare policy have diminished, for example, as various welfare reform proposals have been defeated in the context of polarization of liberals and conservatives. Social

initiatives that propose fundamental innovations in policy, such as new housing subsidies, are likely to be engulfed in controversy. Proposals perceived to make fewer persons dependent on the state arouse less controversy than those widely perceived to create dependency. Welfare, public housing, and public employment programs have consistently been regarded by conservatives at local and national levels of government as discouraging individual initiative, while health, education, and social security programs are often portrayed as enabling people to be more productive or as rewarding individuals for personal initiative.[8]

Polarization can occur as well in social agencies. Proposals to make major changes in agency services often cause polarization, as illustrated in case example 1.1 (see chapter 1). In this instance, Dr. Breeze seeks multiple changes in agency policy, but his reforms alienate those who favor and benefit from traditional services and policies. Polarization is also likely when proposals are perceived to assist some organizational participants and harm others. A proposal may be perceived to expand the programs of one unit of an organization to the detriment of another. Or conflict may be exacerbated by ideological cleavages about the proper mission of the agency. Dr. Breeze and allies want to emphasize social action and services to the poor, in contrast to traditionalists, who favor counseling services to more affluent consumers.

POLITICAL AND ECONOMIC REALITIES

Power and procedural realities influence legitimation outcomes by providing a favorable or unfavorable context for specific proposals. Even proposals supported with considerable external pressure can be sabotaged by powerful, strategically placed opponents, just as measures with scant backing can sometimes be legitimated through the determined, behind-the-scenes support of persons familiar with the intricacies of parliamentary maneuvering.

Power Realities

It is important to determine whether power is concentrated or dispersed in a specific legislative, agency, or bureaucratic arena. A group of political theorists known as *elitists* argues that power is usually concentrated in the hands of relatively few participants or interests, a point of view also favored by Marxists, who argue that powerful economic interests dominate the political process.[9] The chances of securing passage of a specific reform diminish as power is concentrated and as elites oppose it. Such elites may also succeed in diverting available resources to their initiatives and programs so that few resources are left for alternative programs, as illus-

trated by the contention of many reformers that defense-related industries have succeeded in capturing vast portions of the federal budget to the detriment of social programs.

Another group of political theorists known as *pluralists* argues that power is usually dispersed between various interests and participants.[10] When it exists, a pluralist power structure is a favorable sign for reformers, provided that they are able to mobilize citizen and interest group support for specific measures. Even the most ardent pluralist must admit, however, that "interest group democracy" works better for some than for others; the poor, those perceived to constitute a burden on the state, and persons regarded as deviant are less likely than others to benefit from large and well-financed constituencies and interest groups.

Procedural Realities

Policies are constructed in the course of procedural or parliamentary maneuvers. A diagram of the decision-making process in a legislative setting helps one to appreciate the complexity of these procedures (see illustration 6.3). Numerous persons, committees, or deliberative bodies must sequentially assent to successful policies, as illustrated by a bill introduced in the House of Representatives that must normally proceed through subcommittees, committees, and a vote of the full House, a sequence that must usually be repeated in the Senate. A conference committee of selected members of House and Senate is sometimes needed to resolve differences in the House and Senate versions as a prelude to final approval by the president. (A two-thirds vote of both House and Senate is required to override a presidential veto.) Many parliamentary techniques exist for circumventing specific steps in this process, but they require considerable support from other politicians if they are to succeed.[11]

The more complex the decision-making process, then, the more likely that opponents can find methods of defeating or diluting policy proposals. When proposals are initiated, it is necessary to ask which persons control the decision-

ILLUSTRATION 6.3   Route Followed by One Bill in the Federal Congress

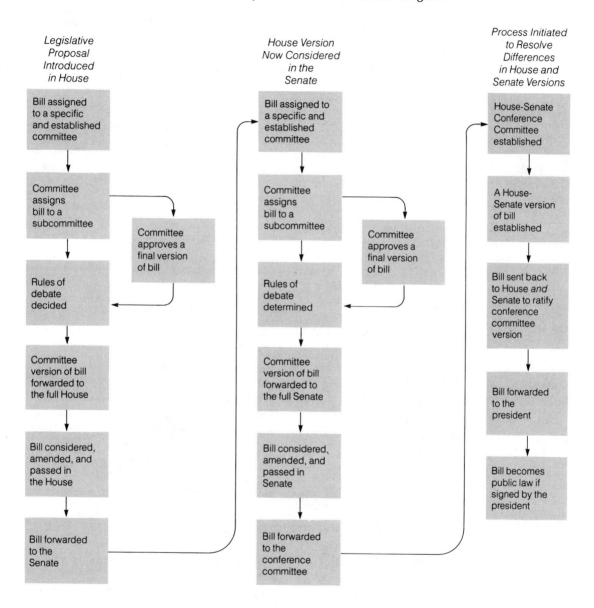

making apparatus at specific points, whether they favor the proposal, and whether proponents will be able to overcome opposition. In the case of the Senate during the early years of the presidency of Ronald Reagan, Republicans obtained a majority of Senate seats and held the position of chairperson in the various Senate committees. These Republican chairpersons, moreover, worked in liaison with White House staff members, who assisted them by mobilizing party support for those bills that were given priority. Disgruntled Democrats discovered that many of their legislative initiatives never made it beyond these committee gatekeepers. They also found that many bills that were approved in the House, where Democrats were chairpersons in the various committees (their party held a majority of House seats), were referred to Senate committees that promptly defeated or rewrote them.

Procedures for decision making are less routinized in many social agencies than in legislative arenas. Boards of directors possess ultimate oversight functions, but many decisions derive from discussions of executives, supervisors, and direct service staff. Both complex and simple decision procedures exist. In the former, a staff member, staff committee, or executive can initiate a proposal, e.g., to develop a new agency program. The proposal may be developed by a staff committee, come to the full staff for consideration, and be taken to the board of directors by the executive. The board may then refer it to a board committee as a prelude to taking a final vote. (In some cases, funders may also be included, particularly when the board wants their participation to ensure funding for the program.) While many major revisions in agency policy are considered through complex decision procedures, simpler options sometimes also exist. For example, a hospital social service director who wants to develop social work services on the neurology ward may assign a staff person quarter-time and subsequently obtain formal clearance from a hospital administrator to station a social worker half-time on the service. (She may reason that approval is more likely after the quarter-time social worker has demonstrated success.)

Skill is needed to carefully consider when, where, and how to introduce suggestions for policy changes.[12] Use of complex decision routes may be required in some cases but not in others. Sensitive choices must be made about whom to consult and when, since staff who violate official agency protocol by breeching official channels can antagonize potential support.

CULTURAL AND VALUE FACTORS

When analyzing whether a specific proposal can succeed, social workers often analyze predisposing orientations of key decision makers. Do they favor or oppose the proposal or are they undecided—and how strongly do they hold these positions? Someone may mildly oppose a policy proposal but be amenable to reconsideration when given new evidence. Others may be unalterably opposed. Naturally, a participant is most interested in assessing positions of those participants who will make or contribute to final decisions within the decision route chosen.[13]

In the development of strategy, it is also important to analyze the salience, or importance, that persons attach to a policy proposal. Its chances of passage decrease, for example, as powerful persons are not only irreversibly opposed to it but also willing to commit time and resources to its defeat. Its chances increase as supporters are willing to invest resources to secure its passage.[14] External pressures often influence levels of salience. A politician is likely to attach importance to a policy he believes to be favored by many constituents yet may be apathetic to a policy when he is not subjected to constituency pressures.

The prognosis for passage also becomes more favorable as participants perceive specific issues to be associated with win-win rather than win-lose politics.[15] In the former case, participants believe that they can collaborate to produce policy proposals, as illustrated in bipartisan collaboration on legislation to provide national research funds for child abuse, legislation in which both sides receive political credit for helping abused children.

But win-lose orientations are common in legislative and some agency settings. Traditional in the legitimation phase are rivalries between political parties, between spokespersons for specific policy positions, and between competing units of a bureaucracy. In win-lose politics, rivals mutually fear that they will lose political ground to the extent that the other side wins. Members of one political party, for example, may fear that substantial numbers of elderly persons will vote for candidates of the opposing party if that party succeeds in passing a proposal to assist that population. Or conservative politicians may fear that passage of a liberal social reform measure will make them "lose credit" among their conservative constituents and also allow liberal politicians to strengthen their political standing among relatively liberal constituencies. The prognosis for issues embroiled in win-lose politics is usually bleak unless supporters possess far more political resources or skill than their opposition.

GAUGING FEASIBILITY

As a prelude to developing strategy, social workers often assess whether a specific proposal can be passed or approved by combining various kinds of information about background factors, political and economic forces, and cultural and value realities. A negative prognosis does not necessarily mean that proponents retreat—they may proceed because they believe that the issue is so important that action is needed, or they may modify their proposal to make it more feasible. Alternatively, they may decide to wait for a more favorable time if events are unfavorable. The need for skill in developing and implementing legitimation strategy is most acute, of course, when the prognosis for a measure is bleak.

When gauging the feasibility of a proposal, social workers engage in a diagnostic process that combines information about the various contextual factors discussed up to this point (see illustration 6.4). The prognosis is favorable, for example, if (1) key decision makers are besieged by external pressure from mutiple interest group, consumer, professional, and provider sources, (2) pressure is unremitting and intense, (3) pres-

ILLUSTRATION 6.4   Diagnosing Background Realities

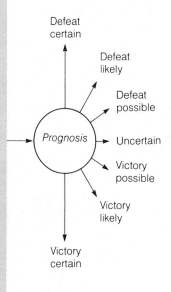

External Pressures and Realities	Decision Arenas and Decision Makers	Predisposing Orientations of Key Decision Makers
• number of sources of pressure • intensity of pressure • direction of pressure • extent of polarization • breadth of consensus • extent to which background situational factors are supportive	• if power is concentrated, do proponents possess high-level support? • if power is dispersed, do supporters possess resources to mobilize support from disparate sources? • if complex decision routes are required, do proponents possess required procedural skills and allies?	• what importance (salience) is attached to a measure? • to what extent is a measure associated with win-win or win-lose orientations of key decision makers?

Prognosis:
Defeat certain
Defeat likely
Defeat possible
Uncertain
Victory possible
Victory likely
Victory certain

sure is largely favorable to the proposal and polarization is minimal, and (4) power is dispersed in the setting but allies have access to key leaders and committee members who can facilitate parliamentary or procedural success.[16] The prognosis is improved when key decision makers also have favorable orientations toward the proposal, want to invest major resources in it, and believe that win-win strategies are possible. Background events may also facilitate passage, as when strategically placed persons in legislative or agency arenas decide that it will enhance political or agency interests, or when the policy agenda contains no competing or distracting issues.

Background realities are rarely this favorable. Substitute a negative contextual factor for any of the positive ones in the preceding example, and the prognosis becomes less favorable. When many of the factors are unfavorable, passage is unlikely—a fact to be used in deciding whether to proceed and in devising strategy.

POWER RESOURCES IN STRATEGY

Someone who decides to proceed with a policy proposal should develop a strategy or game plan that defines actions and steps to be taken to facilitate its passage. Power considerations are basic to strategy. While many definitions exist, most theorists define power as a resource to be used to influence the activities or positions of others by inducing them to engage in activities or take positions that they would not normally have engaged in or taken.[17] The nature of power—and its use in political strategy—is clarified by an examination of the various kinds of power resources.

Resourceful participants in the legitimation phase realize that many sources of power exist. A necessary and often difficult part of political strategy is deciding which kind or source of power to use and when and with whom to use it. A distinction between person-to-person, process, procedural, and substantive power is useful.

Person-to-Person Power

Participants often try to modify the policy positions of others by directly interceding with them. Common kinds of person-to-person power are described in table 6.1.[18] Coercive power, for example, involves the use of sanctions or threats to modify positions or activities, in contrast to reward or expertise power. In the case of legitimation power, participants use their administrative or professional credentials to convince others to modify positions. An executive might suggest to staff, for example, that she "has ar-

TABLE 6.1　Varieties of Person-to-Person Power

Kind of Power	Examples
coercive power	use of actual or threatened sanctions or penalties
reward power	use of actual or promised rewards, such as promotions, pay increases, *quid pro quo* arrangements
expertise power	use of personal credentials and (presumed) knowledge
legitimation power	use of administrative or other authority or professional roles to elicit support
charismatic power	use of personal attributes to elicit support

rived at a policy position only after carefully surveying the overall needs of the agency and based upon long years of administrative experience."

When devising strategy, participants need to consider which kinds of person-to-person power to utilize and with whom. Consideration should be given to the question of who should take the lead in trying to modify policies or activities of others. Rather than personally intervening, for example, someone might convince a friend or colleague to broach a policy innovation to an agency executive. In case example 6.1, opponents of housing subsidies to middle-income consumers try to convince a leading conservative to influence others not to vote for the subsidies and to support existing subsidies for low-income consumers.

Process Power

Some persons are adept at choosing and implementing strategies to shape the nature of political interaction so that it is favorable to their proposals (see table 6.2). A social worker in an agency may decide that a policy change can best be initiated in behind-the-scenes discussions with the executive director, since publicizing the issue would bring extensive opposition from those traditionalists who do not want to modify existing policy. Therefore, she might pursue a behind-the-scenes (i.e., low-conflict) strategy. In other circumstances, she might employ a more public strategy that would heighten conflict. Assume, for example, that the executive director opposes a change in agency policy but that all line staff members favor it. She might decide that open discussion of the policy is required in order to induce the executive to reconsider the issue.

Process strategy often involves the development and use of coalitions.[19] By pooling resources, members of different groups can be more effective than solo advocates (see guest editorial 6.1, where Chauncey Alexander, the former executive director of the National Association of Social Workers, implores members of the profession to initiate and join broader coalitions to counter funding cutbacks of the Reagan Administration).

Procedural Power

Social workers can try to influence the course of events by making and implementing key procedural choices that often require cooperation from others. Decisions about when to initiate proposals (i.e., timing) are often crucial determinants of ultimate outcomes. If an agency staff member initiates a proposal when agency finances and leadership are unfavorable, the proposal may be doomed to failure, but the same proposal may succeed if introduced six months later. Procedural power also involves choices regarding leadership and parliamentary strategy during formal deliberations (see table 6.3).[20]

TABLE 6.2 Varieties of Process Power

Kinds	Options
influence speed of deliberations	speed up or delay
influence number of participants	increase or decrease scope of conflict
influence level of conflict	escalate or deescalate conflict
influence extent to which persons work together	form or block formation of coalitions
personal role	assume leadership role or background role
proactive or reactive role	initiate or block a proposal

GUEST EDITORIAL 6.1

Social Workers Should Battle Social Welfare Reductions

By Chauncey Alexander

The scenario for the current American scene comes straight from *The Empire Strikes Back.* Sinister forces, with a series of lightning-like rays, are attempting to destroy programs created in forty years of struggle and designed to provide some minimum security for the nation's citizens.

It is not science fiction to say that a *Star Wars* has been conducted by the former movie star from California, who is using the mass-media technology to overwhelm the meager communication resources of children, the poor, disabled, elderly, unemployed, and other victims of societal dysfunction.

Led by the "Darth Vader" of the Reagan "Empire," David Stockman, perpetrators of the budget blitzkrieg have thrown the federal government back 127 years and resurrected the policy of President Franklin Pierce. In 1854, President Pierce vetoed a bill that had finally passed both houses of Congress as a result of a six-year campaign by Dorothea Lynde Dix. It preserved 12,225,000 acres of public land for the benefit of the "indigent insane, as well as the blind, deaf and dumb." In a striking parallel to oil corporations' rip-

offs today, the land-grabbing railroads had stolen public resources for their own private use, which stimulated Dorothea Dix to undertake legislative action.

President Pierce vetoed the bill on the grounds that Congress did not have the power to make provisions of an eleemosynary character outside the limits of the District of Columbia. He used the alarmist argument that if Congress could provide for the indigent insane, it has the same power to provide for the indigent *not* insane and would thus "transfer to the federal government the charge of all the poor in all the states." His interpretation that the "general welfare" clause of the Constitution does not allow the federal government to take responsibility for the welfare of its citizens dictated public policy for the next eighty-one years, until the passage of the Social Security Act.

Only the organized effort of human service coalitions and the mobilization of concerned professional, labor, religious, civil rights, and social welfare groups across the country kept a few programs—such as the recent child welfare services legislation and the Education for All Handicapped Children Act—from being swallowed in block grants. They also helped

Substantive Power

Decisions about the substance of policy proposals are also crucial in the legitimation phase (see table 6.4). When using substantive power, participants develop the substantive content of proposals to enhance support.[21] Assume, for example, that two persons favor providing low-income housing subsidies. One wants the subsidies to be given primarily to persons falling beneath poverty standards; the other wants subsidies to go to a broader group. The initiator of a housing subsidy proposal might decide not to define precise income levels within the legis-

make it possible to build a few safeguards into the block grants, such as adequate notice and public hearings on state plans.

Despite the general success of the second Reagan stampede, these few protections offer the means for countering the overall impact of the radical reductions. The formation of state-level coalitions of human service advocates could influence governors to make rational and equitable use of their meager funds. Otherwise, there will be gladiatorial contests among health and social services agencies scrambling for a share of the greatly reduced funds for human service programs.

Even though social services, those whom they help, and social workers themselves are targets of this massive governmental turn-around, the situation presents a significant challenge and opportunity to the social work profession. So, demoralization is out and optimism is in!

Social work, of all the social sciences, knows that the reality of individual and social inequities cannot be covered over or denied forever. On 5 February 1981, President Reagan, in a speech to the American people, selected the following as our principal economic problems: inflation, regulation, taxes, budget deficits, and spending growth. He did not refer to unemployment, usurious interest rates, outrageous prices and profits, and the continuing escalation of military expenditures —the most significant economic problems for the American people and the prime causes of the probems he cited. Therefore, social workers can perform an important public service by keeping people's attention focused on the real problems and demonstrating their impact as seen in professionals' experience. What more direct way to interpret social work to agency boards, civic leaders, and the public at large?

Millions of people in our country are in for some hurtful times. As a result, there will be manifestations of anxiety, anger, and undoubtedly violence. Public officials, frustrated by inability to respond to these symptoms appropriately, will continue to turn to more repressive measures. Social workers can turn many away from such a dead-end approach by offering positive alternatives drawn from their own experiences. Information networks can be established to replace the social data collection mechanism now being destroyed by the Reagan/Stockman/Schweiker axis.

Social workers and NASW are rapidly becoming key founders of coalitions, committees, and caucuses, seeking to build a unity of purpose and action among participants in a group resistance to the destruction of the economic and social security of America.

Optimism is often labeled "Pollyannaism." But it is built upon some measure of personal security and integrity, and a recognition of social reality—and a belief in the basic honesty and generosity of the American people.

Chauncey Alexander was executive director of the National Association of Social Workers.
SOURCE: Copyright 1981, National Association of Social Workers, Inc. Reprinted with permission from *NASW News*, Vol. 26, No. 9 (October 1981), p. 24.

lation in hopes that the two would vote for it. (Both participants might vote for the legislation and hope that administrative guidelines issued after passage by federal officials would favor their respective positions.) In other cases, support for a proposal can only be obtained when specific provisions are strengthened or clarified.

Advocates of low-income housing might insist, for example, that eligibility details be defined in the legislation to ensure allocation of housing units to the poor. Sometimes proposals include contradictory provisions to appease various factions.

Ethical dilemmas are often encountered in the

TABLE 6.3   Varieties of Procedural Power

Kinds	Options
timing of proposals	initiate now or wait for more favorable events
deciding which decision route to employ	use one or another committee or choose one or another part of the organization or decision apparatus when initiating a proposal
specific parliamentary tactics	seek amendment of a proposal or work to defeat it
specific parliamentary tactics	seek immediate approval of a proposal or try to refer it back to committee
specific parliamentary tactics	accept a given committee or meeting as an appropriate place to consider a measure or seek to refer it to another committee with "proper jurisdiction" over the matter
specific parliamentary tactics	develop an autonomous measure or try to attach it to another measure
specific parliamentary tactics	seek to defeat a measure or try to water it down by making key substantive changes

TABLE 6.4   Varieties of Substantive Power

Kinds	Options
influence content of proposal	delete or add measures
influence sharpness of resolution	develop highly specific and detailed provisions or seek ambiguity and lack of detail
influence size of measures	develop pilot or incremental changes or seek major and ambitious reforms
influence relationship between one measure and another	attach a proposal to another measure or detach a provision from a larger proposal
influence content of proposal	seek a highly consistent proposal or add extraneous or inconsistent measures, as when compromises are accepted

use of substantive power. When should participants agree to compromises in order to appease opponents? When do compromises represent unacceptable abdication of principle? Pejorative labels are often used in the legitimation phase to denounce those who have made errors, including terms like *opportunistic, idealistic, inflexible, unrealistic,* and *unprincipled.* Substantive decisions are often difficult to make and depend on weighing substantive issues in the context of professional, value, and political considerations.

Bowled Over by GOP Teamwork, Democrats Change Their Game Plan

By Richard E. Cohen

WASHINGTON—Democrats have been badly battered this year, but still have some fight left, as they showed last week when Congress returned from its August recess.

Most of them recognize that it is too late to reverse the major spending and tax cuts Congress has approved this year. But they intend to score some political points this fall by mounting vigorous political attacks against President Reagan for high interest rates and big federal deficits. . . .

The Democrats, who have suffered—in the seasonal parlance—from repeated squabbles in their huddle, poor play selection and untimely fumbles in execution, hope they can regain momentum by calling attention to similar foul-ups by their political opponents.

That's bad news for Reagan, who also has to worry these days about growing splits on federal spending among his own Cabinet members and House and Senate Republicans as well as the sinking confidence of the business community in Reaganomics. The economic turbulence may ease as Reagan and his GOP cohorts identify additional spending cuts to provide more visible proof that they are sticking closely to their promise to balance the federal budget in fiscal year 1984. The tem-

porary political uncertainty, however, is giving Democrats a welcome opportunity to throw blocks at the Republicans, who seemed invincible only a few weeks ago in strong-arming the Democratic attack.

The apparent result is that the latest economic problems mean an end to the Reagan honeymoon, a return to a more routine "business as usual" conflict between the President and Congress, and tougher public questioning of Reagan's actions.

It remains to be seen how well the Democrats take advantage of the changing fortunes. Many of their tacticians—especially in the House where they hold nominal control—are all too well aware they thought they had Reagan stopped several times since he took office, only to see him take the offensive and defeat their challenge—most notably, on the budget and tax bills.

In those cases, House Speaker Thomas P. (Tip) O'Neill Jr. (D-Mass.) encouraged his committee chairmen to work with committee members in preparing alternatives to the Reagan proposals. After a lengthy series of meetings—both among Democrats and with the GOP members—committee leaders repeatedly moved a long way toward Reagan's policies without winning his support.

"We ended up offering 75% of what Reagan wanted, not something different," said a

DEVELOPING STRATEGY OR GAME PLANS

In case example 6.3, elements of the strategy or game plan of Democrats are discussed in the wake of extraordinary legislative successes by Republicans. Prior to this point, Democrats "suf-

fered . . . from repeated squabbles in their huddle, poor play selection, and untimely fumbles in execution" but tried to evolve strategy effective in countering the strategy of Republicans. President Reagan, leader of the Republican party, had achieved striking political successes but feared "growing splits over federal spending among his

top aide to a key House Democrat. But Reagan then undercut the Democratic actions by saying they had failed to address his proposals and emphasizing the stark contrast between the two sides. His last-ditch drives to win the crucial votes of conservative Democrats and a few wavering moderate Republicans succeeded because of Reagan's personal lobbying, his speeches to the public and the support he won from influential local constituents.

The Democrats also suffered because they were not organized in either their party philosophy or political strategy. Despite pleas starting early this year from some of their House and Senate members, party leaders did little to urge the rank and file to develop and support positions consistent with Democratic principles.

"We have been so anxious to win at any price that we've been willing to paper over our differences and give away the interests of our traditional constituencies with statements that can be interpreted in any way and really

do not say anything," said Rep. Theodore S. Weiss (D-N.Y.) "We have to decide what our party stands for."

Weiss and a growing number of liberal and moderate Democrats believe the time is overdue for Democratic leaders to stop acting as though they are responsible for the fate of Reagan's programs. Instead, they argue, Democrats should stake out their own positions and highlight the differences from Reagan without worrying about whether they can push their alternatives through the House or Senate.

On Social Security, for example, Democrats increasingly are saying that it is in their political interest to let the Republicans, who have a majority in the Senate, take the heat by dealing with Reagan's plan, including a controversial reduction in benefits for recipients who retire at age 62 instead of 65. Although most Democrats familiar with the problems of the Social Security system agree that something must be done by next summer to keep the old-age trust fund solvent for the next few

Cabinet members and House and Senate Republicans as well as the sinking confidence of the business community in Reaganomics." Democrats decided not to take the initiative in developing Democratic budget alternatives to Republican budget cuts because they preferred to "let the President take the heat" (a substantive power resource). Some wanted to develop new party leadership to increase cohesion in party ranks (a coalition or process political resource); many sought direct appeals to voters to shore up party strength in upcoming elections, perhaps with extensive use of the mass media (a process political resource).

Strategy or game plans are also used by social workers in agency settings. In many cases, they employ game plans that combine low-conflict,

behind-the-scenes, and incremental reform options, as reflected in the aforementioned example of a social worker who sought gradual expansion of her department's services to various new units of the hospital. In other cases, social workers use high-conflict strategies when they believe that no alternatives exist and defects in agency services are glaring. More common than high-conflict strategies are those involving moderate conflict, such as negotiations in staff or board meetings.[22]

Strategies or game plans, then, require definition of a set of coordinated and sequenced activities that are adapted to political realities, and need to be revised as background factors, political and economic realities, and other contextual factors change. When developing strategy, social

years, they figure there is no reason to play Reagan's game again by coming up with their own solution and having it become the new center of debate.

Many Democrats say they should take the same approach on the growing federal deficit for 1982. Rather than identify specific defense programs or social services that can be pruned a few billion dollars, they may gain greater political mileage by giving the Republicans that responsibility. Then, of course, they can attack Reagan and the GOP for whatever decisions they make or avoid. . . .

The strategy carries some hazards. Most obviously, perhaps, the Democrats risk being called obstructionists at a time when Reagan retains high political support across the nation. They also know they must be careful not to associate themselves too closely with spending or regulatory programs that are easy targets of critics.

As Democrats explore tactics to improve their legislative performance, many are focusing on the performance of their party leaders.

Although no shakeup is imminent, grumblings by rank and file Democrats are on the rise and speculation about successors to the current leadership is rampant.

The most frequent target of criticism is House Speaker O'Neill. Although he remains a source of affection and respect to most Democrats, many are saying he should retire next year in the interest of the party. They cite his inability or unwillingness to call out a distinct party position in response to Reagan, his weakness in communicating with the public, especially on television, and perhaps more importantly the fact that Republicans have made him their prime symbol of what they want to change. . . .

Although their spirits have been lifted by Republican difficulties with the federal budget and with GOP political vulnerability to high interest rates, the Democrats must become more aggressive in convincing the voters that the Reagan program won't work, and that they can address the nation's economic and defense problems more effectively.

Richard E. Cohen is congressional correspondent for the National Journal. SOURCE: This article first appeared in the *Los Angeles Times*. Reprinted by permission of the author.

workers need to avoid such common dangers as excessive or insufficient confidence or assertiveness, unbalanced use of conflict, and failure to develop power resources.

Avoiding Overconfidence and Underconfidence

The twin dangers of over- and underconfidence exist when constructing political strategy. Those who are overconfident underestimate the political resources and skills of opponents. Underconfidence can also be damaging, as when someone who falsely believes that a proposal faces an uphill battle can waste time and political resources in mobilizing coalitions and other supports. In some cases, such overorganization ac-

tually arouses opposition from those who believe that they too should join the fray.

Avoiding Overassertiveness and Underassertiveness

Underassertive participants minimize personal power resources as well as resources of potential allies. To be able to use the various kinds of power described in this chapter, participants need to recognize personal power resources and convert them into effective power. In many cases, participants need to convince nonassertive but potential allies that they too can make an important contribution.

Overly assertive participants sometimes create difficulties for themselves by overestimating

POLICY PRACTICE CASE 6.1

A Social Work Intern Tries to Develop a Preventive Program in a Mental Health Agency

It is curious that the Mountain View Child Guidance Clinic considers itself an advocate for the mental health needs of children when it neglects the children of the psychiatrically hospitalized parent. Such children are in crisis and experiencing extreme family disequilibrium at the time of the parent's hospitalization. They need immediate assistance in understanding and dealing constructively with feelings and thoughts associated with this experience. It is preferable that this intervention occur at or near the time of the crisis, when defenses are most fluid and before maladaptive patterns of functioning have been solidified. To meet this need, I am trying to develop, as an addition to the existing structure of brief services offered by the clinic, a crisis group for children of psychiatrically hospitalized parents.

I am hoping that the program can proceed on the eight-week crisis model currently adhered to by the clinic; however, several alternatives in programming are possible. A fixed membership group composed of children experiencing the recent hospitalization of a parent could be used, with the number of children in the group to be based on demand, with an upper limit of ten. Referrals and screening for the group could be accepted up to one day prior to first meeting, but, once the group has started, no new members would be added. Such groups would be offered at overlapping intervals of four weeks. Alternatively, an ongoing open-ended group with children rotating through an eight-week membership could be used so children could be accepted into a group as soon as they were referred, a strategy that would avoid any delays and limits on membership.

Implementation of this program would be based on referrals from local psychiatric hospitals. The coordination and cooperation necessary for such a program would be a landmark in the clinic's history. Although cooperative interrelations with other mental health agencies in the area is a stated goal, the

their power resources and inadvisedly championing a measure that is doomed to defeat. The skillful participant, then, is aware of the limitations of power resources as well as their strengths.

Balanced Use of Conflict

In some cases, participants use conflictual strategies because they believe behind-the-scenes or other nonconflictual approaches will not be effective. In such cases, strategists develop coalitions, utilize coercive power, and enlarge the scope of conflict by such techniques as mass-media publicity.

However, conflictual strategies carry dangers. Losers may face reprisals, and outcomes are often uncertain when protagonists engage in conflictual politics, since both sides may resort to extraordinary tactics. Therefore, participants may choose instead to use less conflictual strategies in which relatively unobtrusive use is made of various kinds of person-to-person, process, procedural, and parliamentary resources. Important changes can sometimes be wrought in official policy in such a way that others are hardly aware that the changes have occurred. As an example, an innovative but rather unobtrusive pilot project may eventually lead to other changes in the direction of agency services. Such strategies often do not require the heavy investment of time and resources required in conflictual politics and

clinic is openly competitive in its relationships with other child-related services. Providing this new service would add to the clinic's prestige in the community. Its success would depend on the referrals of psychiatrists who assist patients admitted to various public and private psychiatric hospitals in the area. Should the clinic bypass the authority of the doctor and accept referrals directly from the social service departments, it would alienate some physicians.

Announcements could be sent to the hospitals, their social service departments, and specific doctors. The service must be offered as a support service for both the doctor and the hospital.

The politics of this agency dictate, alas, that the new program not be called preventive lest funders and policymakers not favor it. Since they believe that no room exists in the budget for prevention, this program will be called crisis intervention.

Four local hospitals could be approached with announcements of the new clinic program. A follow-up phone call would add a personal touch and hopefully clinch the process. As a staff member, I would person-ally persuade doctor-friends of its merit while soliciting membership and support.

A number of barriers frustrate change in this agency. The clinic focuses its energy on the quantity rather than the quality of services. Of primary importance to the executive director is avoidance of a waiting list. To this end, he mobilizes all forces, and any program change that would deter this aim is automatically shelved. Further, staff are usually inundated with work and so have little time to create innovative services. Similarly, the agency values efficiency in programming and expenditures. Clinic executives believe that they cannot afford to risk any revenue by applying funds to areas other than those directly funded and approved. Another barrier to innovation is disinclination of the agency staff to participate in program development, which deprives the agency of new program ideas. Staff members come to work to glean what fulfillment is available through the clients themselves but leave the business of the clinic to the bureaucracy.

I am only a student intern in this agency, but I want to get this innovation off the ground prior to the end of my field experi-

are less likely to lead to animosity between persons and factions.

Flexibility in use of conflict, then, is needed. In some cases, political realities require conflictual strategies. In other cases, they are counterproductive and can increase opposition to specific measures.

Developing Potential Power

Skillful strategists view power as consisting of current and potential resources. In this perspective, they try to enhance personal power resources by increasing personal expertise, credibility, reliability, and other attributes likely to enhance future effectiveness. Emphasis is placed upon developing relationships with key persons inside and outside a policy arena, relationships useful when subsequently building coalitions and seeking support for policy reforms.

POLICY PRACTICE IN THE LEGITIMATION PHASE

Even in developing a relatively small pilot project in policy practice case 6.1, the social work intern has to carefully devise methods of obtaining support and decreasing opposition. Indeed, development and use of power often require as much skill in agency as in legislative settings.

ence. Considering the nature of the agency, it is essential to introduce the change in an administratively sanctioned way through approved channels. Therefore, I initially broached the idea of the innovation to the director of outpatient services, Mr. Jones, who is my preceptor for short-term and intake cases. On first mentioning the plan, I was careful to make it appear as an idea that I had developed in the course of discussions with him. I interpreted it as consistent with comprehensive mental health care for children, an ideal he had often espoused. Underscoring the validity of the time-limited approach, which he likes, and stressing its efficiency in terms of the waiting list, I ventured to actually propose a pilot plan. He groaned and suggested that I "write it up," with no explanation as to what that meant. Rather than irritate him further, I did not mention the project for several weeks. I then told my regular field instructor that I was discussing with Mr. Jones a new program for children of hospitalized patients, and I received her approval to use this as a learning experience in program design.

Several weeks later, I found that Mr. Jones had totally forgotten my plan. But, in further discussion, he expressed strong interest and even brainstormed an initial strategy with me that would allow the innovation to gradually gain support in Mountain View Child Guidance. He argued that we should develop a two-phase strategy. In phase 1, I would develop a pilot project as a student intern that would not need formal clearance from high-level executives or the agency board. (He would notify the executive that a student intern was establishing a pilot group-treatment program for children of institutionalized persons.) He urged a "low profile" during this initial period. Subsequent to initiation of the project, he would develop a strategy for formal program proposal that would go to the executive director and (hopefully) eventually to the board, a strategy that would require

formal earmarking of agency funds for the program. He hoped that my experience in devising a pilot project would provide useful information that could be used when writing the formal proposal and making a case for it in oral presentations to the executive and the board. He concluded with the statement "You know that you will have to do the entire program in the pilot phase. All the screening and everything." He seem tantalized by the idea of obtaining increased service with no additional expenditure of staff time.

To date, I have succeeded in involving Mr. Jones in planning sufficiently to encourage his sense of investment in the program. I have abided by the rules of the game in recognizing his authority and decision-making powers and in deemphasizing my own initiative. My short-term strategy, then, is to begin the program myself. But a number of obstacles could still interfere with program acceptance by key decision makers even during the pilot phase.

One obstacle is the issue of community coordination. Currently, the clinic engages in superficial coordination with local mental health agencies, only exchanging cases sporadically on a case-by-case basis. No clear plan exists for coordination of services. This program will necessitate an intermediate type of coordination: a case-planning coordination organized into a whole-family approach. The current fragmentation in treatment of families with a disturbed member would be a danger in this program, since it would undermine the purpose of comprehensive care. What are the factors involved in this coordination process?

First is the issue of goal conflict. On the surface, there appears to be little; both the psychiatric hospitals and the clinic serve and are concerned with the mental health needs of families. But is that really the case? In fact, the hospitals view treatment of the parent-patient from a pathology model rather than a family systems perspective. In that case, they may choose to refer the child not for group but for individual treatment as an "impaired" family member. It will be important to impress on these staff members that the crisis groups that I form help the child in crisis rather than providing long-term therapy. With regard to the power relationships between agencies, the major snare seems to be the doctors' autonomy. The administrators of area psychiatric hopitals may also perceive the group for children as highlighting their own program deficiencies and choose instead to provide a similar service themselves.

At present, the agencies do not consider themselves to be interdependent. Instead, they coexist in separate realms of the psychiatric community and rarely communicate. More positively, though, they may cooperate with this project not only because of the obvious needs of the children but also because child and adult agencies are in fact complementary services in the community that do not usually compete for the same clientele.

To alleviate some of the tension between agencies and to facilitate the common goal of improved community mental health, I will plan individual visits to each hospital's social service department. Possibly I will be invited to present this program to the monthly medical staff meeting, a direct encounter with most of the staff doctors. In addition, I will invite representatives of each hospital to the clinic for an orientation and open house, which should improve relationships between clinic and hospital and emphasize the community nature of the project.

Within the clinic itself, a political process will ensue in the initiation of this program. When Mr. Jones seeks its offical approval, he must submit to the medical director for confirmation; he in turn takes it to the executive committee for approval, and they then present it to the board of directors for final approval. However, since Mr. Jones is the most powerful person in the agency, his approval should lead to its acceptance. A complicating factor is the director of training, Ida Brown. To be candid, she does not particu-

larly like Mr. Jones and often opposes any proposals initiated by him.

She may interfere in the decision-making process by pushing for a nondecision; i.e., she may suggest the plan be initiated only after lengthy study or pending location of special sources of external funding. Further, many in the agency focus on the child as patient, a focus that clashes with the program's preventive mission.

I also see several other groupings developing. One is composed of the senior administrator and the chief of program development (also the director of support services). These two men are allied in their unstated mission of increasing clinic prestige and influence in the community. They will probably support the program from their positions of stated commitment to enriching the quality of service available to the community. This would appear reasonable and underscore the senior administrator's interest in the efficient business operation of the clinic.

The executive director himself will probably support the program in deference to Mr. Jones, to whom he defers on all issues pertaining to the outpatient part of the agency. The outpatient service functions virtually independently from the day treatment and other components of the agency.

The medical director is also a figurehead, whose medical degree is valued by the agency. He will most assuredly remain neutral lest he find himself in the middle of a political battle. He appears to have little power in the agency.

The board of directors also has little power in this agency. They are most concerned with what mural is painted on which wall and how chairs are grouped in the waiting room. Program development is not their expertise, and they usually abide agreeably with decisions made by the executive director.

In implementing this program, Mr. Jones will want a strong evaluation component. A before-and-after study can easily be incorporated into the proposal. The instrument used requires ratings of the child by parent and by therapist. Further, evaluation of parents is possible. Consider a parent whose spouse has just been hospitalized and is left to care for the children alone. Such a parent would almost certainly benefit from receiving some group services.

In the future, I see this program as an integral part of the clinic's services, if it can survive pilot and approval stages. The children served during their first experience with a parent's hospitalization may choose to return themselves for assistance at the time of a rehospitalization. And children who have experienced numerous parental hospitalizations will be able to compare previous episodes with the one eased by clinic services. We may then see self-referrals by children and fami-

lies, reducing the need for referrals by doctors.

Another possibility is the development of similar programs within the area hospitals themselves as part of their social services to families. In this case, the clinic could serve those children whose parents have been recently discharged from the hospital, i.e., after the hospitals have discontinued services. An enlargement of the program is therefore possible to assist the returning parent to readjust to his or her family.

Mr. Jones wants me to assist him in writing the formal proposal after my pilot project has been in operation for five months. The project has made me realize that good clinical skills need to be supplemented by program design and legitimation skills. How else can social workers develop and institutionalize innovative services?

SOURCE: This case is adapted from one developed by Stacy Stern, M.S.W. Names and locations have been altered.

Conceptual Skills

Before they develop strategy, social workers need to be able to identify specific background, political, economic, cultural, and administrative factors that provide the context for specific proposals. These contextual factors allow judgments about the probable ease or difficulty of obtaining approval from decision makers. In policy practice case 6.1, the social work intern decides that she can obtain clearance for her proposal but fears that a number of contextual factors will complicate or even imperil the project. (Because she has identifed those factors, she is able subsequently to devise strategy to offset or counter them.)

On the negative side, she fears that many staff members might object to a proposal that would mandate a preventive program, an approach incongruent with prevailing emphasis by the agency upon curative programs. The scarcity of agency funds as well as their provision by funders who prefer traditional therapy programs is hardly a positive factor. Further, she does not know whether other agencies, much less her

own, will want to enter into collaborative arrangements, given the lack of interagency coordination.

Still, many contextual factors suggest that change is feasible. The agency staff would benefit from prestige associated with development of an innovative project, one that would receive considerable publicity in the network of community mental health agencies and institutions. The project would assist children, a group emphasized by the agency. Initial staffing by a student intern makes the project feasible on a pilot basis. Support for it by an influential staff person, Mr. Jones, is a favorable sign, even if some others in the agency can be predicted to oppose it.

If one conceptual challenge in the legitimation phase is to identify important contextual factors and gauge feasibility, another is to identify relevant power resources that can reduce opposition and increase support. In this case, the social work intern uses various kinds of person-to-person, process, and procedural power resources. She uses persuasion with her preceptor and her field instructor (person-to-person power). Were she able to find research studies or descriptions of similar projects elsewhere, she might achieve even more credibility. Although the matter is not mentioned in this case, she becomes acquainted with the agency executive because he is often present in the agency when she holds a special evening group. Indeed, at a key juncture, she speaks with him about her work on the project for children. Even during its pilot phase, the student intern hopes that knowledge about it will subsequently lead him to support its expansion and formalization. Social workers should be particularly adept at using person-to-person power because they possess knowledge of psychosocial factors; i.e., they can decide what kinds of person-to-person power are likely to be effective with specific persons.

The social work intern uses process power when she decides to implement a pilot project collaboratively with Mr. Jones before trying to secure high-level agency approval for an ongoing project. In light of the traditional nature of agency programs and probable resistance to a preventive program, this choice may be a wise one, even if it means a substantial delay before official sanction is sought. She also chooses to initiate the project proposal with a person who has substantial power in the agency, Mr. Jones.

Practical realities during the legitimation phase should be noted. In many cases, social workers do not know with great certainty how a proposal will be received by key decision makers. Projects are often launched even when their initiators do not feel that they can gauge their political feasibility; indeed, some policy practitioners may err on the side of caution by not taking risks. No one likes to be associated with a losing cause, but many good ideas would never be tested if all persons waited until they believed success to be certain.

Furthermore, conceptual work continues throughout the legitimation phase. Although social workers may try to gauge feasibility before launching a proposal, they often need to make new estimates and develop new strategies as the proposal moves toward and through decision arenas. In some cases, unexpected sources of opposition develop that need to be addressed in the give-and-take of political interaction. In many cases, strategy plans have to be drastically changed in response to the actions of others. A social worker may believe, for example, that a specific policy can be legitimated in low-conflict, behind-the-scenes deliberations but may decide to use a conflictual strategy when others launch a public and emotional attack against the proposal.

Value Clarification Skills

The student intern in policy practice case 6.1 wrestles with a variety of ethical dilemmas commonly confronted in the legitimation phase. She wants to develop and secure high-level sanction for a preventive project and suffers misgivings when she decides to portray it as a pilot crisis intervention project. It is difficult to decide in many cases whether, when, and to what extent to dilute or modify proposals during the legitimation phase. On the one hand, social workers often want to obtain legitimation for policies as they ideally prefer them to be but realize, on the other hand, that this approach can imperil approval. Two kinds of errors are possible, errors that virtually all practitioners will make at one time or another. First, policy practitioners may underestimate the extent of real opposition and not make sufficient compromises to secure passage, an error that can lead to post mortem guilt about having wanted too much. Second, they many overestimate opposition and prematurely accept compromises, an error that can lead to guilt about excessive timidity. These kinds of errors are commonly made because of the intrinsic difficulty of predicting the nature and extent of opposition to specific proposals. Either error is preferable to a third, however—excessive caution that leads to noninitiation of any proposal when a social worker believes that existing policies are clearly defective.

The social work intern must also ponder ethical issues associated with implementation of her political strategies. She wonders, for example, whether it is ethical to initiate a proposal with her preceptor prior to informing her field supervisor—or whether behind-the-scenes development of an informal strategy with Mr. Jones somehow violates canons of openness, which she values. (He specifically advises her not to inform others about their intention to secure official agency sanction for the program because he fears that agency opposition might be aroused.)

As she thinks about these issues, she begins to develop some ethical resolutions based on her own ethical reasoning. Outright lying or deception is rarely warranted, she decides, and can often be counterproductive. But canons of honesty do not require divulging information to others when they do not specifically solicit it. In this instance, her decision not to inform other staff members does not constitute an ethical transgression, she decides, although she does conclude that her student role obliges her to discuss the project with her field instructor. (She might find herself in an ethical quandary if she believes that her field instructor would rally opposition to the project.) A distinction can be made, she decides, between acts of commission and acts of omission. Acts of commission include deliberate falsification and lying; acts of omission include decisions not to divulge information. In the latter case, Mr. Jones's warning not to tell seems ethically justified in light of potential opposition to the project within the agency.

In ethical reasoning during the legitimation phase, then, social workers have to decide whether specific actions violate ethical principles. As in value clarification in other phases, some issues require complex balancing of alternative values. Approval of a specific policy that will, it is believed, ultimately help consumers may require certain actions that violate ethical principles of openness or candor. In some instances, resolution is relatively simple; in others, social workers need to make difficult choices. Frank discussion of options with a trusted colleague can assist ethical decisions during the legitimation phase.

Interactional Skills

Strategy that rests on a good conceptual base can hardly succeed if proponents lack interpersonal skills. If the social work intern were unable to obtain Mr. Jones's support for the project, she probably would not have much chance of obtaining eventual approval for the proposal. Social workers often develop, staff, and participate in coalitions in agency, community, or legislative settings. Many persons are reluctant to join specific coalitions, however, because they fear that they could become locked into a course of action, become associated with a losing cause, or be required to commit extensive time to coalition meetings. Sometimes coalitions experience internal conflict when persons compete for leadership or disagree about policies and political strategy. When membership is heterogeneous in values and interests and leadership is weak, inordinate time can be spent developing goals and strategy. In some cases, leaders of coalitions take positions without fully consulting membership, a practice that can quickly undermine group confidence in its leaders.

Even with these problems, coalitions stemming from collective action for (or against) specific policies are invaluable in developing power resources. Coalitions allow persons and interests to pool their power resources and to increase their chances of success. Though most obvious in community and legislative settings, coalitions can be important in agencies as well. In policy practice case 6.1, for example, Mr. Jones might decide to establish a task force to explore program options for the families of institutionalized patients. This task force might then lead to a broad base of internal support for programs like the one initiated by the social work intern. Alternatively, an advocate of mental health patients could initiate a community coalition to pressure mental health agencies to devise programs for this population, perhaps working in conjunction with the local mental health association.

Political Skills

No matter what the setting, social workers who try to obtain support for specific proposals must often decide what level of conflict or controversy is most likely to enhance their success. In many cases, they use nonconflictual strategies if they fear controversy will lead to activation of powerful opponents who become alerted to a specific issue. In policy practice case 6.1, the social work intern and Mr. Jones decide that a low profile is needed. Low-conflict strategies also have the advantage of not usually requiring the investment of time and resources and the jeopardizing of personal relationships often associated with conflictual strategies.

In some cases, however, social workers decide that they have to incite controversy. Someone may believe that change is needed but that high-level and powerful persons systematically impede any departures from existing policies. Particularly when they believe that important issues are at stake, social workers may believe that they have no ethical alternative to conflictual strategies. In community and agency settings, many trade unionists, tenant organizers, and civil rights groups often adopt confrontive strategies to publicize issues and mobilize constituencies. In some cases, social workers incite controversy even when they believe imminent successes are not likely, since they perceive controversy to be an educational tool that is needed to sensitize others to important issues.

Decisions about the use of low- or high-conflict strategies require ethical reasoning in the context of political realities. Use of conflictual strategies can pose personal risks because social workers may encounter the ill will of superiors who resent confrontation. In some cases, moderate-conflict strategies can be used, strategies commonly associated with negotiation, in which contending interests try to fashion policy settlements in a give-and-take atmosphere. Yet some issues require confrontive strategies, and social workers may need to use them on occasion.

Political skills are required to implement low-, moderate-, and high-conflict strategies. In policy practice case 6.1, for example, the social worker uses substantive and process power resources to minimize controversy. She does not use emotionally charged words, portray the project as a radical departure from existing policy, or try to "open up the issue" by including many persons in the political process.

Position-taking Skills

The social work intern used various kinds of person-to-person, process, and procedural

power resources in policy practice case 6.1. Position-taking skills require use of substantive power; i.e., power that derives from using arguments and positions that are effective in obtaining support from a specific audience. She uses substantive power when she portrays the project as a pilot project that emphasizes crisis intervention services. She believes that opposition might increase if she labels it as a major or preventive program. Were the proposal to come before the agency's board, care would need to be taken to present it as an innovation that would be perceived in positive rather than threatening terms; thus, emphasis could be placed upon the positive effects of the new program for the agency, including its utility in increasing referrals to ongoing clinical programs of the agency. Details of proposed interventions with the families could be highlighted to a professional audience with use of supportive social science and professional theory.

SUMMARY

During the legitimation phase in agency, community, and legislative settings, policy options are considered for collective approval. The legitimation phase can be better understood if placed in the context of background factors, political and economic realities, and cultural and value considerations. These various contextual factors influence the kinds of strategies chosen by social workers who seek reforms.

Sources, direction, and amount of external pressures shape policy choices of decision makers in agency and legislative arenas. The prognosis for specific policy reforms usually improves as intense positive external pressures predominate and as proposals are not associated with polarization between parties or factions. Many political and economic realities also influence outcomes during legitimation. The prognosis for specific proposals usually increases as strategically placed persons favor them, procedural realities do not give opponents numerous possibilities to defeat them, and proponents successfully choose procedural options that minimize opposition.

Cultural and value factors are also important, as reflected in the predisposing orientations of key decision makers. The prognosis for specific proposals usually improves as such decision makers attach importance to them and associate them with win-win rather than win-lose politics.

When gauging the feasibility of a proposal as a prelude to developing strategy, social workers engage in a diagnostic process that combines information about background, political, economic, and value factors. When developing political strategy, skillful practitioners recognize the existence of multiple power resources, including person-to-person, process, procedural, and substantive power. When developing strategy game plans, these practitioners avoid both overconfidence and underconfidence, overassertiveness and underassertiveness. They make balanced use of conflict and recognize that effective strategy requires development of potential power resources. Finally, as in other policy phases, social workers who wish to participate effectively in legitimation need interactional, conceptual, political, position-taking, and value clarification skills.

Key Concepts, Developments, and Policies

Ethical issues
Sources of external pressure
Amount of external pressure
Direction of external pressure
Polarization
Power realities
Pluralists
Elitists
Procedural realities
Predisposing orientations
Salience
Win-win politics
Win-lose politics

Gauging feasibility
Power resources
Sources of power
Person-to-person power
Process power
Procedural power
Substantive power
Strategy or game plans
Overconfidence and underconfidence
Overassertiveness and underassertiveness
Balanced use of conflict
Potential power
Practice in the legitimation phase

Main Points

1. Ethical issues pertaining to the definition of policy objectives and strategies must be addressed and resolved during participation in the legitimation phase.

2. The legitimation phase, during which binding or collective choices are made, is crucial to policy development.

3. Sources, intensity, and direction of external pressures on important decision makers must be analyzed when gauging the feasibility of specific proposals.

4. Many issues are associated with polarization between competing factions. A number of factors determine why some and not other issues are associated with high levels of conflict.

5. Political and economic realities, including matters of power and procedure, influence legitimation outcomes.

6. In an examination of the predisposing orientations of key decision makers, it is important to assess how much importance, or

salience, they attach to an issue and whether they associate it with win-win or win-lose politics.

7. The feasibility of securing passage of a specific policy proposal is determined by combining various kinds of information about background, cultural, and value factors and about political and economic realities.

8. Power resources are used to facilitate passage of a proposal, i.e., to induce others to engage in activities or take positions that they would not normally have taken.

9. Many varieties of power exist, including person-to-person, process, procedural, and substantive power.

10. Strategy or game plans are developed as persons plan a set of coordinated and sequenced activities that are adapted to political realities.

11. Various dangers need to be avoided when developing strategy, including underconfidence and overconfidence, overassertiveness and underassertiveness, indiscriminate use of conflict, and failure to develop potential power.

12. Multiple practice skills are needed in the legitimation phase.

Questions for Discussion

1. Review case example 6.1, assuming the role of persons defending housing subsidies for low-income consumers. What favorable or unfavorable background factors did they encounter in terms of the source, amount, and direction of external pressure? What favorable or unfavorable political and economic realities did they encounter, including those related to power and procedure? What favorable or unfavorable value or cultural factors did they encounter in terms of salience and the orientations of key decision makers?

2. What kinds of person-to-person, process, procedural, and substantive power resources did advocates of low-income housing subsidies use in case example 6.1?

3. In case example 6.3, discuss the strategy or game plan of the Democrats. Comment in particular on their reasons for deciding to use low-conflict strategies. Did their strategy seem to be advisable?

4. Discuss the statement "Social workers are often uncomfortable with power and often think that its acquisition and use are extraneous to professional practice."

5. In some agency or organization with which you are familiar, discuss the feasibility of obtaining collective approval for a specific policy

reform or change that you have identified. What options exist in terms of the kind of game or strategy plan you might devise?

6. In the preceding question, discuss kinds of policy skills you might need if you were to seek legitimation for the policy reform.

7. In policy practice case 6.1, discuss the following dilemmas, tasks, and realities encountered by social workers during the legitimation phase:
   a. It is often difficult to predict in the early stages whether a specific project is feasible.
   b. "It is difficult to decide in many cases whether, when, and to what extent to dilute or modify proposals during the legitimation phase."
   c. Social workers sometimes overestimate opposition and prematurely accept compromises.
   d. "Strategy that rests on a good conceptual base can hardly succeed if proponents lack interpersonal skills."
   e. Coalitions are often difficult to form and maintain.
   f. In many cases, social workers use low-conflict strategies if they fear controversy will lead to activation of powerful opponents.

Suggested Readings

Bachrach, Peter, and Baratz, Morton. *Power and Poverty* (New York: Oxford University Press, 1970). The introductory chapters of this book provide a discussion of power and of the intricacies of the decision-making process.

Brager, George, and Holloway, Stephen. *Changing Human Service Organizations* (New York: Free Press, 1978). The authors discuss concepts and strategies relevant to efforts to change policies in agency or organizational settings, using many examples from social work practice.

Coplin, William, and O'Leary, Michael. *Everyman's Prince* (North Scituate, Mass.: Duxbury, 1976). The authors provide useful information about methods of gauging the feasibility of specific policy proposals.

Deutsch, Morton. *The Resolution of Conflict* (New Haven: Yale University Press, 1973): pp. 351–400. Controversy and attendant conflict is not inevitable in social welfare policy but is more likely when associated with various factors, which are discussed by Deutsch.

Freeman, Jo. "Resource Mobilization and Strategy: A Model for Analyzing Social Movement Organization Actions." In Mayer Zald and John McCarthy, eds., *The Dynamics of Social Movements* (Cambridge, Mass.: Winthrop, 1979): pp. 167–190. Political strategies used by community-based social movements are analyzed, strategies relevant to efforts by feminist and other cause-oriented groups that seek fundamental changes in social policies.

French, John, and Raven, Bertram. "The Bases of Social Power." In Dorwin Cartwright and Alvin Zander, eds., *Group Dynamics: Research and Theory* (New York: Harper & Row, 1968): pp. 259–269. A classic article that discusses coercive, expertise, and other forms of person-to-person power.

Patti, Rino, and Dear, Ronald. "Legislative Advocacy: Seven Effective Tactics." *Social Work*, 26 (July 1981): 289–297. Practical suggestions are provided for enhancing support of specific legislative proposals.

Peabody, Robert, et al. *To Enact A Law* (New York: Praeger, 1972). The authors provide an excellent introduction to legislative politics.

Redman, Eric. *The Dance of Legislation* (New York: Simon & Schuster, 1973). A first-person account of the intricacies of obtaining passage of a policy proposal in Congress.

Schattschneider, Eric. *The Semisovereign People* (New York: Holt, Rinehart and Winston, 1960). A classic and concise discussion of the nature of the political process.

Notes

1. Brager and Holloway, *Changing Human Service Organizations*, pp. 25–28, 141–146.

2. Schattschneider, *The Semisovereign People*, pp. 1–46.

3. Dear and Patti, "Legislative Advocacy."

4. Yeheskel Hasenfeld, "The Implementation of Change in Human Service Organizations: A Political Economy Perspective," *Social Service Review*, 54 (December 1980): 508–521.

5. Coplin and O'Leary, *Everyman's Prince*.

6. Deutsch, *The Resolution of Conflict*, pp. 351–400.

7. See Warren Miller and Donald E. Stokes, "Constituency Influence in Congress," *American Political Science Review*, 57 (March 1963), 45–56.

8. Richard Fenno, *The Power of the Purse* (Boston: Little Brown and Co., 1966), pp. 390–413.

9. C. Wright Mills, *The Power Elite* (New York: Oxford University, 1956).

10. See Robert A. Dahl, *Pluralist Democracy in the United States* (Chicago: Rand McNally, 1967), and Banfield, *Political Influence* (New York: Free Press, 1961).

11. Lewis Froman, *The Congressional Process: Strategies, Rules, and Procedures* (Boston: Little Brown, 1967).

12. Brager and Holloway, *Changing Human Service Organizations*, pp. 157–192.

13. Coplin and O'Leary, *Everyman's Prince*.

14. Ibid., pp. 16–17.

15. Deutsch, *The Resolution of Conflict*, pp. 351–400.

16. See Coplin and O'Leary, *Everyman's Prince*.

17. The concept *power* is discussed by Bachrach and Baratz, *Power and Poverty*, pp. 17–38.

18. See John French and Bertram Raven, "The Bases of Social Power," pp. 259–269.

19. Nancy Humphreys, "Competing for Revenue-Sharing Funds: A Coalition Approach," *Social Work*, 24 (January 1979): 14–20.

20. Varieties of procedural power are discussed by Lewis Froman, *The Congressional Process: Strategies, Rules, and Procedures.*

21. Substantive power involves not only the content of policy positions but also the style of presentation. See Milan J. Dluhy, "Policy Advice-Givers: Advocate? Technicians? or Pragmatists?," in Tropman et al., eds., *New Strategic Perspectives* (New York: Pergamon, 1981), pp. 202–217.

22. Alternative political strategies are discussed by Brager and Holloway, *Changing Human Service Organizations*, pp. 129–152.

CHAPTER 7

The Implementation Phase: Troubleshooting Operating Programs

Many policies fail because they rest on a poor conceptual base, e.g., on faulty definitions of social problems in the scanning phase. In many cases, however, shortcomings can be attributed to organizations, staff, and resources associated with their implementation. Sometimes reformers achieve pyrrhic victories when their legislative gains are subsequently sabotaged during implementation. Social workers need to:

Understand ethical issues that commonly arise during the implementation phase

Be able to identify indicators that suggest that operating programs are defective

Understand a range of background, political, economic, and ideological factors that influence implementation processes

Identify various high-level or societal factors that impede implementation of specific policies

Identify various regional and agency factors that impede implementation of specific policies

These various topics are discussed in this chapter. At the end of the chapter, a policy practice case is presented to illustrate the troubleshooting activities of a social worker in a social agency.

Case example 7.1 discusses implementation issues of a state agency that funds programs for the aging. Critics allege that implementation processes are so flawed that many consumers receive inadequate services, an allegation challenged by the director of the agency. The various controversial issues presented in this case often arise during the implementation process.

ETHICAL ISSUES IN IMPLEMENTATION

Personal policy preferences of professionals are often at variance with official policies, as when official policies are perceived to be harmful to consumers. Social workers often dislike deterrent policies, i.e., those that focus on controlling and punishing consumers who are perceived to violate social norms. Few would argue that penalties, sentences, and withdrawal of assistance are never needed, but application of deterrence to consumers who are innocent victims, as in the case of many unemployed welfare recipients, can be questioned on both ethical and pragmatic grounds. Critics of deterrence in welfare policy

---

CASE EXAMPLE 7.1

How Well Is California Providing Services for the Aged?

Mystery of the Missing Millions

By Hal Rubin

Every year there are 400,000 more Americans over the age of 65 than there were the year before. In California, 10 percent of today's population is 65 or older. And if current projections are correct, one-fourth of all Californians will be over age 60 four decades from today.

Such statistics suggest one reason why senior citizens' political clout is growing, both in Sacramento and Washington. Another reason is that they are proportionately better voters than their children and grandchildren. Any proposal for aiding the elderly is difficult for a politician to oppose. For example, there are about 100 different state programs benefiting older people in one way or another, administered by 42 various departments and agencies.

But the agency directly responsible for helping the elderly with their nonmedical needs is the Department of Aging (CDA) in the Health and Welfare Agency. Relatively small (115 positions) by bureaucratic standards, the CDA nevertheless has an ever-growing supply of federal dollars to spend on its programs. In 1971–72, the department received a modest $680,000 from Washington; by 1975–76 it was getting $20 million; and in 1980–81 it will get $66 million.

So rapidly have the federal dollars grown, in fact, that CDA is apparently unable to spend them all. In hearings this summer, legislators heard again of an embarrassing surplus of millions of dollars which have been allocated for programs for the California aged—mainly in nutrition services—but never spent. Even though federal policy requires its grants to the department to be spent in the fiscal year allocated, Washington has been reluctant to take back its unused dollars. The political backlash when even one feed-the-aged program closes is enough to discourage federal bureaucrats from leaning too heavily on the Sacramento department.

Ironically, this political sensitivity to the powerful senior citizens' lobby may be a major reason why the state's elderly are not better served by the CDA. Despite years of problems and charges of mismanagement, the department and its senior-citizen director, Janet J. Levy, age 66, seem almost immune from significant efforts at reform, either by state officials or Washington purse-string holders.

A Curious Relationship

Here is how this curious relationship has developed:

CDA is charged with receiving and administering funds allocated to the state under the federal Older Americans Act. Passed in 1965, this act is intended to help older people secure equal opportunity to acquire suitable housing, adequate income, restorative services, job opportunities and a dignified retirement. The act emphasizes maximum independence and dignity in a home environment for older persons capable of self-care with appropriate supportive action. Effort is made to keep seniors out of institutions, and special attention is given to the "vulnerable" elderly—those with the greatest economic or social needs.

The performance of the CDA in pursuing these goals has been drawing fire for years. The agency responsible for California's elders went through five reorganizations and as many directors between 1967 and 1975, before it settled down under its current director.

California gets 11 percent of the Older Americans Act appropriation according to a formula based on the state's percentage of persons over 60. Nutrition services account for a major portion of the spending: $37.6 million during 1979 for 50,000 daily meals for the elderly—an average of $2.89 a meal. The federal share was $1.84; the remaining $1.05 came from local sources, including county funds. Older persons may voluntarily contribute all or part of the cost of a meal. About 12 percent of the meals were home-delivered and the rest were served in a group setting.

Other services provided by the CDA include subsidized employment in community activities for low-income elderly (the Senior Companion Program and the Foster Grandparent Program), financial assistance for the purchase and renovation of community senior centers, transportation, training, information referral services and other programs. The department's current budget includes $3.1 million from state funds, in addition to the federal and local sources.

The CDA negotiates thousands of individual grants with contractors and subcontractors throughout the state's 33 planning and service areas. The local-level network involves 15 Area Agencies on Aging (Triple A's). Eighteen more Triple A's will be added next month in response to federal requirements.

On the federal level, the CDA is monitored from San Francisco by Region IX of the Administration on Aging in the Department of Health and Human Services, formerly HEW. On the state level is the California Commission on Aging, composed of 25 members appointed by the governor, the speaker of the Assembly, and the Senate Rules Committee. It acts in an advisory capacity to the CDA and serves as the principal state advocate in behalf of older persons. Rounding out the bureaucracy is the Assembly Committee on Aging, with Norman Waters as chairman. Waters succeeded Henry J. Mello in April.

Since Levy took over at CDA six years ago, she has been questioned and criticized regularly on dozens of fiscal, accounting and management issues. Everyone from the federal Administration on Aging to the Assembly members on the Aging committee have taken swipes at Levy's department—but little change has occurred, and the federal dollars keep growing.

Charges against the CDA include:

Delayed reporting procedures. During the past two fiscal years CDA reports were late in all eight reporting periods, and their contents failed to indicate that past inadequacies had been corrected.

Inadequate information. "The department is

not getting timely information to make some very basic management decisions about allocations of funds," says John F. McCarthy, regional program director for the federal Aging Administration. "We think they should know exactly what has been expended by all projects in the state, so they can judge if people are meeting the expected operational level of the program—and not finding out about it three to five months later."

Huge unspent allocations. Estimates differ, but CDA critics agree that millions of dollars have been sent to California in recent years, and that CDA has only made a dent in spending them. . . .

How big is the department's surplus? The auditor general reports that between 1974 and 1979, CDA received $157.6 million for nutrition and social services and spent $132 million, leaving an unexpended balance of $25.6 million. In February 1979 the CDA estimated its unexpended balance at only $3.1 million. But in November CDA's estimate was revised to $11.2 million, and in December it raised the estimate to $15.5 million.

The legislative analyst's office has said that the CDA has not yet demonstrated a capacity to spend its annual allocation of federal funds. Because it has failed to comply with federal reporting deadlines and because its accounting and reporting systems are still inadequate, CDA could lose its federal funding in the future, the analysts have warned.

Inadequate programs. The Health Committee of the California Commission on Aging reported recently that the CDA nutrition program is performing poorly. "Continued fiscal conservatism on the part of the department not only ignores the needs of many older persons, but also calls into question California's need for federal funds that it cannot or will not spend," the committee charged. "It (the CDA) has discouraged the use of federal funds for expanded home-delivered meals."

John Riggle, executive secretary of the Commission on Aging, says such fiscal conservatism punishes the homebound elderly, who are among the most needy. More than 20 other states, operating the kind of nutrition service they were directed to provide, got additional funds when they ran out, according to Riggle. If the CDA does not spend what has been allocated, Congress concludes there is less need among the elderly in California, he says.

Last June the auditor general reported to the Joint Legislative Audit Committee that many of the state's nutrition programs were also operating in violation of health and safety codes. The standards most frequently violated included improper food preparation, improper sanitation in food storage and preparation, and improper sanitation in the distribution of meals. . . .

Scandals and abuses. A 1980 General Accounting Office review of contracts granted by the CDA revealed other problems. The Rio Hondo Action Council had its contract terminated and went out of business amid allegations of fraud and misuse of funds. A contractor involved with community housing did not provide the required services and failed to refund more than $44,000 due from a prior contract. . . .

The Older Americans Act prohibits means testing because the act is not intended to operate as a welfare program and its services are not restricted to those with incomes below the poverty line. Other than for nutrition, the act does not specifically provide for contributions for services. But that has not stopped some contractors. In Los Angeles County last year, six of 26 grantees had a means test or eligibility criteria that limited program participation by the elderly. This year four were still using a means test. A contractor who ran a bus service for the elderly was charging a fare of 75 cents while operating a federally funded transportation service.

Lack of mission. Critics in and out of the Commission on Aging charge that the CDA has followed passive and conservative policies and that its lack of advocacy is behind many of its problems.

Levy's Responses

To all of these charges, Levy responses are consistent: There are no missing millions of dollars—only allocated funds that have not yet been spent. The problems with contractors are minor and generally caused by flawed management at the local level. And most of the criticism of her department is politically motivated.

The issue of surplus dollars is exaggerated, she insists. "Ever since the Department of Aging was established six years ago, there has been a persistent but erroneous myth that there exists a large and readily available treasure chest of surplus nutrition funds that the CDA is somehow unwilling to release." It is true, she says, that since 1973 "the influx of money was more than the Aging network

could absorb at one time." And because some local programs were not able to spend all the money allocated to them, the accrued funds piled up. . . .

Some of the department's problems resulted from a lack of staff, Levy says, and most of them were inevitable but temporary growing pains. Yet late in July Levy came under fire again when the CDA refused to provide financial help to keep open the Sacramento Senior Health Day Care Center. When pressure was applied by Governor Brown's office and area legislators, money was found in the CDA budget. The *Sacramento Bee* commented editorially, "The incident brings to light troubling attitudes and policies that transcend Sacramento's program . . . More fundamentally it raises questions about the very purpose of the Department of Aging when it becomes the obstacle instead of the advocate and provider of services articulating the needs of the aging." . . .

SOURCE: *California Journal,* September 1980, 361–363. Reprinted by permission.

argue, for example, that rolls can best be reduced by providing jobs and training rather than by punishing recipients.

Professionals may also disagree with official policies on any of the seven core issues discussed in chapters 1 and 2. For example, they may disagree with the priority given specific social problems in an agency (core issues 1 and 2), with policies that prescribe certain interventive approaches (core issue 3), with specific eligibility policies (core issue 4), or with specific policies that shape agency decision making and program evaluation (core issues 6 and 7).

Ethical dilemmas often arise when personal policy preferences are at variance with official policies; possible ways of resolving such dilemmas are various. Some staff members grit their teeth and *implement disliked policies* even while seeking to change them. Alternatively, avoidance, undermining, and confronting strate-

gies are used. In *avoidance* approaches, agencies decline funds and staff members avoid roles that require implementation of disliked policies. Staff members may resign when they are in basic disagreement with prevailing policies. In *confronting* approaches, staff members openly criticize official policies even at risk of sanctions such as demotion or loss of employment. In *undermining* approaches, they create conditions or take actions that sabotage implementation of disliked policies, as when staff members overlook or do not obtain information that would disqualify a consumer from a program.[1]

Social workers encounter difficult issues when deciding which strategy to use. At what point does halfhearted compliance constitute outright and perhaps illegal defiance? In what circumstances can compliance be questioned as unethical? When should social workers risk their jobs to criticize policy? Answers to these questions depend on the nature of the objection to formal policy, on personal and professional values, and on the likelihood that prevailing policies can be changed.

DEFECTS IN OPERATING PROGRAMS

Professionals scrutinize operating programs as a prelude to deciding whether changes need to be made in their policies, funding, or administration. Defects in implementation often exist when there is a lack of correspondence between official and implemented policy, when excessive variations exist in programs funded by the same source, and when programs are ineffective or inefficient.

Correspondence of Official and Implemented Policy

Discrepancies often exist even when official policy is unambiguous. In case example 7.1, some providers choose to use means tests when serving elderly consumers even when these are prohibited by high-level policy. Such discrepancies can stem from many factors. Providers may not be acquainted with the content of legislation or regulations, they may lack resources or skills, or they may choose not to implement policies that are not monitored by funders. Whatever their causes, discrepancies between official and implemented policy often suggest that policy reforms are needed.[2]

Variability in Implementation

Official policies established by county, state, or national legislatures are not always implemented in similar fashion by all providers. Many studies suggest that the operating programs of different providers differ significantly even when they receive funds from the same source. Such variability is not necessarily an evil, since providers need to be able to tailor programs to the specific needs of their consumers. A staff that implements a nutritional program in an area with sub-

stantial numbers of home-bound senior citizens, for example, may emphasize meals-on-wheels services, whereas a staff in another jurisdiction may place more emphasis on out-of-home (i.e., congregate) nutritional programs.

Still, variability often suggests defects in implementation. Existence of sexism, racism, or agism among local officials may cause restrictive policies in some jurisdictions, and some rural or inner-city jurisdictions may lack the fiscal resources or professional staff to implement policies specified in national legislation.[3]

Program Efficiency

Providers are subject to criticism when they waste scarce program resources. In case example 7.1, critics allege that the state department of aging did not invest sufficient resources in program monitoring to prevent misuse of funds. In other cases, providers devote excessive funds to overhead costs.

More difficult to assess than wastage is the extent to which providers fail to focus resources on consumers who truly need services or program benefits. In the case of a mental health agency that focuses services exclusively on relatively affluent consumers, few would deny that these consumers need assistance, but serious questions could be raised about the exclusion of low-income or multiproblem clients. Such misdirection of resources may occur because staff members do not like to work with certain kinds of consumers, refuse to modify helping techniques to the needs of specific groups, or do not develop outreach programs to locate consumers who might not otherwise use programs.

Program Effectiveness

Programs may not effectively address the social problems of consumers for reasons not specifically related to implementation. Perhaps official policies devised in national legislation require deterrent services that do not meet the basic needs of consumers. Or perhaps, insufficient funds are allocated to allow local providers to develop quality services. Nevertheless, implementation realities also contribute to the ineffectiveness of certain programs. Staff members may lack required skills, for example, or they may not invest themselves in their work because their morale is low.

OVERVIEW OF IMPLEMENTATION

A central task of professionals who assume a troubleshooting role during the implementation phase, then, is to identify defects in operating programs and to locate factors that cause those defects. A variety of background, political, economic, and ideological or value factors influence troubleshooting activities of staff and executives, as portrayed in illustration 7.1.

Background Factors

Funding and policy, basic inputs in the implementation process, provide both opportunities and restrictions to implementers. Limits are established through the procedural, eligibility, organizational, and service prescriptions that usually accompany funds from government or private sources. An agency providing services mandated by the federal Older Americans Act, for example, is limited by official restrictions contained in the legislation as well as by administrative and policy guidelines issued by federal officials charged with distributing funds available under the act. When federal funds are channeled through state or local agencies, as illustrated in case example 7.1, state or local officials

ILLUSTRATION 7.1　An Overview of the Implementation Phase

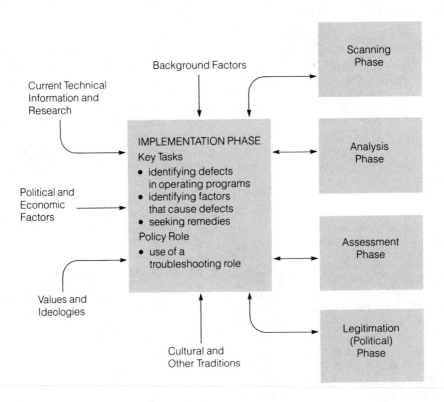

also issue policy guidelines. Further, activities of providers are restricted by the amount of funds provided them by government and other sources, especially in periods of funding cutbacks.

However, the extent to which providers are restricted by government policy varies. In the case of the federally funded Food Stamps program, for example, policy restrictions are so numerous and detailed that providers have little discretion; restrictions define in precise terms who is eligible, the amount of food subsidies, and procedures to be used in determining eligibility. In other cases, the funds given agencies have relatively few strings attached. Federal authorities, for example, may provide monies for services to home-bound elderly persons but give agency providers considerable discretion regarding the content of services.

Political and Economic Realities

Implementation of specific policies is uncertain if powerful organized interests oppose them (see guest editorial 7.1).[4] As an example, federal officials hoped that Medicare would facilitate provision of free medical services to many elderly citizens. During the process of implementation,

however, many physicians charged consumers at rates above the maximum reasonable fees allowed by federal authorities—and then required elderly consumers to pay the difference. (A loophole in the legislation made this permissible, but many officials did not realize how common the practice would become.) In similar fashion, nursing homes, profit-oriented daycare centers, and a host of other interests maintain powerful lobbies in Washington and state capitals that resist efforts to limit their autonomy during implementation of publicly funded programs. Some argue that the prevalence of these interests makes it even more important that legislation be written to clarify minimum standards and policy objectives to empower those who monitor policies.[5]

Value and Ideological Factors

Values influence implementation at numerous points in the process, as illustrated by the orientations of agency staff members, who often share policy preferences that together form "agency mission." These shared preferences and objectives stem from many sources, including program traditions; socialization of new staff; use of agency sanctions (e.g., promotions and pay in-

---

GUEST EDITORIAL 7.1

The Confessions of an Unrepentant Federal Regulator

By Joan Claybrook

My first day on the job—April 8, 1977. It was the beginning of President Carter's bold experiment—appointing public-interest activists rather than the usual industry officials (who pass through the revolving door from industry to government and back to industry) to head the federal regulatory agencies. I was

administrator of the National Highway Traffic Safety Administration.

Would the new crop—from state governments, congressional staffs, consumer and environmental organizations and universities—be shrewd enough to survive the anti-regulatory political pressures? Knowledgeable enough to manage large bureaucracies? Or would the industry beat us down?

The resources, while an improvement over the skimpy funding of the nonprofit organizations I was used to, were insufficient to properly address the massive public health problems of 50,000 highway deaths and 4 million injuries, vehicle and factory exhaust emissions, chemical pollutants choking our rivers and lakes, drugs of questionable safety or efficacy, contaminants in meat, fish and poultry, overuse of pesticides, carcinogenic substances in the workplace, transportation and disposal of toxic materials. And the resources were further limited by the rules, regulations and bureaucratic reviews for managers of government agencies, which far exceed any applied to industry.

Carter's 1982 budget allocated about $2.5 billion, or three-tenths of 1%, of the federal budget for the health-and-safety regulatory agencies to forge remedies or limits for the pervasive threats to public health. (The new Reagan budget has targeted these agencies for cutbacks, seriously inhibiting disease and injury-prevention research for future generations of Americans.)

Members of the Business Roundtable were not pleased with the new breed of regulators Carter appointed. Sid Terry, Chrysler's vice president for public responsibility and consumer affairs, called my nomination "appalling."

Most disturbing to the business community was the new vision we public-interest regulators brought to government. We came with a strong determination to curb industry abuses. Although we favored removal of government price and license regulations that shielded the trucking and airline and communications industries from competition in the marketplace, we would fight for government to play a primary role where the public's health and safety were at stake.

We learned in short order that America's industrial chieftains have a different philosophy. They generally view government through balance-sheet spectacles. Loan guarantees or tax subsidies are welcome; they enhance profits. New requirements from Uncle Sam to prevent harm to the environment or the citizenry, even when they are cost-effective for consumers or valuable in saving lives, are seen simply as a reduction in profits.

During the next four years a struggle took place over who would govern the risks imposed on the public by U.S. manufacturing and commerce: the government regulators or the business executives. The regulated industries launched ferocious attacks on issue after issue to dismantle or delay various health-protection standards: vehicle emissions limits, control of benzene and cotton dust in the workplace, automatic restraint systems in cars, stopping-distance requirements for truck brakes, proper disposal of industrial wastes, labeling of cosmetics and processed food.

Although our statutory assignment was to issue health and safety standards, between the bureaucratic limitations and the corporate critiques we had time to fight for only a few very high-priority issues, those in which major health scourges could be mitigated by available technology. Other important but lower payoff projects had to be abandoned.

Even when we limited our agenda, however, and accommodated the requests for more lead time, the industry would often tactically maneuver to avoid the final implementation of a safety standard. General Motors and Ford accomplished this in their opposition to improved automatic restraints, such as air bags or automatic belts. Since the mid-1970s, when GM produced a few thousand highly successful cars equipped with air bags, consumers have not been able to buy them. The companies have complained about one technical problem after another, all of which have been shown to be fallacious. To further discourage consumer interest, last summer they jacked the price of air bags from $193 in 1977 to between $500 and $800, far above the cost of manufacture. The air bag requirement is scheduled to take effect with 1982 models, but the auto companies have just asked again for it to be reconsidered.

Surviving politically was also a challenge for us newcomers. Even with support in the White House, our programs could be defeated or maimed in Congress unless we could dispel myths and enhance public knowledge of the benefits our programs supplied. I learned to explain auto regulation as follows:

Myth: There is too much regulation.

Reality: In the last 10 years, only three vehicle-safety standards have taken effect which cost consumers more than $10. The existing standards have saved about 70,000 lives and thousands of injuries since 1968, according to the Government Accounting Office. Auto crashes are still the largest killer of Americans under age 34, the largest cause of paraplegia, and a major cause of epilepsy. If all cars had improved occupant restraints, such as air bags or automatic belts, side impact and rollover protection and exteriors less harmful for pedestrians, about 15,000 lives would be saved each year. The necessary technology has been available for more than five years. In fact, the Department of Transportation has an experimental car that is lightweight, fuel efficient and crashes safely at speeds up to 50 m.p.h. It would cost about $7,000 in mass production.

Myth: Regulations stifle innovation.

Reality: The past four years, as the auto industry engineers will tell you, have been the most exciting because the new safety, fuel economy and emissions requirements have challenged their scientific ingenuity. The new systems developed not only save precious lives and fuel, but as the United Auto Workers' president Douglas Fraser has said, also create jobs and are an essential part of our nation's progress.

Myth: Regulations cost too much.

Reality: Like an ounce of prevention, health and safety regulations are an investment in America's future. Auto crashes cost more than $50 billion each year in human and property damage (assuming a human life is valued at only $300,000!). The existing auto safety and bumper standards cost consumers (including profits to industry) about $300 per car, or $3 billion, although the companies indicated in 1976 that they would, on the average, reduce car prices by only about $80 if all the safety standards were removed. Also, without the standards, insurance rates would be increased.

The final scorecard for the public-interest regulators? We were certainly persistent. Most of us completed our full terms in office. We used our political and communications skills to advance our programs. We listened to the regulated industries, but we did not bow to their wishes. Somehow we pushed some safety and advancements through the bureaucratic and political jungle.

Our philosophy is based on the rule of law, which, as Henry Ford III admitted on "Meet the Press" in 1977, was the reason this nation has seen improvements in vehicle safety, fuel economy and emissions. But it was perhaps best expressed by columnist George Will that year when he wrote: "Government exists not merely to serve individuals' immediate preferences, but to achieve collective purposes for an ongoing nation. Government, unlike the free market, has a duty to look far down the road and consider the interests of citizens yet unborn. The market has a remarkable ability to satisfy the desires of the day."

Joan Claybrook was administrator of the National Highway Traffic Safety Administration from 1977 to 1980. SOURCE: This article first appeared in the *Los Angeles Times*. Reprinted by permission of the author.

creases) that reinforce certain kinds of beliefs; and fear that movement in a new direction may lead to practical problems, such as loss of agency funds. Agency mission shapes: attitudes of staff toward the kinds of consumers given preference; helping techniques; the extent to which the agency collaborates with other agencies; and the use of preventive programs. In the example of congregate rather than home-based nutritional programs, organizational mission supportive of home-based services might make agency staff resistant to initiation of congregate services even when those services are favored by funding sources. Or staff members might so resent congregate programs that they would implement them inadequately. Mission, then, is important not only as it leads staff to resist some policies but also as it influences staff investment in particular programs.[6]

It is not easy to modify organizational mission. In some cases, organizational goals change after changes in agency funding and programs. In the case of the Young Men's Christian Association (YMCA) of metropolitan Chicago, change in mission occured only after an innovative executive initiated some pilot projects to assist juvenile delinquents.[7] (Prior to this point, staff and board were unwilling to consider new projects that departed from traditional recreation programs.) In many cases, executives provide a policy model for organizational staff; by emphasizing some and not other policy preferences in program, hiring and promotion, and other decisions, they foster change (or traditionalism) in agency mission. External funders influence internal mission both by mandating specific policies and by monitoring agency programs, particularly when they provide a dominant share of agency resources.

The importance of values and ideology are equally obvious in government settings. As an example, many highly placed officials appointed to various government positions by President Ronald Reagan shared his distrust of the federal government and were thus unwilling to enforce administrative regulations issued by the prior administration. Favored policies and programs receive priority in any presidency, whereas others are relegated to secondary status.

Identifying Obstacles to Implementation

Social workers who believe that specific programs need to be improved must identify factors that detract from program success. In some cases, a specific factor may appear to assume central importance, as when a social worker decides that the staff needs in-service training. In other cases, many obstacles, both internal and external to the agency, contribute to program difficulties. In the following sections of this chapter, macro (government), mezzo (regional), and micro (agency) obstacles are discussed.

OBSTACLES: MACRO FACTORS

Agency staff members and executives are often criticized for providing poor services; however, mandates, resources, and tasks given to them by government authorities often contribute.[8] In addition, government agencies frequently fail to monitor local programs or to provide their staff technical assistance.

Policy Clarity

Official policy can be so vague that providers do not know what is expected of them. In the case of the state department of aging in case example 7.1, critics allege that it often gives funds to local agencies in the absence of detailed policy guidelines. Lack of clarity in official policy contributes to variations in programs that are offered by different agencies and funded from the same source.[9] An example of lack of policy clarity is the mandatory reporting law enacted in California to encourage reporting of child abuse cases. In this instance (see case example 7.2), many jurisdictions do not insist on reporting of cases by local professionals, and widespread variations exist in reporting practices.

Policy Tasks

When official policy prescribes complex tasks, correspondence between official and implemented policy is less likely.[10] Some policy tasks are relatively simple, as when funds are distributed to agencies to provide specified nutritional services to senior citizens. Complex tasks often require the collaboration of a number of agencies and the use of sophisticated technology, as illustrated by legislation prescribing (1) establishment of living centers for the elderly that provide a continuum of living arrangements, extending from independent to nursing home care, and (2)

CASE EXAMPLE 7.2

Child-Abuse Prevention—A $100 Million Failure

Social Service Versus Law Enforcement

By Cynthia Willett

Last year, during the International Year of the Child, the state Legislature joined the worldwide observance by adopting a resolution stating that "freedom from abuse" is a basic right of all children. Yet child neglect and abuse are severe problems in California. Between 60,000 and 70,000 cases are reported to authorities annually; estimates of the actual incidence of child abuse range from four to 12 times higher than that.

But as disturbing as these statistics may be, the state and local systems for dealing with abuse cases constitute an almost equally great cause for concern. Each of California's 58 counties has its own way of handling child abuse—a situation that has led to wide disparity in services provided. "We don't have a statewide system for handling child abuse and neglect cases; we have 58 systems that are basically autonomous," says Michael Wald, former head of the State Advisory Committee on Child Abuse. Contributing to this autonomy has been the state's failure to set concrete guidelines for programs and to enforce minimum standards.

Many of the problems stem from the vaguely written law on mandatory reporting. Enacted in 1963 out of a growing concern over the "battered child syndrome," the law requires certain specified professionals (doctors, teachers and others) to report suspected cases of child abuse or neglect. But the law allows reports to be filed with three different agencies: the local police, the county welfare department's Child Protective Services (CPS) or the juvenile probation department. Whichever agency gets the first report must file it with the police.

And the law also fails to specify how a case should be handled after it's reported. It is unclear which agency should assume primary responsibility. As a result, police and social service agencies traditionally disagree over the way child abuse cases should be handled. Child abuse is a crime and, particularly for the more serious forms of physical and sexual abuse, many officials want to treat it as such. The question is whether rehabilitation or criminal prosecution serves society better.

The mandatory reporting law does nothing to clarify which approach, rehabilitation or punishment, should take precedence. Because of this, the system demands a high degree of cooperation between child-protection workers and law-enforcement personnel. Many counties have established interagency coordinating councils to promote information-sharing and consistency in process. But there are still several counties without such councils. . . .

SOURCE: This is an excerpt from an article that appeared in the *California Journal* (October 1981), pp. 402–403. Reprinted by permission.

provision of financial, recreational, medical, and social services. Regardless of their competence, local providers find that the difficulty of these tasks inhibits correspondence between official and implemented policies.

Requisite Resources

Americans have a penchant for developing programs that have sweeping objectives but are not coupled with the necessary resources. In the absence of necessary staff or facilities, programs often fail. Then, too, technical assistance may not be available to providers. In an extended study of federally funded community mental health centers conducted in the 1970s, for example, researchers found that federal officials gave centers minimal consultative assistance—no wonder then, that such complex tasks as keeping track of and providing services to released mental patients were not implemented.[11] In the case of living centers for the elderly combining a variety of living arrangements and services, cooperation is needed between zoning authorities, federal housing officials who provide rent subsidies, local social service agencies, and hospitals—complex requirements unlikely to be met if technical assistance and sufficient financing are not available.

Transmission of Policy

Complex patterns of transmission can imperil implementation of specific policies. Funds provided under the federal Older Americans Act are often funneled through state departments of aging, which in turn can use local area agencies on aging (AAA's) to develop contracts with specific agencies. In this instance, funds and policies are filtered through four layers of authority; at each point in the transmission process, miscommunication of official policy can occur, and political interests may thwart policies inimical to them. One solution is to reduce the number of different authorities that participate in the policy transmission process by increasing the role of either federal or local authorities.[12]

Then, too, some argue that more resources should be devoted to the monitoring of policy.

Monitoring is a messy business that is often ignored. Sometimes government and other officials do not detect obvious fraud, as in case example 7.1, but minor infringement of policy can be even more difficult to detect. Monitoring often consists of brief visits to projects and inspection of summary statistics, but both provide uncertain sources of evidence, as reflected in the carefully orchestrated testimonials that often greet site visitors or the manipulation of program statistics to make local programs appear to comply with official policy. Even in the case of obviously defective programs, government agencies can be subjected to intense political pressure from agencies and communities when they propose termination or reduction of funding. For maximum impact, monitoring activity should be coupled with technical and consultative assistance to providers in implementing policies.[13]

OBSTACLES: MEZZO BARRIERS

Some critics argue that implementation of policy is frustrated by absence of regional coordinating and planning mechanisms. Many problems arise during implementation of programs, including distribution, access, outreach, and interorganizational difficulties that cannot be addressed by distant state and federal officials and agencies (see table 7.1). Regional bodies have the potential, they argue, to identify some of these problems because of their proximity to local agencies. To be effective, regional authorities need legal mandates, research capabilities, and staff to troubleshoot problems, provide technical services, and initiate programs.[14]

But many regional bodies are underfunded, and local governments and agencies often view them as competitors likely to take from them major policy and funding roles. Regional authorities must contend with myriad programs that have various funding sources beyond the control (or even influence) of regional bodies. In the case of the elderly, funds from the Older Americans Act, including the Meals-on-Wheels program, are channeled through state departments on aging and regional area agencies on the aging. But the latter may have no influence over medical or

TABLE 7.1 Mezzo (Regional) Policy Issues

Selected Issues	Regional Implications
Maldistribution of agencies and staff	Disproportionate program resources are located in specific locations within regions to the detriment of underserved populations.
Referral blockages	Inadequate definition of referral networks so that many consumers do not receive needed services.
Lack of continuity in services	Nonarticulation of sequences or combinations of programs so that the frail elderly and others do not receive a range of services.
Duplications	Inefficiencies derive from unnecessary duplication.
Lack of preventive services	Lack of analysis of regional preventive needs leads to nonimplementation of preventive services.
Inflexibility of services	Lack of identification of populations with unique service needs—with resulting failure to develop innovative or different services for distinctive populations.

housing programs, which are provided by wholly different agencies. Even when they identify serious problems, regional authorities often lack legally prescribed powers to intervene.

OBSTACLES: MICRO FACTORS

When macro and mezzo factors are conducive, implementation of specific policies can still be stymied by local providers. At worst, some agencies flagrantly waste or misuse funds; however, partial or inadequate implementation of policies is more common because of the various intraagency factors presented in the following sections.

Organizational Design

One central problem is to match program tasks with organizations that can effectively implement them.[15] The array of organizations providing services includes self-help organizations, large public agencies, agencies that give staff considerable autonomy, and organizations that develop endless, carefully defined procedures. In the words of the architect Frank Lloyd Wright, "form should follow function"; i.e., organizations should be designed to implement specific kinds of tasks. In the ensuing discussion, merits and problems of bureaucratic and nonbureaucratic models are delineated, as are the kinds of tasks for which they are suited (see table 7.2).

Bureaucratic Organizations. In its technical sense, *bureaucracy* describes specific features of organizations.[16] First, persons within organizations make a distinction between *personal* possessions and interests and *organizational* requirements. Materials purchased by organizations belong to them and not to their staff, just as time on the job is devoted to organizational rather than personal business. Second, bureaucracies commonly link occupational positions to specific

TABLE 7.2 Comparison between Bureaucratic and Nonbureaucratic Models

Selected Organizational Characteristics	Bureaucratic Models	Nontraditional Models
staff participation in decision making	minimal	extensive
specialization in jobs	marked division of labor	emphasis on generic skills and sharing of tasks
use of procedures to routinize work of staff	extensive use of procedures	deemphasis on protocol
centralization	highly centralized	decentralized
use of supervision	supervision emphasized	low-level staff members given extensive leeway in their work

tasks, so that hiring is based in considerable measure on relevant qualifications and skills. (Hiring based on friendship or familial ties is discouraged.) Third, in a *division of labor*, employees commonly develop expertise in particular tasks. In hospitals, for example, pathologists, X-ray technicians, dieticians, and various medical specialists perform specialized tasks in different departments, bureaus, and divisions. Fourth, division of labor is commonly coupled with a *chain of command* that defines the responsibilities of staff. Boards of directors establish overall policy, executives assume key roles in orchestrating organizational activities, and supervisors in a descending hierarchy assume various kinds of roles in monitoring and overseeing the work of staff. Finally, formal procedures and policies evolve to guide staff activities. Procedures are developed, for example, to guide the work of intake staff members in their interaction with consumers, to establish methods of recording information from case interviews, and to regulate the handling and accounting of funds.

Chain of command, division of labor, and formalization of procedures can contribute to implementation problems in bureaucracies. Executives who only talk with high-level staff do not hear the ideas of line staff or consumers except as they come indirectly from their immediate subordinates. The division of labor can lead to excessive specialization by staff members who fail to see general needs of consumers. Formal procedures can discourage staff from individualizing service or making exceptions to formal policy.

But attributes of bureaucracies also have positive consequences. Imagine an organization where employees regularly pilfer organizational sources because they do not distinguish between their personal and organizational lives; where there is no method of systematically conveying policies downward from the board through executives to other staff members; or where, in the absence of a division of labor, staff members do not develop specialized skills required in a technological society. Finally, imagine an organization where staff has to devise procedures *de novo* every time a new issue or situation arises. Although often portrayed as insensitive to consumers, bureaucracies can often be beneficial to them. Formal procedures make it more difficult for staff to deny services on the basis of favoritism or racism. Consumers often want specialized services for particular problems. They also want to be certain that staff members who assist them were hired because they met certain standards of competence.[17]

Although virtually all organizations incorporate various features of bureaucracy, some emphasize them more than others, as illustrated by large public assistance agencies, Social Security offices, and hospitals, where chain of command, specialization, and formalization of procedures are particularly obvious. Some theorists argue that highly bureaucratic organizations may be needed when routine and standardized tasks are required, as in agencies that dispense income to consumers.[9]

Nontraditional Organizations.   In many cases, however, staffs of organizations do not provide standardized services or perform routine tasks. Many social service organizations must adapt services to changing and often unpredictable consumer needs. Further, many consumers need assistance from teams of staff members representing different professions and possessing multiple skills. Some theorists argue that service organizations are required that tend toward the nontraditional models described in table 7.1. In these organizations, staff members participate more extensively in agency decisions, and top-down communication patterns are modified to enhance two-way consultation between various levels of staff. Although characteristics of bureaucracy remain, formalized procedures, specialization, and chain of command are given less emphasis.[18]

Like their bureaucratic counterparts, nontraditional organizations are not problem-free. At one extreme, the staff in a free clinic that lacks any procedures, leadership, or chain of command can spend an inordinate amount of time in endless intraagency meetings and experience confusion about staff roles. But few would argue that a traditional bureaucratic model should be used by all agencies or that some problems encountered by nontraditional organizations could not be decreased if staff and executives incorporated selected bureaucratic characteristics.

Mixed Types.   Both bureaucratic and non-traditional organizational models have their de-

fenders, but a crucial and difficult task is to decide how to combine elements of both in social agencies. In the case of decision making, some theorists argue that neither the direct service nor the administrative staff should dominate, but it is difficult to determine how much staff participation should be encouraged and whether such participation, if carried beyond some threshold, could endanger the organizational stability engendered by the traditional chain of command. These kinds of organizational design questions arise in attempts to develop mixed types of organizations. Perhaps the central challenge is to construct social agencies that retain positive bureaucratic attributes but are softened with nontraditional innovations. Many consumers would benefit as well were they not confronted with excessive regulations, inflexibility, and specialization, not to mention depersonalization of services (see guest editorial 7.2).

Logistical Factors

Programs can suffer from lack of internal planning to facilitate movement of consumers through the service system and coordination of staff. The costs of inadequate logistical planning are often borne by consumers, as illustrated by endless waits in waiting rooms or repeated visits to agencies when services could be provided sequentially on specific days. In the case of services requiring multiple decision and clearance points—e.g., a project to construct innovative living arrangements for elderly consumers—charts need to be developed for sequences of actions and decisions and for allocation of responsibilities.[19]

Structural Factors

Administrators sometimes experiment with innovative ways of structuring organizations to offset effects of specialization. In many traditional bureaucracies, staff is organized into divisions or bureaus on the basis of function. Some agencies, however, organize staff into matrix arrangements in which individual staff members primarily identify themselves with multi-

GUEST EDITORIAL 7.2

Bureaucratic Heart:
Matter of Life and Death

By Joanne Gonzalez

I work at the senior citizen center in Claremont. It's close enough to my home that I can walk to work, and I usually arrive in good spirits. But this Monday morning, the first call I answer makes me so angry that I feel lightheaded.

The caller is a man. His wife's cousin is critically ill. A month ago, they visited with her. She was fine then. She had just retired from her nursing assistant's job at a local hospital and was out and around, seeing friends and so forth. One month later, they found her unconscious in bed, dehydrated, weighing barely 90 pounds.

"How did this happen?" I ask, picturing the wasted body lying alone in the quiet house.

She knew before retiring that her Social Security income would be only $170 a month, so she applied for Supplemental Security Income. She was eligible as far as assets and income were concerned, but the office staff wanted to see three years' worth of bank statements to confirm this. She went home and searched and found only the most recent statements from 1982. But they wanted the statements from 1979, 1980 and 1981. No one at the Social Security office told her that she

could get copies from her bank. Her application for supplemental income was denied.

On April 12, she did two things: She requested, in writing, an appeal of her case, and she stopped eating.

When her relatives found her, they had her rushed to a hospital.

Her cousin's husband was calling for help in applying for power of attorney so that some bills could be paid and legal consent for medical procedures could be given. I gave them a form for her to sign, and I wrote to the Social Security office requesting immediate reconsideration of the denial.

The woman never woke up to sign the paper; she died April 30. She died because she couldn't find three years' worth of paper. She died because she had $170 a month coming in and $38 in her savings account, and the years ahead were too awful to face, and she didn't know how to get help.

I felt that I had failed her. My only comfort is the memory of the people I have helped—the elderly men and women who needed assistance with pages and pages of forms, and the ones I've accompanied to the Social Security office, the place they dread most, next to a nursing home.

The two Social Security offices I've dealt with for 3½ years tend to be staffed by people

---

professional teams rather than with specialized units (see illustration 7.2).[20] Like most innovations, matrix organization is hardly a panacea. Professionals in health settings may miss the stimulation of placement in specialized units, and considerable tension may build between

members of different professions as they vie for leadership or ignore contributions of others. Still, some theorists believe that matrix approaches deserve serious consideration because they foster collaborative efforts between members of different professions.

whose attitude can best be described as sullen. They don't like dealing with a "welfare clientele," which is how they describe people who need supplemental benefits.

"We don't conduct interviews, we conduct interrogations," a a Social Security employee told me.

Calvin M. will never forget that attitude. In 1976, he was declared permanently disabled. He remembers the judge, confirming his eligibility, saying, "You will never again have to worry about how you are going to feed your children." He started worrying, all right, when his disability benefits were cut off in December, 1980; his file was "lost," and no money came in for 15 months.

I appealed the decision, and in response the Social Security Administration wrote to Calvin, who has an artificial hip, walks with a cane and has a useless arm that hangs by his side: "Although you state bending was frequent on your specific job, the work does not usually require a lot of bending. You have the capability needed to work as a machinist."

We asked for a hearing; fortunately, the decision was reversed by an administrative law judge. Calvin and his family got a check for 15 months' back disability benefits.

I have been told that I get too emotionally involved with the people I help. Yes, I do get involved; I really care. Is that wrong? Do people who have been confused by official letters from the Social Security Administration and patronized by sullen clerks need to confront one more cold fish when they find their way to my desk? Sometimes, when I go to the regional offices, I lose my temper. "How can you do these things? How can you ruin people's lives like this?"

These are some responses that I've gotten: "We are not social workers; we are here to administer funds." "This is a pass/fail system: One penny over and you're out." "The nature of the program is not such that humaneness counts."

How can humaneness not count when you are dealing with the frail elderly, with the physically and mentally disabled, the sick, the tired, the survivors of a lifetime of hard work and misfortune? Don't they deserve more than a "pass/fail"?

I want to see some of the regulations changed. I don't like to see an 86-year-old lady told that she will lose her monthly check because she owns a burial plot worth $250. I don't like to see a 92-year-old, crippled with arthritis, told that she will lose her benefits if she doesn't personally come to the Social Security office for a redetermination of her status.

Maybe every Social Security office needs an ombudsman, a liaison, a person who will work on the people's side, to make things easier. Of the Administration's thousands of employees, surely there are enough who still have a heart—people who will squeeze a hand and kiss a cheek, who will really listen, who will say, "I know just what the problem is, and I know how to help you." And mean it.

It's a matter of life and death.

Joanne Gonzalez is director of information and referral for the Senior Citizens Activity Center in Claremont. SOURCE: This article first appeared in the *Los Angeles Times*. Reprinted by permission of the author.

Decision Making

Agency decision-making mechanisms are crucial to implementation of many policies, including use of agency planning and boards. In some cases, agencies cannot implement specific policies because their boards do not favor them or because they lack backup planning capabilities.

Agency Planning. Although governmental and regional planning has been discussed in considerable detail, less attention has been given to

ILLUSTRATION 7.2   Organizational Structure

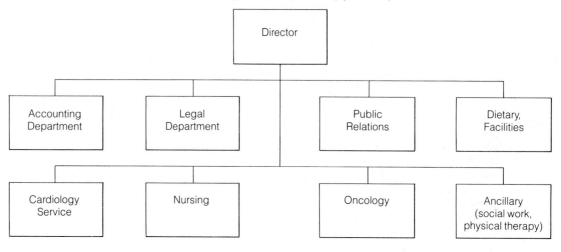

Traditional Organizational Structure (by function)

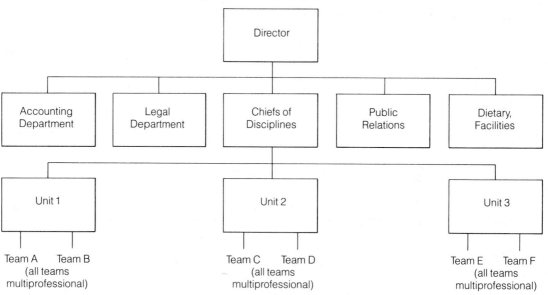

Matrix Organizational Structure (by unit and team)

agency planning. In some cases, absence of planning frustrates inplementation of policies, as illustrated by policies mandating provision of preventive services. Unlike traditional curative or remedial programs, agencies that emphasize prevention must locate consumers who are believed to be at risk but who have not yet developed any or significant social problems—a task requiring collaboration with hospitals, courts, schools, and other community agencies with access to consumers who might benefit from preventive programs. Since methods of providing preventive services are not as fully developed as more traditional curative services, planning is required to develop intervention strategies. Data from a recent research project suggest that agencies with relatively insignificant planning are far less likely to implement preventive services than those with relatively detailed planning—a finding that underscores the importance of planning for implementation of complex tasks.[21]

Agency Boards.   Boards not composed of representatives sympathetic to specific policies are hardly likely to insist on their implementation. For example, many boards place little pressure on staff and executives to implement preventive services because they are more accustomed to traditional clinical services. Many boards in the nonprofit sector are composed of persons influential in the community who may be disinterested in outreach to or services for disadvantaged populations. When public agencies have boards at all—many public executives report directly to higher-level government officials—they may be composed of political appointees who favor politically palatable programs but not major innovations. Even boards composed of talented and innovative citizens may be manipulated by executives who may not keep them fully informed, may insulate them from agency programs, and may limit their recruitment of new members to those unlikely to question prevailing policies.[22]

Agencies can nonetheless improve implementation by making creative use of citizen contributions and by engaging in fund raising. Consumer advisory boards, for example, can be developed to publicize agency programs to underserved groups and to develop new program ideas. Rotation of board membership coupled with deliberate inclusion of a range of citizens from various social classes and ethnic groups can enrich and diversify deliberations. Executives can develop training and decision-making materials to elevate skills and deliberations of boards, but they must first believe that citizen contributions will enhance agency policy.

Staff Factors

Direct service and supervisory staff are crucial to implementation of policies because they provide resources and services to consumers. In many cases, official policies are inadequately implemented because a variety of staff factors are not conducive.

Staff Morale.   Disagreement exists about how to define and measure morale and its implications for implementation. Still, many policies do suffer during implementation because staff members are dissatisfied with their work or their administrators. For example, staff members in a large nursing home for the elderly may receive low wages and believe that owners want to skimp on services to residents in order to increase profits—realities not conducive to high morale. These staff members may experience burnout or may become socialized to prevailing orientations of management. Rapid turnover of staff can also frustrate service delivery.[23]

Many antidotes to low morale have been proposed. A large group of theorists suggests that participatory management may be an antidote to low morale. Surely, they aruge, involvement by staff in the fashioning of agency decisions is likely to facilitate enhanced self-esteem and identification with agency programs. Other theorists question participatory approaches on grounds that they are often used to promise staff roles in decision making, promises often not kept or violated when participatory-minded executives are succeeded by those with more traditional perspectives.[24] Others belive that morale can be raised by increasing (where possible) staff remuneration, modifying jobs to make them more challenging, or giving staff members more autonomy in their work.[25]

Staff Skills.   Training programs are needed in many settings to enhance staff skills as they pertain to implementation of specific policies. Staff members may need training to work with specific minority communities, provide a range of community services such as outreach, use group interventions, and provide preventive services. But presence of requisite skills does not insure implementation when funding and other supports are not provided. Provision of in-service training, for example, may be a symbolic gesture not supplemented by ongoing technical, resource, and other supports necessary for implementation of policies.

Informal Networks and Official Policy. Staff members develop informal associations within formal organizations that can promote or hinder policy implementation. A distinction is useful between *official* and *unofficial* policies. Unlike the former, unofficial policies are developed by the agency staff in the course of its work. Official policy in a nursing home may state, for example, that the staff should "provide services to enable residents to maintain their maximum level of independence and movement as a prelude (where possible) to early release." Suspecting that management would prefer not to encourage early release in order to maximize profits, staff in one

institution may choose instead to place most residents in wheelchairs soon after admittance, regardless of their physical and mental capacities. New staff members are quickly socialized to this unofficial wheelchair policy, and it is reinforced by the informal organization; e.g., those who deviate may be subjected to cynical comments or scapegoating.

No simple methods exist for making unofficial policies congruent with offical ones. Efforts by management to directly influence the informal organization by firing "destructive leaders" or obtaining secondhand information about its norms and leadership are usually counterproductive. Probably the best approach is to involve staff directly in discussion of discrepancies between official and unofficial policies as a prelude to devising corrective action.

Structure of Jobs.   Although specialization is needed, more consideration should be given to

POLICY PRACTICE CASE 7.1

A Social Worker Diagnoses a Self-Help Center

Political conflict and difficulties generated by the uncertainty of funding sources have long been facts of life at the self-help center (SHC). Recent and unprecedented situational influences and staff and leadership changes have resulted in radical organizational changes (and, to an extent, organizational chaos.) This time period can be divided into two segments. First, the SHC experienced significant changes between January and November 1978 due to receipt of a major grant. Second, from November 1978 to the present, the SHC has had three executive directors, each representing, at least in part, different leadership styles and abilities.

January 1978, when the SHC was awarded a general revenue-sharing grant (matched county and federal funds administered by Mammoth county), marked a dramatic turn-

ing point in the nature of the SHC. Prior to that time, the SHC was funded by a number of smaller grants allowing for a paid staff of only five at a low salary scale. Most of the staff and professional workers were volunteers attracted to the SHC philosophy of providing an alternative (some would say, "counterculture") model for quality community medical care. The atmosphere was described as "free," "open," and "informal." Bureaucratic structure, rules, and regulations were kept to a minimum. Staff members had considerable input into the decision-making process. Meetings tended to be informal affairs, with attention paid to ideological issues, political concerns, and innovative ideas. Conflict tended to be resolved by face-to-face confrontation and discussion within a context of mutual respect and trust. It is reported that the staff felt

methods of broadening the responsibilities of staff members in order to challenge them to develop new skills. Rotation of staff members to different assignments can also facilitate staff development, as can efforts to expand their administrative responsibilities.

POLICY PRACTICE IN THE IMPLEMENTATION PHASE

Policy practice during implementation is particularly important to social workers, since they are well situated to address defects in operating programs. A troubleshooting role may be used in this phase to supplement ongoing direct service and supervisory roles. In policy practice case 7.1, a social worker discusses the implementation issues he faces in a self help center (SHC) that is experiencing considerable chaos, which in turn seriously undermines services in the agency.

Specifically, he fears that policy objectives that originally formed the mission of the SHC have been replaced by more bureaucratic, establishment objectives.

Value Clarification Skills

When clarifying values, social workers have to decide which services and programs their agency should provide and which fall beyond its purview. It would be fine, of course, if agencies were able to implement all programs desired by their staffs and boards, but fiscal and other realities require difficult choices that are based on values. In policy practice case 7.1, for example, the social worker wants the SHC to emphasize nontraditional services that emphasize advocacy, free services, team services, and extensive use of volunteers—services given in an informal atmosphere that contrasts with traditional social agencies. He believes that movement of the SHC

very much like a family, with the SHC administrator and the board organically involved in the SHC as a whole.

The SHC administrator (who was to become executive director #1) had been a part of the clinic almost since its inception, rising through the ranks from patient to volunteer to psychological counseling administrator to clinic administrator. He was highly committed to a sense of organizational mission that saw the patient as the number one priority of the clinic operation. Although it was indicated that, to a degree, he was afraid of power, it seems fair to say that, during his tenure as leader, his stature in the clinic was almost mythical.

The sudden influx of grant monies in January 1978 had a profound impact on the various indices of organizational functioning, an impact that could have been predicted along Weberian lines: increased bureaucratic structure, i.e., more formalized staff-adminis-

tration relations; the development of a more hierarchical administrative structure; rules regulating staff conduct; and written formulation of administrative rules and decisions. In fact, the grant allowed for a tripling of the number of paid SHC staff members. The number of administrative positions also increased, creating a greater sense of bureaucratic structure. The SHC administrator assumed the newly created position of executive director, whose functions would include public relations, grant writing, and the role of liaison between the board and the staff. The position of SHC administrator, involving direct contact with and supervision of the staff and the day-to-day activities of the SHC, was given to a long-time SHC volunteer. The size, nature, and experience of the staff changed. Many without any previous association with the SHC were hired. More complex staffing patterns developed in what had been an agency with a relatively simple structure.

And, because of the grant's extensive demands for accountability, much effort had to be directed toward retaining it.

The change in the SHC was dramatic: staff meetings became more formal and tended to involve matters of money, time, etc., rather than innovative programming suggestions and philosophy. Regulations related to accountability were handed down, and statistics and time-sheets were required. Decisions were increasingly made on an executive level by the executive director, board president, and executive committee of the board. Even department administrators were sometimes bypassed in decisions affecting their departments. And communication within the center became less direct and effective, with conflicts no longer resolved by face-to-face discussion. Further, conflict and disagreement no longer seemed to occur within a context of mutual trust and respect.

On an administrative level, increasing polarization developed between board and staff. The board now tended to view staff members as their paid employees and themselves as having license to make demands on staff energy and time. Gone was the feeling of the center as a family. Additionally, the board evidenced significant concern for making the center acceptable to the "establishment," a source of conflict with original staff members, many of whom tended to see themselves as counter-culture. Also, the executive director, although still considering himself a staff member, increasingly supported board positions against the staff.

Imposition of accountability regulations, decreased staff input and involvement in decision-making, formalization of administrative structure, and a marked tendency in the direction of authoritarian leadership by both the executive director and the board resulted in conflict, job dissatisfaction, and a lowering of morale.

As might be expected, the staff resisted implementing accountability measures. In particular, some of the "old guard" were opposed to statistical requirements on the grounds that they were contrary to the spirit of the SHC. Even at this point, however, the board seemed unable to understand why they were encountering staff resistance to their decisions. They tended to label it as "childish" and as evidence that the staff did not care about the SHC as much as they did. Understandably, staff morale suffered, as did job efficiency: the amount of nonproductive small talk increased and program innovation declined.

Executive director #1 had to retire because he suffered a serious illness. His successor, an interim appointee who had briefly held a part-time administrative position at the SHC, was selected by the board the following day. No staff input was solicited. As might be expected, this interim director was in a precarious position, subject to dismissal at any time by the board. It became clear at this point that the power of the organization was in the hands of the board president.

Under this executive director (#2), bureaucratic structures and procedures developed even further, although resistance was by this time largely centered in a few of the original staff. The sense of formality in the SHC was further increased when the center moved to new, larger, and in some ways more sterile quarters a few days after #2 took office.

Intraagency communication suffered under #2, who reportedly had difficulty dealing with groups of people and was weak in the areas of human relations and administration. On the positive side, however, this executive was able to tolerate criticism from staff and from other administrators; possessed good administrative, public relations, and grant-writing skills; and allowed for some autonomy on the part of department administrators.

He was removed from his position after about six months. The exact reasons for this seem unclear, although personality factors and the inevitable comparisons with his predecessor seem to have played a role. His difficulty in the areas of communication and sensitivity to human problems were stressed by the staff through their one representative on the personnel committee. With executive director #3, SHC organization and functioning approached the level of organizational chaos. In choosing this leader, the board looked for a non-SHC person. Unlike previous directors, he had no SHC experience, nor did he seem to be committed to SHC philosophy; rather, he had a managerial orientation (most recently as administrator of a private hospital). From the board's perspective, he was a director they thought they could control.

Initially, the staff had high hopes that this executive would stand up for staff positions against the board. Such hopes seemed justified when he proclaimed his intentions to revise the personnel code and solicit staff input into decision making. In fact, these hopes proved to be unfounded, since there ensued a complete breakdown of communication, at least as far as the staff and most administrators were concerned. Access to the director was limited to two friends on the staff. Even his executive secretary had to make an appointment to meet with him. Criticism and disagreement were neither encouraged nor well received. Much decision making was unilateral; department administrators were often not even consulted on decisions affecting their departments. The quality of these decisions suffered noticeably from lack of necessary information and input.

At this point, the board still seemed blind to staff unrest and maintained their paternalistic attitude toward those who complained. Further, the executive, together with the board, brought about the precipitous firing of five staff members. The reasons for these terminations ranged from anticipated financial shortages to trivial administrative complaints. It seemed abundantly clear, however, that personal dislikes were major issues; those fired seemed to be staff members who were particularly bright, experienced, knowledgeable, and effective in their areas. Some of them were strong personalities and quite out-

spoken, and it is easy to see how a leader with a low sense of self-esteem could feel threatened by their presence. Indeed, he promoted some staff members that many regarded as less competent than those who had been fired.

Five months after assuming the position of executive director, the executive was fired by the board (or at least pushed to the point of offering his resignation). The board feared that they lacked sufficient control over the director and his decisions. Issues of his effectiveness and the chaotic condition of the clinic seem not to have been crucial determinants of their action. Indeed, one of the director's qualities that the board found attractive when he was hired was his public relations skill, which, no doubt, they felt would stand the SHC in good stead with community and funding sources. Part of their disillusionment may well have been due to his failure to achieve the desired results with the funding agencies.

The costs paid by the SHC in this chaos included low staff morale, with its effects on job efficiency and effectiveness, nondevelopment of innovative changes in SHC programs, and the departure of good workers from the organization. Further, the policy objectives or mission of the original center seem to have been replaced by a new ethos more akin to that of establishment agencies.

A number of steps seem to be necessary if this organization is to function on a more satisfactory and productive level. First, change is required in the style of leadership exercised by the executive director. Improvement in communication with both staff and board and an openness to innovative suggestions and constructive criticism are crucial. The director ought to have and project a significant degree of autonomy from board pressure in order that he might truly serve as a liaison rather than as an apologist for board dicta. This would allow support of staff positions on particular issues and serve, to a degree, as a check on the board's involvement in regular SHC activities. Additionally, if the present staffing structure is maintained, the executive director should properly be concerned with the acquisition of funding, public relations, and community activities, with the day-to-day management of the SHC in the hands of a qualified and capable administrator.

Second, the person occupying the position of SHC administrator must necessarily be a competent, confident, and trustworthy individual able to make decisions and deal in a fair and sensitive manner with staff members both as a group and as individuals. This presumes, however, that the executive director would not feel threatened by dissenting points of view.

Third, staff rights should be strictly guaranteed, with particular emphasis on due process in hiring and firing procedures. Greater autonomy should be provided for department administrators, and a mechanism should be set up to allow for and encourage input by administrators and line staff into the making of decisions that affect their departments. Staff meetings should be conducted on a regular basis for administrative purposes, input into decision making, or resolution of conflict. Additionally, a grievance mechanism (a committee, ombudsman, etc.) should be set up to address problems that mutual problem-solving techniques seem unable to handle.

Reduction of emphasis on rules and regulations would also be a step in the direction of a better-functioning organization and the attainment of stated SHC goals. Also, the cost of maintaining some of the relatively trivial staff requirements should be reevaluated.

Perhaps such a realignment of SHC priorities would help to shift the focus of staff discussions and meetings back to more ideological and philosophical concerns, with exploration of the program changes and innovative methods needed to realize the organizational mission. Hopefully, this would involve a resurgence of concern with community health care issues and increase social activism.

Fourth, board members should involve themselves in areas in which they are uniquely qualified, particularly areas involving organization of community support for SHC funding and activities. The attempt by influential board members to involve themselves in the running of the SHC itself might be a diversion of their energies from more necessary and productive tasks.

Fifth, a structure ought to be established for the organization of the many volunteer workers and professionals who are crucial to SHC functioning. A director of volunteer services is needed, someone who could identify the needs of volunteers, coordinate their training and scheduling, and represent their interests to the SHC administration. This position would hopefully allow for the development of a power-base for volunteers.

Finally, since the staff is so demoralized by all the changes, an outside consultant should be hired who can facilitate the development of problem-solving groups. This would allow identification of the areas of conflict experienced by individuals, exploration of organizational assumptions and values, and frank discussion of changes that have occurred in the organization in the context of the funding turbulence of the 1980s. And people would be compelled to discuss current political realities of the SHC, its present values, and its administrative personnel, perhaps even to assume a troubleshooting role to devise methods of coupling self-help and bureaucratic models.

It is impossible and undesirable to turn the clock back to the early days of the SHC "family," as appealing as that notion might be to some. It does appear possible, even necessary, to subject the present SHC structure and operation to critical analysis and diagnosis in order to identify strategies for change.

SOURCE: This case has been contributed anonymously. Names and locations have been altered.

to a more bureaucratic model jeopardizes the "distinctive mission" of the SHC, a contention disputed by other agency participants who believe that the SHC must move toward more traditional models of service delivery in order to be able to obtain grants from traditional funding sources.

Instrumental values influence the kinds of organizational structures and procedures that specific social workers favor. In policy practice case 7.1, the social worker likes the "family atmosphere" of the original SHC, in which heavy reliance is on the use of unpaid volunteers. Other participants in the SHC apparently favor more traditional models of organization, including more extensive use of professional and salaried staff, an option made feasible when the SHC receives a large grant. When deciding whether specific procedures and policies are meritorious, social workers often have to calculate trade-offs. As an example, program manuals may bring red tape and inflexibility yet protect rights of consumers or allow an agency to meet specific priorities of its funders or its board. These trade-off calculations often require difficult value choices in the context of fiscal realities. Should the SHC, when faced with a funding crisis, for example, institute a sliding fee schedule with its attendant means test in order to be able to focus free services on low-income persons? Or would this policy seriously jeopardize the accessibility and informality of services that made the SHC a distinctive agency in the first place?

Sometimes social workers have to decide during implementation the extent to which their agencies should make service concessions in light of funding realities. In policy practice case 7.1, some of the old guard staff wonder whether grantsmanship projects require them to modify traditional programs excessively to meet the needs and requirements of funders. Yet social workers often must make concessions to funders if they want their agencies to continue or expand.

Value dilemmas discussed earlier in this chapter are obvious in policy practice case 7.1. Some social workers in the agency confront agency administrators, a strategy that leads in some cases to demotions or even loss of employment. When should social workers try to change disliked policies even when they experience personal risks? Some social workers in the SHC also leave the agency to avoid change-oriented projects. When is flight an acceptable resolution, and when does it represent unwarranted abdication of responsibility? Such complex issues require careful weighing and balancing of competing personal and professional objectives that all social workers have to make at one or another point in their careers.

Conceptual Skills

A major task during implementation is to identify macro, mezzo, and micro factors that frustrate achievement of policy objectives in a specific setting. The social worker in policy practice case 7.1 seeks to identify factors leading to reduced staff investment in work as well as decreased emphasis by the SHC on nontraditional services to consumers. In this agency, as in many agencies, numerous factors have to be considered. Funding instability, a macro factor, contributes to agency instability. He also identifies many micro factors that, he believes, foster poor services, including inadequate organizational leadership, lack of internal communication, excessive regulations, and lack of adequate grievance procedures.

An important conceptual task is to devise priorities when establishing troubleshooting strategy. Which specific macro, mezzo, or micro factors should be remedied initially? In complex situations like the SHC, it is difficult to know where to begin because so many, often interacting factors contribute to implementation problems. In policy practice case 7.1, for example, funding instability is partially responsible for the growing use of regulations within the SHC, since administrators hope to impress more traditional funders accustomed to more bureaucratic modes of organization.

In many cases, of course, priorities are established by assessing the feasibility of modifying specific macro, mezzo, and micro factors. Because he cannot address the external (i.e., macro) funding problem, the social worker in policy practice case 7.1 chooses the micro factors listed at the end of the case. Many of these factors could not be addressed, however, without the leadership of an executive who could obtain the confidence of both the staff and the board in an agency where these two groups had become polarized. A frustrating but common dilemma, then, is to identify factors that can be addressed in a relatively brief time frame, even when this requires frank recognition that more basic factors must be addressed subsequently. Perhaps the social workers in the SHC need, at a minimum, to rally behind some initial policy change, if only the establishment of a more explicit grievance procedure for managing dismissals and promotions more equitably.

In one sense, troubleshooting during implementation is analogous to direct service interventions with individuals. Various personal, familial, and environmental factors are identified that contribute to dysfunctional outcomes, and a strategy is devised for addressing one, several, or many of the factors in an initial time frame. As suggested earlier, social workers often begin with relatively simple strategies to obtain some immediate successes, even when they know that more basic factors need to be addressed eventually. During troubleshooting, social workers also need to diagnose organizational settings and operating programs to ascertain why they are not achieving specific policy objectives and then to devise interventions that allow development of changes that will improve existing services.

Political Skills

Social workers who have decided that specific macro, mezzo, or micro factors can be changed in a specific setting must then initiate an intervention strategy. They usually encounter political realities like those described in policy practice case 7.1, where any proposed changes in agency policies are likely to encounter the opposition of one or more persons. In many cases, persons become enamoured with existing policies, even when persuasive arguments are presented that suggest the need for policy change. A sort of inertia develops in which standard operating procedures are perceived as ends in themselves rather than as instrumentalities to be retained only as they contribute to quality services.

Then, too, specific persons and organizational units often benefit from existing policies and fear that policy changes will diminish their roles or prestige. Such fears are most obvious when social workers propose shifting a program to another unit, decreasing the size of one program to facilitate enlargement of another, or shifting administrative responsibilities from one person to another. Within as well as between organizations, turf rivalries occur in which persons and agencies jealously guard their programs and their administrative roles.

Clearly, then, intervention strategies during the implementation phase often require a return to the legitimation phase discussed in the last chapter, in which power realities are assessed and political strategies developed to reduce opposition to changes in policy that have the promise of improving implementation. Various kinds of person-to-person, procedural, substantive, and process power must be used, often together, to obtain modifications of implementation policies.

Distinctions between legislative and organizational change are worth noting. Conflict between contending factions is often obvious in legislatures; indeed, politicians often want to discredit opponents so that they can consolidate their own constituency support and diminish electoral support for current or potential rivals. In organizations, however, staff members are not usually accustomed to extreme conflict. Unlike legislatures, organizations usually exclude outsiders from controversies. Staff members have to work together on a daily basis and fear that immersion in conflict could jeopardize ongoing interpersonal relationships. Finally, executives possess considerable power in organizational settings that can sometimes be used to foster compliance with existing policies.

Considerable skill is required, then, to develop and secure changes in agency policies, where subtle use of power is often needed. In some cases, social workers need to persuade other strategically located persons to initiate changes, as when a direct service worker convinces an executive director that a specific policy is misdirected. In many cases, changes must be defended on their intrinsic merits to decrease the likelihood that others will perceive them as disguised efforts to increase the power of specific units or individuals. Sometimes informal coalitions can be developed that allow a number of persons in staff and personal contacts to develop support for policy changes. Where unions exist, their support for modifications of policy can be obtained, particularly when issues have some bearing on the working conditions of staff. Sometimes, of course, conflictual strategies are needed when no recourse exists and when staff are willing to accept possible personal and organizational repercussions. In policy practice case 7.1, the social worker seems to believe that confrontation between staff and board might eventually become necessary if some improvements cannot be otained by using less conflictual strategies.

In some cases, external or macro policies impede realization of specific policy objectives, as when funds allocated to an agency are insufficient to allow staff to adequately address consumer needs. Or staff may be asked to implement policies that they believe to be misdirected, as in the case of deterrent policies toward welfare recipients. In such cases, agency staff members need to join other persons and institutions to seek changes in macro policy even when immediate successes are not assured. When reimbursement procedures prevented free clinics in one state from receiving reimbursement for many of their services from state health and mental health programs, they formed a statewide coalition that hired a lobbyist who successfully modified many of these policies.

Interactional Skills

Social workers often use interpersonal, group, and community skills when trying to troubleshoot agency services. In some cases, staffs in service organizations believe that candid discussion of agency policies is taboo; thus, social workers need to assume a role in encouraging

examination of dysfunctional policies. Sometimes persons who initiate changes in program policies have reason to believe that they could suffer personal risk, but, in many other cases, persons overestimate the extent to which they will be branded as troublemakers. When sound professional reasons exist for questioning policies, agency executives and board members are often receptive. Indeed, interpersonal skills are needed not only to sensitize others to the need for change and to accurately assess the risk involved but also to communicate to decision makers a convincing rationale for examining specific policies.

Group skills are needed for participating on agency committees and task forces that examine specific policies. In some cases, social workers need to help these groups brainstorm alternative policies, particularly when innovations are prematurely dismissed or not even considered. When task forces or committees do not exist and important policy issues need to be addressed, social workers can sometimes urge the formation of such groups and try to secure the representation of persons who have creative suggestions for change.

Interactional skills are also needed to develop and use consumer and community contributions to agency policies and programs. As suggested by the extensive use of volunteers and community residents in the agency in policy practice case 7.1, community persons can make important contributions by supplementing professional services, drawing neglected populations into service, and participating in fund-raising projects. In most agencies, community liaison roles should be established at the service delivery level to develop community involvement, roles that should be supplemented by executives as they broaden community representation on agency boards.

Indeed, membership of agency boards needs to include perspectives of consumers and neglected populations but should also include persons adept at fund raising with traditional funders. The social worker in policy practice case 7.1 believes that the board neither assumes major fund-raising capabilities nor develops perspectives that would make the agency responsive to its consumers. Agency executives also need to help boards develop their policy roles. Boards should not be rubber stamps; i.e., they should examine and establish agency priorities and monitor agency performance. Yet they should not become enmeshed in internal workings of agencies to the point that they deprive executives and staff members alike of their professional roles.

Position-taking Skills

When trying to convince others within an agency or service delivery system that organizational changes are needed, social workers have to present positions in a manner that attracts support from specific audiences. In some cases, specific fears need to be addressed. Some persons may fear, for example, that their roles or prestige will be diminished by development of new procedures. Others may fear the unknown. Administrators may wonder if changes in procedures and policy will lead to major increases in costs.

The kind of presentation that is used must be carefully tailored to the specific audience. In the case of persons who are experts, technical and research evidence is often useful, while pragmatic considerations are usefully emphasized with administrators. In some cases, visual aids that allow graphic documentation of operations of new procedures or programs are useful. Formal and relatively lengthy presentations may be effective in some circumstances, whereas relatively brief and informal discussion may be more effective in others.

SUMMARY

Troubleshooting roles are assumed by participants whenever they identify and try to correct errors during implementation. When deciding whether, when, and how to respond to disliked policies, participants encounter serious ethical issues. They need to decide, in the context of values and political resources, whether to use an avoidance, confronting, or undermining strategy. Defects in implementation are often indicated by a lack of correspondence between official and implemented policy, variability in implementation, undue waste of resources, and ineffective services or programs.

Obstacles to implementation include macro (high-level), mezzo (regional), and micro (agency) factors. Problems in implementation often occur when high-level policy is exceedingly vague, poses tasks that exceed capabilities of providers, is not accompanied by needed resources, is transmitted through multiple layers of authority, or prescribes regulations that run counter to interests of powerful groups. In many cases, high-level funders contribute to implementation problems by not monitoring programs.

Mezzo and micro barriers also contribute to implementation problems. Americans have not developed effective regional organizations that detect and troubleshoot problems in the program delivery system. A key issue in micro settings is to decide when to use features of bureaucratic, nontraditional, and mixed organizational models. To be asked is, Which facets of the various models contribute to investment of staff in service delivery and facilitate provision of specific kinds of programs? Logistical and structural factors and organizational mission also need to be scrutinized. Some agencies try to improve programs by developing planning capacities and using contributions from consumers and community representatives in decision making. Careful attention is needed in agency settings to methods for increasing staff morale, enhancing their skills, and developing informal associations supportive of quality services.

Troubleshooting requires a variety of value clarification, political, conceptual, and interactional skills. Direct service and other staff should assume important roles not merely in providing services but also in initiating changes within their agencies.

Key Concepts, Developments, and Policies

Ethical issues

Avoidance, confronting, and undermining strategies

Defects in operating programs

Discrepancy between official and implemented policy

Variability in implementation

Program efficiency

Program effectiveness

Background factors

Discretion during implementation

Political realities

Agency or program mission

Obstacles to implementation

Macro obstacles

Policy clarity

Policy tasks

Requisite resources

Transmission of policy

Mezzo obstacles

Regional authorities

Micro obstacles

Organizational design

Bureaucratic organizations

Nontraditional models

Mixed types

Chain of command

Division of labor

Formalization of procedures

Logistical factors

Structural factors

Matrix organizations

Decision making

Agency planning

Agency boards

Staff morale

Participatory management

Staff skills

Informal networks

Job structure

Policy practice skills in implementation

Main Points

1. Ethical issues are often encountered by social workers when they must decide whether to use avoidance, confronting, or undermining strategies in implementing disliked policies—or whether to implement them at all.

2. Defects in implementation often exist when there is lack of correspondence between official and implemented policy, variation in programs funded by the same source, or evidence of inefficiency or ineffectiveness of programs.

3. Legislative mandates and funding, basic inputs in the implementation process, may leave providers with considerable or little discretion.

4. Political and economic realities often influence the implementation process.

5. Value and ideological factors influence implementation, as suggested by the importance of "agency mission."

6. When assuming a troubleshooting role in the implementation phase, social workers need to identify factors, including macro, mezzo, and micro barriers, that detract from the success of specific programs.

7. Macro barriers include lack of clarity in policy mandates, overly complex or difficult policy tasks, especially when combined with inadequate resources, and multiple layers of authority in the transmission of policy.

8. Many mezzo, or regional, issues arise in social welfare programs, issues that can be addressed by regional authorities.

9. When examining possible micro, or agency, factors, social workers need to wrestle with organizational design issues when they decide whether to use bureaucratic, nontraditional, or mixed types of organizations.

10. Other micro factors that need to be considered during implementation include logistical, structural, decision-making, and various staff factors.

11. Various skills are needed by social workers who engage in policy practice in the implementation phase.

Questions for Discussion

1. In case example 7.1, identify various indications that implementation processes are defective, i.e., require reforms.

2. Under what circumstances might a social worker decide not to implement an official policy? When have you used undermining, confronting, or avoidance strategies, and why?

3. What macro obstacles or barriers to implementation exist in case example 7.1? What changes would you make if you were director of the state agency on aging?

4. Critically discuss the statement "Most problems during implementation can be traced to lack of constructive attitudes on the part of staff."

5. Some theorists appear to argue that staff can only be productive when nontraditional organizations are used. To what extent do you think that bureaucratic modes of organization can or should be altered? What kinds of services or resources should be delivered through (a) bureaucratic organizations? (b) nontraditional organizations?

6. Critically discuss the statement "Regional authorities constitute yet one more layer of bureaucracy and should be avoided."

7. Someone recently argued that "most policies of agencies are dictated nowadays by external funders and officials, so social workers within agencies have relatively little role in policymaking during the implementation phase." Do you agree? To what extent should legislation be written to allow local providers considerable autonomy in making implementation choices?

8. In some agency or organization with which you are familiar, identify micro, mezzo, and macro factors that: (a) facilitate implementation of specific policies; (b) frustrate their implementation.

9. Discuss the following dilemmas, tasks, and realities encountered by social workers during implementation in policy practice case 7.1:
   a. Trade-offs often have to be considered during implementation, as reflected in decisions regarding use of fees.
   b. Social workers often have to decide to contest disliked policies, even when personal risks are involved.
   c. Social workers often have to establish priorities when devising troubleshooting strategy, since many factors impede implementation of specific policy objectives.
   d. Unlike members of legislatures, where conflict is common, persons in organizations perceive controversy as unusual, a fact that should be considered when devising strategy to change organizational policies.
   e. Consumers need to be more fully involved in fashioning agency policies, yet agency executives often give them limited policymaking roles.

Suggested Readings

Chu, Franklin, and Trotter, Sharland. *The Madness Establishment* (New York: Grossman, 1974). The authors present an excellent case example of the discrepancy between official, or enacted, policy and implemented, or operational, policy.

Hasenfeld, Yeheskel. "The Implementation of Change in Human Service Organizations." *Social Service Review,* 54 (December 1980): 508–521. The author provides a theoretical perspective that identifies various political and economic factors that shape the development of policies and programs in social agencies.

Montjoy, Robert, and O'Toole, Laurence. "Toward a Theory of Policy Implementation." *Public Administration Review,* 29 (January 1980): 465–477. Many factors relevant to policy implementation are discussed.

Patti, Rino. "Organizational Resistance and Change: The View From Below." *Social Service Review,* 48 (September 1974): 367–383. The author provides analysis of the power resources of direct service agency staff members as they try to modify agency policy.

Perrow, Charles. *Complex Organizations* (Glenview, Ill.: Scott, Foresman, 1972). Various alternative theories of organizational behavior and functioning are identified and critically discussed.

Pressman, Jeffrey, and Wildavsky, Aaron. *Implementation* (Berkeley: University of California Press, 1974). This classic analysis of implementation processes spurred further attention to an important but neglected phase in the policy cycle.

Williams, Walter. *Government by Agency* (New York: Academic Press, 1980). This book presents a detailed analysis of regional agencies in the contemporary period, including case studies.

Williams, Walter. *The Implementation Perspective: A Guide for Managing Social Service Delivery Programs* (Berkeley: University of California Press, 1980). The author provides a concise and insightful discussion of governmental, political, and other factors that influence the implementation process.

Notes

1. The considerable power resources often possessed by line workers is discussed by Michael Lipsky, "Standing the Study of Public Policy Implementation on its Head," in Walter Burnham and Martha Wagner, eds., *American Politics and Public Policy* (Cambridge, Mass.: M.I.T. Press, 1978), pp. 391–402.

2. See Robert S. Montjoy and Laurence J. O'Toole, "Toward a Theory of Policy Implementation," pp. 465–477.

3. Variations in administration of public welfare policy are discussed by Martha Derthick, *The Influence of Federal Grants* (Cambridge, Mass.: Harvard University Press, 1970).

4. Political realities during implementation are discussed by Eugene Bardach, *The Implementation Game* (Cambridge, Mass.: M.I.T. Press, 1977).

5. Theodore J. Lowi, *End of Liberalism* (New York: W. W. Norton, 1969).

6. Richard H. Hall, *Organization, Stucture, and Process* (Englewood Cliffs, N.J.: Prentice-Hall, 1972), pp. 79–103.

7. Mayer Zald, *Organizational Change: The Political Economy of the Y.M.C.A.* (Chicago: University of Chicago Press, 1970).

8. Chu and Trotter, *The Madness Establishment.*

9. Ibid.

10. Montjoy and O'Toole, "Toward a Theory of Policy Implementation."

11. Chu and Trotter, *The Madness Establishment.*

12. Pressman and Wildavsky, *Implementation.*

13. Herman Somers and Ann Somers, *Medicare and the Hospitals* (Washington, D.C.: Brookings Institution, 1967), pp. 204–225.

14. James Sundquist, *Making Federalism Work* (Washington, D.C.: Brookings Institution, 1969).

15. Perrow, *Complex Organizations,* pp. 166–170.

16. Ibid., pp. 1–60.

17. Positive attributes of bureaucracy are discussed by Victor Thompson, *Without Sympathy or Enthusiasm* (University: University of Alabama Press, 1975).

18. For one discussion of nontraditional organizations, see Rensis Likert and Jane Likert, *New Ways of Managing Conflict* (New York: McGraw-Hill, 1976).

19. Logistics of the implementation process are discussed by Allen Spiegel and Herbert Hyman, *Basic Health Planning Methods* (Germantown, Md.: Aspen Systems, 1978), pp. 239–287.

20. C.E. Teasley and R.K. Ready, "Human Service Matrix: Managerial Problems and Prospects," *Public Administration Review* (March–April 1981): 261–267.

21. Bruce S. Jansson, "The Ecology of Preventive Services," *Social Work Research and Abstracts,* 18 (Fall 1982): 14–22.

22. Nancy R. Dinkel et al., "Citizen Participation in CMHC Program Evaluation: A Neglected Potential," *Community Mental Health Journal,* 17 (Spring 1981): 54–66.

23. Robert A. Guest, *Organizational Change: The Effect of Successful Leadership* (Homewood, Ill.: Irwin, 1962).

24. Perrow, *Complex Organizations,* pp. 97–143.

25. Lyman Porter et al., *Behavior in Organizations* (New York: McGraw-Hill, 1975), pp. 274–311, 341–367.

PART 4

The Assessment Phase, Policy Positions, and Policy Research

Chapter 8 continues our discussion of the various phases of the policy formulation process. It describes strategies—including value-based, professional, administrative, consumer-oriented, and outcome approaches—commonly used to assess programs. Social workers need familiarity with the strengths and weaknesses of alternative strategies in order to participate intelligently in the assessment phase.

Chapter 9 is devoted entirely to discussion of position taking skills, since the development, presentation, and defense of positions is central to social welfare policy. Indeed, as discussed in chapter 9, the prominence of position taking in social welfare policy distinguishes it from allied disciplines of administration, community organization, and research. Social workers need to be able to identify preferred policies, develop coherent positions, criticize policies proposed to others, and present positions effectively to a range of different kinds of audiences. In the concluding part of the chapter, methods of obtaining evidence for policy positions are described, including the use of various library and government sources.

CHAPTER 8

The Assessment Phase: Error Detection Role

Social welfare programs have been under attack in the last several decades partly because many persons believe them to be ineffective, overly costly, or unnecessary. These beliefs are reflected in statements like the following: "Social programs of the Great Society did not reduce the size of welfare rolls"; "Agencies and professionals use their program resources to enrich themselves rather than to help consumers"; "Many social programs are used by middle-class persons who do not really need them." Defenders of social programs retort that many have been successful or that negative assessments are sometimes based on inadequate empirical evidence.

As in other policy phases, conclusions of one faction can be roundly contested by others. The many and sometimes conflicting approaches used to assess social programs are discussed in this chapter. Further, persons who disagree about the basic objectives of specific programs tend to disagree about their relative effectiveness. Like scanning, analysis, implementation, and legitimation, then, assessment is often associated with controversy.

The major task in the assessment phase is to develop and present evidence or arguments pertinent to decisions regarding termination, modification, or expansion of programs. This basic task requires completion of other, related tasks: defining objectives of specific programs, developing measures of their relative success in achieving objectives, obtaining information or evidence, and defining the implications of findings. As noted in this chapter, social workers need to develop proficiency in a variety of quantitative and qualitative assessment techniques to enable them to participate fully in the process of evaluating specific programs. They need to be able to answer questions like the following:

Can social welfare policies be evaluated exclusively through value-oriented assessments, or are other evaluation strategies needed?

What cultural, technical, and political realities influence assessments of specific programs?

How is the assessment phase linked to other policy phases?

What alternative professional, administrative, consumer-oriented, and outcome assessment strategies exist, and what are the relative merits of each?

What kinds of outcome studies exist, and what are some of their pitfalls or dangers?

These issues are discussed in this chapter as a prelude to examination of a policy practice case dealing with monitoring strategies used in Pennsylvania to oversee daycare programs.

GUEST EDITORIAL 8.1

Defending the Welfare State

No One Should Expect Kindness to Be Efficient, and Ordinarily No One Does

By Glenn Tinder

The current retreat from the welfare state cannot be stopped merely by reaffirming the liberal faith. Defenders of the welfare state cannot evade the self-criticism that present conditions demand of them, and this self-criticism must take place on the philosophical as well as the pragmatic level.

The truth is that there are good reasons— although not necessarily sufficient ones—for this country to retreat from the welfare state. The most obvious of these is that many welfare programs have not worked as they were supposed to. Milton Friedman, in *Capitalism and Freedom*, notes with contemptuous assurance and brevity the perversions and failures affecting the reforms of recent decades: regulatory agencies devised to protect consumers in fact are controlled by the interests that were supposed to be regulated; the income tax sup-

posedly is to redistribute income in favor of the disadvantaged, but actually is "a facade, covering loopholes and special provisions that render rates that are highly graduated on paper largely ineffective"; the agricultural program, set up "to help inpecunious farmers," has "wasted public funds, distorted the use of resources, riveted increasingly heavy and detailed controls on farmers . . . and withal . . . done little to help the impecunious farmer"; housing programs have "worsened the housing conditions of the poor, contributed to juvenile delinquency, and spread urban blight"; the social security system, created to provide basic security for everyone, has to be supplemented by mounting welfare doles. The list is not exhaustive. Nor, in its general purport, is it controversial or partisan. Hardly anyone now claims that the welfare state works very well.

Another good (but perhaps not sufficient) reason for withdrawing from past humanitarian commitments is that they have turned out to be in conflict with other values, above

IS ALTRUISM ENOUGH?

As Tinder notes in guest editorial 8.1, social programs can be defended, apart from any other rationale, as acts of altruism or charity. Assistance to persons in trouble as an end in itself is supported by Judeo-Christian traditions and by moral philosophers who contend that society, in the absence of altruism, would resemble a jungle in which individuals ignore the suffering of others as they seek personal gain.[1] Many liberals and socialists contend, for example, that the welfare state is required to reduce extremes of social inequality and to assist individuals who experience social problems. Not to provide mental health, medical, economic, or other services and resources to persons on grounds that we lack necessary knowledge and expertise represents, some would argue, callous indifference.

Selected Moral Principles

Moral principles pertinent to assessment derive from many sources and extend to many facets of social programs. A theorist in medical ethics may argue, for example, that a series of basic moral principles can be identified (see table 8.1) from religious traditions or from the writings of moral

---

all with price stability and with national defense. In the Johnson years it was widely assumed that the United States had enough money to avoid irresolvable dilemmas and tragic choices. But the climate of public feeling suddenly has changed. It is now generally assumed that large-scale public expenditures cause inflation; and it is recognized by everyone that inflation washes away the foundations of social order and that its consequences are harsh for the poor as well as for the prosperous. . . .

Underlying explicit criticisms of the welfare state, one may suspect the presence of implicit doubts—unstated, or even unrecognized, misgivings about its moral legitimacy. For example, while old-fashioned charity encouraged condescension, the welfare state would, if it could, reduce humanitarianism to administrative routine. That may be desirable on the whole, but it would still take something important out of human relationships. . . .

But if we abandoned the welfare state, the result would be political demoralization in the full sense of the term: the loss in our political life not only of *morale* but of the sanction of *moral law*. Human beings cannot for long accept a concept of politics that severs all connection between government and ultimate values. They insist on linking their temporal and spiritual concerns. The prophets of ancient Israel, Plato and his ideal of philosophic kingship, and medieval theocracy testify in diverse ways to this determination. The modern welfare state, in its own way, does so as well. The dangers inherent in joining the realms of Caesar and the spirit are obviously great. But completely separating them is intolerable. Political life unrelated to our understanding of the highest good must be either trivial or brutal; and an understanding of the highest good that is unreflected in the public realm must be academic and sterile. The welfare state is a relatively humble spiritualization of the public order. It symbolizes the idea that government should serve justice and kindness. If we give up trying to invest our politics with that modest amount of spiritual significance—if fiscal responsibility comes in effect to be our understanding of the highest good—what will remain in our public life to command respect?

It is because the retreat from the welfare state has been prompted by good reasons, however, that reiterating old liberal argu-

philosophers who develop them through a reasoning process.[2]

These principles have an obvious bearing on efforts to assess social programs. The *principle of autonomy* suggests the need to incorporate tenets of self-determination in social programs. The *principle of honesty* suggests that social workers and other helpers need to give consumers sufficient information to enable them to participate in making service decisions. A consumer who does not realize that he or she has a terminal condition, for example, cannot participate intelligently in decisions regarding further surgery. The *principle of contract keeping* requires that information given by consumers to helpers be kept confidential unless nondivulging of information could lead to serious injury to the consumer or others. As an example, a social worker may decide to inform police that a client wants to kill his wife because the social worker believes the spouse to be in real danger.

The *principle of justice* is basic to social policy. Specific social programs can be supported on the moral grounds that they are required to

---

ments and appealing to traditional liberal sentiments will not be enough. The welfare state must be reconceived.

The issue is not primarily one of practicality. It is risky to rely on trying to show that welfare policies can be, or have been, more effective than appearances indicate. It is risky also to concentrate on arguing the compatibility of social welfare with economic stability and national security. Such tactics cannot be wholly spurned: if the welfare state were completely unworkable it would be morally indefensible. But probably not all issues of practicality can be resolved in favor of the welfare state; and some of the misgivings about the welfare state—that compassion will be wholly bureaucratized, that life will be institutionally bound to mere material well-being—are not practical. Indeed, a disproportionate concern for practicality is what has led to the present crisis of the welfare state. Practicality should be subordinated to considerations of a different order. The welfare state can be rendered defensible only by being resituated, only by being put on better foundations than the pragmatic and optimistic concept of life that liberals traditionally have accepted.

The process of rethinking the welfare state can conveniently begin with the standards of justice and kindness. Among individuals, these prescribe relationships that are assumed to be valuable in themselves. Consequences do not count, at least not decisively. If someone restores a lost wallet to the owner we do not ask how the money it contained will be spent in order to determine whether this was an appropriate act. If someone helps save a friend from unemployment and poverty and the friend later dies of drink we do not conclude that the original assistance was unwise. Indeed, a strict sense of justice is apt to be severely indifferent to consequences and genuine kindness is often connected with a charitable awareness of human failings and perversities. Moreover, in personal relationships it never occurs to us that the imperatives of justice and kindness might be invalidated by coming into conflict with other values. It is taken for granted that to do all we should may sometimes require sacrifices and may sometimes be impossible.

Is there any reason why such attitudes should not prevail in the public realm? If they did, if just and kindly relationships were assumed to be worthy in themselves and not to require justification by their consequences, much of the disillusionment and confusion

help some particular segment of society attain equality with other segments. Programs to aid those in medical need, those with mental health problems, and conflict-ridden families are linked by the common motive of assisting persons who encounter material, physical, mental, or other inequalities. The principle of justice also suggests that preventive programs should be established for populations with an inordinate risk of developing material, mental, or physical problems, since the absence of these programs consigns racial minorities, women, the poor, and other out-

groups discussed in chapter 1 to continuing high levels of risk.

Problems with Value-Oriented Assessments

One method of assessing social programs, then, is to determine whether they adhere to basic ethical or moral principles. But altruism is, some argue, an uncertain basis for assessing programs. First, as discussed in chapter 1, persons differ in their basic values, differences that foster dis-

---

now surrounding the idea of the welfare state probably would not have arisen. Such has been the liberal confidence in our powers of action, however, that human suffering came to be conceived of primarily, not as a demand on thoughtfulness and common humanity, but as a problem to be solved. Thus the aim of acting justly and kindly was replaced by that of taking appropriate remedial measures. The vision of history as a compassionate sharing of human troubles became instead the vision of a process leading to the elimination of troubles. Relationships in the public sphere came to be evaluated not according to their intrinsic qualities but according to their results.

This is not to say that liberal pragmatism is wholly wrong. We cannot evade practical considerations, and justice and kindness must aim at eliminating the distress to which they respond. But to count on eliminating distress leads to a derangement of priorities. Practicality takes the place of morality. This happened; as a result the welfare state was made vulnerable to charges of being ineffective and overly costly once it faced the practical difficulties that were sure to arise.

The argument exemplifies what I believe is the most compelling objection to the whole neo-conservative movement. The case against

capitalism is not primarily one of inefficiency. Here Marxism, no less than liberalism, misleads us. In the last few years we have discovered not only that the welfare state sometimes does not work very well but that capitalism sometimes does. Liberals would not have been thrown so far off balance by this discovery if they had not gotten in the habit of assuming that possessing worth and working well are about the same. But the case against capitalism rests on our communality. Even if the market were as wondrous in its working as enthusiasts of free enterprise suppose, we could not allow our relations with one another to be set and controlled exclusively by a mechanism.

Recent criticisms of the welfare state are, as noted, mostly reasonable. But they are seen to be inconclusive once the welfare state has been resituated on firmer grounds than those provided by liberal pragmatism. In a polity giving justice and kindness priority over practicality, we could admit the ineffectiveness of many welfare measures without fearing that the whole idea of the welfare state would become invalid. Our aim is not to construct a problem-free social order but to live humanely in history.

Glenn Tinder teaches political science at the University of Massachusetts (Boston). SOURCE: Glenn Tinder, "Defending the Welfare State," *New Republic* (March 10, 1979), pp. 21–23. Reprinted by permission.

TABLE 8.1   Selected Moral Principles

Principle of Autonomy: Consumers should make major choices about treatments or other social interventions given them by social programs except where they are so physically or mentally incapacitated that choices must be ceded to family members, guardians, or other responsible persons.

Principle of Honesty: Consumers should expect professionals and other providers to tell them important facts about their physical or mental condition so that they (consumers) can make informed choices about their treatment and life options.

Principle of Contract Keeping: Consumers should expect that personal information given to professionals or providers not be divulged to others except when helpers have cause to believe that specific consumers or others could be harmed.

Principle of Justice: Consumers who suffer marked inequalities in income or who experience physical, emotional, or other forms of acute suffering should receive services and resources from socially sanctioned programs.

These principles are discussed in more detail by Robert Veatch in *A Theory of Medical Ethics* (New York: Basic Books, 1981).

agreement about the desirability of specific programs. Liberals might support major public employment schemes to assist the unemployed, only to meet opposition from conservatives who contend that efforts to equalize job opportunities represent unwarranted interference in the economy. Similarly, liberals and conservatives often differ when attempting to decide what level of charity is required in a moral or just society. Unlike many liberals, conservatives favor only a "safety net" that extends services and resources to persons desperately in need.

Second, values provide little information about how best to provide social programs. Many would agree that society should try to assist persons who abuse their children, for example, but they would like to obtain information about relative merits of alternative strategies. Interest in assessing alternative approaches is spurred by a healthy desire to spend scarce resources wisely. Many critics of medical services argue, for example, that development of preventive programs would allow Americans to reduce the extraordinary costs of existing medical interventions, savings that could in turn be used to fund new medical programs to underserved populations. It

is necessary, then, to study other assessment techniques to supplement those that rely on the use of values or ethical principles.

OVERVIEW OF THE ASSESSMENT PHASE

Activities during assessment are influenced by a range of situations or societal factors (see illustration 8.1). These factors are discussed as a prelude to analysis of alternative sources of evidence commonly used during assessment.

Cultural Factors

To what extent should social programs be subjected to systematic evaluation? What kinds of evidence should be collected when such programs are assessed? What criteria should be used in decisions as to whether to retain or terminate them? Answers to such questions are influenced by cultural factors, as trends in evaluation practices in the United States suggest. Prior to the 1960s, relatively little use was made of quantitative techniques for evaluating programs,

ILLUSTRATION 8.1   Overview of the Assessment Phase

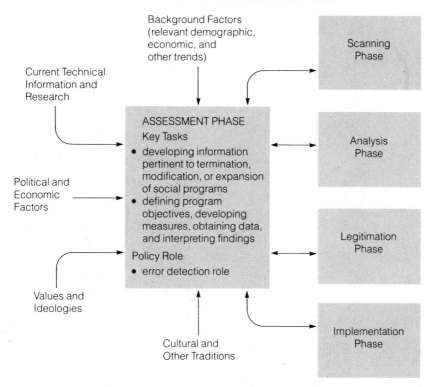

partly because computer and research technologies were not developed and partly because social welfare programs generally were perceived to provide emergency and short-term services and resources that were not expected to solve basic mental health, drug, juvenile delinquency, unemployment, and other social problems. As programs are perceived to solve problems, evaluation becomes a vital enterprise, since their relative success can only be gauged by studies that ascertain the extent to which they have in fact solved those problems.

The specific kinds of evaluation techniques used can also be influenced by cultural factors, such as evaluation fads. In the 1960s and 1970s, successive use was made of a number of techniques, including planning, programming, and budgeting systems (PPBS), cost-benefit analysis, zero-based budgeting, and management by objectives (MBO). It is beyond the scope of this discussion to analyze these various techniques, but their very number suggests that choice of specific techniques depends on current trends.[3]

In social agencies, use of evaluation is also influenced by orientations of staff and decision makers. In some settings, executives are favorably disposed to evaluation projects, including the extensive use of quantitative methods. In other settings, no tradition of evaluation exists, and the staff is actively opposed to its use. Research suggests that a variety of attitudinal and program factors influence evaluation.[4]

Technology

Development of computers has stimulated greater use of empirical studies since researchers can now process enormous quanitities of data.

In addition, advances in research technology provide researchers with technical tools for reducing error in evaluation projects.

Growth of technology in medical, mental health, and other sectors has indirectly fostered research by allowing new treatment options that invite systematic evaluation. In the 1940s, for example, many mental patients were confined to institutional settings. Now researchers are examining the efficacy of a variety of counseling, medication, and community strategies for persons able to reside in community settings because of the development of mood-altering drugs.

Political Realities

Decisions about whether, when, and how to assess programs are frequently influenced by political realities. In some cases, programs are declared successes by powerful persons or interests even though little systematic evaluation has occurred (illustration 8.2). Or empirical evaluations may in fact be whitewashes because highly placed persons commission or perform one-sided or haphazard evaluations. In other cases, opponents of programs develop evaluative projects that seem designed to discredit a program by limiting assessment to a specific facet of the program or using ill-advised research techniques. Some researchers wish that assessment could somehow be delegated to dispassionate and highly trained staff members who would place assessment above politics, but the assessment phase is inextricably entwined with politics, because the kinds of assessments made of specific programs have profound implications for program funding.[5] Negative evaluations can hardly improve the chances of increased funding, particularly during a period of scarce resources.

Linkages between Assessment and Other Phases

The assessment phase is linked to the scanning, analysis, legitimation, and implementation phases (see illustration 8.1). In one sense, assessment serves to validate or reject choices made in other phases. Examination of the relative effec-

ILLUSTRATION 8.2

"By The Powers Vested In Me, I Hereby Declare Each Of You A Success"

From *Herblock's State of the Union,* Simon & Schuster, 1972. Reprinted by permission of Herblock Cartoons.

tiveness of program interventions can suggest that basic causes of social problems were incorrectly identified during the scanning phase, that ill-advised policy choices were made during the analysis phase, or that choices made during program implementation detract from the effectiveness of a program. A program's lack of success can be caused by a series of errors that may not be detected until evaluators try to examine the relative effectiveness of programs during the assessment phase.

ALTERNATIVE ASSESSMENT STRATEGIES

Moral arguments used during the assessment phase have already been discussed. This section will describe the use of professional, administrative, consumer-oriented, social impact, and consumer-outcome sources of evidence.

Perspectives of Professionals

Programs are sometimes assessed in terms of whether they incorporate procedures or approaches favored by specific professions. Social workers can assess mental health programs, for example, by examining whether their staff members engage in appropriate process recording of cases, whether credentials of staff reflect training in accredited schools of social work, or whether staff members receive adequate supervision or in-service training. In some cases, professionals assess agencies by analyzing whether specific kinds of services are offered, such as crisis intervention or group therapy. Then, too, the work load of the staff can be examined; when burdened with excessive work, some reason, staff members can hardly be expected to provide quality services.[6]

Few doubt that the accumulated practice wisdom of professionals ought to assume a major role in assessment. Despite the development of research technology within professions and in the social sciences, many (some would say most) program interventions are devised by staff members who draw on personal and professional practice skills that often involve as much art as science. Professionals are often more sensitive to the effects of work load and other practical considerations upon the quality of programs than external program evaluators.

Undue reliance on professional standards, however, can lead to biased assessments of programs. For example, a free clinic staffed by volunteers and paraprofessionals may provide needed and quality services but rank low on many professional standards. In addition, professions can impose standards that others regard as self-serving, as when physicians refuse to accredit or give hospital privileges to midwives, despite evidence that they can provide quality out-of-hospital childbirth services that are also less expensive than those of obstetricians. Then, too, different professions develop divergent standards. Many physicians, for example, give scant importance to the use of social services in medical settings, in contrast to social workers, who insist that environmental, familial, and personal interventions are required to hasten recovery of many patients.

Administrative Standards

Critics of specific programs sometimes argue that they should be terminated or modified because they are poorly administered, as evidenced by wastage of funds, lack of administrative controls, or favoritism in hiring and promotion. As an example, officials in the administrations of Presidents Richard Nixon and Gerald Ford argued that federally funded neighborhood health centers were inefficient and proposed sharp reductions in their funding.[7]

But administrative criteria may provide misleading evaluations. Defenders of these neighborhood health centers argued, for example, that they appeared to be inefficient only because they were assessed according to efficiency standards of traditional medical programs in hospital settings. The neighborhood centers were providing innovative and needed outreach, preventive, community work, and multiprofessional services, which made them appear inefficient when compared to hospitals. In similar fashion, as suggested in chapter 7, theorists often differ in their views of the attributes of good administration, as reflected in different leadership styles of executives and alternative methods of structuring agencies.

Still, few would doubt that efforts to scrutinize the quality of the administration of programs ought to assume a role in their assessment. When national officials do not devise some minimal guidelines, local programs may be more subject to wastage of funds or outright misdirection of program activities away from those intended by legislators. In specific programs, low morale, absenteeism, and staff turnover are often indicators of poor management.

Consumer Preferences

Another method of assessing programs is to analyze consumer response. Consumers can "vote with their feet" by seeking certain kinds of programs and avoiding others. Experienced social workers obtain important information about specific agencies, for example, by observing activity there—in contrast to others, innovative programs are often unusually busy.

Consumers can often discriminate between poor and quality services, as reflected in responses to questions about agency services before, during, and after receipt of services. Reputational surveys suggesting that most consumers do not know about a program or have erroneous impressions of the kinds of services offered by its staff can prompt greater use of outreach by agency personnel as well as other reforms.

Some assessments examine whether programs are used by intended or specific populations.[8] In some cases, professionals do not serve low-income consumers or those with particularly difficult problems. Some studies also suggest that services offered by programs and those desired by consumers often do not match. For example, consumers who want help with tangible economic, housing, and employment needs are frustrated when program staff members only provide therapeutic services.[9]

But consumer preferences are no certain guide to assessment. Some researchers note that many

---

GUEST EDITORIAL 8.2

Exploding Some Myths about Social Programs

Common American Criticisms of Social Welfare Programs

By Vernon Jordan

Federal social programs are under heavy attack. They are widely believed to have failed in their objectives, to be designed to help only blacks, and to cost more than the economy can afford.

All those beliefs are false.

Federal social programs have worked. Some are among the most successful endeavors of government. Despite an enormous budget, the Pentagon demonstrated that it cannot land helicopters in the Iranian desert, but, despite pinched funds, social programs have alleviated hunger, improved the education of the poor and trained many young people for productive jobs.

The food stamp program is an example of how a federal program can make a direct attack on malnutrition and hunger. Before the program was instituted, a congressional investigation found widespread hunger in parts of the country. Recently, a followup study found that, thanks to the food stamp program, extreme hunger has largely been eliminated. Sure, the program isn't cheap. But its rising costs are directly due to the rise in food prices, an inflationary development that makes food stamps even more necessary for the poorest among us.

Head Start is another success. It got a bad press in its first few years. But a recent study that followed children from Head Start through young adulthood found that they performed better in school, and were more interested in going to college and less likely to get into trouble than children with similar backgrounds who did not have the benefit of the program. The lesson of Head Start is that social programs should be seen as investments—by spending on pre-school education, the government saved later and

consumers, on client satisfaction surveys, automatically give positive ratings to programs because they fear that negative reports will lead to termination of service, do not want to harm staff members who have assisted them, or do not realize that better services exist elsewhere.[10] Heavily subscribed agencies may use public relations gimmicks or be situated in areas where consumers lack other service options.

Impact and Outcome Studies

Many evaluators ask whether specific programs produce sufficiently positive benefits for society (impact) or for their consumers (outcomes) to merit retention or expansion. In many cases, these questions are answered in the course of empirical studies using research methodology. In guest editorial 8.2, Vernon Jordan, past president of the National Urban League, argues that considerable empirical evidence exists that can be used to defend major social programs, evidence suggesting both that many consumers are assisted (outcomes) and that society often saves money by investing in programs that avert welfare and other costs (impact).

Impact Studies.   In impact studies, research-

---

larger expenditures on remedial classes, law enforcement and training costs.

The Job Corps is another Great Society program that gets little credit. But it is a success—70% of corps graduates land jobs in the private sector, and most of the rest go into the military or continue their education. Not bad, since most of their peers are still pounding the streets looking for work.

There are plenty of other successes, ranging from Social Security and Medicare programs that have boosted most of the elderly out of poverty, to housing-subsidy programs that help millions of people improve their living standards.

And the big secret is that most of the beneficiaries of federal social programs are white. The big lie that these are "black" programs is defeated by statistics.

The majority of people on welfare are white. Half of food stamp recipients are white. Four out of five recipients of social and nutritional services for the aged are white. Ninety-two percent of Social Security funds go to white recipients. Four out of five Medicare participants are white. The majority of CETA jobs are held by whites. Whites are two-thirds of the beneficiaries of the Section 8 housing-subsidy program, the program that accounts for nearly all current housing subsidies.

That list can be extended further. The plain fact of the matter is that not only are many federal social programs successful in that they accomplish what they set out to do, but that they also often serve many more whites than blacks.

The third leg of the stool of falsehood is that those programs are bankrupting the country. Again, that's not true. Social programs may account for a large share of the federal budget, but so do other government functions. No one is proposing to disband the military because it will cost some $200 billion next year.

It is wrong to see social programs solely as costs, without assessing their considerable benefits. They constitute an investment in America's human resources.

Programs that develop skills, provide basic life supports and bring hope are indispensable to a civilized society. And anyone who says that these functions can be performed without government intervention is, at best, just plain wrong.

SOURCE: Vernon Jordan, past president of the National Urban League. Reprinted by permission of the National Urban League. This article first appeared in the *Los Angeles Times*.

ers examine the relationship between the social impact and the cost of specific programs. *Social benefits* of a mental health program may include, for example, enhanced productivity accruing from reduction of suicides, drug addictions, alcoholism, and institutionalization. In this case, society not only averts welfare costs but also benefits because many persons pay taxes who would not otherwise obtain employment. Further, a host of secondary benefits should not be neglected. Parents of the mentally ill experience reduction in stress and stress-related conditions when the mental problems of children are alleviated or when society allows them respite from daily interaction with their children. *Social costs* are the expenses incurred by society when funding programs, including expenses related to staff, program benefits, and facilities. The *benefit-to-cost ratio* measures the extent to which the benefits of a program exceed its costs.

Benefit-to-cost studies contribute to informa-

tion about relationships between benefits and costs of specific programs. They can facilitate reductions in funding for trivial programs and expansion of merited ones. But these studies are bedeviled by many technical problems—and some ethical problems, as well. Researchers often cannot accurately measure benefits to society, e.g., reduction in the number of suicides or the number of alcoholics frequently cannot be traced to a specific mental health program. (Suicidal and drinking behaviors can be influenced by a host of genetic, familial, community, and economic factors.) Long-term benefits may accrue to society that cannot be gauged in the short term, as when children who receive preschool services fare better, years afterward, in high school studies and in employment. Some services can be justified on the humanitarian grounds that they reduce suffering, even if no empirical evidence exists that they produce measurable social benefits.

CASE EXAMPLE 8.1

Science and Public Policy—Who Is Served?

By Lee Dembart

Times Science Writer

Every year if not every day we have to wager our salvation upon some prophecy based on imperfect knowledge.—Oliver Wendell Holmes, 1919

Does saccharin cause cancer? How clean should the air be? What is the threat of acid rain? Is fumigated fruit dangerous? Is nuclear power safe? How much benzine may workers be exposed to? What should be done with toxic wastes?

In a scientific and technological world, these and similar questions are increasingly coming before legislatures, regulatory agencies and the courts.

More and more, however, scientists and scholars who follow these debates are concluding that the scientific arguments at the heart of them are inconclusive and probably cannot be resolved.

Proposals have been made to establish "science courts" to rule on the scientific facts of a dispute. But scientists have generally been wary of such panels because they would create an orthodoxy alien to the traditions of science and because of doubt that they indeed would resolve many disputes.

Area of Uncertainty

In any case, observers say, the scientific evidence is only one of many factors that go into making public policy on many controversial issues.

"In virtually all cases you find that the sci-

Outcome Studies. In other cases, researchers ask, "Can we study those who use specific social programs to see if they benefit from participation?" Inquiry can be directed toward *subjective* or *attitudinal* outcomes, as when researchers wonder if consumers are less depressed because they participated in a mental health program. Researchers can also probe *behavioral* outcomes, as when they ask if consumers who participated are more likely to obtain work, not to return to state institutions, not to engage in violent behavior, or not to commit suicide.

BALANCED APPRAISAL OF OUTCOME STUDIES

Outcome studies have multiplied rapidly during the last several decades, partly in response to the growth of computer and research technology.

Some argue that agencies and policymakers should routinely conduct empirically based outcome studies of major programs. But others wonder whether these studies yield accurate assessments of many programs. Perhaps a balanced perspective is needed toward this and other assessment techniques.

Both the promise and the limits of outcome studies can be better understood by placing them in the context of broader issues regarding the relationship between science and social welfare study (see case example 8.1). Despite advances in research technology and data processing in the social sciences, nagging questions persist about the accuracy of findings when noted researchers who analyze the same data reach strikingly different conclusions. Indeed, as discussed in case example 8.1, some persons suggest the formation of scientific courts where panels can examine findings and discuss their implications for specific policy issues.

---

entific facts are inconclusive," said Clifford Grobstein, professor of biology at UC San Diego. "What is known is always less than you would like to know."

"The scientific information is rarely decisive on its own," said Tony Robbins, former head of the National Institute of Occupational Safety and Health and now a member of the staff of the House Energy and Commerce Committee.

"In almost every case, after you have the best inputs that scientific experts are able to provide, you are left with a substantial area of uncertainty," said Harold Green, director of the Law, Science and Technology program at George Washington University.

"In resolving that area of uncertainty," he said, "the only way you can do it is through value judgments."

The Reagan Administration has made clear its intention to reduce the amounts of technological regulation both in recently created

agencies, such as the Environmental Protection Administration and the Occupational Safety and Health Administration, and in older, well-established agencies, such as the Food and Drug Administration.

How, then, are these disputes to be resolved, and how is the public to be protected when and where it needs protection? Under the "science court" idea, a body of experts would be empaneled to hear the conflicting arguments on scientific issues and reach a conclusion at least as to what the facts are.

In this process, advocates would testify and would have the opportunity to cross-examine their opponents.

Science Courts

Last year, when he was running for President, Ronald Reagan told the magazine Physics Today that he would explore the feasibility of establishing science courts to assist the government in decision making.

Outcome studies provide useful information both before and after their completion. Because most of us believe that phenomena like mental illness, poverty, alcoholism, and child abuse do not randomly occur, we try to isolate their causes as well as the components of social programs that appear useful in addressing them. Outcome studies challenge social workers to ask questions like "What are the major components or approaches used in our social interventions?" "Which components are most crucial when addressing specific kinds of social problems?" and "What alternative approaches might be used that are not currently reflected in our programs?" By fostering critical analysis of programs, outcome studies challenge program personnel to examine prevailing assumptions and consider program options.

But nagging questions persist about the accuracy of many social science and outcome studies. This section discusses promising approaches in evaluation research as well as persistent sources of error.

Varieties of Outcome Studies

Outcome studies can be used to analyze the global effectiveness of programs, as when someone asks whether consumers benefit sufficiently from a given program to warrant its being retained. Other studies are used to compare alternative strategies for assisting consumers. An agency serving elderly persons might try, for example, to compare congregate (i.e., center-based) nutritional programs with home-based "meals-on-wheels" programs.

"The science court would draw a line between what we think we know and what we don't know," said Arthur Kantrowitz, a professor of engineering at Dartmouth College, who first proposed the idea.

"It would not manufacture knowledge where knowledge didn't exist before," he said. "What it would do would be to draw a line between what has stood the test of attempts to tear it down and what has not."

A related proposal, put forward by Joel Yellin, associate professor of environment, technology and law at the Massachusetts Institute of Technology, would set up a committee of scientific and technically trained people to advise federal courts on the facts of a dispute as well as on the larger, non-scientific issues involved.

"The evidence is that the courts have not been able to deal well with scientific and technological issues and that the adversary process, which is at the root of what the courts do, has not been helpful," Yellin said.

But the science court and similar proposals have been attacked on the grounds that they would create a scientific orthodoxy that is not in keeping with the aims or process of science.

The history of science shows many discoveries that were scorned when first proposed, but later accepted as fact. Science court proposals also are challenged as attempting to dispel the uncertainty that is an irreducible part of all knowledge.

"I do not think it is possible except in a Soviet-type dictatorship for somebody to decide what is correct and that decision makes it correct," said Green of George Washington University.

As to Kantrowitz and Yellin, Green said, "They are people who want correct decisions, and I don't think there are any correct decisions."

Retorted Kantrowitz: "I shudder at the notion of an officially imposed set of facts, but I also find the present situation chaos, where access to the facts for laymen is impossible. . . ."

"The role of the court is not to decide whether one view of science is to prevail over

Some evaluators suggest that projects that analyze alternative strategies are more useful than those that attempt global assessments. Since it is difficult to measure all possible outcomes accruing from a major social program, a program that is ineffective in meeting some of its objectives may be prematurely terminated. An evaluation of the federally funded preschool program known as Head Start found that Head Start graduates did not experience short-term "cognitive gains," a finding that led some to argue for termination of funding. Other researchers subsequently found that Head Start enrollees experienced many additional nutritional and medical gains and that Head Start graduates were not as likely as others to drop out of school—outcomes not explored in the earlier national study.[11] Further, many evaluators caution that it is haz-ardous to generalize about global success or failure of major national programs from studies conducted at specific program sites because of variations in program quality.[12]

When comparing alternative program strategies, then, evaluators do not try to establish whether entire programs should be retained but try instead to facilitate choices between program options. Alternative service methodologies, intervention strategies, program designs, and project implementation can be analyzed (see table 8.2).[13]

Some Methodological Options

The variety of technical approaches that can be used in outcome studies have advantages and disadvantages in terms of their cost, the kinds

---

another view of science," said David Bazelon, senior circuit judge of the U.S. Court of Appeals in Washington.

The court's job, he said, is "to make sure that the agency has given complete notice, afforded an opportunity for anybody who has a point of view to be heard and considered."

Agencies, Bazelon said, should "be very explicit about why one scientific view is rejected" and should also be "explicit about where it is relying on inferences from hard science and technology."

But if the courts are to consider the merits of a dispute, who should they rely on for the facts?

Expert witnesses?

"Expert witnesses are whores," Green said.

Many others agreed, though not in such a colorful way. Expert witnesses, they said, are chosen not for their wisdom or sagacity but for their willingness to say in the simplest, clearest, least tentative way what a particular side wants said.

All of which leaves the basic problem unresolved. As a result, what emerges from scientific disputes in the public arena are political decisions in which the scientific evidence is weighed against the needs and interests of different segments of the public.

"Regardless of what the scientific facts are, you have to accommodate values that are conflicting," Grobstein of UC San Diego said.

"The resolution of conflict is essentially a political decision," Green said. "I don't know of any better way to do it."

"Merely relieving us of scientific uncertainty would not produce political conclusions," said Donald Kennedy, president of Stanford University and former commissioner of the Food and Drug Administration.

"Even if we could do animal tests as easily and accurately as we do analytical chemistry; even if we could assess human risk to the third decimal place; even if we could measure medical benefits with great precision," he said, "most of our difficulties would remain."

SOURCE: Copyright 1981, *Los Angeles Times*. Reprinted by permission.

TABLE 8.2   Selected Foci in Comparative Studies

> *Alternative Service Methodologies:* Group versus individual counseling approaches; self-help versus professional interventions; services from individual professionals versus services from multiprofessional teams.
>
> *Alternative Intervention Strategies:* Psychosocial versus behavior modification approaches; familial versus individual interventions; provision of cash benefits versus provision of social services; short- versus long-term services.
>
> *Alternative Program Designs:* Storefront versus centralized services; waiting-list versus immediate-service options; paraprofessional versus professional services; combined versus single (i.e., autonomous) programs.
>
> *Alternative Implementation Strategies:* Services offered by highly specialized versus generic workers; workers who receive frequent supervision versus those who receive traditional supervision and those who receive peer supervision; agencies that emphasize planning and research projects versus those that rely on conventional wisdom.

SOURCE: Scarvia Anderson and Samuel Ball, *The Profession and Practice of Program Evaluation* (San Francisco: Jossey-Bass, 1978), pp. 30–33.

of error they minimize, and the ethical issues they pose.[14]

Experimental Studies. In many outcome studies, comparison groups are established that consist of (1) persons receiving one kind of program service or benefit and (2) persons receiving no or different services or benefits. Comparisons of members of the different groups provide valuable information about the effects on consumers of services and benefits. When consumers who receive services appear no better off than those who do not, for example, evaluators may conclude that a specific counseling program is not effective.

Even when differences between comparison groups exist, however, evaluators must be cautious in attributing those differences to use of services, since background factors can independently influence outcomes. As an example, some persons may not improve when receiving counseling services not because they receive poor service but because they become unemployed.

In experimental studies, consumers are randomly assigned to comparison groups to increase the equivalence of those groups and thereby

minimize the likelihood that nonprogram factors will contaminate findings (see case example 8.2). In the preceding example, random assignment would diminish the likelihood that persons suffering loss of employment would be concentrated in the group receiving counseling services. More probably, such persons would appear in comparison groups in roughly equal numbers, thereby reducing the influence of this background factor.

Quasi-experimental Studies. Alternatively, a researcher may decide that it is not to be feasible to use random assignment when establishing comparison groups. In some cases, the program staff may believe it to be unethical to deny services to some consumers in order to compare them with others receiving assistance. Then, too, consumers often relocate or terminate, which frustrates efforts to make comparison groups equivalent. The term *quasi-experimental* is used, then, to describe evaluation projects that do not use random assignment (see case example 8.3). In such studies, it is more difficult to rule out the effects of background events that influence lives of persons in the study independent of social

An Experimental Outcome Study

A mental health executive decided to conduct an experimental study to determine whether persons who were suicidal could be better helped by intensive individual counseling or through intensive small-group approaches. He used a standard test that measured "level of depression" as well as one that probed "life satisfaction." Consumers who approached the agency were assigned randomly to experimental (intensive group) and control (intensive counseling) groups. He planned to administer the tests one month after the consumers had completed the treatment programs.

Even in the planning stage, the executive feared that the tests, although yielding im-portant information, might not probe key facets of the consumers' mental health. Should he test the extent to which others believed that the consumers had improved or deterio-rated in their mental health? Should "real world" indicators of mental health be mea-sured, such as job- or family-related behavior? Even if those receiving one kind of inter-vention improved relative to others in the short term, would they retain this im-provement for long periods of time?

Even in the planning phase, then, the exec-utive realized that his experimental strategy would not eliminate all sources of error. But he decided to proceed to obtain useful infor-mation about treatment alternatives.

programs. Further, attributes of consumers can themselves influence outcomes. For example, if persons receiving treatment from a mental health program are older than those in another group not receiving assistance, differences in group outcomes may be influenced by age. (Older persons may be less likely to recover rapidly from some kinds of mental problems.) Had random assignment been used, attributes like age would be less likely to assume a role, since members of comparison groups would be more likely to have similar characteristics.

Correlational Studies. Some outcome studies do not follow consumers as they receive assistance but analyze program effects after assistance has been received. In the aforementioned evaluation of Head Start, evaluators compared children who had already graduated from Head Start with children who had never attended the program (see case example 8.4). Many technical problems in correlational studies frustrate efforts to interpret findings, including (as in quasi-experimental studies) the separation of program effects from innumerable background events and personal attributes.

Pitfalls in Outcome Studies

In quasi-experimental and correlational studies, many potential sources of error are difficult to eliminate. But even in experimental studies, many realities can frustrate outcome studies and embroil them in controversy. Indeed, as portrayed in illustration 8.3, evaluators run a kind of obstacle course. Persons who do not have knowledge of these dangers may prematurely accept findings of an outcome study suggesting that a program should be terminated or may believe that positive findings necessarily indicate that a program is effective.

Accuracy of Measures of Program Success. Imagine a series of interlocking circles arranged in a vertical pattern. The top circle represents a program objective stated in relatively general

A Quasi-experimental Outcome Study

A mental health executive wondered if brief institutionalization of suicidal clients coupled with intensive services might prove to be a useful intervention strategy. She reasoned that "many suicidal persons may need a complete respite from current familial and job-related stress," a respite that could be provided in an institutional setting. Therefore, she decided to plan a study in which she would compare levels of depression and life satisfaction of suicidal consumers who receive institutional services coupled with social services and those who only received outpatient services. She planned to administer a pretest (i.e., to compare levels prior to receipt of treatment) and a posttest (i.e., to compare levels after receipt of treatment).

She realized that it would not be possible in this study to randomly assign consumers to the experimental (institutional) and control (outpatient) groups because many consumers would not want to be institutionalized. But she realized that many possible sources of error could make it difficult to determine the accuracy of study findings. Those choosing institutional services might be persons already "better off" than those relying on outpatient services. Thus, even if their posttest scores were higher than the scores of others, the researcher would not be certain that this result was not due to their personal attributes. Further, the experimental group might be more affluent than the control group, since more affluent persons might be more willing to relinquish employment when institutional assistance was sought. Such consumers might experience less stress than poorer consumers, a fact that could influence mental states independent of program effects.

In spite of these fears, she decided to proceed with the study in hopes of obtaining preliminary information about outcomes associated with institutional and outpatient interventions.

A Correlational Outcome Study

An executive of a county mental health department wanted to examine drug dependency of consumers who had utilized a variety of programs offered in public agencies in the county. Therefore, she decided to conduct a survey of recent graduates of counseling programs, institutional services, and programs that offered drug substitutes, such as methadone. Many of the graduates could no longer be located, but sufficient numbers could, she hoped, to make the study feasible. She hoped to obtain information about the relative success of the various strategies by examining drug dependency of the graduates.

But she soon realized that she encountered many formidable obstacles. Since persons had not been randomly assigned to counseling, in-

terms, such as "improving the mental well-being of consumers." Evaluators need to develop specific and concrete measures that can be used to determine to what extent the program is achieving this objective. They may choose behavioral or attitudinal measures (see illustration 8.4). But the concrete, or operational, measures of success represented in the lower circles may not truly measure the general program objectives represented in the upper one.[15] As an example, the

ILLUSTRATION 8.3 Evaluator's Obstacle Course

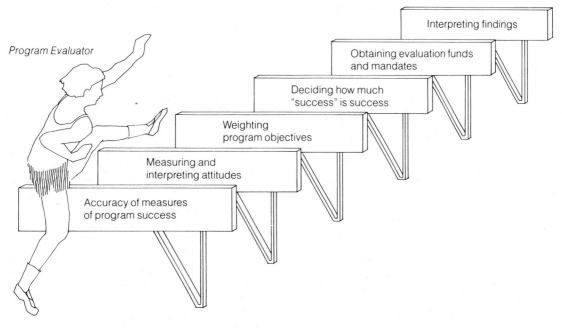

stitutional, and drug substitute programs, it was likely that there were systematic differences between members of the program by age, social class, ethnicity, and other factors that might influence outcomes. Further, she realized that the kinds of services given to addicts in the counseling programs varied widely, that institutional services also varied widely, and that some drug substitute programs coupled medical services with a range of other services, whereas others did not. She wondered if she would be able to compare the three kinds of services with one another in light of variations within each intervention approach.

A research consultant suggested that she not undertake the study but try instead to use an experimental or quasi-experimental approach to enhance the validity of findings. However, she decided to proceed in order to obtain a "first reading" of drug dependency outcomes associated with the various interventions.

ILLUSTRATION 8.4   Movement from Broad to Operational Measures of Success

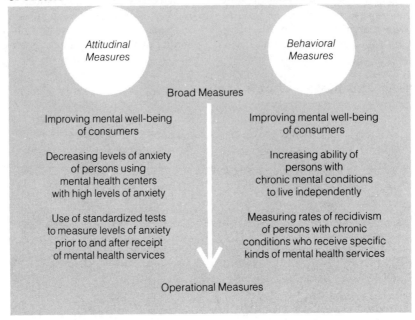

Attitudinal Measures

Behavioral Measures

Broad Measures

Improving mental well-being of consumers

Improving mental well-being of consumers

Decreasing levels of anxiety of persons using mental health centers with high levels of anxiety

Increasing ability of persons with chronic mental conditions to live independently

Use of standardized tests to measure levels of anxiety prior to and after receipt of mental health services

Measuring rates of recidivism of persons with chronic conditions who receive specific kinds of mental health services

Operational Measures

recidivism rate of patients in mental hospitals is one possible behavioral measure of program success. An evaluator would not necessarily conclude that services were effective if fewer persons who received them returned to state hospitals than persons who received no mental services. Perhaps many desperately ill persons are not readmitted who should be (current laws in most states restrict commitments to those in imminent danger of harming themselves or others). Or perhaps those who seek and receive mental health services are already not as mentally ill as those who do not receive services, thus accounting for their lower rates of recidivism. Moreover, staff members in some mental health programs may discourage enrollees from returning to institutions if they believe that this will improve their program's chances of receiving a positive evaluation.

Measuring and Interpreting Attitudes. Subjective states of mind are difficult to measure and interpret. When program staff members are asked to rate the mental condition of consumers before, during, and after treatment (a practice used in some outcome studies), they can unconsciously (or consciously) rate them as having progressively lower levels of anxiety, depression, and other adverse conditions because they want to believe they have provided successful services. Levels of mental health are difficult to measure or interpret even when outside raters are used. What level or threshold of anxiety, for example, suggests that an individual is mentally ill? Definitions of mental health can be influenced by cultural and social class factors. As noted in chapter 2, the culture of Japanese Americans stresses the nondivulging of anxiety; thus, apparent low levels of anxiety may reflect this cultural propensity rather than mental health. In short, evaluators need to exercise caution when measuring or interpreting subjective states of mind—and even more when using them in assessing the success or failure of specific programs.[16]

Weighting Program Objectives. As noted previously, the fact that many programs have multiple objectives makes evaluation more difficult. Is a mental health program to be judged by its immediate effects on those who use services, by the effects of services on family members, by the effects of consultation given by program staff to others in the community—or should it be judged according to some combination of these or other objectives? Findings of a specific evaluation project are vulnerable to attack by those who argue that evaluators ignored or neglected to attach sufficient importance to key program objectives. In other cases, critics may allege that evaluators only analyzed immediate benefits and ignored possible long-term effects.[17]

How Much Success Is Success? Evaluators must make judgments about the amount of success required to indicate that a program should be retained or expanded. In the case of mental health programs, they have to determine how much reduction in anxiety, depression, and recidivism is required. If objectives are overly modest, so little may be expected of programs that even those producing negligible gains are declared successes.

Unrealistic expectations are also a danger. Some argue that is unrealistic to expect programs to effect marked changes in the lives of consumers because no single (or even relatively long-term) intervention can be expected to bring dramatic changes in lives influenced by many forces and events, including economic realities, situational factors, and behavior of immediate family members. Indeed, life prospects of many consumers may best be improved by the combined effects of health, mental health, housing, community, employment, and other programs. Evaluators with unrealistic expectations, then, can inadvertently use research findings for conservative purposes. Declaring many specific programs to be unsuccessful because they do not effect dramatic improvements, such evaluators may suggest their termination or reduction and, in the process, eliminate combined amenities that could improve the lives of many.[18]

Obtaining Evaluation Funds and Mandates. In many cases, evaluators find that program staff members and executives do not want evaluations. It is easy to dismiss such persons as defensive. But outcome studies remain an uncertain science, and who can blame those who do not want to risk their programs or their jobs when negative findings, perhaps not fully warranted, could lead to funding cuts? In some cases, evaluators with highly developed technical skills lack communication and interactional skills to involve staff members and consumers in the process.[19]

Evaluators may also encounter ethical dilemmas. Some executives may want evaluations that are structured to vindicate a program, but the evaluator may recognize that such an evaluation would violate research precepts. Should the evaluator proceed in hopes of generating important information or withdraw from the project?

Outcome studies and supporting social science research are vulnerable to loss of funds. As suggested in case example 8.5, evaluation funds and mandates are subject to political forces. To some, social science research is "soft research" that lacks the exactitude of research in the physical sciences. The Reagan Administration slashed funds for many kinds of research, including long-standing projects that probe basic social trends and the causes of phenomena like poverty, partly because some of its officials were contemptuous of social science research. Persons who favor major use of program evaluation studies, then, encounter serious political obstacles in many settings. They can often successfully argue, however, that failure to conduct empirical research can seriously undermine efforts to rigorously scrutinize existing programs.

Interpreting Findings. Findings of evaluation studies are often difficult to interpret.[20] Suppose that an outcome study strongly suggests that a program is not succeeding, as in the case of the Head Start program that did not appear to produce cognitive gains for its graduates. At first glance, a negative finding such as this would ap-

CASE EXAMPLE 8.5

White House Uses Social Sciences, but Cuts Funding for Research

By Philip J. Hilts
Washington Post Staff Writer

The Reagan administration has begun a social science hour at the White House.

Twice a month, the president, vice president, Cabinet and senior White House staff view charts and graphs. They listen to statisticians sketch profiles of our changing society. The object is to understand the background social facts against which policy will be mapped.

The Reagan team is building a reputation for a more sophisticated appreciation of social science research than any previous administration. Yet even as the social science hour gets under way, budgeteers at the other end of the White House are ordering huge cuts in the programs that produce the very data the administration wants to use.

This seeming contradiction prompted one administration social scientist to comment: "Where the hell do they think these numbers come from? They don't fall out of the sky. They are taking these numbers and these ideas, and throwing out the programs that produced them. It's unbelievable."

Of all the hundreds of Reagan budget cuts, few have appeared to be so ideological. Few seem so contradictory to the style of the administration. Few that are so small have engendered so much concern and protest even from friends of the administration.

And few others have the distinction of appearing to be perhaps a simple blunder.

Office of Management and Budget Director David A. Stockman and others have complained for years that social sciences produce little or nothing useful, and that their studies are often used to support liberal social programs.

Sociologists admit there is biased social science in government, mission-oriented studies that discover exactly what the bureaucrats wanted to hear about their programs.

But that is not what has been cut by Stockman.

Although the intention apparently was to cut the loose, often partisan, mission-oriented social science carried on in some parts of the government, the cuts will kill the hardest, most neutral and most useful basic work in the social sciences. At the National Science Foundation in particular, the research is basic social science, the best in the field by all accounts.

At the NSF, basic research in three fields—social, behavioral, and economic science—costs little more than half the price of maintaining the Pentagon's military bands. Nevertheless, social science has been hacked and the bands remain. Stockman listed cuts in NSF grants for social, economic, and behavioral research—studies of everything from the gross national product to the origin of man—from $49 million in 1981 to $16 million in 1982.

All new social science grants at the Alcohol, Drug Abuse and Mental Health Administration (ADAMHA), between $10 million and $20 million, are targeted as well.

The fields of study being hit include economics, political science, sociology, cognitive psychology, linguistics, anthropology, and social and developmental psychology. In three areas—anthropology, economics and political science—the NSF is the only U.S. government agency that gives grants for basic research. Basic work in those sciences will be almost wiped off the federal government's books.

The Institute for Social Research in Ann Arbor, Mich., houses racks of brown plastic tape containing extraordinary volumes of data about this country—how Americans work, how they vote, look for houses, buy food, spend the minutes of their days, and make do when the money runs low. Thousands of questions and cross-questions about American behavior and feeling are logged here.

Now half its $15 million budget, and similar amounts at other major research centers, are threatened by the Reagan administration. The budget cuts will wipe out one-quarter to one-half of the entire field of basic research in social science, according to estimates by Harvard statistician Frederick Mosteller and others. . . .

Here are a few recent examples of the Reagan administration's use of all this research:

• The agency that made the drastic cuts in social science research, the president's Office of Management and Budget, uses it constantly.

Recently, OMB wanted to know about income trajectories—how people's income rises and falls over time; the ISR study on this is the only source of such information, and it now may be shut down.

On another occasion, the OMB wanted to know about the effects of budget cuts: What cities and what regions would be hit? The most accurate, accessible record of where federal dollars are spent is at the ISR, where they got the call just as they were getting ready to shut down the study because of the OMB cuts.

• The administration's most important use of social science, however, may be at the new social science hour. The White House's chief planner, Richard Beal, started the sessions.

"It's a system for providing social and demographic information to the policy people in a systematic and regular way, in advance of policy debates," Beal says. "If we are going to look at health care, then a month ahead we'll have a briefing on the way the health care system works. It's like the briefings we give the president on international situations. . . .

"The baby boom, the enormous change in population that we are getting, affects every piece of domestic legislation we deal with. . . . You've got to know how the pig is moving through the python. . . ."

At the Institute for Social Research, F. Thomas Juster, its director, says more than half the budget comes from threatened long-term data base programs such as the national election and income dynamics studies. Tracking the same questions year after year, these are to social science what the telescope is to astronomy. Without such data it is impossible to follow change in society, to mark new trends or identify fundamental, unchanging rules. . . .

The long-term study of income dynamics has interviewed annually for 14 years more than 5,000 families. The families over that time have come together and have split, have aged, and have sent off new, young families on their own. It is a tiny nation, counted, questioned and tabulated. All are asked about income and expenditures, their jobs, how they raise their kids, about housework and about food, about the age when the kids leave home, and when the grandparents return to it.

"After many years of following these people, you can't find anything about their behavior patterns, or their attitudes, or anything else, that has anything to do with their economic success or failure. It looks like a random event," says James Morgan, the ISR researcher in charge.

"Now that's an important issue for people who believe that the poor are poor because of their own indolence, nefariousness, or neglect.

"We also find that there really are two very different categories of poor people. There is a vast difference between the people who stay poor all the time and the people who are poor only once in a while," Morgan says. "That's important because we wasted a billion dollars in the 1980 census . . . they're counting the wrong thing!"

The federal statistics make no distinction between those who slip into poverty one year only and those who live in it all their lives. Distinguishing the two kinds of poor would allow money to go to the right places— poverty money to the hard-case poor, and unemployment, training, and other programs to the temporarily poor.

Not only will this information be lost if the studies are closed, Morgan says, but it is unlikely that they will ever be restarted because of the difficulty in putting such projects together.

"You're not going to start another like this in a hurry," he says. ". . . now, to keep it going, the cost is $1 million a year. The first year, starting from scratch, you'd be in for $10 million before you turned around."

These anxieties at Ann Arbor are matched at other research centers and major universities across the country.

At eastern universities, two researchers who had followed the lives of heroin addicts for decades have found that users commit crime when they are high, but not when they aren't. And they are caught less than 1 percent of the time.

While one wing of the Reagan administration is intrigued by social research days, another is explaining that social sciences are far less important than the natural sciences of biology, physics and mathematics. Those so-called "hard" sciences were given budget increases because they are more productive in the economy, says Frederick Khedouri, OMB associate director in charge of science. . . .

A year before he became budget chief, Stockman, then a Michigan congressman, joined with Texas Democrat Phil Gramm (now better known as cosponsor of the

pear to warrant termination of the program. These findings, however, could also be used to support massive increases in funding if an evaluator believed that the program's services were not sufficiently intensive. Perhaps Head Start could foster cognitive gains if children were enrolled for twelve months rather than receiving only summer-long services. Such a possibility could prompt an evaluator to interpret negative findings as suggesting the need for a fourfold increase in program funding.

Evaluators may also encounter ethical dilemmas when presenting findings. In some cases, politicians or executives choose only to disclose certain portions of data—or actually distort data. The findings of some studies are suppressed when they run counter to the needs of powerful interests.

WHICH ASSESSMENT APPROACH IS BEST?

Up to this point, value-based, professional, administrative, consumer-oriented, social impact, and outcome approaches to assessment have been discussed. The mutiplicity of assessment approaches returns us full circle to the controversial nature of social welfare policy. Theologians, moral philosophers, professionals, administrators, researchers, and politicians participate in assessment. In some cases, they speak in dif-

Gramm-Latta budget resolution) to draft an alternative budget. Stockman and Gramm wrote that "soft" research produces no breakthroughs:

". . . Research in the social sciences, education, and economics may produce long-run improvements in social program design and operation, [but] there is a strong case to be made that overreliance on the pet theories of econometricians, educationists, and social science 'fixers' has *created* the vast gulf between federal spending and resultant social benefit that we now seek desperately to close. Given present fiscal realities, such research is a very low priority, and funding should be cut back drastically in the short term."

With these lines Stockman connects basic research in the social sciences with social programs such as those of the Great Society. Then he reduces social science research to "pet theories" that waste money and do not produce the social benefits promised. . . .

Stockman apparently relied on his earlier budget paper to make many cuts. "We were instructed to cut science education by half and to reduce support for the social sciences by [three-quarters]," says a budget officer. . . .

In their own defense, social scientists say their studies of human behavior are easy targets for nonscientists who feel competent to criticize behavioral psychology or sociology but wouldn't dare try to judge biology or physics or astronomy. Aside from the lay criticism, however, some social scientists are prepared to concede that the practical results of their disciplines are unimpressive.

"I am afraid the record is a poor one. . . . We do not have any theories that allow us to predict events with more accuracy than intelligent laymen," says Allen Mazur of Syracuse University.

"Nor do we have any theories that allow us to construct better social systems—schools, police forces, cities, nations—than can be constructed by laymen. . . . I would not go so far as to say that professional social science has made no contribution at all, but what has been made is a little hard to find. Do not expect much from the social sciences. We are trying, but it is very hard work."

SOURCE: Philip J. Hilts, "White House Uses Social Sciences, but Cuts Funding for Research," *Washington Post* (June 29, 1981), pp. 1, 8, 9. Reprinted by permission.

ferent languages, as when theologians or philosophers defend or attack programs in strikingly different terms than the researcher. Sometimes they are contemptuous of one another. Researchers may believe that professionals are well-meaning but fuzzy-minded persons who are unable to scrutinize social programs objectively. In other cases, some use the language and perspectives of others, as when social workers develop, conduct, and use sophisticated outcome studies.

In fact, none of the assessment approaches is clearly superior to the others. Research has considerable promise but is sufficiently costly that only a minuscule fraction of social programs, and then only limited facets of them, can be subjected to rigorous scrutiny. Even in the case of technically sophisticated studies, accuracy and implications of findings are often questionable.

Note has already been made of the promise and the limitations of professional, administrative, value-based, and consumer-oriented approaches to assessment. Values like altruism are useful in defining ultimate objectives but provide little information about how best to achieve them. Professional wisdom contributes to assessment as it draws on the experience and theories of those who directly interact with consumers, but it can reflect outmoded or incorrect approaches and even protect professional vested interests. Preferences of consumers provide useful information, but client satisfaction surveys and consumer utilization patterns do not always serve as guides for distingishing poor programs from good ones. Administrative criteria offer useful benchmarks for analyzing implementation of social programs and detecting extremes of inefficiency, but no consensus exists as to how best to administer social programs.

Discussion returns at this point to the five Es discussed in chapter 2: effectiveness, efficiency, equity, equality, and externality criteria.[21] As noted in table 8.3, those who use the various approaches to assessment often emphasize different criteria: perhaps a balanced perspective suggests that the various approaches each yield different and useful information about the workings of specific social programs but that none is a certain guide.

Notwithstanding the multiple approaches to assessment, social workers should continue to develop projects to subject their interventions and social programs to empirical evaluation. Irrespective of whether such studies are used to provide funders with information about the relative effectiveness of programs, social workers need empirical studies to develop and test intervention strategies. They need to use empirical information to develop innovative projects that are rigorously assessed.[22] If the profession does not aggressively seek empirical data about outcomes, it risks placing undue reliance on traditional approaches or on the numerous intervention fads that arise with regularity. At the same time, social workers need proficiency in all the assessment approaches discussed in this chapter so they can use other assessment techniques when empirical ones are not feasible. They also need to be able to critically analyze how other persons develop their assessment strategies and recommendations, since any of the assessment approaches can be used in erroneous fashion to recommend discontinuation or modification of a program or policy.

POLICY PRACTICE IN THE ASSESSMENT PHASE

Officials in the Office of Children and Youth of the Pennsylvania Department of Public Welfare, in conjunction with other officials, developed a

TABLE 8.3 Alternative Assessment Approaches

Professional Approaches: tend to emphasize *effectiveness* of programs in addressing consumer needs. Research may be used, as may concepts from seminal leaders or schools of thought (e.g., Gestalt therapy).

Value-Oriented Approaches: tend to emphasize *equity* and *equality* considerations as well as other moral precepts drawn from religious or philosophical traditions.

Administrative Approaches: tend to emphasize *efficiency* of services as well as other administrative considerations.

Outcomes-Oriented Approaches: tend to focus on *effectiveness* of services when examining outcomes for specific consumers. But attention may also be given to combining effectiveness and efficiency criteria when research is used to identify intervention approaches that yield the most positive outcomes for the least funds.

Impact-Oriented Approaches: tend to emphasize measurement of externalities of social programs, e.g., the extent to which they increase productivity and reduce dependency.

Consumer-Oriented Approaches: tend to focus on *equity* (fair treatment) and *effectiveness* criteria. Typically, consumer use of and satisfaction with programs is taken as a proxy for equity and effectiveness.

method of obtaining information about operations of daycare centers in the state (see policy practice case 8.1). This monitoring approach is not an outcome or impact assessment study of the kind discussed earlier in this chapter, since it does not focus on measuring the behavioral or attitudinal changes that accompany receipt of daycare services by children or family members.

But it allows periodic measurement of implementation (by providers) of (1) administrative standards established in state and federal policy, including standards pertaining to facilities, equipment, and sanitation, and of (2) required standards, including child-to-staff ratios, credentials of staff, and use of parent advisory boards.

POLICY PRACTICE CASE 8.1

How Well Has Pennsylvania's System Performed?

Overview of Pennsylvania's Day Care Monitoring System

The instrument-based program monitoring system developed by Pennsylvania is known as the Child Development Program Evaluation (CDPE). The system was implemented in day care centers in 1978 and has been used continuously since then as the principal basis for licensing all centers in the state.

Pennsylvania is one of a handful of states that requires both private and publicly funded day care centers to comply with a single set of state requirements in order to be licensed. The CDPE thus includes both items that are designed to ensure compliance with basic health and safety requirements (covered under licensing requirements in many states) and items that focus on program criteria (described under program development in many states).

The CDPE questionnaire measures compliance with state regulations in Pennsylvania. The regulations are very specific with regard to required practices and standards and are grouped into seven categories: administration, nutrition, social services, transportation, health, child development and environmental safety. The complete instrument, which consists of 279 items that are each clearly linked to a particular regulation, is administered annually to all day care centers. Each of the items on the CDPE is assigned a weight based on its

importance in reducing risk to children. The questionnaires are precoded for easy scoring and entry into a computerized data processing and information system, or for manual processing.

Recently, Pennsylvania has developed a shorter version of the CDPE, referred to as an indicator checklist, which includes selected items from the complete questionnaire and can be used to predict performance. The short form that is now being tested contains only 18 items. It is anticipated that the indicator checklist could be used on an alternating basis with the comprehensive instrument, that it would be a good predictor of program performance, and that it would reduce monitoring costs to the state. Pennsylvania's experience with developing the indicator checklist has indicated that similar methodologies can be applied to reduce the length of many different types of state licensing and monitoring questionnaires, while preserving the validity of the questionnaire's measures of compliance and program quality.

Pennsylvania is particularly advanced in having linked the CDPE system with the state's financial and statistical reporting systems. The beneficial effects of this linkage have already been described in terms of Pennsylvania's ability to make sensitive policy decisions and reduce costs based on accurate and timely information.

What Is the Regional Compliance Picture?

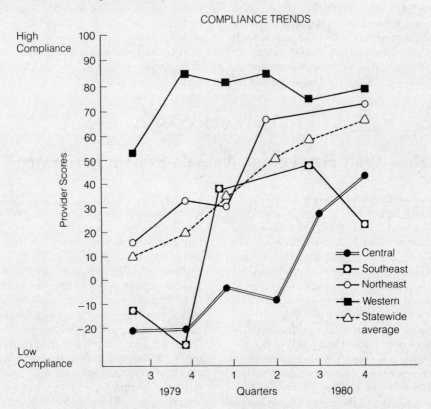

An IPM can provide readily available, quantitative information for analyzing compliance trends for sections (e.g., regions) within a state. Using compliance scores from IPM system reports, Pennsylvania was able to demonstrate substantial improvements in the quality of care provided by day care centers. (See figure.)

Having regional scores grouped by component area (e.g., administration, environmental safety), the state was able to target training in health for day care center staff in the Southeast region and in both health and administration for providers in the Central region.

Components of the CDPE

The CDPE system has five basic components that are described in detail in Volume 2 of this series. The components are:

- Pennsylvania's day care regulations;

- The CDPE questionnaires (long and short versions);

- CDPE coding manual;

- Pennsylvania's system for assigning weights to specific CDPE items; and

- forms for reporting CDPE results.

These components are all essential features of the CDPE system. The items on the questionnaires are, in many cases, simply rephrased from particular regulations (see Exhibit A). The coding manual is used to score the CDPE responses from a day care center and to ensure consistency in the way the CDPE is administered. The weighting system is used to score the responses; weights reflect important policy considerations with regard to items on the CDPE, such as those pertaining to safety, that cannot be compromised and which are sufficient grounds for denying a day care license. The reporting forms drive the system and make monitoring possible by providing regular measures for program quality, health, and safety at both the provider and regional/state levels.

Types and Level of Information Generated

The CDPE system generates three levels of information:

- provider information;

EXHIBIT A   Generic Classification Framework for Day Care Monitoring Activities*

Goals of Monitoring	Generic Monitoring Functions	Examples of States' Terms
Protecting the health and safety of young children	Perform health, sanitation, fire, and safety inspections Review health and immunization records of children and staff Check staff knowledge and skills with respect to health and fire safety procedures Check records for availability of emergency phone numbers and health precautions Check adequacy and nutritive content of meals Check safety of vehicles and transportation procedures Enforce child abuse prohibitions Develop corrective action plans for deficiencies	Licensing Supervision Registration Approval Regulation Corrective Action Technical Assistance Delegation/Coordination (e.g., of all agencies involved in licensing)
Promoting positive child development	Check provision of program of activities Check provision of toys and activities equipment Verify levels of staff interaction with children Check levels of parental involvement Ensure staff qualifications and capabilities Encourage improvements in service (e.g., provide information, training, technical assistance) Check staff-child ratio and group size Verify existence of plans for each child Check for mainstreaming and special activities to include handicapped children in program Develop corrective action plans for deficiencies	Quality Assessment Regulation Licensing Supervision Registration Certification Technical Assistance Training Providers Corrective Action State Participation in Public Groups (e.g., professional associations, local community groups) to Promote Child Development Public Education Interagency Cooperation Program Enrichment Program Development

*List not intended to be comprehensive.

(continued)

EXHIBIT A   (continued)

Goals of Monitoring	Generic Monitoring Functions	Examples of States' Terms
Assuring compliance with contracts	Verify delivery of contracted levels of service (e.g., enrollments, attendance) Verify compliance with other terms of contracts (e.g., nondiscrimination, minimum wage) Check quality of statistical and financial information and conduct fiscal audit Develop corrective action plans Check determination of eligibility for children	Contracting Reporting Billing and Paying Auditing (fiscal and program) Periodic Reviews of Contract Performance Provider Selection Administration/Judicial Review Procedure Contract Compliance
Managing resources efficiently and effectively	Short-range and long-range planning Allocating resources Recruiting and developing staff Developing new provider resources Evaluating day care system Developing procedures and systems Developing and monitoring policy	Legislation Regulation and Policy Development Planning Budgeting and Financial Control Personnel Management Funds Development (e.g., Titles XIX and XX) Technical Assistance in Managing Programs Facilities Development Systems Development Program Research and Evaluation Staff Development Resource Development (e.g., provider recruitment)

- regional information; and
- statewide information.

Basically, the system produces information needed to make all of the monitoring decisions about a particular *provider*. Provider information includes scores for each of the seven categories of regulation covered by the CDPE and a composite score on the CDPE. It is possible to obtain historical trends for the performance of a particular provider and to perform analyses of the extent to which performance in one category (e.g., social services) is correlated to performance in others (e.g., child development).

The CDPE also generates summary information on category scores and composite scores by *region*. Comparisons among providers are possible both by type of provider (e.g., non-profit, for-profit) and by general statistics for the region (e.g., score ranges, average scores by category).

Statewide category scores and composite scores provide perspectives on whether providers are improving in general and on the effects of changes in regulations and policy. Relative improvements in monitoring efforts in various regions can be observed. When CDPE results are linked to financial and statistical information systems, an even broader range of policy questions can be addressed.

Each of these levels and types of information is readily available to the state staff who make use of the information. For example, monitors at the regional level may obtain rapid feedback on performance of particular providers. Regional managers have a basis for evaluating the performance of providers in their region as compared with those of other regions. Central office staff, state budget personnel, and legislators have convenient access to general state levels of performance as these change over time.

The Implementation Process in Pennsylvania

Use of the CDPE questionnaire began in 1978. The implementation process, however, is ongoing, with constant improvements being made in the basic system. Pennsylvania staff estimate that it took roughly 18 months to establish a functioning system. The total cost for developing Pennsylvania's system has been estimated at $400,000, including the development of data processing systems. This development cost could be substantially reduced for a state interested in transferring Pennsylvania's technology and methodology and adapting them to its own requirements.

Pennsylvania's cost of monitoring day care using the CDPE is estimated at $400,000 per year. This figure includes costs related to the state's entire system, such as staff, travel, data processing, report production, and maintenance of the CDPE in light of policy and regulation changes. These costs will vary substantially for another state, depending on the caseload size, the background and training of

the monitoring staff, frequency of monitoring visits, size of the state, travel time to reach provider sites, and, of course, the number of providers in the state. Each of these cost areas requires important policy decisions that must be made by legislators and administrative decisions made by central-office day care managers.

These annual monitoring costs represent a saving compared to Pennsylvania's costs before the CDPE was introduced. Further improvements to the CDPE are likely to reduce these costs even more. For example, if the short version of an instrument like the CDPE is used, additional cost savings would occur.

In addition to the time and costs involved, two factors were especially critical in Pennsylvania's implementation process: the involvement of providers and the level of state commitment to implementation. From the very beginning of the project it was felt that development of the system required the involvement of providers and state, regional and central office program staff. The involvement of providers served both to enhance the quality of the items on the questionnaire and to minimize the suspicion and distrust that are often aroused when major administrative and regulatory changes are made. Continuous participation of providers in designing the questionnaire, assigning weights to items, and conducting field trials helped to ensure a high level of acceptance when the questionnaire was first used for licensing and funding purposes.

Pennsylvania's level of commitment to implementation was high, and the degree of commitment was a key element in the success of the implementation process. The substantial costs and the long duration of the implementation effort required careful planning and execution on the part of day care staff and trust on the part of state legislators and executives. The establishment of the CDPE was clearly not a quick panacea but a comprehensive and thoughtful solution to particular concerns that

Pennsylvania faced in its monitoring effort. A lower level of state commitment would have endangered the entire concept of an IPM system.

Pennsylvania's experience with the CDPE suggests many of the issues that other states will need to address in implementing an IPM. These issues are presented briefly in the next section.

How Do Instrument-Based Systems Improve Day Care Monitoring?

How is instrument-based program monitoring performed? Instrument-based program monitoring relies on the use of a detailed questionnaire or checklist based on explicit state regulations to determine how well a day care provider is meeting state requirements. When the assessment and questionnaire are completed, the results are scored using a common scoring manual for all providers of a given type (for example, day care centers), and coded for entry into an information system, either manual or automated. The results are used to determine whether the state needs to intervene in order to improve conditions at specific provider sites. The providers' scores on the questionnaires are also used to support state decisions concerning

Can IPM Systems Increase the Effectiveness of State Monitoring Efforts?

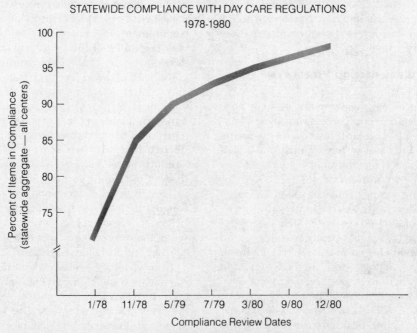

STATEWIDE COMPLIANCE WITH DAY CARE REGULATIONS
1978-1980

The most basic question that state day care administrators must address is whether efforts to gain compliance with state requirements are producing desired results. Pennsylvania's IPM system has provided periodic, accessible information to demonstrate that the state has made substantial progress in improving compliance since the IPM system (called the Child Development Program Evaluation system in Pennsylvania) was introduced in 1978.

These results have created support for the IPM system at all levels of the state government and have been effective in persuading policymakers to maintain current day care monitoring efforts.

the granting and renewal of licenses and state funding. Aggregate, statewide scores can be used as a basis for broad policy decisions directed at improving the general quality of day care and setting state funding levels.

Objectives and characteristics of the IPM approach. IPM systems are more comprehensive, objective, and consistent than the narrative report approach. They are also easier to read and understand. They are ideally suited to achieve the following objectives of a day care monitoring system:

- *Ensure equitable, enforceable monitoring of day care to meet a desired level of child health and safety.* Most states have requirements concerning the health and safety of day care centers. It is essential that health and safety standards be clearly specified, clearly understood by providers, easily evaluated, and consistently enforced by the state.

- *Ensure that day care promotes child development.* Typically, a state is concerned that children who are served by publicly funded day care providers (or all providers in some states, such as Pennsylvania) receive positive experiences from their day care in terms of their individual growth and development.

- *Provide for efficient and cost-effective funding and monitoring procedures.* States need to achieve the benefits of monitoring as efficiently as possible and at the minimum necessary cost.

- *Permit sound policy decision making.* States are concerned that their funds are spent in a way that ensures the best possible day care services. To address this concern, state policymakers need consistent, objective, quantifiable indicators of how many individuals are being served by day care and what funding levels are required to serve these individuals at different levels of program quality. Further, policymakers require an information base for deciding how policy should evolve in the future and for developing and maintaining appropriate legislation, regulations and policy guidelines.

Achieving these objectives requires timely, reliable, concise information about a state's day care program. An IPM system can provide this kind of information and has the following additional beneficial characteristics:

- *Quantitative and objective.* Using a program monitoring instrument produces clear, specific, and objective information about programs. The use of highly structured questions and records of on-site observations minimizes ambiguous results and biased observations. Questionnaire items lend themselves to quantitative analyses and produce readily summarized and easily interpreted data that are of value to policymakers.

- *Easily administered and consistent.* The questionnaires can be administered by monitors with varying academic backgrounds who have been trained to gather information quickly and with a minimum of interference with the ongoing activities of the provider. While much of a questionnaire may deal with evaluative and programmatic information, responses from various providers and monitors are highly consistent.

- *Supportive of providers.* Many providers welcome the use of such instruments because they know what specific areas are covered and they can structure their programs to meet state expectations. Involvement of providers in developing the questionnaire further ensures that the questions will be comprehensive without being burdensome. The use of questions that explicitly cover all regulations, and establish a uniform set of requirements, increases the providers' perception that the requirements are equitable, necessary, and desirable with respect to improving day care.

- *Focus on results.* The design of the questionnaire reduces undersirable bias that may result from differences in temperament and child care philosophy between the provider and the state monitor. The IPM focus is entirely on the services provided and how they affect children.

- *Based on state-of-the-art child development research.* The questionnaire items can be designed to reflect current "best practice" in day care. In this way, the questions may be used to encourage providers to experiment with and adopt successful approaches that have been shown to be effective in research in child development. IPM can be used to improve day care, and not just regulate it to ensure that minimum requirements are met.

- *Easy to modify and improve.* The questionnaire format with specific and unambiguous responses is easily adapted to changing developments in child care practices and state policy requirements. State requirements can be easily communicated to funded providers by incorporating new or revised questions on which assessments will be made. It is also easy to incorporate any federal requirements that may exist.

Desirable results from using IPM: Pennsylvania's experience. The positive features of IPM that have been described above may have particularly beneficial results for a state, if Pennsylvania's experience is a guide. Since Pennsylvania's system was introduced in 1978, it has produced the following improvements:

- *Cost reductions.* By linking the results of their IPM to the state's information system, officials in Pennsylvania have been able to identify high-cost, publicly funded providers who offer services only marginally better in quality than those of lower-cost providers. The state was able to set a ceiling on day care funding that did not jeopardize program quality, and used the funds that were formerly given

Hardly a panacea, monitoring in state, regional, county, municipal, and agency settings nonetheless allows funders and public officials to assess whether operating programs conform with minimum standards defined to protect consumers from inferior services. While outcome and impact studies are also needed, even minimal information about the kinds of services received by consumers has often been lacking, information that can be used to provide technical assistance to providers who are not meeting basic standards.

Conceptual Skills

In policy practice case 8.1, state officials first have to define minimal standards of daycare programs. In some cases, these standards are defined in the administrative guidelines accompanying federal and state childcare funds or in existing licensing regulations. In other cases, state officials have to define them in the course of discussions with providers and childcare experts. Were the state to attempt an outcome study that examined the effects of specific pro-

to high-cost providers to improve services of other providers on a targeted basis. The state saved approximately $5 million in day care funds while maintaining the quality of day care services, and it did so without major resistance from the provider groups.

- *Improved program performance.* Providers' scores on the monitoring questionnaire have improved over time as providers focus on meeting the state's clearly defined expectations. Because these expectations reflect both program quality and basic licensing standards, these improved scores indicate that the state-funded day care services have become markedly better in a short period.

- *Improved regulatory climate.* By involving providers in all stages of the development and improvement of the questionnaire, and by using the questionnaire to create clear expectations of providers, officials responsible for day care monitoring have reduced the tension and legal conflicts that often arise in regulated industries. Providers are satisfied that

the questionnaires are fair and that they are administered consistently and without special treatment given to particular providers.

- *Improved information for policy and financial decisions.* By linking the results from the IPM system to information systems that provide financial and statistical information on day care, officials in Pennsylvania have been able to make financial decisions about cost ceilings without much of the conflict that usually accompanies such decisions. The state is also in a strong position to complete the implementation of unit costing and competitive procurement systems in a way that explicitly considers program quality. Ultimately, the information provided could be used to answer such basic policy questions as: "Does state-funded day care really enhance the development of children for whom it is provided?" In the meantime, policymakers are receiving concise, quantitative, useful, and timely information to support difficult decisions with respect to trade-offs among state services in a period of tight resources.

SOURCE: Materials excerpted from Richard J. Fiene and Mark G. Nixon, *An Instrument-Based Program Monitoring System* (Washington, D.C.: Children's Services Monitoring Transfer Consortium, 1981), pp. 3–4, 7–9, and Richard Fiene, *A Conceptual Framework for Monitoring Children's Services* (Washington, D.C.: Children's Services Monitoring Transfer Consortium, 1981), pp. 12–13.

grams on children and their families, it would similarly have to specify the kinds of outcomes to be measured, such as growth in interpersonal skills, school readiness skills, or extent of participation by parents in childcare advisory boards. No matter the kind of study used, then, a conceptual task is to develop specificity when defining the attributes of programs to be measured or their effects on consumers and their families.

In many cases, of course, difficult choices have to be made. In policy practice case 8.1, for

example, officials develop a shorter questionnaire that is alternated with the longer one because providers cannot be asked each time about 279 facets of their programs. In outcome studies, researchers have to decide which attitudinal or behavioral outcomes are most important to examine, a difficult task in light of the large number of instruments that have been developed to measure various aspects of the mental, emotional, and developmental characteristics of children.

Another conceptual task is to select research, statistical, and computer techniques that are best suited to obtaining and processing information. Pennsylvania officials have to decide whether to draw a sample of all centers in the state or use questionnaires with selected centers, whether to use lengthy or relatively brief questionnaires, and whether to rely on mailed responses or make on-site visits. Further, as suggested earlier in this chapter, researchers have to decide in outcome studies whether to use experimental, quasi-experimental, or correlational designs.

Value Clarification Skills

Decisions about the focus of monitoring or outcome studies can only be made if value-based choices are made about the relative importance of various program objectives. When devising the brief questionnaire of 18 items that is alternated with the longer questionnaire of 279 items, state officials have to decide which 18 items are most crucial. In outcome studies, researchers must similarly decide which objectives receive primacy in their studies; should an evaluation measure cognitive gains of children, their interpersonal skills, developmental gains, or parent participation on advisory boards?

Interpretation of findings is also influenced by values. State officials might decide, for example, that noncompliance with one specific program regulation is not particularly serious but that noncompliance with others suggests that program funds should be withheld, particularly if demonstrable improvements do not quickly occur. In the case of noncompliance, officials have to decide how much noncompliance (and for what time period) is sufficient grounds for withdrawing funds from a program. In the instance of outcome studies, researchers have to decide how much success (and what kind) is required for a program to be labeled effective.

Persons also differ in the value they attach to accountability. Some providers and professionals believe that government officials and funders should provide them with resources but not insist that they demonstrate that their interventions meet prescribed standards or produce positive outcomes. Others retort that this autonomous orientation leads to wide variations among programs, with some not meeting even minimal standards—a problem, for example, when childcare programs provide services in facilities that do not even meet fire and sanitation standards. Still, excessive regulations and evaluations can stifle providers, who sometimes encounter a barrage of inspectors from many departments. Some balance is needed between the twin needs of accountability and autonomy—although many critics believe that autonomy often takes precedence, to the detriment of accountability.

Political Skills

In the absence of high-level support, assessment projects of all kinds are likely to founder. Officials in the Pennsylvania Departments of Public Welfare, Human Services, and Education want to develop monitoring procedures that ensure minimal standards to protect children, assist them in allocation decisions, and forestall political pressure emanating from periodic scandals associated with programs that do not meet minimum standards.

Advocates of assessment projects, then, have to convince key decision makers of the need for expenditures of resources on those projects. In policy practice case 8.1, local providers are given technical assistance from state officials in the wake of monitoring, a strategy that leads them to perceive monitoring as a constructive rather than punitive activity. In similar fashion, outcome studies are more likely to be used if executives believe that they will facilitate choices between alternative intervention strategies.

Many decision makers fear that assessment projects are not feasible, i.e., require so much time and so many resources that they are not practical. In the case of Pennsylvania, a top management firm is hired to provide needed technical consultation so that a time-limited and feasible monitoring project can be developed. Difficult choices must sometimes be made when balancing feasibility with research objectives. As an example, classic experimental studies are sometimes not feasible within specific time and resource constraints. Therefore, alternative designs need to be used even when researchers know that their use entails certain sacrifices. In similar fashion, on-site visits to all childcare centers in policy practice case 8.1 would provide better data than use of mailed questionnaires, since interviewers could personally inspect centers to see if respondents are providing accurate information. But, because state officials realize that on-site visits cannot always be made because of their cost, they may decide to use a combination of mailed questionnaires and on-site visits.

Social workers sometimes participate in the politics of assessment when they seek inclusion of specific social work standards in licensing, accreditation, and reimbursement standards. As an example, social workers have sought to tighten standards of the Joint Commission on the Reaccreditation of Hospitals so that social work services are more routinely supplied in hospital settings. Social workers can buttress such efforts, of course, as they develop outcome studies demonstrating that social work services enhance the well-being of consumers, studies that could be used to counter arguments that inclusion of social work services is not needed.

Interactional Skills

Interactional skills are needed by social workers during the planning, implementation, and interpretation phases of assessment projects. In planning phases, support for specific assessment projects has to be generated by developing strategies to include staff, administrators, consumers, and others in their design. Similarly, consumers and staff are not likely to participate in the data-gathering phases if they believe that the assessment project is gathering unimportant or inaccurate information. In policy practice case 8.1, providers could sabotage the monitoring project if they believe that the questionnaire is just another form to be filled out. A challenge to researchers is to obtain and then maintain the trust of administrators, staff, and consumers throughout the research cycle.

Many fine studies come to naught because little attention is given to the interpretation phase of research projects. Researchers need to involve a range of persons in this phase since people tend to ignore findings if they do not have to personally grapple with their implications. Do negative findings suggest that a program should be terminated or restructured? Are the data sufficiently precise to warrant major and far-reaching conclusions, or should less ambitious implications be identified? In the case of contradictory findings, as when a program is successful in obtaining one but not another outcome, which of the findings should receive most attention? These kinds of questions, often leading to divergent interpretations, need to be faced honestly and openly.

Position Taking Skills

Social workers participate in position taking during the assessment phase as they develop implications of research for existing policies and programs. In some cases, research findings suggest that existing services need to be modified or even discontinued, while modest changes are suggested in other cases. In many cases, findings of evaluation projects are inconclusive; i.e., present evidence may suggest that specific programs meet certain objectives but not others.

Social workers sometimes initiate positions that are suggested by research findings, but they also need to be able to respond to positions that are developed by others. When someone interprets policy implications of an evaluation project in simplistic or erroneous fashion, social workers should not hesitate to question the position. Someone might suggest that a program be discontinued, for example, because it failed to meet specific cost objectives, but ignore many other positive findings. Or someone might urge discontinuation of a program on the basis of its effectiveness in achieving one objective, yet ignore many other and equally important objectives.

SUMMARY

The major task in the assessment phase is to develop information pertinent to decisions about termination, modification, or expansion of social welfare programs. Because evaluations of programs can contribute to their demise or growth, assessment projects assume major importance in social welfare policy. In one sense, the assessment phase serves as a check on choices made during other policy phases. The effectiveness of program operation is likely to be diminished if social problems are not carefully defined in the scanning phase, if incorrect program design options are chosen in the analysis phase, or if ill-advised administrative approaches are used in the implementation phase.

Those who participate in assessment variously use professional, administrative, consumer-based, social impact, or outcome strategies when evaluating programs. In addition, some argue that social programs can be defended for meeting such value-based objectives as furthering social justice. Each of these assessment strategies can contribute useful information about strengths and weaknesses of social programs, but each can also lead to biased or incomplete evaluations. The practitioner should be familiar with all of them.

There has been a burgeoning of evaluation efforts that use research and computer technology to assess operating programs, efforts often directed toward measuring consumer outcomes associated with specific social programs. Such projects can contribute to program assessment both before they are completed (they lead to critical scrutiny of current programs) and after findings are issued (they can identify aspects of programs that appear to further or hinder program effectiveness). Outcome studies are hardly panaceas, however, as revealed by the widespread controversy they engender.

Whatever the assessment approach used, political realities often intrude. In some cases, decision makers choose to ignore important studies, distort the findings, or commission studies that do not incorporate widely accepted research techniques. Periodic cuts in national funding for basic and evaluative research reflect their vulnerability to political forces. Social work participants in assessment need political skills as they critique existing studies and initiate projects of their own, including empirical studies that analyze and test interventions and theory. They also need value clarification, interactional, position taking, and technical skills during initiation, implementation, interpretation, and dissemination phases of assessment projects.

Key Concepts, Developments, and Policies

Moral principles pertinent to program assessment

Perspectives of professionals in program assessment

Administrative criteria in program assessment

Consumer preferences in program assessment

Outcome studies

Subjective or attitudinal outcomes

Behavioral outcomes

Methodological options

Experimental studies

Comparison groups

Social impact studies

Cost-benefit analysis

Random assignment

Quasi-experimental studies

Correlational studies

Accuracy in measuring program success

Concrete, or operational, measures

Measuring and interpreting attitudes

Weighting program objectives

Determining required levels of success

Political realities in obtaining evaluation mandates and funds

Interpreting findings

Policy practice skills in assessment phase

Main Points

1. The major task in the assessment phase is to develop and present evidence or arguments pertinent to decisions regarding termination, modification, or expansion of specific programs.

2. Moral principles, including autonomy, honesty, contract keeping, and justice, can be used in assessing programs but need to be supplemented by other assessment tools, since they do not give sufficient information about merits of alternative intervention strategies.

3. Cultural, technological, and political realities influence whether and how key decision makers evaluate social programs.

4. The assessment phase can serve to validate or reject policy choices made in other policy phases.

5. Perspectives of professionals are useful in assessment strategies, since accumulated practice wisdom can yield important information about social interventions. But undue reliance on professional standards and wisdom can also yield biased assessments that are, for example, skewed toward acceptance of traditional approaches.

6. Administrative criteria can be used to assess programs and to detect poor administration but can skew assessment toward premature rejection of nontraditional programs that do not conform to existing standards.

7. Consumer preferences and assessments often yield important information about the merits of specific programs but can also yield incorrect information, as when many consumers decline to criticize programs in client satisfaction surveys.

8. Impact studies assess the extent to which a social program has positive implications for society—e.g., by decreasing the severity of a social problem. Cost-benefit studies specifi-

cally examine the ratio of program costs to savings to society that accrue from the program, as reflected in averted welfare costs, increased productivity, and other results.

9. Outcome studies can focus on attitudinal, or subjective, outcomes or on behavioral outcomes. They can also provide empirical information about the effects of programs on consumers and their problems.

10. Outcome studies can be used to make global assessments of programs or can be directed toward assessing alternative intervention strategies.

11. Methodological options can be categorized as experimental, quasi-experimental, or correlational, depending on whether they use comparison groups or random assignment and whether they are conducted after the fact or at the time that services or resources are delivered to consumers. (Experimental studies are subject to fewer sources of error than the other options.)

12. Even in experimental studies, researchers encounter a number of obstacles, including those pertaining to the accuracy of measures of program success, accuracy of measurements and interpretations of attitudes or other states of mind, weighting of program objectives, decisions as to how much success is success, and interpretation of findings.

13. Evaluators often encounter political problems when seeking mandates and funds for projects or when persuading decision makers to accept or use project findings.

14. Social workers need to use outcome studies both to advance their own knowledge and to assess social programs. Other approaches to assessment also have merit, but none is a certain guide.

15. Social workers need to develop various skills that are useful during the assessment phase.

Questions for Discussion

1. Do you agree with the following assertion in guest editorial 8.1: "If just and kindly relationships were assumed to be worthy in themselves and not to require justification by their consequences, much of the disillusionment and confusion now surrounding the idea of the welfare state probably would not have arisen"? If a moral case can be made for a social program, why also obtain empirical data about its effectiveness?

2. Take a specific social program or agency as your point of departure and list some of the kinds of assessment questions you would pose were you using (a) professional standards or criteria, (b) administrative standards or criteria, (c) consumer preferences or choices, and (d) outcome studies. Then list some disadvantages and some advantages associated with each strategy.

3. Assume you want to evaluate the extent to which a new, multiprofessional suicide prevention project is more effective than a traditional crisis counseling program. Discuss alternative methodological options you could use when analyzing outcomes of the two programs.

4. Imagine that you are evaluating the Head Start program in a specific agency. The agency board is interested in a number of outcomes, including parent involvement, improved self-esteem of children, and enhanced school readiness of enrollees. Using this example, discuss issues you might encounter in (a) devising accurate measures of success regarding one of the above objectives, (b) measuring and interpreting attitudes of children, (c) weighting program objectives, (d) deciding how much "success" is success, and (e) interpreting findings.

5. Discuss the following assertion: "Negative findings may sometimes mean that a program should be expanded."

6. Why is the assessment phase, seemingly dominated by social scientists, often embroiled in politics?

7. Discuss the statement "Social workers should make far more use of empirical studies to evaluate social programs."

8. Discuss the following dilemmas, tasks, and realities illustrated in policy practice case 8.1:

   a. A difficult task in assessment projects is to decide which program objectives are most important.

   b. Practical realities often preclude selection of research techniques that would provide the most accurate information.

   c. A balance is needed between the twin needs of accountability and autonomy.

   d. "In the absence of high-level support, assessment projects of all kinds are likely to founder."

   e. Although technical skills often receive most attention during the assessment phase, interactional skills are often crucial to the initiation, implementation, and use of assessment projects.

Suggested Readings

Anderson, Scarvia, and Ball, Samuel. *The Profession and Practice of Program Evaluation* (San Francisco: Jossey-Bass, 1978). The authors discuss methodology as well as ethical and technical issues in program evaluation.

Levy, Charles. *Social Work Ethics* (New York: Human Sciences, 1976). The author provides an introduction to ethical issues commonly confronted by social workers.

Posavac, Emil, and Carey, Raymond. *Program Evaluation: Methods and Case Studies* (Englewood Cliffs, N.J.: Prentice-Hall, 1980). This is a book for readers with some knowledge of research, but it is very readable and includes many case examples.

Riecken, Henry, and Boruch, Robert, eds. *Social Experimentation: A Method for Planning and Evaluating Social Intervention* (New York: Academic Press, 1974). An advanced discussion of methodological issues in program evaluation.

Tripodi, Tony, et al. *Differential Social Program Evaluation* (Itasca, Ill.: Peacock, 1978). The authors discuss many varieties of evaluation stud-

ies that measure outcome, cost, and administrative factors.

Weiss, Carol, ed. *Evaluation Action Programs* (Boston: Allyn & Bacon, 1972). The author provides an interesting array of case examples of program evaluations as well as discussion of the limits and potentials of quantitative evaluations.

Weiss, Carol. *Evaluation Research* (Englewood Cliffs, N.J.: Prentice-Hall, 1972). This is an excellent book for the reader with relatively little research knowledge.

Notes

1. John Rawls, *A Theory of Justice* (Cambridge, Mass.: Harvard University Press, 1971), pp. 258–333.

2. Robert Veatch, *A Theory of Medical Ethics* (New York: Basic Books, 1981).

3. A number of these techniques are discussed in Murray L. Gruber, ed., *Management Systems in the Human Services* (Philadelphia: Temple University Press, 1981).

4. Differences in orientations toward "search activity" in agencies are suggested in empirical findings presented by Bruce S. Jansson and Samuel H. Taylor, "Search Activity in Social Agencies: Institutional Factors That Influence Policy Analysis," *Social Service Review* (June 1978): 189–201. Also see Jack Rothman, *Using Research in Organizations* (Beverly Hills, Calif.: Sage, 1980).

5. Carol Weiss, "Where Politics and Evaluation Research Meet," *Evaluation*, 1 (1973): 37–46.

6. J. Richard Woy et al., "Quality Assurance in Human Service Program Evaluation," in C. Clifford Attkisson et al., eds., *Evaluation of Human Service Programs* (New York: Academic Press, 1978), pp. 411–445.

7. Karen Davis, and Cathy Schoen, *Health and the War on Poverty* (Washington, D.C.: Brookings Institution, 1978), pp. 163–172.

8. U.S. National Institute of Mental Health, *A Working Manual of Simple Program Evaluation Techniques for Community Mental Health Centers* (Washington, D.C.: Government Printing Office, 1976), pp. 124–180.

9. Daniel Katz et al., *Bureaucratic Encounters: A Pilot Study in the Evaluation of Government Service* (Ann Arbor: Survey Research Center of the University of Michigan, 1975).

10. U.S. National Institute of Mental Health, *A Working Manual*, pp. 230–232.

11. Marshall S. Smith and Joan S. Bissell, "Report Analysis: The Impact of Head Start," *Harvard Educational Review*, 40 (1970): 51–104.

12. J. S. Bissell, *Implementation of Planned Variation in Head Start: Review and Summary of First Year Report* (Washington, D.C.: Office of Child Development of U.S. Department of Health, Education, and Welfare, 1971).

13. Anderson and Ball, *The Profession and Practice of Program Evaluation*, pp. 30–33.

14. See Carol Weiss, *Evaluation Research*, pp. 60–91.

15. Robert Mayer and Ernest Greenwood, *The Design of Social Policy Research* (Englewood Cliffs, N.J.: Prentice-Hall, 1980), pp. 121–154.

16. Earl R. Babbie, *Social Research for Consumers* (Belmont, Calif.: Wadsworth, 1982), pp. 90–91.

17. Edward Suchman, "Action for What? A Cri-

tique of Evaluation Research," in Carol Weiss, ed., *Evaluation Action Programs*, pp. 52–85.

18. Anderson and Ball, *The Profession and Practice of Program Evaluation*, pp. 110–125.

19. Posavac and Carey, *Program Evaluation*, pp. 40–46.

20. Anderson and Ball, *The Profession and Practice of Program Evaluation*, pp. 110–125.

21. For discussion of research directed toward the various "five Es," see Tripodi et al., *Differential Social Program Evaluation*.

22. Jack Rothman, *Social R and D: Research Development in the Human Services* (Englewood Cliffs, N.J.: Prentice-Hall, 1980).

CHAPTER 9

Policy Positions, Presentations, and Research

Position taking skills are needed by social workers in the various policy phases. Indeed, position taking is integral to social welfare policy formulation, since the central objective of policy making is to develop and defend substantive positions that can lead to changes in existing policies. Position taking is so important to policymaking that this entire chapter is devoted to it.

Social workers develop and defend positions in many kinds of forums. Direct service staff members develop policy positions in their agencies and convey them in written or oral form to other staff members, supervisors, and executives. Social work executives scrutinize agency policies and develop positions for presentation to boards, funders, and legislators. Social workers often help professional committees and coalitions develop and present positions to government officials and legislators. In some cases, social workers are members of or staff consumer groups that develop advocacy positions for specific communities or disadvantaged groups. When developing positions, social workers need to be able to answer questions like the following:

What substantive content should be included in positions?

What alternative formats can be used when presenting positions?

What skills are needed in communicating positions?

What research tools are needed when developing and defending positions?

POSITIONS AS POLICY PRODUCTS

Position taking skills are needed both to develop the substantive content of policy recommendations and to present them in a manner that increases support for them. Position taking skills are closely linked to other skills and roles in the policy making process. Positions cannot be developed without use of value clarification, conceptual, political, and interactional skills. A social worker who assumes the problem recognition and definition role in the scanning phase, for example, might use value clarification, conceptual, political, and interactional skills to develop the position that his agency should commit more resources to addressing mental health needs of adolescents. He could then assume a program and policy design role in the analysis phase and develop a program proposal to serve this population. (Positions are also developed in implementation, assessment, and legitimation phases.)

A position, then, is an action-oriented statement that recommends specific policies with supporting arguments and evidence and is used to convince others that specific action and approvals are needed. Such positions are characteristically developing during the various policy phases as a prelude to their formal introduction to decision makers in the legitimation phase. In many cases, however, positions are developed or modified during the legitimation phase in the course of political interaction.

Positions are thus policy products or statements fashioned in agency, community, and legislative settings in each of the policy phases and with respect to any social problem. The importance of positions in social welfare policy distinguishes it from other allied methodological disciplines. *Researchers*, for example, use methodological skills and techniques for establishing and testing hypotheses and for collecting empirical data, but these techniques are specifically used in social welfare policy to obtain informa-

tion that can eventually be used to construct policy positions. During the scanning phase, for instance, policy practitioners use research methodology to obtain information about the prevalence of specific kinds of social needs in communities as a prelude to developing certain positions, e.g., that new or expanded programs are needed to address unmet needs. *Administrators* use various organizational, budgeting, and personnel concepts and techniques to develop and maintain agencies. But these concepts are used by the policy practitioner to develop positions about how to improve the operations of existing programs so that they more fully implement specific policy objectives. Administrative concepts are useful, for example, in designing programs in the analysis phase or troubleshooting them during implementation. *Community organizers* have developed techniques for developing and staffing community groups, task forces, and committees, methodologies that are specifically used by policy practitioners to help groups to develop and defend positions in any of the policy phases.

Policy practitioners, then, borrow from other disciplines as they assume different roles in the various policy phases, but they use these techniques and concepts in the process of developing, defending, and securing support for policy positions. Borrowing from other disciplines is so extensive that boundaries between those disciplines and social welfare policy may sometimes become blurred. Indeed, preceding discussion suggests that policy practitioners have to borrow concepts and techniques as they develop and obtain support for policy positions. In this sense, discussion in chapters 3 through 8 of this book serves as an introduction to the practice of social welfare policy, practice that can be enriched by knowledge about other, related disciplines.

Devised to address diverse issues and presented to many kinds of audiences, policy positions can take many forms. Whether making a presentation to a legislative committee, preparing a proposal for a foundation, writing a policy memorandum, or writing a policy research paper in an academic setting, social workers need to be familiar with alternative forms of positions. This section of the chapter discusses the content and format of policy positions as a prelude to an examination of the practical realities that need to be considered by policy practitioners as they plan presentations of their positions. When constructing positions, policy practitioners need to plan direction, focus, and content.

Direction of Positions

The direction of policy positions depends on whether policy practitioners initiate proposals or react to those that have been developed by others. In *affirmative positions,* practitioners develop their own policies and defend them by offering supportive evidence and arguments. In *negative positions,* social workers criticize the positions or policies of others, as illustrated by an attack on a proposed cutback in program funds or a deterrent policy toward welfare recipients.[1] Affirmative and negative positions characteristically developed in the policy phases are described in table 9.1.

Social workers need familiarity with both affirmative and negative position taking in each of the policy phases. In some respects, affirmative positions are more difficult to develop, since the burden of proof has to be assumed by those who develop new and untried policies. The policy practitioner who develops a negative position, by contrast, can often pinpoint flaws in the arguments and evidence used by others, sometimes a simpler task than developing a positive rationale for proposed policies. In national policy arenas, affirmative and negative positions are frequently developed by professional associations, such as the National Association of Social Workers, as they propose new policies, such as national health insurance, and criticize cutbacks and other restrictive policies.

Focus of Policy Positions

In oral and written presentations alike, a diffuse and rambling quality conveys the impression that the position taker has not given sufficient thought to the subject matter. Admittedly, social welfare policy issues are often complex and re-

quire consideration of large amounts of information, but understanding becomes even more difficult if a clear focus is not established at the outset. Social workers need to specify the social problem, choose specific policy arenas, select a time frame, and emphasize one or more policy phases.

Selecting a Social Problem. Care needs to be exercised in focusing on manageable problems. Major social problems, such as poverty, are so multifaceted and complex that they do not provide sufficient focus for most policy research projects, much less for specific positions. Many social problems can be subdivided into smaller ones. Poverty can be discussed, for example, as it is experienced by *specific groups* in the population —families with a single head of household, migrant laborers, unemployed persons, recently divorced women, or members of specific minority groups. In addition, *geographic limits* or boundaries can be used to establish a social problem focus, as in positions regarding poverty-stricken persons in Appalachia, inner cities, or areas devastated by the loss of industry. In some cases, social workers develop positions pertinent to different *forms* or *manifestations* of a social problem, as illustrated by positions regarding persons experiencing long-term or chronic poverty in contrast to those experiencing short-term poverty. Finally, a social problem focus can be achieved by developing positions pertinent to persons experiencing a social problem for *specific reasons or causes.* For example, a research project might focus on poverty occasioned by physical disability, mental illness, job-related discrimination, or absence of job-related skills. In many cases, of course, a focus is achieved by using a number of the preceding classifications. A feminist might wish, for example, to develop policy positions pertinent to women (social group) who have recently been divorced (specific cause) and are experiencing poverty (kind of deprivation).

Choosing a Policy Arena. Various policy arenas were discussed in chapter 1, including agency, professional, nonprofit, government, regional, and legislative settings. Policies are fash-

TABLE 9.1   Affirmative and Negative Positions in Various Policy Phases

	Affirmative Positions	Negative Positions
Scanning phase	A specific condition in the external world merits designation as a social problem	A specific condition in the external world is wrongly defined to be a social problem
	A specific condition in the external world merits more attention or higher priority	A specific condition in the external world merits less attention or lower priority
	Statement of the causes, scope, or prevalence of a specific social problem	Critique of a statement of the causes, scope, or prevalence of a social problem
	Statement of an intervention strategy for addressing a social problem	Critique of a prevailing or proposed strategy for addressing a social problem
Analysis phase	Defense of a policy option pertaining to the staffing, locus, or content of a social problem	Critique of a policy option pertaining to the staffing, locus, or content of a social program
	Defense of some specified relationship between agencies providing specific services or benefits or of specific policies that guide funding or oversight of social programs	Critique of some specified relationship between agencies providing specific services or benefits or of specific policies that guide funding or oversight of social programs
Implementation phase	Defense of specific policies in macro, mezzo, or micro arenas that will improve or facilitate implementation of specific policies	Critique of specific policies in macro, mezzo, or micro arenas that detract from or impede implementation of specific policies
Assessment phase	Development of some strategy for assessing a specific social program	Critique of a specific strategy for assessing a specific social program
	Development of funding and policy implications of an assessment project	Critique of funding or policy implications drawn from an assessment project

ioned in all of these, but the policy researcher often chooses one or several for primary emphasis. In some cases, social workers write positions that focus on policies in their agencies. Alternatively, as illustrated by testimony presented to a legislative committee, social workers can seek changes in policies in government arenas, whether local, state, or national.

Combinations of arenas are often chosen. In the case of a position presented to legislators, a social worker might need to consider changes in a state statute that have important repercussions for policies and procedures of social agencies implementing programs funded under the statute. If state officials were to decide that state-funded mental health clinics should be required to provide certain kinds of preventive services, for example, the social worker would also need to consider the policy changes required in the local agencies.

Choosing a Time Frame. Some policy positions are developed in the course of *historical* research. A social worker might study the development of public works during the Great Depression, for example, to derive suggestions for current policymakers. He could argue that a public works project like the Civilian Conservation Corps (CCC) should be revived to address high rates of unemployment among contemporary youth. In other instances, simplistic or erroneous strategies used in the past can be identified, as illustrated by ill-conceived projects to reduce welfare rolls by requiring women with young children to take jobs in the absence of job creation, daycare, and training.

Many position takers provide historical perspectives but emphasize *current* policies. Or they can develop current positions by anticipating *future* trends and developments. A position taker in an agency that serves blind consumers, for example, could develop a position recommending current policy changes in light of projected changes in the characteristics of agency clientele. In some cases, position takers develop scenarios in which they try to model or simulate future developments.

Selecting Policy Phases. A focus for positions can be developed by emphasizing one or several of the policy phases discussed in chapters 2 through 8. A social worker might discuss current problems of malnutrition among the elderly (scanning phase) as a prelude to developing policy proposals for new or expanded programs (analysis phase). A policy practitioner could examine how a specific program is not achieving specific policy objectives in order to develop ideas for modifying agency procedures (implementation phase). Someone could explore the politics associated with welfare reform in Congress in order to develop possible compromise positions to make passage more likely (legitimation phase). Or a practitioner could discuss alternative methods of evaluating a social program (assessment phase).

However, issues in one phase often cannot be neatly separated from issues in other phases. When constructing proposals in the analysis phase, for example, social workers often consider political realities likely to be encountered in the legitimation phase. Further, most positions require examination of prevailing policies and the contextual political, ideological, and economic factors surveyed in the preliminary policy phase discussed in chapter 2.

Illustrative Positions. The following four examples illustrate the tools presented thus far for classifying specific policy positions by their substantive focus.

1. A social worker is interested in the problem of malnutrition among the elderly (social problem) as discussed in the Congress (policy arena) during the 1970s (time frame). He wants to examine the kinds of legislative proposals devised to address the problem during this period (analysis phase) in order to identify policy options that might be useful during the 1980s.

2. A social worker wants to examine how policies enacted at the state level to assist victims of forcible rape (social problem) have been implemented (policy phase) in a specific county

(policy arena). She wants to conduct this study in order to be able to make recommendations for improving and tightening policies.

3. A social worker decides to examine the extent of poor housing in rural areas (social problem). He wants to examine various research documents and census reports to determine the seriousness of this problem (scanning phase) as a prelude to developing policy recommendations for Congress (policy arena).

4. A social worker decides that major national legislation is needed to help battered women (social problem) and decides to try to develop facets of a proposal (analysis phase) to be presented to a sympathetic legislator (policy arena). Aware that conservatives have defeated measures in the past, she wants to be certain to collect substantial information about the politics associated with such measures so that she can use this information to develop politically feasible options (here she is using information from the legitimation phase).

Elements of Policy Positions

Positions commonly contain certain elements, including orienting content, the presenting policy issue, perspectives, policy alternatives, preferred policy choices, and implications. These elements are present in policy practice case 9.1, a policy memorandum prepared by a social worker for a

---

POLICY PRACTICE CASE 9.1

Memorandum for the Commissioner

SUBJECT: Deinstitutionalization: Recommendation for planning

PREPARED BY: Dr. Marcia Mabee

I. Policy Issue

In the context of the development of the next series of five-year plans, what should be the role of state hospitals for the mentally ill and state schools for the mentally retarded in comprehensive community care? Specifically, should DMH care for its remaining institutionalized clients totally within existing institutions, totally in the community through the mechanism of purchase of services (POS), or somewhere in between? How can the department shape its personnel policy accordingly?

Recommendation: DMH's goal for its mentally retarded clients should be total deinstitutionalization, liquidation of existing state schools, and implementation of a total POS system of community care. The goal for mentally ill clients should be liquidation of exist-

ing state hospitals, leaving a residual role for small institutions, one in each of the seven regions to serve violent patients. The proposed facilities would be operated by private auspices under state contract. Community care services should be totally POS. DMH's personnel policy should be, implicitly, a policy of attrition. Explicitly, DMH should work closely with unions to arrange for three options: (1) early retirement, (2) training and transfer to other state positions, (3) training and transfer to a limited number of community service settings under public auspices to preserve vesting but without civil service protections, e.g., municipal hospitals, state university–sponsored settings, etc.

II. Summary and Analysis of Issues

The impetus for deinstitutionalization is founded on a belief, buttressed by research findings, that large institutions inhibit and discourage potential for independent func-

department of mental health. The author provides *orienting content* when she establishes a time frame in the initial sentence and a policy arena in the second; i.e., she alerts the reader that the memorandum focuses on development of a five-year plan by the Department of Mental Health (DMH). The *presenting policy issue* is discussed in the first paragraph and amplified in the second when she tells the reader that "DMH's goal for its mentally retarded clients should be total deinstitutionalization, liquidation of existing state schools, and implementation of a total POS system for community care." *Perspectives* are outlined in the third paragraph, which gives a brief overview of deinstitutionalization in the context of legislative, legal, and funding realities.

The middle section of the memorandum discusses three broad *policy options* as well as their relative merits. A *preferred policy choice* is identified after the author has discussed the available options and has prepared the reader by presenting their positive and negative attributes. In the concluding *implications* section, she discusses political and implementation factors that require further attention should officials adopt her preferred policy alternative.

These elements are usually present in policy positions, whether they are presented in written or oral form, brief memorandums or longer research reports, informal discussions or formal presentations. Indeed, as discussed in the next section, social workers need familiarity with a

---

tioning for mentally ill and mentally retarded individuals. This belief, particularly prevalent for the past twenty years, underlies passage of the Community Mental Health Centers Act of 1963 and various subsequent presidential directives to reduce the rolls of public institutions for the mentally retarded. Legal developments, especially several Supreme Court decisions, have hastened deinstitutionalization by prohibiting involuntary commitment without provision of treatment. Social programs such as Medicaid, Medicare, Title XX, and SSI have provided heretofore absent funding sources for community services. The result of these developments has been a nationwide census reduction of 370,000 in a twenty-year period (1955–1975) in public mental hospitals and 24,000 in an eight-year period (1967–1975) in public "schools" for the retarded. In Massachusetts, corresponding reductions have been 7,000 in the state hospitals, 1971–1978, and 1,100 in the state schools for the retarded, 1971–1977.

Current situation—What has happened to deinstitutionalized clients? It is a well-known fact that many "deinstitutionalized" individuals have been "reinstitutionalized" in nursing

homes without resources, and frequently inclination, to meet the needs of mentally disabled residents. Many other individuals reside in substandard boarding houses, do not receive rehabilitation or treatment services, frequently decompensate and are readmitted to state hospitals. Still other individuals are simply "lost to follow-up."

This situation is the result of three factors: (1) gaps in services in the community for a deinstitutionalized population; (2) presence of funding sources for services not tailored to the needs of the mentally disabled individual but offering a protective environment; (3) pressure from mounting costs and a desire to avoid legal suits to deinstitutionalize quickly, thus precluding planning to fill service gaps and foster receptive community attitudes.

What should the optimal community care system look like? What is needed? The literature abounds with descriptions of successful and unsuccessful community care programs for the deinstitutionalized mentally disabled. The same essential program elements emerge again and again as keys to success or failure. They are: (1) targeting of chronic patients: a priority commitment; (2) linkage with other resources, e.g., vocational rehabilitation, etc.; (3) functional integrity: provision in the community of the full range of functions that are associated with institutional care; (4) individually tailored treatment; (5) cultural relevance and specificity: programs tailored to the realities of local communities; (6) specially trained staff attuned to the unique survival problems of mentally disabled clients living in non-institutionalized settings; (7) hospital liaison: public or private beds; (8) internal evaluation.

The problem at hand is how to move states like Massachusetts from their current situation of half-filled institutions and inappropriately and underserved community-based clients to a fully community-based model incorporating the eight key program elements.

III. Available Options

Option 1: Don't try. Discontinue deinstitutionalization—devote scarce resources to upgrading institutions.

- *Pro:* This option has appeal for those who doubt the potential for growth of mentally disabled individuals and who, due to concern or contempt, want them off community streets. It is administratively simpler, leaving the state in complete control. However, it is likely to be more costly, since community-based programs can utilize federal funding sources such as SSI and Medicaid.

- *Con:* Research offers strong support that large institutions reduce individualization, thereby decreasing opportunity for ego development necessary for the establishment of independent functioning. Current concern for civil liberties will not tolerate this option, particularly in regard to the mentally ill.

Option 2: Develop a total community care system incorporating the eight key program elements using POS.

- *Pro:* A major criticism of POS has been that the state loses control and is dominated by providers. However, this has largely been due to a lack of state planning, an abundance of direct service oriented and trained personnel versus management-trained personnel, and a state "inferiority complex." These deficiencies can be altered. State legislatures must be persuaded to continue to provide funds to support institutional care as well as new funds for the development of community services. Once community settings are in place, institutional expenditures can be converted to community expenditures, and further new funds can be discontinued. This interim support of two systems provides the hiatus needed for important planning efforts. Administrative personnel can be retrained and direct service personnel phased out. Liquidating property assets, converting direct service expenditures into POS monies, provides the state with buying power it need not be afraid to exercise; community mental health centers and other financially distressed community service settings will welcome state funding.

- *Con:* Community programs, exemplifed by community mental health centers, reject the chronically mentally disabled as "unrewarding." Community residents reject the mentally disabled out of fear and disgust and concerns about property devaluation. Although some programs may welcome state funding, delayed payment creates prohibitive cash-flow problems.

Option 3: Develop a community care system incorporating the eight key elements using POS but reserve a residual role for small regionally located state institutions for the treatment of violent mentally ill individuals. The proposed facilities would be privately managed and staffed. Develop a limited number of direct service community programs under other public auspices, such as municipal hospitals and state university–sponsored settings. Staff them with transferred institutional personnel.

- *Pro:* This option is particularly suited to the mentally ill. Violent patients frequently cannot safely be treated in community hospital settings. Presence of small, secure institutions in each region will provide more humane, cost-effective care than preserving and maintaining large institutions for this purpose. The rationale for private administration, as for POS versus direct services, rests on the assumption that personnel currently serving in the state institutions are so imbued with the institutional practices that suppress client development that they would simply recreate those negative practices in the proposed institutions. Literature describing successful retraining of institutional personnel into community settings refers to early deinstitutionalization efforts. Most of the best personnel have now left the state systems. Private community programs are fiercely resisting incorporating the remaining state personnel, even the professionals. However, because unions are strong and have influence with state legislators, and out of a sense of fairness, employee concerns about jobs and retirement benefits must be attended to. Three options may meet the needs of state personnel while preserving the state's policy of attrition: (1) early retirement benefits, (2) training and transfer to other state positions, (3) training and transfer to community settings under other public auspices. The latter option is designed for those who are vested and lack mobility. It is hoped exposure to more privatelike adminis-

tration without civil service protection will encourage either positive change or resignation.

- *Con:* Any residual institutional role is dangerous, as it will be overutilized. The incentives needed to attract private management and professional staff for the proposed secure facilities would outweigh any cost-effectiveness smaller facilities would provide. The assumption that all state personnel are recalcitrant and "untherapeutic" is unfair and untrue.

Recommendation: Choose option 2 for the mentally retarded and option 3 for the mentally ill.

Rationale: Although deinstitutionalization is a goal for both the mentally retarded and the mentally ill, differences in the nature of their disabilities and in existing funding sources call for differences in policy.

Mental retardation, by and large, is a stable condition. Research has shown that individualized educative efforts can significantly improve the functioning of many retarded children and adults. To encourage individualized growth, in 1972, the federal government authorized Title XIX reimbursement for small, fifteen-bed facilities that supply occupational, socialization, and physical therapy as well as psychological, social work, medical, and dental services. The funding provision for these facilities under Title XIX in conjunction with the relatively stable condition of mentally retardation permits planning for a totally contracted community care system. The ICF/MRs are frequently the first step for many retarded individuals to less restrictive settings, such as group homes and supervised apartments. Much of the success of currently functioning ICF/MRs and group homes is due to the intense vigilance and advocacy of the parents of retarded individuals.

The mentally ill, by contrast, have few if any advocates (families are often nonexistent for one reason or another), lack federal support for settings comparable to the ICF/MRs (in fact, if more than 50 percent of a nursing home's residents are found to be mentally disabled, federal support ceases), and suffer from a frequently fluctuating disease process requiring a range of different treatment methods. As a result, standby inpatient beds, as noted in the eight key program elements, must be available, and some of these beds must be in a secure setting to protect others from violent patients and suicidal patients from themselves.

The personnel issue is the same in both cases, and the recommendation described applies to both.

IV. Implementation Factors

How can legislators be persuaded to continue to support both an institutional system and development of community-based services? They must be impressed with the horrors of a poorly planned deinstitutionalization process. Plenty of examples exist, probably even locally. Use them to gain crucial planning time.

How can unions be persuaded to comply with an implicit policy of attrition that will no doubt be perfectly explicit to them? The state administration must impress on local legislators, i.e.,

those whose areas are most affected by deinstitutionalization, that institutions are inhumane, anachronistic relics that must be abolished (I understand a Senator Backman has been vocal in this regard; this can be pointed out) but that the state wishes to be fair to employees caught in the middle.

DMH management should be sure to broaden the base when dealing with unions. Don't meet just with union leaders; involve rank and file and respected professionals. DMH should be sensitive to employee anxieties and commited to retraining and relocation efforts. New York State has been successful in this area and offers a good model.

What about the future? Should the state's goal be permanent dismantling of all direct care services? No. Once the current system has been dismantled and POS has been in operation for a while, DMH should evaluate the cost-effectiveness of providing direct care services versus POS, especially for outpatient services. Prof. Barry Friedman of the Heller School at Brandeis offers an excellent analytical model to this end. It is the stigma and ingrained practices of the current state system that must be destroyed. There is no reason why DMH, instituting the proper incentives, could not rebuild a direct care system under a new philosophy of care.

SOURCE: Dr. Marcia Mabee

---

number of these formats when presenting their positions.

ALTERNATIVE POSITION FORMATS

The format of a position is determined by its length, by whether it is written or delivered verbally, and by whether it is presented formally or informally. Alternative formats include extended papers, memorandums and brief position

papers, personal discussions, and formal oral presentations.

Extended Policy Papers

In academic and some bureaucratic settings, positions are developed in extended papers when position takers have the time and mandate to conduct in-depth explorations of policy issues. Such papers benefit from clarity of expression, clear sequencing of topics, logical progression, and adequate documentation. (Sources of evi-

The Research Grant Application

An Exercise in Scientific Writing

By George N. Eaves

A Nobel laureate recently stated that writing project proposals had filled his whole scientific life with agony. While agony may represent a somewhat extreme response, I am sure that most scientists consider the preparation of research grant proposals at least a discomfort. Since the preparation of research grant proposals is an activity which involves so many scientists, perhaps we should consider why we need to write grant applications. While the question is largely rhetorical, it is a question that must be answered occasionally. An obvious answer is that the grant application is the only effective way we have found whereby a large number of scientists can compete for limited funds for research. A less obvious answer is concerned with the spending of public funds. The National Institutes of Health must protect the public's funds that are appropriated for health-related research by seeing that they are allocated wisely and that the public is thereby assured of an optimum return for its investment. The worthiness of projects for support

from public funds is judged by qualified scientists in terms of the most promising research in a special investigative field. The basis for the judgment is the grant application. . . .

In 1977, about 5500 applications were reviewed by the Study Sections of the Division of Research Grants during the October-November 1977 meetings. The increased number of applications restricts the attempts of the Executive Secretary—the scientist administrator who coordinates the initial review for scientific merit—to devote special, personal attention to each application. Yet, as the number of applications has increased, the overall care with which the applications have been written has diminished. Nevertheless, the members of the Study Section have to rely primarily on the information presented in the application and on any additional materials submitted by the applicant in support of the proposal. . . .

With the increasing number of applications to be reviewed, we will more and more have to depend solely on the application as it is submitted. The importance of a complete and lucid application is therefore now more critical than ever. The author of the project-grant application must convince his peers of his

---

dence that can be used to build bibliographies and obtain information are discussed at the conclusion of this chapter.) These qualities are particularly important because the position taker often presents papers to persons or groups with considerable knowledge of the subject matter.

Clarity of Expression.   Clarity of expression is enhanced by avoiding excessive verbiage, unneces-

sary jargon, and overly complex sentences. When readers have difficulty comprehending the meaning of sentences, their attention is distracted from the ideas contained in the paper. Clarity can be achieved by developing basic writing and editing skills for improving successive drafts of the paper. In guest editorial 9.1, a government official who has reviewed many requests from researchers for government grants

knowledge, ability, specific intentions, and accomplishments in his chosen sphere. How does he start?

An investigator who is well informed about the peer review process has an advantage. Indeed, as Peter Woodford has emphasized in his manual on the teaching of scientific writing, the author of a project proposal must learn all he can about those who will read his proposal and keep those readers constantly in mind as he writes. Although that is certainly a basic consideration for any kind of scientific writing, many of our applicants have depended on the questionable reliability of word-of-mouth descriptions of the procedure for the review of project-grant proposals, without knowing exactly who the readers of the application will be. Since a description of the peer review process employed by the NIH is readily available, let us go to the next step and examine the basic skills needed to write the application.

Lucid writing and logical organization offer the most difficulty in the formulation of an effectual research proposal. I believe that many scientists are better than their applications indicate and that their chief weakness lies in their inability to describe and communicate the work that is so close to them. There are many reasons why one is not able to communicate in writing. An obvious reason is a lack of proficiency in clear, direct exposition. Highly developed writing skills alone, however, do not insure a successful grant application; it is the quality of the science that determines the success of an application. Nevertheless, the most meritorious science

can be misunderstood if the proposal is not written clearly and accurately. Some of the serious barriers to effective writing may not be obvious because they have become so closely identified with published reports of scientific experimentation. For example, the style of most scientific journals, in English, incorporates a tradition of indirectness, which is exemplified by the unwieldy passive voice that reflects the investigator's function as a mere reporter, as if he had nothing to do with the experimentation that he reports. In contemporary scientific writing, the passive voice is presumably retained as a means of directing the emphasis to the substance of a report, rather than to the experimenter. Yet, few scientists can write unambiguously in the passive voice.

Consider, for example, the vagueness of the simple expression encountered so frequently in the discussion section of a report: "the results are believed to support the authors' hypothesis." Is this believed by the scientific community in general, by all of the scientists whose research is based on the same hypothesis, by the authors and their present and former colleagues, or by only the authors? Were these results presented at a national meeting before they were published, and do the authors therefore know something about the acceptance of the data that the reader does not know? Comparable vagueness in a statement related to a scientific procedure, method, or result also forces the reader to presume the intended meaning. Is it any wonder, then, that there can be so many interpretations of the same report?

discusses the importance of clarity of expression in applications for research funds, but his comments apply to any policy document.

Clear Sequencing of Topics. Because of the complexity of many policy issues, writers need to develop an organizing scheme for papers. Orienting materials and perspectives provide required background materials, which can then be followed by discussion of the relative merits of various policy options and development of a policy position. Writers should use a range of centered and indented headings to identify the content of specific sections of the paper. Transition

All aspects of the communication of science depend on precision, as does scientific experimentation. Consequently, any style of writing that results in ambiguity should be abandoned in favor of a means of expression that insures clarity. If the authors of a report believe that their results support their hypothesis, they could simply state clearly and directly that "we believe our results support our hypothesis." Do not be concerned with what you may think is acceptable because it is traditional. Use a style of writing that permits you to communicate clearly.

We must become aware of the importance and the necessity for the development of basic skills in writing. Unfortunately, we can find few models to guide us in our attempts to develop effective writing skills. The education of a scientist includes little or no instruction in the precision of expressing ideas or of summarizing data. Instead, graduate students in the sciences and medical students must teach themselves by imitating reports already published, even though the published reports used as models are also links in a chain of mimicry. In fact, the entire historical concept of reporting scientific data has become so enshrined with an inviolable mysticism that the chain is rarely broken. While the sagacious scientist can usually wade through the ambiguity and eventually presume an author's intentions, no scientist should be subjected to this inconvenience. In the case of the grant application, however, the convenience of the reviewers is not the primary consideration; the research grant application must reflect how the investigator thinks, and it must convey unequivocally his plans for the proposed project. If the application is obscure and ambiguous, are the reviewers unreasonable to expect that the author's approach to science may share the same deficiencies? The written communication of scientific data is as much a part of the scientific endeavor as the experiment itself. . . .

While a reader's accurate comprehension depends largely on the author's skill in communicating, the most careful attention to the construction of individual sentences cannot expiate poorly organized material. Planning and organizing are as essential in writing as they are in efficacious experimentation. Yet, the inability to organize material into an effective application or report represents a stumbling block for many scientists. In the formulation of a grant application, logical organization is not limited to the concepts of order and arrangement, but involves judgment about the appropriateness and relevance of data and background information that should be included in the proposal. Good organization not only enhances the comprehensibility of a proposal but also reflects an investigator's judiciousness, critical insight, and understanding of his field of research.

Throughout the career of a scientist, he must write: manuscripts for publication, grant applications, internal reports, progress reports to granting agencies, letters of recommendation, and critical reviews for journals and for granting agencies. The development of skills in communicating science will not be easy, but an awareness of the problem should provide us with an appropriate beginning. . . .

SOURCE: Reprinted with permission from *Grants Magazine*, Vol. 1, No. 1, March 1978; copyrighted by Plenum Publishing Corporation.

sentences at strategic points allow readers to progress from one topic to another.

Logical Progression. It is sometimes tempting in policy papers to include more content than is truly needed. The writer needs to establish priorities for identifying important content. Many decision makers want to be able to understand the essential argument of a policy writer rather than to be inundated with unimportant or trivial information.

A carefully devised sequencing of topics allows the writer to avoid unnecessary repetition. Points developed in early portions of papers do not need to be discussed at length in subsequent sections, although writers may wish to refer readers back to preceding discussion. The organizing strategy must have logical coherence. A policy position should emerge as the writer gives information in sequential steps.

Writers sometimes omit information that is vitally important to a policy issue, or they introduce it belatedly. In the case of policy issues associated with political controversy, for example, writers should include extended discussion of political realities in orienting and perspectives sections as well as in subsequent sections where they discuss policy options and preferred policies. When analyzing such issues as work incentive policies for welfare recipients, writers have to grapple with technical material, such as the findings of recent and major research projects that analyze the extent to which generous welfare payments encourage (or discourage) employment by welfare recipients. When discussing many policy issues, writers need to identify relevant core and instrumental values that influence the policy positions of others and the policies preferred by the writer. For example, a paper on federal policy regarding abortions by Medicaid recipients would be incomplete if it ignored difficult and important value issues.

Memorandums and Brief Position Papers

In many cases, writers have to develop relatively brief memorandums that succinctly define issues and propose recommendations. These are written for an audience that is not receptive to longer documents, as in the case of an executive who wants a brief and concise report to highlight policy options. Policy memorandums can serve many functions. They can establish a need to place a policy issue on the agenda at an upcoming meeting, develop outlines of a policy position to stimulate further discussion at the meeting of a task force, or sensitize persons to policy options that have been previously ignored.

A challenge in writing brief policy documents is to present considerable material in a con-

densed format. Brief documents can never present all relevant material or develop positions or arguments at length, but their writers need to appear knowledgeable about the subject matter.

Grant Proposals

Grant proposals are policy documents because they require definition of the policy objectives associated with programs that are scrutinized by funding foundations, corporations, government officials, and other funders. Indeed, grant proposals draw on concepts and issues of the various policy phases discussed in preceding chapters. The California Department of Mental Health, for example, requires applicants for funds to define relevant community needs (scanning phase), community input and program strategies (analysis phase), staffing and administrative considerations (implementation phase), and evaluation plans (assessment phase) (see case example 9.1). Note how state officials score or rate proposals based on how successfully they deal with these issues.

Good proposals contain innovative service approaches. A cooperative project may be described that teams staff from various agencies; innovative technologies may be proposed, such as educational approaches in preventive programs; or services may be specifically tailored to the needs of groups in the population that do not find existing services responsive. In each of these cases, the proposal suggests that its writer has developed an innovative strategy that could serve as a model to other providers.[2]

Audience realities need to be carefully considered when developing proposals. The policy preferences and priorities of specific funders need to be investigated before applications are submitted. Foundations usually have particular program preferences, as illustrated by a foundation that only funds projects in the health care system. As mentioned in chapter 5, discussions with program staff prior to submission often provide additional information about foundations.

Corporations usually want to be certain that adequate fiscal and administrative controls and

CASE EXAMPLE 9.1

Criteria for Grant Review

Total Score _____

Total Average Score _____

Rated by
(initial) _____

Applicant _____

Project Title _____

Criteria	Approp. Page*	Weight	For Committee Use Only						Score W × R
			Rating low					high	
			0	1	2	3	4		
A. NEED									
1. Community need for the proposed services		3							
2. Services aimed at priority mental health problems(s)		3							
3. Services directed to high-risk populations in terms of age, economic status, geographic location, etc.		3							
4. Evidence of how the proposal fits the County Short-Doyle Plan or supplements it		3							
5. Existing services will not be unnecessarily duplicated		3							
6. Relevance to today's mental health issues		2							
7. Application in accord with state plans and priorities		3							
8. Applications in accord with local priorities		3							

Subtotal _____

Average _____

*Instruction to Proposal Reviewer: Please indicate page(s) in application where each item is addressed.

| | | | For Committee Use Only | | | | | | |
| Criteria | Approp. Page* | Weight | *low* | | Rating | | *high* | Score |
			0	1	2	3	4	W × R
B. COMMUNITY INPUT								
1. Linkage with appropriate resources		3						
2. Evidence of community support and involvement		3						
3. Evidence of coordination with present community resources		3						
4. Volunteer involvement in planning, service delivery, and decision-making		2						
5. Consumer involvement in planning, service delivery, and decision-making		2						

Subtotal _____

Average _____

| | | | | | | | | |
C. PROGRAM								
1. Alternative methodologies have been considered		1						
2. Service availability, accessibility and responsiveness to consumer		3						
3. Budget appropriateness		3						
4. Project encourages continuity of care		3						
5. Methods are feasible and appropriate to the objectives		2						
6. Services include prevention		2						
7. Innovativeness		2						
8. Physical facilities are adequate		1						
9. Appropriate and necessary license requirements and standards met		1						

Subtotal _____

Average _____

Criteria	Approp. Page*	Weight	For Committee Use Only					Score
			Rating low				high	W × R
			0	1	2	3	4	
D. STAFF								
1. Competence of personnel		3						
2. Staffing is appropriate and available		2						
3. Utilization of paraprofessionals		1						
4. Utilization of volunteers		1						
5. Opportunities for training and career development		1						
6. Receptivity to receiving consultation		1						
7. Evidence of commitment		3						
8. Evidence of good communication patterns		3						

Subtotal _____

Average _____

Criteria	Approp. Page*	Weight						Score
E. FOLLOW-THROUGH								
1. Planning for utilization and dissemination of outcome(s)		3						
2. Procedure for continuation, if program proves successful		2						
3. If program is part of a larger structure, how does it fit into program emphasis and/or priorities		1						
4. Receptivity to doing consultation		1						

Subtotal _____

Average _____

Criteria	Approp. Page*	For Committee Use Only						Score
			Rating					
			low				high	
		Weight	0	1	2	3	4	W × R
F. EVALUATION AND RESEARCH								
1. Evaluation and review of the problem (literature, visitations, etc.)		3						
2. Coherence—clear and logical relationships within the proposals		2						
3. Goals and objectives are clearly defined and measurable		2						
4. Evaluation and progress report procedures are adequate		3						
5. Credibility—are the methods and procedures generally accepted?		2						
6. Replicability		2						
7. Built-in procedure for on-going evaluation and/or research								

Subtotal ______

Average ______

Comments: ______________________________

SOURCE: This grant review drew heavily from:
a) California Areawide Comprehensive Health Planning Agency-Basic Criteria for Grant Review
b) United Way of Los Angeles Agency Rating
c) Factors Influencing the Success of Applied Research, NIMH Report on Contract 43-67-1365.

procedures exist when funding projects. They are sometimes more willing than foundations to give resources for ongoing administrative costs but may prefer donation of supplies or machines. Government funders are limited by the specific mandates given to them by legislation and policy guidelines. Social workers who want to develop skills in proposal writing and submission should consult reading and technical materials that are widely available (see selected readings at the end of chapter 5).

Personal Discussions

Personal discussions with decision makers are often used by position takers, whether to solicit policy perspectives, provide information about a current policy issue, or mobilize support. In these discussions, social workers draw on knowledge of psychological, social, and other factors. Personal discussions with legislators, for example, should be planned with sensitivity to the legislators' perspectives and time constraints. Social workers sometimes feel intimidated in approaching public officials when they believe that their perspectives will not be taken seriously. In policy practice case 9.2, a social worker discusses his experience contacting legislators when seeking state subsidies for persons with kidney disorders. He finds that he is most effective when he presents concise positions that can be supported with backup technical information.

Social workers are most likely to be effective with legislators when they are perceived to be credible, i.e., possess good information, present balanced points of view, give timely assistance, and are responsive to requests for further information. Social workers also must be willing to make strategic compromises that appear reasonable in the context of political realities.[3] In addition, they need skills in identifying strategic legislators who can be most helpful with their legislation because of committee or party membership, expertise, or alliances. In many cases, aides of legislators as well as government officials with relevant expertise can provide important technical and political information.[4]

It is important not to assume that someone will or will not support a policy proposal because they have taken certain positions in the past. True, a staunch conservative is unlikely to support a major new social program. But situations change, and current realities may have an entirely different impact on positions than similar situations previously encountered. In some cases, mere consultation with persons may decrease the likelihood of their opposing a policy proposal, particularly when they are asked to contribute their suggestions.

Formal Presentations

Social workers often make formal presentations to staff meetings, agency boards, community groups, professional associations, and legislative committees. In some cases, they also give policy views on radio and television or to reporters from the news media. These presentations require careful planning.

Most importantly, the audience needs to be assessed. A technical presentation is likely to be effective with an audience that is already knowledgeable about an issue but ineffective with an audience that expects a call to action. A presentation that emphasizes value-laden, emotional content is not likely to be effective with a group of moderate, pragmatic legislators who want to know if a specific policy proposal is fiscally feasible in an era of scarce resources.

When making formal presentations to legislative committees, social workers need to be thoroughly versed in the substantive issues associated with the particular piece of legislation. How do its provisions differ from current laws? What are positive and negative attributes of specific provisions in terms of equity, effectiveness, efficiency, externality, and equality criteria? What effects do provisions have on existing providers? How much would provisions cost?

Analysis of legislation needs to be coupled with understanding of committee membership. When a faction of a legislative committee assumes particular importance, arguments should be developed that will be convincing to its members. Policy perspectives of members should be analyzed so that specific questions can be anticipated.[5]

Fortunately, social workers can obtain background information about legislative committees from many sources, including aides to legislators, staffs of state agencies, lobbyists for groups like the National Association of Social Workers and the League of Women Voters, and discussions with persons who are knowledgeable about certain kinds of policies. Honest and balanced testimony is needed, including frank admission that the testifier does not have specific technical information or a ready answer to specific questions.[6] Whenever possible, support and technical information should be obtained from the state agency that will administer a proposal.

Social workers who make formal presentations should also carefully consider their length. In legislative testimony, for example, oral presentations are usually brief and highlight major issues. Testimony is often supplemented by brief written materials that present somewhat ex-

POLICY PRACTICE CASE 9.2

A Social Worker Approaches Legislators

Social workers may ask, How do you approach a legislator? In fact, they are generally not green-eyed monsters ready to pounce on you and put you down. They are human beings—sometimes hassled, sometimes short, sometimes friendly or arrogant, intelligent or ignorant, sympathetic or discouraging. They are busy and are pushed and pulled in a thousand different directions by numerous constituents and groups. How, then, should you approach them?

First, prepare yourself thoroughly before setting up your appointment and meeting with the legislator. State your problem in an easy-to-understand manner. Put it in writing so that the legislator can go over it and present it to his aides and resource experts for evaluation. Present any supporting documentation you may have to substantiate your assessment of the problem. Express clearly and directly your proposal for the legislative solution. Use graphs or charts that can simplify an explanation of the problem or solution.

It is often helpful to seek expert assistance in preparing your presentation of the problem and proposed solution. Even when you believe you have come up with the ideal solution, check it out with the specialists. They may find loopholes or point out affected client groups you may not have realized would be involved.

In our case, we found a technical expert in a department of state government. This resource person met with us on several occasions and made invaluable technical suggestions, even though the department would not officially support our project because a conservative governor feared that our efforts would require considerable state resources. Naturally, we would have preferred the backing of this department, since it would have added political support for our proposal. Still, the behind-the-scenes technical advice of the resource person was invaluable.

From the beginning, it is imperative to build a strong relationship with the legislator and his or her key staff persons. Although it is important to stay in contact with the legislator, much guidance, paperwork, research, and contacts can be effectively handled through a staff person. In our case, we met with the assemblyperson only twice and spoke with him directly by phone only once or twice until the bill was actually introduced into the state legislature, but we were in regular contact with the staff person.

SOURCE: Michael Cervantes, M.S.W.

panded discussion of issues covered in testimony. Both oral and written materials often emphasize an overall philosophy or point of view, since legislators are not likely to read overly complex documents. (Such documents may also have the disadvantage of locking the advocate into detailed positions that may need to be modified in the give-and-take of policy compromises.)

In other cases, social workers make fuller presentations that use graphic, technical, case study, and audio aids. Here, too, care must be taken not to deluge an audience with material or to use overly complex tables or charts that make the subject matter difficult to understand. Presenters should be well enough versed in their subject matter to look directly at their audience during the presentation.

No matter how well planned, unforeseen developments complicate the work of presenters. Perhaps a certain individual has an ax to grind

and proceeds to ask a series of difficult questions meant to place presenters on the defensive. It is important before presentations to try to anticipate possible sources of opposition as well as the kinds of information likely to be requested. As noted in the previous discussion, many audiences appreciate honesty when presenters do not have technical information and lack answers to specific questions.

Public Media

In some cases, social workers present policy positions to the public media through responses to editorials on radio or televsion, participation in talk shows, or briefing discussions to reporters. A response to an editorial on radio or television, for example, requires highlighting of policy perspectives and issues in a condensed format. In policy practice case 9.3, for example, a social

POLICY PRACTICE CASE 9.3

Feedback: Workfare

Announcer: In a recent editorial, the management of WBZ opposed the current workfare plan presented by Governor King to Washington. Here with some further comments on the issue is Constance Williams of the Massachusetts chapter of the National Association of Social Workers.

Williams: Workfare will have negative consequences for labor in general by providing a pool of workers who can be forced to work in poor conditions for low wages.

Support for the work ethic is not the issue. Studies show that most recipients prefer working. But, with continually rising unemployment, the jobs simply do not exist.

The typical adult receiving AFDC is a young, unskilled mother. A single mother not only must earn a living wage but also needs adequate daycare. Workfare must cover the

costs of both in addition to the costs of training programs that are expensive and result in few permanent jobs. Actually, only a minority of welfare recipients never work. One-third of all AFDC recipients go off welfare each year.

What needs to be addressed, then, is growing unemployment, shrinking educational and training opportunities, and insufficient childcare. Workfare is a punitive smokescreen to make it seem as if government is doing something useful. In reality, it will only serve to increase despair in the lives of many women and children and create more family problems.

The task of expanding work and training opportunities and meeting childcare needs of low-income people is difficult, but workfare is clearly not the solution.

SOURCE: Constance Williams.

worker supplements a radio station's editorial with further reasons for opposing a "workfare" proposal supported by a public official. She succinctly identifies economic, value, and administrative objections to workfare and portrays it as "a punitive smokescreen to make it seem as if government is doing something useful." In the process, she also conveys a problem-solving perspective when she suggests that panaceas would not suffice when dealing with complex issues, an orientation likely to appeal to persons seeking practical solutions.

The press can also be an ally when social workers are able to obtain the assistance of reporters willing to feature policy problems, issues, or events such as demonstrations. In some cases, reporters can be called by social workers for extended briefings that eventually lead to full-length stories uncovering, for example, abuses in nursing homes. Social workers can also call press conferences on important and timely topics, but they need to arrange sponsorship of them by one or more community groups or agencies. In some cases, professionals can give members of the press important information about specific policies or programs that can contribute to the development of columns or features.

Social workers should participate on talk shows that discuss social issues like child abuse to sensitize the public to the issues and to relevant policy options. Attempts should be made to identify the kinds of technical information and questions that are likely to be encountered. A talk show host, for example, often briefs participants in advance about the format of the show, the kinds of questions that will be asked, and the perspectives of other participants. Preparation is particularly important when different points of view are represented in a debate format.

REALITIES THAT SHAPE POSITIONS AND FORMATS

Decisions about the content and format of policy positions must be based on the objectives of the position taker, the audience, and practical realities, such as the time available for preparation.

These various contextual factors are encountered in agency, community, and legislative settings.

Objectives of the Position Taker

In some cases, position takers want to open up an issue for discussion rather than present specific and well-formulated policy proposals. A policy practitioner may believe that an existing policy needs to be examined because it may be defective. In such case, positions are developed that emphasize orientations and perspectives, but the position taker does not try to develop a preferred policy or solution. A social worker may document general discontent with an existing policy in an agency, for example, but not develop a policy alternative in hopes that others will agree that further deliberations are needed.

In other cases, position takers want to educate others as a prelude to changing existing policy. In an agency setting, for example, a position paper or a verbal presentation can be used to introduce staff to alternative policies and programs that are employed in other agencies in hopes that such information will spur them to reconsider existing policies. In this example, a position taker could emphasize orientations and perspectives and introduce selected policy alternatives.

Position takers often want to mobilize support of or opposition to specific policies. In such cases, they provide a full range of content but emphasize the merits of preferred policy options in contrast to less attractive ones.

Audience

Position takers must also consider the kind of audience that is reading or hearing their positions. Audiences variously consist of single persons, such as executives or legislators; groups, such as staffs or boards; or some sequential set of audiences, as when a policy proposal progresses from a staff meeting to an executive to an agency board. If the response of an audience to a policy position is unfavorable, its chances may be imperiled, particularly if it includes decision makers who will eventually assume an important role in approving or dismissing it. Presentations, then, need to be adapted to the interests and orientations of specific audiences. For example, a distinction can be made between advocate, technical, and pragmatic presentations.[7]

Advocate Positions.   In some cases, audiences have already decided the kinds of actions needed to resolve a specific policy problem, as in the instance of a Gray Panther audience that is concerned about funding cuts in a nutrition program for elderly persons. Here a position taker does not dwell on numerous policy options but moves rapidly toward presentation and defense of preferred policies, often appealing to perspectives and values that are shared by the audience and the position taker. Position takers also discuss political or implementation implications, as when, for example, a presenter suggests developing a coalition to convince legislators to rescind funding cuts.

Technical Positions.   Position takers sometimes encounter technically sophisticated audiences, such as experts who are deeply versed in the nuances and subtleties of policies associated with a specific issue. In such cases, they do not usually dwell on orientations or perspectives, since the audience is already familiar with them. Considerable attention is given instead to identifying policy options and comparing their relative merits, sometimes with considerable discussion of trade-offs associated with specific policy choices. Although underlying values may be discussed, positions must be substantially grounded in research and technical considerations.

Pragmatic Positions.   In other cases, position takers make presentations to administrators, legislators, or direct service staff members who are interested primarily in fiscal, administrative, or professional implications of specific positions. They want to know if changes in policy are feasible in light of current realities, knowledge that is important to them because their work requires them to discard policy options that prove too costly or difficult to implement. Positions must appear reasonable to such audiences. Since politicians want to know, for example, whether a certain position will allow them to build constituency support, the position taker must convince them that widespread support exists for specific policies.

Dilemmas in Position Taking.   Position takers sometimes experience unpleasant dilemmas. Someone may wish to present a policy likely to be unpopular with an audience, as when a social worker is asked to address an audience that is suspicious of a reform proposal. Or someone may wish to present an advocate position to a group of pragmatic executives insensitive to the needs of a certain group of consumers. In such cases, position takers may choose to be openly confrontive in hopes of persuading some persons to modify their positions. But confrontive approaches can be counterproductive and should therefore be used with an understanding of their risks.

Time Realities

Position takers sometimes have the luxury of spending substantial time developing their positions, as illustrated by a task force that devotes several years to intensive examination of a specific issue. In such cases, numerous policy options can be carefully explored, with preferred recommendations resting on a solid base of research.

But other positions must be constructed hurriedly. Some legislators, for example, have to develop positions on complex issues at the last minute before an important committee hearing or floor debate. Professionals sometimes have to respond to proposals that are delivered without advance notice in agency or board meetings. Position takers, then, have to develop skill in presenting their positions in brief periods and formats.

OBTAINING EVIDENCE

Whether social workers prepare memorandums, extended papers, or oral presentations, they need skills in obtaining information that can be used to build and defend positions. The amount of evidence required varies from project to project. More materials are available for some topics than for others. In some cases, time considerations preclude an exhaustive inventory of available sources of information.

Specifically, they need to be able to build bibliographies; i.e., lists of sources of information that include books, government publications, and journal articles. They need to be able to obtain important policy documents such as government reports. In some cases, written evidence is supplemented with interviews.

The precise sequence followed in obtaining information varies from project to project. In some cases, position takers interview knowledgeable persons prior to conducting library research. More commonly, however, they use the kind of sequence outlined in the following discussion, in which they begin with general library materials, locate more specialized documents, and then obtain information from persons in the field who can provide firsthand perspectives.

Classifying Problems and Issues

As a prelude to building bibliographies, social workers need to be able to classify problems, i.e., identify key words that enable them to find available reading material. In many cases, relevant information is listed under a number of headings. In the case of policies pertaining to the issue of rape, for example, a policy researcher might want to examine literature pertaining to women's issues, family violence, crime, and sexual harassment. Literature might also be discovered under other headings that describe specific kinds of rape (e.g., "incest") or special kinds of institutions or staff members that encounter or address the problem (e.g., "hospital emergency rooms" or "free clinics"). In some cases, information can be discovered in literature that explores more general subjects, such as feminism, women's rights, or crimes of violence. Finally, relevant information can be found by examining literature that explores related topics, such as deviance, crime, criminology, and sexism.

Policy researchers need to be creative, then, in brainstorming a variety of concepts and words that subsequently lead to important streams of research and writing. In some cases, their work is facilitated when a specific problem or issue is relatively narrow or focused, since literature is likely to be concentrated under a relatively small number of headings. In the case of policies to assist children with reading disorders, for example, a policy researcher might discover most information under headings like "education," "dyslexia," "handicapped children," or "reading disorder." Other broad problems, such as poverty, are classified under a seemingly endless list of headings and subjects. Even a seemingly specific problem like alcoholism may be discussed in the literature on a number of topics, including substance abuse, addiction, mental health, crime, accidents, mortality, health, and occupational disease, not to mention specific populations such as adolescents and women.

Preliminary Search

With key concepts and words identified, policy researchers can quickly identify an array of information sources by conducting library research; i.e., using indexes and abstracts, finding relevant bibliographies, searching card catalogues, and scanning footnotes in seminal articles and books. In initial library research, a useful strategy is to identify relevant titles under various key concepts and words by using (1) the card catalog that identifies holdings under subject headings, and (2) the *Library of Congress Subject Headings* (two volumes) to see if additional key concepts or words are listed that appear important to the policy (these volumes are catalogs of subject headings used in card catalogs). Further, book-length bibliographies are often found in the card catalog under specific subjects, as illustrated by a card with the heading "Child Abuse—Bibliography." A reference librarian should be consulted during the process of preliminary search for assistance in locating bibliographies and other reference aids that are useful to beginning research on a topic.

Policy researchers are often surprised to find

that they can readily find a series of important books merely by browsing shelf holdings near a relevant volume, because library books are shelved according to their subject matter. A book on women's issues, for example, is shelved next to other books covering similar material, though books relevant to this topic are also found in other locations in the library. When books are not on the shelf because they are missing, have been checked out, are on reserve, or are in a pre-shelving area, researchers should inquire at the circulation desk.

After identifying books on a topic by using the card catalog and browsing the shelves, researchers can use indexes and abstracts to identify journal articles. Indexes are publications, usually published at regular intervals, that list citations under subject and author headings. In the *Social Science Citation Index*, for example, articles from over 2,000 journals in the social sciences published during specific time periods are arranged by subject matter and author. Specialized indexes exist as well, as illustrated by the index *Child Abuse and Neglect Research*. Abstracts list books and articles and provide a brief description of their content, as illustrated by *Social Work Research and Abstracts*, a compilation of material from social work and related literature. (See Table 9.2 for a selective list of abstracts and indexes that often prove useful in social welfare policy research projects.)

As policy researchers soon discover, indexes and abstracts can be a curse as well as a blessing. They provide quick access to many titles but use different subject headings and often inundate the researcher with excessive material. The problem of inundation is particularly acute if the researcher opts for a computer search of literature, a technology now available in most libraries at relatively modest cost. As an example, titles and abstracts of articles listed in 780 educational journals can be obtained through the computer-based Educational Resources Information Center (ERIC) or through 120 different but similar files in the Lockheed Dialogue system, which covers, among others, the Social Science Citation Index and the Public Affairs Informational Service. These computer searches can sometimes lead to

identification of large numbers of articles, so care is needed to choose relatively narrow terms that allow the researcher to restrict titles to those specifically germane to the policy topic.

Another approach for generating titles is to use the indexes of journals that specialize in issues or topics relevant to the researcher's inquiry. A policy researcher, for example, might wish to examine annual indexes of journals like *Public Interest*, *Social Policy*, and *Public Welfare*. In the case of popular literature on current events, the annual and monthly update volumes of the *Reader's Guide to Periodical Literature* can be consulted.

Finding Seminal Works

Although titles of relevant books and articles are helpful, the researcher often needs to locate pivotal or seminal works that provide an overview of the policy topic, including historical and other information about the policy context, and information about specific facets of the topic. In some cases, the researcher can obtain listings of important works from someone—a reference librarian, a researcher, or a participant in policy development—who is deeply versed in the literature associated with a specific policy topic.

Examination of footnotes and bibliographies of recent books and articles can lead to identification of basic works that are referenced more frequently than others. Journals publish critical book reviews that often allow identification of the perspectives of authors, reviews that can be located by referring to the *Book Review Digest*, *Book Review Index*, or the *Social Sciences Index*.

The collected writings of important authors can be identified by using the card catalog in the library or referring to author listings in specific indexes or abstracts. In some cases, researchers may wish to begin their research by reading a few well-chosen seminal works and then proceed to development of more extensive bibliographies. They can also consult basic reference books, such as the *Encyclopedia of Social Work*, to obtain initial information about a policy topic. Other useful reference books include the *International Encyclopedia of the Social Sciences*, *Dictionary of the So-*

TABLE 9.2 User's Guide: Abstracts and Indexes Frequently Used in Social Welfare Policy Research

Abstracts on Criminology and Penology

American Statistical Index (AIS)

Congressional Information Service (CIS)

Crime and Delinquency Abstracts

Crime and Delinquency Literature

Cumulated Index Medicus

Cumulative Index to Nursing and Allied Health

Current Index to Journals in Education (ERIC)

Current Literature on Aging

Developmental Disabilities Abstracts (formerly Mental Retardation Abstracts)

Dissertation Abstracts International (used in conjunction with Comprehensive Dissertation Index)

ERIC (Educational Resources Information Center)

Excerpta Medica

Government Reports Index

Human Resources Abstracts (formerly Poverty and Human Resources Abstracts)

Index of Economic Articles

Journal of Human Service Abstracts

Medical Socioeconomic Research Sources

Monthly Catalog of U.S. Government Publications

New York Times Index

Poverty and Human Resources Abstracts

Psychological Abstracts

Public Affairs Information Service

Readers Guide to Periodical Literature

Rehabilitation Literature

Research in Education (ERIC)

Research Relating to Children

Selective Index to Health Literature

Social Science Citation Index

Social Sciences Index (formerly Social Sciences and Humanities Index)

Social Work Research and Abstracts (formerly Abstracts for Social Workers)

Sociological Abstracts

United Way of America: Digest of Selected Reports

Women's Studies Abstracts

Ruth Britton assisted in developing this list.

cial Sciences, Dictionary of Sociology, Encyclopedia of Psychology, and the Encyclopedia of Bioethics.

Policy Commentary

In many cases, policy researchers supplement bibliographies with readings from newspapers and journals that discuss current issues. Annual indexes and periodic updates are available in most libraries for major newspapers such as the New York Times, the Christian Science Monitor, the Washington Post, the Los Angeles Times, and the Wall Street Journal. Timely articles on current policy issues in these publications are often available on microfilm and provide a wealth of material drawn from interviews with strategically placed participants in policy or program arenas. The National Journal provides excellent coverage of current policy issues and includes frequent update indexes to facilitate location of a range of articles on health and welfare issues. At the state level, researchers should consult indexes of major newspapers in their particular state as well as policy journals such as the California Journal. Information about public opinion on public issues can be found in various publications listed under the Gallup Report and the Harris Survey.

Current Legislative Developments

The Congressional Quarterly Almanac is an indispensible and easy-to-use resource for current policy papers, since it provides a yearly summary of legislative developments in the Congress. At the end of each volume, a subject index allows location of discussion of (1) legislative developments associated with particular pieces of legislation and (2) an overview of developments in health, public welfare, and related sectors. (As noted later in this chapter, the Almanac is particularly useful because it allows ready identification of congressional publications that present public hearings held by congressional committees on specific pieces of legislation.) The researcher who is interested in legislative developments that occurred after publication of the most recent edition of the Almanac can consult weekly editions of the Congressional Quarterly

Weekly Reports. The Congressional Quarterly's Guide to the Congress is a reference book that discusses Congressional procedures. Another useful book is the Almanac of American Politics that includes profiles of important elected officials as well as their voting records.

Government Deliberations

While secondary accounts are useful, policy researchers often want to read transcripts of legislative deliberations, such as committee hearings or debates on the floor of Congress. (Important policy documents are often inserted into these transcripts as well.) Committee hearings are printed and distributed to many libraries; they can be easily located by locating the name of the relevant committee and dates of the hearings in the aforementioned Congressional Quarterly Almanac or in the Congressional Information Service (CIS) that indexes hearings, committee publications, and legislation. Government and Congressional publications are sometimes cataloged under a section of the author card catalog beginning with "U.S." As an example, perusal of the 1971 volume of the Congressional Quarterly Almanac indicates that childcare provisions of welfare reform legislation introduced by President Richard Nixon were discussed before the Finance Committee of the Senate on September 22, 23, and 24, 1971. This particular committee hearing had been bound by the library; its call number was located by looking in the author card catalog under the heading "U.S., Congress, Senate, Finance Committee, Hearings on S. 2003, Child Care Provisions of H.R. 1." In some libraries, government documents do not appear in the card catalog, but appear in a separate catalog or in listings maintained in the "hearings section" of the government documents room. (A reference librarian should be consulted to ascertain how government documents are cataloged in a specific library.) For titles of very recent committee hearings, the researcher should consult issues of the Congressional Quarterly Weekly Report.

Annual volumes of the Congressional Record contain transcripts of deliberations in the House and Senate. A researcher who wanted to exam-

S. 4106

91st Congress, 2d Session

In the Senate of the United States, July 21, 1970

Mr. Magnuson (for himself, Mr. Jackson, Mr. Cranston, Mr. Hughes, Mr. Kennedy, Mr. Nelson, Mr. Randolph, and Mr. Williams of New Jersey) introduced the following bill; which was read twice and referred to the Committee on Labor and Public Welfare

A Bill

To amend the Public Health Service Act in order to provide for the establishment of a National Health Service Corps. *Be it enacted by the Senate and House of Representatives of the United States of America in Congress assembled,* That this Act may be cited as the "National Health Service Corps Act of 1970".

Sec. 2. Title III of the Public Health Service Act is amended by adding at the end thereof a new part as follows:

"Part J—National Health Service Corps, Establishment of National Health Service Corps; Functions

"Sec. 399h. (a) There is established in the Service a National Health Service Corps (hereinafter in this part referred to as the 'Corps') which shall be under the direction and supervision of the Surgeon General.

"(b) It shall be the function of the Corps to improve the delivery of health services to persons living in communities and areas of the United States where health personnel, facilities, and services are inadequate to meet the health needs of the residents of such communities and areas. Priority under this part shall be given to those urban and rural areas of the United States where poverty conditions exist

and the health facilities are inadequate to meet the needs of the persons living in such areas.

"Staffing; Term of Service

"Sec. 399i. (a) The Surgeon General shall assign selected commissioned officers of the Service and such other personnel as may be necessary to staff the Corps and to carry out the functions of the Corps under this part.

"(b) Commissioned officers of the Service in the Corps and other Corps personnel shall be detailed for service in the Corps for a period of twenty-five months. An individual detailed to the Corps may voluntarily extend his service in the Corps for a period not to exceed an additional twenty-five months. An individual shall have the right to petition the Director (appointed pursuant to section 399j of this part) for early release from service in the Corps at the end of twenty-four months of service therein.

"Director of the National Health Service Corps

"Sec. 399j. The Corps shall be headed by a Director who shall be appointed by the President, by and with the advice and consent of the Senate. It shall be the responsibility of the Director to direct the operations of the Corps, subject to the supervision and control of the Surgeon General.

"Authority of Secretary to Utilize Corps Personal

"Sec. 399k. The Secretary is authorized, whenever he deems such action appropriate, to utilize commissioned officers of the Service and other personnel detailed to duty with the Corps to—

"(1) perform services in connection with direct health care programs carried out by the Service;

"(2) perform services in connection with any direct health care program carried out in whole or in part with the Department of Health, Education, and Welfare funds or the funds of any other department or agency of the Federal Government; or

"(3) perform services in connection with any other health care activity, in furtherance of the purposes of this Act. Should services provided under this subsection require the establishment of health care programs not otherwise authorized by law, the Secretary is authorized and directed to establish mechanisms whereby recipients of such services shall pay, to the extent practicable, for services received. Any funds collected in this manner shall be used to defray in part the operating expenses of the Corps.

"National Health Corps Advisory Council

"Sec. 399l. (a) There is established a council to be known as the National Health Corps Advisory Council (hereinafter in this section referred to as the 'Council'). The Council shall be composed of twelve members appointed as follows:

"(1) three members from the Department of Health, Education, and Welfare, serving outside the Corps, to be appointed by the Secretary;

"(2) three members appointed by the Secretary from private life;

"(3) three members detailed to duty with the Corps, at least two of whom shall be commissioned officers of the Service, to be appointed by the Secretary; and

"(4) three persons who have received more than minimal health care services from the Corps, to be appointed by the Secretary after the Corps has been in operation for a period of at least one hundred and twenty days and to be appointed from geographically dispersed areas to the extent practicable.

"(b) Members of the Council shall be appointed for a term of three years and shall not be removed, except for cause. Members may be reappointed to the Council.

"(c) It shall be the function of the Council—

"(1) to establish guidelines with respect to how the Corps shall be utilized and to consult with and advise the Director generally regarding the operation of the Corps;

"(2) to assist the Surgeon General, at his request, in the selection of commissioned officers of the Service and other personnel for assignment to the Corps, and to approve all assignments of Corps members;

"(3) to establish criteria for determining which communities or areas will receive assistance from the Corps, taking into consideration—

"(A) the need of any community or area for health services provided under this part;

"(B) the willingness of the community or area and the appropriate governmental agencies therein to assist and cooperate with the Corps in providing effective health services to residents of the community or area;

"(C) the prospects of the community or area for utilizing Corps personnel after their tour of duty with the Corps:

"(D) the recommendations of any agency or organization which may be responsible for the development, under section 314(b), of a comprehensive plan covering all or any part of the area or community involved; and

"(E) recommendations from the medical, dental, and other medical personnel of any community or area considered for assistance under this part.

ine testimony in the Senate on specific legislation could find the dates it was discussed in the *Congressional Quarterly Almanac* and then proceed to the appropriate dates in the bound volume of the *Congressional Record*. A *Congressional Index* is published each year and is indexed by subject matter, enabling a researcher to quickly find floor testimony on specific issues that arose during the year (periodic updates allow location of recent hearings).

Legislation and Regulations

Many policy papers require examination of legislation, whether proposed bills or enacted public laws. Proposed legislation is usually included in the text of hearings of committees in the House or Senate as well as transcripts of floor debates in the *Congressional Record*. In case example 9.2, a bill that proposes amending the Public Health Service Act to establish a National Health Service Corps—legislation that was eventually enacted—is included in this chapter because some readers may want to examine Eric Redman's excellent case study of its development and passage.[8] In this particular example, the bill proposes adding a section to existing public law (i.e., "Part J—National Health Services Corps"). Note how the legislation discusses a number of the core policy issues discussed in this book, including those pertaining to staffing of the National Health Service Corps, its financing, and establishment of decision-making procedures through formation of a National Health Corps Advisory Council. Many policy details are also not defined in the legislation, details that had to be addressed subsequently in administrative regulations. Redman and his allies chose not to include detailed policies concerning eligibility, for example, to avert controversy.

Proposed bills become public laws when they are formally approved by the legislature and the President. Major provisions of public legislation laws are summarized in the *Congressional Quarterly Almanac* as well as the *Congressional Quarterly Weekly Reports*.

Within a year of enactment, public laws are printed in a series of books published by West Publishing Company known as the *U.S. Code Annotated*, as well as in the *U.S. Code* published by the U.S. Government Printing Office. Enacted legislation is classified under one of fifty titles that correspond to specific subjects. Thus, for example, additions to and amendments of the Social Security Act are placed under Title 42 of the *U.S. Code*.

The policy researcher often wants to examine regulations pertinent to implementation that are issued by government authorities in the wake of passage of legislation. The *Code of Federal Regulations* contains rules that are in force at the time it is published each quarter and has fifty titles like the *U.S. Code*, to assist the reader in locating regulations that correspond to specific pieces of enacted legislation. An excerpt from the *Code of Federal Regulations* presented in case example 9.3 discusses the use of social workers in skilled nursing facilities. Often technical and uninteresting in appearance, these administrative regulations can have profound implications for consumers, providers, and professionals. Policy researchers who want to examine recent or proposed regulations can examine daily issues of the *Federal Register* and its quarterly index. (All proposed regulations have to be printed in this publication prior to their adoption to allow interested persons to comment on them.)

Statistical Information

The *Statistical Abstract of the United States* annually summarizes crime, health, and other selected statistics published by government agencies. Thus, the researcher need only search the index of this publication for relevant trend data. At periodic points in this book, charts are used that are drawn from *Social Indicators III*, the third in a series of publications of the U.S. Bureau of the Census. Census data is summarized in the *U.S. Census of Population*. The Bureau of the Census also publishes many *Current Population Reports* that draw on census and other studies. The beginning researcher can often consult a reference librarian and ask about the availability of trend data relevant to such policy topics as child abuse, malnutrition, infant mortality, and poor hous-

CASE EXAMPLE 9.3

Code of Federal Regulations;
Title 42, Public Health;
Chapter IV, Health Care Financing Administration;
HS of October 1, 1980

405.1130 Condition of participation—social services. The skilled nursing facility has satisfactory arrangements for identifying the medically related social and emotional needs of the patient. It is not mandatory that the skilled nursing facility itself provide social services in order to participate in the program. If the facility does not provide social services, it has written procedures for referring patients in need of social services to appropriate social agencies. If social services are offered by the facility, they are provided under a clearly defined plan, by qualified persons, to assist each patient to adjust to the social and emotional aspects of his illness, treatment, and stay in the facility.

(a) *Standard: Social service-functions.* The medically related social and emotional needs of the patient are identified and services provided to meet them, either by qualified staff of the facility, or by referral, based on estab-

lished procedures, to appropriate social agencies. If financial assistance is indicated, arrangements are made promptly for referral to an appropriate agency. The patient and his family or responsible person are fully informed of the patient's personal and property rights.

(b) *Standard: Staffing.* If the facility offers social services, a member of the staff of the facility is designated as responsible for social services. If the designated person is not a qualified social worker, the facility has a written agreement with a qualified social worker or recognized social agency for consultation and assistance on a regularly scheduled basis. (See § 405.1121(i).) The social service also has sufficient supportive personnel to meet patient needs. Facilities are adequate for social service personnel, easily accessible to patients and medical and other staff, and ensure privacy for interviews.

ing. The *American Statistical Index* lists titles of all government publications that provide statistical information as well as the agencies that issue them (from which copies can be obtained). Other books that provide statistics include the *Handbook of Labor Statistical Yearbook,* the *Historical Statistics of the U.S., Business Statistics,* the *Statistical Yearbook,* and the *Demographic Yearbook* (the latter two publications are issued by the United Nations).

Additional Resources

As policy researchers obtain familiarity with the resources discussed thus far, they can use other

resources as well. For example, titles, abstracts, and the names of sponsors of proposed legislation can be obtained by using the *Digest of the Public General Bills and Resolutions* published by the Congressional Research Service of the Library of Congress or the *Congressional Index* published by the Commerce Clearing House. Persons who want information on recently enacted legislation that has not yet been published in the *U.S. Code* can consult the *United States Code Congressional and Administrative News.* Government publications can also be accessed by referring to the *Monthly Catalog of U. S. Governmental Publications,* a rich repository of titles of publications that are relevant to many policy topics. (Libraries designated as "depository libraries" are required to have many of these government publications in their holdings.)

Whether using these or other resources discussed in this chapter, policy researchers should not be intimidated by the plethora of resources or their seeming complexity. Researchers who begin with the easy-to-use and indispensible *Congressional Quarterly Almanac* can easily obtain additional information about other sources from reference libraries, and librarians in law libraries can assist them in locating copies of legislation or relevant administrative regulations.

Many researchers need to obtain legislation and administrative guidelines enacted at the state level. Each state has a series of volumes that present state laws as well as administrative regulations. (Consult a reference or law librarian to obtain references applicable to a specific state as well as transcripts of committee and legislative deliberations.)

Interviewing

No substitute exists for interviewing persons who, because of their strategic location, know about important facets of policy. Line staff, supervisors, and administrators can discuss issues associated with implementation of existing policies. Aides to legislators and staff in government agencies can provide invaluable information, whether in local, state, or federal arenas.

Preparation for interviews is essential. In many cases, the policy researcher should already have invested considerable time in library research to enable more productive use of the interview, including a focusing of questions on topics not discussed in written materials. Although relatively open-ended or unstructured questions are often used, the researcher should carefully develop a set of questions to be used during a portion of the interview that direct attention to important facets of the policy topic. Similarly, time should be given to developing an initial list of interviewees who (1) represent several or more perspectives on the policy topic and (2) are positioned to provide specific kinds of information about it.

Persons who conduct interviews on sensitive policy topics soon realize that good fortune is required to find key informants willing to discuss controversial issues. Some interviewees are extremely guarded in divulging information and personal perspectives; others not only assist the researcher but provide names of additional interviewees.

In order to increase the likelihood that interviewees will share information, researchers should maintain a posture that is relatively neutral yet supportive, even with informants whose personal perspectives diverge markedly from their own.[9] Interviewers from academic settings should not cut off exchange of information with moderate or conservative interviewees by appearing to fit liberal academic stereotypes.

SUMMARY

Position taking skills are needed to develop substantive policy recommendations in the various policy phases and arenas we discussed in chapters 1 and 2. Positions are "action-oriented statements that recommend specific policies with supporting arguments and evidence" and are used to persuade others that specific actions or approvals are needed. Indeed, position taking is so integral to social welfare policy that it can be used to distinguish it from other disciplines, including research, administration, and community organization.

When constructing positions, social workers plan their direction, focus, and content. Both affirmative and negative positions are used as social workers develop and defend (affirmative positions) or criticize (negative positions) specific policies. A focus for positions is developed by carefully selecting a social problem, choosing a policy arena, identifying a time frame, and selecting a policy phase. Most positions contain orientations, issues, perspectives, and implications, but the central portion of many positions is comprised of discussion of available policy options and preferred policy choices.

Many formats can be used to present positions, including extended papers, proposals, memorandums, and brief position papers. Written materials are often supplemented by oral materials, whether personal discussions or formal presentations. In some cases, social workers make presentations to the public media that can sensitize the broader public to policy issues.

When selecting the content and format of policy positions, social workers need to consider their own objectives, the orientations of the audience, and practical realities, such as the amount of time available for preparation and presentation. As an example, formal presentations to legislative committees are typically brief and supplemented by concise written materials that highlight issues and identify preferred policies.

Social workers need to be familiar with techniques for gathering evidence that can be used to develop and buttress policy positions. When a topic has been chosen, policy researchers often identify key concepts that can be used to access various sources of information. Researchers typically move from general to more specific, focused sources. General sources include various indexes, abstracts, encyclopedias, and dictionaries, which usually generate a wealth of article and book titles that appear to be relevant to the policy topic. Additional titles can be identified by perusing the subject portion of the card catalog and by browsing library shelves in proximity to a specific book that is relevant to the policy topic. Computer searches can also be useful, particularly in extended and relatively ambitious policy research projects.

Current information about specific topics can be obtained from articles in newspapers or national journals. Many researchers use the *Congressional Quarterly Almanac* or the *Congressional Quarterly Weekly Report*, publications that not only summarize key policy developments but also provide references to committee hearings and floor debates. Inspection of the transcripts of deliberations of legislators, whether hearings of congressional committees or floor debates printed in the *Congressional Record*, provides useful information about policy issues. Researchers also find policy documents published by government agencies or commissions to be useful as cataloged in the *Monthly Catalog of U.S. Governmental Publications.*

Copies of proposed bills, enacted legislation, and regulations obtained from transcripts of congressional hearings, the *Congressional Record*, the *U.S. Code,* or the *Code of Federal Regulations* often allow policy researchers to be more precise in their discussion of policy issues. Interviews with key informants can supplement library and government materials with important information and perspectives, just as inclusion of statistical information can illuminate the nature of the social problems and issues that first occasioned policy initiatives.

The policy puzzle is rarely completed, however, until the researcher has articulated a policy position that identifies preferred strategy for addressing social problems in one or another of the policy phases. Even in historical studies, policy researchers usually develop judgments about the merits of specific policies sometimes coupled with discussion of implications for contemporary policies. In studies of contemporary issues, policy researchers delineate problems as well as solutions that have been proposed by others but usually develop their own recommendations, which sometimes coincide with positions already articulated by others. As policy researchers develop positions, they become participants in policy controversy, since their perspectives, even when developed in the course of arduous research, are likely to be questioned by persons with divergent values, interests, and technical opinions.

Key Concepts, Developments, and Policies

Policy positions
Affirmative positions
Negative positions
Focus of policy positions

Elements of policy positions
Formats for positions
Extended papers
Memorandums and brief position papers

Proposals
Personal discussions
Formal presentations
Legislative committees
Media presentations
Objectives of position takers
Audiences
Advocate, technical, and pragmatic positions
Time realities
Classifying problems and issues
Preliminary search
Indexes
Abstracts
Library of Congress List of Subject Headings
Shelf holdings and catalog

Author catalog
Subject catalog
Computer searches
Journal indexes
Seminal works
Congressional Quarterly Almanac and
　Weekly Reports
Congressional Record
Government hearings
Bills
Public law
Code of Federal Regulations
U.S. Code
Interviews

Main Points

1. Policy positions are important products in the various policy phases and arenas. They are "action-oriented statements that recommend specific policies with supporting arguments and evidence." Position taking skills are needed to develop, present, and defend them.

2. Social welfare policy can be distinguished from other allied and methodological disciplines by its emphasis on positions and position taking. Still, policy practitioners use techniques and concepts from research, administration, and community organization when developing, presenting, and defending policy positions.

3. Policy practitioners need to plan the direction, focus, and content of policy positions.

   a. The direction is determined by whether the position taker develops and defends policies (affirmative positions) or criticizes policies developed by others (negative positions).

   b. A focus is developed for positions by specifying social problems, choosing a policy arena, selecting a time frame, and choosing a policy phase.

   c. Content of positions includes orientations, issues, perspectives, policy options, preferred policies, and implications.

4. Alternative formats for positions include extended papers, memorandums and brief position papers, proposals, personal discussions, and formal presentations.

5. When planning the content and format of policy positions, social workers need to consider practical realities, including personal objectives, the nature and orientations of the audience, and time considerations.

6. Audiences include staff meetings, executives, boards, the public media, consumer groups, legislative committees, and professional associations. Technical, pragmatic, and advocacy positions are variously used, depending on the objectives of the position taker and the perspectives of the audience.

7. An initial step in policy research is to classify problems and issues, i.e., to identify key words and concepts that allow researchers to find data in library sources.

8. In preliminary search, researchers identify an array of information sources by using in-

dexes and abstracts, finding relevant bibliographies, scanning footnotes, using card catalogs, and conducting a shelf search.

9. Early in the research process, researchers try to identify seminal or basic works that provide perspectives and an overview.

10. Articles in the press and national policy journals provide important information on current developments.

11. The *Congressional Quarterly Almanac* and *Congressional Quarterly Weekly Reports* provide an overview of current legislative developments as well as references to congressional committee hearings and floor debates. Transcripts of committee hearings and committee reports are available in many libraries and provide important testimony on policy

issues, as do transcripts of floor debates in the *Congressional Record*.

12. Discussion of proposed bills and enacted legislation can be found in committee hearings and the *Congressional Record*. Various legal references can be used to find the text of legislation.

13. The *Code of Federal Regualtions* and the *Federal Register* contain important administrative regulations, both operational and proposed.

14. Various sources of statistical information can be used to provide data about social issues and trends.

15. Policy researchers often interview persons who, because of their strategic location, are knowledgeable about specific facets of policy topics.

Questions for Discussion

1. For purposes of discussion, choose a policy issue or topic that interests you and identify several different kinds of positions you might develop by choosing (a) different methods of defining the social problem, (b) different policy arenas, (c) different time frames, and (d) different policy phases.

2. Choose any current controversial policy issue in the nation or in an agency and then develop (a) an affirmative position and (b) a negative position. Do you agree with the assertion "It is far easier to criticize someone else's policy preferences (a negative position) than to have to defend your own (an affirmative position)"?

3. How does social welfare policy differ from such related disciplines as research, administration, and community organization? Do these various disciplines overlap?

4. Identify a policy issue in a social agency with which you are familiar. Then choose an audience to which you might conceivably make a presentation after you have developed a policy position. What format would you use for your presentation? How would your objec-

tives, the perspectives of the audience, and time realities shape your choice of format as well as the content of your position?

5. What are some major differences between advocate, technical, and pragmatic positions? Discuss audience realities and personal objectives that might influence your choice of one rather than another of these positions.

6. Take some policy issue or topic and brainstorm a list of key concepts and words that might be useful when seeking articles and books relevant to the topic. Then find which subject headings are actually used (a) in the card catalog (use the *Library of Congress Subject Headings*) and (b) in three relevant indexes or abstracts.

7. Indexes and abstracts can be both a blessing and a curse. Discuss this statement as well as how you might deal with the problem of excessive amounts of information pertaining to the policy topic you have chosen to research.

8. Discuss how you would use the *Congressional Quarterly Almanac* and the *Congressional*

Quarterly Weekly Reports to obtain references to congressional deliberations relevant to a specific policy topic.

9. Choose a policy area and list various kinds of information that would be important to locate in library sources. Then outline the library sources you would use to find the various kinds of information.

10. You decide to interview someone for a research project who has opinions diametrically opposed to yours (e.g., an overtly sexist or racist person who nonetheless can provide valuable information). What strategies might you use to obtain information? What dilemmas might you encounter during the interview itself?

Suggested Readings

Brock, Bernard, et al. *Public Policy Decision Making* (New York: Harper & Row, 1973). Methods of establishing and defending policy positions and of criticizing alternative policies are discussed in this book on debate strategy. (Any book on debate strategy is applicable to position taking in social welfare policy, as are such programs as the McNeil-Lehrer evening report on public television.)

Coplin, Merry. *Library Research for Public Policy Issues* (New York: Learning Resources in International Studies, 1975). A concise discussion of various data and information sources that are useful to those undertaking policy research projects.

Dexter, Lewis. "Role Relationships and Conception of Neutrality in Interviewing." *American Journal of Sociology,* 62 (September 1956): 153–157. This article is an excellent introduction to policy interviewing, with discussion of difficulties in obtaining information from persons with perspectives that differ from the researcher's.

Dluhy, Milan. "Policy Advice-Givers: Advocates? Technicians? or Pragmatists?" In John Tropman et al., eds., *New Strategic Perspectives* (New York: Pergamon, 1981): pp. 202–217. The author suggests that the style or approach used in presenting policy positions must be adapted to the audience.

Dunn, William. *Public Policy Analysis* (Englewood Cliffs, N.J.: Prentice-Hall, 1981): "Modes of Pol-

icy Argument," pp. 64–94. An advanced discussion of alternative methods of presenting and defending policy positions.

Hatry, Harry et al. *Program Analysis for State and Local Governments* (Washington, D.C.: Urban Institute, 1976): Appendix B. Two illustrative outlines of an issue paper are presented.

Mayer, Robert, and Greenwood, Ernest. *The Design of Social Policy Research* (Englewood Cliffs, N.J.: Prentice-Hall, 1980): "History of the Policy Problem," pp. 98–121. An excellent discussion of various sources of data and information for policy research projects.

Mullins, Carolyn. *A Guide to Writing and Publishing in the Social and Behavioral Sciences* (New York: Wiley, 1977). The author analyzes writing style as it pertains to publishing articles, monographs, and texts in the social sciences, but her comments on style apply to the writing of many policy documents and papers as well.

Rusher, William A. *How to Win Arguments* (Garden City, N.Y.: Doubleday, 1981). A readable discussion of debate strategy by one of the major participants in the popular "The Advocates" program on public television.

Turman, Barbara. "Critical Sources for the Examination of Current Policy Debates." In W. Joseph Heffernan, *Introduction to Social Welfare Policy* (Itasca, Ill.: Peacock, 1979): pp. 300–310. A listing and abstract of major sources of information relevant to public welfare research projects.

Notes

1. Affirmative and negative positions are discussed by Brock et al., *Public Policy Decision Making*.

2. Proposal writing is discussed by Craig Smith and Eric Skjei, *Getting Grants* (New York: Harper & Row, 1981).

3. Rino J. Patti and Ronald B. Dear, "Legislative Advocacy: One Path to Social Change," *Social Work*, 20 (March 1975): 108–114.

4. Cecilia Kleinkauf, "A Guide to Giving Legislative Testimony," *Social Work*, 26 (July 1981): 297–306.

5. Ibid.

6. Ibid.

7. Dluhy, "Policy Advice-Givers: Advocates? Technicians? or Pragmatists?" in Tropman et al., eds., *New Strategic Perspectives* pp. 202–217.

8. Eric Redman, *Dance of Legislation* (New York: Simon & Schuster, 1973).

9. Lewis Dexter, "Role Relationships and Conception of Neutrality in Interviewing," *American Journal of Sociology*, 62 (September 1956): 153–157.

PART 5

Policies, Programs, and Issues in the Contemporary Period and in Four Policy Sectors

Parts 1 through 4 have presented *general* concepts for understanding and participating in the formulation of social welfare policy. Now, the chapters of part 5 will link these concepts to policy formulation in *specific* policy sectors in which many social workers become involved: child and family, economic security, health, and mental health.

Each chapter in part 5 begins by presenting guiding orientations that reflect values and theoretical orientations that are frequently espoused in social work literature. Then, normative frameworks are used to assess existing policies in terms of effectiveness, efficiency, equity, and equality.

Social workers also must be able to identify relevant political, economic, and ideological factors that will impede or support the modification of existing policies, so each chapter contains a brief analysis of the historical evolution of policy in the sector being considered.

Selected reform proposals that have promise of significantly improving existing policies are discussed in each chapter; specific policy roles that social workers can assume are identified.

In conclusion the policy framework that was developed in chapter 2 is used at the end of each chapter in part 5 to summarize prevailing policies, the shortcomings of existing programs, selected reform options, and the roles of policy practitioners.

To be certain, some reforms are remote possibilities in the conservative tenor of this decade. Still, a historical perspective suggests that social reformers will again obtain major changes in existing policies. As discussed in this part, a reform era occurred relatively recently, during the presidencies of John Kennedy and Lyndon Johnson in the 1960s. In that decade, the federal government assumed major roles in funding of economic security, child and family, mental health, and health programs for the first time. While the tenor was conservative in the 1970s under the presidencies of Richard Nixon, Gerald Ford, and Jimmy Carter, major advances occurred in consolidation and expansion of job training and public employment programs, expansion of the

Food Stamps program, revisions in Social Security payments so they rose with inflation, and federalizing payments for elderly indigent persons. Proposals to reform welfare and health care systems were defeated but nonetheless received serious attention.

President Reagan launched an unprecedented attack on social welfare programs in the 1980s as he sought both to limit their funding and to divest the federal government of major policy roles in favor of delegation of expanded roles to state and local governments. He was remarkably successful in his conservative strategy in the first two years of his presidency, but then many politicians of both parties resisted further cuts as they became more aware of the magnitude of social needs that were not being addressed by American society as it headed toward the next century.

Indeed, it is during conservative eras that social workers need to be particularly active in social welfare policy formulation; i.e., to develop skills in assuming the various policy roles discussed in this book. They need to use these roles and skills to develop reforms in child and family, economic security, health, and mental health sectors to assist consumers who lack the resources or good fortune to obtain assistance from existing programs.

Policy in the Child and Family Sector

Few would disagree that children and families are vital national resources, yet government policies often contribute to the serious social problems they encounter. Many critics argue that Americans lag behind Europeans in ensuring basic income, health, and nutritional standards for the nation's families and in providing needed daycare services at a time when large numbers of women seek employment. Social workers need to be familiar with existing policy issues in this sector because they often work with families with children, whether in specialized child welfare agencies or in their practice in health, mental health, and economic security sectors. They need to be able to:

Identify normative positions that identify minimum economic and social supports, supplements, and substitutes that should be available to families

Pinpoint defects in existing programs and policies that undermine or impede the extent to which they meet effectiveness, efficiency, equity, equality, and other criteria

Understand the evolution of American policies in the child and family sector prior to 1965, in the period 1965 to 1968, and during the current era of policy uncertainty

Articulate and obtain support for a variety of contemporary policy proposals to improve existing policies

Have familiarity with a variety of policy roles that

social workers can assume in the various policy phases as they seek policy reforms

These topics are discussed in this chapter to provide a foundation that can be used to inform the policy practice of social workers in the child and family sector.

Social workers are often caught in the middle, as reflected by the comment of Frischella Smith in case example 10.1:

"They think they can give me a schizophrenic, drug addict, incorrigible and I am supposed to change him in three months." Overworked and underfunded, staffs in child welfare departments often do not have the luxury of providing a spectrum of services to troubled families. American economic and social policies also contribute to family breakdown by not providing employment, medical, nutritional, and economic supports.

CASE EXAMPLE 10.1

Foster Homes

A Huge System with Major Problems

By Celeste Durant

Times Staff Writer

Fifty-seven tattoos were sanded from her body when she was 17—a record in pencil lead and skin of boredom, frustration and weakening sanity, a legacy in self-mutilation during 14 years in foster care.

She remembers drawing most of them to while away the hours she spent in solitary confinement in the 37 juvenile institutions she was placed in during her late childhood and adolescence.

Before, during and after the institutions there was a series of 30 foster homes where she also spent time, shuffled from family friends˚and relatives to homes licensed by the county.

And during her odyssey from one home to another, one institution to another, she watched herself progress from a lonely child looking for love to a person anesthetized to new people and new hopes.

She became hardened, difficult to handle, a chronic runaway who ended up spending four years of her life—two weeks here, three months there—in solitary with only two or

three years of formal education and a nervous breakdown to show for it.

And when she left the system at age 18, she went out into the world, had three children and became a child abuser—a woman capable of dragging a child across the room by its hair, hurling a child through the air in a fit of rage or attempting to strangle one.

Her children also ended up in foster care; one of them, a son, she put up for adoption.

She is now 37, has two of her children back with her and is a foster mother.

Her name is Jolly K. and she is the founder of Parents Anonymous, a self-help group for child abusers. . . .

There are more than 10,000 foster children in Los Angeles County ranging in age from infancy to 18; they come in all sizes, colors and sexual preferences and are spread out from one end of the county to the other. . . .

The county's foster child population changes from day to day, week to week; some stay only a few days while others spend their entire childhoods.

They have been removed from their homes either to protect them from their parents or because they have committed crimes.

Where they live, how long they stay and

CHILD AND FAMILY: A NORMATIVE POSITION

In traditional perspectives, the family is a castle that should not be subjected to interference by government. Certainly, values, religious perspectives, and many child-rearing and discipline practices should not be dictated by external authorities. Carried to an extreme, however, "home is a castle" ideology ignores harsh realities. In industrial society, families require economic support; without it, they cannot provide material necessities to children, much less daycare, preschool, health, homemaker, and other services. Parents need a variety of supports not required in traditional societies with extended families, since they often cannot use contributions of grandparents and other kin in the child-rearing process. When pathological family relationships develop or parents are unable, for

---

what happens to these children is the responsibility of a sprawling, chaotic, fragmented system that the Los Angeles County government calls "out-of-home placement."

As county governmental systems go, "out-of-home placement" is awesome—it meanders over three separate county departments, employs about 2,800 county workers, utilizes the services of over 4,000 private households and more than 500 group homes and large institutions.

Its total budget hovers in the neighborhood of $118,117,631 a year with $40,204,880 of it coming from federal funds.

The system suffers from all the expected frailties of large bureaucracies—mountains of paper work, limited funds, inadequate resources and a general lack of communication among its various parts.

It also labors under the additional burdens that arise when a bureaucracy gets involved in the business of dealing with people's lives.

Although there have been many changes in the system since Jolly K. was a child, she feels many of the problems are still there.

"I would like to tell you that I am an exception," she said. "On a scale of 1 to 10, I am toward a 10 but there are a lot of kids on the 5, 6 and 7 level. They haven't had as many placements as I had, but what's the arbitrary number before you break their hearts, minds and souls? . . ."

"The quality of placements vary from very good to average to not so good and Probation and DPSS (the Department of Public Social Service) from time to time close down sub-par ones but when you get to the lower end of the spectrum you are between a rock and a hard spot—you need bed spaces and you can't afford to be choosy," said Judge Peter Smith, presiding judge of the Juvenile Court. . . .

Social workers and probation officers for DPSS and Probation conduct home investigations and interviews and then recommend what should be done with the children in question.

It is then up to the judges or commissioners in the Los Angeles County Juvenile Court and dependency court to decide what should happen to the child on the basis of these recommendations and any evidence presented by the parents' or children's attorneys.

Once children are admitted to the system, there are three types of living situations available to the county:

—An individual foster home which is a private residence licensed by the county to take from one to six children and provide the environment of a natural family;

—A small group home, licensed by the state to take between six and 15 children in a homelike setting but with some professional staff to provide counseling;

—A large facility which takes from 15 youngsters on up, licensed by the state and is supposed to have highly trained staff and strong rehabilitative programming for youngsters with serious emotional, behavioral or educational problems that require special treatment.

If children are being placed in the system and forgotten, as some critics contend, it is largely because of what is generally considered the system's major stumbling block: a shortage of trained social workers and an overabundance of case loads.

Children's services workers have an average case load of about 58–60 youngsters and probation officers have about 35 or 40.

The Child Welfare League of America recommends a maximum of 25–30 placed children per worker.

With the studies and court reports required from workers, there is very little, if any time left over to perform the primary function of the job, which is to counsel the children and their families.

In addition, workers feel unappreciated and under constant pressure.

"They never mention the children's services worker—our role," said a worker in the San Fernando Valley, "we are confronted with doors, (of hostile families) lawyers in court, dealing with judges and the constant emotional nature of our job."

"We deal with a lot of disturbed parents. We have to have unlisted telephone numbers because of calls from people," she continued.

Many admit that the day-by-day confrontations with the chaos of other people's lives wears them down and makes them less responsive to the needs of their clients—they suffer from what they call "burnout."

Burnout can take many forms—fear of the next home visit or investigation or it can be exhibited in cynicism and cruelty to clients.

Workers in DPSS say the burnout sufferers in their ranks are legion.

Another common complaint is about paper work. Said one DPSS worker:

"You have to prove your existence by producing paper, and this job doesn't lend itself to that. It's hard to prove what you have done in establishing trust with a child on paper."

Foster parents are paid on a sliding scale depending on the age of the child, between $185 (for ages 0–4) to $282 (for ages 15 and up) a month with a once-a-year allowance for school clothes that ranges from $43 to $85.

The money is not intended to be payment for foster parent services but for the maintenance of the child in the home. If it were considered salary, Mrs. Kloempken said, "we would get 27 cents an hour in remuneration."

Why then, do people volunteer to be foster parents?

"The saccharine types will say that it's the first time they call you momma—maybe that does it," Mrs. Kloempken said. "I get a real satisfaction in watching a child's intellectual and emotional progress.

"To see children who have had no exposure to music and books get interested. They see me carrying a book with me every time I go to the bathroom and they say 'Um, there must be something to that.' Pretty quick they have a book out of the bookcase and you have got them reading and interested and that excites me."

Foster parents say that if the child is to be raised like the other children in the home, the foster parents must reach into their own pockets.

"The attrition rate of foster parents is growing," said Mrs. Kloempken, who lives in Rowland Heights and was president of the Los Angeles County association before she became head of the statewide group. "We had 5,000 (in the county) two years ago and we are now under 4,000.

"The quality of care is going down—the better people are getting out because there are so many bureaucratic hassles. I think it's the lack of services and the lack of assistance when you are in need—the increased lack of skills in the professional staff and the under-staffing."

"Unfortunately," Mrs. Kloempken said, "there *are* a lot of rotten foster parents—well, if they think there are now, just wait a little.

"When you make a job more and more difficult, the only people who will remain in it are the people who are in it for the wrong reasons."

The kind of abuse that Mrs. Kloempken and others say is in the system is not malicious physical abuse but simply a failure to provide a "nurturing and enriching atmosphere."

"Some of these kids are living with a family but they never take them anywhere," said a foster mother from the Central City chapter of the association. . . .

The group facilities used by the county range from large single-family homes in the middle of Los Angeles to large idyllic lodges in the San Bernardino Mountains with numerous variations in the middle.

Both the large and the small facilities are supposed to provide therapeutic environments for youngsters that are too difficult to be handled in an individual foster home.

The smaller homes try to achieve a family-like atmosphere through house parents with some trained staff (usually someone with a master's degree in clinical social work) providing counseling on a formal or informal basis.

The six or more youngsters in the house are encouraged to function as a family, eat together, go on trips, participate in house activities and chores. . . .

Said Frischella Smith, director of the Storm Centers for Teenagers in the mid-Wilshire district of Los Angeles, "I am supposed to be a miracle worker. They think they can give me a schizophrenic, drug addict, in-corrigible and I am supposed to change him in three months—I am good, but I am not that good."

—Some administrators also complain that social workers and probation officers sometimes withhold information about a particular child because they don't want the agency to reject the child.

—Others say the county's diagnostic workups are not thorough enough and many times they find a child's problem is not what the county said it was.

"We have had evaluations that were done by professional people for the county that were very, very poor," said Edward Boyle, of the Edward C. Boyle Home in Los Angeles.

—Some complain that medical cards and other important records are often late in coming from the county, which only delays treatment. Some smaller homes, which operate without large cash reserves, say that youngsters' payment checks are often late, as well.

With a large number of severely mentally disturbed youngsters to be placed, the county has been under extreme pressure to find suitable facilities.

Youngsters who are assaultive or mentally ill but not sick enough to be committed to mental institutions, can sit around in holding facilities like MacLaren Hall or Eastlake Juvenile Hall for months because no facilities will take them.

"It is not unusual for difficult to place youngsters to spend six months in Juvenile Hall," said one probation officer.

A recent court decision said that in order for a minor to be committed to a state psychiatric hospital that child must be found to be dangerous to himself and others. . . .

The system is making changes, trying to improve.

Officials say they are increasing their efforts to try to keep youngsters in their homes. To do this, DPSS has just held the first Civil Service examinations in seven years for the position of children's services worker and plans to hire 50 new ones.

The new employees will help to lighten case loads and allow workers more time to counsel families and children.

The department also says it is clamping down on voluntary placements of children by parents and is reviewing case loads more often so that more children can be referred to the Department of Adoptions rather than remain in foster care limbo.

mental or physical reasons, to undertake child rearing, parents and particularly children need a range of services and resources.

Permanent Parental Relationships

Many theorists argue that children need a sense of security that is best provided when they have secure relationships with one or more parents.[1] Impermanence of foster-care placements, as discussed in case example 10.1, can deprive children of the basic security needed for healthy development.

Tangible Supports for Families

If parents lack economic resources, they often cannot obtain basic medical, nutritional, mental health, and other services. Apparent neglect of children may be a symptom of economic deficits. A supportive family ecology should include recreational space, decent housing, financial resources, steady employment by heads of households, affordable or free medical services, mental health services, and nutritional supplements (illustration 10.1). Tangible supports are particularly needed by those families that have limited economic resources, reside in unwholesome environments, such as crowded tenements, or live in areas with high rates of crime. Families where both parents work or with only one parent require daycare service. When a number of these conditions are present, families may require assistance from several programs.

Quality of Familial Interaction

Permanency of relationships needs to be supplemented by loving, supportive, and constructive relationships with parents that allow children to develop a sense of competence, interactional and coping skills, and self-esteem. It is difficult to describe or measure such relationships. At one extreme, case example 10.1 describes destructive

ILLUSTRATION 10.1

"MAN DOES NOT LIVE BY SCHOOL LUNCH PROGRAMS ALONE!"

Paul Conrad, © 1982, *Los Angeles Times*. Reprinted by permission.

relationships both within natural families and in foster homes, as illustrated by the life of Jolly K., who grew up in many foster and institutional placements that did not provide her with constructive relationships and parenting. Definition of the basic minimum attributes of families is needed to identify pathological families and to allow construction of standards to guide daycare, preschool, foster-care, and other out-of-home arrangements.

Concepts drawn from prominent theorists allow definition of desirable attributes of families as well as attributes of destructive relationships (see table 10.1).[2] Any definition of normalcy in families must consider the extent to which basic material needs are met, trusting relationships are developed, autonomy and initiative are encouraged, and constructive discipline is provided. Cultural and class bias can lead to mistaken judgments, as when professionals mistakenly view divergent methods of disciplining children as child abuse. Careful assessments are necessary, then, to ascertain whether specific families cause multiple, continuing, or extreme deficiencies that are likely to lead to temporary or permanent damage to children.

Family Supplements and Substitutes

When children are in danger, society should intervene rapidly and with the best available technical resources. No policy problem deserves more careful consideration, since interventions (or the lack of them) have crucial implications for the lives of unfortunate victims, both children and adults. *Early detection* capabilities are needed to locate troubled families as early as possible. When such families are identified, *timely* and *intensive* interventions are required to ascertain whether children are physically endangered and whether family pathology can be reduced by providing services, educational knowledge about child rearing, economic assistance, or medical aid. Well-defined *plans* must be made soon after the point of initial contact and at successive and identified points thereafter to prevent children and families from entering an ill-defined state of limbo, as illustrated by the case of Jolly K. in case example 10.1. Whether family foster care, institutions, or group homes, substitute arrangements should have the attributes of a healthy family described in table 10.1.[3] Children damaged by traumatic experiences need medical and

TABLE 10.1 Selected Positive and Negative Attributes of Families

	Relationship between Parents and Child	Extent to Which Personal Initiative Is Fostered	Extent to Which Child Is Allowed Autonomy	Extent to Which Authority Is Used Constructively	Material Security
Negative Factors	Basic mistrust, suspicion, animosity	Child's initiative systematically thwarted; no recognition of personal accomplishments	Either child given excessive autonomy (neglect) or autonomy overly stifled	Excessive use of coercion or authority	Deprivation of child in terms of food, clothing, and other necessities
Positive Factors	Basic trust, love, affection	Child's initiative systematically encouraged; praise of personal accomplishments	Autonomy encouraged, but not to the point of neglect	Discipline used for reality reasons, but not to excess	Basic material needs met

mental health services during this intervention process.

Child and Family Rights

The natural parents of children should have access to legal representation whenever decisions are made to seek removal of their children, just as parents who voluntarily relinquish their children must be fully informed of the consequences of their decisions. Such decisions and choices are so crucial to the lives of parents and children alike that procedural safeguards are required.

DISSATISFACTION WITH CURRENT PROGRAMS

Although no one would claim that government can legislate love, affection, or human bonds, it can foster them by creating indirect financial and other supports for families, providing supple-

mentary resources such as daycare, and funding programs that provide sensitive and skillful interventions. Considerable dissatisfaction exists regarding the extent to which current policies meet the effectiveness, efficiency, equity, and equality criteria discussed in chapter 2.

When existing policies and programs in the child and family sector are assessed, it is useful to examine the extent to which they (1) support natural families, (2) supplement them with daycare and other services, and (3) provide substitute services when natural families cannot cope with their children. In the following discussion, existing policies and programs are assessed as to whether they provide these three kinds of services and resources effectively, efficiently, and equitably.

Effectiveness

Family Supports.   Preceding discussion suggests that absence of tangible supports increases fam-

---

GUEST EDITORIAL 10.1

Budget-Hackers Take Aim at the Defenseless Poor

By Marian Wright Edelman

When the Reagan Administration's budget-cutters wield their axes, an utterly defenseless group—children, especially black children—will be among their prime targets.

Even now, before the cuts start, black children are twice as likely as white children to suffer from poverty, parental unemployment, inadequate schooling and poor health.

Many black children already are ineligible for services that they badly need. Millions

more are not receiving services for which they are eligible, simply because programs fail to adequately deliver services to the black community. Capricious eligibility standards and poor administration of benefits keep black families from getting the help that they need before their problems become serious, requiring costlier solutions.

A result of this deplorable situation is that a black child today has nearly one chance in two of being born into poverty, is more than 2½ times as likely as a white child to live in

ily tension, makes normal parenting more difficult, and makes it more likely that children will suffer lasting physical and mental health problems. In guest editorial 10.1, Marian Wright Edelman, director of the Children's Legal Defense Fund, underscores the economic plight of many black families, the absence of basic nutritional and medical services for many children, and high rates of unemployment among minority teenagers. Other "at risk" families include those with single heads of households, since they are far more likely than others to experience poverty.

Family-planning services are neglected in the United States, particularly among the poor. By denying free or low-cost abortions to many low-income women and by underfunding family-planning services, Americans indirectly encourage the formation of vast numbers of teenage families as well as unwanted children in other families.[4] Economic hardship, stress, and physical and mental health problems of child and mother are frequent outcomes of these policies.

Family Supplements. The effectiveness of American daycare programs has been sharply challenged by many critics. Most American daycare is provided through informal arrangements with relatives or neighbors or through "family daycare", in which a care giver cares for several or more children in his or her own home. In addition, a substantial number of parents leave children, particularly those of school age, unsupervised at home. When hundreds of thousands of parents resort to unregulated daycare, problems are likely. Conflict may exist between the interests of children and the profit motives of providers who find profits reduced as they add more staff or decrease child-to-staff ratios. Further, society places women and their spouses in a moral dilemma when it fails to provide free or subsidized daycare. Daycare that is more than custodial is expensive and absorbs much (in some cases all) of the personal earnings of women. Therefore, many families skimp on daycare for economic reasons, sometimes with horrible consequences (see guest editorial 10.2).[5]

---

dilapidated housing and is twice as likely to be on welfare.

What is being created is a growing permanent "underclass" in American society. It should come as no surprise to anyone that young people unfairly treated grow up lacking respect for the premises of equality espoused by adults. Their alienation and resentment are built-in time bombs that threaten all of us. And the prospects are not good.

Almost 41% of all black children are recipients of Aid to Families With Dependent children, a federally funded program whose payments are already abysmally low. The national average, which typically covers a mother and two children, is $241.35 per month, or $2.74 a

day per person. Moreover, despite rhetoric about the importance of keeping families together, many states deny support to families unless no unemployed father lives in the home.

Richard S. Schweiker, the new secretary of health and human services, has proposed turning AFDC into a bloc grant to states and tightening eligibility requirements. Both these policies would take children off the AFDC rolls, and could reduce payments even further.

Health care is another area that could suffer with social-program cuts. Twice as many black as white women now lack prenatal care at almost every stage of pregnancy, and there is a high correlation between a lack of such care and infant mortality and illness. A black infant is twice as likely as a white infant to die during the first year of life. Growing up, black children are more likely to be sick. One of seven black children under age 15 lacks a regular source of health care. Two out of every five black children from ages 5 to 9 in central cities are not immunized against polio, tetanus, diphtheria and whooping cough—diseases that we know how to prevent.

Eligibility for Medicaid and the services that it offers varies from state to state. In 17 states, Medicaid does not cover prenatal care during the first pregnancy. In more than half the states, a family in which the father lives at home is ineligible.

Medicaid's preventive program to find and stem children's health problems before they become serious serves only about one-fourth of all eligible children. Other support services that would enable parents and children to use this and other federal and state programs are poor.

If Medicaid eligibility requirements become even stiffer, or if AFDC eligibility is tightened, poor black and pregnant women will receive even fewer services and less timely medical care than they do now. They will cost the taxpayers thousands of dollars in unnecessary last-minute treatment in hospital emergency rooms.

The other crucial area at stake for poor children is nutrition. On any given day, among 6-to-11-year-old black children, one in 10 eats less protein than the established minimum standards. One in five black children does not get enough calcium; two in three do not get enough iron.

Approximately one out of every two black AFDC families does not receive free school lunches for their children; more than one in four do not get food stamps—this, despite the fact that their income would make them eligible for these programs.

Schweiker and John Block, the secretary of agriculture, have suggested cutting back the food-stamp program by reducing the number of beneficiaries. Senate Finance Committee Chairman Robert Dole (R-Kan.) wants to do this without depriving the really "needy." One would hope that the many poor black children and their families who depend on food stamps to eat will qualify for Dole's needy list.

There are specific federal budget cuts and changes that can be made without denying people important benefits. For example, a black child is three times as likely as is a white child to be labeled educable mentally retarded. Besides being unfair to the child, this overrepresentation is costly to taxpayers. Also, when Congress considers reauthorizing the Vocational Education Act, it should ensure that funds are targeted at youths with the highest risk of unemployment.

Reforms such as these can set us on the road to fiscal soundness. But scissors-happy public officials should eschew belt-tightening that is more show than substance. Each year that black children lack adequate food, health care and other items needed for survival will cost the nation billions of dollars in lost productivity and expensive remedial efforts. We must factor that future cost into any ostensible "savings" that we hope to achieve now at the expense of the poor.

Marian Wright Edelman, a lawyer, is president of the Children's Defense Fund in Washington.
SOURCE: This article first appeared in the *Los Angeles Times*. Reprinted by permission of the Children's Defense Fund.

GUEST EDITORIAL 10.2

The Moralizers Breathe Fire at Another Lonely Victim

By Alber Reingewirtz

Dist. Atty. John Van de Kamp was wise in deciding not to file murder charges against Jeanette Williams, whose two young children died in a fire in their ghetto home while she was at work. If he had prosecuted this unfortunate young woman on even the lesser charge of child-endangering, he would have had to arrest every one of the thousands of single parents in this county. We have all stretched ourselves at times in trying to raise our children alone while also trying to keep a job so that we can support them. The only difference between her and us is that we've been lucky; her tragic bad luck was hardly justification for adding a trial to her suffering.

If it had come to that, she would have been judged by a jury of peers, but we who are her equals in this situation already knew that she was not guilty. This pre-judgment aside, I would have been glad to stand as Jeanette Williams' peer, even though I am a divorced, 46-year-old, white male.

Six years ago, when my predicament started, my daughters were 6, 8 and 10. Like everybody else, I had to earn a living, but I could not afford a baby sitter on a daily basis. So, every day after school, they came home and waited for me, all by themselves.

I had many fears about what would happen, and after a while I found some help that I could afford, a lady who spoke only Spanish and about whom I knew little. She looked after the girls, cleaned the house and even cooked for us. She was not used to the American diet, so half the time we hardly ate, but

the house was a little cleaner and I worried a little less. At least an adult was with my children. Then she left, and again I was alone and full of worries until I found another lady and then a succession of other ladies.

In between, I stretched myself pretty thin, as any single mother would. There is no choice.

Single parents do not need a law to tell them not to leave their children alone. It is elementary. Caring for our children is like breathing. We can hold our breath for a while; likewise, when we are forced by circumstances, we can leave a child unattended. All of us do at one time or another. If the state cannot arrest all of us, it should take the law off the books, for what good is it?

The society that makes these laws is the same society that praises motherhood, and fails miserably in making that praise meaningful.

Jeanette Williams, the reports say, had her first child when she was 15, still in high school. I do not know, of course, what her thoughts were then. But I do know that our society is full of moralizers who say that this is what a girl should do in her predicament. But they were not present when a baby sitter was needed, nor would they help her put food on the table. After the birth, the moralizers had left to victimize another future mother. Jeanette Williams was of no interest to them anymore. They expected her to fulfill the requirements of the law. They complained when she stayed home to do that, because then society had to support her and her children. And, when she did the "right" thing and got a job in a society that will not provide child care, they complained that she was neglecting her children.

The moralizers have so much power in this society because they have managed to put human problems into absolute terms: Abortion is murder! Welfare is cheating! We must preserve the sanctity of life! Well, I say to the moralizers, you gave birth to Jeanette Williams' children, and their deaths are your responsibility also. You should be on the stand, not only for the lost lives of two children but also for destruction of their mother's youth and life. But, no, you are like buzzards, attracted by pain and agony and not about to leave until no life is left in your prey.

This sounds extreme, but it is from the heart of another parent who has had to raise children alone. Like Jeanette Williams, I struggled; like her, I stretched myself thin; like her, I worried, always alone. But I want her to know that she is not alone. There are thousands, millions of us. We don't often speak out about our sorrow, our pain, our fears, our loneliness. But every one of us who saw ourselves when we looked at Jeanette Williams on the television screen through a blur of tears, we all must speak out. We must ask this question of the moralizers, the legislators of bad laws, the absent parents, the bystanders: Was the death of Jeanette Williams' children in society's interest?

Alber Reingewirtz works as a salesman in Los Angeles. SOURCE: This article first appeared in the *Los Angeles Times.* Reprinted by permission of the author.

Preschool programs are also inadequate in many areas, especially for low-income and blue-collar families. Affluent persons have purchased nursery school services for decades as a supplement to family child rearing. Hardly a panacea that can transform children or remedy family deficiencies, preschool programs nevertheless provide a useful respite from parenting and facilitate social interaction and school readiness. The Head Start program (discussed later in this chapter) assists low-income families and gives medical and nutritional services but reaches only a fraction of poverty-level preschool children.

Family Substitutes. Many criticisms have been levied against American programs that serve as a substitute for natural homes. (See a flowchart of family substitutes in illustration 10.2.) Virtually all commentators agree that children should remain with their natural parents whenever possible. Yet local authorities seldom fund sufficient child welfare or social service staff attached to juvenile or family courts to allow intensive assistance to families, as suggested by

discussion of lack of sufficient staff in the Los Angeles County child welfare agency in case example 10.1. Large numbers of shelters, homemakers, and day centers where family members can receive short-term intensive services are also needed, as illustrated by programs that allow live-in or residential services to families who have engaged in child abuse. (Pilot programs have been effective in rehabilitating families and have saved taxpayers enormous sums by obviating the need for extended foster-care or institutional placements, but these interventions require substantial and ongoing funding.)[6]

All too often, social workers are presented with extreme instances of abuse, neglect, and delinquency. Programs are needed to educate the public as well as physicians, the clergy, and schools to the early signs of family pathology. Also needed are self-help groups for parents who have abused their children.

With child welfare departments understaffed, juvenile courts provide a precarious foundation for children's services in many jurisdictions. Since few areas have consolidated divorce, custody, probate, adoption, and child welfare functions in so-called family courts, individuals must deal with a bewildering number of agencies and courts. Juvenile courts occupy a central role when children are removed from their natural homes. They are seldom funded to hire sufficient social service staff to compensate for the lack of staff in child welfare departments. Judges typically lack training in child welfare and have inordinately large case loads. As important, courts lack the ability in many jurisdictions to follow and monitor children placed in foster homes or residential facilities.[7]

Despite promising developments in "tracking" children and in establishing periodic plans for their care, some children are not adequately monitored in out-of-home placements. (One observer wryly remarked that it is sometimes easier to locate a stray pet than a specific child.) Courts have also been remiss in appointing temporary or permanent personal guardians for children who are separated from natural parents, guardians who could monitor their progress and serve as their advocates. Whether individuals or agencies, guardians assume many of the prerogatives of natural parents.[8]

ILLUSTRATION 10.2 Typology of Placement Options in Child and Family Sector

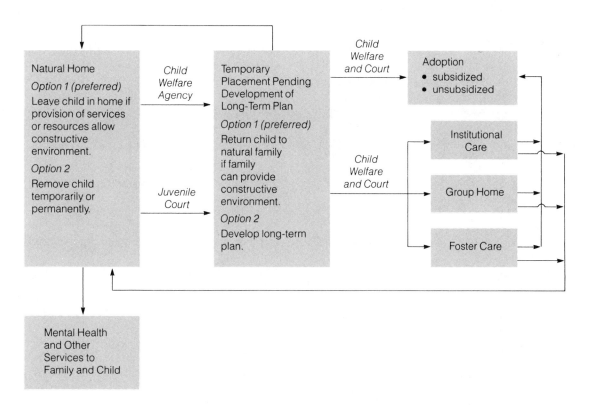

Case example 10.1 highlights problems in many foster-care placements. Foster parents receive relatively low remuneration for their work, seldom receive training prior to or during their work, lack technical assistance for children with specific problems, and often lack ongoing social service supports from hard-pressed child welfare staff.

Finally, although many quality nonprofit children's institutions exist in the United States, some want only to serve less disturbed or nonpoor children and relatively few develop smaller community-based group homes that lessen the stigma and impersonality often associated with larger institutions.[9]

Efficiency

Family Supports. Many critics believe that preventive medical, nutritional, and income programs could reduce subsequent costs of social and medical emergencies. Evidence suggests that infant and maternal services, for example, can decrease incidence of medical problems of mothers and children. By decreasing unwanted children, premature marriages, and teenage parenting, family planning and subsidized abortions can avert subsequent costs. From a preventive perspective, systematic targeting of health and nutritional programs to "at risk" low-income and single-parent families is needed; even prior to dramatic cutbacks by the Reagan administration, these services were available only to relatively few families.[10]

Family Substitutes. Costs for foster and institutional care of children removed from their natural families could be markedly reduced by providing subsidies for adoptions of children who have not traditionally been adopted, i.e., children from racial minorities, children with physical and mental handicaps, and older children. Research indicates that these children can be adopted and can have constructive relationships with their new parents. Aggressive recruitment of potential parents is needed, especially those from minority backgrounds, as well as subsidies to cover short-term medical and other services

and to defray general costs to the adopting family. (Subsidies can be offered for an initial period or over a longer period.) Despite innovative programs by states like Illinois and passage of federal legislation in 1980 providing some federal funding for subsidized adoptions, existing programs at the local level are insufficient.[11]

Although institutional placements are needed by some children, many critics support drastic reduction of institutional services in favor of group homes and foster placements. As an example, Massachusetts closed virtually all of its institutions for delinquent children in favor of community placements both to save funds and to offset negative attributes of large institutions.[12]

Equity and Equality

Family Supports. Although Americans stress equality of opportunity, they have not used this doctrine to equalize medical, daycare, recreational, economic, or preschool options for children. The plight of low-income black families in obtaining these services has been discussed, but blue-collar families also experience acute problems. Often lacking eligibility for free or subsidized medical, nutritional, daycare, and preschool programs, many of them must try to purchase these services when already experiencing economic difficulty.

Family Supplements. Some families discover informal and quality daycare arrangements available from neighbors or relatives that also fit their personal work schedules and budgets. Many others are not so fortunate because of the absence of systematic daycare planning in American society. From an equity vantage point, reliance on consumer payments for daycare is not advisable, since relatively affluent persons are better able to afford it than their poorer counterparts. Linking of daycare subsidies to welfare status is also questionable because poor and blue-collar persons do not qualify for them even though their needs are similar to those of welfare recipients. (As discussed later in this chapter, public daycare subsidies are largely restricted to existing and potential welfare recipients.)

Family Substitutes. White children are more likely than those from racial minorities to be adopted and so to avoid the limbo of endless foster placements. In addition, some residential institutions have been reluctant to accept minority and low-income children. Other subtle forms of discrimination are alleged in some jurisdictions, including premature separation of children from black families by white workers who sometimes mistake authoritarian child rearing for abuse or who underestimate rehabilitation possibilities in families plagued by economic misfortune.[13]

AMERICAN TRADITIONS: POLICY PRIOR TO 1965

Lack of major national funding for many child and family programs cannot be understood apart from deep-seated American traditions. Although a series of cautious and limited reforms have been enacted, a major breakthrough in national funding parallel to those in medical and educational sectors has not occurred.

Early Reforms

Life was difficult for children in the nineteenth century. Extraordinary rates of infant and child mortality existed even among affluent classes. In the absence of child labor regulations, many children worked in textile, agricultural, and other enterprises for miserable pay and under dangerous conditions. When parents were destitute, children were often placed in local poorhouses or "contracted out" to families who cared for them, often in return for their work.

Modest reforms did occur, however. Sectarian groups rescued some children from poorhouses by developing a variety of institutions for deaf, blind, and other children. An ambitious project initiated by Charles Brace led to placement of roughly 30,000 orphaned, poor, or wayward children from Eastern cities in homes on the frontier between 1853 and 1929, although critics argue that families were often not screened and many used children for cheap labor. In the early part of

this century, some states developed so-called mothers' pensions to enable poor children to remain with their mothers. (A sort of moral means test was used, however, that often limited the pension to "deserving widows" rather than to women who were divorced, abandoned, or not married.) Juvenile courts were established in many states in the early part of this century to keep delinquent, neglected, and abused children from having to associate with adult offenders. In 1912, a national agency known as the Children's Bureau was established that assumed major research and reform roles but did not fund social programs. Finally, a small maternal and child health program existed between 1920 and 1929 (the Sheppard-Towner Act) but was not renewed by Congress in 1929.

In the era preceding the Great Depression, then, Americans clearly perceived child and family programs as belonging to local and state jurisdictions or as the province of voluntary and often sectarian agencies. Even at the local level, no public funding existed for daycare programs or preschool programs for the poor. Disinclination to establish publicly funded programs was further bolstered by the 1917 Supreme Court ruling that the federal government could not regulate child labor.[14]

Reforms of the 1930s

While poverty of the Great Depression fell heavily on the nation's children, no systematic strategies were developed to assist them. The Aid to Dependent Children program was enacted as Title IV of the Social Security Act of 1935, but it was a relatively restrictive income maintenance program that subsequent amendments have only partially improved. (It was renamed the Aid to Families with Dependent Children, or AFDC, program in 1950 when the parent was included in the grant.)

A federal–state matching program, AFDC gave grants to children of families that had only a single head of household. Impoverished families with two parents were excluded from grants by the original legislation and had to use relatively austere general assistance programs funded by localities. This defect was partially addressed by passage of the AFDC-U program in 1961, which gave states the option of including two-parent families in grants that contained an unemployed father, but most states continue not to exercise this option even today. States were also allowed to set the eligibility criteria of the program, a provision that allowed poor or conservative states to use extremely restrictive standards. Virtually no one anticipated that AFDC would become a multibillion dollar program, since its founders viewed it as a program, like mothers' pensions, that would assist small numbers of widows. Yet despite its massive growth, it has hardly provided sufficient economic supports for most low-income families.

Several other developments of the 1930s are noteworthy. In a reversal of prior decisions, the Supreme Court finally upheld the Fair Labor Standards Act of 1938 that prohibited child labor for children under sixteen and forbade employment for those between sixteen and eighteen in specified hazardous industries. Title V of the Social Security Act included federal funding for local maternal, child health, and crippled children programs as well as assistance to states for administrative and training costs associated with child welfare programs, but pathetically small sums were authorized for implementation. Substantial daycare was provided under public works programs in the 1930s and then for children of women workers during the Second World War, but federal funding of daycare was terminated soon after the war ended.[15]

ERA OF CAUTIOUS REFORMS: 1965–1968

Americans, then, had developed few national programs for families and children prior to 1965. Support was limited to the relatively harsh federal-state AFDC program. No federal funds were used for family supplementation programs like daycare and preschool programs, and family substitute programs received virtually no federal assistance, since foster and institutional care were funded by private agencies and local authorities.

Various background events, particularly the soaring rate of employment among women, made federal involvement in the child and family sector imperative.[16] Women first experienced massive employment during the Second World War, when millions worked in wartime industries. Although many were displaced by returning veterans, women's employment continued to rise during the 1950s, 1960s, and 1970s (illustration 10.3). Although those with preschool children generally refrained from employment until the youngest child entered the first grade, this trend has changed so markedly that roughly 33 percent of women with preschoolers currently work. There have also been sharp increases in the numbers of families with single parents, families far more likely to experience poverty and need daycare, health, and other supports. This trend has been exacerbated by the fact that by 1980, nearly one-third of all marriages were ending in divorce. The rate of teenage pregnancies has also soared in the last de-

ILLUSTRATION 10.3 Workers, by Sex, 1955–1995

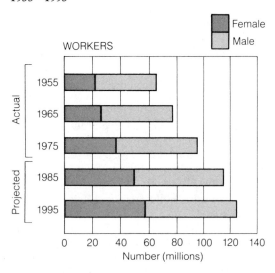

SOURCE: U.S. Department of Commerce, Bureau of Census, *Social Indicators III*, 1980, p. 319.

cade, and teenagers were more likely to use alcohol and drugs in the 1970s and 1980s than in previous eras.

Family Support Reforms

A number of reforms provided health benefits to low-income mothers and children. Maternal and infant care projects of Title V of the Social Security Act were markedly expanded and used to fund prenatal nutrition and health projects for mothers, follow-up health services for infants, and health services for children—projects that demonstrated that significant reductions in infant mortality and birth defects could result from preventive health services targeted to at risk groups.[17]

It has long been recognized that low-income youth suffer high rates of eye, ear, malnutrition, and other health problems. When Medicaid passed in 1965, it included a little-noticed provision that required the state to implement routine medical screening and treatment of low-income youth by 1975. A series of bureaucratic errors, disinterest by local and national officials in providing funds for screening and treatment, and lack of medical resources led to nonimplementation of the legislative mandate until well into the 1970s. Inadequate as they were, the screening programs demonstrated that health problems of hundreds of thousands of low-income children could be identified and treated.[18]

Family Supplements

When the problem of mounting AFDC rolls was addressed in the early 1960s, attention was focused not on strategies to make women work but rather on strategies to decrease desertion by men. Theories about the ill effects on children of maternal deprivation were commonly used to oppose the widespread employment of women with children, whether they were on welfare or not. To provide assistance to welfare families, particularly to provide services to keep them intact, a liberal "federal match" for social services to AFDC recipients was made available to the states under amendments to the Social Security Act in 1962 that provided three federal dollars for every dollar the state allocated to services.

If daycare was incidental to deliberations in 1962, the contrary was true in 1967, when many legislators wanted to make women on welfare work in order to arrest fantastic growth in welfare rolls. Amendments to the Social Security Act in 1967 established that all AFDC women, even those with preschool children, were now required to work. Under the so-called Work Incentive program (WIN) under Title IV of the Social Security Act, AFDC women were provided with job training and daycare and required to participate in both at the risk of losing their grants. But daycare was often of low quality, as reflected by average annual daycare subsidies of $390 per child in 1971.[19]

However, another stream of funding existed for daycare for welfare recipients; namely, funds from Title XX of the Social Security Act. To understand the development of Title XX, it is necessary to review the AFDC program. Mounting concern had developed by 1962 about rapidly increasing numbers of women and children receiving welfare under the AFDC program, as discussed above. A "services strategy" was employed whereby Congress added to Title IV of the Social Security Act provisions that payed states for 75 percent of the costs of services provided to AFDC families, services that were presumed to offer hope of reducing rolls by giving recipients assistance from social work staff. This service strategy was at best naive, because it did not address the need for jobs and training that were needed by AFDC recipients. Furthermore, by the late 1960s, many states realized that they could use this federal service money for a variety of programs, including daycare. Because of escalating federal costs of Title IV services and outright abuse of the program (some states used the service funds for programs like highway construction), the services were transferred in 1975 from Title IV to a newly established Title XX of the Social Security Act that was to provide a variety of services to existing and potential welfare recipients. Daycare was the single largest program chosen by states and localities under Title XX and continues to use roughly 20 percent of the program.[20] (Some daycare continues to be provided under Title IV for AFDC recipients who are receiving training.)

As noted earlier in this chapter, many reformers believe that the nation has erred in linking national daycare to welfare programs—or even to Title XX—that limit its use to existing or potential recipients, since this policy restricts access by nonwelfare families. Some also doubt that many welfare departments can devise or oversee innovative daycare programs, since welfare officials often favor using large public and nonprofit daycare centers rather than developing or using the small family daycare programs preferred by many mothers. In some cases, too, welfare planners are preoccupied with reducing the cost of daycare to the detriment of its quality.

With direct public subsidies restricted to welfare recipients and with most women using nonlicensed, informal arrangements, daycare is a phantom activity in the United States. No one knows its overall quality or even the economic burdens it imposes on women. One major survey suggests that over 90 percent of women would prefer the protections of daycare licensing; i.e., they do not like to use out-of-the-home family daycare that is subject to no public standards, as is currently the case in many jurisdictions. Most would probably favor more public subsidies so that they would not have to choose between employment and quality (and expensive) daycare.[21]

Government subsidies for daycare in many European countries have evolved from movements to increase economic equality of women. In the United States, however, women's liberation groups have been so preoccupied with the Equal Rights Amendment, discriminatory hiring and promotion practices, and sex discrimination that they have given scant attention to daycare.[22] Although tax credits for daycare costs represent grudging acknowledgment of the financial burden involved, the major impetus for direct federal subsidies has come through welfare policy, a fact that makes public subsidies unavailable to most working women.

For decades, the nonpoor have sent their children to nursery schools in churches and other settings and have paid the required fees. Project Head Start, initiated under Office of Economic Opportunity legislation (OEO) in 1965, became a poor persons' nursery school that also provided medical screening and nutritional services, encouraged parent participation in program administration and activities, and provided a mixture of summer and year-round programs. (Some Head Start projects also provide daycare.) Because OEO officials were desperate for an easy-to-implement and popular program that would offset political controversy associated with many of the other OEO programs, Head Start became the single largest program funded by OEO in 1966 although its funding stabilized thereafter in the vicinity of $500 million (in 1980 dollars). Conservatives were hardly likely to allow the program to grow to massive proportions, however, and found support from a large research project in 1968 that alleged that Head Start did not lead to lasting cognitive and interpersonal changes in enrollees, a study attacked on methodological grounds by Head Start supporters, who also pointed to subsequent research favorable to the program.[23]

Family Substitutes

A major innovation in the 1960s was an amendment in AFDC legislation that allowed federal authorities to pay a portion of costs of foster-care placements for children who were removed from their natural families by court order. Prior to this reform, these services were wholly funded by local authorities and private philanthropy, funding hardly adequate to finance mounting child welfare case loads. Many localities still lack resources to fund foster and institutional care at needed levels, as illustrated by case example 10.1 at the start of this chapter, which describes funding crises experienced by one metropolitan county.

ERA OF UNCERTAINTY: BEYOND 1968

Despite the conservative tenor of the 1970s, some important policy breakthroughs occurred in the child and family sector, including provision of federal funds for adoption subsidies, services for juvenile offenders, and family planning. Reformers also encountered many distressing developments, however, including cuts in many programs in the 1980s that threatened hard-won gains of previous decades.

The need for adoption subsidies to ease financial burdens is particularly apparent with low-income and blue-collar adoptive parents. Some states began to use Title XX social service funds for this purpose in the 1970s, but thousands of minority children remained mired in long-term foster and institutional care. With passage of the Adoption Assistance and Child Welfare Act of 1980, the federal government (1) provided, under Title IV-E of the Social Security Act, funds for adoption subsidies for children already in institutions and foster care; (2) required states to make reports on all children in foster care; and (3) provided federal money for foster care even for children not under court-ordered placement, although a ceiling was placed on these funds to provide local governments with an incentive to seek adoptions. Unlike adoption subsidy programs passed in many states, the federal subsidies were to be paid on the basis of the child's need rather than the financial status of the family, and subsidies were to continue until the children reached eighteen. This legislation received scant support from the Reagan Administration, however, and many feared that it would be placed in a block grant, which might lead to its demise, particularly because few jurisdictions appeared to aggressively seek subsidized adoptions for minority children even with the federal subsidies.

One notable post-1968 reform was the Juvenile Justice and Delinquency Prevention Act of 1974. Juvenile courts, it will be recalled, were established to isolate youth from adult offenders. By the 1960s, however, it became clear that many status offenders—i.e., youth who had committed no misdemeanor or felony but had become runaways or truants—were stigmatized by association with the juvenile courts. Further, many reformers hoped that children who had committed misdemeanors could be diverted

from the court through referrals to social agencies or special "juvenile diversion" projects. This diversion strategy was favored to avoid punitive treatment of children and to save costs of juvenile court proceedings and subsequent institutional care. The 1974 legislation gave grants to local juvenile diversion projects on the condition that runaways be referred to shelters or agencies apart from those used for delinquent children. Further, localities were to cease the still common practice of placing delinquent children in detention and other facilities used for adult offenders.

A final policy development in the 1970s concerned family violence. Increasing attention was given to the phenomenon of child abuse in the 1960s, and all states by 1972 had adopted mandatory reporting laws. In 1973, the Child Abuse Prevention Act passed, legislation that established research funds to be disseminated to universities and to pilot projects as well as a national clearinghouse for dissemination of research and practice interventions. But the legislation did not establish federal funding for operating programs, so that child welfare units in most public agencies were unable to provide needed services to mounting child abuse caseloads.

Indeed, many commentators argued that family violence was not restricted to children but posed a serious problem for many wives. By 1980, many shelters for battered women had been established. Most had a precarious funding base, however, and had to rely on an assortment of foundation and government funds to survive. Conservative legislators blocked efforts to secure major federal funding for the programs on grounds that family matters belong exclusively to the jurisdiction of local governments.

As for family planning, federal funding was made available under the Family Planning Services and Population Research Act of 1970, legislation that assisted 4 million low-income women by 1980, including 1.3 million teenagers. Still, funding for these programs was inadequate to meet the needs of most low-income families. Further, members of the so-called Moral Majority, a coalition of fundamentalists and conservatives, opposed expanded funding because they feared family planning somehow contributed to promiscuity, especially among teenagers. They persuaded the Reagan Administration to develop regulations, subsequently subject to litigation, that required clinics to inform parents when their teenagers sought birth control materials. They also sought a constitutional amendment to rescind the landmark 1973 Supreme Court decision that declared state laws unconstitutional that prohibited abortions during the first trimester of pregnancy. Funding of abortions for low-income women under the Medicaid program was terminated in the late 1970s at the insistence of these groups, a policy that penalized the poor, since affluent persons were able to purchase abortions from physicians.

In the Reagan Administration, funding of programs for children was drastically cut. Cuts in food stamps and Medicaid programs that importantly assist low-income families and children, are discussed in chapters 11 and 12. The purchasing power of grants under the AFDC program had already declined in real terms by 29.4 percent between 1969 and 1981, and these grants were subjected to further cuts in 1981. Indeed, the Reagan Administration proposed another $2.3 billion in cuts for 1983. A variety of school and summer nutritional programs to assist low-income and other children were cut 20 to 80 percent in 1981. Designed to assist low-income pregnant women and infants, the Woman, Infants, and Children supplemental food program (WIC) was reduced in funding in 1981 and was slated for a 35 percent cut when the Reagan Administration proposed that it be placed in a block grant.

Children bore the brunt, then, of a major share of cuts in funding enacted in the early 1980s. Although definitions of poverty vary, the Bureau of Census reported that 11.4 million children, or two-fifths of the total poverty population, lived beneath official poverty standards.[24] As noted previously, children were most likely to experience poverty in families with single parents, families growing at such a rapid rate that some commentators argued that "feminization of poverty" was rapidly becoming a reality.

Reformers in the child and family sector also feared that a number of federal-state categorical programs would be placed in block grants and that many local units would divert these funds for other programs or would target their funds to families that did not need assistance as urgently as low-income families. Thus, under the Omnibus Budget Reconciliation Act of 1981, a series of block grants were created by the Reagan administration to replace fifty-seven categorical programs. These grants included a maternal and child health block grant ($373 million) and a social services block grant ($2.4 billion). Reformers feared that adoption subsidies that had been established by 1980 legislation would be placed in the block grants and that many jurisdictions would cease to use the funds for facilitating adoptions of children from racial minority backgrounds. Further, Title XX social services had required focusing of resources on existing or potential welfare recipients, a requirement relaxed in the new social services block grant where the Title XX funds were placed.

REFORMING CHILD AND FAMILY POLICY

Reformers in the child and family sector contend with background ideological and political realities that discourage major reforms when they try to address many of the deficiencies of existing policies.

Mobilization of Bias

Many barriers frustrate efforts to obtain major national commitment to daycare, preschool, health, family subsidy, and nutritional programs, as illustrated by an ill-fated effort in 1971 to obtain a major funding breakthrough. Various federal legislators initiated schemes in 1969 and 1970 to use federal funding to establish drastically expanded preschool programs and to develop planning agencies for fragmented children's program. By 1971, both the House and Senate had developed and approved child development legislation that proposed multibillion dollar national funding of preschool, daycare, nutritional, and other programs for low-income and blue-collar families.[25]

There were signs, however, that President Nixon might not approve the legislation; in fact, he issued a veto message that both reflected and incited ideological opposition to any major national legislation. Although the message contained various criticisms of administrative provisions, its principal contention was that the legislation would take the family from "its rightful position as the keystone of our civilization" and would "commit the vast moral authority of the federal government on the side of communal approaches to child rearing as against the family-centered approach." This veto message was important because it made explicit a conservative rationale for opposing future initiatives. Although welfare daycare was needed to decrease rolls, President Nixon argued, other efforts to provide major federally funded services for the family (or children) represented intrusion into the privacy of the family. He also argued that programs to fund daycare for non-welfare families encouraged parents to abdicate parenting functions.

When the president's objections to child development are supplemented by the opposition of many conservatives to federal participation in family planning, provision of abortions, and shelters for battered women, it becomes clear that reformers encounter formidable barriers. To these barriers must be added the sheer cost of subsidizing daycare, foster-care, and preschool services, particularly as blue-collar and middle-income families are made eligible. (Quality daycare alone costs upwards of $3,000 per child per year.) Disagreements also exist about the desirable attributes of daycare and other services. For example, many reformers favor relatively high staff-to-child ratios, such as one staff person to every five children in a daycare center. But critics ask, "How do you know that children will be harmed if the ratio is reduced to one staff member for every fifteen children?"

A consequence of various barriers to reform is that Americans resort to symbolic measures but give them little funding. As noted in guest editorial 10.3, Americans pride themselves on benevolence toward children. But benevolence stops short of committing major funds to health prevention, family-planning, early education, or income programs that truly raise economic standards of many low-income families.

To secure children's legislation, strong national organizations with grass-roots constituencies need to be formed in coalitions that rally support for specific policies, since children do not vote. Coalition building is made difficult, however, by fragmentation between preschool, daycare, foster-care, and institutional programs and supporters.

Selected Reforms in Scanning and Analysis Phases

The central task facing reformers is to develop public and legislative awareness of a range of children's problems beyond limited daycare, preschool, foster-care, and institutional services now subsidized by public authorities. Until children's programs are widely perceived as pertinent to relatively broad numbers of families, including blue-collar and middle-income families, legislative interest is likely to be minimal.

Progress must be made in decreasing the extent to which the problems of children are defined in narrow (i.e., categorical) terms. Those who drafted comprehensive child development legislation in 1970 and 1971 deliberately did not list many of the traditional classifications of children's programs in order to decrease fragmentation between preschool, daycare, foster-care, and other services. Of course, specialized programs are needed for children and families with specific problems, but program linkages can be developed. As an example, daycare services can be used not only for children of working parents but also as resources for child welfare staff who want to provide respite for families currently unable to care for their children. Some foster-care homes might also provide some daycare services, and preschool programs might add daycare children to their programs. (Planned overlapping implies the need for regional referral and information centers that can also develop resources.)

Child-Centered No More

Harsh Policies Belie Our Image of Benevolence

By K. C. Cole

More than a year ago, I was hired as a consultant to a federal panel on child health. When I took the job, I admitted that it wasn't a subject I particularly warmed up to.

Not that I don't warm up to children. Like any parent, I'm quite concerned about my own child's health. But it's hard to shake the impression that children in this child-centered society are already coddled and spoiled, and that parents could and should care for their own. In a time of high taxes and inflation and worries about nuclear war, focusing on kids seemed like kid stuff.

Obviously, a lot of Americans out there agree with me. We've been cutting kids' programs right and left with hardly a whimper. Education has suffered from property-tax cutbacks all over the country. My 12-year-old stepdaughter in California is missing out on music programs, art programs and athletic programs because the adults in her affluent community want to live high off the hog.

Maybe we're not as child-centered as we'd like to think. Every time I hear elderly politicians pronounce that we don't have to protect the environment because we have plenty of this or plenty of that, I note that they always add, "to last until the year 2000." And then I wonder if they have grandchildren.

Nowhere is our low investment in children more dramatic than in the matter of health. For example, out of $15 billion spent on Medicaid in 1976, only $2.6 billion was spent on kids. In the same year, only 13% of children's

health costs were paid out of the public till, as opposed to 59% of the cost of older people. The major federal program providing services to poor mothers and children (Title V of the Social Security Act) spent only $400 million on all projects, while the Department of Defense spent twice that on health care for dependent minors of military personnel.

The truth is that more children live in poverty than people of any other age group.

Clearly, this doesn't add up to "coddling." But do children warrant a major national investment? It's hard not to be convinced that they do.

Our population is growing older. If we don't support our children today, who will support us in our old age? Who will earn the incomes that will pay our Social Security? As one child psychologist pointed out, the empty school benches of today are the empty workbenches of tomorrow. And yet we treat children with the same lack of respect that we show toward other resources like land and oil.

One reason that child health expenditures are relatively low is that children are relatively healthier than older people. But even apparently healthy children can carry the seeds of serious, even deadly, adult disease. Obesity, for example, which is a major contributor to heart disease and strokes, often begins in infancy; early malnutrition can cause a whole plethora of developmental problems. Children are particularly susceptible to toxins and carcinogens because they are small and growing.

In addition, child-health dollars are small because we get what we pay for. And what we pay for, through Medicaid and private insurers, is anything but the preventive care that children need. In fact, only 4% of our multibillion-dollar health budget pays for preventive care. Half of private insurance plans exclude prenatal care; half leave major gaps in coverage during the critical first few days of life.

Our stingy policies toward children are far more inefficient than even the federal bureaucracy itself. When it comes to education, for example, we seem to understand intuitively that to be effective, it should begin at the earliest possible age. Witness the success of Head Start. But when it comes to health, we throw all our dollars at the older age groups, patching up after the preventable, and often irreversible, damage has been done. In the same way, we spend billions for high-technology intensive-care units to save babies born with birth defects, children maimed in car accidents and teen-agers shot in gun accidents, but we won't spend the millions needed to prevent the causes of those problems.

Everyone knows that prevention is the health idea whose time has come. But it's an idea that seems to be stamped "adults only." We stuff ourselves on health foods and jogging while letting our kids eat Twinkies and feeding them a steady diet of violence on TV. We worry a lot over whether we should eat cyclamates or cholesterol, but we don't bother to seat-belt our children into cars. We spend dollars that don't end for our own defense, but hardly a penny for our defenseless and vulnerable children.

Many health conditions that leave children dead or disabled or retarded appear during pregnancy or birth, and low birthweight babies are in the gravest danger. Most such babies are born to teen-age mothers. One half to two-thirds of pregnant women in poverty are malnourished.

We pay billions in welfare and health costs to support these children of children; billions more to support their economically dependent mothers. But we don't spend the little that is needed to provide family-planning services that have been proven to reduce unwanted pregnancies. We don't provide the support services that would allow teen-age mothers to stay in school, to become productive, to gain options other than the prospect of giving birth to yet another unhealthy, unwanted child.

With child abuse on the rise and some 600 children in this nation murdered by their own parents last year, it is instructive to know that studies in other countries have found that the single most effective measure against child abuse is family planning.

Nutrition is especially easy to dismiss as a frill. To an adult, good nutrition makes the difference between a trim figure and ugly extra pounds of fat. But for children, it is often a matter of life or death. Children who go unfed or underfed are prone to a plethora of physical and mental health problems. They do poorly in school, poorly in life, and do not add to our national productivity.

And then there's the matter of medical care. More than half of indigent children receive essentially no well-child care at all, which means no preventive care—which means that by the time minor illnesses are treated, they are serious and expensive. Congress is cutting funds for inoculation programs in an effort to "save" money; yet a $180-million measles vaccination program recently saved an estimated $1.3 billion in medical care resulting from complications such as deafness and mental retardation.

There's a lot more than money at stake. I don't want my small son growing up in a society whose citizens are mental and physical cripples because they were not cared for as children. I don't want to grow old in such a society myself.

K. C. Cole is a science writer living in Washington. Her commentary is from *Newsday*. Reprinted by permission of *Newsday*.

CASE EXAMPLE 10.2

In Defense of Anti-Spank Law

Swedish Describe Efforts at Child Abuse Prevention

By Harriet Stix

SAN FRANCISCO—"One thing is perfectly clear," said Bertil Ekdahl, the author of Sweden's so-called "anti-spanking law," as he described life with his three children. "I cannot raise my hand."

He smiles when he says that, but in Sweden it is widely accepted that even apparently minor mistreatment may impair a child's healthy development. The anti-spanking law says "a child may not be subjected to physical punishment or other injurious or humiliating treatment." When the Swedish Parliament adopted it, not quite two years ago, the vote was a close-to-unanimous: 259 for, 6 against.

Recently, four Swedish spokespersons for children's rights toured this country and Can-ada, holding one-day seminars on the prevention of child abuse and neglect. Their visit was sponsored by the Swedish embassies in Ottawa and Washington and the Swedish Information Service in New York, in cooperation with the Children's Defense Fund. San Francisco was the last stop of a trip that included Ottawa, New York, Washington and Chicago.

Educational Campaign

In an interview, Ekdahl and his colleague, Swedish children's ombudsman Bo Carlsson, explained that the anti-spanking law carries no penalties; the person who smacks a child does not in turn get smacked. Rather, the new law is perceived as part of a massive educational campaign against physical punishment.

It is a concept that seems to run counter to

More attention should be given to families in their community settings. Existing programs emphasize providing daycare, preschool, medical, and other benefits to children, but services should also assist families. In some cases, families fail because they reside in intolerable community environments, because a parent is unemployed, or because parents are alcoholic. Terms like *child welfare* or *childcare* should be modified to terms like *family welfare* or *family care*. Even when children are removed from natural families, the decision should be made only after intensive work with both natural and adoptive or foster-care families.

In terms of effectiveness and efficiency of children's programs, even more attention should be given to family supports that allow many natural families to remain intact; to subsidized adop-tions to place national emphasis on permanent adoptions for as many children as possible; to juvenile diversion projects to emphasize out-of-court services to status offenders and those who commit minor offenses; and to community group-care homes and family daycare homes as useful supplements to institutional services. Massive employment and training projects are also needed for unemployed and underemployed teenagers.

Although these policy options have been frequently discussed, they are unlikely to be implemented if there is not a major national commitment to funding for them. Family supports require funding of competent staff with adequate time and access to a range of community employment, health, homemaker, educational, daycare, preschool, and other community services. Sub-

increasingly punitive-minded currents in this country. "Lawyers, especially, can't understand how a thing can be forbidden and still be without punishment," Ekdahl commented, "but, in fact, it has been rather successful. The aim is not to prosecute. After all, a single slap is not so awful."

Carlsson reacted sharply to that characterization of a slap: "But it's not OK from my point of view," he objected, explaining that even a slap carries the message that people "have a right to use physical abuse," a message he rejects.

He likes a cartoon that shows "Mother Bear," having just spanked her child, explaining "I do it out of love." Baby Bear is thinking, "I wish I could show my love."

Said Carlsson, "Everyone remembers a spanking. It's funny that there are not more youngsters revolting against their parents."

No Legal Rights

The children's ombudsman is employed by Radda Barnen—the Swedish Save the Children Organization—rather than by the government. Carlsson believes this is a good thing, although he has no legal rights of intervention. "I think it is an advantage," he said. "The ombudsman is not bound by being part of a governmental body, and also can influence opinion more."

As in the case of the anti-spanking law, the main function of the child ombudsman's office is seen as educational. Mostly it is involved in informing professionals, legislators and the general public about the needs and rights of children.

Carlsson suggested that although "it's easy to get a rosy picture of Sweden," with its affluent population and enormous social welfare apparatus, its children still are in need of protection. "It is clear that you can't see the wounds on the outside, but you find them inside the children." He cites some statistics:

During a study of children in five countries (Sweden, Spain, Israel, Algeria and Ethiopia) 11% of Swedish 11-year-olds said that no grown-up had ever liked them. No children in the other countries gave this answer.

In a survey of Swedish 4-year-olds, it was

---

sidized adoptions require major funds for subsidies and competent staff who can recruit new parents and provide them with skills to help children with mental, physical, and other handicaps. Juvenile diversion projects require sustained work with families of runaways, truants, and those who have committed minor offenses as well as the skills necessary to do follow-up work with youngsters. Community group-care and family daycare homes require staff who can provide technical assistance and monitoring. Commitment to a set of nationally funded policies that can accomplish these objectives is unlikely in the near future. Those interested in such changes will need to work at them one by one in local jurisdictions and agencies.

The setting of standards for daycare programs is a particularly vexing problem. Optimally, many advocates for children would prefer center-based daycare regulated by national standards, but budget-conscious officials and conservatives stoutly resist such policies on both cost and ideological grounds. The current reality is that many states have vague standards that are often not enforced, and most daycare arrangements, such as family daycare, fall outside their purview. Inclusion in most states of family daycare under state licensing or regulation is worthy of consideration.[26]

Reforms to provide a more favorable environment for families are also needed, including public policy directed toward reducing exposure to violence. An interesting example is provided by the Swedish government, which developed legislation forbidding corporal punishment (see case example 10.2) Projects are also needed

found that 20% to 25% showed signs of psycho-social problems.

Another indication that all is not comfortable, Carlsson said, is the use of alcohol among youngsters, 60% of whom have at least tasted it. Ten percent of 13-year-olds say they have a drink once a week.

More than half of Swedish mothers of children under 7 work at least half time, and 20% of the children live in single-parent families. The day-care arrangements that result mean "kids between 2 and 7 meet a lot of children and adults, with few stable relations," Carlsson said. "In six years, a child can meet 100 adults, and change all his peers."

"The old family doesn't exist—today's family is something quite different, and the

concept of childhood is quite different," Carlsson said. And he believes this is true in every industrialized country.

Besides its research in education projects, the ombudsman's office also operates a telephone service for individual cases, which is used both by professionals and the public.

Spanking on Decrease

The effect of the new law, and the Swedish belief that education is more effective than punishment, will not be clear for several more years, but Ekdahl said, "we believe spanking has decreased."

Said Carlsson: "The most important thing is that it has started people talking, thinking.

to reduce exposure of children to violence on television.[27]

Basic reforms in American tax, employment, and income maintenance programs are also needed. Serious consideration should be given to a family allowance similar to those currently provided in Canada and in many European and some third-world countries, in which income is given to all families, either as a flat per-child grant or as graduated grants that vary with family income. Full employment policies are needed so that teenagers from minority families do not continue to bear a disproportionate burden of unemployment.

Selected Reforms in Implementation and Assessment Phases

Regional authorities need to be established that can serve a variety of administrative and planning functions in the implementation phase, whether to provide information and referral services for parents, assist in the development of new daycare centers and homes, or develop interagency collaboration. More ambitiously, they

could assume certain licensing and funding responsibilities, i.e., actually participate in the program delivery system. Like area agencies for the aging, they could serve as one focal point in the community for a particular issue—in this case, services for children. They could also assume ombudsman functions, such as ensuring that children are not lost in the maze of existing foster placements.

POLICY ROLES OF SOCIAL WORKERS

The following case example illustrates the policy roles of social workers in the child and family sector. A state law specified that status offenders —i.e., curfew violators, truants, incorrigibles, and runaways—be kept in unlocked facilities separate from juveniles who had committed penal code violations. To implement the law, officials in one county took a vacant juvenile facility that had been used for delinquents and assigned staff from the county probation department. The problem with this approach was

It will take time to change, certainly, but to start that process is important."

Ekdahl commented that, possibly, people in Sweden are more accepting of the government's getting involved in such issues, traditionally considered family matters, because "we pay so much in taxes." It is a matter of getting something in return for all that money.

Certainly in Sweden, so much smaller and more homogenous than this country, the issues are different. But in comparing the two countries, Ekdahl concludes that perhaps, after all, there are "not so many differences. What's in the best interest of the child . . . there are not so many differences."

In Sweden, he said, the anti-spanking law was never particularly controversial, "but it certainly has been in the U.S., and in other countries." He described some "funny misunderstandings" around it—the headline in an American paper that read, "Sweden: Heaven for Naughty Children and Nightmare for Parents" and the English cartoon of a child who has just been spanked and is muttering, "If this had been Sweden, you would be rotting in jail for this."

Swedes, in particular Swedish children, know about the law, and approve it. At one point, to spread the good word, information was printed on all four sides of milk cartons.

"I can just imagine," said Ekdahl, "the conversations around breakfast tables."

that a law-and-order attitude prevailed, an approach underlined when the presiding judge of the juvenile court issued a memorandum stating that any status offender who left the facility without staff permission would be reclassified as a delinquent and placed in a locked juvenile home. (Though later struck down by an appeals court, the edict illustrated the prevailing punitive orientation of staff members.)

Survey Role

The social worker in this case had to decide in the early phases of the project whether a "mobilization of bias" existed that would make policy reforms virtually impossible. She noted that many officials and departments were wedded to traditional and punitive policies toward runaway youth but also noted many favorable signs. Extensive national interest existed in developing nonpunitive alternatives to institutionalizing runaway youth. Further, recent state legislation mandated development of innovative policies that could also save the state funds by averting the high costs of institutionalization.

Problem Recognition and Definition Role

A social worker in the regional office of the county mental health department developed an approach to the runaway problem different from that of the juvenile court judge. Instead of a law-and-order problem, she conceptualized it as a family problem that could best be handled through a shelter administered by the mental health department. Funding came from the national Law Enforcement Assistance Administration (LEAA) and from mental health funds, with referrals not only from the juvenile court but also from the schools, parents, and other social agencies. A voluntary rather than a custodial or deterrent approach was used: youngsters were told that they were free to leave whenever they wished, but informed that the center had services and resources that they might find helpful. (A commitment to family and individual counseling was a condition, however, for staying at the home.)

Initial experience suggested three major groups of runaways. Some were in the midst of adolescent developmental crises exacerbated by difficult family relationships; some wanted independence prior to age eighteen even though forbidden by law to leave their families; and some were impulsive, often antisocial loners or misfits. Different intervention strategies appeared useful for the three groups of runaways. For those with developmental crises, intensive family and personal counseling was helpful. Ongoing shelter and vocational services were planned for those desiring independence. And for those with basic personal problems, long-term assistance was used. The social worker, then, went beyond the limited definitions of the juvenile court judge and sought to develop family and community services geared to specific needs of various groups.

Program and Policy Design and Troubleshooting Roles

The social worker, then, proposed a variety of programs under the aegis of the shelter, including satellite hospices for youngsters unable to return home, longer-term residential treatment placements for youngsters with deep-seated problems, and outpatient referrals to the children's service division of the community mental health center. The proposal soon ran into opposition from child welfare staff in the department of public welfare, who feared a lack of sufficient counseling staff, and from court officials, who feared lax treatment. Although funds were promised initially, the various departments did not contribute sufficient funds to allow satellite centers to be used. Meanwhile, a series of independent private, profit-oriented agencies were forming and promised the courts to be able to deliver "less expensive services."

The social worker formed a planning committee composed of officials from the various departments and helped them develop an understanding of the complexity of the problem and of the need to develop a joint strategy to fund the shelter's multifaceted programs. In addition, a private foundation made a three-year grant providing major funding for staff in the project, which increased the credibility of the effort. The court agreed to contract with the shelter for services to a specified number of youngsters but wanted an evaluation of the project within two years. Specifically, they wanted to know how many of the youth engaged in status offenses upon release. In turn, the community mental health agency detached staff from their children's division to work in the shelter, as did the child welfare department. They too wanted results of an evaluation project, with emphasis on analysis of family counseling services.

Error Detection and Change Agent Roles

In this case example, the social worker realized that well-conceived evaluation information needed to be obtained, including baseline data about the number of children served and the number who again engage in status offenses as well as an estimate of the unmet service needs in the area. Cost realities also needed to be examined to determine whether it was less expensive to contract shelter services to private providers or to continue to provide them directly.

Change agent roles were also required at numerous points. The social worker had to develop support from other agencies, the courts, the child welfare department, and the county board of supervisors in order to secure approval of specific policies that governed referral systems, funding, and assessment procedures.

SUMMARY

An overview of discussion in this chapter is provided in illustration 10.4, which utilizes the policy framework developed in chapter 2. Prevailing policies provide the starting point for policy, since they describe existing strategies for assisting children and their families. A normative framework facilitates critical analysis of prevailing policies in terms of effectiveness, efficiency, equity, equality, and other criteria. Selected reform options provide an agenda for professional advocacy within scanning, analysis, implementation, assessment, and legitimation phases.

Permanency of relationships needs to be supplemented with caring relationships with par-

ILLUSTRATION 10.4   Policy in the Child and Family Sector

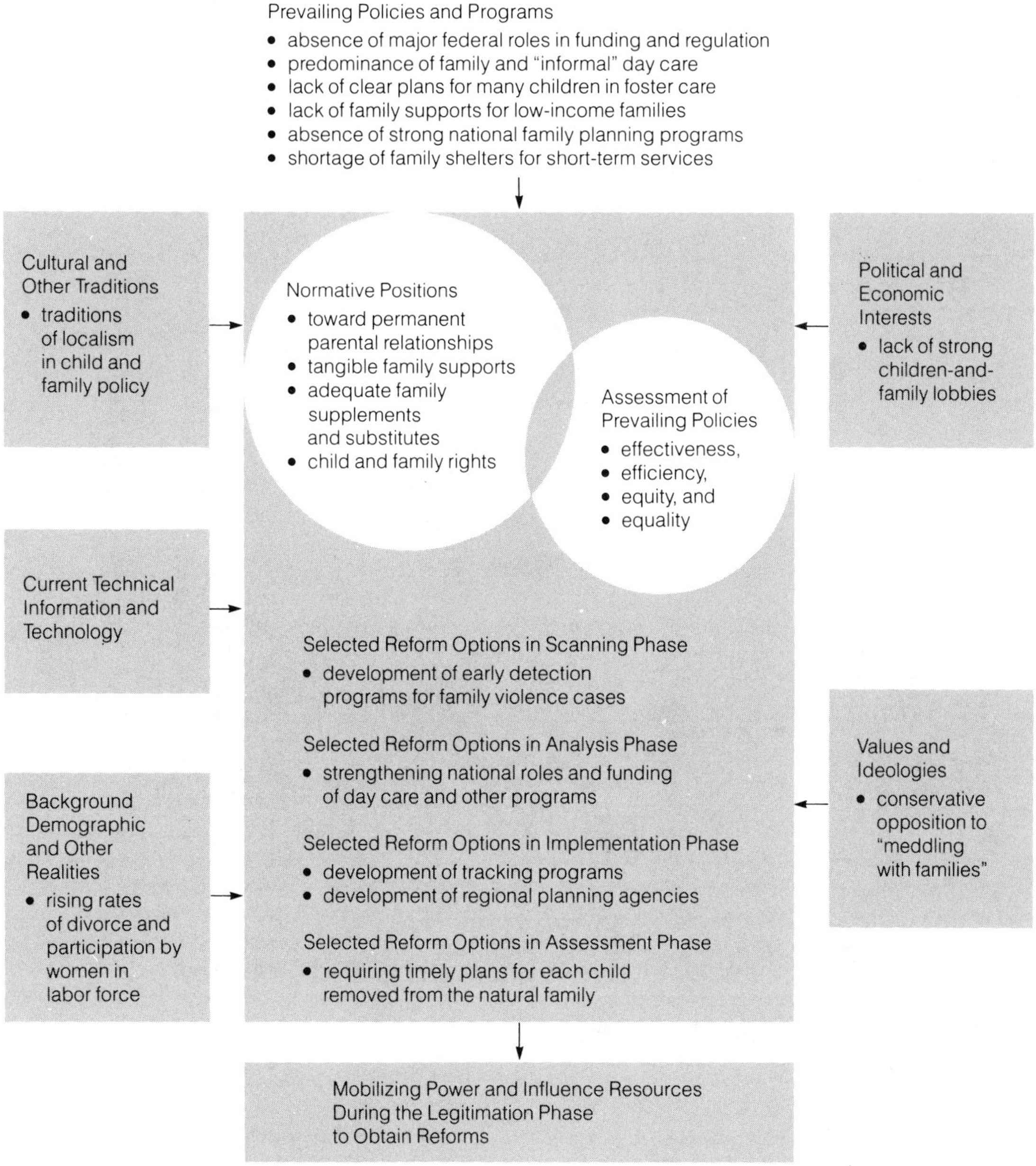

Prevailing Policies and Programs
- absence of major federal roles in funding and regulation
- predominance of family and "informal" day care
- lack of clear plans for many children in foster care
- lack of family supports for low-income families
- absence of strong national family planning programs
- shortage of family shelters for short-term services

Cultural and
Other Traditions
- traditions
  of localism
  in child and
  family policy

Normative Positions
- toward permanent
  parental relationships
- tangible family supports
- adequate family
  supplements
  and substitutes
- child and family rights

Assessment of
Prevailing Policies
- effectiveness,
- efficiency,
- equity, and
- equality

Political and
Economic
Interests
- lack of strong
  children-and-
  family lobbies

Current Technical
Information and
Technology

Selected Reform Options in Scanning Phase
- development of early detection
  programs for family violence cases

Selected Reform Options in Analysis Phase
- strengthening national roles and funding
  of day care and other programs

Selected Reform Options in Implementation Phase
- development of tracking programs
- development of regional planning agencies

Selected Reform Options in Assessment Phase
- requiring timely plans for each child
  removed from the natural family

Values and
Ideologies
- conservative
  opposition to
  "meddling
  with families"

Background
Demographic
and Other
Realities
- rising rates
  of divorce and
  participation by
  women in
  labor force

Mobilizing Power and Influence Resources
During the Legitimation Phase
to Obtain Reforms

ents and peers that allow children to develop a sense of competence, interactional and coping skills, and self-esteem. Families require income, housing, community, medical, daycare, and pre- school supports in an industrial society that places the major burden of raising and support- ing children on parents. When children are in danger, early detection, intensive interventions, and well-defined and time-limited plans are required that can draw on a range of community resources. Whether foster family care, institutions, group homes, or adoptions, substitute arrangements should meet carefully defined standards. Further, children should not be left in limbo in these settings but should, whenever possible, be returned to natural families or linked to adoptive parents.

Considerable dissatisfaction exists regarding American policies in the child-and family sector. Low-income children and families suffer multiple income, medical, nutritional, and other deficits. Family-planning services are insufficient, and denial of subsidies for abortions by low-income women is, at best, a short-sighted policy. Because Americans have not constructed a national system of daycare or preschool services, many parents must suffer the economic hardship of expensive, quality services. Despite incremental improvements, child welfare services are largely reactive and understaffed and lack a range of community service options. Far more use should be made of preventive medical and social services, subsidized adoptions, and community alternatives to institutions.

Other than the AFDC program, Americans did not develop major national programs to assist children until the 1960s. A series of cautious and incremental reforms ensued, including the Head Start program, daycare under Titles IV and XX of the Social Security Act, the Juvenile Justice and Delinquency Prevention Act, the Child Abuse

and Prevention Act, and various maternal, infant care, and children's health programs funded under Medicaid and Title V of the Social Security Act. But legislation to develop major national funding for children's programs was defeated in 1971 and at successive points during the 1970s.

Deep-seated ideological and political opposition exists to the development of major national programs and to the provision of family planning and subsidized abortions. Those who favor expanded programs need to engage in social action to draw on the power resources of organizations with strong grass-roots support. Reforms are needed that develop public subsidies for children from diverse economic classes, break down narrow categorical definitions, focus services to family units, and provide staff and other resources required to implement innovations. During implementation, continuing attention needs to be given to developing tracking systems to keep children from being lost in the foster and institutional care system.

Social workers can assume a variety of policy roles in the child and family sector, including redefining problems in terms of their family and community context; establishing interorganizational linkages; devising assessment strategies to gauge the effectiveness of alternative strategies; and developing political resources and strategies to increase pressure on legislators to consider major changes in policies to provide more adequate supports, supplements, and substitutes for American families and their children.

Key Concepts, Developments, and Policies

Family supports
Family supplements
Family substitutes
Child and family rights
Family planning
Daycare
Preschool programs
Natural home
Adoptions

Institutional care
Foster care
Group homes
Temporary and permanent placements
Child abuse and neglect
Juvenile courts
Child welfare departments
State of limbo
Infant and maternal services

Adoption subsidies

Sectarian and nonprofit agencies

Charles Brace

Children's Bureau

Sheppard-Towner Act

Title IV of the Social Security Act (Aid to Dependent Children)

Title V of the Social Security Act

Fair Labor Standards Act

Maternal and infant care projects

Medical screening under Medicaid

Services under Title IV-A of the Social Security Act

Work Incentive program (WIN)

Title XX of the Social Security Act

Family daycare

Daycare licensing and standards

Head Start

Child development legislation

Family Planning Services and Population Research Act

Supreme Court ruling on abortion

Woman, Infants, and Children Supplemental Food program

Adoption Assistance and Child Welfare Act

Omnibus Budget Reconciliation Act of 1981

Main Points

1. Although governments cannot legislate loving, supportive, and constructive relationships, they can facilitate them by providing supports and supplements to families.

2. When families do not provide a positive environment for their children, supports, supplements, and in some cases substitute arrangements are needed, but with due regard for the rights of children and their parents. As much as possible, a state of limbo should be avoided.

3. The effectiveness of American child and family policies is open to question: they do not provide minimum supports to many families; they deny family-planning services to many persons; they do not provide affordable and quality daycare; they do not monitor progress of children placed in substitute arrangements; and they provide insufficient staff in child welfare agencies.

4. The efficiency of American child and family policies is open to question: Americans do not provide preventive medical and nutritional services to "at risk" families and children, do not provide adoption subsidies to facilitate adoptions of hard-to-place children, and fail to fund community alternatives to institutions.

5. Equity and equality criteria are not satisfied by American child and family policies, since they promote or allow great disparities in economic resources and in access to medical, daycare, and other services.

6. Prior to the Great Depression, the federal government assumed minor roles in the child and family sector, with most services provided by nonprofit and sectarian agencies.

7. Major policies enacted in the Great Depression included Title IV and Title V of the Social Security Act, which initiated, respectively, the Aid to Dependent Children program (subsequently renamed the Aid to Families with Dependent Children program) and services for maternal and child health and crippled children. (Title V also gave the states funds for training and administration in child welfare.)

8. Major policies enacted in the 1960s included Head Start, new programs under Title V of the Social Security Act, daycare and work incentives under Title IV of the Social Security Act, special nutritional progams for mothers and infants, AFDC subsidies for court-ordered foster-care placements, and medical screening for children under Medicaid.

9. Even with these reforms, no funding breakthrough occurred in the federal government for programs specifically directed to children and their families. Conservative opposition was exemplified by the message of President Richard Nixon when he vetoed child development legislation in 1971.

10. In the current era of uncertainty, some legislation has been obtained, including the Family Planning Services and Population Research Act of 1970, the Adoption Assistance and Child Welfare Act of 1980, and the Juvenile Justice and Delinquency Prevention Act of 1974. Further, the Supreme Court in 1973 declared state laws prohibiting abortions in the first trimester of pregnancy to be unconstituional.

11. Drastic funding cuts in many programs that provide supports to low-income children and their families were enacted during the presidency of Ronald Reagan. Further, under the Omnibus Budget Reconciliation Act of 1981, he devised social services and maternal and child health block grants to decrease policy roles of the federal government.

Questions for Discussion

1. Review case example 10.1. Critique the American foster-care system in this metropolitan area in the context of effectiveness, efficiency, equity, and equality criteria.

2. Critically discuss the statement "Since government cannot legislate parental love, society is extremely limited in its role in the child and family sector."

3. In case example 10.1, identify policy changes that you think could be made to improve services offered to children.

4. Discuss barriers to the emergence of major federal funding and policy roles in the child and family sector.

5. Discuss major reforms enacted for children in the Great Depression and then during the 1960s.

6. Preventive strategies are particularly effective in the child and family sector and ought to be greatly expanded. Discuss.

7. Why do you think that many of the cuts in programs during the Reagan Administration were directed toward programs providing supports to low-income families?

8. What kinds of difficulties could you imagine occurring as local child welfare departments try to implement the adoption subsidies legislation to increase adoptions of hard-to-place adolescent and multiproblem children?

Suggested Readings

Bakal, Yitzhak, and Polsky, Howard. *Reforming Corrections for Juvenile Offenders* (Lexington, Mass.: Heath, 1979). The authors provide critical discussion of institutional strategies for delinquent children and suggest community alternatives.

Brown, June, et al., *Child/Family/Neighborhood: A Master Plan for Social Service Delivery* (New York: Child Welfare League of America, 1982). The authors present a concise discussion of service, policy, community, and administrative components in child and family services and suggest a new model for service delivery.

Costin, Lela. *Child Welfare: Policies and Practice* (New York: McGraw-Hill, 1979). This book provides an excellent overview of existing policies and programs in the child and family sector as well as historical perspectives and promising policy reforms.

Goldstein, Joseph, et al., *Beyond the Best Interests of the Child* (New York: Free Press, 1973). Drawing on research and professional knowledge, the authors discuss developmental needs of children, such as their need for permanency in relationships, and use this discussion to develop policy positions for child welfare programs.

Kadushin, Alfred. *Child Welfare Services* (New York: Macmillan, 1980). This classic book is particularly strong in its coverage of traditional child welfare issues and services.

Kamerman, Sheila, and Kahn, Alfred. *Social Services in the United States* (Philadephia: Temple University Press, 1976). This book provides excellent coverage of policies, programs, and issues pertaining to childcare, child abuse and neglect, children's institutions, and family planning. Critical analysis of existing programs is used to generate discussion of needed reforms.

Levitan, Sar, et al., *Work and Welfare Go Together* (Baltimore, Md.: Johns Hopkins University Press, 1972). The authors provide a concise overview of the AFDC program as well as consideration of issues and possible reforms.

Steiner, Gilbert. *Children's Crusade* (Washington, D.C.: Brookings Institution, 1976). The author discusses the ill-fated effort to obtain child development legislation in the early 1970s and, in the process, identifies many political realities and troublesome issues confronting reformers.

Steiner, Gilbert. *The Futility of Family Policy* (Washington, D.C.: Brookings Institution, 1981). This book addresses certain knotty conceptual and ethical problems as they pertain to a host of childcare, family violence, and family-planning issues. Interesting international perspectives are provided.

Streib, Victor. *Juvenile Justice in America.* (Port Washington, N.Y.: Kennikat Press, 1978). A brief introduction to services and issues in the juvenile justice system.

Notes

1. Goldstein et al., *Beyond the Best Interests of the Child*, p. 98.

2. See, for example, Erik Erikson, *Childhood and Society* (New York: Norton, 1963).

3. Goldstein et al., *Beyond the Best Interests of the Child*. The distinction between support, supplemental, and substitution programs was established by Kadushin, *Child Welfare Services*.

4. Steiner, *Futility of Family Policy*, pp. 82–88.

5. See Carole Joffe, "Daycare Services," in Neil Gilbert and Harry Specht, eds., *Handbook of the Social Services* (Englewood Cliffs, N.J.: Prentice-Hall, 1981), pp. 50–66. Discussion of a range of family supports is found in Kamerman and Kahn, *Social Services in the United States*, pp. 25–140.

6. An overview of supplemental services is provided by Kamerman and Kahn, *Social Services in the United States*, pp. 141–312. A

case for institutions is made by Martin Wolins, "Observations on the Future of Institutional Care of Children in the U.S.," in Alfred Kadushin, ed., *Child Welfare Strategy in the 1980s* (Washington, D.C.: U.S. Department of Health, Education, and Welfare, Office of Human Development Services, 1978), pp. 90–130.

7. See Terry Jones, "The Juvenile Justice System," in Elizabeth Huttman, *Introduction to Social Policy* (New York: McGraw-Hill, 1981), pp. 253–268.

8. Steiner, *Futility of Family Policy*, pp. 130–155.

9. Geoffrey Pawson, "Organizational Variables Affecting the Deinstitutionalization of Residential Treatment Centers," unpublished doctoral dissertation, University of Southern California, 1980.

10. See discussion of family planning in Kamerman and Kahn, *Social Services in the*

United States, pp. 387–435. Infant and maternal services are discussed by Karen Davis and Cathy Schoen, *Health and the War on Poverty* (Washington, D.C.: Brookings Institution, 1978), pp. 120–160.

11. Costin, *Child Welfare,* chapter 9.

12. Ibid., p. 60.

13. The classic book on discrimination is Andrew Billingsly, *Children of the Storm: Black Children and American Child Welfare* (New York: Harcourt Brace Jovanovich, 1972).

14. Costin, *Child Welfare,* pp. 27–36, 83–94, 157–159, and 185–190.

15. Ibid., pp. 415–416.

16. William Chafe, *The American Woman: Her Changing Social, Economic, and Political Roles* (New York: Oxford University Press, 1972).

17. Davis and Schoen, *Health and the War on Poverty,* pp. 120–160.

18. Ibid., pp. 84–86.

19. AFDC policy in the 1960s is discussed by Gilbert Steiner, *State of Welfare* (Washington, D.C.: Brookings Institutation 1971), pp. 31–121. Also see Levitan et al., *Work and Welfare Go Together* (Baltimore: Johns Hopkins University Press, 1972).

20. Martha Derthick, *Uncontrollable Spending for Social Services Grants* (Washington, D.C.: Brookings Institution, 1975).

21. Costin, *Child Welfare,* pp. 397–433.

22. See Susan and Martin Tolchin, *Clout: Women Power and Politics* (New York: Coward, McCann & Geoghegan, 1974), p. 230.

23. Bruce S. Jansson, "The History and Politics of Selected Children's Programs," unpublished doctoral dissertation, University of Chicago, 1975, pp. 60–142.

24. "Reagan's Polarized America," *Newsweek* (April 5, 1982), pp. 20–28.

25. Steiner, *Children's Crusade.*

26. Costin, *Child Welfare,* pp. 424–425.

27. Societal policies to reduce violence are discussed by David Gil, *Violence Against Children* (Cambridge, Mass.: Harvard University Press, 1977).

Policy in the Economic Security Sector

Social workers have traditionally assumed major policy roles in the economic security sector, as reflected by their roles during development of the Social Security Act in 1935 and during subsequent implementation of various programs established by that legislation. Some critics fear, however, that the profession may disengage itself from this sector and hence from its traditional interest in the plight of poverty-stricken persons, whose ranks are again swelling after marginal reduction of poverty in the 1960s and 1970s. Indeed, all social workers should:

Be able to articulate normative standards and positions that define goals for reducing social inequality and allow critical assessment of deterrent policies that support increasing disparities between incomes of the rich and the poor

Be able to identify and analyze a variety of short-term approaches to reducing economic inequality and meeting needs of the poverty-stricken

Have familiarity with a variety of long-term approaches for helping poor persons improve their economic position

Be able to identify basic defects in existing policies and programs in the economic security sector that prevent them from meeting effectiveness, efficiency, equity, and quality criteria

Possess knowledge of the evolution of American policies in the economic security sector during the 1930s, during the 1960s, and during the current era of policy uncertainty

Be able to develop reforms that can improve existing policies and programs in this sector

These topics are discussed in this chapter to provide background and conceptual materials that can be used in the practice of policy in the economic security sector.

POVERTY: A NORMATIVE POSITION

Poverty exists in rural as well as urban settings, but it is most obvious in inner-city communities because of the sheer number of poverty-stricken persons living there in close proximity, often in blighted areas. Poverty in inner-city settings is discussed in guest editorial 11.1, an article that raises a number of difficult questions. How much economic inequality should exist? What strategies, singly or together, appear to be effective in redressing this inequality? Why have Americans succeeded in reducing the numbers of persons

---

GUEST EDITORIAL 11.1

Life in the Cities: Separate, Unequal

By Robert Scheer
Times Staff Writer

A rather neat thing happened on the way to an integrated society. Neat in the sense of tidy, that is. Most of the poorer blacks and Hispanics ended up contained in the central cities—out of sight and out of mind.

It therefore is not true that the cities are no longer needed or terribly useful. They increasingly perform the function of vast holding cells for society's rejects: 60% of unemployed blacks, 60% of welfare recipients, 70% of robbers and the victims of robberies, 90% of youth gangs.

The civilization of the cities is marked by the life experiences of an underclass—people without options—children whose parents

have never held a steady job, who themselves and whose own children most likely will not.

The cities, with their growing underclass, are ever more separate and unequal. . . .

The situation is similar throughout the country. The white "civilization" is located increasingly in the shopping malls, tract homes, country clubs, factories, new corporate headquarters and school systems of the suburbs. . . .

The burgeoning black middle class is also involved in flight from the cities' underclass but, because of racial prejudice, it's not easy for them to get away.

Racism associates all blacks with, and holds them accountable for, the problems of the ghetto. Whites tend to hold all blacks responsible for urban crime and violence, but

who fall beneath official poverty-line standards but not decreased economic inequality in the nation? As in other policy sectors, normative issues and perspectives often shape policy choices and analysis; thus, a number of issues and perspectives are discussed in this section of the chapter as a prelude to critical analysis of existing policies.

Reducing Economic Inequality

When analyzing poverty, as described in guest editorial 11.1, a policy analyst might choose two related but different objectives. Attention could be given to policies that allow inner-city blacks and other poverty-stricken persons to obtain sufficient economic resources to purchase minimum amounts of food, housing, medical, and other amenities—i.e., to raise them from *absolute poverty*. Alternatively, policies could be pursued

to allow them to make economic gains relative to whites in surrounding suburban communities— i.e., to decrease *relative poverty*.[1] Difficult and controversial as it may be, the central task facing the nation is to reduce relative poverty, as suggested by the following philosophical and moral arguments.

Philosophical Considerations. Many theorists argue that no moral basis exists for supporting extreme economic differentials between social classes.[2] Some inequality is inevitable, but the extreme inequalities prevalent in the United States seem unnecessary, particularly in light of the substantially lower levels in West Germany, Japan, and Scandinavian countries. The top quintile (one-fifth) of the population currently possesses roughly 42 percent of national income, in comparison to 6 percent for the lowest quintile. Economic inequality is even more obvious

---

there is no such association of innocent whites with white criminals. White suburbanites are not held responsible for their children who turn up junkies or teen-age prostitutes in the big cities.

Blacks are still caught by their skin color. Ernest Green, one of the black children who walked into that school in Little Rock in 1957 and who grew up to become an assistant secretary of labor in the Carter Administration, reports his own experience:

"You get on the elevator in your suit and tie and briefcase with somebody that is white, particularly a white female, and you immediately see fear in their eyes."

Even when blacks have the money, racial barriers make it more difficult for them to get out of the cities. Harvard social psychologist Thomas F. Pettigrew estimates that while only 8% of Chicago's blacks live in the suburbs, according to the 1970 census, 46% should be expected to live there on economic grounds

alone. But middle-class blacks are slowly but surely leaving the central cities and when they stay, are tending more often to use private schools, further isolating the minority underclass.

The progress of blacks into the ranks of the middle class has been real and substantial and fully 25% of black families had an income of more than $16,000 per year in 1976 (as compared to 50% for whites). But there are also just as many poor black families and twice as many blacks out of work today as there were 10 years ago. These are the blacks who form the enduring underclass.

That underclass is marked by female-headed households and children born out of wedlock. In 1976, one-fourth of all black children were in families headed by women who were unemployed or not in the labor force as compared to 18% in 1969. In 1976, 28% of blacks were said to fall below the poverty line.

As the Labor Department's Green put it:

"You have a class breakout. I mean, some of those—that's not true of all middle-class blacks—but some of those who have made it reply back much like some whites do; that (poor) people are in the condition they're in because it's their own fault. . . .

"I think the gap has widened. It seems to me what the country hasn't focused on is that the issue in the '60's clearly was that no blacks, regardless of economic class, could do certain things . . . Now legally that's been thrown out and what that did was to open up access for those who had a certain amount of income and economic security. But still, for large numbers of people that didn't matter. Making that legal change didn't gain them any more access than they had before."

The type who hasn't benefitted, according to Green, is "a black kid who can't find the support, can't find formal education, can't get out to where the jobs are in the suburbs, doesn't know how to deal with the system. Then you've got a continuous, swirling black underclass that never understands how to manipulate the system."

A recent Washington Post series celebrated the fact that blacks are cast as typical Americans in television commercials and programs and cited this as proof of the nation's progress toward an integrated society. But in real life, when whites think of blacks, it is most often the ghetto underclass black whom they think about and whom they fear.

A Harris Poll conducted for the U.S. Department of Housing and Urban Development showed that crime and poor schools were the most important reasons for people's rejection of life in the cities. And the two are obviously connected.

Urban crime, in particular urban school violence, is a reality. The most recent national study of school violence, for example, revealed that principals in one-quarter of the senior high schools in large urban areas reported that vandalism, theft and attacks represented a fairly serious or very serious problem. . . .

The FBI: "Robbery is primarily a large city crime. Seven out of 10 robberies in the United States occurred in the cities with more than 100,000 inhabitants. These cities experienced 521 robberies per 100,000 people."

Almost 60% of those arrested for robbery in 1976 in the entire nation were what the FBI still chooses to call Negro. Blacks accounted for 52% of the prostitution arrests, 55% of all arrests of gambling, 40% of weapons violations, 47% of rape and 53% of murder.

While arrest figures may be misleading, in urban areas where blacks represent a higher percentage of the population, the proportions are substantially higher.

It is also true that blacks account for a disproportionately high number of the victims of such crimes—47% of those murdered, for example. Blacks are the main victims of urban violence and they are the ones who must live near it.

It is not that blacks are, by nature, more violent than whites or that there are few white criminals. (Whites account for 69% of all burglary arrests, 65% of larceny arrests and 51% of rape arrests.) And it is not that most blacks today are violent.

But a disturbing number of chronically unemployed and otherwise deprived young blacks have come to view violent, criminal behavior as an option for advancement in a way that seems wildly irrational to one who has other, more acceptable, options.

This bleak picture of ghetto life did not shock Georgia state senator and civil rights veteran Julian Bond, who said:

"I go out to the federal pen here a lot and people tell me that the age has just dropped so radically. The average age of the prisoners used to be in the late 30's. Now it's in the mid-20's. This is the federal system we're talking about, not the state system. The black-white ratio has almost reversed from being about 20% black some years ago to being 40% white now.

"And you see it in all these young guys out there—Vietnam vets, bank robbers, drug people and such. Small time—all of them small time. The prison used to be filled with organized crime figures. Now it's filled with bank robbers. It used to have a lot of moonshiners in it—white country moonshiners. Now it's got black bank robbers. Bank robbery is the crime of choice among black youth. Big money. And that's what happens to those people."

Those people are only a small minority of the black population and certainly of the urban one, but they seriously affect the civilization that is possible in the modern city, from the graffiti on the trains to the life-styles in the schools. It would be stupid—and futile—to deny it.

Which is precisely why the courts ordered desegregation in the first place—to permit minority children an escape from total immersion in that grinding ghetto life. If ghetto poverty remains frozen in place at the heart of America's cities, if the schools present no real options, it is to be expected that hundreds of thousands of young people will grow up unable to do anything but make life miserable for themselves and their neighbors.

It is as if the "urban crisis" has become an acceptable euphemism for racial problems at a time when government officials are all too aware that most white Americans no longer have any patience or tolerance for dealing with race. . . .

The various government strategies for saving urban America beg this key point—that white flight is not a response to the physical decay of the cities but rather to the fact that poor people have been trapped there. Obviously, most Americans feel that they neither need, nor can afford to associate with, the poor and their problems.

We reject the cities because we reject the poor. If a neutron bomb were suddenly dropped on the poor of St. Louis, New York City or central Los Angeles, the housing stock would be rediscovered by affluent home buyers as quaint, conveniently located and architecturally fascinating and they would pour in money to rehabilitate those structures that are now rejected.

A less drastic people-removal process is under way in a number of cities and it's called neighborhood restoration. But the brownstones and Victorian houses that are restored in Washington, D.C., New York or San Francisco become valuable only because the neighborhood is changing. Which means that the balance has swung toward more affluent and white residents, and that a security zone has been thrown up around the "new" neighborhood.

The people-removal part of urban renewal was not accidental to the policy. It was the policy.

By 1967 urban renewal had removed 400,000 housing units from U.S. cities and built only 12,000 new units of public housing for the people displaced.

The cities, more often than not, have been victims of federal programs designed to ensure their progress. The urban renewal of the '50's—the bulldozer tactic—left deserted areas in one side of town and overcrowding in the other.

Public housing projects of immense proportions planned as alternatives to the ghettos became ghettos themselves, further isolating the poor and minorities from the rest of the population.

Shortlived and underfunded poverty programs did little more than raise expectations and then deny them. The much-touted War on Poverty never cost more per year than what the government is now planning to spend on two aircraft carriers, according to Rep. Ronald V. Dellums (D-Calif.).

when shares of national wealth are compared, i.e., current income, including returns from economic holdings and appreciation of unsold assets, such as real estate and stocks. The highest quintile of the population possesses 76 percent of the wealth, in comparison to only one percent for the lowest quintile, and long-standing economic disparities between highest and lowest quintiles have not diminished (see illustration 11.1).[3]

Economic inequality is defended on the pragmatic grounds that it is required to preserve the work ethic, to persuade talented people to compete for and endure sacrifices associated with difficult and time-consuming jobs, and to allow accumulation of funds that can be used to fuel investments to promote economic growth. (The latter rationale was used by the administration of President Ronald Reagan to support decreases in

ILLUSTRATION 11.1   Median Family Income and Lowest and Highest Fifths of Family Income: 1947–1978

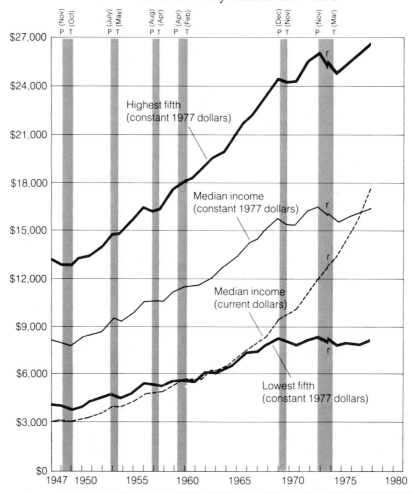

SOURCE: U.S. Department of Commerce, Bureau of the Census, *Social Indicators III*, 1980, p. 435.

taxes of the affluent relative to those of the poor.)

Three kinds of comparisons suggest that considerable reductions in inequality would not be accompanied by dire consequences and might even increase work incentives and economic growth.[4] First, some societies with far less inequality have more productive economies, including West Germany, Japan, and Sweden. The work ethic appears not to have declined in these countries, and their citizens do not appear to need extraordinary reimbursement to seek challenging positions in science, technology, or the professions.

Second, recent studies of effects of a guaranteed income do not demonstrate across-the-board reduction in motivation to work, even when persons are given relatively generous income supplements. Finally, persons in specific groups within the American population that primarily compete with one another in labor markets often do not appear to need extreme economic differentials in income to motivate them to seek challenging positions. In comparison to others, for example, white employed males have relatively equal income. Yet, despite this relative equality, considerable competition exists among them for positions in fields like medicine and business. Further, some professions draw willing applicants even when pay is not munificent—an assertion that any underpaid college professor will readily support. Liberal critics appear on target, in short, when they argue that conservatives use a sort of economic metaphysics to impute dire consequences that will follow some, even major, reductions in economic inequality.

Survival Standards vs. Redistribution. How much inequality should exist however, is difficult to determine. Should shares of income and wealth of the various quintiles be modestly or drastically different? Many participants in policy accept a relatively conservative course that involves (1) defining some minimum "market basket" of foods, housing, clothing, and other amenities that constitutes minimal but acceptable living, (2) ascertaining how many Americans fall beneath this standard, and (3) devising income

and other programs to bridge the poverty gap. In 1964, officials in the Department of Agriculture computed that roughly 30 percent of household budgets was devoted to food purchases and so priced out a market basket of an acceptable, if minimal, diet for a family of four. An official in the Department of Health, Education, and Welfare then multiplied this sum by roughly three to achieve an official poverty line. Corrected periodically for inflation and further refined, this base line by 1981 was $9,290 for a family of four.

Considerable success has been, achieved in reaching this objective, since large numbers of Americans were catapulted above the official poverty line by welfare, Food Stamps, Medicaid, Medicare, Social Security, housing, and other programs during the 1960s and 1970s. But earnings, private pensions, real estate, and investment holdings, magnified by tax loopholes, allowed the nonpoor to equal or surpass the gains made by the poor. The poor's relative share of national income and wealth, then, did not markedly increase.

Further, reduction in absolute, or survival-line, poverty does not mean that the poor perceive themselves as more affluent. Many American poor persons would be regarded as relatively affluent in India but perceive themselves to be out of the economic and social mainstream because their point of reference is their relative economic deprivation within this country. As discussed in case example 11.1, many inner-city blacks compare their lot with whites in suburban communities and with affluent blacks, who often leave inner cities for upper-class neighborhoods and private schools.[5]

From this perspective, then, a major anti-poverty challenge is to increase economic resources of the poor relative to the affluent (a position eloquently supported by the late English Theorist Richard Titmuss).[6] Reduction of relative poverty should be a primary objective that also leads to reduction in survival-line poverty.

Two Remaining Moral Arguments. Two additional arguments are often used to counter efforts to redistribute massive resources to the poor.

Some persons perceive poverty to be synonymous with moral fault, i.e., with laziness and lack of personal sacrifice. Others argue that persons should be able to retain their personal wealth in a free society; in this perspective, policies to redistribute resources from the affluent to the poor reduce the freedom of the individual and are thus to be strenuously resisted.[7]

Both of these moral arguments ignore economic and social realities. Neither poverty nor wealth are simple consequences of personal lifestyle but result from good fortune, possession of credentials, inherited wealth, contacts, and job-seeking skills. Further, achieved wealth is associated with many social and governmental factors that favor some persons and not others. Since children of affluent persons inherit wealth simply because they are fortunately situated, is it deprivation of their rights to redistribute some of it to others who are not so fortunate? In similar fashion, federal and local income tax policies bestow generous tax deductions and shelters to wealthy persons, generosity not conceded to the poor (see illustration 11.2).

Setting Objectives. Americans, then, should devise welfare objectives that reduce economic inequality by raising the shares of poorer members of society. The economist Lester Thurow argues that policies should be devised to make the distribution of income among employed members of society roughly equal to the current distribution of income among white employed males. To achieve this goal, incomes of minorities and women would have to be markedly increased relative to white males. For elderly and other members of society who cannot work, he argues, welfare payments should raise their income to one-half the current median income, since polls suggest that many citizens regard this level as a suitable minimum economic standard.[8] Even this modest objective would require major increases in welfare payments, however, since such payments usually fall below one-half the 1980 median income of roughly $18,000 per family of four. Finally, he contends, society should create employment to ensure that all unemployed persons can obtain jobs at competitive salaries.

ILLUSTRATION 11.2

"We're All In The Same Boat"
4/11/73

From *Herblock on All Fronts*, New American Library, 1980. Reprinted by permission of Herblock Cartoons.

Promoting a Random Distribution of Poverty

If some economic inequality has to exist, surely it would be best if it were distributed randomly among the population, so that no single group had to bear a disproportionate burden. But data suggest that the burden of poverty is not randomly distributed (see illustration 11.3 for comparisons of income of white and black families). The average black family's income is only 61.5 percent of the income of the average white family. Women, on average, earn roughly one-half the wages of men, a figure that has decreased since 1948. Families headed by single women are far more likely than the general population to experience poverty because they must also raise children on low wages generally re-

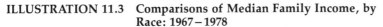

ILLUSTRATION 11.3 Comparisons of Median Family Income, by
Race: 1967–1978

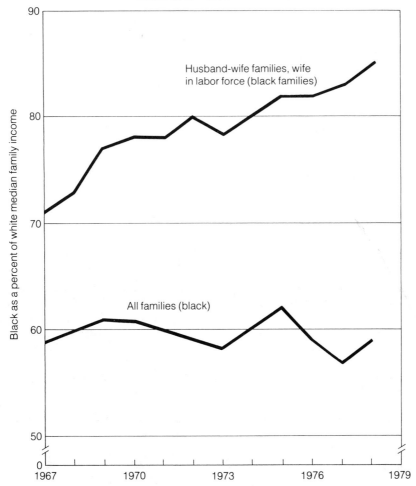

SOURCE: U.S. Department of Commerce, Bureau of the Census, *Social Indicators III,* 1980,
*Words in parentheses have been added by the author.

ceived by female workers. Policies are needed, then, that specifically target jobs, social programs, and tax policy to populations that experience economic deprivation.

MULTIPLE STRATEGIES: SHORT-TERM APPROACHES

Both short- and long-term strategies are needed to reduce relative poverty (see table 11.1). In the short-term, income redistribution can be accomplished through reforms of federal and local taxes, development of income maintenance programs, reforms in service or resource programs, and creation of jobs. (Long-term strategies are discussed later in this chapter.)

Tax Policies

The tax system can be a powerful governmental tool for redistributing income when tax policies

TABLE 11.1   Short- and Long-Term Poverty-Reduction Strategies

Short-Term Strategies	Long-Term Strategies
major revisions in tax policy	increasing competitive capabilities of specific groups
revisions of means-tested income maintenance programs	decreasing job-related discrimination
revisions in social insurance (income) programs	developing appropriate fiscal and monetary policy
revisions in means-tested service and resource programs	
revisions in social-insurance service and resource programs	
use of affirmative action and quota policies	
creation of jobs by government	

impose relatively higher rates on the rich than on the poor. The poor can be given special *tax deductions* to reduce their taxable income or *tax credits* (i.e., direct payments) to enable persons who have income beneath a specific floor to receive government payments rather than pay taxes. A scheme was enacted in 1973, for example, that gives tax credits to families earning less than $4,000 per year. An expansive scheme known as the negative income tax (NIT) is supported by many theorists because families receive benefit payments directly from the Internal Revenue Service to raise their income to a certain threshold rather than experiencing the stigma associated with welfare programs.[9] Decisions about the size of benefits given poor families are influenced by basic values. The conservative economist Milton Friedman proposed a relatively low floor, for example, in contrast to liberal economists.[10]

Means-Tested Income Maintenance

Income maintenance programs, commonly called welfare or public assistance programs, distribute income to persons who meet specific income and other criteria. As an example, care takers and their children who fall beneath specified income and asset tests receive funds under the Aid to Families with Dependent Children program

(AFDC), a program that is discussed subsequently. Other programs, discussed subsequently, include the Supplementary Income Program (SSI) and the local general assistance programs (GA). The SSI program provides welfare benefits to indigent persons over age sixty-five as well as indigent disabled persons and is federally funded and administered unlike the AFDC program. General assistance programs are wholly funded and administered by states and localities and provide welfare benefits to indigent persons who do not qualify for assistance from federal-state programs such as AFDC and SSI. Benefits under these local programs are usually very limited; their caseloads include many single non-elderly persons as well as many families in those states that have not expanded their AFDC programs to include two-parent families.

Means-tested income maintenance programs can assume a relatively less important role in American social welfare policy if other remedies, such as the negative income tax, social insurance, or public works, are used to give income to the poor. A case can be made that tax and job remedies should be drastically expanded in the United States to give demeaning and politically unpopular welfare programs somewhat less prominence. In any society, however, many persons need income supplementation through major income maintenance programs.

Social Insurance Income Programs

Means-tested income maintenance programs are financed by government revenues and reach only those persons who meet specific eligibility criteria. Social insurance programs, by contrast, are financed by payroll deductions of employees and employers and given to citizens, regardless of income, who encounter certain life events, such as retirement or disability (Social Security), unemployment (unemployment insurance), or work-related injury (workman's compensation). These insurance programs are typically geared not to providing resources to meet basic and ongoing living expenses but to cushioning the economic hardship that often accompanies such circumstances.[11]

One advantage of social insurances is that many recipients perceive them to be earned benefits, which are not as stigmatizing as welfare programs. Also, by providing benefits to rich and poor alike, they draw support from a broad spectrum of the population. Unlike means-tested programs, however, they do not emphasize redistribution to the poor, since the poor often pay relatively high rates of payroll taxes in comparison to the rich and bear a disproportionate burden of the higher prices passed on to consumers by employers to finance their share of payroll taxes. Still, the poor often obtain a larger share of benefits from many of these programs because they experience higher rates of such life events as unemployment and disability.

Participation in social insurance programs is mandatory for most citizens. Although some conservatives view mandatory participation as an infringement of personal rights, a case can be made that many consumers would not otherwise set aside funds in anticipation of distant or catastrophic events. Social insurance programs, then, are crucial elements in income policy.

Means-Tested Service and Resource Programs

Many social programs distribute services or goods to the poor through means-tested programs. In the case of the Medicaid program, for example, persons who meet income eligibility standards established by state governments receive cards that enable them to receive specified medical services from participating providers, who then bill the government. In other cases, consumers receive funds or money substitutes like food stamp coupons that are given to businesses or providers for specified services or goods. (The Food Stamps program is discussed subsequently.)

The advantage of these programs is that government authorities can directly influence what services or goods are distributed to or used by the poor. Food stamps, for example, can only be used to purchase food. Since poverty-related income eligibility is used, as in means-tested income programs, these programs also focus resources on the poor. In addition, programs like Food Stamps and Medicaid are politically acceptable to many Americans because they emphasize basic necessities and draw on the support of specific interest groups, such as farmers and physicians, who benefit from them.

Many policy analysts favor turning these service and resource programs into cash and using their funds to increase grants under income maintenance programs to give consumers more choice in the use of resources and reduce the stigma associated with identification cards or food stamps.[12] A case can be made on political grounds, however, that these programs should be continued and expanded. Since Americans have never been prone to provide generous funds for means-tested income maintenance programs, why not distribute some resources to persons through Food Stamps, Medicaid, and other in-kind programs?

Social Insurance Service and Resource Programs

Some social insurance programs provide goods or services rather than cash. In the case of Part A of Medicare, for example, persons over sixty-five who have participated in the Social Security program qualify for specified (and limited) hospital benefits. Like cash benefits under Social Security, benefits are financed by funds paid by employers and employees. This kind of program redistributes resources to the poor only insofar as

Playing Politics with Minorities' Last Hope

By Roger Wilkins

For five decades, blacks have viewed the federal government as the principal guarantor of their rights and the most powerful force for opening opportunities to those whose lives had been stunted by racism and its offshoots, discrimination and neglect of the plight of the minority poor. Now blacks and their allies watch with a kind of impotent dismay as the Reagan Administration and some of its staunchest allies in Congress display a grim and comprehensive intention to destroy the government's capacities to carry that fundamental and humane task to its logical conclusion: an America that keeps its constitutional promises to all its citizens.

The reliance of blacks on the federal government is understandable. Racism and its results are so deep and broad a part of American culture that no power in the American environment other than the government, acting as the better part of the conscience of the whole people, could possibly stop it and eradicate its pervasive effects in our society.

Over the years, the government gave hope to minorities by undertaking that task. There are some memorable milestones. The social programs of the New Deal, which included blacks as beneficiaries, gave them a sense that they were at last a part of the nation's concerns: President Harry S. Truman's order desegregating the armed forces took the issue several steps forward, and the Supreme Court's 1954 decision ruling that segregated education is unconstitutional was the first fundamental tender of full constitutional citizenship to blacks. Later, there were the passage of laws and the establishment of structures to enforce those laws, all of which gave blacks an umbrella of hope and ties that bound them to society.

Among the most important of those events were the establishment of the U.S. Commis-

they make greater use of their benefits than others or do not bear a disproportionate burden of payroll taxes. (Since affluent persons tend to live longer than poor persons and use Medicare over longer periods, its redistributive effects are not obvious.) Still, Medicare is a highly popular program because it, like the Social Security program, is perceived to provide earned benefits.

Affirmative Action and Quotas

One method of assisting the poor or groups that have experienced disproportionate poverty is to increase their relative share of jobs, either by setting quotas or by devising plans to gradually increase their numbers in specific work settings

through affirmative action. These policies are politically explosive because white and male citizens can lose opportunities as minorities and women gain them, especially in a nongrowth economy. Further, some fear that these policies imperil standards because traditional testing and credential requirements are sometimes waived, a charge rebutted by those who contend that testing and credentialing are often subject to class and cultural bias and do not necessarily predict on-the-job competence.[13]

Government authorities have pursued affirmative action strategies under the Civil Rights Act of 1965 to bring legal action against universities and corporations with public contracts. The many class-action law suits levied against cor-

sion on Civil Rights in 1957, the passage of the Civil Rights Act of 1964 and the Voting Rights Act of 1965, the formation of the Equal Employment Opportunity Commission, the Office of Federal Contracts Compliance, the Civil Rights Division and the Community Relations Service in the Department of Justice. Under successive Republican and Democratic Administrations, these laws and structures were developed and enhanced, as were the remedies of affirmative action and transportation of pupils to achieve desegregation.

Those developments gave blacks, no matter how difficult the remaining problems they faced, a sense that they were an integral part of a caring nation that was struggling with its conscience.

The current Administration is changing all that. The dismissal of Arthur S. Flemming as chairman of the U.S. Commission on Civil Rights, while far from the most important of the steps the Administration has taken, stands almost as a metaphor for its actions and attitudes. The commission was established as a monitor of the civil-rights posture of the United States, including the enforcement ef-

forts of the federal government itself. While the President appoints the members of the commission, the legislation creating it envisioned an independent analyst, not a policy arm of any particular Administration.

Flemming, a distinguished Republican public servant, was appointed by President Richard M. Nixon and has continued to serve under Presidents Gerald R. Ford, Jimmy Carter and Ronald Reagan. In a move unprecedented in the commission's 24-year history, Reagan has announced that he intends to appoint Clarence M. Pendleton, president of the San Diego Urban League, in his place.

The White House says that Flemming is not being replaced because it is unhappy with what the commission has been saying lately. But the commission has been critical of the Administration for pulling back on affirmative action and abandoning the use of pupil transportation as one of the means to achieve school desegregation. In addition, the commission has cited the use of deadly force against minorities by some police departments as a significant national problem, while presidential counselor Edwin Meese III has

porations have led to substantial back payments as well as promotions for women and minorities. It is not realistic to assume that racial minorities and women can achieve parity in sectors of the economy where they are grossly underrepresented unless government requires the use of affirmative action or quotas in the current hiring decisions of corporations, universities, and government authorities (see guest editorial 11.2).

Creation of Jobs by Government

Government can create jobs in government and nonprofit sectors by directly subsidizing all or part of their cost. Two major experiments with job creation indicate that it can successfully pro-

vide millions of jobs to unemployed persons but that it is likely to draw conservative opposition that leads to its demise. In the Great Depression of the 1930s, various public works programs encountered criticism that public jobs competed with private industry, provided political patronage, and created make-work positions. After their demise in 1941, no further programs were enacted that created jobs on a massive basis until the Comprehensive Employment Training Act (CETA) of 1973; subsequently, under Title VI, hundreds of thousands of persons were hired by public and nonprofit agencies in public service jobs that could not last more than one year. Although training components of the act remained, public service employment succumbed to the

been critical of critics of the police. Flemming's proposed replacement opposes busing and affirmative action, and is a friend of Meese. Blacks now wonder just how independent the commission, which has been a conscience for the nation, will continue to be.

At the Justice Department, busing and affirmative action have been cast aside as remedies for school segregation and illegal employment discrimination, and the attorney general and the assistant attorney general for civil rights have been enunciating a school policy that sounds remarkably like the separate-but-equal doctrine that the Supreme Court ruled unconstitutional 27 years ago. Civil-rights enforcement initiatives have all but stopped in Justice, and principles of litigation designed to protect against discrimi-

nation, which have been forged in a bipartisan fashion, have been abandoned.

The Equal Employment Opportunity Commission has been allowed to languish. Of five commissionerships, only two are filled, leaving the agency without even enough members to form the quorum required to make policy decisions. The Administration has nominated William M. Bell, a black Detroiter, to chair the commission. Civil-rights and women's groups have taken a look at Bell's qualifications for running an agency with more than 3,300 employees and a $140 million annual budget, and have found it wanting. He runs a personnel-placement agency of which he is the only employee and that, he admits, has placed no one in the past year. His earnings last year were $7,000. Privately, black

budget cutting of the Reagan Administration, when objections surfaced similar to those levied against public works in the 1930s. (CETA is discussed in more detail subsequently.)

Certainly no programs are perfect, but CETA public service jobs served as one vehicle for expanding employment opportunities in an era of high unemployment. Although income, service, and resource programs are important, government can assist those who need work only if it provides or otherwise subsidizes employment when the private market is insufficient. Many lament that the poor are lazy; few are willing to put this hypothesis to the test by offering them enough jobs to eliminate long-term unemployment.[14] (A proposal initiated by Rep. Augustus Hawkins and Sen. Hubert Humphrey in the 1970s to require massive creation of jobs when the national unemployment rate reached excessive levels was defeated.) This inconsistency is yet more glaring when government authorities themselves create unemployment by using economy-slowing fiscal and monetary pol-

icies to fight inflation, policies that place disproportionate burdens on low-income persons.

MULTIPLE STRATEGIES: LONG-TERM APPROACHES

Various short-term approaches can be supplemented with policies for creating societal and labor-force changes likely to enhance the income of the poor. Because these policies promise only distant changes in income and employment redistribution, they are not substitutes for short-term strategies.

Increasing Competitive Capabilities of Specific Groups

Americans have been more willing to fund job training than job creation schemes because they are consonant with American values that prize pulling oneself up by ones bootstraps. Training can be placed on a continuum extending from

leaders are enraged that so unqualified a person would be nominated by the President for such an important post.

The Labor Department is considering curtailing drastically the ability of the Office of Federal Contracts Compliance to enforce the executive order requiring that organizations doing business with the federal government not discriminate in their employment practices.

On Capitol Hill, Republican allies of the Administration have produced a blizzard of proposals to curb busing, affirmative action and the jurisdiction of the Equal Employment Opportunities Commission. The attorney general, traditionally the government's chief civil-rights enforcer, gives lip service to the idea of achieving equal justice for minorities, but his department and his colleagues in government are actively engaged in dismantling the structures, procedures and programs that have in the past provided both progress and hope for blacks and other minorities.

As a former director of the Community Relations Service in the Department of Justice, I am often asked whether this record and the social program cuts dictated by Reagan's economic policies will produce another wave of unrest in the nation's cities. I do not know the answer to that question, and I believe that it is irresponsible to predict riots. I do know this, however: No good social consequences can flow when the federal engines of justice are throttled back and the strands of hope and trust to which people have clung for five decades are peremptorily severed.

Roger Wilkins, now a journalist, was director of the Community Relations Service in the Department of Justice from 1966 to 1969. SOURCE: This article first appeared in the *Los Angeles Times*. Reprinted by permission of the author.

general remedial education to specialized on-the-job training. A host of job training programs have been used, including vocational education programs funded largely by state and local units that often "cream" more highly skilled persons to the detriment of others. Job skills programs were initiated in the 1960s in institutional settings and consolidated in the Comprehensive Employment Training Act of 1973, which funds skills training in institutional centers administered by local authorities. Other training programs include the residential Job Corps program, the Work Incentive program (WIN) for unemployed adult recipients on AFDC rolls, and vocational rehabilitation programs that provide services to the physically handicapped.[15]

Still, American commitment to job training has been halfhearted in comparison, for example, to West Germany. In coming decades, racial minorities and women are likely to encounter marked difficulty in obtaining positions in such rapidly growing technical fields as computer programming, not to mention workers who are dis-placed by structural changes in automobile, steel, and other basic industries. Massive job training efforts need to be established, with priority given to groups in the population that are disproportionately unemployed or lack access to critical industries.

Decreasing Job-Related Discrimination

Note was made of federal monitoring of agencies with federal contracts to promote affirmative action. An Equal Employment Opportunity Commission (EEOC) was created to enforce Title VII of the Civil Rights Act of 1964, which bans discrimination on the basis of race or sex in both private and public organizations. The EEOC brings lawsuits against violators, which are in turn supplemented by legal action of employees. In addition, the Office of Federal Contract Compliance Programs requires firms using federal funds not to discriminate and to develop affirmative action strategies. The precise effect of these various monitoring and legal strategies is unknown, but few would doubt that continuing scrutiny of job-related discrimination is needed.[16]

Fiscal and Monetary Policy

The ultimate victims of high rates of unemployment are racial minorities and women, just as those with low wages or fixed assets, such as the poor and the elderly, suffer from high rates of inflation. Americans have been notably ineffective in recent years in using either fiscal policies (i.e., those pertaining to spending and taxation) or monetary policies (i.e., those pertaining to banking, credit, and the supply of money) to create a healthy economy. As in Japan and West Germany, innovative fiscal and monetary policies are needed that encourage diversion of resources from real estate and nonindustrial ventures to those that expand the productive

capacity of the nation. Many economists also believe that the national government should assume a more aggressive role in developing American industries in high technology fields to make Americans more competitive in world markets.[17]

DISSATISFACTION WITH PREVAILING POLICIES

At no point since the 1930s have policies in the economic security sector been fraught with so much controversy. Conservatives have recently sought major cuts in existing programs, whereas many liberals have contended that existing policies have not reduced economic inequality.

Effectiveness and Equality

The tax system appears to be progressive at first glance, since tax levels increase as income rises.

ILLUSTRATION 11.4 Average Monthly AFDC Payments per Family, by State: 1977

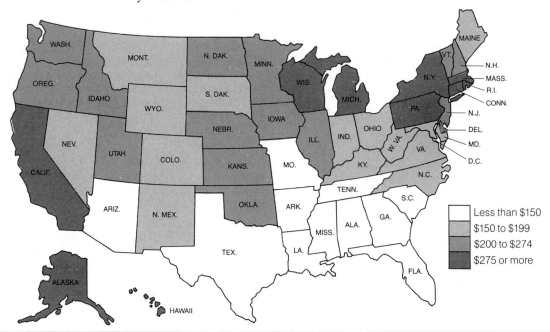

SOURCE: U.S. Department of Commerce, Bureau of the Census. *Social Indicators III*, 1980, p. 387.

In practice, however, it is not progressive, since rich and poor persons tend to pay, on average, roughly similar proportions of income to the government because of the large number of tax loopholes that favor affluent persons. Further, the size of intergenerational transmission of wealth is suggested by the fact that Americans levy an average tax of 3 percent on estates, a policy that clearly favors affluent families. Much as they have grown, social programs are meager in comparison to the economic effects of the tax system. Therefore, Americans are ill-advised to expect ADFC, Food Stamps, and similar programs to reduce inequality in the absence of tax reform.[18]

Redistribution is also deterred by eligibility criteria that often do not equal official poverty standards. As discussed earlier in this chapter, major reduction in distribution of wealth requires development of programs that raise incomes of the nonworking poor to at least one-half the median income, or about $9,000 per family of four in 1980. Many income assistance programs provide benefits beneath the official poverty line, which is roughly equal to one-half the median income. In the case of AFDC, payments vary widely between the states (see illustration 11.4).

SSI benefits are established nationally at 75 percent of the official poverty line. Although many persons are raised above official poverty lines because they also receive Social Security, Food Stamps, and other benefits, many still do not receive enough to allow them to approach one-half the national median income.

Nonparticipation in programs also limits their effectiveness. Three-fourths of the eligible poor do not use means-tested income programs like AFDC because they are unaware that they qualify, do not know how to apply, or fear stigma associated with welfare programs.

Americans have in fact had considerable success in raising Americans above official poverty lines, even when they have not redressed relative economic inequality. The number of elderly persons and children in poverty has been markedly reduced (see illustration 11.5). These gains reflect major increases in the minimum benefit levels allowed working recipients of AFDC, establish-

ment of national minimum eligibility standards in the SSI and Food Stamps programs, procedural reforms in the Food Stamps program that drastically increased enrollments, and major increases in Social Security benefits.[19] Gains have also occurred because many persons use several programs in conjunction. For example, persons on AFDC and SSI rolls automatically qualify for the food stamps and usually receive Medicaid benefits.[20]

Efficiency

One method of gauging the efficiency of social programs is to scrutinize the size of their administrative overhead costs relative to their overall budgets. Many critics argue the use of such strategies as the negative income tax, which distributes income resources through the internal revenue system, could markedly reduce the need for welfare bureaucracy—hence for administrative overhead—in local jurisdictions. Although difficult to calculate, some efficiencies could perhaps be obtained by centralizing certain income maintenance functions in Washington.

Another method of assessing the efficiency of social programs is to ask what proportion of program benefits are focused on those persons who most need them—in the case of income maintenance and insurance programs, on the poverty-stricken population. From this perspective, a highly efficient program would deliver benefits largely to persons who are beneath official poverty lines. On this count, many American programs in the economic security sector appear quite efficient, since they are means-tested at relatively low eligibility levels.

In contrast, the Social Security program, although it raises more persons above the poverty threshold than any other program because if its sheer size, is relatively inefficient, since a large proportion of its benefits go to nonpoor persons. As Americans tax Social Security benefits and put proceeds in the trust fund, as advocated by former HEW secretary Joseph Califano and signed into law by President Reagan in 1983, the program becomes more efficient because the poor elderly, who pay relatively low taxes,

ILLUSTRATION 11.5 Children under 18 in Families below the Poverty Level, by Type of Family and Race of Householder, Selected Years: 1959–1978

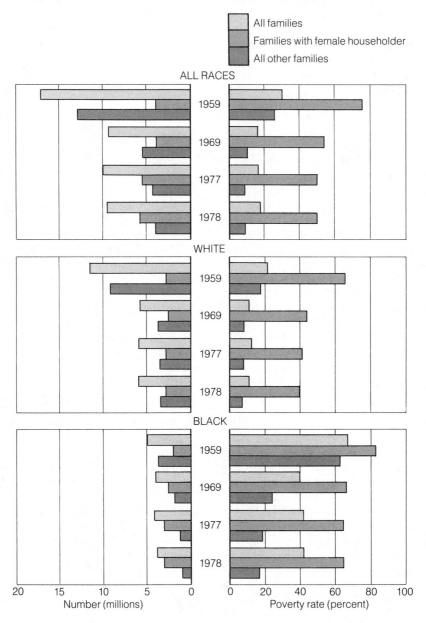

SOURCE: U.S. Department of Commerce, Bureau of the Census, *Social Indicators III*, 1980, p. 462

pay fewer taxes on their benefits than the non-poor elderly.[21] Similarly, some conservatives favor changes in the Medicare program to focus more resources on poor rather than affluent consumers.

The efficiency of American income, service, and resource programs is problematic, however. As programs become more efficient, i.e., focus benefits and income on the poor, nonpoor persons become more likely to perceive them as irrelevant. Perhaps Social Security and Medicare should remain relatively inefficient, since they reinforce and contribute to the notion that the nation has a commitment to the social welfare needs of all its citizens.

Equity

Regional variations in eligibility and benefits under many means-tested programs are common in the United States because the federal government cedes key policy decisions under AFDC and Medicaid programs to local units. These policies contribute in turn to problems of equity because citizens with identical problems and resources but living in different jurisdictions often receive strikingly different services or benefits. Further, taxpayers and officials in jurisdictions that are relatively generous in benefits and eligibility often fear that their relatively munificent programs will attract citizens from other jurisdiction, a fact that contributes to political pressures in these jurisdictions to cut benefits and restrict eligibility. Critics argue that efforts by President Reagan to emphasize localism through block grants exacerbate problems of equity by encouraging variability in program benefits in different jurisdictions.

ERA OF POLICY BREAKTHROUGH: THE 1930s

Despite many and recent reforms, continuities in policy are obvious in the evolution of American welfare policy. In the codification of existing statutes and practices that comprised the English Elizabethan Poor Laws of 1601, local overseers of the poor were instructed to fund programs for the destitute, to treat the "undeserving" or employable poor in relatively harsh fashion in comparison with the unemployable poor, and (when possible) to use austere institutional or indoor relief. This tradition guided American policy, so despite development of mothers' pensions, workman's compensation, and unemployment insurance in many states in the first third of this century, major federal roles had to await the Great Depression.

The foundation of social welfare reform was the Social Security Act of 1935. Seminal books on the politics of the act by economist Paul Douglas and welfare administrator Josephine Brown suggest that it represented a retreat from more radical approaches to income redistribution, especially the Federal Emergency Relief Administration (FERA) and major public works programs.[22]

Two massive programs, the FERA and the Civilian Works Administration (CWA), represented the first responses to the widespread unemployment and poverty of the 1930s. Headed by social worker Harry Hopkins, the FERA was remarkable in many ways, even by contemporary standards. During its brief existence from 1933 to 1935, it distributed income to both the unemployed and working poor, indeed, roughly one-half of its recipients were employed. Further, the legislation required states to establish FERA offices and state administrative machinery separate from the existing network of poor houses and local welfare agencies to avoid a punitive orientation. It also mandated use of trained social workers in supervisory positions and gave federal adminstrators veto authority over top administrative appointments to guard against political patronage. The FERA was supplemented by the CWA, which led to the employment of millions of persons in its two years of existence.

If the FERA and CWA were emergency responses, it remained to be seen what ongoing programs would be developed by President Franklin Roosevelt. The Social Security Act provided the answer, representing both a major victory for those who wanted an ongoing federal commitment to economic security programs and a strategic retreat in response to mounting conservative opposition to work and income programs; Roosevelt's reluctance to ensnare the federal government in ongoing major welfare roles; and fears that the Supreme Court would declare far-reaching programs unconstitutional. Instead of programs like the FERA to cover broad portions of the population, highly specific and separate means-tested income programs were developed for the elderly (Old Age Assistance [OAA]), the blind (Assistance for the Blind [AB]), and children with only one parent (ADC). It was widely assumed that each of these groups would be very small and that OAA would "wither away" when elderly persons began receiving their Social Security checks. Major eligibility and level-of-benefit decisions in these programs were left to the states, with federal authorities assuming major funding roles. (States were required, however, to devise plans that established uniform eligibility standards as well as grievance or fair hearing procedures.)

If welfare programs received scant attention, the pillars of the act were social security and unemployment insurance provisions. Insurance programs were more tolerable to Americans because they were self-funding through payroll deductions and represented earned benefits rather than handouts. Although not widely discussed, financing of both programs fell decidedly on low-income workers, since employer shares were indirectly borne by consumers, especially those with low income, in the form of higher prices. (Payroll deductions for unemployment insurance were exclusively borne by employers, whereas equal shares were contributed by employers and employees in Social Security.) Many workers were excluded from coverage, notably agricultural workers, including large numbers of blacks and Hispanics in the South and Southwest.

Public works projects were excluded from the Social Security Act because Roosevelt did not want to institutionalize them. The Works Progress Administration (WPA) replaced the CWA and gave localities greater roles in project selection and administration but continued to arouse controversy, was subject to periodic cutbacks, and was finally terminated in 1941.

The nation emerged from the Great Depression, then, with an array of limited but needed programs. The Full Employment Act of 1946 was a symbolic measure that pledged the nation to maintain full employment but offered no assistance to victims of unemployment. During the conservative era of the 1950s, federal welfare authorities tried to make the most of their limited legal powers in the Social Security Act to stop Southern jurisdictions from using subjective and racist standards to exclude blacks from AFDC rolls, to prevent localities from publicizing names of recipients, and to upgrade standards of administration.[23]

ERA OF EXPANSION: 1962–1968

Many reforms were enacted between 1962 and 1968 that addressed various needs of low income persons. A number of these are discussed in more detail in other chapters including changes made in the AFDC program (chapter 10) and medical reforms (chapter 12).

Enacted in 1964, the Food Stamps program was initiated by Democrats and built on a series of pilot projects run by the Kennedy Administration. It was widely known that many poor families lacked resources to obtain sufficient food, as reflected in documentation of malnutrition in many low-income areas. The Department of Agriculture distributed some surplus foods to the poor, an approach that was cumbersome because of the logistics of storing and then transporting food to distribution points. Some reformers wished that the various states would increase welfare budgets so poor persons could directly purchase food, but many states retained very low welfare grants. Further, many low-income persons chose not to apply for welfare even when eligible. A solution to widespread malnutrition, then, was to devise a system for providing food stamps or coupons to families that purchased them at a sum considerably less than their retail value at those stores that would accept them.[24] Families on welfare were automatically eligible, but many poor families not on welfare could also be certified by local welfare departments. Localities were given the option of participating in the program with the Department of Agriculture paying the entire cost.

A major problem with the program was that it did not reach poor families who lacked the funds or knowledge to make the periodic payments necessary to purchase the stamps. Further, participants were stigmatized because they became highly visible as poor persons when purchasing food with the stamps. Many localities chose not to participate or set restrictive eligibility standards. Reforms in the program in the 1970s corrected some of its faults, including setting national eligibility standards in 1971, making the program mandatory in 1973, and developing methods in 1978 that allowed recipients to receive coupons without having to make cash payments. (In 1968, the program was given open-ended authorization, i.e., Congress pays all costs of the program each year.)

The multifaceted Office of Economic Opportunity (OEO) legislation (the so-called War on Poverty), which spearheaded programs to address the needs of inner-city and rural victims of poverty, had two major components. First, it provided funds for development of community action agencies (CAAs) that were to plan and coordinate services for the poor in specific geographic areas—cities, counties, or clusters of counties. Applications from various nonprofit organizations were forwarded to Washington, which then decided which applicants were designated as official community action agencies for specific geographic areas. Second, it funded a variety of service programs. The most popular of these was the Head Start program, which provided educational, nutritional, child development, advocacy, parent participation, and other services to low-income children and their families. The Job Corps and Neighborhood Youth Corps programs were also important: the former provided residential training to low-income youth in rural settings and some urban

sites; the latter provided part-time employment for low-income teenagers. OEO also funded legal aid, job training for welfare recipients, and programs in special health clinics in low-income areas.

The War on Poverty provided important services to low-income populations but encountered so many political and administrative obstacles that it was effectively dismantled by 1968. The community action agencies were most controversial. A clause in the legislation requiring "maximum feasible participation" of the poor on boards of the CAAs slipped through the legislative process virtually unnoticed. In many jurisdictions, extensive wrangling took place over the composition of the boards, with civil rights and citizen groups often vying with established political interests. In some cases, multiple applicants from specific areas sought official designation. When CAAs engaged in advocacy against entrenched politicians like Richard Daley, powerful mayor of Chicago, political uproars ensued. Then, too, administrative and logistical problems were encountered in starting hundreds of CAAs in a short period of time, problems that led to charges of fraud and mismanagement. As nonprofit agencies outside government, CAAs found it difficult to influence local programs or policies and were in many cases coopted by local politicians and agencies to the detriment of their planning or advocacy roles.

Confusion was widespread about the relative importance of community action agencies and service programs, on the one hand, and the various OEO service programs, on the other. A large percentage of OEO funds was earmarked for the Head Start program, much to the chagrin of those who emphasized the role of the CAAs. Some of the service programs were themselves controversial, as illustrated by charges that residential Job Corps training in rural areas did not effectively prepare inner-city youth for the job market.

OEO met its demise in the early years of the Nixon Administration when most if its programs were transferred to other units of government. Perhaps its most important legacy is a series of programs that focus services upon low-income populations including Head Start, the Job Corps, and neighborhood health centers. Critics wonder whether it should have placed more emphasis upon job creation and income redistribution measures that could have materially improved the lives of low-income persons.[25]

ERA OF UNCERTAINTY: BEYOND 1968

Surprisingly, a number of reforms in the economic security sector occurred during the relatively conservative period of the 1970s. During this period of policy uncertainty, the Comprehensive Employment and Training Act of 1973 was passed, the Supplementary Security Income program was devised, Social Security benefits were "indexed" to rise with inflation, procedural changes were made in the Food Stamps program so that more persons would receive coupons, and social services were expanded under Title XX of the Social Security Act. Major proposals to revamp the American welfare system by Presidents Richard Nixon and Carter, while defeated, introduced important policy options.

Still, reformers were disheartened by many developments in the 1970s and particularly by policies enacted by the Reagan administration. As discussed in more detail subsequently, revenue sharing and block grants were used to decrease policy roles of the federal government while they enhanced roles of state and local government. Major cuts were made in funding of many social programs in the early years of the 1980's to the point that many critics feared that substantial gains made in reducing poverty in prior decades would be erased.

New Federalism

Many reforms of this current era are part of the so-called *new federalism,* a movement fueled by suspicion of federal roles, the financial straits of local jurisdictions, and the desire to avoid the fragmentation associated with hundreds of cate-

gorical programs.[26] Although local governments were given many policy roles in Great Society legislation, funding and policy powers of the federal government increased markedly in the wake of Great Society reforms, a trend hardly palatable to conservatives or local officials who resented federal restrictions.

One solution was to develop granting or funding approaches to give local and state governments unrestricted federal funds, as reflected in the development of unrestricted grants (*general revenue sharing*), block grants that provided lump sums to governments for use in general areas such as housing (*special revenue sharing*), and *grant-in-aid* programs for services that gave localities even more autonomy than traditional categorical programs.

General revenue sharing was established by passage of the State and Local Fiscal Assistance Act of 1972, which provided approximately $30 billion to local governments during its first five years of operation and was subsequently renewed. The federal government placed virtually no restriction on the use of funds to finance municipal improvements or the ongoing costs of government. (Less than 3 percent of these funds were used for social services.) Special revenue sharing was also established by the 1972 legislation in transportation, rural community development, urban community development, manpower training, education, and law enforcement sectors. Relatively few restrictions were placed on localities in their use of these funds as well.

Critics argue that general and special revenue sharing funds are often not used for programs that directly benefit the disadvantaged or for social services. As an example, one community proposed using its community development funds for construction of a municipal golf course, hardly a priority for those concerned with appalling conditions in the inner city. Supporters of general and special revenue programs cite the real economic needs of local jurisdictions as well as the opportunity to develop programs specifically designed to meet local needs.

President Reagan proposed applying the principles of the new federalism to existing social welfare programs by drastically reducing roles of the federal government for federal-state categorical programs. Under the Omnibus Budget Reconciliation Act of 1981, the administration devised a series of block grants that included social services ($2.4 billion); community services ($398 million); alcohol, drug abuse, and mental health ($491 million); preventive health services ($95 million); maternal and child health ($373 million); community development ($1.08 billion); and primary health care ($284 million). These various block grant funds, totalling $7.6 billion, were obtained by eliminating fifty-seven specific categorical programs and pooling their funds into consolidated grants to the states. He also proposed in spring 1982 an even more massive expansion of state social welfare policy roles when he sought to give states the responsibility for operating and funding Food Stamps, AFDC, and forty-three other programs to be funded in part by giving states access to certain federal revenue sources, such as excise taxes on cigarettes. (This proposal was ultimately blocked by many liberals and local officials both because they feared powerless groups would receive scant attention from local officials and because they believed localities lacked sufficient resources even with access to excise taxes.)

A number of issues arose as block grants were implemented.[27] First, the federal government placed $1.2 billion less in block grants than had been allocated to now-defunct categorical programs in 1981. Second, despite restrictions placed on them in the block grant legislation, states were given greatly expanded powers. Because many state legislatures are dominated by agricultural and suburban interests, many critics feared the gradual erosion of funding for programs that targeted resources to inner-city and poverty populations.

Third, since states were no longer required to pay matching funds for many social programs, many critics feared that their contributions to social welfare would be reduced, a possibility that would exacerbate already enacted federal cutbacks. Finally, some feared competition among the have-nots for scarce block grant funds. Agencies that had received federal funds from the old categorical programs, often as a result of lengthy applications to the federal government, now would have to compete with a host of new providers, including those in affluent communities. Some critics also doubted whether state governments possessed the technical expertise to discriminate intelligently between quality and inferior programs, much less to monitor them.

Economic Security Reforms

The Comprehensive Employment and Training Act of 1973 (CETA) provided training and public service employment for persons in public and nonprofit agencies. Title VI of the act provided jobs for unemployed persons who had skills for specific public service positions, but funding for this portion of the legislation was terminated by President Reagan. Both training and employment benefits are limited to one year to avoid permanent subsidy of persons and positions. Like public employment programs of the 1930s, CETA encountered numerous criticisms, including arguments that it subsidized make-work jobs, was poorly managed, and passed over chronically unemployed persons in the training programs. Realities of massive unemployment in the current era, especially in minority communities, have forestalled termination of training components of the program.

Another policy innovation of the 1970s was the placement of three programs (Aid to the Blind, Aid to the Disabled, and Old Age Assistance) in one program to be administered by the Social Security Administration rather than local welfare departments. This reform was supported by those wishing to reduce the stigma to the elderly and the disabled of receiving financial assistance from traditional welfare agencies and to increase levels of grants by having federal authorities assume the entire cost. A national minimum standard was established that was higher than standards in many states under the old programs. Despite administrative changes, the program (the Supplementary Security Income program [SSI]) focuses benefits on the very poor, since consumers obtain eligibility only if they pass a restrictive means test.[21]

The Family Assistance Plan

In retrospect, however, the boldest reform proposals of this period were not enacted; namely, efforts by presidents Richard Nixon and Jimmy Carter to achieve major reforms in the welfare system. These proposals deserve discussion because they suggest important policy options and highlight political barriers to major policy changes in American welfare programs. Social reformers were further chagrined at the magnitude of economic security program cutbacks enacted during the presidency of Ronald Reagan (cutbacks also discussed in this chapter).

To the surprise of liberals and conservatives alike, President Nixon developed a welfare reform plan that included AFDC families, families with two parents, childless couples, and nonelderly individuals and set a national annual benefit floor of $1,600 per family of four (1969 dollars). While this national floor was less than welfare benefits in some industrial states, it far exceeded prevailing benefits in many rural states. His Family Assistance Plan (FAP) also proposed allowing recipients to keep 50 percent of their earnings rather than only the 33 percent allowed by 1967 work incentive legislation. The work incentive concept was based on the belief that many recipients who could not keep a major portion of their earnings and continue to receive some welfare benefits would not have sufficient incentive to work. (Otherwise, it was argued, they might terminate employment to receive welfare benefits that virtually equaled their take-home pay, particularly in low-paying jobs.) When work incentives were combined with a national income floor, vast segments of the population would have been eligible for benefits from the Family Assistance Plan, including almost 40 percent of the population of states like Mississippi.

FAP failed to be enacted because it was caught in the vortex of ideological politics. Nixon and his adviser Daniel Moynihan hoped to attract a moderate coalition consisting of Democrats and Republicans who favored the simplification achieved by a plan that consolidated AFDC and local general assistance, encouraged work by providing even larger work incentives than the 1967 legislation, and reduced inequities between states and regions.[28] Any welfare reform proposal also draws support to the extent that it promises fiscal relief to state and local governments. For this reason, FAP drastically increased the federal share of welfare funding, particularly in Southern and some Midwestern states. Nixon hoped, then, to consolidate support from moderate politicians and buttress it with sufficient liberal and conservative support to make a winning coalition.

Conservatives were the strongest initial dissenters. Many objected to the national minimum benefit, wanted stronger work requirements, and objected to requirements that jobs taken by recipients had to pay a minimum wage. They were able to seize on a host of technical errors in the original plan, most importantly the fact that many working FAP recipients would disqualify themselves from Food Stamps, Medicaid, and many other programs as they reached maximum benefit levels, which could serve as a disincentive to employment. As the administration made successive changes to appease conservatives, it alienated liberals who feared that it was selling out to conservatives. Emboldened, many liberals insisted on even higher national minimums, more public jobs, and greater fiscal relief for Northern states. Caught in this vortex, FAP was eventually defeated, an outcome hastened by the president's decision to turn to other issues.

Program for Better Jobs and Income

In some respects, the welfare reform proposal of President Jimmy Carter was even more ambitious than FAP, since it envisioned merging the AFDC, SSI, and Food Stamps programs. A three-tiered system was envisioned. The first tier was to be composed of unemployable persons, including the elderly, the chronically disabled, and women with children under age fourteen (changed in a subsequent version to age 7), who were to be included in a means-tested program with a national benefit floor of $4,200 per year for a family of four, a floor roughly the same as FAP when corrected for inflation. A second tier was composed of nonworking but employable persons, who were promised a public job if one could not be located after a reasonable search. (The Carter Administration envisioned creating 1.4 million public service jobs, an unprecedented objective.) The third tier included the working poor in the private sector, who would receive assistance up to a ceiling of $8,400 in earnings. The plan established somewhat higher payments for tier 3 than for tier 2 to encourage persons to seek private employment at the earliest possible point.[29]

The Carter proposal was even less successful politically than FAP; indeed, HEW Secretary Califano likened welfare reform to "Middle Eastern politics." Conservatives such as Sen. Russell Long (D., La.) pushed the administration to require all AFDC women to work, even those with preschool children. Meanwhile, liberals in the House and Senate wanted higher income floors and more fiscal relief for localities. If FAP benefited from the support of Wilbur Mills, then chairman of the crucial House Ways and Means Committee, the Carter plan was vigorously opposed by Mills's successor, Al Ullman. In addition, many legislators wondered if it was feasible to create 1.5 million public jobs for relatively uneducated and low-income persons.[30]

Restrictive Policies

Although the percentage of Americans living beneath official poverty lines declined during the 1970s, the poverty population grew alarmingly from 1978 to 1982. (The percentage of Americans living beneath poverty lines rose from 11.5 percent to 16 percent in those four years.) An economic downturn was partly responsible, but so too were severe cuts in the budgets of many social programs and regressive tax changes.[31]

To many critics, the administration of President Ronald Reagan used its antigovernment ideology to curtail programs for the poor while maintaining those that served more affluent persons and providing the affluent as well with large

reductions in taxes (see guest editorial 11.3). Social Security, Medicare, and programs for veterans, comprising roughly 95 percent of so-called safety net programs, suffered some but modest cutbacks—yet almost four-fifths of the recipients of these programs are nonpoor. In contrast, Food Stamps, Medicaid, AFDC, and rent subsidy programs, a high percentage of whose beneficiaries are poor, suffered massive cuts.

Devastating cuts were also experienced by public employment programs. While urging all Americans to seek employment, the administration pursued economic policies that increased unemployment to the highest levels since the Great Depression while simultaneously cutting CETA public service jobs and job training programs. (CETA jobs were eliminated altogether and job training programs were halved.) Paradoxically, the administration also removed work incentives for AFDC recipients, a group portrayed by administration officials as not wishing to work. Work incentives installed in 1967 enabled working recipients to keep a portion of their take-home pay while continuing to receive some assistance. In order to cut AFDC costs, the Administration sought to lower eligibility standards by moving back toward pre-incentive policies. Further, restrictions on eligibility for Medicaid and other programs meant that persons who earned even minimal amounts also lost access to many public programs. The effect was to reduce the incentive to work, since working AFDC women often earned less than those who did not work, a fact hardly likely to promote employment by persons who were already desperately poor.[32]

Reagan's use of supply-side economics, discussed in chapter 4, stressed giving across-the-board tax cuts, but with disproportionately high cuts for affluent persons. His tax reforms, which proposed a series of tax measures extending into the mid-1980s, were enacted in summer 1981. Their effects in increasing economic inequality are suggested by estimates by the Congressional Budget Office that the 1983 tax cut, when coupled with cuts in social programs, would leave the average family that earns more than $80,000 per year with $15,000 in additional income—and

GUEST EDITORIAL 11.3

Misguided Federal Budget Ax

Safety Net Isn't Catching Those Who Need It Most

By Bob Greenstein

With one round of budget cuts behind us, and another round to be announced by President Reagan in January, it is time to examine what has happened to the much heralded "safety net."

The President announced in February that the "truly needy" would be protected because seven programs would be immune from budget cuts. The seven were Social Security, Medicare, veterans' programs, Supplemental Security Income for the elderly and disabled, free school lunches, summer jobs for youth, and Headstart.

What the President did not say, however, was that 95% of the money in this "safety net" is allocated to three programs—Social Security, Medicare and veterans' programs—in which most recipients are not poor. More than four of every five recipients of Social Security or Medicare, for example, have incomes above the poverty line. This is because these three programs primarily serve elderly persons and veterans, regardless of their income level.

By contrast, nearly two-thirds of the 29 million Americans who do live in poverty either receive no protection at all from any of these seven programs or at most receive a free lunch, hardly a safety net by itself. The basic support programs that millions of families with low incomes depend on most—such as food stamps, Aid to Families with Dependent Children, Medicaid (which, unlike Medicare, is restricted to poor families and individuals) and rent subsidies—were precisely where the Administration asked for, and got, some of the deepest cuts.

A new Census Bureau study shows that households covered by Medicaid have average gross incomes of $6,000 a year. Those receiving rent subsidies have average incomes of $5,000. The latest Agriculture Department survey finds average incomes of only $325 a month in households on food stamps. Average income for AFDC mothers is even lower than that.

These families who live below the poverty line will now receive less welfare and fewer food stamps, and at the same time frequently have to pay more for rent, heating bills and medical costs.

The poverty-support programs that have been heavily cut consume far less of the federal budget than programs like Social Security, Medicare and veterans' assistance, where the cuts were, on a proportionate basis, much smaller. Social Security, Medicare and veterans' programs cost more than $200 billion a year. The poverty-support programs ac-

the average family that earns less than $10,000 per year with $240 less income.

Apart from their distributive effects, the president's tax cuts threatened funding of social welfare programs by drastically cutting federal tax revenues, which already had diminished due to stagnation of the economy. Indeed, budget deficits exceeding $100 billion were estimated by

count for only about one-fourth as much spending. The reason is simple: The poverty programs cost less because they are restricted to those with low incomes.

Contrary to popular impressions, eligibility for these programs has been tightened in recent years. Food stamp income limits, for example, have been cut three times since 1979, and about 90% of all recipients now have gross incomes below the poverty line while on stamps. The new census report confirms that, even before the Reagan Administration took office, these programs were targeting increasingly on the poor rather than expanding into the middle class. If the programs were growing, it was not because more middle-income Americans were managing to qualify, but because more Americans were poor. The census data show that last year the number of Americans living in poverty jumped by 4 million, one of the biggest increases in the past 20 years. With unemployment now rising, the number in poverty will soon pass the 30 million mark.

What should we make of all this? First, as even David A. Stockman has now acknowledged in the much-publicized Atlantic Monthly article, there are serious questions about the basic fairness of the first round of budget cuts. The programs on which poor families are most dependent are where the biggest cuts were made.

Second, we must ask hard questions about future budget policy. If military spending is to grow massively, and since interest payments on the national debt and cuts in Social Security are off limits, nearly all additional cuts that the Administration wants will have to come from the same one-third of the federal budget that absorbed the earlier cuts. Details of the Administration's new budget proposals that have leaked out make clear that the same poverty-support programs that were cut sharply before will be asked to bear the brunt of the next round of cuts as well.

With food stamp benefits averaging 44 cents per person per meal, and with average welfare benefits having declined 24% (after being adjusted for inflation) since 1969, the real safety net for impoverished families was not in strong shape before Reagan took office. After the major budget cuts of this summer, there is great danger in slashing further in these areas. The abortive effort by the Administration to reduce school lunch portions for poor children and call ketchup a vegetable illustrates that there is little extravagance left in these programs.

We would do better to reexamine the lush tax cut—which reduces government revenues a staggering $750 billion over the next five years, provides 35% of all tax breaks to the richest 5% of our society, and hands major tax breaks to the oil companies and other corporations—and to take a hard look at a military budget that increases funds for military bands while nutrition aid for the poor is being cut, rather than to slice a second chunk out of basic subsistence programs for our nation's poor.

Bob Greenstein is a former administrator of the U.S. Agriculture Department's Food and Nutrition Service. He is establishing a new institute in Washington to study the effect of Reagan policies on low-income persons. SOURCE: This article first appeared in The *Los Angeles Times.* Reprinted by permission of the author.

1983, with escalation in succeeding years to $200 billion. These deficits, most economists agreed, contributed to high interest rates that in turn impeded economic growth. The deficits provided the administration with a convenient rationale for further reducing social program funding. (Reagan was unwilling to cut defense spending and had in fact initiated increases in military spending unprecedented during peacetime.) A "guns versus butter" debate arose as in the Vietnam era, but, unlike the administration of President Johnson, the Reagan Administration decidedly favored guns.

Resistance to the Reagan initiatives was surprisingly modest during 1981 when the aforementioned policies were enacted. Split by defections from Southern Democrats and a lack of leadership, the Democratic party lacked policy alternatives and feared a groundswell of support by blue-collar and other traditional constituents for cutbacks in government. By summer 1982 and through 1983, however, considerable opposition began to develop even among Republicans to the administration's proposals for further cutbacks in social welfare funding, expansion of block grants to include new programs, and increases in defense spending. It was too early to tell when the pendulum would swing back toward liberal perspectives, but few doubted that such a swing would eventually take place in response to the magnitude of the nation's social problems and extraordinary economic inequality.

REFORMING ECONOMIC SECURITY POLICY

Preceding discussion suggests that those who seek reforms in economic security policies confront many barriers. Ideological barriers are obvious, since neither liberals nor conservatives in the United States seem to favor major reduction in relative poverty. Although interest groups champion specific programs, a strong lobby does not exist that advocates a package of tax, income maintenance, social insurance, and public works programs that could radically redistribute wealth in a nation characterized by extremes of affluence and poverty.

Selected Reforms in Scanning and Analysis Phases

As preceding discussion suggests, combinations of proposals are required if the extraordinary in-

equality prevalent in the United States is to be reduced.

Making Explicit a Redistributive Agenda. Americans have not generally made explicit economic objectives that include reduction in economic inequality. National redistributive objectives are needed, such as those identified by the economist Lester Thurow, who argues that the nation should reduce inequality to the point that the distribution of income in the general population approximates that currently enjoyed by white employed males. In absence of such redistributive objectives, economic security reforms are likely to be piecemeal, at best.

Including the Working Classes. Since many members of the Reagan Administration were distressed at the numbers of nonpoor persons (i.e., blue-collar workers) receiving benefits from Food Stamps, CETA, and AFDC programs, they proposed reforms to reduce eligibility levels. But redistributive objectives lack political feasibility if persons near but above the poverty line are not assisted by income, training, and employment programs.

Establishing National Floors. Although national floors were established in the SSI and Food Stamp programs, variations between states continue in the AFDC and general assistance programs. There is no reason why accidental factors, such as location, should cause some to live in abject poverty while others receive far higher subsidies.

Selective Consolidations. Some persons believe that all existing service and resource programs should be "cashed out" (i.e., dissolved and turned into cash) and perhaps ultimately replaced with a negative income tax. Certainly, some simplification of the American welfare system is needed, since many programs exist with different eligibility criteria and administering agencies. Still, the merits of continuing various categorical programs should not be ignored. Were most of them replaced by a single cash assistance program, opponents of income redistribution would only need to attack one program rather than myriad separate categorical programs like Medicaid and Food Stamps. Further, many special interests favor and defend existing categorical programs, as illustrated by support of Food Stamps by agricultural interests. From the vantage point of the poor, why end these special programs when Americans are not likely to generously fund a consolidated program? In short, some balance is needed between (1) simplification and consolidation of existing programs and (2) continuation of popular and needed categorical programs.

Recognition of the Tax System as Social Welfare. Most attention has focused on social welfare programs like Food Stamps and AFDC to the detriment of major reforms in the tax system that could foster economic equality. The tax system should be explicitly recognized as a social welfare program, and tax reforms should be initiated to make it more progressive.

Massive Creation of Public Jobs. Automatic "triggering" of public jobs during period of high unemployment is needed. The poor want to work no less than others yet often cannot find positions. Not only should jobs be created by government, but they should pay wages competitive with the private sector to increase their redistributive potential.

Selected Reforms in Implementation and Assessment Phases

As in scanning and analysis phases, major reforms are needed in implementation and assessment if relative poverty is to be reduced.

National Roles. Poverty is no longer a local problem, since national economic trends and policies cause unemployment and low wages. National authorities should assume even larger funding roles, devise national floors, and monitor programs to ensure that they meet national standards.

Relationship of Services and Income. Prior to the 1970s, services were provided in the course of determining eligibility and distributing welfare benefits. Trained social workers were integral to income programs and visited homes of recipients to assist with referrals, crises, tangible necessities, and familial problems. By the mid 1970s, most public welfare offices placed services in offices separate from eligibility and payment offices. As social work professor Norman Wyers notes (see guest editorial 11.5), separation has had negative consequences, including diminution of the social services often needed by poor persons beset with situational, employment, and other pressing problems. A compromise position might involve placing social workers at the intake division of the public welfare agency where they would develop criteria to be used to place some recipients in caseloads of social workers who would offer services on an optional basis. Although it is difficult to determine which consumers most need services, trained social workers assume a screening and service function in medical, child welfare, and other settings. Many persons and families subject to extreme poverty require assistance in obtaining access to tangible resources and in developing personal and family strategies to cope with economic deprivation.

Outreach. Only a fraction of eligible consumers actually use current income and service programs. Failing approval of a negative income tax, far more attention should be given to methods of outreach to encourage eligible consumers to actually use them. Renewed attention should be given to the so-called negative income tax, in which persons earning less than a specified amount receive automatic payments from the Internal Revenue Service.

Redistribution Impact Statements. When any new policy proposal is considered, formal estimates of its impact on economic inequality should be required much as environmental impact statements are required for other proposals. Although not a panacea, such a policy might sensitize Americans to the social consequences of

GUEST EDITORIAL 11.4

Unanticipated Consequences of Policy Change

The Separation of Social Services from Income Maintenance in Public Welfare

By Norman Wyers

The separation of social services from income maintenance was mandated by the Department of Health, Education, and Welfare in 1972, capping intense activity during the previous several years. States were to submit plans for separation by October of that year and to implement their plans by January 1, 1972. The mandate was rescinded three years later. During that three-year period, the majority of states formally separated social services from public assistance. While most of those states remain in the posture of separation, many are considering a return to the merged model.

The manifest reasons for separating social services were twofold: first, to eliminate use of coercion on recipients to use social services; and, second, to clarify the division of labor among public welfare eligibility and service welfare workers. Laudable as these purposes may have been, it is not clear that they have been realized. Indeed, the single empirical study conducted to assess alternative models of service delivery suggests greater utilization of services and greater satisfaction by both recipients and service providers with the pre-separation model.

The field of income maintenance has been neglected by social work during the past decade, perhaps partly because many social work functions have been downgraded in the wake of separation. Only in the past several years have some social work observers begun to engage in analysis of possible problems that have resulted from separation. These problems, largely unanticipated in 1972 on the eve of separation, include deprofessionalization of income maintenance workers thoughout the country; loss of organizational status and professional respect experienced by service workers; conflict between social service and income or eligibility staff; and increasing rates of staff turnover and "burnout" by service workers. Indeed, some suggest that income maintenance and eligibility determination are highly complex tasks that cannot be performed adequately by clerks or untrained technicians.

More research and evaluation are needed in the immediate future to explore various models of providing services within public assistance settings. It is premature to advocate return to the merged model. But it is likely that many consumers, often those from desperately impoverished families, need a host of advocacy, social, referral, educational, and preventive services that appear to be denied to most of them within current public assistance programs. Some have argued that social workers are steadily "disengaging" from the poor. Not to develop research and policy positions relevant to low-income consumers who receive public assistance, positions that articulate methods of humanizing programs by supplementing income with social services, is to abdicate a traditional and important social work function.

Norman Wyers is Associate Professor at the School of Social Work of Portland State University in Portland, Oregon.

policies that increase inequality in a society that already tolerates gross economic disparities.

PRACTICE OF POLICY IN THE ECONOMIC SECURITY SECTOR

A social reform project of a social worker illustrates use of the various policy roles in the economic security sector. The social worker was able to modify statutes in one state so that persons with chronic kidney disease were not economically penalized when they tried to obtain employment. The social worker and others in the state had tried to encourage these patients to resume employment in the wake of major health problems, since they believed their recovery often hinged on their reintegration into the community. They soon discovered that existing policies often made resumption of employment impossible for many patients, a discovery that spurred them to seek reforms in state statutes.

Survey Role

In the early phases of this policy change project, the social worker had to examine prevailing policies and political realities to ascertain whether reform was possible. He decided that it would be difficult to obtain policy changes because state funds would be required in a period of scarce resources. But he anticipated many favorable forces, including widespread interest by conservatives and liberals alike in fostering employment of disabled persons. Further, he believed that widespread public support could be mobilized for persons with such desperate medical problems who wanted to better their condition.

Problem Recognition and Definition Role

Members of Congress recognized that persons with chronic kidney disease could not usually afford extraordinary and ongoing costs of kidney dialysis and medications, not to mention surgery and postoperative treatments in the case of kid-

ney transplants. An amendment was added to federal Medicare legislation in 1973 that extended Medicare coverage to such persons even though most had not yet reached sixty-five. Since coverage of major medical costs for these kidney patients, however, included only 80 percent of the cost of dialysis, hospitalization, and physician fees, many consumers had to resort to subsidies from the means-tested Medicaid program to cover the balance of their medical fees.

Social workers in a dialysis unit of a hospital discovered that many patients encountered a predicament. Encouraged to seek employment by social workers, they often found that their earnings disqualified them from participation in the means-tested Medicaid program. When they had to pay 20 percent of their medical costs from their earnings, they often were in serious economic straits—with less income than if they had remained unemployed and continued to receive Medicaid subsidies. In addition, many patients lost eligibility for the means-tested federal disability funds under the Supplementary Security Income program funds, also withdrawn when persons obtained employment.

The social workers in this unit contacted many others and found that the problem was widespread. Statistics obtained from the state's department of health yielded information about the number of persons who experienced kidney disease and received various kinds of public subsidies. They discovered that they had identified a major social problem that could only be addressed by modification of state laws. The seriousness of the problem was underscored when social workers reported that many patients who did not resume employment seemed devastated by feelings of dependency, aimlessness, and guilt. These negative orientations appeared to impede their physical recovery and even their survival rates.

Program and Policy Design Role

Alternative strategies were explored to correct the problem, including revisions in regulations governing the Medicaid program and development of new legislation that would extend state-funded subsidies to employed kidney patients. Assistance from a state official in the department of health was invaluable to the social workers as they gradually decided that the latter course was required. They had to devise a sliding subsidy formula that caused state subsidies to decline as income rose, a solution that lowered costs to the state and made employment even more attractive to patients because they could continue to improve their economic condition even as their wages increased. (Earned income plus state subsidies were pitched so that total resources always exceeded total resources of unemployed patients, a policy that appealed as well to conservative lawmakers who wanted strong work incentives.) In writing the legislation, the social workers continued to benefit from the behind-the-scenes technical consultation of the state official, who now gave it secretly because the director of the state department opposed the scheme.

Change Agent Role

The social workers had by now found a "lead legislator," i.e., one with important committee and political connections who was willing to assume a leadership role in promoting the legislation. They also developed a statewide constituency of kidney patients, providers, and professional associations that began to rally support for the legislation among health professionals and in the larger community. A statewide newsletter was developed to publicize the issue, and extensive coverage was obtained in the mass media about specific persons who had not been able to resume employment because existing policies penalized them.

The social workers maintained close contact with aides of the lead legislator as they obtained sponsorship of the legislation from other important lawmakers, orchestrated testimony at public meetings of the committees considering it, and kept track of its movement through the legislature. They had to be particularly vigilant because the state department had officially op-

posed the legislation in testimony, alleging that it would be overly costly. Because they had done careful technical work, the social workers were able to demonstrate that the state would recover substantial sums from the tax payments of employed patients, sums that partially offset the cost of the program.

Troubleshooting and Error Detection Roles

On passage of the legislation, social work staff members assumed roles in informing hospital staffs about the new subsidies available to employed kidney patients. They also planned to monitor the subsidy program to see if adjustments were necessary in subsidy formulas and amounts. Perhaps, some wondered, more generous subsidies were needed. The social workers also wanted to be certain that kidney patients were given more assistance from staff in the local offices of the state's rehabilitation department, which was charged with providing counseling, job training, and placement services to disabled persons.

SUMMARY

A summary of discussion in this chapter is provided in illustration 11.6, which draws on the policy framework developed in chapter 2. Prevailing policies, a normative position, assessment of prevailing policies, and selected reforms are portrayed, as well as various background, political, and ideological factors that impinge on policy development in the economic security sector.

A case can be made that economic inequality in the United States can be substantially redressed without reducing economic growth or work incentives. More attention should be given to reducing relative inequality or poverty so that the economic gap between the lowest and highest quintiles of the population is reduced. Both short- and long-term strategies can be used not only to reduce inequality but also decrease the

ILLUSTRATION 11.6 Policy in the Economic Security Sector

Prevailing (Current) Policies and Programs
- multiple and fragmented means-tested income programs
- local policy roles in shaping eligibility of AFDC and general assistance programs
- lack of progressive income tax system
- disinclination to develop ongoing and large public employment schemes
- variation between states in eligibility criteria for many means-tested welfare programs
- preoccupation with reducing absolute rather than relative poverty

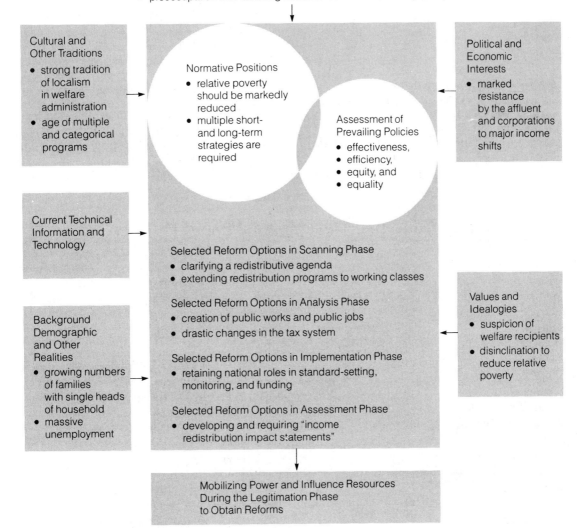

Cultural and Other Traditions
- strong tradition of localism in welfare administration
- age of multiple and categorical programs

Political and Economic Interests
- marked resistance by the affluent and corporations to major income shifts

Normative Positions
- relative poverty should be markedly reduced
- multiple short- and long-term strategies are required

Assessment of Prevailing Policies
- effectiveness,
- efficiency,
- equity, and
- equality

Current Technical Information and Technology

Selected Reform Options in Scanning Phase
- clarifying a redistributive agenda
- extending redistribution programs to working classes

Selected Reform Options in Analysis Phase
- creation of public works and public jobs
- drastic changes in the tax system

Values and Idealogies
- suspicion of welfare recipients
- disinclination to reduce relative poverty

Background Demographic and Other Realities
- growing numbers of families with single heads of household
- massive unemployment

Selected Reform Options in Implementation Phase
- retaining national roles in standard-setting, monitoring, and funding

Selected Reform Options in Assessment Phase
- developing and requiring "income redistribution impact statements"

Mobilizing Power and Influence Resources During the Legitimation Phase to Obtain Reforms

extent to which poverty is disproportionately shouldered by racial minorities and women. Short-term strategies include expanded means-tested income, resources, and service programs; continuation and expansion of social insurance programs; reforms in the tax system; and initiation of job creation programs that add millions of jobs to labor markets. Long-term strategies include reductions in job-related discrimination, programs to increase employment capabilities of the poor, and use of fiscal and monetary policy to increase jobs.

Widespread dissatisfaction exists with current policies. Their failure to reduce relative inequality has been obvious, even though far fewer Americans now live beneath official poverty lines. Inequity exists when persons living in certain states or two-parent families receive lower benefits than persons in other jurisdictions or in families with single heads of households.

The relatively limited policy reforms of the 1930s were supplemented by a host of reforms in the 1960s and 1970s that led to large increases in social welfare spending. Further efforts to extend reform, however, met marked resistance, as reflected in opposition to successive efforts in the Nixon and Carter administrations to secure major welfare reforms. Officials in the administration of Ronald Reagan mounted an assault on social programs unparalleled in the contemporary period, including elimination of public employment programs.

A host of policy options merit consideration, even though many are controversial and certain to draw widespread opposition from conservatives. These include setting of specific redistributive objectives, inclusion of working classes in many programs, establishment of national floors, selective consolidations of separate programs, massive creation of jobs, and explicit definition of the tax system as a social welfare program. Careful scrutiny should be given during implementation to the current separation of services and income in welfare agencies as well as to the lack of outreach.

Key Concepts, Developments, and Policies

Absolute poverty
Relative poverty
Quintiles
International comparisons
Redistribution
Moral arguments for and against redistribution
Random distribution of poverty
Short-term strategies
Tax policies
Negative income tax
Means-tested income programs
AFDC
General assistance
Social insurance income programs
Social Security
Means-tested service programs
Cashing out
Social insurance service programs

Medicare
Affirmative action and quotas
Public service jobs (CETA)
Humphrey-Hawkins legislation
Institutional training
Job Corps
Work Incentive program (WIN)
Equal Employment Opportunity Commission
Office of Federal Contract Compliance
Long-term strategies
Fiscal and monetary policy
Inheritance taxes
Food stamps
Median income
Supplementary Security Income
Elizabethan Poor Laws
"Deserving and undeserving" persons
Federal Emergency Relief Administration

Civilian Works Administration
Old Age Assistance
Aid to the Blind
Works Progress Administration
Full Employment Act of 1946
Family Assistance Plan

Work incentives
National floors
Program for Better Jobs and Income
"Indexing"
Omnibus Budget Reconciliation Act of 1981

Main Points

1. Although it is important to reduce absolute poverty, a more difficult but equally necessary task is to reduce relative poverty.

2. International comparisons, analysis of work motivation of white employed males, and research projects do not support the conservative contention that drastic reductions in economic inequality in the United States would reduce the work ethic or national productivity.

3. A strong moral case can be made for reducing the extraordinary economic inequality that exists in the United States. If poverty has to exist, better that it be distributed randomly than concentrated among racial minorities, women, and other specific groups.

4. Various short-term approaches can be used to redress economic inequality, including tax reforms, expansion of means-tested income and service programs, expansion of social insurance income and service programs, use of affirmative action and quota policies, and creation of jobs by government.

5. Various long-term strategies can be used to redress economic inequality, including programs to increase the competitive capabilities of specific groups, programs to decrease job-related discrimination, and use of fiscal and monetary policy to spur economic growth.

6. The effectiveness of American economic security policies can be questioned, since the distribution of income and resources does not lead to a lessening of disparities of wealth between highest and lowest quintiles. American income maintenance programs are subject to low payments, regional variation (see AFDC), and lack of participation by

many eligible citizens. Still, large numbers of Americans were catapulted above official poverty lines in the 1970s by combined improvements in social insurance, income maintenance, and other programs.

7. American income and service programs focus resources on low-income populations, but such efficiency may imperil broad-based support for them.

8. Problems of equity are exacerbated when income and resource programs are administered by local units of government.

9. Many programs were initiated during the Great Depression, including various titles of the Social Security Act, various work programs, and the Federal Emergency Relief Administration (FERA). Still, public works did not survive, and the Social Security Act in some respects represented a strategic retreat from policies of the FERA.

10. Many income and service programs were enacted in the 1960s, and additional reforms were obtained even in the conservative era of the 1970s, as reflected by passage of the Comprehensive Employment Training Act (CETA).

11. Two major welfare reform plans failed to obtain passage; the Family Assistance Plan and the Program for Better Jobs and Income. Both would have established national floors, consolidated various programs, and created jobs for low-income persons.

12. Major cuts occurred in many means-tested income and service programs during the administration of President Ronald Reagan. He also extended the principles of the new fed-

eralism to social welfare programs with establishment of block grants under the Omnibus Reconciliation Budget Act of 1981.

13. Many reforms should be considered, including development of a redistribution agenda, inclusion of the working classes in social programs, establishment of national floors, selective consolidations, tax reforms, massive creation of public jobs, retention and expansion of federal roles, outreach, and clarification of the relationship of services to income.

Questions for Discussion

1. Review guest editorial 11.1. Discuss the "web of policies" that together perpetuate existence of an "underclass" of low-income persons.

2. Why is the policy objective of reducing absolute poverty a relatively conservative one when contrasted with the objective of reducing relative poverty? How have Americans fared in reducing absolute poverty? In reducing relative poverty?

3. Identify philosophical, pragmatic, and moral arguments used by conservatives to justify and support marked economic inequality. Discuss them critically and in the process present relevant evidence that suggests that reduction in inequality would not necessarily bring dire economic consequences.

4. Critically discuss the assertion "Government should primarily assist low-income persons by providing job training programs, since that is the best strategy for getting them into the economic mainstream."

5. "Since Social Security provides major benefits to affluent persons, it should be abolished." Discuss this statement critically.

6. Discuss pros and cons of "cashing out" means-tested income and service programs; i.e., abolishing them and giving cash directly to consumers.

7. What negative consequences might flow from President Reagan's proposal to give states the responsibility of administering and funding AFDC and Food Stamps programs?

8. Why is tax reform so elusive, particularly when most people agree that current tax policies do not redress economic inequality in the United States?

9. Discuss pros and cons of affirmative action and quota policies, and critique the lack of enforcement or implementation of these policies by the Reagan Administration.

10. Discuss central objectives of welfare reform proposals like the Family Assistance Plan and reasons for their political defeat.

11. Why have Americans been reluctant to maintain major programs that create or subsidize jobs such as those developed during the Great Depression and under the CETA program—particularly when most Americans agree that adults should have access to jobs?

Suggested Readings

Aaron, Henry. *Politics and the Professors* (Washington, D.C.: Brookings Institution, 1981). This is a provocative account of the development of poverty and welfare reforms in the 1960s and 1970s as well as discussion of poverty-related research.

Barth, Michael, and others. *Toward An Effective Income Support System* (Madison, Wis.: Institute for Research on Poverty, 1974). The authors discuss numerous issues pertaining to work requirements, coverage, and program mergers in welfare programs.

Brown, Josephine. *Public Relief, 1929–1939* (New York: Holt, 1940). The classic account of the emergence of public welfare programs in the 1930s.

Califano, Joseph. *Governing America* (New York: Simon & Schuster, 1981). The author provides first-person accounts of the policies and politics of Social Security and welfare reforms in the Carter Administration.

Dobelstein, Andrew. *Politics, Economics, and Public Welfare* (Englewood Cliffs, N.J.: Prentice-Hall, 1980). A readable introduction to existing public welfare programs, their administrative structure, and current issues.

Fuchs, Victor. "Redefining Poverty." *Public Interest*, 8 (Summer 1967): 88–96. In this classic article, the author presents a rationale for using relative rather than absolute or "market basket" definitions of poverty.

Haveman, Robert, ed. *A Decade of Antipoverty Programs* (New York: Academic Press, 1977). Various income, training, and equal opportunity programs are discussed from a range of viewpoints.

Heffernan, W. Joseph. *Introduction to Social Welfare Policy* (Itasca, Ill.: Peacock, 1979). The author provides detailed discussion of public welfare programs and issues and of historical perspectives.

Lekachman, Robert. *Greed Is Not Enough: Reaganomics* (New York: Pantheon, 1982). A liberal economist criticizes the way in which policies of the Reagan Administration increased economic and social inequality.

Levitan, Sar. *Programs in Aid of the Poor for the 1980s* (Baltimore, Md.: Johns Hopkins University Press, 1981). A succinct review and analysis of contemporary American social welfare programs.

Levitan, Sar, and Taggart, Robert. *Promise of Greatness* (Cambridge, Mass.: Harvard University Press, 1976). A sympathetic portrayal and analysis of major social welfare reforms enacted in the 1960s and early 1970s by two authors who contend that inordinate attention has been given to "the least successful attempts at social improvement with their attendant horror stories."

Moynihan, Daniel. *The Politics of a Guaranteed Income* (New York: Vintage Press, 1972). In this first-person account of the politics and controversy associated with the Family Assistance Plan in the Nixon Administration, the author is not reluctant to lambaste liberal and conservative opponents of the legislation.

Ozawa, Martha. "Income Maintanance Programs." In Neil Gilbert and Harry Specht, eds. *Handbook of the Social Services* (Englewood Cliffs, N.J.: Prentice-Hall, 1981): pp. 353–380. The author provides a concise overview of programs and issues in the public welfare sector.

Stein, Bruno. *Social Security and Pensions in Transition* (New York: Free Press, 1980). This book is an excellent starting point for persons who want to obtain knowledge of the intricacies of Social Security and pension issues and programs.

Thurow, Lester. *The Zero-Sum Society* (New York: Basic Books, 1980). Chapters 1, 4, and 7 provide discussion of many tax, public employment, and income maintenance issues from the perspective of an economist who believes that major redistribution of resources to the poor is not incompatible with economic growth.

Notes

1. For discussion of relative and absolute poverty, see Victor Fuchs, "Redefining Poverty."

2. John Rawls, *A Theory of Justice* (Cambridge, Mass.: Harvard University Press, 1971), pp. 60–65.

3. For international comparisons, see Thurow, *Zero-Sum Society*, pp. 1–9.

4. Ibid., pp. 155–190.

5. Ibid., pp. 155–190.

6. Richard Titmuss, *Commitment to Welfare* (New York: Pantheon, 1968), pp. 124–137.

7. See Marc F. Plattner, "The Welfare State Versus the Redistributive State," *Public Interest*, 55 (Spring 1979): 28–49. For a liberal perspective, see William Ryan, *Equality* (New York: Pantheon Press, 1981), pp. 37–96.

8. Thurow, *Zero-Sum Society*, pp. 194–200.

9. Heffernan, *Introduction to Social Welfare Policy*, pp. 170–174.

10. Milton Friedman, *Capitalism and Freedom* (Chicago: University of Chicago, 1962), pp. 161–177.

11. Eveline Burns, *Social Security and Public Policy* (New York: McGraw Hill, 1956), pp. 27–55, 112–126.

12. Gilbert Steiner, *State of Welfare* (Washington, D.C.: Brookings Institution, 1971), pp. 318–319.

13. S.M. Miller, "The Case for Positive Discrimination," *Social Policy*, 4 (November-December 1973), 65–72; and Neil Gilbert and Joseph W. Eaton, "Favoritism as a Strategy in Race Relations," in Jack Rothman, ed., *Issues in Race and Ethnic Relations* (Itasca, Ill.: F.E. Peacock, 1977).

14. Thurow, *Zero-Sum Society*, pp. 200–211.

15. Job training programs are discussed in Sar A. Levitan, *Programs in Aid of the Poor for the 1980's*, 4th ed. (Baltimore, Md.: Johns Hopkins University Press, 1980), pp. 115–143, and in Sar A. Levitan et al., *Human Resources and Labor Markets* (New York: Harper & Row, 1980).

16. Levitan, *Programs in Aid of the Poor*, pp. 126–128. Also see James M. McPartland and Robert L. Crain, "Racial Discrimination, Segregation, and Processes of Social Mobility," in Vicent T. Covello, ed., *Poverty and Public Policy* (Cambridge, Mass.: Schenkman, 1980), pp. 97–126.

17. Thurow, *Zero-Sum Society*, pp. 26–154.

18. An overview of income maintenance programs is provided by Sar Levitan et al., *Work and Welfare Go Together* (Baltimore: Johns Hopkins University Press, 1972). For discussion of the tax system, see Joseph A. Pechman, *Federal Tax Policy* (Washington,

D.C.: Brookings Institution, 1977), and Joseph A. Pechman and Benjamin A. Okner, *Who Bears the Tax Burden?* (Washington, D.C.: Brookings Institution, 1974).

19. Alma W. McMillan and Ann Kallman Bixby, "Social Security Expenditures, Fiscal Year 1978," *Social Security Bulletin*, 43 (May 1980): 3–17.

20. See Morton Paglin, *Poverty and Transfers In-Kind* (Stanford, Calif.: Hoover Institution Press, 1980).

21. Califano, *Governing America*, pp. 268–402. Distributive effects of various income and insurance programs are discussed by Ozawa, "Income Maintenance Programs," in Gilbert and Specht, eds., *Handbook of the Social Services*, pp. 365–369.

22. Paul Douglas, *Social Security in the United States* (New York: McGraw-Hill, 1936), and Brown, *Public Relief, 1929–1939.*

23. Winifred Bell, *Aid to Dependent Children* (New York: Columbia University Press, 1965), pp. 76–92.

24. Gilbert Steiner, *State of Welfare* (Washington, D.C.: Brookings Institution, 1971), pp. 191–236.

25. For discussion of the War on Poverty, see James L Sundquist, *Politics and Policy, the Eisenhower, Kennedy, and Johnson Years* (Washington, D.C.: Brookings Institution, 1968), pp. 111–154. A critical account is given by Daniel Moynihan, *Maximum Feasible Misunderstanding* (New York: Random House, 1973), while a more sympathetic discussion can be found in Sar Levitan, *Promise of Greatness.*

26. An overview of the new federalism is provided by Robert S. Magill, *Community Decision Making for Social Welfare* (New York: Human Sciences Press, 1979).

27. Rochelle Stanfield, "Picking up Block Grants—Where There's a Will, There's Not Always A Way," *National Journal*, 15 (April 10, 1982): 616–620.

28. One discussion of FAP can be found in Daniel Moynihan, *Politics of a Guaranteed Income*

(New York: Random House, 1973). Also see Heffernan, *Introduction to Social Welfare Policy*, pp. 241–255.

29. Califano, *Governing America*, chapter 8, and Heffernan, *Introduction to Social Welfare Policy*, pp. 259–266.

30. Ibid.

31. "Reagan's Polarized America," *Newsweek* (April 5, 1982), pp. 20–28.

32. Robert Lekachman, *Greed Is Not Enough: Reaganomics* (New York: Pantheon, 1982), p. 100.

Policy in the Health Care Sector

Medical care programs and services dwarf all other social welfare programs. Americans spend approximately $118 billion per year from all sources on medical care, or 8.3 percent of the gross national product, and about $50 billion from local and federal government revenues. (This last figure may be compared with the roughly $15 billion spent by the two largest publicly financed welfare programs and the roughly $4 billion spent by the federal government on publicly subsidized housing programs.) The staggering size of the medical industry and the sometimes life-and-death consequences of policy decisions mean that policy choices in this sector assume major importance for consumers, providers, and taxpayers.

The roles of social workers in the health care sector are expanding, as illustrated by growing numbers who work in various hospital and clinic settings. The funding cuts of medical care programs for the poverty-stricken in the early 1980s as well as intrinsic defects in traditional medical programs suggest that social workers will need to assume an even larger role in developing policy reforms in this sector, requiring social workers to be able to:

Articulate normative positions about the kinds and levels of health care that should be available to all consumers, including health-related preventive and counseling services

Identify defects in existing services in the health care sector as they impede achievement of effec-

tiveness, efficiency, equity, equality, and other criteria

Understand the evolution of American policies in the health care sector as they evolved prior to 1920, in the period from 1920 to 1960, during the 1960s, and during the current period of policy uncertainty

Articulate a variety of policy reforms that have promise in improving existing programs

Identify a variety of policy roles that social workers can assume in the health care sector

These topics are discussed in this chapter, and concepts are provided that can be used in the practice of policy in the health care sector.

Guest editorial 12.1 discusses a number of defects in existing programs and policies and specifically identifies a variety of problems likely to be exacerbated by the health care cuts enacted in the early 1980s. Indeed, as subsequent discussion suggests, many critics argued that the American health care system failed to provide

sufficient preventive services or health care to the poor even before these cuts.

HEALTH CARE: A NORMATIVE POSITION

In traditional perspectives, medical care involves technical interventions by physicians to address already developed medical problems. Consumers recognize symptoms, seek assistance, are diagnosed, receive surgical or pharmaceutical assistance, follow medical regimens, and (hopefully) recover. But traditional perspectives and services need to be supplemented by broader notions of health care.[1] Indeed, the term *health care system* is used in this discussion instead of *medical system* to underline the need for services that supplement traditional ones. Any health care system should (1) address mutiple causes of illness, (2) eliminate multiple barriers that impede use of services, (3) provide preventive

---

GUEST EDITORIAL 12.1

Let Them Eat Placebos

Reagan Health-Care Program Would Ravage Services for Poor

By Geraldine Dallek

Congress frequently behaves as if its budget debates were a matter of life and death. This week they may be, as the House takes up President Reagan's proposals to eliminate billions of dollars in federal health-care financing. Rep. Henry A. Waxman (D-Los Angeles), whose health subcommittee is holding hearings on the cuts, has pledged to oppose this effort.

The Administration's proposals, which would reduce the health-care budget by more than $2 billion, would seriously cut into

nearly every medical program for the disadvantaged: Medicaid, community and migrant health centers, the National Health Service Corps, maternal and child health, lead-poisoning prevention, infant-care programs, rat control and high-blood-pressure control, to name only a few.

Cutback decisions were made not on the basis of failure or inefficiency. They seem to meet one criterion only—they serve the poor. Federal health programs for the middle and upper classes, such as income-tax exemptions for medical care, remain intact.

The Administration has not adequately explained why so many indigent health-care programs are on the chopping block. Cer-

services, and (4) provide consumers and their representatives with major roles in decision making. Regardless of income, race, or place of residence, all Americans should have access to quality care.

Multiple Causes of Illness

In traditional perspectives, illness is caused by bacterial, viral, physiological, and genetic factors. Current research also implicates a host of

---

tainly there is room for improvement in the operation of some. But, on the whole, the Administration has ignored the fact that these programs have worked very well.

Consider the Community and Migrant Health Centers Program, which supports public and private non-profit organizations. The centers provide care to medically underserved populations with high rates of infant mortality and a shortage of physicians.

These 1,000 centers serve 6 million impoverished and elderly people. In California, more than 75 centers provide care for almost 700,000 persons. Los Angeles County has six centers that provide care to an estimated 177,000 residents.

The Administration proposes to cut the program by 25% and give the remaining money to the states. Individual states will not be obligated to use the money to fund the program. Inflation and state administrative costs will bring reductions to 35% or 40%.

The National Association of Community Health Centers estimates that, if the Reagan proposal passes, 450—almost half—of the nation's community and migrant health centers will be forced to close.

Furthermore, other programs on which these centers depend are also being reduced, increasing the odds against center survival.

These centers are economical: In fact, they reduce the use of expensive emergency-room care and cost 33% to 60% less than outpatient departments and emergency rooms. Studies show that community and migrant centers reduce hospitalization rates for center users by 25% to 66%. The amount of money thus

saved exceeds the cost of the entire $373-million program.

The centers have been effective. In New York City, prenatal and neonatal mortalities dropped 41% and premature births declined 29% over four years in the area surrounding one health center. Centers in Boston were responsible for a 60% decrease, over 10 years, in the incidence of rheumatic fever.

These centers remain indispensable to the poor. The circumstances that led to their establishment—lack of health-care providers in rural and inner-city areas—persist.

If half or even a third of the health centers are lost as a result of the budget cut, who will care for the tens of thousands of poor Californians unable to secure medical care when ill?

How many people will face a plight similar to those who use the Southern Lassen Rural Health Center, which depends on federal funds? The only health-care providers in south Lassen County are the full-time nurse practitioner and the part-time doctor employed by the health center. If the cuts are passed, its 2,500 clients, many of whom are elderly poor, will again have to travel about 45 miles north to Susanville or 45 miles south to Reno for medical care.

The Clinica de Salud del Pueblo operates three health centers, two in Imperial County and one in Riverside County. Half their funding comes from the health-centers program. These centers are the primary providers in their areas, with 30,000 patient visits a year. According to center director Manuel Gonzales, 85% of the center patients are migrants and their families, and almost all are ex-

additional factors, including life-style, diet, poverty, malnutrition, and occupational and mental factors. If illness were only caused by bacterial and related physical causes, disease would be distributed randomly across the population.

But certain *kinds* of persons are far more likely to die at a relatively early age or to encounter serious illness. As noted in guest editorial 12.1, the average life expectancy for migrant laborers is forty-nine years. Poor persons and members of

---

tremely poor. Facing a 30% to 40% cut in federal funding, the centers will be hard-pressed to survive.

Migrant farm workers have an average life span of 49 years, and suffer from pesticide poisoning and many other disabling illnesses. Is the Reagan Administration suggesting that California's migrant-health centers are no longer needed?

Five primary health-care centers in East Los Angeles face a possible $700,000 reduction in federal funds. Directors estimate that these centers would have to reduce the number of clinic visits by 80,000 and drastically cut preventive, family-planning and nutrition services. (There are few private physicians in East Los Angeles—only one obstetrician-gynecologist for 87,000 persons, only one pediatrician for every 47,500 persons.)

"The saddest thing," says Castulo de la Rocha, executive director of La Clinica Familiar del Barrio in East Los Angeles, "is that federal, state and local cuts will mean that patients are going to have nowhere to go. Too many will suffer. Conditions which could have been treated early will develop into costly emergencies."

The Watts Health Foundation, the oldest and largest community health center in California, operates three clinics and provides care for 40,000 people in South Los Angeles. The foundation estimates that cuts will mean the closure of at least one facility, a sharp reduction in hours and elimination of optometry, dental, hypertension and sickle-cell-screening services.

Some Administration voices claim that

such centers are "government clinics" that compete with private physicians. Although these centers do depend, to one degree on another, on federal subsidies to operate—after all, they care for the sick, poor and uninsured—the vast majority are private, nonprofit health-care providers. They were built because of community effort, employ community workers and must, by law, have a community board of directors. Centers can serve as examples of local control, something highly valued by the Administration. Further, these centers operate in communities in which there are not enough physicians and other health providers available to meet community needs. They would not be eligible for federal funds otherwise.

Last March, as Republicans sharpened their ax, Waxman introduced a bill that is an alternative to the Administration's 25% cut and the state bloc-grant proposal. Under the Waxman proposal community and migrant health centers would receive less federal support in fiscal 1982 than they got in fiscal 1981, but the reduction would be far less severe than the proposed Reagan cuts and would permit most centers to survive. Introducing his bill, Waxman noted that community and migrant centers "have worked" and "are making quality primary care available to millions who otherwise go without."

Needy Americans have been promised a "safety net" of programs, but in the area of health that net is illusory. The poor are standing on a precipice—and it looks as though the Reagan Administration is about to shove them off.

Geraldine Dallek is associated with the National Health Law Program, Inc. SOURCE: This article first appeared in the *Los Angeles Times*. Reprinted by permission of the author.

racial minorities experience far higher rates of illness and infant mortality than others. Persons who experience sudden changes in their lives, including death of a spouse, change of residence, loss of a job, and even promotion are more likely to become ill. Married persons fare better in health terms than those who are single, and single males are particularly susceptible to serious illness. Persons who work in certain occupations suffer unusually high rates of illness and mortality. Most obvious is the smoking hazard: despite extensive publicity about the risk, millions of Americans smoke heavily. Many theorists believe that a strong association exists between stress and illness. Health systems should place priority on identifying "at risk" populations and targeting medical services, health education, outreach, and advocacy to them.[2]

Multiple Barriers to Utilization

Traditional medical services are predicated on the assumption that consumers are rational, i.e., that they recognize symptoms, seek technical assistance, and follow medical regimens. But many researchers have emphasized the nonrational aspect of consumer health behavior. All of us use denial mechanisms at one point or another to discount the importance of specific conditions. Cultural preferences influence whether consumers recognize dangerous symptoms, delay treatment, or trust physicians.[3] Some consumers are relatively fatalistic when they experience certain health problems, as evidenced by research indicating that blacks tend to believe that cancer is necessarily a terminal condition.[4]

Social and economic barriers also frustrate utilization of services. Research indicates that a variety of inconveniences retard use of medical services, including lack of money and transportation. Nearly 30 million Americans have no medical insurance, and roughly 40 percent of American medical bills are paid out-of-pocket. Many low-income and rural Americans have to travel long distances because physicians and providers tend not to locate services in low-income areas. In Chicago, for example, there are 210 doctors per 100,000 persons in affluent areas but only 26 per 100,000 in low-income areas.[5]

Preventive Services

Discussion of multiple causes and barriers in health care underlines the need for preventive services that systematically identify and address them (illustration 12.1). In the case of primary prevention, major attention should be given to smoking, alcohol consumption, occupational hazards, pollution, and other causes. Since income and health status are closely related, income redistribution can be regarded as a health prevention measure. Methods of identifying and reaching consumers who are in "at risk" groups are also needed. For example, since pregnant women who also drink heavily are far more likely to have infants with birth defects, outreach services are needed to find and help them.

Secondary prevention is also needed, as illustrated by efforts to find consumers in the early

ILLUSTRATION 12.1

"Could You Hurry And Find A Cure For Cancer? That Would Be So Much Easier Than Prevention"
1/9/77

From *Herblock On All Fronts,* New American Library, 1980. Reprinted by permission of Herblock Cartoons.

TABLE 12.1   Selected Sources of Illness Amenable to Prevention

Sources	Associated Health Problems	Prevalence
Smoking	Cancer of the lung, lip, oral cavity, esophagus, bladder; chronic bronchitis and emphysema; arteriosclerotic heart disease; and specified noncoronary cardiovascular diseases	Per capita consumption of cigarettes for 18+ population for 1974 was 4270.
Alcohol	Cirrhosis of the liver; various cancers (particularly if combined with smoking); malnutrition; lowered resistance to infectious diseases; gastrointestinal infections; muscle diseases; and damage to the brain and peripheral nervous system	More than 100 million Americans drink, and 9 million are classified as alcoholics or alcohol abusers.
Inadequate or excessive food consumption	Malnutrition is associated with obesity, atherosclerosis, vitamin deficiency, anemia, and diabetes. Obesity is associated with diabetes, hypertension, arthritis, pulmonary dysfunction, angina, gall bladder disease, and increased complications from surgery.	Malnutrition is common in low-income areas and among the elderly; as many as 30 percent of Americans may suffer from obesity.
Motor vehicle accidents	Motor vehicle accidents are associated with fatalities and disabling injuries.	Over 50,000 deaths and 2,000,000 disabling injuries occur each year.
Mental illness and poverty	Although causality is difficult to demonstrate, stress and mental illness have been found to be associated with coronary heart disease, some forms of cancer, and a host of other illnesses. A striking relationship exists between poverty and health status; death rates, infant mortality, and morbidity rates are higher for lower economic groups.	It is estimated that 10 percent of the population (20 million people) suffer from some form of mental illness.
Environmental pollution	There is greater prevalence of chronic bronchitis, emphysema, and lung cancer in areas with high air pollution. A host of pesticides and other chemicals have been linked with many diseases.	Air pollution and other forms of environmental pollution are prevalent in all major cities.
Genetic factors	Genetic factors are associated with mental retardation, developmental abnormalities, schizophrenia, diabetes, heart disease, and hypertension as well as cystic fibrosis, Tay Sachs disease, sickle cell anemia.	Genetic diseases account for many of the hospitalizations (20–29 percent) in pediatric and adult populations.

SOURCE: U.S. Department of Health, Education, and Welfare, Public Health Service, *Forward Plan for Health, FY 1977–1981* (Washington, D.C.: U.S. Government Printing Office, 1975).

stages of illness and draw them into services. Clinics discussed in guest editorial 12.1 encourage early use of health care by low-income persons who might otherwise defer use because of inconvenience in traveling to distant public hospitals, because of lack of funds or lack of knowledge of the seriousness of various symptoms, or because of lack of trust in health professionals.

Consumers in Decision Making

Sums spent on health care by Americans are expected to increase dramatically as the population ages and as the use of expensive technology increases. These costs are ultimately borne by consumers, whether through insurance premiums, out-of-pocket costs, or tax payments.

In the face of these rising costs, difficult decisions must be made. Should highly expensive procedures be given to all who want them, or should they be rationed? Should costs of medical services be contained to decrease mounting costs? To what extent should more physicians be located in low-income areas? Consumers or their elected representatives should participate in these decisions, since they are the ultimate funders and users of health care services.

Equality of Access and Utilization

There should be equal access to curative and preventive medical services regardless of income or place of residence. Guest editorial 12.1 suggests that Americans are far from achieving equal access. Middle- and upper-class citizens usually see private physicians who have surgical and other privileges at local nonprofit hospitals. Poor persons are more likely to use underfunded public hospitals or clinics or to use foreign-born private physicians who lack official connections with local hospitals. (When the poor need surgery, many of them are referred by these physicians to public hospitals, where hospital-based physicians provide surgery). In short, two American medical systems exist.[6] Because of the greater remuneration and prestige involved, a disproportionate number of highly trained staff persons choose the affluent system. And the poverty system of medicine, described in guest editorial 12.1, is continually subject to cutbacks in funds by politicians representing middle- and upper-class Americans with no personal stake in the medical system used by the poor.

DISSATISFACTION WITH THE HEALTH CARE SYSTEM

Many criticisms have been made of the health care system in terms of effectiveness, efficiency, equity, and equality criteria.

Effectiveness

It is difficult to gauge the effectiveness of an entire health care system. Many environmental factors other than medical services influence the health of a population, including poverty, stress, and life-style factors. To further confound matters, researchers have not been able to discover obvious medical reasons for decreases in incidence of stomach cancer and some other diseases. Alternative measures can be used to measure health status, including extent of absenteeism, life expectancy, and incidence of various kinds of disease, and it is not always clear which measures should be used. Still, international comparisons suggest that American health care could be markedly improved (see illustration 12.2). Differences in health status of American and Swedish populations for example, exist partly because low-income persons in Sweden are more able to obtain preventive and other services. The medical economist Victor Fuchs also makes a convincing case that the Swedish are more healthy because they experience fewer illnesses and deaths deriving from life-style or the environment, illnesses that include heart disease, cirrhosis of the liver, accidents, homicides, and motor accidents.[7]

Among the poor and nonpoor alike, effectiveness of the health care system would also be increased, many argue, by making more systematic linkages between mental health and medical services. If stress and mental illness are major causes of illness, consumers need to have access to social work and allied services at many points in the health care system. Further, many health conditions, such as cancer, severe heart disease, arthritis, and stroke, severely restrict life options, and recovery is likely to be delayed if consumers do not receive supportive services. Yet few physicians have training in mental health services, and many are disdainful of them, despite the fact that emotional disorders rank second only to upper respiratory conditions in illnesses reported in the practices of family physicians.[8] In addition, social work and allied services are seriously underfunded in most hospitals.[9]

Efficiency

The efficiency question asks whether sufficiently positive outcomes result from the vast sums

ILLUSTRATION 12.2   **Infant Mortality Rates, Selected Countries:
1971—1976**

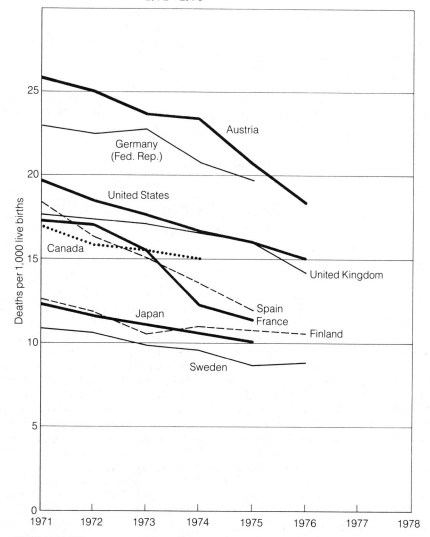

SOURCE: U.S. Department of Commerce, Bureau of the Census, *Social Indicators III*, 1980, p. 89.

Americans spend on health care. This concern about efficiency is hardly academic, since some local governments are on the brink of bankruptcy because of soaring medical payments, many consumers find it difficult to finance required out-of-pocket medical expenditures, and some employers are hard-pressed to meet insurance premiums of employees.[10]

Soaring costs of medical care in the United States can be attributed in part to the use of advanced technology (see guest editorial 12.2). Medical innovations have increased the effectiveness of services, but they have also caused problems. For example, some American doctors perform surgeries of questionable utility, including tonsillectomies, hysterectomies, radical mastectomies for breast cancer, and a variety of other procedures. Indeed, some technologies can be counterproductive. As an example, the use of elaborate equipment to monitor the health status of the unborn fetus has been widely questioned because it leads to far higher use of caesarean sections in the United States than in other countries. American doctors, more than their European counterparts, routinely order enormous numbers of tests, X-rays, and other procedures, partly in response to the threat of malpractice

suits. Although development of so-called miracle drugs has revolutionized medicine, side effects often cancel positive effects, and combinations of drugs bring additional medical problems.

Inefficiency is increased, some critics argue, by the noncompetitive nature of the American system and the inability of government officials and insurance companies to regulate costs. In a truly competitive system, consumers compare services and choose those that are relatively inexpensive. Because of the prevalence of third-party

---

GUEST EDITORIAL 12.2

Medical Technology Runs into a Solid Wall of Costs

By Daniel S. Greenberg

The Administration is counting on heartless economizing to hold down health-care costs, but ticking beneath its medical strategy is a binary political bomb that's sure to blow the lid off any containment strategy.

The first ingredient is our aging population. Though only 11% of Americans are over 65, that segment of the citizenry runs up about one-third of the nation's health-care bills.

The second ingredient is a medical revolution built on electronics and molecular biology. In combination, they are providing health care with wizard-like techniques that sometimes relieve suffering and extend life— but always run up immense bills.

Put together, the factors of age and technology will further intensify medicine's already grisly conflict between money and service, inevitably to the political detriment of anyone who can be tagged for denying the

wonders of medicine to a substantial and increasingly well organized bloc of voters.

The effects of modern science on medical practice are to be seen all along the life span, from premature birth to ancient age. And more innovations are on the way, while newly certified ones rapidly become commonplace in hospital wards. While some developments, such as the new ulcer-treatment compounds, markedly reduce costs by forestalling the need for expensive and dangerous surgery, the trend is toward more elaborate procedures, at higher costs.

Thus, cardiac-bypass surgery has evolved from a medical novelty into a standard treatment with ever-increasing patient loads. The refinement of drugs for suppressing tissue rejections has hugely improved the odds for successful organ transplants, even to the point where once-unthinkable heart-lung transplants have been successful. Meanwhile, that much-debated symbol of super-expensive medical technology, the computerized

insurance, consumers have incentives to purchase medical services up to the limit of coverage. Since most insurances cover prevailing medical fees, no incentive exists to seek the least expensive services.[11]

For physicians, there are no economic incentives to cut fees or to provide only those surgeries, drugs, or services absolutely needed by consumers. Since physicians and hospitals are reimbursed for the procedures they perform by insurance companies and government author-

ities, the more procedures they perform, the higher their income. This fee-for-service method of paying doctors is not used as extensively in other countries, where more doctors are salaried or remunerated according to the number of patients in overall patient loads. However, alternative methods of reimbursing physicians are perceived by many Americans to constitute socialized medicine.

Incentives to overprovide are often exacerbated by the threat of malpractice. Since mal-

---

scanner—a sophisticated X-ray device of unique diagnostic power—is now gaining recognition as a standard item for any respectable hospital. Long criticized by medicine's cost-controllers as an example of gold-plated technology that should be limited to specialized regional centers, the scanner is winning approval just as even more versatile and expensive models are being developed. The old ones cost $200,000 to $1 million apiece; some new models run more than $1 million.

What's ironic about this flourishing of medical technology is that many thoughtful physicians have deep doubts about its medical effectiveness, humanity and cost. But, given medicine's historic devotion to extending life, it is difficult to resist the new technology, even when it breaks the bank and leaves many of its supposed beneficiaries dead or just barely alive.

In many instances, the routine application of intensive-care techniques has been found to be positively harmful, according to a study recently published in the Journal of the American Medical Assn. Writing on "Medical Intensive Care for the Elderly," a team of physicians who studied nearly 2,700 successive admissions to intensive-care units (ICUs) concluded that the use of these high-cost facilities

was often unjustified in terms of doing the patients any good. Nonetheless, the authors found that "the care of the elderly has become a major function of general medical ICUs." Citing a respected British study, they noted that a group of heart-attack patients "treated at home actually did better than their (hospitalized) counterparts."

The critics of onrushing medical technology are confronted by the fact that, while some of it works and some of it doesn't, the medical culture is naturally inclined to whatever is new and promising. Delays for adopting the new are shunned for fear of being slow in applying beneficial techniques. Meanwhile, doctors, who are the ones who provide customers for hospitals, are notorious for pressuring hospital administrators to trade up for the latest equipment.

The press is often attracted to cases of fargone patients who want to be spared the dubious benefits of high-technology medical care. But far more common are patients, in alliance with their families, who believe in medical miracles, and who want the whole armory deployed in their behalf.

Their numbers are increasing, and so is the armory. How do you fit that into a cost-containment plan?

Daniel S. Greenberg is editor and publisher of an independent Washington-based newsletter,
Science & Government Report. SOURCE: This article first appeared in the *Los Angeles Times.*
Reprinted by permission of the author.

practice claims are processed in the courts in the United States, patients and lawyers have an incentive to seek ever-larger settlements. Physicians not only perform unnecessary tests and procedures to ward off possible claims but pass on to consumers the high costs of malpractice insurance. (In many other countries, malpractice claims are settled by public or quasi-public boards that make awards on the basis of a fixed schedule of payments.)

Many also argue that medical economics do not usually correspond to competitive models. As more physicians are added, evidence suggests, they increase demand for services by referring patients back and forth or by providing even more tests and surgery. Hence, prices and fees do not diminish (see guest editorial 12.3).[12] Some critics question as well the extraordinary incomes and revenues of physicians and hospitals that are ultimately reflected in the fees and insurance premiums paid by consumers.

Equity and Equality

A troubling criticism of the health system is that persons with similar medical problems receive markedly different kinds of medical treatment and have different kinds of service options. Serious issues have been raised about differences of

---

GUEST EDITORIAL 12.3

Doctors, in Oversupply, Create New Demand

By Daniel S. Greenberg

The futurologists of medical manpower had me worrying about what we're going to do with that tidal wave of doctors coming out of the medical schools. But then I spotted a help-wanted ad in a recent national medical journal, and I knew at once that the doctors will get by. It read:

"Physician wanted for established weight-control center. Offering annual salary of $72,000 . . . 3½ days per week; vacation with pay and other possibilities."

Worthy of notice here, apart from the ample pay, truncated work week, and "other possibilities," is that medicine, in the best entrepreneurial spirit, is expanding its market share by moving into a field formerly dominated by moonlighting gym instructors. And

it's not just in the weight wars that this is happening.

In similar expansionist fashion, medically supervised skin-care centers are popping up to compete with the wrinkle-fighting services of the old-fashioned beauty salon.

Closer to the core of traditional medicine, advertisements are popping up announcing separate walk-in clinics for minor health emergencies, plastic surgery, alcoholism and guidance for the sick as well as those with an ailing heart.

Management companies offer marketing advice and financing for launching these clinics, some of which are franchised in fast-food fashion.

Meanwhile, for the physician who wants to practice without managerial burdens—and more and more doctors fit that discription— profit-seeking hospitals offer career oppor-

medical care and options between men and women, rich and poor, urban and rural residents, and patients with acute and chronic conditions. It is difficult to demonstrate the precise role that medical care assumes in contributing to disparities between the health status of groups such as members of white and minority populations, since many other life style and economic factors contribute. But critics argue that disparities like those depicted in illustration 12.3 could be significantly reduced if inequities in coverage and access were reduced.

Feminists note the lack of women in obstetrics and gynecology, high rates of hysterectomies and other surgeries, and overmedication of many women. The rise of free clinics for women, pressure on medical schools to accept more women applicants, efforts to obtain more women members in male-dominated medical specialties, and pressure to obtain legal sanction for use of midwives to deliver babies all stem from dissatisfaction with existing services.[13]

Elderly persons with disabilities and chronic conditions like arthritis and heart disease often receive inferior services, as do many who need primary care. American medical trainees have flocked in great numbers to the numerous medical specialties. Even including specialists who provide only some primary care (such as internists, pediatricians, obstetricians, and gyne-

---

tunities. Shrewdly located and strong on marketing, these hospitals, along with other doctor-run health-care businesses, are prospering to the point where the editor of the New England Journal of Medicine has expressed concern about the relative balance of commercial and medical values. He's arguing, in effect, for a return to a purity that probably never flourished. But whatever the ethical state may be of the medical marketplace, the odds are that the long-warned-of doctor surplus is going to add to the commercialization of medicine.

Revealing clues about where things are headed are to be found in statistics, compiled by the American Medical Assn., that show that doctors respond to competition by working less and charging more. From 1978 to 1979, the association reported, the average work week of office-based physicians declined by nearly one hour, and the weekly average number of patients dropped from 130 to 122. In the same period, average income went from $65,500 to $78,400.

As more surgeons come into practice, individual surgeons are operating less and charging more. Overall, however, there's more surgery, for no apparent reason other than that there are more surgeons.

President Reagan's medical planners contend that cost-cutting will inevitably follow when deregulation and competition are introduced into American medicine. What they overlook is that regulation is more talked about than present in American health care. Doctors have always been quite sovereign and could order up whatever they deemed desirable—with faraway insurers footing the bill.

As for competition, it may trim some costs by offering cheaper, stripped-down insurance that will make the customer more cost-conscious. But that doesn't address the health industry's market-expansion drive.

The big change in American medicine is that doctors are no longer content to wait for the patients to show up. Like other smart sellers on the American scene, medicine has graduated to arousing demand.

Daniel S. Greenberg is editor and publisher of Science & Government Report, an independent, Washington-based newsletter. SOURCE: This article first appeared in the *Los Angeles Times.* Reprinted by permission of the author.

ILLUSTRATION 12.3   **Life Expectancy at Birth, by Race and Sex:
1900–1977**

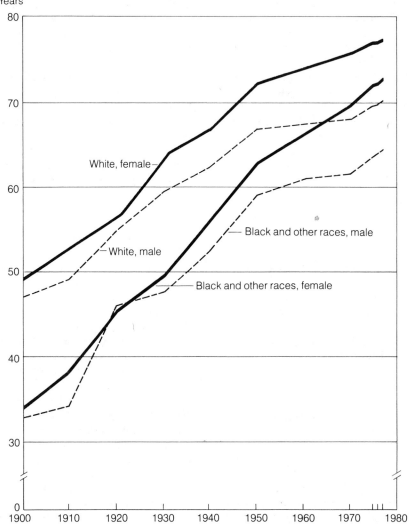

SOURCE: U.S. Department of Commerce, Bureau of the Census, *Social Indicators III*, 1980, p. 72.

cologists), only 47 percent of U.S. doctors emphasize primary care, in contrast to 74 percent in Great Britain. The United States lacks a network of family physicians who can provide early detection services, treat relatively routine conditions, and be accessible to the increasing number of Americans who suffer from chronic conditions. Further, the shortage of general practitioners has meant that many specialists provide patients with community services for which they lack training and then charge exorbitant specialist fees.

ERA OF COMPETING PROFESSIONS: PRIOR TO 1920

Americans have created a private entrepreneurial health care system strikingly different from those in other industrialized nations, a system where relatively few American physicians are on salary, the government assumes a minimal role in regulating or planning health care, and considerable autonomy is given providers.

Prior to this century, health care in the United States was not dominated by any particular profession. Most medical procedures were provided in offices of doctors or in homes of consumers. In absence of scientific knowledge about germs, viruses, genetics, and physiology, no clear basis existed for deciding who should be licensed to provide health care. The result was a proliferation of health care professions that included osteopaths, chiropractors, naprapaths, spondylotherapaths, mechanotherapaths, neurotherapaths, naturotherapaths, iridologists, and magnetic healers.[14] A strange variety of herbs, potions, and other remedies were used, including leeches to let blood from unfortunate victims. Typhoid, malaria, cholera, and other plagues were rampant in this period, as were a host of childhood diseases, such as scarlet fever, influenza, diphtheria, enteritis, and whooping cough.

ERA OF MEDICAL AUTONOMY: 1920–1960

At the turn of this century, it was unclear how Americans would structure and finance health care services in the wake of major surgical and pharmaceutical advances. Health care is unique in its "Russian roulette" uncertainty: although many consumers can finance routine procedures, they rarely know in advance when they will need major funds for serious illnesses. Some mechanism was needed for cushioning these periodic, unpredictable, and often large expenditures.

Answers to these questions were provided in the push and pull of politics. A relatively weak association known as the American Medical As-

sociation (AMA), representing one set of health care professionals, began a multipronged strategy that led to its virtual domination of health care in the United States by 1920. After initial misgivings its leadership championed, more aggressively than rival professions, the technical innovations of the period from 1880 to 1920, most importantly germ theory, surgical procedures, drugs, and innoculations. As medical innovations based on these advances proved effective, many consumers and politicians saw physicians as technically superior to other professionals. Political clout was needed, however, to persuade the various state legislators to pass licensing laws restricting medical practice to physicians. Historians have chronicled the process by which the AMA developed a strong grass-roots base linking county chapters with state and national organizations.[15] Although membership in the AMA was not a prerequisite, the organization was able to persuade legislatures to restrict medical practice to those who had attended AMA-accredited, university-based medical schools and had passed AMA-approved state examinations. (Prior to these developments, most practicing physicians received training in proprietary medical schools, often of dubious quality.) Although chiropractors and osteopaths survived, physicians became the dominant providers and the American Medical Association the major political force in the health system.

Physicians further consolidated their status by dominating staffs of the rapidly emerging network of nonprofit hospitals. By 1920, most hospitals limited "privileges" (i.e., the right to use their premises for surgery and other medical procedures) to physicians accredited under state law. Further, physicians achieved considerable roles in deciding which hospitals would be accredited.[16]

By 1920, then, the American Medical Association had become the dominant force in medical politics and aggressively opposed efforts to modify fee-for-service and entrepreneurial medicine. Whereas considerable attention was given in England and Germany to various governmentally mandated and financed insurance schemes, leadership of the AMA believed government in-

tervention would threaten the doctor–patient relationship and represented socialist or "Prus-
sian" policies. Many American consumers and
their political representatives also became convinced that good medicine was free-enterprise
medicine in which consumers (often in conjunction with employers) arranged their own insurance schemes and were responsible for their
medical bills, even if this required making considerable out-of-pocket payments.[17]

The development of private insurance to assist
consumers deserves futher discussion. Although
corporations had begun to develop insurance
plans for employees prior to the Great Depression, most nonpoor Americans financed medical
care from personal resources. The Depression
made glaringly clear that insurance was needed,
since many consumers could not pay even minimal medical bills. Nonprofit insurance companies were created in the 1930s and 1940s in most
states to cover hospital costs (Blue Cross) and
fees of physicians (Blue Shield). Once created,
campaigns were organized to convince employers to offer insurance financed by joint contributions of consumer and employer and to convince consumers to purchase insurance policies
directly from "the Blues." The campaign was remarkably successful; by 1950, 8.5 percent of total
personal health expenditures were paid by private health insurance, a figure that had risen to
25 percent by 1965. Physicians and hospital providers dominated the boards of the Blue Cross
and Blue Shield companies, which in turn dominated the health insurance industry. A nongovernment insurance mechanism had been established that was controlled by providers
themselves, a mechanism that continued to insulate the medical system from government intrusion and softened pressure for government
subsidies.

During the Great Depression, considerable
pressure also developed for some form of national health insurance, again because many consumers could not pay medical bills. Mass-based
trade unions in automobile and other basic industries experiencing major growth in the 1930s
favored major federal subsidies to health care.
But leadership of the AMA continued to oppose

"socialistic medicine." President Franklin Roosevelt decided at the last moment to delete health
insurance from the Social Security Act because
he feared controversy might endanger its passage.[18] (President Harry Truman backed national
health insurance but lacked sufficient support.)

American health care, then, is quite different
from its European counterpart. In England,
many physicians were on salary to trade unions,
consumer groups, and local governments even in
1900, and, in 1911, the English developed a major
scheme to provide national subsidies for health
care of workers. By 1948, the English had evolved
a full-fledged nationalized health care system
with (1) a national network of public hospitals,
(2) physicians on salary to the hospitals, (3) community physicians providing family services under contract with the government, and (4) free
health care for all citizens. Regional planning
mechanisms were developed to ensure that major policy choices in various regions were made
by boards with political and consumer representatives in liaison with national health authorities.
Although differing in details, many other European countries developed similar public financing and controls over the medical system, in
contrast to the entrepreneurial system of the
United States, where federal authorities have
only recently begun to assume financing and regulatory roles.[19]

One final accomplishment worth noting in
American health care in the early part of this
century was the establishment of local departments of health as well as construction of
sanitation and health codes, policies crucial in
averting disease in American cities. Social workers assumed leading roles in this public health
movement as they documented the need for
public health measures and lobbied for their
enactment.

ERA OF FEDERAL SUBSIDY:
1960–1968

When Americans finally did give the federal government a major role in health care in 1965, they
chose not to make major reforms but rather to

provide funds to elderly and impoverished consumers to purchase services from those providers in the existing system who chose to serve them. A majority of physicians in many states chose not to serve poverty-stricken consumers because public authorities set ceilings on fees. As for elderly consumers, physicians and hospitals were allowed to charge more than federally approved fees and to collect additional payments directly from them over and above subsidized payments.

Medicare

Widespread recognition of the plight of elderly citizens, many of whom had no health insurance because they were no longer eligible for insurance at their place of employment, triggered development of various health insurance proposals in the 1950s by Democrats and Republicans. Their versions differed, and a political stalemate developed.

A series of events turned the tide in 1965, roughly fifty-four years after the English had initiated a government insurance plan. Although John Kennedy ran in 1960 on a platform supporting national health insurance for the elderly, he was not successful in obtaining its passage. But President Lyndon Johnson and congressional leadership were able to fashion a compromise plan in 1965 that coupled elements from both Democratic and Republican versions. Part A of the Medicare legislation was mandatory for all elderly persons covered by Social Security and established an insurance pool financed from premiums paid by workers and employers to cover specified hospital costs. Participation in Part B was voluntary, reimbursed specified services of physicians, and was financed by a combination of relatively modest premiums paid by elderly participants (approximately one-half of total costs) and contributions from the federal government (the remaining costs).[20]

The Medicare legislation only covered short-term or acute medical conditions and procedures rather than the long-term, chronic conditions often experienced by the elderly; reimbursed only a maximum of 60 days in the hospital; did

not reimburse out-of-hospital nursing home costs; and only covered 100 days of convalescent care. In many cases, elderly persons, after exhausting Medicare benefits, had to delve into personal savings and assets. (Only when these were depleted could they qualify for Medicaid payments.)

Medicaid

States and localities had complained about the medical costs of welfare recipients and had received limited federal assistance for medical services of public assistance recipients in 1950. In 1959, a federal match of medical expenditures was passed that provided for the "medically indigent elderly," i.e., those elderly persons who did not qualify for the federal–state Old Age Assistance program but who could not pay medical bills. Participation was voluntary, and most states chose not to join. Since no federal subsidies existed for poor persons who were not elderly and not on welfare, many of these medically indigent persons used overcrowded county and municipal hospitals or did not use medical services at all. Some sort of program was needed that would provide federal assistance to welfare recipients and medically indigent persons, whether elderly or not.

The Medicaid program, or Title XIX of the Social Security Act, provided subsidies to low-income consumers who continued to use existing physician and hospital services. In order not to undercut traditional local responsibility for health needs of the poor, wide latitude was given to states not only to determine eligibility but also to decide precisely what services would be covered. All participating states were required, however, to offer five basic services: outpatient and inpatient hospital care, lab and X-ray services, skilled nursing home care, and physicians' services. Ten additional optional services were named that were to be phased in by 1975, including home health care, clinic services, physical therapy, drugs, dentures, preventive screening, and eyeglasses. It was assumed that Medicaid would be a relatively modest program and that most states would restrict eligibility and services to minimize their share of program costs. (In most states, welfare departments conduct means tests.)[21]

Other Health Measures

More modest initiatives of the 1960s also merit attention. One innovation was to establish neighborhood health centers that used federal funds to develop and provide community-based services in low-income or rural areas. Many of these offered outreach, bilingual, and other innovative services, but only 125 of the projected 1,000 centers had been built by 1976 because Congress did not appropriate needed funds.[22] (Many private medical providers were fearful that these centers would compete with them.) Another innovation was to set up special maternal and infant care programs as well as special clinics for low-income children known as the children and youth projects funded under Title V of the Social Security Act. Like neighborhood health centers, these programs were insufficient in number to meet more than a fraction of medical needs in underserved populations.[23]

Though not developed in the 1960s, the extensive programs of the Veterans Administration (VA) also deserve mention. Created by the Serviceman's Readjustment Act of 1944, the VA has 166 hospitals located in all states except Alaska and Hawaii and gives medical services to more than 100,000 patients every day. The VA also maintains many outpatient clinics as well as home care and nursing home services. Apart from public hospitals, these programs represent the only socialized or government approach to medical care in the United States. But even the programs of the VA do not constitute a major breach in American entrepreneurial medicine. Although millions qualify, most nonpoor veterans use private physicians and insurance because the VA system, like the public hospital system, is widely perceived to provide "poor persons' medicine."[24]

Health Care Planning

During this period, federal and congressional officials tried to introduce planning into the health care system, but their efforts were often ineffectual. The Hill-Burton legislation of 1949 required development of state plans for hospitals in return for federal construction assistance, and regional planning schemes were used on a small scale in the 1960s. Not until 1974 did the National Health Planning and Resources Development Act mandate a national network of planning agencies in which any self-constituted group, whether nonprofit or public, could apply to the federal government to be designated as the official health systems agency (HSA) in one of 218 health districts established by federal authorities. (Those chosen received staff and administrative funds.) These agencies were given authority to veto some of the expansion decisions and the major equipment purchases of hospitals and were given a more general mandate to undertake surveys of health needs and to seek cooperation of local providers in meeting those needs. The legislation did not include authority over distribution of physicians, regulation of their fees, or authority to require physicians and hospitals to serve the poor. Despite some successes, the HSA's were not able to overcome opposition of many providers to central planning, surmount rivalries between hospitals, or develop innovative preventive programs.

ERA OF UNCERTAINTY: BEYOND 1968

As in other policy sectors, major cuts in health programs were proposed by the Reagan Administration in spring 1981, the largest being directed at the already underfunded Medicaid Program. Although not accepting Reagan's specific proposal, the Congress approved a 3 percent cut in federal Medicaid expenditures in 1982, another 4 percent cut in 1983, and a 4.5 percent cut in 1984. The administration proposed elimination of HSAs, but the Congress continued them while halving their funding. Modest cuts in Medicare were enacted, including $1 billion in funding cuts in 1982 and a substantial raise in consumer payments. The administration proposed massive cuts in Medicare for 1983 and succeeding years, but the Congress balked in summer 1982 because its members worried that they might experience political losses if they slashed the politically popular program.[25]

The Congress also devised three major health block grants in summer 1981 under the Omnibus Reconciliation Budget Act: preventive health services, primary care, and maternal and child health care. These block grants not only terminated many categorical programs but were also accompanied by drastic funding cuts. The primary health care block grant, for example, funded the neighborhood health centers in low-income areas, but their funding was slashed from $456.2 million in 1981 to a proposed budget of $347.5 million in 1983. In 1981, the administration proposed including migrant labor health centers and family planning in this block grant, but Congress rejected the proposal to protect these programs from the vagaries of politics at the local level.

Maternal and child health care programs funded under Title V of the Social Security Act as well as seven other programs were placed in the maternal and child health care block grant. Here, too, the President proposed cuts in funding from the $456.2 million allotted to the various categorical programs in 1981 to $347.5 million for the 1983 block grant. The president also proposed reductions in various programs placed in the preventive health services block grant, programs already deemphasized in American health care.

These various cuts, many of them directed at programs that assisted low-income populations, occurred at a time when 22 to 25 million Americans were covered by no medical insurance (see case example 12.1). Further, the administration had not developed reforms to address the causes of the medical cost inflation that continued to plague all consumers of health services. While arguing that government should withdraw to allow the private market to prevail, the administration continued tax concessions to consumers and employers resulting, when coupled with Medicare, in $55 billion in health subsidies to families earning more than $16,000, a sum roughly equivalent to the public subsidies provided to families earning less than that amount.[26] Some officials in the administration wanted to convert Medicare benefits into vouchers paid to

elderly consumers at the start of a year, but this market strategy was unlikely to obtain support in a Congress that did not want to appear to be dismantling the program. Critics argued, then, that the administration undercut services for low-income consumers without providing any larger strategy to reform health care, much less to develop some national health insurance scheme to assist the millions of persons not covered by medical insurance.

REFORMING MEDICAL CARE

Considerable "mobilization of bias" exists against basic reforms in the American medical system. Although their power diminished somewhat in the wake of their unsuccessful and massive lobbying effort to defeat Medicare and Medicaid, national and local chapters of the American Medical Association remain a formidable obstacle to any reforms that regulate physicians in their fees, services, location, or choice of consumers. Measures to require physicians to serve the poor or to locate practices in underserved areas, for example, have been strenuously resisted. The American Hospital Association expends millions of dollars in lobbying against measures to control or regulate hospital fees. These political and economic interests are supplemented by the disinclination of many Americans to consider basic reforms, such as national health proposals, that would drastically increase funding, planning, and regulatory powers of the federal government. Whether due to tradition or to the masterful public relations of providers, many Americans continue to believe that basic reforms represent socialized medicine, a spector associated with the destruction of the doctor–patient relationship. (Despite higher life expectancy and lower mortality rates in many European countries, most Americans assume that, because those countries use socialized models, they must provide inferior medical care.)

Basic reforms are also impeded by the lack of visibility of medical costs in the United States. If consumers had to directly pay for their care, they might insist upon development of less costly alternatives, including preventive programs. But

CASE EXAMPLE 12.1

22–25 Million Not Covered, Study Finds

Health Insurance

By Harry Nelson
Times Medical Writer

A federal study has set at between 22 million and 25 million the number of Americans who have no health insurance of any kind.

Investigators at the National Center for Health Services reported an analysis of the study here Tuesday at the annual meeting of the American Public Health Assn.

The question of how many Americans lack health insurance has been an issue in Congressional debate on a national health insurance program. Forces that favor such a program have estimated that up to 25 million people have no health insurance. Opponents contended that the figure is too high.

Another Group Identified

In addition to a group of about 18.2 million individuals who are always uninsured, the researchers have identified for the first time about 16 million others who are insured only during part of the year. It is from this group that at any one time as many as 7 million persons may be added to the always uninsured group to make a total of 25 million.

Gail R. Wilensky, a senior research manager at the center, said that until now, it had not been possible to separate the occasionally insured group of 16 million from the group of 18.2 million that is always uninsured.

She said the controversy that has persisted over the number of uninsured persons has been due largely to the group which at various times of the year swings between insured and uninsured status, depending largely on their employment status.

Impact on Care Use

Another facet of the study, Wilensky said, middle- and upper-class consumers are not aware of medical costs, because their insurance premiums are partially or wholly paid by employers. The costs for employers of providing health fringe benefits for employees are, in turn, diminished by tax laws that allow them to deduct them from their income tax; i.e., to receive an indirect and hidden subsidy totalling roughly $10 billion for the whole nation per year. Many critics argue, then, that policy makers in socialist countries are more likely than Americans to confront and make difficult policy choices because they directly encounter overall costs of their medical care systems in the form of their national health care budgets.

In the longer term, mobilization of bias against basic reforms may erode. Since the number of elderly persons is rapidly increasing, the cost of medical care is likely to escalate dramatically. Exotic technology will further escalate costs. In addition, although a major surplus of physicians is predicted by 1985, costs will not necessarily decrease, since physicians create demand (as previously noted). The American poor, while accustomed to a separate and unequal medical system, are likely to become restive in light of continuing cutbacks. Finally, many theorists believe that major reductions in illness and mortality require self-care (i.e., sensible lifestyle) and correction of environmental and oc-

was to learn the relationship between the lack of insurance coverage, the use of outpatient medical service, and disability.

The finding was that sick people tend to see the doctor more when they have health insurance than when they lack coverage. This was particularly true for minorities and for the poor who are insured only part of the year.

The 179 million Americans who are always insured have the highest rate of health care use. Their rate of use is nearly double that of the 18 million who are never insured.

The part-time insured have the highest rate of medical care use when they have insurance.

There were some striking racial differences in insurance coverage. Among whites, for example, 91% of all those in the highest income bracket are always insured, but only 79% of all high-income Latinos are insured. Among high income blacks the figure is 87%. Wilensky said she could not explain why Latinos did not buy insurance as frequently as blacks or white.

The study was based on extensive interviews involving about 40,000 persons in the recently completed National Medical Care Expenditure Survey. According to Wilensky, it provides the best national picture of health care insurance and use.

Another aspect of the study was to look at access to medical care among nonwhite aged persons. Based on the survey, it was estimated that while 72.6% of the white elderly have private insurance to supplement Medicare coverage, only 32.1% of the nonwhite elderly have that coverage.

The findings, according to Amy B. Bernstein and Marc L. Berk, also indicated that the nonwhite elderly are more likely than whites to report poor health status.

A difference was also found in the type of care received by whites and nonwhites. For example, nonwhite elderly are more likely than white elderly to report that their usual source of care was at a site other than a physician's office—a clinic, for example.

The survey also showed that the minority aged wait an average of almost an hour before receiving care—much longer than the waiting time experienced by other age and racial groups.

cupational hazards. As these changes occur, a medical system that expends more and more resources on surgeries, expensive tests, and drugs is likely to come increasingly into question.

Reforms in Scanning and Analysis Phases

Expanded Services. Outpatient visits, comprehensive mental health services, preventive health services, consumer health education services, outreach services, home health care services, and ombudsman or advocacy services are often not covered by insurance companies, Medicare, or Medicaid. These are precisely the kinds of services, however, that have the potential to prevent illness and to reduce inequities in health care utilization. Policy makers need to carefully scrutinize these kinds of services, select those with the most promise for preventing illness, and then secure adequate funding for them from public or nongovernmental insurance sources. In the process, the roles of nonmedical staff who provide these kinds of services, such as social workers and health educators, need to be markedly expanded.

Alternatives to Fee-for-Service. Instead of receiving fees for services rendered, physicians can be given salaries or reimbursed according to the size of their patient loads (a capitation method of payment). Health maintenance organizations (HMOs) can also be used in which groups of physicians and other health professionals provide services to consumers who enroll by paying an annual fee. As an example, an HMO charges a family of four $1,000 for medical care during a year even if costs of that care exceed the annual fee. (Annual fees are set so that the HMO recovers its overall costs.) Despite variations between HMOs in methods of paying physicians and in scope of services, they share certain advantages.[27] First, they make insurance companies unnecessary, since the HMO acts, in effect, as an insurance company for its enrollees. Second, the set annual fee gives the HMO an economic disincentive to overprovide, since its staff does not want to operate at a deficit and wishes to increase enrollments by charging competitive fees. (In some HMOs, surpluses at the end of the year are returned to staff in the form of bonuses.) Third, the use of annual fees can enhance competition among providers, since consumers can compare fees and services of alternative HMOs. Many HMOs also have an incentive to provide preventive services to enrollees in order to reduce annual treatment expenses.

HMOs are not panaceas. Some find it difficult to enroll consumers because many Americans prefer more traditional forms of medical practice. If not regulated, unscrupulous organizations can collect fees for promised services and then not provide them. Although only 4 percent of Americans belong to HMOs, enrollments have grown rapidly. (The Health Maintenance Organization Act of 1973 provides seed money and requires employers who offer medical insurance plans to offer HMO coverage, when available, as one alternative.)

Direct National Funding.   Americans have not had to address difficult cost and program choices because funding of medical services is splintered between employers, consumers, and the government and because costs are hidden by extensive use of private insurance. If, like many other peoples, Americans funded medical care from a national budget, they would be more likely to scrutinize services and devise methods to make services more effective, efficient, and equitable. Funding could occur from some combination of Social Security payments, direct federal contributions, state and local payments, and consumer contributions.

Reforms in Implementation and Assessment Phases

Mainstreaming the Poor.   Medical care for the poor is likely to be shortchanged as long as they receive it from different providers than the nonpoor and as long as their care is financed separately from the medical care of the broader population. Many physicians and other health care staff members are drawn disproportionately from ranks of the nonpoor and prefer working with affluent populations, to the extent that many facilities serving low-income populations find it difficult to attract highly qualified staff. A first step, some argue, is to develop nationally funded health insurance that funds most medical care from general revenues and enables the poor to use the same medical system as other citizens. Some critics also favor regulations that prohibit "patient dumping," i.e., denial of service to low-income consumers.

Government Regulations.   Existing medical providers are fond of arguing that they suffer from excessive government regulation, but, by international standards, they enjoy considerable autonomy. They are able to establish fees in absence of government regulations and are not subject to regulations limiting choices about their locus of practice. American hospitals have traditionally had considerable antonomy in setting their fees, expanding their facilities, and purchasing equipment despite periodic attempts to regulate them. (By contrast, hospitals in many other countries are administered and regulated by public authorities.)

Critics of regulations argue that market strategies will suffice. Better, they say, to terminate regulations so that the silent working of the market will lead to more efficient, effective, and equitable services. The problem with this argument, supporters of regulations retort, is that the American medical system has used a market strategy grounded in fee-for-service and entrepreneurial practice, but this strategy has not resulted in equitable or efficient services.

Regional Planning. In many European systems, health budgets are devised for geographic regions where regional authorities decide what facilities, providers, and services are needed to meet the health needs of the population. These regional authorities often control funds and so can influence local programs. Americans have no such "regional accounts," however, since private insurance companies, government, and consumers pay large portions of health care bills but are not organized in regional fashion. Further, insurance companies and government do not use their funding leverage to influence services or sites of practice of providers. Many critics believe that Americans would benefit from greater use of regional authorities to offset the fragmentation of existing services.

NATIONAL HEALTH INSURANCE

Perhaps the most basic policy issue confronting Americans is whether and how to establish national health insurance. Governmental, expanded coverage, and market models have been advanced.[28] Sen. Edward Kennedy is the leading exponent of a *governmental model* (see case example 12.2), although a proposal modeled on the English system has also been advanced by congressman and social worker Ron Dellums.

Senator Kennedy favors direct government subsidies of a wide array of health services financed by payroll deductions of employers and employees and funds from general revenues. He emphasizes mainstreaming of the poor, since all citizens in his mandatory plan would receive coverage for the same services at the same fees. Regional planning bodies would be given central planning and regulatory roles. Representative Dellums advocates a government system of health care that gives even stronger roles

to regional authorities, which could hire physicians directly or reimburse them through the capitation method of payment (i.e., by the numbers of persons they serve rather than for the specific services or procedures they provide to individuals). Most social workers find versions like those of Senator Kennedy and Representative Dellums to be more consonant with personal and professional values than expanded coverage or market models, since all citizens receive identical coverage under one publicly funded plan.

Expanded coverage plans proposed by both the Nixon and Carter Administrations emphasize (1) use of federal regulations to require employers to offer employees private health insurance with specific minimum benefits and (2) continuation of programs like Medicaid and Medicare to assist unemployed and elderly persons. A major problem with these plans is that they finance services for low-income persons differently from services for more affluent persons. Consequently, the affluent would have no more personal stake in them than they have in the current Medicaid program, a fact that could lead to inadequate funding for programs serving the poor.

In *market models*, such as the Medicredit scheme of the American Medical Association, consumers would be provided with cash, tax deductions, and tax credits that allow them to purchase the services they need on the open market. The major problem with market schemes is that they do not propose major changes in the current medical system, which is beset with defects in effectiveness, efficiency, and equity.

POLICY ROLES OF SOCIAL WORKERS

The medical sector provides rapidly expanding job opportunities for social workers, who are called on to assume problem recognition, program design, troubleshooting, error detection, and change agent policy roles in hospital, community clinic, community, and legislative arenas. But social workers must come to terms with the fact that they are not the dominant profession

CASE EXAMPLE 12.2

Health Care Weaknesses Outlined

Hearing Headed by Kennedy Compares U.S., Canadian Systems

By Harry Nelson
Times Medical Writer

GARDEN GROVE—Some of the major weaknesses of the American health care system were graphically illustrated here Friday in a hearing chaired by Sen. Edward M. Kennedy (D-Mass.), Congress' leading spokesman on national health insurance.

Nearly 1,000 persons jammed the Garden Grove Community Center to hear a group of U.S. patients describe their problems with the health system—problems that a group of comparable Canadian patients flown here for the hearing said are nonexistent in their country, which has had national insurance since 1968.

Even members of the U.S. health professions—a group not on the friendliest terms with Kennedy on health matters—would have agreed that the problems outlined during the hearing generally were valid.

But whether the national health insurance plan envisioned by Kennedy would solve the problems without creating newer ones that may be equally undesirable—an assertion made by his critics—is unknown, since his plan is untried.

The six U.S. witnesses—all Californians—recited tales of bankruptcy, canceled private health insurance policies, lifetime savings spent in a week for sickness care, loss of insurance coverage after loss of a job and red tape problems with Medi-Cal.

Gary Thompson, a 41-year-old Los Angeles radio engineer, said he was forced into bankruptcy to avoid collection agencies trying to collect more than $10,000 that his health insurance did not cover for the care of his prematurely born child.

Pat Ambrose, a 60-year-old Napa real estate salesman, said he must pay $8,378 a year for his wife's kidney dialysis—despite the fact that she has coverage by two insurance policies plus Medicare.

Mrs. Kenneth Pelgrim of Santa Barbara said her doctor had advised her to have an X-ray procedure to diagnose heart disease but that she has declined to do it because she is afraid "of what might come afterwards" in the form of expensive surgery or other care.

Her husband said they have no health insurance because no company will cover his wife's preexisting health condition, which is the underlying cause of her heart disease.

Elizabeth Wehn of Fullerton said her husband has been in a hospital and nursing home

in the medical sector: attitudes, preferences, and traditions of the medical profession shape programs and services in virtually every setting. This fact ought not to suggest, however, that social workers cannot have a major impact on development of policies and services. In many hospitals, for example, social workers have succeeded in modifying traditional policies to enable

victims of cancer, heart disease, and many other problems to receive social services. Social workers need to develop skills in communicating with physicians, nurses, and other professions in the health sector and in persuading them that traditional medical services need to be expanded to provide counseling, educational, advocacy, and community services.

for the last five years, she said their group policy was cancelled the day he became unable to work, and that she has spent all their savings and life insurance policy accruals.

She said she applied for Medi-Cal coverage, the health program for the poor, in September but has not heard from them since.

The patients from Canada—all of whom had medical problems similar to the U.S. residents—said the Canadian insurance program paid their medical costs with only minimal insurance premium cost to workers and out-of-pocket expense.

A key feature of Kennedy's plan, which is expected to be introduced to Congress in several months, is that it combines cost controls with universal, comprehensive health insurance—the only insurance proposal to do so.

Dr. William H. Thompson, president of the Orange County Medical Society, who addressed the hearing, said the way to control health costs is for the public to adopt a "better life-style to decrease their demand" on health services.

Thompson was booed by the audience of nearly 1,000—largely senior citizens—when he said the health care delivery system in this country is "the best in the world."

At a Los Angeles press conference, Dr. Richard F. Corlin, president of the Los Angeles County Medical Assn., said "Kennedy's claim that national health insurance will keep costs down is refuted by everything government has done."

"If health costs are capped without reducing demand, rationing (of health services) will result—which is what has happened in England and Canada," Corlin said.

Christine P. Burr, a UCLA school of nursing faculty member, said the present system forces patients to "inappropriately" go to doctors in order to get the care paid for by insurance when their real need is health education or direct preventive health care by professional nurses, neither of which is covered by insurance.

Dr. Greg Anderson, a resident physician at County-Harbor General Hospital, said it is not uncommon for persons hospitalized in private hospitals to be sent to county hospitals when their private health insurance runs out.

While opponents of Kennedy's plan agree on the need for comprehensive health coverage, agree that many persons have inadequate health insurance, that prevention should be emphasized, and that costs must be controlled, they do not agree on the means proposed by Kennedy for correcting these deficiencies.

Main disagreements are on the respective roles of government and the private sector; whether cost control should be voluntary or compulsory; whether the system should be financed with taxes or other means and the timetable for implementing a program.

Change Agent Role

Social workers, physical therapists, and occupational therapists are often termed ancillary staff in medical arenas, a designation that underlines the difficulties involved in their securing expanded roles in the medical sector. Whether working in hospitals, community clinics, the community, or legislatures, social workers need to develop and use power resources to obtain policies that help turn "medical care" into "health care." In health care, many professions collaborate in meeting the physical, psychological, social, and community needs of consumers.

Since change often occurs in incremental

steps in clinics and hospitals, social workers need a combination of assertiveness and sensitivity to political realities. Assertiveness is needed to plan and implement innovative services. In many cases, mandates to provide social services in the health setting are achieved only after the utility of social work services has been demonstrated, i.e., after physicians and nurses have been shown that social work interventions speed recovery of patients and facilitate the work of other health care professionals. But a frontal attack on prevailing policies or physicians is often counterproductive; skillful social workers incrementally build services and staffs by carefully seizing opportunities and demonstrating competence.

In the broader community, social workers need to participate with professional and community organizations to build consumer-oriented health coalitions to act as a counterforce to established interests. Such coalition-building is particularly necessary to offset cuts in preventive programs as well as in those that serve low-income populations, including public health programs, neighborhood health centers, and maternal programs. In some cases, social workers need to develop skillful strategies for insisting on accreditation and licensing standards that mandate full inclusion of social workers in hospitals, clinics, and other health care programs.

Survey Role

Social workers need to identify ideological, political, economic, and technical factors that provide the context for projects to modify existing policies. A social worker in a hospital who wants to expand social work roles, for example, needs to identify the extent to which a mobilization of bias exists against policies that would allow social workers to provide services. Perhaps personnel and policies in one section or service of the hospital, unlike those in another section or service, suggest that reforms would be difficult. When seeking changes in state and national policies, social workers similarly need to be familiar with prevailing policies and existing realities that

may, for example, make major expansion of preventive programs difficult.

Problem Recognition and Definition Role

A central task of social workers is to sensitize other health care professionals to expanded definitions of health problems. Community, family, and mental factors need to be identified that place some consumers in high-risk health categories and entitle them to receive social services as well as preventive programs. Although physiological factors are certainly important, recovery of many patients is facilitated when the whole person is made the focus of health care services. Persons who lack adequate living arrangements, who do not have employment, who lack family and community supports, or who have not "worked through" feelings that accompany illness may find their recovery delayed by mental stress and conflict.

Indeed, an ecological perspective is needed that addresses personal, family, community, and environmental factors that influence the well-being of consumers.[29] Social workers are uniquely positioned within the health care system to provide this perspective and to implement it by including a range of social and preventive services in hospitals and other settings.

Program and Policy Design Role

Social workers should participate both in intradepartmental and facilitywide planning projects, not to mention community and professional task forces. "Programmatic assertiveness" is needed in which social workers take the initiative in defining policy options neglected by others. Increased attention must be given to community outreach and prevention services as well as to linkages between health services and a variety of community agencies.

Social workers can seek policies supportive of multiprofessional teams, mandatory visits by social workers to certain kinds of consumers (e.g., victims of rape), use of group services, and encouragement of self-help groups for victims of cancer and other traumatizing conditions. Social workers should also urge expansion of ombudsman and patient advocacy services to ensure that the poor or those with specific kinds of problems do not receive inferior services and that consumers are given expanded roles in selecting medical procedures.

Troubleshooting Role

Many practical factors frustrate delivery of humane health care services, including rivalries between different professions, staff burnout, disinclination of many physicians to share power and services with others, lack of defined policies and procedures, lack of funds for innovative programs, and lack of community linkages of hospitals and clinics. Social workers should assume troubleshooting roles to identify factors that impede effective services and to identify strategies for removing those impediments.

Error Detection Role

In many cases, evaluations in medicine focus on effects of specific medical technologies without consideration of the emotional, familial, and community factors that influence outcomes. As an example, a researcher found that patients on cardiac wards often show signs of improvement simply when assured that financial burdens will be managed. A host of other interventions provided by social workers are also worth assessing, including tangible assistance with finances, referrals to other services, direct crisis intervention, advocacy, explanation of medical realities and issues, encouragement of family participation in medical choices, follow-up in nursing and convalescent homes, and provision of group services. Social workers need to develop projects to assess these kinds of assistance, since medical staff members are unlikely to perform this task for them.

SUMMARY

An overview of discussion in this chapter is presented in illustration 12.4, which is derived from the policy framework presented in chapter 2. This illustration summarizes prevailing policies, normative positions, assessment of prevailing policy, and selected reform options in the health care sector, as well as a variety of ideological, political, and technical factors that influence policy development.

The medical system should be transformed into a health care system that gives attention to multiple causes of illness, multiple barriers to utilization, and preventive services. Dissatisfaction with the existing medical system is considerable and growing; many critics note neglect of prevention, environmental and personal causes of illness, and outreach to groups who use services belatedly or not at all. American health care is exorbitantly expensive. Soaring costs are attributable in part to reliance on fee-for-service financing and to overuse of drugs and some technologies. Also, the widespread use of insurance gives consumers little incentive to economize. The separate and unequal set of services that exists for the poor is subject to cutbacks because the nonpoor have no personal stake in them.

Not until 1965 did Americans develop major federal funding for health care, but even Medicare and Medicaid subsidized the existing system rather than reforming it. Major reforms of the American medical system have been impeded by vested interests of providers as well as by widely held beliefs that expansion of government roles would lead to "socialized medicine." In scanning and analysis phases, policies should be considered that promote health prevention, expanded roles for social workers, alternatives to fee-for-service, and direct national funding of health care. In implementation and assessment phases, scrutiny should be given to mainstreaming, regulatory, and regional planning options. Governmental, expanded coverage, and market models of national health insurance have been proposed, but chances for short-term passage are slight. In clinic, hospital, community, and

ILLUSTRATION 12.4 Policy in the Health Care Sector

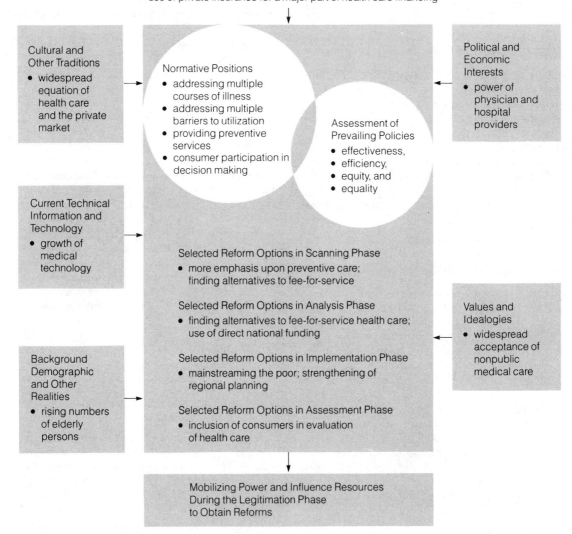

Prevailing (Current) Policies and Programs
- reliance on fee-for-service medical practice
- separate and unusual system of care for the poor
- limited government involvement in the health care system
- emphasis upon preventive services
- limited roles for social work and other ancillary staff
- use of private insurance for a major part of health care financing

Cultural and Other Traditions
- widespread equation of health care and the private market

Normative Positions
- addressing multiple courses of illness
- addressing multiple barriers to utilization
- providing preventive services
- consumer participation in decision making

Political and Economic Interests
- power of physician and hospital providers

Assessment of Prevailing Policies
- effectiveness,
- efficiency,
- equity, and
- equality

Current Technical Information and Technology
- growth of medical technology

Selected Reform Options in Scanning Phase
- more emphasis upon preventive care; finding alternatives to fee-for-service

Selected Reform Options in Analysis Phase
- finding alternatives to fee-for-service health care; use of direct national funding

Values and Idealogies
- widespread acceptance of nonpublic medical care

Selected Reform Options in Implementation Phase
- mainstreaming the poor; strengthening of regional planning

Background Demographic and Other Realities
- rising numbers of elderly persons

Selected Reform Options in Assessment Phase
- inclusion of consumers in evaluation of health care

Mobilizing Power and Influence Resources During the Legitimation Phase to Obtain Reforms

legislative settings, social workers can assume a variety of change agent, survey problem recognition, program design, troubleshooting, and error detection roles. By assuming these roles skill-fully and energetically, social workers can play a leading part in reforming the existing medical care system.

Key Concepts, Developments, and Policies

Multiple causes of illness
Multiple barriers to utilization
Medical insurance
Consumer payments
Maldistribution of providers
Primary and secondary prevention
Privileges
Measures of health status
Infant mortality rates
Technology
Third-party insurance
Fee-for-service reimbursement
Malpractice
Chronic and acute conditions
American Medical Association
Licensing
Doctor–patient relationship
Blue Cross and Blue Shield
National health insurance
Socialist systems of health care
Entrepreneurial systems of health care

Medicare, Parts A and B
Medicaid
Coverage
Neighborhood health centers
Maternal and infant care programs
Children and youth projects
Veterans Administration
Hill-Burton
National Health Planning and Resources
  Development Act
Health systems agencies
Catastrophic health conditions
Medical inflation
Preventive health services block grant
Primary-care block grant
Maternal and child health block grant
Health maintenance organizations
Capitation
Health Maintenance Organization Act of 1973
Alternative models of national health insurance

Main Points

1. Traditional medical or disease-oriented models are inadequate in light of multiple causes of illness and multiple barriers to utilization.

2. Many critics believe that major improvements in the health status of Americans require the use of preventive programs.

3. Great disparities exist in access to medical services between low-income and rural citizens on the one hand, and more affluent and urban citizens, on the other.

4. Serious questions have been raised about the cost-effectiveness of American health care. Despite far larger per capita outlays of funds, Americans continue to rank behind many other countries on various measures of health status.

5. Rising costs of American health care appear to be associated with the prevalence of third-party insurance, the sometimes excessive use of technology, the fee-for-service method of reimbursing physicians, and "defensive medicine" in response to malpractice suits.

6. There continues to be a shortage of general or family practitioners and medical services for elderly persons with chronic problems. Feminists charge that sexism is still common in medical services and staffing patterns.

7. The American Medical Association gained enormous power in the early part of this century and used it to block numerous proposals to enlarge funding and policy roles of state and national governments. Although its power has been somewhat eclipsed in the

wake of its unsuccessful effort to defeat Medicare in 1965, it continues to wield considerable power, as does the American Hospital Association.

8. Americans developed a fee-for-service entrepreneurial model of medical practice that continues to prevail. By contrast, many other countries have either developed governmental models or greatly broadened government regulatory and financing roles.

9. Americans have made major use of nonprofit and profit-oriented insurance mechanisms and hospitals.

10. Medicare and Medicaid represented the first major health care funding commitment of the national government. Medicare assisted elderly consumers and was financed by a combination of payroll deductions, premiums, and general revenue funds. It was designed to assist elderly persons with hospital and physician costs associated with acute rather than chronic health conditions.

11. Medicaid is a state–federal matching program that finances medical care for welfare recipients and medically indigent persons. States were given major policy roles in determining eligibility and establishing which

services are covered, a fact that has led to marked variations in programs.

12. Special programs created during the 1960s included federal financing of neighborhood health centers in low-income areas, maternal and child health programs, and children and youth programs.

13. Despite passage of the National Health Planning and Resources Development Act of 1974, regional health planning has not been emphasized in the United States. Budget cuts of the Reagan Administration have further weakened roles of the health systems agencies.

14. Major cuts in Medicaid, Medicare, and many other public health programs were enacted during the Reagan Administration. Various categorical programs were consolidated into preventive health services, maternal and child health care, and primary-care block grants.

15. Serious consideration should be given to expanding the role of health maintenance organizations; to expanding preventive health programs and programs that target resources to low-income and "at-risk" populations; and to enacting national health insurance.

Questions for Discussion

1. Review guest editorial 12.1. Discuss how cuts in neighborhood health services and other programs could further detract from effectiveness, efficiency, and equity of American health care.

2. Some critics argue that major gains in health care must now come from development of preventive programs. Discuss.

3. Is a fee-for-service and entrepreneurial model of medicine intrinsically better than governmental models in terms of effectiveness, efficiency, and equality of outcomes? Discuss.

4. Identify various factors that together contribute to runaway costs in the medical sector.

5. "Although Medicare and Medicaid programs have assisted many consumers, they have

hardly brought major structural reforms in the American medical system." Discuss this statement, and, in the process, review the basic features of those programs.

6. "Programs for poor persons are likely to be poor programs." Discuss the implications of this statement for national health insurance programs and for the Medicaid program.

7. What distinctive perspectives can social workers bring to hospitals and clinics that provide medical services?

8. What are positive and negative features associated with health maintenance organizations? Do you think they should be given far larger roles in the American health care system?

Suggested Readings

Anderson, Odin. *Uneasy Equilibrium* (New Haven, Conn.: College and University Press, 1968). The author provides an overview of American policies in the health sector.

Bracht, Neil. "Social Services in Medical Care Systems." In Neil Gilbert and Harry Specht, eds., *Handbook of the Social Services* (Englewood Cliffs, N.J.: Prentice-Hall, 1981): pp. 311–336. The author provides a concise overview of the use of social services in the medical care system in hospital, clinic, and community settings, with particular reference to social work roles.

Coulton, Claudia. "Person–Environment Fit as the Focus in Health Care." *Social Work*, 26 (January 1981): 26–36. The author shows how social workers bring to health care institutions ecological perspectives that can significantly improve services offered to consumers, and she provides a normative framework that is useful in analyzing health care policies.

Davis, Karen. *National Health Insurance* (Washington, D.C.: Brookings Institution, 1975). The author identifies critical issues in the controversy surrounding national health insurance and describes and critiques alternative forms of insurance.

Davis, Karen, and Schoen, Cathy. *Health and the*

War on Poverty: A Ten-Year Appraisal. (Washington, D.C.: Brookings Institution, 1978). An excellent overview of the variety of health reforms enacted in the 1960s, with critical discussion of their effectiveness in improving the health of low-income, elderly, and rural citizens.

Fuchs, Victor. *Who Shall Live?* (New York: Basic Books, 1974). In the context of international comparisons, the author raises searching questions about policies and programs to be used to enhance the nation's health.

Marmor, Theodore. *The Politics of Medicare* (Chicago: Aldine, 1975). This book is an account of the evolution and passage of Medicare legislation, with particular emphasis on political and institutional realities.

Roemer, Milton. *Comparative National Policies on Health Care.* (New York: Dekker, 1977). The author identifies basic issues that must be addressed by a health care system and then contrasts American policy choices with those of other nations.

Stevens, Rosemary. *Welfare Medicine in America: A Case Study of Medicaid* (New York: Free Press, 1974). The origins, passage, and implementation of Medicaid legislation are discussed in this excellent and detailed book.

Notes

1. Traditional medical perspectives are discussed by William R. Rosengren, *Sociology of Medicine* (New York: Harper & Row, 1980), chapter 4.

2. Rudolf H. Moos, "Social Ecological Perspectives on Health," in George C. Stone et al., eds., *Health and Psychology* (San Francisco: Jossey-Bass, 1979), pp. 523–549.

3. Andrew C. Twaddle, *Sickness Behavior and the Sick Role* (Boston: Hall, 1979).

4. U.S. Department of Health, Education, and Welfare, Public Health Service, *DHEW Publication No. (HRA) 79-627*, pp. 104–105.

5. U.S. Department of Health, Education, and Welfare (Washington, D.C.: U.S. Government Printing Office, 1976), *Trends Affecting the United States Health Care System*, [1976], pp. 104–116.

6. The dual system is discussed by Dorothy A. Kupcha, "Medicaid: In or Out of the Mainstream," *California Journal*, 10 (May 1979): 181–183.

7. For discussion of evaluation of American health care, see John H. Dingle, "The Ills of Man," in *Life and Death and Medicine* (San Francisco: Freeman, 1973), pp. 49–56; Steven

Jonas, "Data for Health and Health Care," in Steven Jonas, ed., *Health Care Delivery in the United States* (New York: Springer, 1977), pp. 40–60; and Fuchs, *Who Shall Live?*, pp. 30–55.

8. David Rogers, "The Challenge of Primary Care," in John Knowles, ed., *Doing Better and Feeling Worse* (New York: Norton, 1977), pp. 81–105.

9. In a survey conducted by Bruce Jansson, June Simmons, and Candyce Berger, one-third of a sample of fifty nonprofit hospitals in Los Angeles County in 1980 were found to have one or fewer social workers in their social work departments.

10. John K. Inglehart, "Health Care Cost Explosion Squeezes Government Programs and Insurers," *National Journal Proceedings of National Leadership Conference on American Health Policy* (April 1976): 4–11.

11. Davis, *National Health Insurance.*

12. Linda Demkovitch, "Cutting Health Care Costs—Why Not Let the Market Decide?", *National Journal*, 11 (October 29, 1979): 1796–1801.

13. Claudia Dreyfus, ed., *Seizing Our Bodies: The Politics of Women's Health* (New York: Vintage, 1977).

14. James G. Burrow, *Organized Medicine in the Progressive Era* (Baltimore, Md.: Johns Hopkins University Press, 1977).

15. Burrow, *Organized Medicine,* and Ronald L. Numbers, *Almost Persuaded: American Physicians and Compulsory Health Insurance, 1912–1920* (Baltimore, Md.: Johns Hopkins University Press, 1979).

16. Rosemary Stevens, *American Medicine and the Public Interest* (New Haven, Conn.: Yale University Press, 1971), pp. 85–92.

17. Numbers, *Almost Persuaded.*

18. Anderson, *Uneasy Equilibrium.*

19. For international comparisons, see Brian Abel-Smith, "Major Patterns of Financing and Organization of Medical Care in Countries Other than the United States," in Subcommittee on Social Policy for Health Care ed., *Social Policy for Health Care* (New York: New York Academy of Medicine, 1969), pp. 13–17; and Milton Roemer, *Comparative National Policies on Health Care* (New York: Dekker, 1977.)

20. For discussion of Medicare and its evolution, see Theodore Marmor, *The Politics of Medicare;* and James L. Sundquist, *Politics and Policy: The Eisenhower, Kennedy, and Johnson Years* (Washington, D.C.: Brookings Institution, 1968), pp. 275–308.

21. For discussion of Medicaid, see Stevens, *Welfare Medicine in America.*

22. For discussion of the neighborhood health centers, see Davis and Schoen, *Health and the War on Poverty.*

23. Ibid.

24. Robert Morris, *Social Policy of the American Welfare State,* (New York: Harper & Row, 1979), p. 88.

25. Various policies of the Reagan Administration are discussed in issues of the newsletter of the American Public Health Association; see, for example, *The Nation's Health, 12 (February 1982): 1.*

26. *"Reagan's Polarized America," Newsweek* (April 5, 1982): 20–28.

27. For discussion of HMOs, see Demkovich, "Cutting Health Care Costs," pp. 1796–1801; and U.S. Department of Commerce, *Trends Affecting the U.S. Health Care System,* pp. 221–261.

28. Davis, *National Health Insurance.*

29. Coulton, "Person-Environment Fit as the focus in Health Care."

Policy in the Mental Health Sector

Persons who suffer severe anxiety or depression, are unable to resolve conflicted relationships, or suffer a myriad other psychological problems often turn to mental health services. In most cases, they seek assistance for acute (i.e., short-term) problems. In other cases, they suffer severe, often chronic conditions that place them in ongoing contact with mental health institutions and services.

Social workers have attained prominence in various service roles in the mental health sector, roles that should in turn facilitate their increasing involvement in the development of policy proposals to improve programs in this sector. Social workers need to:

Develop normative positions that prescribe the kinds of services that should be provided by programs in the mental health sector and define distinctive roles for social workers

Identify defects in existing policies and programs in the mental health sector as they impede achievement of effectiveness, equity, equality, and other objectives

Understand the evolution of American policies in the mental health sector during the nineteenth century; during the era of institutions preceding 1950; during the era of deinstitutionalization between 1950 and 1968; and during the current era of policy uncertainty

Be able to develop policy reforms that can improve existing programs

Develop knowledge of a variety of policy roles that social workers can assume in the mental health sector

These topics are discussed in this chapter to provide concepts useful in the practice of policy in the mental health sector.

As illustrated in case example 13.1, many controversial policy issues exist in this sector. Critics complain that hundreds of thousands of Americans have been "dumped" from institutions into the community with few supports or services, that poor persons are likely to lack the insurance or personal resources necessary to allow them to obtain outpatient services, and that services of many clinics and professionals are irrelevant to groups such as the elderly, the poor, and racial minorities.

CASE EXAMPLE 13.1

The Latest Crisis in Care for the Mentally Ill

By Kathryn Maney

In 1849 the brig Euphemia lay docked off the shore of San Francisco, its hold serving as both the mental institution and jail for the community. Today, a growing number of mentally ill persons are once again being held in the jail system, due to bed shortages and inadequate planning of mental care facilities.

"As supportive services and outpatient facilities face cutbacks, patients become much more visible," says Al M. Loeb, director of the state Department of Mental Health. "The state and society will pay in one way or another. Law enforcement officials will pick up those creating a nuisance, hallucinating or loitering, and they'll end up in the jail system. It's a very uncomfortable issue."

Jailing of the mentally ill occurs most often in large urban areas:

- In Los Angeles County, the number of "mercy bookings" has steadily increased over the last two years. (Jailing of the mentally ill is often called mercy booking, because it is frequently the only alternative to leaving the patient on the street where he or she may be a danger to self or others.)

- A recent study by the Los Angeles County Mental Health Department showed that during a four-week period, the County-University of Southern California emergency room turned away 271 acutely ill patients. Countywide, 430 were turned away.

- San Francisco's director of jail psychiatric services, Suzanne Tavano, admits that "the number of mentally ill prisoners in the Hall of Justice, accused of serious crimes, has grown 70 percent in the past year—and that figure is rising steadily."

- On a normal day, one prisoner in 12 in San Francisco's jail system is classified as mentally ill. Mentally ill prisoners number over 100 among the 760 or so prisoners who are confined at the Hall of Justice.

The Department of Mental Health estimates that of the 3.45 million persons in California needing mental health care each year, nearly one-fifth—690,000—are not served by the system. The reasons: unrecognized or undiagnosed illnesses, clients' inability to meet commitment standards or lack of facilities and bed space.

MENTAL HEALTH SERVICES: A NORMATIVE POSITION

In this as in other policy sectors, policy practitioners need to develop normative positions that provide a foundation for their work, positions that define the kinds and amount of services that should be available to consumers.

An Ecological Approach

Mental health is enhanced as security, affection, task accomplishment, creativity, and sexual needs are met. But persons can hardly satisfy these needs if they lack a positive relationship with their environment. Unemployed persons, for example, cannot meet task accomplishment needs; persons embroiled in conflictual, de-

Out of the Institutions

The roots of the current problem can be traced back to the mid-1950s, when a "deinstitutionalization" movement grew nationwide. Its goal was to move the mentally ill from institutional settings to less restrictive communitycare facilities. The belief that mentally disordered persons could be treated more effectively and humanely in their own communities became federal policy with the passage of the National Mental Health Act and the Community Centers Act. The latter bill provided seed money to the states to create community-based facilities to replace the state hospitals as primary mental health care centers.

But only one-third of all community health centers projected for California were funded, and the federal funds to keep the centers afloat for the first 10 years have now run out. That leaves county health officials scrambling for money to maintain those centers that have remained public. (About one-half of California's community health centers are privately owned and operated.) Yet the statewide statistics on deinstitutionalization are dramatic. State hospitals held 37,000 patients in 1957; today that population stands at just over 5,000. The decline was actually a result of a combination of factors. There was natural attrition as elderly patients died and other aged patients who formerly would have been

placed in state hospitals were directed into nursing homes. Then three state hospitals were closed over a four-year period: Modesto's in 1970, Dewitt's in 1972 and Mendocino's in 1973. Most important, legislation aimed at shifting the population to community based facilities (the Short-Doyle Act) and restricting conditions for commitment (Lanterman-Petris-Short Act) resulted in significantly reduced hospital populations.

The Short-Doyle Act was passed in 1957 and initially required equal funding from both local and state levels. That was part of the reason for the community health centers' slow rate of growth, because if a county chose to treat a patient in a community program, the county had to pay 50 percent of the cost. If that same patient was placed in a state hospital, the state paid 100 percent of the cost. The disincentive was eased in 1967 by the Lanterman-Petris-Short (L-P-S) Act, which shifted funding for community care to a 90 percent share for the state, 10 percent for the county. And since the passage of Proposition 13, the Legislature has had to waive the counties' share due to their inability to pay it.

In addition to changing the funding structure, L-P-S became known as the mental health patient's bill of rights because of the changes it required in confinement proceedings. The law restricted commitments to those persons who were either gravely disabled and unable to provide for their own maintenance or dangerous to others. Unless one of those two conditions is met, mentally disturbed persons can be held against their will for only 72 hours. Some mental health officials are dissatisfied with L-P-S because they feel too many mentally ill persons are not receiving treatment because of the commitment standards. They are now reexamining L-P-S and hope to propose modifications soon.

The patients first released from state to local programs did not seriously overburden community resources. They included those least disabled and best prepared to function in the community, plus the elderly who were placed in nursing homes with federal support. As deinstitutionalization accelerated, however, it became obvious that few communities were sufficiently equipped to handle the acutely ill. These persons required extensive after-care services which either did not exist or were poorly funded in most counties. Many patients had been institutionalized for long periods of time and lacked the social skills and community supports to assist in the transition.

The Pendulum Swing

Now the pendulum appears to be swinging in the opposite direction: There is a small but growing body of professionals who think deinstitutionalization may no longer be a realistic goal. "I think we're looking at a new chapter in the deinstitutionalization story," says Paul Gorman of the state Department of Mental Health. "The state is coming to the end of its policy to return state hospital patients to the communities. Community programs are inadequate and more expensive. There's an economy of scale at work here. State hospitals can maintain a sizeable staff: the cost of their physical plant is nominal compared to buying new buildings, and their occupancy is always at least 90 to 95 percent. There's simply no cheaper way to go."

Once the primary provider of mental health services, the state hospitals have evolved from patient warehouses into total care facilities serving only those patients who cannot be adequately served in the local communities. The hospitals were plagued with problems in the 1970s, including state investigations of 1,000 questionable deaths of patients, understaffing, deteriorating facilities, loss of accreditation, use of shock therapy and involuntary sterilizations. But the hospitals have undergone extensive scrutiny as a result and there has been some improvement in conditions and administration.

There is new awareness among mental-health officials that current hospital populations may be close to an irreducible minimum. Even though Governor Brown's 1981–82 budget calls for a 200-bed reduction, and a department study projects an additional 600-bed reduction over a three-year period, Mental Health Director Loeb says it is doubtful that such reductions will occur. County directors have told him the figures are much too optimistic. The post-Proposition 13 funding crunch precludes building facilities for the released patients, and many of the acutely ill could not function in any setting other than a hospital.

Another factor often overlooked is the growing number of penal code patients whose release is unacceptable to the public. About 40 percent of mentally ill patients in state hospitals are committed by the courts as criminally insane. These include those judged to be not guilty by reason of insanity, incompetent to stand trial and mentally disordered sex offenders.

"I don't think people realize the large number of patients who are criminally insane when they talk about reducing the state hospital population." says Mike O'Connor, director of Napa State Hospital. "The public's not ready to receive these people back into the communities. I don't like to admit this fact, but I have to be realistic."

O'Connor cites an example: "A few years back, we had a patient who was transferred here from Atascadero (one of the state's two hospitals housing only the criminally insane), where he'd been sentenced following conviction for child molesting. He was a model patient and after eight years of hospitalization, we felt he was ready to re-enter society. We called his home—a small Northern California county—and they told us there was no way they would ever take him back there. They're just not ready to trust them (the criminally insane) again."

Critics of the state hospital system argue against the restrictive, isolated environments, their excessive reliance on drugs and their chronic understaffing problems. The isolation and drug dependency are counterproductive to preparing the patients to re-enter society, according to Tony Hoffman, spokesman for the Families of Disabled Children. "Putting a mentally ill person in a state hospital and expecting him to get well is like putting a person in the desert and expecting him to learn how to swim. It's just not possible," Hoffman's opinion is buttressed by the recidivism rates of state hospital patients: Of all patients admitted to state mental hospitals in one recent year, about 60 percent had been there at least once before.

Scandals and Dollars

State hospitals treat only about 10 to 15 percent of the state's acute mental patients, according to Department of Mental Health statistics. The great majority are in community facilities—skilled nursing homes and board-and-care homes. And many of these facilities have recently been charged with the same abuses that state hospitals were accused of in the mid-70s. "There have been cases of overdrugging and mysterious deaths," says Hoffman. "They thought they'd break up the scandals by removing patients from the state hospitals, but the problems followed the patients."

The state is currently involved in a major federal audit of mental care in nursing homes. Primarily serving the elderly, nursing homes attract Medi-Cal patients due to the restrictions on Medi-Cal that preclude payments for patients in total mental care facilities. Funding problems are also anticipated because of President Reagan's proposal to fund Medi-Cal at current levels plus 5 percent. Inflation in medical care is running at 15 percent annually.

Board-and-care operators, who receive direct federal funding in the form of Supplemental Security Income (SSI) for each patient, are finding it hard to stay afloat on the $402 per patient per month they receive. Responsible for about 25,000 mentally ill patients in California, the operators have been going out of business or switching their clientele to the aged or developmentally disabled, who are easier to care for and more highly subsidized. The department estimates that over the last three years 400 beds were closed in San Francisco alone. Licensed by the state Department of Social Services, board-and-care homes are residential facilities providing 24-hour care for a small group of patients, usually about six.

One of the continuing complaints about facilities for the mentally ill are their dependency upon drugs to keep patients manageable. A recent survey of 123 Parents of Adult Mentally Ill (PAMI) members in California revealed that drugs were used in 94 percent of the cases. Each patient was administered an average of 5.2 different drugs at one time or another. Most mentally ill patients in state hospitals also receive other kinds of medication, according to Napa Hospital Director O'Connor.

In the 1960s, some serious side effects from such drugs began to be identified. The PAMI survey revealed that 74 percent of the subject patients had experienced side effects from the drugs, and 44 percent of the patients felt the drugs weren't properly monitored.

SOURCE: *California Journal*, July 1981, pp. 239–241. Reprinted by permission.

pendent, or dominating relationships are unlikely to satisfy affectional needs; and those who live in blighted neighborhoods marked by high rates of crime are not likely to meet security needs.

An ecological perspective is useful because it emphasizes relationships between persons and their environment. A major function of mental health practitioners, agencies, and institutions is to help consumers develop positive rather than negative relationships with their environment to increase the extent to which their basic needs are met.[1]

The concept of stress is important to an ecological perspective. Stress arises when persons cannot develop constructive relationships and fulfilling activities within family, occupational, and community settings. Some stress is functional, such as the self-generated stress that one experiences when one initiates and wants to

ILLUSTRATION 13.1   An Ecological Framework

STRESS

Groups Likely to Experience Stress
- persons with marked physical or mental handicaps
- members of groups that encounter discrimination
- poverty-stricken persons
- persons with prior destructive familial or personal relations
- isolated persons
- persons who have suffered traumatic losses

Indicators of Stress
extent to which:
- discrepancy exists between personal objectives and environmental opportunities
- persons experience continuity and security in environmental setting
- person is part of supportive community and familial networks
- person possesses skills to navigate environment
- internal conflicts prevent person from understanding and coping with external world

Environmental Context
extent to which:
- environment is turbulent
- environment provides security
- environment is oppressive
- key components of environment can be altered

Personal Attributes
- coping skills
- cognitive skills
- level of physical health
- familial and community resources
- interpersonal skills
- material resources
- survival skills
- personal objectives

Selected Outcomes
- sense of self-esteem
- sense of competence
- mental suffering or anguish
- personal planning or coping behavior
- personal resilience
- appropriate assertiveness
- role fulfillment (in familial, community, and occupational roles)

complete a project, but many theorists argue that excessive levels of stress are not conducive to mental health.

Ecological Interventions

The following discussion outlines a number of interventions suggested by an ecological framework (see illustration 13.1).

Helping Persons Negotiate Their Environments. In some cases, persons are frustrated by personal objectives that lead them to develop dysfunctional relationships or make ill-advised choices. A person may enter a marriage, a job, or a personal relationship with unrealistic expectations, only to encounter a series of disappointments. Or a person may believe that he or she can achieve occupational success far beyond personal possibilities, an expectation that may foster a continuing sense of personal defeat. In other cases, persons may have overly modest objectives, as when one who expects never to be promoted creates a self-fulfilling prophecy. In similar fashion, some persons set occupational objectives so low that they never seek work that challenges or satisfies them. Mental health practitioners often *help persons develop objectives* conducive to establishing positive relations with persons and institutions in their environment.

In some cases, mental health practitioners help persons *work through destructive experiences* as those experiences influence current coping. For example, someone subjected to abuse by a parent may need help in fulfilling positive parenting roles as an adult. Another task of mental health services is to *provide consumers with skills* to cope with aspects of their environment. Nonassertiveness, for instance, may contribute to personal victimization by family members, employers, and others. In such cases, services are used to help the consumer develop new methods of relating to others. Or consumers may lack knowledge of available services and resources that in turn are useful in developing contacts, skills, or needed information.[2]

Mental health practitioners often help consumers *modify destructive habits,* as illustrated by projects to help persons with phobias, destructive health habits such as smoking, or obsessional thought patterns. In some cases, learning or behavioral strategies are effective, as when consumers receive positive reinforcement to modify habits and activities.[3]

Environmental Modification. In many cases, consumers need assistance in *developing new or modified environments.* A social worker may help a consumer establish residence in a halfway house or a physically disabled person find a living situation in which spatial arrangements do not jeopardize personal coping. In some cases, environmental modification involves efforts to help persons avoid or leave destructive relationships, as when a mental health practitioner helps a person terminate an ill-advised marriage. Persons may also be linked to community supports, as illustrated by referrals to self-help groups.

Social action activities should be integral to mental health services. If blighted communities, poverty, discrimination, and other destructive environmental factors create stress, then substantial effort should be given to modifying these influences. Consumers often need personal *advocacy* from mental health staff as well to assist them in obtaining benefits and resources to which they are entitled. In many cases, *consultative services* are offered to staff and community persons to facilitate additional supports for persons experiencing high levels of stress. In this perspective, mental health staff modify environments by helping police, hospital staff, court personnel, and family members to assist and relate with sensitivity to persons with mental problems.

Ecological Framework and Mental Health Policy. The ecological framework suggests that mental health staff members need to provide a range of services to help consumers develop constructive relationships, opportunities, and skills within their environmental context. Although persons are also assisted in discussing personal conflicts and past family relationships, emphasis is placed on helping them develop positive and growth-inducing interaction with their environment. Many mental health agencies and practitioners, by ignoring practical realities that intrude on consumers, ignore as well the economic, physical, political, peer, and community variables that precipitate and perpetuate current mental health problems.

Variability of Services

Although interpersonal, security, and other needs are shared by persons of all cultures, mental health interventions risk imposing values on others if deliberate effort is not made to shape them to the needs of different social classes, age groups, and racial, ethnic, and sexual minorities.

Persons with severe and chronic mental problems require different services than persons with temporary difficulties.

An ecological perspective must be adapted to the specific needs of individuals and groups. Since individuals differ profoundly in the level and kinds of stress they can tolerate, personal attributes must be considered when helping others obtain a satisfactory relationship with their environment. Considerable research suggests, for example, that schizophrenics cannot tolerate normal levels of stress in interpersonal, occupational, or family settings. Thus, a mental health worker who exhorts a schizophrenic to enter an occupation or training program that far

CASE EXAMPLE 13.2

The Cost of Money

Increasing Signs of Violent Discontent Seen among Teen-Age Children of the Privileged

By Blaine Harden
Washington Post Staff Writer

Out in America's promised land, in the suburbs and villages where the moneyed classes raise their families, there are increasing signs of a self-destructive, violent and perverse discontent among the children of privilege. . . .

In Potsdam, N.Y., the 24-year-old son of a prominent chemistry professor came home from his wanderings last fall and entered his parents' spacious home with a knife. Glenn Goodrich, a bright but aimless young man who friends said was always dwarfed by the brilliance of his father, stabbed Frank C. Goodrich in the heart as he lay asleep and forced his mother into the master bedroom to stare at the body. "Poor dad, I was proud of my father," Goodrich told his mother, as they stood beside the bed. Then, with his father's

blood, he wrote on the wallpaper above the bed: "The Horror."

Outside the Washington Hilton last March, another aimless young man from a privileged family allegedly attempted the ultimate American horror. John W. Hinckley Jr., who had failed to measure up to the success of his brother and sister, who had shrunk from the pressures of high school, whose name went unspoken when his oil-executive father talked of his successful children, stands charged with trying to kill the president of the United States.

Behind these spectacularly tragic examples of privileged kids gone wrong there is growing statistical evidence and near unanimity among mental health experts across the country that growing up affluent can be a curse as well as a blessing.

In the suburbs of major U.S. cities, the home of about 70 percent of the 3 million

exceeds his or her personal stress tolerance level may unwillingly encourage a traumatic setback. Similarly, persons differ in their notion of acceptable living arrangements; attachment to career; level of participation in neighborhood groups; and kinds of family arrangements that fulfill affectional and security needs. In addition, cultural differences influence the use of problem-solving techniques. As an example, Hispanics in the Southwest accord the father an extremely important role in family decision making; hence, noninclusion of the father in counseling with other family members can be a serious blunder.[4]

Staff in mental health agencies also need to adapt their services to the unique needs of persons from different social classes.[5] The insensitivity of many mental health staff members to the needs of poor persons has been widely documented. But affluent consumers also need services tailored to their needs. Mental problems of affluent adolescents are often ignored, for example, until suicides, drug abuse, or even homicides are committed. Although the affluent often have funds to seek assistance from psychiatrists and private mental hospitals, stigmatizing of children as black sheep often precludes the use of such services (see case example 13.2). Like low-income communities, then, affluent communities need outreach and early detection pro-

---

American families with annual incomes of more than $50,000, the curse seems to be getting increasingly destructive.

The rate of adolescent suicide has more than tripled in the United States since 1955, with even greater increases among white males in the affluent suburbs of Chicago, New York, San Francisco and Los Angeles.

In three villages on Chicago's North Shore "suicide belt," where 39 teen-agers took their lives in a recent 18-month period, the teen suicide rate has jumped 250 percent in the past decade and leads the rest of Illinois.

Drug and alcohol abuse among middle- and upper-class teen-agers has increased more rapidly than among the less wealthy. Sexual activity among unmarried white teenage girls has increased more sharply than among unmarried black teen-age girls. Upper-class teenagers have increased their participation in extremist cults.

The statistics suggest an unpublicized, poorly understood misery that lives underground in the suburbs amid carefully pruned appearances. Respectable families try to keep the neighbors from knowing about drug abuse, family violence, even suicide attempts.

But the parents and the teen-agers, the ones who survive, never forget the misery. And, for the most part, they'll talk only when promised anonymity.

Psychiatrists, sociologists, guidance counselors and juvenile court officials from affluent suburbs of Washington, New York, Boston, Chicago, Los Angeles and the super-rich enclave of Palm Beach, say that in the past 10 years they have seen a dramatic erosion in the ability of parents to control their adolescent children, combined with an increase in social and economic pressure on affluent teen-agers.

The experts offer a confused and confusing explanation of why things seem to be going wrong for an increasing number of middle- and upper-middle-class teen-agers: parents are too self-centered, too caught up in proving themselves to give their children love and attention. Tyrannical peer pressure forces adolescents to either follow a stifling, conformist track to professional success or to chuck it all, abandoning their ambitions to drugs, sex and self-loathing. Cruel economics mean that most affluent teen-agers, in an inflationary, slow-growth economy, will never be able to afford the kind of material luxury they now take for granted. . . .

Rich kids do not suffer in silence. They are far more likely than their less affluent peers to receive psychiatric attention and other professional care. It is the poor, not the middle and upper classes, who are overwhelmingly responsible for teen-age deliquency and crime. Rich kids who do get into trouble with the law are far likelier to avoid criminal prosecution than are the poor. . . .

But, for whatever reasons, a surprisingly large number of affluent adolescents, teenagers blessed with the best in education, health care and material comforts, are falling through the safety net that their parents' money provides. The consensus among the mental health experts who treat suburban teen-agers is that most adolescent failure begins at home.

For the minority of affluent teen-agers who wash out, the seeds of failure may have been sown in infancy, according to many psychiatrists.

The breakdown begins in the first few months of a child's life, when affluent, ambitious and busy parents do not take time to establish a presence for their child that is "consistent, continuous and caring," according to Dr. Eliot Sorel, a cultural psychiatrist and assistant professor of psychiatry at George Washington University Medical School. The failure to establish that bond in infancy colors the trust that children have for their parents throughout their adolescence, Sorel says.

In *Prisoners of Childhood*, a new book about how narcissistic parents deform the emotional lives of their children, Swiss psychoanalyst Alice Miller writes that insecure, confused parents can strip their infants of the chance to ever develop self-confidence. . . .

While it's impossible to isolate the precise causes of suicidal impulses and weak self-images among children, psychiatrists say they do see hazards in the increase in dual-income professional families and in high divorce rates.

According to a recent study by the marketing research firm of Yankelovich, Skelly & White, only 16 percent of all households now "fit the traditional concept of mother, father, and two children, with dad the breadwinner and mother staying home to care for the family."

Mental health experts say the increase in working women is a long-needed and healthy change for American women, but that it can play havoc with child-rearing as married couples are forced to juggle the demands of bosses, bill collectors and housework.

The stress imposed on parents and children in these dual-income families is the major mental health problem in the Washington area, according to Burton L. Kraff, a psychiatrist and director of admissions at the Psychiatric Institute of Washington.

Caught between the conflicting demands on their parents, children in these families are frequently raised by a parade of "surrogate" parents—servants or day-care centers—that reduce the chance of a strong bond developing between parent and child.

"The crisis hits," says Robert C. Weigl, a social psychologist in the affluent Mount Vernon area of Fairfax County, "when the kids become adolescents and their parents find they have no control over the kid because they don't know him that well."

Psychiatrists, school officials and sociologists have always guessed that divorce, with the almost inevitable confusion, insecurity and guilt that it imposes on children, is potentially a major cause of adolescent unhappiness and delinquency.

A sharp increase in the American divorce rate, which the government says has nearly tripled in the past 20 years and which has cut across all socio-economic lines, means there are far more children than ever subjected to divorce-related stress. The Census Bureau says nearly 13 million children live in one-parent homes, and the total is growing by more than a million a year.

Whether parents are divorced or not, psychiatrists interviewed across the country say they've seen a marked decline during the past decade in the quality of parent-child relationshps among many affluent families.

"I see parents who are refusing to be parents, who refuse to stand for something or say to their kids that there is right and wrong," says Dr. Bret Burquest, president of the American Society for Adolescent Psychiatry and a child psychiatrist who treats affluent families in West Los Angeles.

So many of the kids I work with have no specific time that they have to come home, no restrictions on their use of cars or credit cards. When there are no limits, these kids get very nervous," Burquest says.

The nervousness begins, psychiatrists say, when a child grows old enought to appreciate gifts, and soon realizes that there may be no limits to what he can have. Many affluent parents assuage their guilt for not giving more of their time by buying oodles of toys. . . .

On Chicago's North Shore, as in many rich suburban areas, parents constantly compare the grade point averages, scholastic aptitude test scores and advanced placement status of their children, says Isadora Sherman, a family counselor in Highland Park, Ill.

One mother at a recent parents meeting said she was worried about the "social adjustment" of her son because he'd received fewer bar mitzvah invitations than her daughter. In April, when college acceptance letters arrive in the mail, telephones ring continually as parents call around to find out who's been accepted to the Ivy League colleges.

Many affluent suburban parents seem to approach child rearing as if it were a competitive sport, with the final score determined by their offspring's educational credentials and professional income.

"The abysmal experience of being average with super-smart and successful parents puts enormous pressures on a teen-ager. The goals his parents set for him are often so far away that anything he can do will never measure up," says Dr. Dunn, at Springwood Psychiatric Institute in Leesburg. . . .

Part of the squeeze on teen-agers is demographic. Seniors in high school next fall will have the dubious distinction of having been born during the last year of the baby boom—the post-World War II explosion of American fertility that began in 1946 and waned in 1964.

High school seniors, along with all their younger teen-age peers, live in the shadow of the greatest population bulge in American history. Like diners who show up late for the feast, teen-agers and young adults are likely to find many of the tastiest opportunities already gone.

"The last baby boomers will grow up into a world already too crowded for them," writes Landon Y. Jones, in *Great Expectations—America & the Baby Boom Generation.* "Ahead of them, every base will be taken by their older brothers and sisters. . . . Throughout their lives they will face the prospect of salaries that were not quite as large as they hoped, devalued education, and difficult promotions."

The 1980 census found that the median age in America, the age at which half the population is older and half younger, is now 30. Accordingly, Madison Avenue has reaimed much of its pitch at the aging demographic bulge. Pepsi Cola no longer runs commercials "for those who think young." Middle-age women like Natalie Wood, not pubescent California blondes, now sell skin moisturizer on television. Levi Strauss has blue jeans for a 30-year-old market that's thicker around the waist than the skinny and shrinking teen-age market. . . .

Exacerbating the pressure on teen-agers, according to school counselors, sociologists and psychologists, is a move toward conformity in public schools and increasing intolerance of teen-agers who don't share the values of their friends.

Isadora Sherman, who's worked with adolescents in the Chicago suburbs for 30 years, says that teen-agers there have swung from being "cliquish and conformist" in the 1950s to "kicking those values" in the late '60s to an "obsessive concern with being successful" in the past five years.

A UCLA survey of 200,000 college freshmen over the past 11 years indicates that incoming college students are increasingly materialistic and conformist. In the past decade, the number of freshmen who said they are interested in being "well-off financially" doubled. . . .

For affluent teen-agers, especially young men, who either haven't the aptitude or the interest in traveling the narrow track through college and into demanding professional careers, there is growing pressure literally to get lost, according to Harvard sociologist David Reisman.

"There's a relatively small but absolutely large number of these young men who don't go to college. Who take menial jobs or just wander around. No one seems very interested. They are not obviously deprived, but they are obviously unhappy," says Reisman, the well-known author of several books dealing with affluent society, including *The Lonely Crowd*.

Reisman says that Hinckley, the accused assailant of President Reagan, fits the pattern of young men from successful families who fail to measure up to a standard of academic and social achievement and drift off into their own isolated worlds. Hinckley, like other sons of wealthy parents, received sufficient money from his parents to keep wandering.

There are no statistics on how many of these wandering sons of privilege there are across the country, but interviews with mental health authorities in six major metropolitan areas indicate the problem is common. . . .

SOURCE: *Washington Post,* July 4, 1981, pp. A1 ff. Reprinted by permission.

grams sensitive to familial, peer, and cultural factors.

Program Linkages

The ecological approach implies provision of mental health services that also link persons with resources in their environment. Unemployed persons may need career counseling, job training, sheltered workshops, or daycare services. All too often, practical necessities are not offered or are given in a passive manner; i.e., persons are referred from one agency to another without follow-up services. *Case managers* are needed in mental health clinics and agencies to monitor the progress of consumers and ascertain whether linkages have been accomplished. In the case of recurring needs, mental health agencies themselves may wish to supply occupational therapy, sheltered workshops, and other services.

Agency consortia are needed that systematically orchestrate interagency referrals. In some cases, mental health agencies should have funds for contracting with other allied agencies for specific services. The ecological framework suggests the need for *interprofessional teams* in which social workers, psychologists, psychiatrists, psychiatric nurses, and paraprofessionals collaborate. Few would doubt the utility of medications in assisting consumers with conditions like depression and psychosis. Equally obvious, however, is the need to couple medication with ongoing, multifaceted services that help them cope within their environmental context.

Prevention

Like poverty, stress does not occur randomly; certain kinds of persons experience more stress than others (see illustration 13.1). Far more research is needed to identify "at risk" populations and to devise interventions that provide educational and other services to help such populations avert subsequent problems.[6] Even in the absence of research, however, existing social science knowledge suggests that groups subject to high levels of stress include persons who have lost spouses or children, persons experiencing marital conflict, runaways, women seeking jobs after long periods of absence from the job market, persons making major life decisions, such as choosing whether or not to have an abortion, and persons subject to serious health crises. Outreach is needed for persons in these and other "at risk" populations prior to the emergence of mental problems. In some cases, social workers should help consumers develop self-help groups that can provide such populations with educational materials. Services are also needed that assist persons in early stages of problem development, including hot line, crisis intervention, and storefront services.

ASSESSMENT OF EXISTING MENTAL HEALTH SERVICES

Many critics argue that American mental health services require substantial reforms, criticism reflected in the recommendations of the President's Commission on Mental Health in 1978.[7] Various issues in the mental health sector are discussed in the following section of this chapter in the context of prevailing policies and contextual factors.

Effectiveness

No programs are more difficult to evaluate than mental health programs, particularly in light of the numerous treatment approaches and sometimes conflicting assessments of specific patients by different mental health professionals. Divergent opinions about diagnosis and treatment are most evident when psychiatrists offer opposing viewpoints in courtrooms. Still, many critics agree that existing services are defective in their treatment of both chronic and acute problems.

Persons with Severe and Recurring Problems. One major criticism of American services is that apparent successes are often mistaken for major gains. For example, although state hospital patient-care episodes declined from 818,832 in 1955 to 651,857 in 1973, many consumers were transferred to other facilities, including nursing homes and board-and-care facilities, where they often received services just as inferior as those in custodial state hospitals. Many other severely ill persons were returned to families that were unable to cope with their problems.

The ecological framework discussed earlier in this chapter provides little reason to be hopeful about the prognosis for severely ill and often psychotic persons under such conditions. Research suggests that they need an environment that provides sufficient challenges to enable them to gradually develop occupational and interpersonal capacities but that also buffers them from familial, interpersonal, and occupational demands that precipitate relapse. Persons with chronic conditions, then, need careful monitoring of their progress, skillful linkages to employment and community networks, "fine-tuning" of medications to avoid the twin perils of overmedication and undermedication, and halfway and other supportive housing arrangements.[8]

Case example 13.3 suggests, however, that development of halfway houses is often thwarted by political, zoning, and legal barriers. Vocational opportunities are often lacking because many persons with chronic conditions cannot find jobs that do not expose them to high levels of stress. Some persons also encounter discrimination from employers. Americans have developed no coherent set of policies for the chronically mentally ill other than a "hands off" policy that provides them with subsidies for minimal living expenses and requires them to negotiate housing and labor markets by themselves. Critics note as well that numbers of admissions have risen sharply even as the numbers of long-term residents in mental institutions have declined, a "revolving door" phenomena that is exacerbated by the inadequacy of community programs providing mentally ill persons with supportive services.

CASE EXAMPLE 13.3

Mentally Ill as Neighbors—Legal Test

Halfway Houses

By Keith Love
Times Staff Writer

Carolyn Harris and Max Schneier have never met, but they have at least one thing in common: Both have had to cope with mental illness in their families.

But whereas Harris was able to get help for her relative and see the situation stabilize fairly quickly, Schneier got more and more involved—until he became one of America's foremost experts on the rehabilitation of the mentally ill.

Now, they are on opposite sides of a dispute that has gone to the state Supreme Court. The outcome, according to state officials and mental health experts, could have a major impact on the treatment of the mentally ill in California.

Seeds of Dispute

Harris, a supermarket checker, has lived for 30 years in a house she owns on a quiet street in Torrance, a bustling South Bay community dominated by oil refineries and huge manufacturing plants.

Two years ago an organization started by Schneier, a retired businessman, put 15 people suffering from mental illness into a large house—a former nursing home—next door to Harris. The group, Transitional Living Centers, or TLC, is licensed by the state of California and has a contract with Los Angeles County.

Soon after TLC opened, a resident of Harris' street took a petition around and got the support of many people who, like Harris, thought that the halfway house was not good for the neighborhood.

Later, the city of Torrance sued to get the center removed, saying it had not applied for a conditional use permit before moving in its clients.

'A Critical Need'

Transitional Living Centers tries to do what mental health experts believe is the most important thing anyone can do for people who are mentally ill: Give them self-confidence in social situations and teach them marketable skills so that they can lead normal lives. It has been highly praised by state and county officials and by leading authorities in the field of mental health care.

"There is a critical need for transitional, residential rehabilitation programs like TLC," Dr. Richard Elper, director of mental health for Los Angeles County, said. "They would allow us to move more people out of hospitals and therapeutic facilities."

For more than a decade California has been transforming its treatment of the mentally ill, emphasizing rehabilitation in the community and avoiding placement in state mental hospitals if at all possible. On one level, the change has been successful. A decade ago, there were 20,000 people in California's mental hospitals; today there are 5,000.

But on another, more crucial, level, the transformation has run into problems. Few residential areas are willing to let halfway houses like TLC locate in their neighborhoods.

As a result, many mentally ill patients wind up in what is known as a board and care home. While a few of these homes provide a cheerful atmosphere and vocational activities, most are nothing more than warehouses—in semi-industrial areas and poor residential neighborhoods.

The patients in such homes, most of whom are stablized by prescribed drugs, do little more than exist. They watch television all day or sit for hours and stare at the walls. They smoke cigarettes and drink coffee.

By comparison, the Transitional Living Center in Torrance is on a shady block of single-family homes and new condominiums. There is a shopping center nearby, and the bustling shops and offices along Hawthorne Boulevard are less than a mile away.

"Clients," as the patients are called at TLC, must be engaged in some vocational activity as soon as they enter the program. They spend only their nights in the Torrance halfway house, or in a similar house in Hawthorne.

A staff of professionals and paraprofessionals keeps the clients on a structured program at TLC's rehabilitation center in Hawthorne. It includes teaching them clerical and janitorial skills, as well as crafts.

It is this atmosphere that mental health experts believe is vital if the community rehabilitation process is going to work.

"This is normal," Schneier said recently as he walked through the neighborhood in Torrance where TLC's 15-person home is situated. But in most communities, he said, "the attitude toward the halfway houses is, 'Great idea, but not on my block.' "

Dr. James Barter, deputy director for clinical services with the state Department of Mental Health, said, "The state needs to better educate the public in order to destigmatize mental illness.

"There have been significant advances in medications. But once the chronically mentally ill are stablized, they need a supportive environment and appropriate activities."

Typically, Barter said, homeowners confronted with the opening of a halfway house in their neighborhood worry that the value of their property will go down. Some fear that the mental patients may harm them.

However, in the Torrance case, neither fear seems to have materialized.

No Problems Foreseen

Jim Clark, an architect who recently built condominiums on the block where TLC opened its house, said he did not think the center would affect his sales.

"I haven't even thought about it," Clark said, "My problem is high interest rates."

He said that several other condominiums on the block had sold for high prices since Transitional Living Centers moved in.

Another resident of the street, Don Horn, said that when he heard the center had opened, his immediate reaction was, "It shouldn't be on this street." He said he did not know what the center did or what kind of people lived there.

Now, he said, he has not thought about the halfway house for some time. "I believe in live and let live," he added.

Transitional Living Centers has 73 clients in all. Its director, Dr. Kenneth A. Parker, said that after two years of operations, the program is just getting to the point where it can place some clients in their own apartments and ensure that they have steady jobs.

He gave a tour of two other residences in the South Bay area where TLC clients live. One, an apartment in Hawthorne for four women who do not require much supervision, represents the middle stage of the TLC program.

The other is a home in Redondo Beach for six people. Like the clients in the Torrance house, they need supervision at night. Evelyn Echols, the "house mother," described the atmosphere as supportive—"but always with the idea that they must learn to do for themselves."

Most of TLC's clients are in their 20s and 30s, and suffer from schizophrenia and manic depressive illness. Most are on prescribed medication and have their own doctors or see county doctors, and most have also been in California mental hospitals. Parker said the center will not accept people with drug or alcohol problems.

Unlike its experience with the larger home in Torrance, TLC had no trouble with municipal officials over the two smaller residences, probably because state law makes it very hard for communities to bar halfway houses for six or fewer people.

The law is less clear on homes for more than six people. But John McDermott, TLC's lawyer, argues that Section 5120 of the Welfare Institutions Code prohibits discrimination against facilities for outpatient psychiatric care in areas zoned for other health facilities, such as hospitals and nursing homes. . .

Persons with Acute Disorders.   Many mental illnesses can be treated in outpatient facilities, whether by physicians, community agencies, or outpatient hospital departments. Here, too, serious questions have been raised about the effectiveness of services. Some critics question the relevance of the activities of many professionals to persons from low-income and racial minority groups. Many therapies are based on the often mistaken assumption that consumers wish to engage in lengthy verbal interactions with staff members who probe internal conflicts. Repeated surveys in one state suggested that low-income persons are underrepresented in caseloads of many state-funded community clinics, but exhortations and policy regulations from public officials have had little effect.[9]

Primary-care physicians, not mental health professionals, are the major providers of mental health services (see illustration 13.2). Most mental health services are delivered not by psychiatrists, psychologists, or social workers but by physicians who encounter large numbers of depressed, anxious, or otherwise troubled patients. Few of these physicians have had training in mental health services. In many cases, they prescribe medications such as valium without inquiring into the causes and seriousness of mental health problems. Few physicians have recourse to mental health personnel in their practices, and many resist referrals to psychiatrists (still distrusted by many of them) even when patients exhibit bizarre behavior. Policies are needed to facilitate referrals of patients to mental health personnel or to station such personnel within primary care medical facilities.[10]

Prevention.   Little attention is given to preventive services in the mental health system. Even in federally funded community mental health centers, which are mandated to provide such services, only 4 percent of staff time is given to "consultation and education." Mental health services are overwhelmingly biased toward institutional programs or toward "clinical hours" spent with persons with established mental health symptoms, to the detriment of educational, early detection, and outreach projects.[11]

Magnitude of Services.   A telling criticism of mental health services is not that public funds are wasted but that current funding is wholly inadequate to provide more than a fraction of needed services. When Medicare and Medicaid were enacted in 1965, policymakers emphasized that these programs funded traditional medical services. Almost as an afterthought, some minor outpatient funding for mental health was included in the insurance program for the elderly (Medicare), but on terms distinctly less favorable than those for medical or institutional services. Thus, the elderly were limited to $250 in out-

ILLUSTRATION 13.2   **Estimated Percent Distribution of Persons with Mental Disorder, by Treatment Setting, United States, 1975**

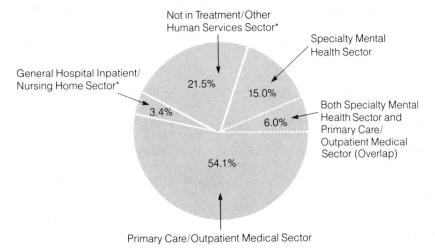

Not in Treatment/Other
Human Services Sector*

Specialty Mental
Health Sector

General Hospital Inpatient/
Nursing Home Sector*

21.5%

15.0%

3.4%

6.0%

Both Specialty Mental
Health Sector and
Primary Care/
Outpatient Medical
Sector (Overlap)

54.1%

Primary Care/Outpatient Medical Sector

Note: Data relating to sectors other than the specialty mental health sector reflect the number of patients with mental disorder seen in those sectors without regard to the amount or adequacy of treatment provided.
* Excludes overlap of an unknown percent of persons also seen in other sectors. SOURCE: U.S. President's Commission on Mental Health, *Report to the President,* Vol. 2, p. 53.

patient mental health subsidies in a particular year and had also to pay one-half the cost of those services. (Compare this with the requirement that they pay only 20 percent of physical health costs or with the fact that Medicare funds a lifetime total of 190 days in psychiatric or convalescent settings.) These minimal outpatient benefits have not been increased since 1965, and inflation has eroded more than 50 percent of their value.

The medical insurance program for the poor (Medicaid) was hardly more munificent. First, only 33 percent of persons living beneath official poverty lines participate in the Medicaid program. Second, federal Medicaid legislation was vague in its mental health provisions, indicating only that states had to supply "outpatient mental health services." But many states have minimized mental health subsidies by sharply limiting the number of outpatient visits covered, insisting that consumers pay a significant fraction of costs, and allowing such low levels of reim-

bursement that most providers refuse to serve Medicaid consumers. As an example, Maryland authorized payments of six dollars per clinical hour with psychiatrists in 1975, a sum far less than prevailing rates.[12]

Despite improvements, mental health benefits in private medical insurance have uncertain status as well. Because most Americans purchase medical insurance primarily for physical illnesses and also want to pay low premiums, certain insurance companies are cautious about extending mental health coverage when competing companies do not. Unlike traditional physician–patient medical transactions that consist of a few brief visits, mental health services are labor-intensive, i.e., require numerous clinical hours. Many insurance companies fear opening Pandora's box even though evidence indicates that mental health visits often decrease utilization of medical services by alleviating stress-induced illnesses and diverting consumers who would otherwise use physicians for mental health services.

CASE EXAMPLE 13.4

Association Hits Changes in Federal Insurance Program

Cutbacks in Mental Health Coverage

NASW has told the House Subcommittee on Compensation and Employee Benefits that recommended changes in the Federal Employees Health Benefits Program are unequitable and discriminatory.

Harold Bussell, president of the Franklin County Mental Health Board in Columbus, Ohio, testifying on behalf of the association, said NASW is opposed to:

- proposed cutbacks in mental health coverage;

- discrimination against social workers and other mental health providers not covered as vendors in some FEHBP plans;

- the contract negotiations process for FEHBP plans which excludes employee representatives;

- an arbitrary shift to a longer interval between FEHBP "open seasons," periods during which non-participating employees may enroll and participating employees may change plans;

- a change which would make Medicare a secondary provider instead of a primary one for those covered by Medicare and FEHBP.

The cutbacks in mental health coverage, backed by Blue Cross/Blue Shield, a provider, and by the federal Office of Personnel Management, which negotiates with insurers for FEHBP coverages, are being considered, according to OPM, because of demand for improvements in dental coverage.

Existing restraints prevent additions of new benefits without corresponding reductions or modification of old ones. NASW understands the program's fiscal restrictions, Bussell told subcommittee members, "but why was mental health singled out?"

OPM claims that mental health benefits coverage is one of the most costly. That, combined with OPM's opinion that "mental conditions do not lend themselves to definitive diagnosis or courses of treatment, making it virtually impossible to effectively control utilization," led to the recommended increases in coverage.

Bussell responded to that justification by saying that while Blue Cross/Blue Shield is quick to point to statistical data on the cost of mental health care, it does not offer comparable data for treatment for other major illnesses such as cancer, heart disease, or childhood maladies. "We are not suggesting," he said, "that benefits should have been reduced for treatment of any specific illness; we are suggesting, however, that a solid case has not been made for the reduction in mental health benefits."

The recommended changes, added Bussell, run counter to recommendations in the President's Commission on Mental Health report, which states that "the federal government also should encourage private insurers to provide mental health benefits comparable to general health benefits . . . There should be minimal patient-borne cost sharing for emergency care. In all other instances, patient-borne cost sharing, through copayments and deductibles for evaluation, diagnosis, and short-term therapy, should be no greater than that for a comparable course of physical illness."

Not only do current plans sell mental health care short, Bussell said, they discriminate against social workers and other mental health professionals. Despite all the available evidence that social work services help relieve mental illness as much as care provided by other mental health professionals, and often less expensively, the Office of Personnel Management refuses to recognize professionally trained clinical social workers as independent, qualified mental health providers.

"Such recognition," said Bussell, "could substantially reduce the cost of providing mental health benefit coverage to federal employees, without reducing the quality of care and treatment."

Bussell then told the subcommittee that it is patently unfair to limit contract negotiations to representatives of OPM and the insurance industry. Federal employees, he said, pay at least forty percent of the program's costs and certainly should have their say. And while it is well documented that the medical profession exerts considerable influence on the insurance industry, other professional provider groups are virtually excluded from the process. "We urge," Bussell said, "that a mechanism be created to provide an opportunity for participation of all parties who have a vital interest in the results of the negotiations."

In opposing a precipitous extension of the period of time between "open season" enrollments, Bussell pointed out that, again, employees have not been privvy to discussions which might foreshadow such a change. The open season is designed in large part to accommodate those who mistakenly enrolled in one FEHBP program or another and wish to drop out or switch. "Prior to any change in open enrollment season," said Bussell, "we recommend the establishment of an improved consumer insurance education program directed at the education of federal employees."

Finally, Bussell attacked the proposed changes in the relationship between Medicare and FEHBP as recommended by the Senate Finance Committee and the House Ways and Means Committee in Congress. Under these changes, FEHBP would become the primary payer for claims filed on behalf of retired federal employees who continue their supplementary medical insurance coverage with one of the participating FEHBP plans.

Such a change would mean savings for the federal government, because federal employees premiums pay a large percentage of the cost for coverage under FEHBP, but nothing under Medicaid.

NASW believes that such a system, by setting aside federal employees as the only group of older Americans whose primary coverage is not Medicare, could be discriminatory. In addition, said Bussell, "we do not know whether advocates for these changes see this as a final step of a plan to reduce the cost of Medicare or a first step in plans to eliminate the federal responsibility in providing health care for all Americans."

Many private insurance companies and public funders also exclude payments to social workers preferring to limit reimbursement to psychiatrists and hospitals. In some states, social workers can be reimbursed for mental health services, but only when they work "under the supervision" of psychiatrists. This vague requirement, one also used by administrators of Medicaid in many states, can be interpreted as requiring work on the same premises as supervising physicians, a restrictive interpretation that impedes use of social work services.[13] (See case example 13.4 for discussion of barriers to mental health coverage for services of social workers under the Federal Employees Health Benefits program.)

Equity and Equality

Preceding discussion suggests the existence of at least three different mental health systems.[14] Affluent persons use private psychiatric hospitals and psychiatrists (*system 1*). To the extent that their insurance does not cover them, they purchase services from personal funds. The very poor have little access to funding for outpatient services and are major users of state hospitals and psychiatric services within county and municipal hospitals (*system 2*). Blue-collar families use the first two systems as well but are also consumers of services of federally funded community mental health centers and social agencies (*system 3*). This latter group, like the poor, cannot afford private psychiatric hospitals and must often use state hospitals. Members of *all* social classes make significant use of physicians to receive various medications for symptoms like anxiety and depression. (The poor must often use emergency room personnel.) The advantage to the affluent of system 1 is that it allows a range of institutional and outpatient services from highly trained professionals, in contrast to the poor, who often have access only to institutional services.

Gross inequalities also exist between regions. There is only 1 psychiatrist per 25,000 persons in rural states like Alabama, in comparison to 1 per 5,000 persons in urban states like New York.

Most psychiatrists and increasing numbers of social workers set up their practices in suburban rather than inner-city areas. As in the provision of medical services, then, persons with identical symptoms often receive strikingly different services depending on places of residence.

POOR LAW TRADITIONS AND THE ERA OF INSTITUTIONS: COLONIAL PERIOD TO 1950

As a brief overview makes clear, American policy in the mental health sector has swung like a pendulum first toward and then away from the use of mental institutions. During the colonial period and well into the nineteenth century, the mentally ill were treated as a subgroup of the poor both because they could not work in an era that emphasized and needed manual labor and because little was known about the treatment of mental illness other than the use of physical restraints and severe measures such as burning or dousing unfortunate victims in water. They were variously placed in almshouses, with families who were paid to take care of them, and in correctional facilities.

Placement of the mentally ill in almshouses was extremely undesirable for a number of reasons—e.g., many were placed in dungeonlike rooms under physical restraints. Dorothea Dix and a series of reformers in the mid–nineteenth century exposed brutish conditions in the almshouses and promoted specialized institutions for the mentally ill. Dix approached legislatures in numerous states, sought state financing of institutions to receive mentally ill persons from local jurisdictions, and was successful in more than thirty states. She failed, however, to obtain donations to the states of federal lands that could then be sold to finance institutions.[15]

These institutional reformers advocated special kinds of institutions that, they hoped, would eventually eliminate mental illness. Mental illness was thought to reflect a sinful and deviant life-style that could be cured only through a regimen of "moral treatment." In relatively small institutions separated from cities to remove occupants from competitiveness and unwholesome influences, a physician superintendent and a cadre of assistants prescribed a schedule of work, recreation, and worship designed to get the mentally ill to voluntarily alter their behavior. The reformers were convinced that their "moral treatment" was far more successful then the still common use of physical restraints and pointed to high rates of discharge. Indeed, many of these residents had a more therapeutic environment than modern schizophrenics left to wander communities without supportive services.[16]

But the promise of institutions was not realized for numerous practical reasons. The "moral treatment" pioneers had envisioned institutions that would help persons from all social classes, including fee-paying consumers. With massive increases in immigration from Europe before and after the Civil War, however, mental institutions were increasingly filled with impoverished immigrants who often were unwilling to tolerate the strict and sometimes religious regimens of superintendents. Affluent persons increasingly used private institutions, and many localities began to refer senile and sick elderly persons from almshouses to institutions—another group unlikely to respond to "moral treatment." Further, many jurisdictions relaxed relatively restrictive laws governing involuntary commitments in the early part of this century, resulting in considerable violation of personal rights both on admittance and in unwarranted retention within the institution.[17] By the turn of this century, then, many state mental health facilities were custodial in nature.

Prior to this century, few outpatient (i.e., community-based) mental health services existed, partly because of the dearth of accepted theory regarding the causes and treatment of mental illness. By the 1920s, however, the theories of the Austrian psychoanalyst Sigmund Freud had taken the United States by storm (he had far less influence in European countries). At last, a seemingly comprehensive theory of human behavior had been developed that could be used for the millions of "neurotic" Americans who needed services but did not need to be institutionalized.

Freud had few competitors in the 1920s. Prior to the First World War, social work theorists like Mary Richmond had developed simplistic but nonetheless ecological frameworks for social intervention, but social workers in the 1920s were as enamored with Freudian theory as psychiatrists. Jane Addams ruefully noted late in the decade that social workers and reformers alike had abandoned social reform and the poor in their fascination with the workings of the inner psyche.[18] In any case, a national network of nonprofit community agencies grew up in the early part of this century, including nonprofit family counseling and child guidance agencies that provided the bulk of community-based, nonphysician services until the establishment of federally funded community mental health centers in the 1960s.

Mental health services were hardly on the agenda of New Deal reformers in the 1930s because their importance was outweighed by economic securities programs like public assistance and public works. The Second World War brought renewed interest in mental health in response to the needs of many soldiers who had suffered wartime mental illnesses and with whom a variety of group, behavioral, and counseling interventions seemed to be effective. Legislation was enacted in 1946 establishing a National Institute of Mental Health to spearhead research into mental illness.

ERA OF DEINSTITUTIONALIZATION: 1950–1968

The federal government assumed a major funding role in the mental health sector for the first time with passage of the Community Mental Health Centers Act in 1963. Many critics wondered, however, whether the act was little more than a bandaid in light of the needs of hundreds of thousands of mentally ill persons who now lived in community rather than institutional settings.

Causes of Deinstitutionalization

Two explanations have been posited for the drastic decline in populations in public mental hospitals in the 1950s and 1960s (illustration 13.3). Some think deinstitutionalization was caused by technical developments and administrative changes. Vast numbers of Americans were able, with the help of symptom-reducing medications, to maintain family and job roles, even though medications did not address the basic causes of illness. Even prior to massive introduction of drugs, administrators of state hospitals had increased rates of discharge by abolishing "chronic wards" where many patients had been placed and given a "no recovery possible" diagnosis. These wards were increasingly eliminated in favor of wards where patients were grouped by their place of origin, a development that decreased the extent of labelling patients as incurable. Finally, some jurisdictions enacted

legislation that placed limits on involuntary commitments; increasingly, consumers could be involuntarily committed only if shown to constitute a physical and imminent danger to themselves or others. "Bizarre behavior," "transiency," threatened suicide, reported hallucinations or delusions, or even verbal threats against others were interpeted by many officials as insufficent grounds for commitment or as grounds for commitment only for a limited period of observation.[19]

A more cynical interpretation of deinstitutionalization is advanced by those who argue that it represented a method of avoiding costly services to assist the mentally ill. Institutional services, even custodial ones, are expensive because of building and staff costs. By providing mental health patients bare subsistence welfare payments, legislators and government officials could send them into unregulated and inexpensive community living arrangements.[20] Indeed, data in illustration 13.4 suggests that decreases in residency in state mental hospitals by white females were offset by increases in numbers residing in nursing homes.

ILLUSTRATION 13.3   Inpatient and Outpatient Care Episodes in Mental Health Facilities: 1955 and 1975

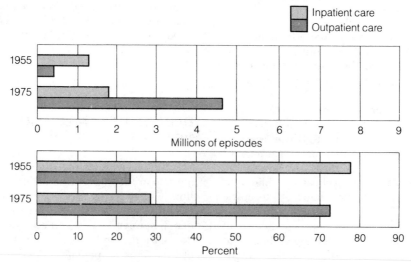

SOURCE: U.S. Department of Commerce, Bureau of the Census, *Social Indicators III*, 1980, p. 68.

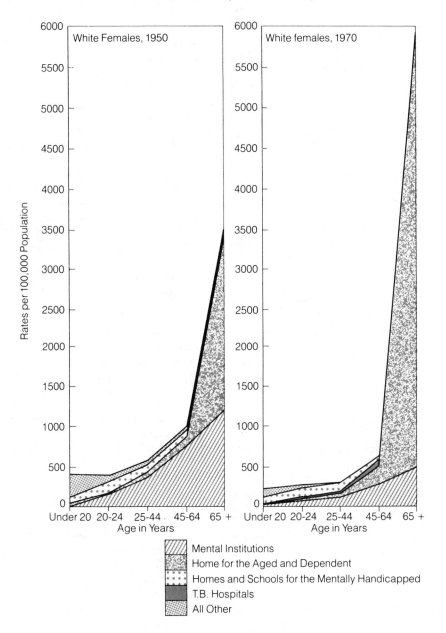

ILLUSTRATION 13.4 Number of Persons in Institutions per 100,000
Population by Type of Institution, by Age:
White Females, United States, 1950 and 1970

White Females, 1950

White females, 1970

Rates per 100,000 Population

Age in Years

Age in Years

Mental Institutions
Home for the Aged and Dependent
Homes and Schools for the Mentally Handicapped
T.B. Hospitals
All Other

Reprinted in U.S. President's Commission on Mental Health, *Report to the President*, vol. 2,
1978, p. 74. SOURCE: U.S. Bureau of the Census, Persons in Institutions, 1950 & 1970.

Deinstitutionalization: The Positive Side

Researchers have documented that many patients develop "institutionalism" when placed in mental hospitals. In the case of schizophrenics, some withdraw permanently into hallucinations, delusions, and dependent behavior. The probability of release also decreases the longer that persons remain in institutions and become accustomed to institutional regimens. Even in inadequate board-and-care homes, consumers at least retain clothing and other symbols of their identity and are allowed to come and go.[21]

Deinstitutionalization: The Negative Side

Whatever its causes, deinstitutionalization was not accompanied by community planning. Unlike the English, who have developed a national system of social services, Americans have not created local cadres of social workers and other staff persons to provide multifaceted, ecological interventions to severely disturbed individuals. Medicaid subsidies allowed the elderly and young to reside in community residential and nursing home placements, and subsidies provided by the federal Supplementary Security Income program covered costs of halfway houses and board-and-care homes as well as the nursing home costs of many mentally disabled individuals. But federal subsidies for community living costs fostered a "quick fix" mentality by many state officials, who often discharged patients, used federal subsidies to replace costs of maintenance of institutions, and then did not provide funding for a range of community services. Nor have federal authorities been willing to supplement Medicaid, SSI, and Medicare living subsidies with massive funding of social services, sheltered workshops, public jobs for the mentally disabled, and construction costs of community residential facilities.

Instead, many private entrepreneurs have taken the initiative in developing board-and-care, hotel, and nursing home residences, many of dubious quality. Further, widespread opposi-

tion to board-and-care and halfway facilities has meant that many are located in blighted areas where persons in need of low-stress environments are subject to criminal assaults, poor housing conditions, and lack of recreational facilities and stable employment. No set of local, state, or national policymakers has wanted to assume responsibility for released patients—they are given subsidies and allowed to use whatever the private market develops. Although some entrepreneurs provide quality services, repeated scandals suggest that many perceive the mentally ill primarily as a source of revenue, and they are seldom equipped, in any event, to help them with the problems of daily living.

In this perspective, deinstitutionalization represents a pyrrhic victory. Some commentators suggest that the percentage of the population in institutions has not really changed; instead, they are now living in various community facilities.

Community Mental Health Movement

Many critics also realized that the nation lacked a network of community facilities that could provide short-term and emergency institutional services, counseling for persons with a wide variety of problems, and preventive services. In 1955, Congress established the Joint Commission on Mental Illness and Health to analyze community services and devise recommendations; although some of its members wanted to upgrade and expand state hospitals, the majority opted for community facilities to provide these services. In its landmark 1961 report entitled *Action for Mental Health,* the commission recommended prompt federal legislation to fund these local services.[22] With the support of President John Kennedy, sensitized to mental health issues because of a developmentally disabled sister, the Community Mental Health Centers Act was passed in 1963 that mandated initial federal funding for centers in catchment areas of between 75,000 and 200,000 persons. Basic services to be provided by these centers included outpatient, limited inpatient, and preventive services. Because the American Medical Association and some conservatives objected, money was authorized only for construction costs, a deficit remedied in 1965 when funds for staff were included.

Strengths of CMHCs. Community mental health centers (CMHCs) now constitute a major source of mental health care in the United States. They serve persons who ordinarily could not obtain private psychiatric services and who often have no insurance coverage (52 percent of CMHC users earn less than $100 per week). Further, they serve persons with a wide variety of mental conditions, including depression (13 percent), neuroses (21 percent), schizophrenia (10 percent), substance abuse (13 percent), childhood disorders (13 percent), and persons with "social maladjustment" (22 percent). Psychiatrists constitute only 3 percent of their fulltime staff, in contrast to social workers (11 percent) and psychiatric nurses (9 percent).[23]

Weaknesses of CMHCs. Intended to provide major services to persons released from mental institutions, to the poor, to youth, and to the elderly, CMHCs have been strikingly remiss on all these counts. Partly because of turf rivalries with state hospitals but also because many of their professionals prefer to work with less disturbed persons, many CMHCs serve few deinstitutionalized patients. In addition, since many centers were established in suburban areas in the wake of passage of the initial legislation and were attached to hospitals under psychiatric leadership, traditional psychiatric interventions were often used rather than interventions relevant to low-income or blue-collar populations. Although 1975 amendments required more services to the elderly and young, only 4 percent of services are given to persons over age sixty-five.[24]

In fairness to the centers, it must be said that many obstacles have been created for them by public authorities. Because no other source of funding exists for mental health services for blue-collar and many middle-class families, they have flocked to CMHCs, making it difficult for overworked staff to conduct outreach to groups less likely to come forward (e.g., the poor, the elderly, and released mental patients). A gradual federal phase-out of funds to specific centers was mandated in the original legislation to promote eventual local funding of centers, but local funds have often not been forthcoming. While exhorting centers to provide preventive services, most funders, federal and state alike, reimburse on the basis of traditional clinical hours, thereby discouraging innovative services, including those very preventive services.[25] The CMHCs encountered hostility from Presidents Richard Nixon and Gerald Ford, who provided funding only reluctantly and insisted that the centers obtain larger shares of funds from fees and insurance payments, policies certain to exclude the poor.

Some deficits of CMHCs have been partially remedied in legislation. At successive points, funding has been continued to centers that had exhausted federal funds, and special funds have been provided for centers in low-income areas. Legislation in 1975 required centers to provide services to the elderly and children and, 1979 amendments mandated greater emphasis on preventive programs, development of consumer advocacy programs, and strengthening of planning by state authorities.

ERA OF UNCERTAINTY: BEYOND 1968

President Jimmy Carter signed the Mental Health Systems Act in 1980, legislation that incorporated many of the recommendations of the aforementioned President's Commission on Mental Illness. The legislation established a series of special grants to the states for programs that targeted mental health services to neglected groups like the elderly, severely disturbed children and adolescents, and chronically mentally ill persons. Funds for the latter group were to be used to help them find housing, provide supportive services, and train personnel to work with them. Further, community mental health centers were required to provide daycare and partial hospitalization, halfway houses, and drug and alcohol abuse programs, services that had previously been optional. They were also required to establish programs for children and elderly persons with mental problems.

Two provisions of the Mental Health Systems Act prompted considerable controversy that almost led its defeat. First, officials who favored increasing the roles of state planning agencies wanted to give state mental health authorities the power to allocate federal community mental health funds, a policy resisted by CMHCs, which had hitherto received funds directly from national authorities. Second, Senators Edward Kennedy and Jacob Javits sought to make states adopt a patient "bill of rights" that would require local providers to explain treatments, their risks, and alternative remedies to consumers and to provide individualized treatment plans, grievance procedures, and freedom from restraint or seclusion for hospitalized patients except in restricted circumstances. Many mental health professionals as well as representatives of mental institutions feared such policies would unduly limit their interventions, a contention questioned by consumer advocates, who insisted that rights of consumers continued to be violated in many jurisdictions. Last-minute compromises averted a stalemate on these two issues. States were given the right to fund local centers, but the latter could appeal to federal authorities if they believed they were being treated unfairly. The legislation was worded to make the patient bill of rights a recommended but strictly optional policy for states.

If the Mental Health Systems Act strengthened policy roles of federal authorities by requiring states to target resources to neglected populations, the policies of the Reagan Administration threatened to give states far greater policy authority in mental health.[26] In the Omnibus Budget Reconciliation Act of 1981, categorical community mental health, alcohol, and drug abuse programs were consolidated in the alcohol, drug abuse, and mental health block grant. While some legislators favored giving states complete autonomy, advocates of the various categorical programs suceeded in placing restrictions on the states that would, at least in the short term, guarantee the continuation of those programs even with the establishment of block grants. States were required to allocate to community mental health programs a substantial portion of their share of the $491 million provided for the block grant and were specifically required to continue funding each community mental health center that had received federal funds in 1981.

Still, many critics wondered if the short-term restrictions placed on states would not eventually be removed, allowing relatively conservative states to withdraw funds from mental health programs. Others wondered if states would target services to neglected populations as mandated by the now-defunct Mental Health Systems Act of 1980. Most serious, though, were sharp funding cuts in the Reagan Administration. The funds allocated to the block grant required local jurisdictions to absorb a 25 percent cut in the funds given to the federal categorical programs. As important, the notion that federal funding of community mental health centers should end after their first eight years of operation was not altered in the Carter or Reagan administrations. Yet recent research suggests that centers that lose major public funding tend to resort to traditional psychiatric models of services reimbursable by private insurance to the detriment of a range of community, preventive, consultative, and other innovative and needed programs.[27]

REFORMING MENTAL HEALTH SERVICES

Many obstacles frustrate efforts to reform mental health policies and funding. As noted in previous discussion, mental health services are labor intensive, i.e., require many hours of staff time per consumer. Therefore, liberalization of insurance coverage or government funding is perceived by many to invite runaway costs. Costs of developing a national network of housing, halfway house, day treatment center, vocational training, and subsidized employment projects for those with chronic and serious mental conditions would be considerable.

Many officials still believe that mental health

services belong to local jurisdictions; even the federal initiative to devise community mental health centers has been perceived by many to represent seed money to be terminated at the earliest possible moment.

Any effort at reform must also address the fragmentation of existing mental health services and funding. Services are provided or funded by Medicare, Medicaid, Supplementary Security Income payments for the disabled (SSI), private health insurance, state mental institutions, nursing homes, board-and-care homes, community mental health centers, private hospitals, outpatient clinics, and tens of thousands of private practitioners drawn from the ranks of the psychiatry, psychology, social work, and counseling professions. No wonder many international observers view American mental health services as chaotic. Despite periodic scandals about conditions in state mental institutions and board-and-care homes, there is a lack of sustained political pressure by those who seek major reforms.

Selected Reforms in Scanning and Analysis Phases

Needed reforms in scanning and analysis phases include development of national programs for those with chronic mental illness, upgrading of funding and services in a national network of community mental health centers, and enhancement of outpatient services.

National Program for the Chronically Ill. Some may object to the word *chronic* when discussing mental problems because it seems to imply that consumers cannot recover. The word has the advantage, however, of underscoring the fact that many consumers experience devastating and ongoing mental problems, including various psychoses and substance abuse. For persons who do not surmount their problems, ongoing services are needed. Several problems impede development of these services. First, policymakers have often assumed that programs that serve those with acute problems should also help those with longer-term problems. However, commu-

nity mental health centers, private practitioners, and many other agencies have provided scant assistance to consumers with long-term problems, partly because their staffs do not like, or feel ill-prepared to assist, this population. Second, funds for various programs for this population come from many disjointed sources that are also not sensitive to the needs of the mentally ill. Medicaid funds residential costs for persons in state or other residential settings who are less than twenty-one or over sixty five as well as mental health costs of some persons between twenty-one and sixty-five in nursing homes. In addition, disability payments from federal authorities through the SSI program fund residential costs of many persons in community board-and-care facilities. Neither Medicaid nor SSI are mental health programs, since their administrators are primarily concerned with the physical health of low-income consumers (Medicaid) or the income maintenance needs of the elderly (SSI). No wonder, then, that SSI payments for board-and-care facilities for the mentally ill are inadequate or that many Medicaid administrators at local and national levels have been impervious to the service needs of hundreds of thousands of persons placed in nursing homes for mental health reasons.

A massive nationally funded program should be established that is specifically directed to the needs of those with major, ongoing, and disabling mental conditions.[28] Some components of a nationally funded program are depicted in illustration 13.5. Funds for this national program for the mentally disabled could be channelled through regional authorities that would take the major initiative in devising and orchestrating a range of services. Many policy and program details would need to be resolved, including precise methods of reimbursing providers and providing the mentally disabled with income maintenance payments. The regional authorities would need extensive licensing, monitoring, planning, research, and contracting roles to truly initiate and sustain a range of services. SSI and Medicaid could continue to fund portions of mental health services for those with chronic problems, but a case can be made that the funds they cur-

ILLUSTRATION 13.5   **Regional Authorities and Services for the Mentally Disabled**

rently spend on the living needs of the mentally ill should be placed in a new, consolidated program.

Community Mental Health Centers. If the chronically mentally ill are underserved, so too are persons with various mental problems who do not normally use outpatient services. The poor, members of ethnic minority groups, persons from blue-collar families, and the elderly have not traditionally used mental health services or find them unresponsive to their needs. Although community mental health centers have proved no panacea, many have served members of blue-collar families. Major expansion of community mental health centers is needed to provide services to underserved populations; needed also is elimination of policies that specify that localities should assume increasing shares of the funding of these centers.

The centers should not be given carte blanche

in developing their services. The ecological perspective discussed at the beginning of this chapter suggests that they should provide a variety of consumer education, counseling, assertiveness training, preventive, and consultative services and should be required to demonstrate that they provide these services in a well-rounded package. (In the absence of monitoring, prior experience suggests that many centers provide traditional interventions directed toward intrapsychic phenomena, sometimes only to middle-class consumers, to the detriment of broader services to expanded populations.) To broaden their image and make them more responsive, centers should be required to earmark some portion of their funds for primary prevention projects, including stress reduction and educational services.

Expanding Other Mental Health Resources. Although national health insurance may even-

. . . But Where Else Have They to Go?

By Barbara Demming Lurie

A movie has been made about the life of Frances Farmer, a 1930s starlet of astonishing beauty who went from the back lots of Hollywood to the back wards of a state mental institution where, during her 10-year involuntary stay, she was reportedly raped, given electroshock treatment against her will and finally, it is speculated, lobotomized.

In reaction to abuses like these, as an out-growth of the civil rights movement and in recognition of the vulnerability of the mentally disabled, came the passage in 1968 of California's Lanterman-Petris-Short Act. This set of laws tightened the elastic standards as to which persons could be given psychiatric treatment against their will, how they could be treated, and for how long. The legislation also spelled out the fundamental rights of all recipients of mental health care, the philosophy being that psychiatric patients don't

tually provide a basic national minimum of outpatient mental health coverage, coverage under Medicaid and Medicare should be expanded in the interim to provide a basic minimum of outpatient benefits rather than the negligible coverage discussed earlier in this chapter. National legislation should be passed requiring private health insurance to provide at least this minimum coverage, since only a minority of states currently require private insurance to cover mental health services. Finally, consumers who lack private health insurance and are not eligible for Medicaid or Medicare should have access to the same package of mental health services under a new federal program.

In all these funding mechanisms, current inequalities between social work, psychiatry, and psychology professions should be eliminated. National legislation should be enacted that equalizes reimbursement of various providers and also clarifies that community mental health centers and a variety of social agencies can receive reimbursement for mental health services. For conditions where medications have shown promise, as in schizophrenia and some forms of depression, consultation with psychiatrists should be required.

Attention should also be given to delivery of mental health services by primary-care physicians, who currently dominate provision of outpatient services. Coverage of mental health benefits provided by primary physicians under public or private insurances should be restricted, and fiscal and regulatory methods should be devised to encourage referrals to professionals trained in mental health services. In addition, regulations should be enacted to curtail the routine prescription of Valium and other mood-altering substances.

Selected Reforms in Implementation and Assessment Phases

Rights of Consumers. No issue is more difficult to resolve than the precise wording of statutes in the various states regarding involuntary commitment to state hospitals.[29] The rights of consumers have been flagrantly violated and individuals deprived of basic liberties in jurisdictions that commit them to institutions when they could be assisted with outpatient services and resources (see guest editorial 13.1).

leave their basic human, civil and consumer rights at the door when they walk into treatment facilities.

In California, being "crazy" is not enough to warrant involuntary hospitalization; rather, the law provides that a person must be dangerous to himself, dangerous to others or unable to provide himself with food, clothing or shelter because of a mental disorder. These three specific conditions were the only ones thought to be of such overriding consequence that they usurped a person's fundamental right to liberty. Thus, the law was in effect saying that the people of California were interested not in an individual's psychodynamics (that is, his hallucinations or delusional systems) but rather in the tangible harm that he could bring to others or experience himself without public intervention.

The 1968 legislation also provides for strict time limitations for involuntary hospitalization: generally an initial 72-hour period for evaluation and treatment and 14 days for intensive treatment. After that if a person is suicidal, he may be confined an additional 14 days (for a total of 31); if he is dangerous to others, he may be detained 90 more days, and, if he cannot provide for his basic personal needs, he may be put on a year-long conservatorship that is renewable. Throughout these periods, the person retains the right to go to court on a writ of habeas corpus to contest the detention.

Many people in the community who have watched the proverbial pendulum swing in the direction of patients' rights and civil rights are now eager for gravity to take its course. Those who see our mental institutions as convenient rugs under which society can sweep its more deviant members complain that the stringent laws interfere with society's housecleaning. Others genuinely concerned about the safety and well-being of the mentally disordered are frustrated because the mental-health laws make it more difficult to put people away for their own protection.

These critics should realize that the reform legislation was not simply the creation of some bureaucrat who had nothing to do on a Monday morning. It was a response to seri-

To safeguard patients' rights, statutes in many areas require evidence of imminent personal harm or harm to others and establish procedures for reviewing cases periodically to ensure that persons are not maintained in institutional settings when they could receive community services. Regional authorities should also provide ombudsman services to be certain that legal protections are honored and that program staff members are informed of safeguards.

But legal protections should not be regarded as a panacea. In many cases, persons who are not committed are denied supportive community services. It is scant comfort to a person experiencing mental anguish to tell her that her formal rights have been protected but that she will not receive services, obtain employment, or find housing. As noted in guest editorial 13.2, some consumers need institutional services who will not voluntarily seek them. Consideration should be given to methods of allowing some involuntary commitment of consumers not perceived to be in imminent danger of killing themselves or others, but with careful safeguarding of their rights.

POLICY ROLES OF SOCIAL WORKERS

Social workers should assume a number of roles in the mental health sector as they assess existing policies and seek reforms.

ous questions about the constitutionality of forced treatment and some very real abuses that plagued the mental-health system. They should also realize that, however long a person is hospitalized, there comes a time when he must return to the community. And community receptivity has been notoriously lacking.

The public attitude, fanned by negative portrayals of the psychiatric population in the news media (titillating headlines, for example about "ex-mental patients" who commit crimes), has erroneously equated mental disorder with dangerousness when, in fact, studies have shown this sub-group to be no more menacing than the population at large. There is also the subtle fear that these people will somehow "taint" us, that mental "illness" rubs off like a bad dye job. Given this atmosphere of discrimination and rejection, is it any wonder that many former patients wind up back in the hospital or in decrepit "mental-patient" ghettos in the worst parts of town?

The reform laws were predicated on the optimistic and ultimately naive assumption that a spectrum of treatment programs in the community would materialize to pick up where giant state institutions left off. This hope was realized only to the extent that there is now a crazy-quilt patchwork of community-based facilities, so fragmented and insufficient that institutionalization in a state hospital or a demeaning existence on the back streets is often an "either/or" proposition. It remains to be seen whether it is any better to lead an isolated life in a deteriorating welfare hotel than in the worst wards of a state institution.

The Lanterman-Petris-Short Act opened the door for psychiatric patients, but, without the safety net of aftercare programs and community involvement, they have nowhere to go, ironically enough. Sadly, this well-intentioned reform has shown that it is possible to legislate freedom, but not acceptance. Those who truly want to do something about our psychiatric population would do well to embrace that mothballed adage about charity beginning at home.

Barbara Demming Lurie is chief of the patients' rights office for the Los Angeles County Department of Mental Health. SOURCE: This article first appeared in the *Los Angeles Times*. Reprinted by permission of the author.

Survey Role

As a prelude to efforts to obtain policy changes, social workers have to examine prevailing policies in specific mental health centers and settings to determine whether specific reforms are possible. As an example, a social worker may want to propose initiation of a preventive program in a mental health center that only provides curative services. The social worker would examine the extent to which a mobilization of bias exists against preventive programs and would use this information when deciding which kinds of preventive projects might obtain support from other staff members and administrators. When seeking major reforms in state and national legislation, social workers need to be familiar with the political, economic, cultural, and technical realities and forces discussed in this chapter, including, for example, the assumption by many legislators that mental health services should be largely funded by local authorities.

Problem Recognition and Definition Role

Mental health services need to be adapted to the distinctive needs of ethnic and racial minorities, women, the poor, and the elderly. Methods of providing outreach to these populations need to be devised to increase the numbers using services. Previous discussion also suggests that social workers can insist that more attention be given to the needs of those with chronic mental

GUEST EDITORIAL 13.2

Some People Do Not Belong on the Street . . .

By Paul Farhi

She staggered down the steps of the apartment building, holding onto the railing with both hands, as if her legs were powerless.

We were about to unload our groceries when we witnessed her uneasy descent that afternoon. From across the street we watched, both of us motionless. "Do you think she's OK?" my wife finally said. "Do you think she needs help or something?"

"I don't know," I said tentatively. "She looks drunk. I think she's OK. She'll just go back up there and sleep it off. Forget it. C'mon."

But neither of us moved.

The woman had crumpled onto the stairway, one hand still on the railing, a look of bewilderment settling across her face. From down the street a man approached and passed beside her. She spoke to him, but the noise of the traffic prevented the words from reaching us. Then, with considerable effort, she extended an arm to him. He kept walking.

She was middle-aged, well-dressed and well-groomed, an attractive woman who apparently lived not 50 yards from us. And here she was staggering down a flight of stairs, dazed, reaching out to a stranger.

My wife and I looked at one another, each of us silently seeking advice about our next move. "It reminds me of what they used to say on 'Naked City,' " I said stupidly. " 'This is the city. There are 8 million stories in it. This is one of them.' "

We stared at the woman for what seemed like a long time. She appeared lifeless. Finally, with quivering legs, she pulled herself to her feet and began to follow an irregular path down the sidewalk. I thought that at any moment she might pitch face-forward into the gutter.

"She could walk into the traffic . . ." my wife said.

"Maybe we could take her up to her apartment," I suggested. But we moved only a few steps closer, still a "safe" distance from her.

---

conditions, persons who obviously need assistance with a host of mental health, community, and housing needs. In many cases, social workers can draw attention to problems not currently emphasized, including services for persons who experience traumatic losses, isolated individuals, and persons encountering life and developmental crises.

Program and Policy Design Role

Innovative programs are needed in the mental health sector. For example, services to the poor and elderly require use of decentralized services, creative use of neighborhood aides, and use of case managers who ensure that specific consumers receive a variety of services. Also, agency services should be supplemented with self-help groups. Social workers should assume leadership in constructing these kinds of interventions.

Troubleshooting Role

Quality mental health services cannot be provided if staff have low morale or are subject to burnout. Interventions in agency and institu-

From the opposite direction, another man approached her.

"Here comes a plot complication," I said, I was relieved. Perhaps, I thought, *this* fellow will spare me some nasty business; perhaps he will help this woman so that I won't have to. Perhaps I won't have to spend the afternoon entangled in a stranger's personal tragedy. Frankly, I didn't want to know about hers.

But the man veered off into his apartment before reaching the spot where the woman had stopped. My heart sank.

The woman approached the other entrance of the building and crumbled in a heap on the stoop.

Suddenly she pitched forward, then listed sideways until her head hit the stairs.

"Stay here," I said to my wife. "I'll go see what's wrong."

The woman was still conscious, "Are you OK? Can I help you?" I shouted. "What's wrong?"

She rolled over with a soft moan, and looked up at me with widened, glassy eyes. In a small, slightly accented voice she managed three words: "Call the Police."

We left her on the stairs and raced to the apartment that the second man had entered. We explained the situation to him and, almost instantly, he escorted us to his phone. I was gratified, and amazed, by his willingness to help. Didn't he realize that we were strangers in the big city?

Two police officers arrived within 10 minutes of our call. They could not see the woman from their patrol car.

"Does she live in this building?" asked one of the cops. "A little woman, red hair?"

"Yes," I said, surprised.

"Let me tell you something," said the cop. "We've committed that lady to the mental hospital three times. The law says you can put them away for 72 hours—that's it. We could do it again, but what good would it do? She'll be out here again in a few days. That's the system."

"So there's nothing that can be done," I said.

"Nothing that'll do her any good," said the policeman. "That's just the way it goes."

We all shrugged. The police officers drove away, and we went back to unloading our groceries. The woman lay in a heap on the stairs down the street.

For some reason, I felt better.

Paul Farhi is a staff writer in Los Angeles for Ad Week. SOURCE: This article first appeared in the *Los Angeles Times*. Reprinted by permission of the author.

---

tional settings are needed to increase staff involvement in their work as well as willingness to use innovative approaches. As part of troubleshooting, social workers should help develop planning committees and task forces to scrutinize operating programs and identify program alternatives.

Error Detection and Change Agent Roles

Social workers can participate in development of multifaceted assessment projects that probe a range of program objectives. Among other topics, assessments should analyze the extent to which specific programs reduce the mental distress of consumers; are relevant to underserved populations, such as the elderly; and provide a range of services, including preventive services and vocational, recreational, housing, and counseling services for the chronically ill.

Mentally ill persons in American society lack political clout in local, state, and federal arenas. Therefore, social workers need to develop broad-based coalitions that demand more adequate funding for institutional and community pro-

ILLUSTRATION 13.6 Policy in the Mental Health Sector

Prevailing (Current) Policies and Programs
- scant coverage of mental health in Medicaid and Medicare legislation
- scant coverage by private health insurance
- absence of articulated community programs for released mental patients
- inadequate funding of state, county, and municipal mental institutions
- network of community mental health centers, but with an uncertain funding base
- separate and unequal services for affluent and poor persons

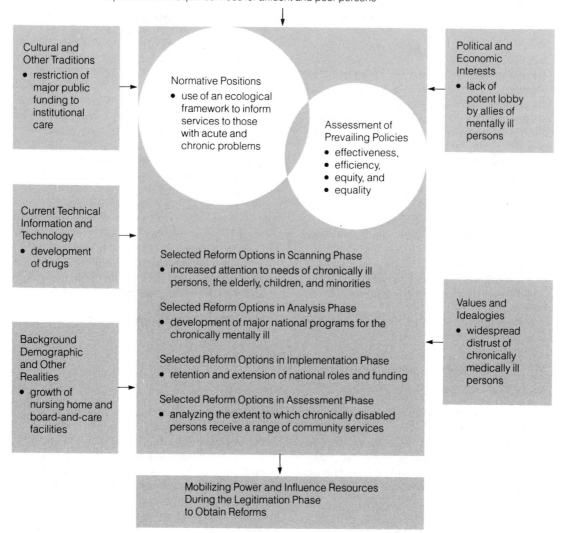

Cultural and Other Traditions
- restriction of major public funding to institutional care

Current Technical Information and Technology
- development of drugs

Background Demographic and Other Realities
- growth of nursing home and board-and-care facilities

Normative Positions
- use of an ecological framework to inform services to those with acute and chronic problems

Assessment of Prevailing Policies
- effectiveness,
- efficiency,
- equity, and
- equality

Political and Economic Interests
- lack of potent lobby by allies of mentally ill persons

Values and Idealogies
- widespread distrust of chronically medically ill persons

Selected Reform Options in Scanning Phase
- increased attention to needs of chronically ill persons, the elderly, children, and minorities

Selected Reform Options in Analysis Phase
- development of major national programs for the chronically mentally ill

Selected Reform Options in Implementation Phase
- retention and extension of national roles and funding

Selected Reform Options in Assessment Phase
- analyzing the extent to which chronically disabled persons receive a range of community services

Mobilizing Power and Influence Resources During the Legitimation Phase to Obtain Reforms

grams. Like welfare recipients and others perceived to violate social norms, persons with mental problems need political assistance from external allies who try as well to educate the public to the potentials of well-funded and enlightened community strategies.

SUMMARY

Illustration 13.6 summarizes discussion in this chapter in the context of the policy framework developed in chapter 2. Prevailing policies, normative positions, assessment of prevailing policies, and selected reform options are portrayed, as are a variety of political, ideological, and cultural factors that influence the development of policy in the mental health sector.

An ecological perspective should inform the delivery of mental health services. Consumers who suffer from acute or long-standing problems need assistance in negotiating their environment, whether by developing realistic objectives, obtaining needed skills, modifying destructive habits, or working through destructive experiences. Environments of consumers need to be modified through social action, advocacy, or consultative services. Services need to be adapted to the needs of specific populations to ensure that middle-class norms are not imposed on the poor or ethnic minorities. Systematic linkages need to be developed between a variety of

agencies, institutions, and programs that assist persons with mental problems, and preventive services need to be provided to "at risk" populations not currently exhibiting mental problems.

American mental health services require numerous reforms. Americans have succeeded in reducing the numbers of persons in institutions but have not developed a network of services and resources for those with chronic and disabling conditions. Wide disparities exist in access to outpatient services for acute disorders, as suggested by the minimal coverage of mental health services offered by Medicare, Medicaid, and private insurance. Services are often dominated by psychiatrists, to the detriment of team practice or provision of services by social work and other mental health personnel. Most outpatient services are provided by primary-care physicans, who often lack rudimentary knowledge of mental problems.

Consideration should be given to development of a major national program that funds a range of halfway house, housing, vocational, day treatment, and recreational programs. In addition, regional authorities should be devised that develop and orchestrate these services. Major national funding should also be provided for a national network of community mental health centers serving populations neglected by traditional agencies and services, including the poor, blue-collar families, racial minorities, and the elderly.

Key Concepts, Developments, and Policies

Ecological approach
Stress
"At risk" populations
Chronic conditions
Acute conditions
Mood-altering drugs
Halfway houses
Deinstitutionalization
Primary-care physicians
Community mental health centers

Coverage under Medicare, Medicaid, and private insurance
Private and public mental hospitals
Three systems of mental health services
"Moral treatment"
Poor Law traditions
Dorothea Dix
Sigmund Freud
Nonprofit agencies
Chronic wards

Involuntary commitment
Schizophrenia
Board-and-care homes
Nursing homes
National Institute of Mental Health
Joint Commission on Mental Illness
Community Mental Health Centers Act

Subsidized employment
Day treatment programs
Supplementary Security Income subsidies
Mental Health Systems Act
Alcohol, drug abuse, and mental health block grant
President's Commission on Mental Health

Main Points

1. An ecological framework provides needed perspectives when policies and programs are being devised in the mental health sector. A variety of services are needed to help persons interact with and modify their environment.

2. Mental health services need to be adapted to distinctive needs, problems, and expectations of specific groups, including women and particular low-income, ethnic, and racial populations.

3. Provision of effective services requires linkages between mental health programs and services provided by other programs as well as the use of case managers and interprofessional teams.

4. Preventive services are needed that target services to "at risk" populations and develop outreach projects and self-help groups.

5. Many problems exist in programs that assist consumers with severe and recurring conditions, such as schizophrenia. Deinstitutionalization has not been coupled with sufficient planning or resources to allow development of a range of community programs, employment opportunities, and housing arrangements.

6. Many problems also exist in services for persons experiencing acute mental health conditions—e.g., the prominence of primary-care physicians, who lack training in mental health, and the lack of funding of outpatient services. Medicare and Medicaid programs give scant funding for these services, and many private insurance policies deemphasize them.

7. Serious inequalities exist in the reimbursement of various mental health disciplines, as suggested by the exclusion of social work providers from reimbursement by many private insurance companies and restrictions on their services under Medicaid and Medicare.

8. At least three different mental health systems exist: different institutions and providers are used by affluent, blue-collar, and low-income families. Serious questions can be raised about equity and equality outcomes in this tripartite system.

9. The "moral treatment" phase brought development of mental institutions, but a variety of factors led to custodial services for many institutionalized persons by the turn of this century.

10. The widespread deinstitutionalization of the 1950s and 1960s was caused by a variety of factors. It can be viewed both as a positive development and as one that often led to inhumane treatment of persons with serious problems. In many cases, persons released from institutions lived in board-and-care and nursing home facilities that did not provide them with a range of needed services.

11. Subsidies from the Supplementary Security Income program and the Medicaid program have provided living expenses for many mentally ill persons.

12. The Community Mental Health Centers Act of 1963 led to creation of a national network of community mental health centers that offer a variety of outpatient and emergency services. The CMHCs have provided many needed services to persons who might not

otherwise have had access to them, particularly persons from lower middle and middle-income families. However, many have provided insufficient services to persons with chronic problems and to low-income, ethnic minority, and elderly consumers.

13. Severe cuts were enacted in CMHCs in the administration of Ronald Reagan. Various mental health and substance abuse programs were placed in the alcohol, drug abuse, and mental health block grant.

14. Consideration should be given to enactment

of a national program for chronically ill persons that consolidates services and funds for this population under the aegis of regional authorities. Funding for community mental health centers should be expanded, as should subsidies for acute services from Medicaid, Medicare, and private insurance sources. Greater equality should be established in reimbursement of various mental health professions, including social work. Right of consumers need to be protected in commitment processes.

Questions for Discussion

1. Review case example 13.1. Identify a variety of factors that contribute to the lack of community services for persons released from mental institutions.

2. A number of social work theorists believe that an ecological model should be used by social workers in their practice. Discuss the kinds of policies suggested by such a model, in contrast with one that emphasizes interventions directed primarily toward exploration of intrapsychic matters.

3. Discuss reasons why preventive services are not emphasized in the mental health sector. What kinds of "at-risk" populations might usefully benefit from them? What kinds of policies would be required in agency settings if such services were to receive greater emphasis? What kinds of changes would have to be made in policies of government funders?

4. Why is it important to adapt mental health services to the distinctive needs of specific populations? Cite examples where mental health providers have not adapted their services.

5. Discuss financial barriers to provision of outpatient mental health services in the con-

text of Medicare, Medicaid, and private insurance.

6. Identify and discuss a range of services needed by persons who have been released from mental institutions.

7. Do you agree with the statement "Since psychiatrists alone possess the ability to dispense medications that are important to the treatment of many persons with mental problems, they should continue to have primary roles in services provided under Medicare, Medicaid, and private insurance"?

8. Discuss the statement "deinstitutionalization in the 1950s, 1960s, and 1970s led, paradoxically, to the reinstitutionalization of many persons in various community facilities."

9. Middle ground is sought by many policy analysts who want to avoid the twin dangers of (1) violating rights of persons during involuntary commitment procedures and (2) making commitment procedures so difficult that some persons who need services do not receive them. Discuss.

10. A case can be made for construction of a special national program for persons with long-term and severe mental problems. Discuss.

Suggested Readings

Bloom, Bernard. *Community Mental Health* (Monterey, Calif.: Brooks Cole, 1977). A readable introduction to community mental health legislation and programs.

Bloom, Martin. *Primary Prevention: The Possible Science* (Englewood Cliffs, N.J.: Prentice-Hall, 1981). Though difficult reading, this book is the most comprehensive discussion available of primary prevention interventions and also probes agency, professional, and policy barriers to preventive programs.

Chu, Franklin, and Trotter, Sharland. *The Madness Establishment* (New York: Grossman, 1974). A readable indictment of the programs and policies of community mental health centers as they failed to achieve the central objectives of the federal legislation that established them.

Mechanic, David. *Mental Health and Social Policy* (Englewood Cliffs, N.J.: Prentice-Hall, 1980). This book is essential reading for those who want relatively advanced analysis of many policy and program issues in the mental health sector.

Meyer, Carol. *Social Work Practice: A Response to Urban Crisis* (New York: Free Press, 1972). The author provides an ecological framework that can be used to inform policy analysis in the mental health sector.

Scull, Andrew. *Decarceration* (Englewood Cliffs, N.J.: Prentice-Hall, 1977). A radical critique of recent policies to empty state mental institutions. The author argues that economic and political motives prompted this policy and attendant nonfinancing of community alternatives.

Segal, Steven. "Community Mental Health." In Neil Gilbert and Harry Specht, eds., *Handbook of the Social Services* (Englewood Cliffs, N.J.: Prentice-Hall, 1981): pp. 168–189. A concise introduction to programs and issues in the mental health sector.

U.S. President's Commission on Mental Health. *Report to the President* (Washington, D.C.: U.S. Government Printing Office, 1978). This four-volume report presents findings of a commission established by President Jimmy Carter. Many readers will find volumes 1 and 2 most helpful, since they summarize and discuss the most important recommendations.

Wing, J. K. *Reasoning About Madness* (Oxford, England: Oxford University Press, 1978). This sophisticated analysis of conceptual and policy issues in mental health by a leading English authority places American policies in international perspective.

Notes

1. Meyer, *Social Work Practice*.

2. Mechanic, *Mental Health and Social Policy*, pp. 112–115.

3. Ibid., pp. 63–65.

4. Adapting mental health interventions to the needs of specific ethnic groups is urged by Wynetta Devore and Elfriede Schlesinger, *Ethnic Sensitive Social Work* (St. Louis: C. V. Mosby, 1981) and Shirley Jenkins, *The Ethnic Dilemma in Social Services* (New York: Free Press, 1981).

5. August Hollingshead and Shirley Fredrick Redlich, *Social Class and Mental Illness* (New York: Wiley, 1958).

6. Bloom, *Primary Prevention*.

7. U.S. President's Commission on Mental Health, *Report to the President*.

8. Careful development of interventions specifically directed to the needs of schizophrenics is urged by Wing, *Reasoning About Madness*.

9. Commission on California State Government Organization and Economy, *A Study of the Administration of State Health Programs* (Sacramento, Calif.: 1976), pp. 198–199.

10. U.S. President's Commission on Mental Health, *Report to the President,* vol. 2, pp. 51–52.

11. Carolyn F. Swift, "Primary Prevention: Policy and Practice," in Richard J. Price et al., eds., *Prevention in Mental Health* (Beverly Hills, Calif.: Sage, 1980), pp. 227–236.

12. U.S. President's Commission on Mental Health, *Report to the President,* vol. 2, pp. 518–527.

13. Ibid., pp. 507–509.

14. For discussion of "four systems of care," see Segal, "Community Mental Health," pp. 185–188.

15. Albert Deutsch, *The Mentally Ill in America* (New York: Doubleday, 1937).

16. Gerald Grob, *Mental Institutions in America: Social Policy to 1875* (New York: Free Press, 1973). Also see David Rothman, *The Discovery of the Ayslum* (Boston: Little Brown, 1971).

17. Ibid.

18. Jane Addams, *The Second Twenty Years at Hull House* (New York: Macmillan, 1930), pp. 188–220.

19. Bloom, *Community Mental Health,* pp. 14–20.

20. Scull, *Decarceration.*

21. Steven P. Segal, and Uri Aviram, "Community-Based Sheltered Care," in Paul I. Ahmed and Stanley C. Plog, *State Mental Hospitals* (New York: Plenum, 1976), pp. 111–127.

22. Joint Commission on Mental Illness and Health, *Action for Mental Health* (New York: Basic Books, 1961).

23. U.S. President's Commission on Mental Health, *Report to the President,* vol. 2, p. 319.

24. Chu and Trotter, *The Madness Establishment.*

25. Various barriers encountered by CMHCs are discussed by Swift, "Primary Prevention: Policy and Practice."

26. See *Congressional Quarterly Almanac,* 1980, vol. 36 (Washington, D.C.: Congressional Quarterly Service, 1980), pp. 430–434. Also see vol. 37, pp. 483–484.

27. J. Richard Woy et al., "Community Mental Health Centers: Movement Away From the Model," *Community Mental Health Journal,* 17 (Winter 1981): 265–276.

28. Although it was never finalized, officials in the National Institute of Mental Health in the Carter Administration developed a plan to provide a range of services and subsidies to persons with chronic and severe mental problems.

29. Commitment issues and laws are discussed by Mechanic, *Mental Health and Social Policy,* pp. 184–214. An extreme libertarian point of view is expressed by Thomas Szasz, *The Myth of Mental Illness: Foundations of a Theory of Personal Conduct* (New York: Harper & Row, 1974).

Index